A Census User's Handbook

A Census User's Handbook

Edited by
DAVID RHIND

Methuen
London and New York

First published in 1983 by
Methuen & Co. Ltd
11 New Fetter Lane, London EC4P 4EE
Published in the USA by
Methuen & Co.
in association with Methuen, Inc.
733 Third Avenue, New York, NY 10017

Printed in Great Britain
at the University Printing House,
Cambridge

British Library Cataloguing in Publication Data
A census user's handbook.
1. Great Britain—Census
I. Rhind, David
304.6 HA1124
ISBN 0-416-30510-5
ISBN 0-416-30520-2 Pbk (University paperback 757)

Library of Congress Cataloging in Publication Data
A Census user's handbook.
Bibliography: p.
Includes index.
1. Great Britain—Census, 1981—Handbooks, manuals, etc. 2. Great Britain—Census—Handbooks, manuals, etc.
I. Rhind, David.
HA1124 1981c 001.4'33 83-8306
ISBN 0-416-30510-5
ISBN 0-416-30520-2 (pbk.)

Contents

List of tables

List of figures

Glossary of abbreviations

Britain	Comprises England, Scotland and Wales; for census purposes, this does not include the Channel Islands or the Isle of Man
COM	Computer Output on Microfilm
CRU	Census Research Unit, University of Durham
DE	Department of Employment
DHSS	Department of Health and Social Security
DoE	Department of the Environment
ED	Enumeration District
GIMMS	Geographical Information Mapping and Modelling System
GRO(S)	General Register Office of Scotland
LAMSAC	Local Authorities Management Services and Computer Committee
NHS	National Health Service
OPCS	Office of Population Censuses and Surveys
OS	Ordnance Survey
PLU	Program Library Unit, University of Edinburgh
RAWP	Resource Allocation Working Party of the National Health Service
RG	Registrar General
RSG	Rate Support Grant
SAS	Small Area Statistics
SASPAC	Small Area Statistics Package (see appendix 7)
SDD	Scottish Development Department
SEG	Socioeconomic group (see appendix 4)
SPSS	Statistical Package for the Social Sciences
SSRC	Social Science Research Council
UK	Comprises England, Scotland, Wales and Northern Ireland; for census purposes, this does not include the Channel Islands or the Isle of Man

Acknowledgements

This book was completed against severe odds. That it was completed is due in part to good fortune but, more particularly, to help, encouragement, advice and information from a very large number of people: they are acknowledged below.

In various universities, Roy Baker, Elisabeth Barraclough, Marjorie Barritt, Michael Coombes, Andy Gillespie, John Goddard, Peter Kemp, Mahes Kirby, David Owen, John Steele, Eric Tannenbaum, and Tom Waugh have, at various times, been invaluable. Present and future academic users of 1981 census data also owe certain of them (and others) a great deal because of their involvement in making census data readily available to academics (see below).

I am particularly grateful for permission to reproduce much OPCS material in this book. In OPCS itself, however, Chris Denham and Barbara Ballard have played a vital role in channelling information and correcting misconceptions. Gerald Boston, Joe Wright and Alex Clarke in the 'sharp end' of OPCS – the data factory at Titchfield – have remained cheerful as well as helpful, irrespective of the pressures upon them. Harry Lawson and Reg de Mellow in GRO (Scotland) have performed equal services. In other government departments, Barbara Rose, Ann Wheatcroft and Ros Whittaker (Department of the Environment) and Ray Harrison and Michael Janes (Manpower Services Commission) have improved our understanding of why they need census data and how they use it for tasks which ultimately touch all our lives. Though contributions have been made to parts of the book by members of government departments, the views expressed throughout the book do not constitute official policy or statements.

Early in 1981, the Social Science Research Council was persuaded to purchase a complete set of Small Area Statistics for Britain and make these available to academic staff and students for *bona fide* research and teaching purposes. It would be remiss not to acknowledge the roles played in this decision by Professors Michael Wise and Brian Robson. So far as SSRC staff are concerned, David Allen and Angela Williams played an essential role in preparing the ground for this major decision.

I occupied many of my non-teaching hours in 1981 working on the

SASPAC project. This, financed by the Local Authorities Management Services and Computer Committee (LAMSAC), produced computer software to handle the 1981 SAS. Designed from the outset to sit on 150 often very different computers in local authorities up and down the country, this was a unique project: even more complications and potential benefits arose by the later addition of universities to this consortium. The 1981 project team, consisting of John Welford and Craig Stott (Program Library Unit, University of Edinburgh) and John Dixon and Peter Norris (University of Durham) achieved by any standards what is a remarkable product. The project continued in 1982 under Marjorie Barritt and Trevor Jones; its results have transformed the way in which the census statistics are used in Britain. We were fortunate in having excellent liaison with LAMSAC via Keith Dugmore, David Hughes and Julia Sullivan. Eivind Gilje of GLC was an excellent chairman of the SASPAC steering committee.

Perhaps more than any others, thanks are due to those ex-colleagues who constituted a loosely bound but effective research team over the years 1973–81. The permanent members of the team were Professor John Clarke, John Dewdney, Ian Evans and myself. Vital contributions were made at different times by Mahes Kirby, Peter Norris, Helen Mounsey, Jane Coulter, Barbara Perry and Dennis Pringle. Professor W.B. Fisher and his successor, John Clarke, sanctioned the use of the departmental typesetter to speed the production of this book.

Finally, the contributions of two women must be mentioned. Without Dinah Michie who typeset, organized, argued, cajoled and generally kept the show on the road, there would have been no such book – or, at least, not yet. My wife is convinced that she has put more effort into it than anyone else: in this she may be right, given the few dishes I have washed and the few leaking taps I have mended over the last year ... she is, of course, *very* much appreciated!

David Rhind
October 1982

The editor and publishers would like to thank the following for permission to reproduce copyright material: OPCS for figures 2.4, 2.5, 2.6, 6.1 and 6.4, tables 2.1, 2.3, 2.4, 2.6, 5.2, 9.1 and 9.5, and appendices 1, 2, 3 and 4; the Post Office for figure 2.2; and the Centre for Urban and Regional Development Studies, University of Newcastle, for figure 2.3. The topographic material in figures 2.4, 2.5 and 2.6 is reproduced from the Ordnance Survey 1 : 50,000 Landranger series map with the permission of the Controller of Her Majesty's Stationery Office, Crown copyright reserved.

Introduction

DAVID RHIND

Censuses of population have a long pedigree; the taking of censuses often has unforeseen repercussions and may lead to policies which greatly affect society. As *The Times* leader (6 April 1981) put it:

> The first *Book of Chronicles* recounts how King David conducted a census, at a time when a graver view was taken of such matters than today, and how a pestilence was visited upon Israel to punish him. The king and his inner cabinet donned sackcloth to a man, and by energetic displays of contrition and diplomacy persuaded God to stay his hand. The chronicler records that as a result of the pestilence there fell of Israel 70,000 men.

Counting people is clearly an ingrained habit, irrespective of the consequences!

The Census of Population is certainly a major decennial event in Britain: the taking of the 1981 Census involved the employment of more than 129,000 people, cost about £45 million and was designed to elicit information from every one of the twenty million or so households in this country. The enterprise of taking the Census contained individual elements of both tragedy and humour: in Northern Ireland, a census enumerator was shot dead as she collected census forms while, on a lighter note, Mrs Beatrice Smith of Weymouth sent a bill for £5 to the Secretary of State for Social Services for the seventy minutes she devoted to completing the census questionnaire. OPCS received no less than 18,000 telephone calls from enumerators and the public over the few days around census night, covering a vast range of queries from the absurd to the arcane.

The results from this census are made available in a variety of forms, chiefly numbers of people or households in specific categories (such as of male old-age pensioners or households lacking a bath) for defined areas of ground; simple arithmetic applied to the 4400 pieces of information available in the Small Area Statistics (SAS) can provide compound indicators of 'goodness' or 'badness', of quality of material surroundings and, with some imagination, of wealth. Such information is available for a variety of different sets of areas – for all counties or Scottish Regions, for all administrative districts, for electoral wards, for the 125,000 enumeration districts (EDs) in Britain and for various others.

These results from the census are the corner-stone of many activities in and outside government, in marketing studies and in academic or private research; the transfer of funds from central to local government is based in part upon the numbers of people in each administrative area; the location of services such as hospitals and clinics provided by health authorities are based in no small part upon the details provided in the census of where old and young people live; arguments over the scale of potential disasters from nuclear power stations or Liquid Petroleum Gas terminals involve intimate consideration of census statistics. We confidently anticipate no less than 10,000 people in Britain making direct use of the 1981 census statistics and decisions arising from some of these uses will ultimately touch the lives of millions.

For many users of statistics produced from the census, detailed local information is vital. Yet it is precisely in these circumstances where the need to maintain confidentiality is likely to affect the results obtained from any analysis; handling Small Area Statistics is not a pastime for the unwary! Furthermore, many users will certainly wish to compare the situation in their area in 1981 with that recorded in the census a decade earlier: this is also not a simple business because of the change of geographical areas for which data have been recorded or because of the different questions asked in the two censuses. Finally, the detailed Small Area Statistics information from the 1981 Census on computer tape will cost only one third of the sum for the equivalent material in paper form; in these circumstances, substantial users of census data need to be or to have access to reasonably skilled computer users.

This book then is designed to be a guide to what is in and what can be obtained from the census; to what is good practice in analysing such data and what is definitely unwise. We set this information into the context of what has been done in the past and, to a small extent, of what is done elsewhere. The use of acronyms – such as OPCS (Office of Population Censuses and Surveys) or GRO(S) (General Register Office of Scotland) – abounds in the book but these are explained in a glossary. Though we cannot hope to cover all the pitfalls specific to every detailed requirement, we do try to establish general guidelines and provide illustrative examples. Specifically, we exclude almost totally any consideration of the Population Census held in Northern Ireland which differed in many respects from that in the mainland part of the United Kingdom. We make no consideration of the Isle of Man and the Channel Islands since no census was held there in 1981. Since we anticipate that users of the book will dip into appropriate sections, rather than read it cover to cover, deliberate overlap has been introduced. As an example, consider the details of the way in which OPCS alter the raw statistics by adding small random numbers so as to protect confidentiality: wherever this is critical to the topic under discussion, a brief description is given of it, plus a cross reference to the main section covering the topic.

No census in Britain is an island, unrelated to its predecessors. For this reason, our opening chapter sets the stage for the 1981 Census by considering earlier censuses, with particular emphasis on the revolutionary 1971 Census. It is written by John Dewdney, Reader in Geography at the University of Durham, who is an authority upon population studies and has previously used data from the 1961, 1966 and 1971 Censuses. The second chapter is a comprehensive description of the statistics emanating and planned to emanate from the 1981 Census by Chris Denham, a Senior Research Officer in OPCS who was intimately involved in the planning of this census, and by the editor. It is followed by a summary of user needs and the main purposes to which census data have been put in the past, written by Peter Norris of the Census Research Unit in the University of Durham and Barbara Ballard of OPCS: we include this because it is our common experience that the work of other people often stimulates us to emulate them or gives us fresh ideas on how problems may be tackled. Their chapter illustrates the way in which the use of census data has permeated much of official planning and some research in Britain.

The next set of chapters of the handbook is concerned with the technical aspects of handling census data. Some colleagues have already suggested that there is little need to incorporate such material in this book since some standard textbooks cover part of what we attempt. The topics are included both because this handbook is substantially 'free standing' and, more important still, because most textbooks encourage readers to use techniques – we actively discourage certain techniques when applied to British census data. Chapters 4 to 6 all take what may be described as a univariate view of the census data, i.e. they describe its analysis one-variable-at-a-time. Thus Chapter 4 by Dr Ian Evans of the Census Research Unit and Department of Geography at Durham University describes how a variety of simple methods may be used to describe the variation across a number of different census areas by using simple statistics such as the median or diagrams such as histograms. After that, Chapter 5 by the editor describes how various simple operations, such as the adding together of information for different age groups to create 'new' composite data, are best carried out. Chapter 6, again by the editor, describes how the same data may be mapped, both by hand and by machine.

Chapters 7 and 8 deal with more complex topics, taking a multivariate (i.e. several variables at-a-time) view of the census data. Dr Evans describes how the relationships between different census variables, given a set of geographical areas (EDs, etc.), can be established and illustrates this with references to work on 1971 data. Dr Stan Openshaw, of the Department of Geography at the University of Newcastle, describes how the converse can best be achieved, i.e. given a set of variables, how geographical areas may be compared and grouped together into clusters of similar characteristics. Peter Norris and Helen Mounsey (also of the Census Research Unit) then describe how and under what circumstances change through time may be defined using census data. This is followed by a chapter by Eric Tannenbaum of the SSRC Data

Archive and by the editor which describes why and how, in theory and in practice, census and other commonly used data sets may be combined for analysis, such as that of medical statistics. The substantive part of the book closes with a chapter describing the substantial advantages all census data users could obtain from microdata, if only that were available (as recently recommended in a White Paper).

It will be obvious to the most casual reader that many of the procedures which we describe are greatly aided by access to suitable computer programs. Indeed, much can be done by simple statistical programs already available on many computers. In Chapters 4 to 8 we have generally assumed the availability of very basic facilities or, alternatively, have suggested sources for the programs (such as those by Dr Openshaw). Selected programs and useful boundary and other data are briefly described in the appendices. Most of the simple analysis in Chapters 4 to 6, however, can be carried out by hand.

In compiling the handbook, we have all been conscious of the desirability to make it available no later than the arrival of the first data from the 1981 Census. Normal commercial practice seems to require about one year between submission of a manuscript and the appearance of the resulting book: this was simply not possible in our case since some details were not finalized until October 1982, by which time much of the Small Area Statistics data were generally available. Inevitably, since the material produced from the census mutates and expands as time goes on, not all of our description will be complete and readers who do not find what they are looking for in this volume should consult either the Office of Population Censuses and Surveys or the General Register Office for Scotland (see appendix 8). The authors are all individually responsible for their material; their employers, while extremely helpful in the formative stages of the book, cannot be assumed to accept responsibility for any statements by their employees. Finally, we all acknowledge the debt we owe to OPCS and GRO(S) and the extent to which we have necessarily drawn on official publications; our interpretations of these are our responsibility.

1 Censuses past and present

JOHN C. DEWDNEY

1.1 Definition and concepts

The term 'census' has been used in many ways and has even been applied to non-demographic data as in 'census of manufacturing' and 'agricultural census'. Thus the term 'population census' is often used for greater clarity. In this volume, the word 'population' is taken as read, following the *Concise Oxford Dictionary* definition of 'census' as 'an official numbering of people with various statistics'.

Thus defined, censuses have a lengthy history covering hundreds if not thousands of years, but most early counts (enumerations) of population were carried out with some specific purpose – such as taxation or military conscription – in mind, were often incomplete and were rarely 'published'. This introductory chapter is concerned only with the modern census, which has been more fully defined (United Nations 1967) as 'the total process of collecting, compiling, evaluating, analysing and publishing demographic, economic and social data pertaining, at a specified time, to all persons in a country or in a well-defined part of a country'.

Implicit in the concept of the modern census is the idea that it should be one of a regular series, though this desirable situation has so far been achieved by only a minority of the countries of the world, of which the United Kingdom is a prime example; equally, censuses have also been held in the United States since 1790. The modern census also involves much more than a simple headcount and the publication of total numbers: it also implies the collection and publication of a great variety of information on the characteristics or 'attributes' of the individual, such as age, sex, marital status, birthplace, economic activity, etc., and the composition of the households among which the population is distributed. British population censuses in the present century have also collected a good deal of non-demographic data appertaining to household tenure and amenities. Since these are collected simultaneously with the demographic data, they can be cross-tabulated with population variables.

Detailed censuses of this kind are essentially a product of the nineteenth and twentieth centuries. A few small European states – Iceland and Sweden for example – held their first censuses in the eighteenth century, but the first modern census of a large population was that of the United States, held in 1790, followed by the first British and French censuses, both taken in 1801. During the nineteenth century, first censuses were held in most European countries, the latest being the Russian census of 1897, and in various parts of 'Europe Overseas': Canada 1851, New Zealand 1851, Australia 1881. A number of Asian territories have an intermittent series of early enumerations but modern census series begin later: India in 1881 and Japan in 1920. China has had only two full modern censuses, held in 1953 and 1982. In Latin America and the Middle East there are several countries with an irregular set of censuses from the mid-nineteenth century onwards, while many tropical African territories did not have their first full census until after the Second World War, e.g. Ghana in 1948, Nigeria in 1952, and the Congo in 1974. A handful of countries still lack a census, notably Ethiopia and Lebanon.

1.2 Origin and development of the British Census

In the United Kingdom, censuses have been held at regular ten-yearly (decennial) intervals since 1801 (1821 in Ireland) with the sole exception of 1941; in 1966 a 10 per cent sample census was held, but a planned 1976 census was abandoned for economic reasons (Clarke 1976). Thus the UK has one of the world's longest series of regular censuses, of which that held in 1981 was the eighteenth.

Generally speaking, successive British censuses have collected and published a progressively larger volume of data, though at times there has been some retreat: the 1931 Census, for example, was less full than that held in 1921, and the 1981 census form contained rather fewer questions than did that of 1971 (see section 2.3.2). The first four censuses (1801, 1811, 1821, 1831) were restricted to a record of the number of males and females in each house and family (Benjamin 1970), with a simple occupational breakdown into five classes: those people in agriculture, trade, manufacturing, handicrafts and 'others'. A question on age was added in 1821 but at first was not compulsory. The 1841 Census involved several important innovations. Enumeration was now carried out by households and the completion of the census form or 'schedule' became the responsibility of the head of household, assisted where necessary by the enumerator. The local conduct of the census passed from the Parish Overseer to the local Registrar of Births, Marriages and Deaths, a post resulting from the establishment of compulsory vital registration in England and Wales in 1837. In Scotland this change was delayed: vital registration was not established until 1855 and the 1841 and 1851 Censuses were organized by the official schoolmaster or 'other fit person' in each parish. Thus it was not until 1861 that the whole of Great Britain had a uniform census organization comprising enumerators responsible to local Registrars, who, in turn, reported to the Registrars-General of England and Wales and of Scotland.

For the censuses of 1841 (England and Wales)/1861 (Scotland) to 1901 inclusive, each enumerator recorded the details from the census schedules in an 'enumerator's book', from which the data could be tabulated for publication; from 1911 onwards, when punched cards were first used for the recording and sorting of census data in Britain, enumerator's books have contained only an administrative record and the headcounts used in the preparation of preliminary population totals. Confidentiality of these books, as of the census schedules themselves, is preserved for 100 years under the provisions of the Census Act of 1920; those of the 1841-81 censuses have now been released and provide an invaluable source of information for detailed studies of the demographic and social structure of the British population in that period (see Chapter 11).

As time passed, a growing quantity of information was recorded. The 1851 Census was considerably more detailed than its predecessors, with questions on age, sex, marital status, relationship to the head of household, birthplace, occupation, education and whether or not the individual was deaf and dumb or blind. In 1891 additional questions were asked on the number of rooms in each household, and the working population was divided into employers, employees and the self-employed ('own-account workers'). In 1911, occupational as well as industrial status was recorded and questions on marital fertility were added, each married woman being instructed to indicate the duration of the marriage, the number of children born alive during the marriage and whether these were still alive at the time of the census.

The establishment of the Local Authority Area as the main areal unit for the publication of results dates from 1911 and has been a feature of all subsequent censuses. The amount and nature of the information demanded continued to change. In 1921, the fertility questions were replaced by one on dependency: each married man, widower and widow was asked to indicate the number of dependent children (below the age of sixteen), whether living with him/her or not. The question on disabilities was dropped, the industrial and occupational classifications were revised (as they have been on several subsequent occasions) and a new question was introduced on place of work, permitting the first studies of 'travel to work' or commuting. Partly for reasons of economy, the 1931 Census was reduced in scope: there were no questions on education, place of work, fertility or dependency but questions on unemployment and usual residence were added.

The twenty-year gap which resulted from the absence of a 1941 Census was only partly filled by the 1939 National Registration data (see Chapter 9). Each head of household was then required to complete a schedule giving the name, age, sex, marital status, occupation and National Service status of every member of the household, and in 1944 a National Register Volume was published showing only the civilian population of each local authority area divided into age and sex groups. As a consequence of this long gap in the succession of censuses and the fundamental changes that had obviously occurred in British society over the two decades after 1931, the 1951 Census was the most detailed to date. In addition to the usual questions on age, sex, marital status, relationship to head of household, birthplace, industry and occupation, questions on fertility, education and place of work were re-introduced. Household amenities were covered in great detail: householders were questioned as to the availability of a piped water supply, a cooking stove with oven, a kitchen sink, a water closet and a fixed bath. The 1961 Census asked also for details of household tenure – whether owned, rented from a local authority or housing association or privately rented (furnished or unfurnished) – and internal migration data, previously restricted to answers to the 'place of birth' question, were strengthened by the introduction of a question asking for each individual's address one year previously. A question on 'usual residents' absent on census night was also added, permitting the calculation of *de jure* as well as *de facto* total populations (see section 2.3.1). In 1971 the main additions were questions of date of entry to the UK if born abroad, address five years ago (first used in the 1966 sample census), parents' birthplace and car availability together with a fuller coverage of educational qualifications. Details of the information collected in 1981 appear in Chapter 2.

1.3 The areal base

Along with changes in the information sought by and subsequently made available from successive censuses, there have also been changes in the areal framework within which the data have been collected and published. Prior to 1841 (1861 in Scotland), data were collected at the parish level, but published only for ancient geographical counties (though some data for these earlier years was subsequently made available for registration districts). From 1841 (1861 in Scotland) to 1901 inclusive, when the unit of data collection was the enumeration district, publication was by registration counties (which did not always coincide with ancient geographical counties), registration districts and sub-districts. Since 1911, however, the main unit of tabulation has been the local authority area, i.e. in England and Wales prior to 1974 the county, county borough, municipal borough, urban district and rural district; and in Scotland before 1975 the county, city, large burgh, small burgh and district. A selection of data was also published at the lower level of wards in urban administrative areas and civil parishes in rural areas. In addition, a considerable range of data has been produced for other types of areal unit. In England and Wales in 1971 these were: standard regions and their subdivisions, conurbations and conurbation centres, hospital regions and area health authorities, and parliamentary constituencies. In Scotland, these other types of areal unit included planning subregions, Scottish Development Department subdivisions and special study areas, (one) conurbation and conurbation centre, hospital regions and area health boards, and parliamentary constituencies. The major change in the system of local authority areas which took place in England and Wales in 1974 and in Scotland in 1975 necessitated the publication of two sets of printed volumes of 1971 results, one in which data were aggregated to the 1971 local authority areas and a second in which they were aggregated to approximate closely to the new units, i.e. counties and districts in England and Wales; regions, island areas and districts in Scotland. Section 2.5 describes the areal base for the 1981 Census and the comparability of areas used in the 1971 and 1981 Censuses.

1.4 Publication

Some idea of the enormous volume of printed material published from the British census may be gained from the following figures, inevitably approximate, for 1971 when the number of printed pages reached its peak. A full set of published volumes for Great Britain amounted to nearly 500 separately bound items containing over 40,000 pages of tables and costing in excess of £1000 at the dates of publication (1971-9). Data of one sort or another were published for more than 22,000 areal units (Hakim 1978b), including wards and parishes.

The figures just quoted refer only to the material provided in the form of bound census reports. The past two decades have also seen major innovations in data provision, particularly the development of the Small Area Statistics (SAS) available on order from (and payment to) the census authorities. Prior to the 1961 Census, it was possible to obtain much of the full range of census data at the level of urban wards and rural civil parishes, even though only a small selection of these appeared in the printed volumes. The development of the present SAS began in 1961 when, for the first time, data at enumeration district (ED) level were made available for selected areas, and was continued in 1966, when data were provided for all EDs; since the 1966 Census was based on a 10 per cent sample of the population, the enumeration districts used in that year were rather larger than in 1961, 1971 or 1981. The supply of SAS was systematized in 1971 by the provision of these data in a standardized format of 1571 variables in 28 tables; for the 1981 Census, SAS comprise over 4300 variables in 53 tables (though OPCS refer to these as 'cells', rather than 'variables'). As we point out in Chapter 2, SAS can now be obtained in various forms – as printed paper sheets to a standard format, on microfilm or on computer-readable magnetic tape – and are produced not only for EDs, wards and parishes but also for all the current local authority and some other areal units.

The most revolutionary innovation of the 1971 Census was the geocoding of the census schedules and the subsequent production of standard SAS for square areas. Enumerators were instructed to label each schedule with a grid reference to 100 m resolution, which permitted the aggregation by computer of each census variable to grid-square totals and the publication of standard SAS for 100 m (in some areas), 1 km, 10 km and 100 km squares of the British National Grid. Thus the data relate to the areas already defined by a grid on all the official, Ordnance Survey topographic maps of Great Britain. This has a number of important advantages (and some disadvantages) compared with enumeration districts (see section 2.5). Statistics for 100 m squares were made available for the whole of Scotland; in England and Wales 100 m coverage was restricted to those areas which had been mapped by Ordnance Survey by 1971 at 1:1250 or 1:2500 scales (see Harley 1975); in all other areas of Great Britain, the maximum resolution available was the 1 km square. Some grid-square data will also probably be produced from the 1981 Census (see section 2.5.9). In both the 1971 and the 1981 Censuses 100 m resolution grid references are attached to SAS data for each enumeration district and define a centroid of the area.

The SAS as developed over the past twenty years have become the basic research tool from British censuses and provide a massive data set. In 1971, for example, there were 147,000 populated 1 km squares and, of these, approximately 54,000 for which the full range of SAS were provided (many of the data were 'suppressed' (see section 2.9.6) in the remainder) giving a data set of more than 100 million items; the data set for EDs was roughly twice as large. The 1981 SAS for the same areal units will be at least twice as big; handling such massive data sets, even by computer, is not a trivial enterprise. The problems of compacting, storing and accessing such data sets have been extensively studied by the Census Research Unit (CRU), Department of Geography, University of Durham (Rhind 1975; Visvalingam 1975; Visvalingam and Perry 1976; Visvalingam 1977; Rhind, Evans and Visvalingam 1980). For most uses, it is imperative to understand exactly how a variable has been compiled; full definitions of all the terms used, together with a detailed explanation of the layout of all 1971 SAS tables, have been published by OPCS (1976, 1977, 1980/8) (see section 2.9.3 for the corresponding information on the 1981 tables).

1.5 The census data

Though lack of space precludes a full description of the panoply of data available from the published Census Reports and Small Area Statistics, their actual use by the research worker reveals their richness and deficiencies (for a summary description of the 1971 data see Dewdney 1981). The great majority of the data are given as simple counts showing, for the area in question, the actual number of persons or households in each category, usually as a cross-tabulation of two or more dimensions (see section 2.6). In a few cases ratios or proportions are given, but in most instances it is left to the census user to devise his own ratio or other measures for his own needs. The CRU, for example, prepared a set of 102 'derived variables' considered to be of particular value in the study of the British population (Rhind, Evans and Dewdney 1977) and have devised their own measures for the analysis and mapping of these variables (Visvalingam 1976; Visvalingam and Dewdney 1977; CRU/OPCS/GRO(S) 1980). Similar work was carried out by others and has been summarized by Hakim (1978a). Chapter 2 considers the structure of 1981 census data in much greater detail, explaining how the Census Offices organize and present the counts.

Thus far, our attention has been concentrated on the historical development of the British census and on the types of data which it provides. Any census, however – and the British census is no exception – takes place within a framework of legal, organizational and other constraints, to which we now turn.

1.6 Census legislation

In Britain, as in most countries, the census is compulsory and is backed by the force of law. In 1981, failure to comply with the census regulations, or the provision of false information, could result in a fine of up to £50. From 1801 to 1911, each successive census required a new Act of Parliament, but the 1921 and all subsequent censuses have been carried out under the provisions of the Census Act of 1920, the most important of which are the following:

i The Act gives power to the Queen to make an order in Council directing that a census be taken. The duty of carrying out the census in England and Wales is laid upon the Registrar-General, who does so under the direction of the Secretary of State for Social Services. The Scottish census is carried out by the Registrar-General for Scotland under the direction of the Scottish Secretary and in Northern Ireland the census operation is now the responsibility of the Census Office of the Department of Health and Social Services. By agreement, the appropriate authorities in the Isle of Man and the Channel Islands, which are not part of the United Kingdom, carry out a census at the same time.

For the 1971 and 1981 Censuses, England and Wales have been under the control of the Office of Population Censuses and Surveys (OPCS). The three Registrars-General and their offices continue to have equal standing in census matters and co-ordinate their work with OPCS through committees and other means, where OPCS often take the initiative on matters relating to Great Britain or the United Kingdom as a whole. These contacts are designed to ensure that the same range of data is collected in each political unit and that their various publications are organized along similar lines. This is most successful in the case of SAS where (in 1981) 42 of the 53 tables are produced to a standard format for the whole of Great Britain. In the case of the published volumes, the majority deal separately with England and Wales, with Scotland or with Northern Ireland and only a few deal with Great Britain or the United Kingdom as a whole. There remain a number of differences between the publications for the several political units, which can present problems for the census user attempting to analyse data for the entire UK.

ii The 1920 Act permits the holding of censuses 'at intervals of not less than five years' (no maximum intercensal period is stated). Thus no new Act of Parliament is required to carry out a census once five years have elapsed since the previous one, and every census since 1921 has been directed by an Order in Council.

iii The Order in Council gives the date when the census will be taken, the persons who are required to make the returns, and the persons to be included in those returns. It also prescribes the questions to be asked but, under the terms of the Act, these must fall within the scope of the following topics:

a name, sex, age;
b occupation, profession, trade, employment;
c nationality, race, birthplace, language;
d place of abode, character of dwelling;
e condition as to marriage, relation to head of family, issue born in marriage;
f 'any other matter with respect to which it is desirable to obtain statistical information with a view to ascertaining the social or civil conditions of the population'.

While this last provision might appear to give the census authorities the right to ask virtually any question whatsoever, the phrase 'social or civil conditions' is held to have a limited scope and any question proposed under this category requires an affirmative resolution in Parliament. In practice, Ministers look in detail at all census proposals which emanate from the Registrars-General before they are laid before Parliament in a draft *Census Order*; the Order is normally debated by both Houses, which have the power to reject them in whole or in part and to raise other matters connected with the census. In the case of the 1981 Census, the *Census Order 1980* (S.I. 1980 No. 702) was laid before Parliament on 20 March 1980, debated in the Lords on 22 April and 6 May 1980 and in the Commons on 29 April 1980 and confirmed on 21 May 1980. *The Census Regulations*, which complete the parliamentary process, govern the detailed arrangements for the conduct of the census and contain copies of the final census form – this is not available to Parliament as a draft. The regulations pertaining to the 1981 Census (S.I. 1980 No. 897) were signed on 30 June and came into operation on 31 July 1980.

The detailed scrutiny given by Parliament to all aspects of the census operation ensures that the public has a strong influence on the nature of the census, particularly regarding the questions to be asked (see section 2.2). In the run-up to the 1981 Census, a proposal was made suggesting the inclusion of an 'ethnic' question and (voluntary) tests of this question were carried out in 1975 and 1977 (Sillitoe 1978). The idea provoked vigorous debates in the press and in Parliament and was eventually abandoned.

1.7 Confidentiality

In addition to these legal and parliamentary restraints on the nature of the information to be collected, there are also major restraints on the way in which it can be made available to the census user. Overriding all other considerations is the basic restraint laid on the census authorities to preserve the strict confidentiality of all the data collected (see Bulmer 1980). This applies not only to the original census schedules and the material accumulated by the enumerators which – as we have seen – is kept secret for 100 years, but also to the published data themselves. Though there is nothing in the Census Act on confidentiality, as it affects output it has become the practice as each census has been taken for the Registrars-General to give undertakings that information about individuals will not be disclosed either directly or in the reports and abstracts. The undertakings have varied in detail and recently emphasis has been put on the security for the census forms and the computing operation as well as on the strict confidentiality of the field operation. Restrictions apply to other government departments and local-government officials as well as to private individuals and organizations. Hakim (1979a) has described in detail census confidentiality in Britain prior to 1981, while a White Paper (HM Government 1981) has described confidentiality and computing aspects of the 1981 Census.

Because published census reports contain statistics for large areas the need for confidentiality constraints is not great. The matter becomes more serious and more complex in the case of SAS, where a few EDs and many of the grid squares are likely to contain very small populations. The confidentiality of the SAS is maintained by two procedures known as 'modification' (or 'adjustment') and 'suppression'. Modification is a relatively simple procedure. In the words of the census authorities (OPCS 1976, 1977)

> In order to obviate any possibility that the population and household data could be used to derive information about an individual, the final figures have been modified by the addition of a quasi-random pattern of +1, –1, 0 to the individual cells. The sum of adjustments within a single ED or grid

square will tend towards zero, as also will the adjustments to any individual cell when accumulated through a number of EDs or grid squares. Any cell containing a zero will be left unadjusted.

This adjustment procedure is applied to all variables for which 100 per cent data are published. Adjustment is unnecessary in the case of data for which SAS are produced on a 10 per cent sample basis, but both types of data are subject to the second procedure, that of 'suppression'. Any statistics from which it might appear to be possible to derive the characteristics of an individual person or household are 'suppressed', that is to say they are not released to the census user. The rules of suppression for both grid square data and ED data in 1971 were as follows:

- i in the case of 100 per cent population variables, all data for areas with fewer than twenty-five inhabitants are suppressed, with the exception of total population, number of males and number of females. In such cases, these three variables are not adjusted, though in unsuppressed areas all population variables suffer adjustment.
- ii in the case of the 100 per cent household variables, all data for areas with fewer than eight households are suppressed, with the single exception of the number of households. This is not adjusted, but in unsuppressed areas all the household variables suffer adjustment.
- iii in both these cases (a and b), higher level figures are obtained by adding together the unadjusted figures from the individual enumeration districts or grid squares. These aggregate figures are then adjusted and are, of course, still subject to suppression in appropriate cases.
- iv in the case of SAS based on a 10 per cent sample, all data are suppressed for any area with only one household in the sample, the figures for the suppressed area being added to the nearest area with one or more households in the sample that is also within the same unit of the next highest level of aggregation.

The objective of all these tortuous procedures is to ensure that, when data are suppressed, a larger areal unit is created for which SAS can be supplied and a list of areas cross-referencing suppressed units to the appropriate 'importing units' is supplied to customers along with their data set.

It should be emphasized that the inaccuracies due to adjustment and suppression are not cumulative: these procedures are carried out from these values anew at each level of aggregation. Nevertheless, the procedures mean that the SAS supplied by OPCS are neither wholly accurate (owing to adjustment) nor complete for every areal unit (owing to suppression). The inaccuracy resulting from adjustment is, of course, generally small; indeed it is likely to be smaller than the inevitable errors in the raw census data. Adjustment effects are likely to be worst in data for small (e.g. ED) rather than large (e.g. county) areas, in areas of low population and in variables with a low mean value. The census user can, however, experience problems as a result of adjustment, particularly if he calculates ratios from adjusted figures. He may, for example, find that the percentage figures for a set of categories – age groups or occupation groups – may add up to more or less than 100 per cent of the total population. Inevitably, the means of maintaining confidentiality differ between the 1971 and 1981 Censuses; the less complex 1981 confidentiality procedures are outlined in section 2.9.6. Full tabulations of the 1971 and 1981 SAS are given in appendices 2 and 3.

In 1971, SAS were suppressed for only a few hundred EDs (out of a total of 125,475 in Great Britain). In the case of grid squares, however, the position may at first sight appear more serious since it produces large numbers of areas for which the full range of data are not available. At the 1 km square level, for example, Great Britain contained 147,685 inhabited squares (CRU/OPCS/GRO(S) 1980) of which 80,139 (54.3 per cent) had fewer than twenty-five inhabitants, 79,264 (53.7 per cent) had fewer than eight households and about 63 per cent were suppressed in the 10 per cent sample data. However, although data were 'lost' for more than half the inhabited area of the country, the suppressed squares proved to contain less than 2 per cent of its total population, mainly in thinly inhabited rural areas.

1.8 Organization of the census

From what has been said so far, it is clear that the organization of a modern census, from pre-census planning through data collection to the publication of the final results, is an extremely large-scale, complex operation.

In Great Britain there is a three-tier hierarchy of personnel concerned with carrying out the census operation, comprising about one hundred Census Supervisors, 2000 Census Officers (with 6500 Assistant Census Officers) and about 120,000 Enumerators. Although the details of organization are somewhat different in England and Wales and in Scotland, the post and role of enumerator are common to both areas and it is the enumerator who is largely responsible for the fieldwork connected with the census.

Unlike the situation in the United States (where they scarcely exist and where part of the census is carried out by mail), very heavy reliance is placed upon use of large-scale topographic maps. The enumerator's tasks, which are designed to extend over a period of four or five weeks, are as follows:

i Prior to the date of the census, he is required to identify and list, within his ED, all buildings, those buildings or parts of buildings which are dwellings and, within each dwelling, each individual household; it is the households thus defined, and separated into 'private' and 'non-private' households, that are the basic unit of enumeration in the British census.

ii Having identified all households within his ED, the enumerator is then required to deliver to each household, some two to three weeks before census date, a leaflet explaining the nature and purpose of the census and indicating what will be required of each household.

iii His next task is to deliver the census form or 'schedule' to each household within a period of ten days before census date. There are different schedules for private and non-private households respectively and slight differences between the schedules for England, Wales, Scotland and Northern Ireland.

In 1971 and 1981, all households in each country received identical schedules, but this has not always been the case. In 1961, for example, it was decided to ask only a limited number of questions of every household and to administer the full range of questions to only a 10 per cent sample of households. Enumerators were provided with packs of schedules in which every tenth schedule asked the full set of questions. This system of 'sampling by enumeration' (Benjamin 1970) contrasts with the system used in 1971 and 1981 when data prepared on a 10 per cent sample basis were produced by selecting a sample of census schedules after the enumeration had taken place.

iv Schedules are collected by the enumerator during the three days following the census. Having collected the schedule, the enumerator is responsible for checking each one for errors and inconsistencies, making return visits to errant households where necessary.

v Finally, the enumerator enters on each schedule the name and full postal address of each household, details of accommodation shared with other households and code numbers for the household, ED and census district. In 1971 he was also required to enter a six-figure grid reference enabling the household to be allocated to the appropriate grid square; for the 1981 Census, grid referencing is carried out in the census offices at a later stage.

Establishments containing more than 100 people (large hospitals, army barracks, etc.) form Special Enumeration Districts and are dealt with by the Census Officer. This individual also trains the enumerators, supervises, checks on the quality and completeness of the information on the census forms and dispatches these forms under strict security conditions to the Census Processing Office.

It is obvious that the completeness and accuracy of the census depends heavily not only on the accuracy of the replies on each schedule filled in by the head of household but also on the care and conscientiousness with which the enumerator carries out his tasks. Such self-enumeration is only possible because the vast majority of form-fillers are able to read, understand and answer the questions. Where difficulties arose because a householder could not understand English, translations of the census form into nine languages were provided in 1981 and interpreters were also available. Completeness and accuracy, however, also depend on the consistent application of the definition of terms as fixed by the census authorities prior to the census. This can be seen, for example, in the definition of 'household' to be used by the enumerator in identifying households in his ED (task (i) above):

> A household is either one person living alone or a group of persons (who may or may not be related) living at the same address with common housekeeping. Persons staying temporarily with the household are included. A boarder having at least one meal a day with the household (breakfast is classed as a meal for census purposes) is included with that household. A lodger taking no meals with the household is classed as a separate one-person household even if he shares kitchen and bathroom. (OPCS 1976)

Equally precise definitions appear in the guidance notes accompanying the census schedule. In answering the question 'How many rooms are there in your household's accommodation?' for example, the respondent was instructed as follows:

> Do not count: small kitchens, that is those under 2 metres (6 ft 6 ins) wide, bathrooms, WCs. Rooms divided by curtains or portable screens count as one; those divided by a fixed or sliding partition count as two. Rooms used solely for business, professional or trade purposes should be excluded. (Census 1981, England; H form for private households)

1.9 Data processing

From all the details given so far, it is clear that a vast amount of data processing is necessary between the collection of raw data on the census schedules and the publication of the Census Reports and SAS. In contrast to the censuses of a few other countries which use some form of 'mark sensed' recording, this involves the coding and manual 'punching' of the data items recorded on the schedules for the production of computer tapes carrying the data set from which the many census tables are eventually produced. Not all the data are fully coded in this manner: names and addresses of residence, for example, are not coded into computer form and a considerable number of 'difficult to code' items such as the addresses produced in response to the question on 'usual address one year ago' were used only on a 10 per cent sample basis in 1971, the sample being 'selected at random from each run of ten private households, and for one person in ten similarly chosen from those not in private households, for each enumeration district (this sample was not reselected on a grid square basis)' (OPCS 1977). Coding and storage, whether 100 per cent or 10 per cent, involves two sets of operations. Aggregation and allocation of the data to a set of areal units, whether EDs, LAAs or grid squares depends on the locational references (e.g. ED ABAA02 or grid reference TQ 297 815) attached to each schedule; allocation of population and household characteristics to the appropriate classes or categories requires coding of the varied information written into the schedule by the head of household.

Some idea of the scale of the operation is provided by the following: in 1971, Great Britain as a whole contained 18.2 million private households, for each of which at least ten pieces of information were available from the census schedules. The total population comprised 53.8 million persons, for each of whom at least ten and possibly as many as twenty-four items were recorded. Thus the complete set of raw census data comprised a total of *at least* 720 ($18.2 \times 10 + 53.8 \times 10$) million items and probably nearer 1000 million.

Moreover, coding is often a complex matter, requiring difficult decisions. In some cases, of course, the information is already classified by the choice of box ticked by the householder on the schedule, for example the answers to such questions as 'How do you and your household occupy your accommodation?' (giving a set of tenure categories) or 'Write the sex of the person (M for male, F for female)'. Other items require transformation during coding: dates of birth given on the schedule have to be translated into ages at census date and then allocated to age groups; places of birth outside the UK have to be grouped by countries or areas, and so on. A third situation is that where answers to questions such as 'What was the name and business of the person's employer (if self-employed the name and nature of the person's business)?' and 'What was the person's occupation?' have to be allocated to the appropriate categories of the pre-existing Standard Industrial Classification and Standard Occupational Classification respectively.

Most complex of all are those cases where items appearing in the census tabulations are derived, during computer processing of the primary coded data, from more than one item on the census schedule. A particularly complex case is that of the 'socioeconomic groups' used in numerous published tables. Individuals are allocated to socioeconomic groups not on the basis of their answers to specific questions on the census schedule but by cross-referencing the answers to several questions on their economic activity and employment status. For example, members of socioeconomic group 5 (intermediate non-manual workers) are defined as:

> 5.1 Ancillary workers and artists – employees engaged in non-manual occupations ancillary to the professions, not normally requiring qualifications of university degree standard; persons engaged in artistic work and not employing others. Self-employed nurses, medical auxiliaries, teachers, work-study engineers and technicians are included.
>
> 5.2 Foremen and supervisors, non-manual – employees (other than managers) engaged in occupations included in Group 6 who formally and immediately supervise others engaged in such occupations. (OPCS 1976)

Not surprisingly, all tabulations involving the seventeen socioeconomic groups are derived from a 10 per cent sample of the schedules.

It should be clear from all this that the 'total process of collecting, compiling, evaluating, analysing and publishing demographic, economic and social data' which constitutes the modern British census is a continuous, large-scale and highly complex operation. The final published volume from the 1971 Census did not appear until 1979, by which time the White Paper (Cmnd 7146, July 1978) heralding the 1981 Census had already been produced, test surveys like that of the proposed 'ethnic' question had been carried out and work was under way on the design of the 1981 schedule, published volumes and SAS. Fortunately, the results of the 1981 Census are being produced rather more rapidly – as Chapter 2 makes clear.

1.10 Conclusion

As has already been indicated, this discussion can give only a glimpse of the wealth and diversity of the material available from the British census. Irritating deficiencies remain: items of interest to the individual research worker are not always available; the areal units used are not always precisely those he requires; data are not wholly compatible between Scotland and England and Wales (Chapter 2); there are many problems associated with tracing change over time (Chapter 9); above all, the cost of obtaining the data may be prohibitive. But no census, particularly one in which confidentiality is always preserved, could possibly satisfy all potential users. The matter of charges to the consumer is a debatable point, particularly when only a small fraction of the cost can be recouped from the sale of data to customers, but the whole question of charging involves government policy and is thus outside the direct control of the census authorities. In general, adverse criticism is far outweighed by praise for the British census as a basic and invaluable source of data for administrative and financial planning and for research of many kinds.

2 The 1981 Census and its results

CHRIS DENHAM and DAVID RHIND

2.1 Introduction

The eighteenth decennial population census of Great Britain was taken on 5 April 1981. It demanded as little from the respondents as any census in the last fifty years and the indications are that the census forms were filled in accurately and without serious deficiencies in coverage. Though the Census was straightforward for the public, it represents the largest resource of statistical data for the social scientists in the 1980s. From each of some 54,128,000 people in Britain (the preliminary count published in June 1981 (HMSO 1981a, 1981b)) came eight to fifteen primary answers. There were six further answers in respect of every household. Further attributes are created from the primary answers, and the basic computer files from which statistics are drawn contain in excess of 2500 million items of information. This information is summarized in the pages of tables in published volumes, but many more statistical abstracts are available in machine readable form; for example, for each of some 130,000 small areas in Britain around 4400 statistical counts will be available.

The aim of this section of the handbook, as is the aim of this handbook as a whole, is to give the census user some understanding of this vast data resource, so that it can be used in an effective and efficient way, and to do this without the user losing sight of research objectives.

Here we explain the unique characteristics of a census and show how the 1981 Census was shaped. Chapter 1 looked briefly at the history of census taking. This section begins by looking in more detail at what happened in the years from 1976 to 1980 when the strategy for the 1981 Census was worked out and its topics chosen. It explains the relationships between fieldwork, processing and statistical output. The way census statistics are presented in cross-tabulations is described, and there is additional information on the geographical basis of the census.

The chapter follows the sequence of events as a census is planned, taken, processed and the results disseminated. It does not deal with the field operation at any length – a complex subject in its own right – but does contain an outline

---

Chris Denham is employed in the Census Division of the Office of Population Censuses and Surveys. The views expressed in this chapter are the author's and do not necessarily represent those of OPCS.

of the topics covered in the 1981 census form. Further discussion of some of the topics occurs in Chapter 3. All this is designed to give the reader an understanding of the background of the census as a whole. But, in particular, it aims to give an understanding of the basic statistical source covered in this handbook – the 1981 Small Area Statistics (SAS) – which is available for the smallest building bricks, as well as for local-authority areas, and as regional and national summaries.

A proportion of the material in this section has been published elsewhere, though in rather diverse sources, and the authors have taken the opportunity to bring it together and make it as up-to-date as possible. The original sources are given in the references to the section, and, where not written by one of the authors, the editor is grateful for being able to draw from these sources.

2.2 Planning the 1981 Census of Population

2.2.1 GENERAL CONSIDERATIONS

The following paragraphs describe the background to modern census-taking and outline the broad range of preparations that were made for the 1981 Census (Census Division 1977, Redfern 1981a).

The census of population is the most important single source of information about the number and condition of the people. The unique value of the statistics from the census arises from: the completeness of coverage because the census is compulsory; the continuity of statistics from census to census, which allows long term changes to be measured; the possibilities of inter-relating various characteristics of the population; the details given by the census about small populations, either in local areas or in minorities through the country; and the comparability of the statistics across the whole country.

A modern census is an elaborate and costly exercise. In 1981, it required some 115,000 enumerators to deliver and collect the census forms from every household in Britain; and it needs complex computing facilities to process the results. The total cost of the 1981 Census will be around £50 million at 1981 Public Expenditure Survey prices. A census is very much a cyclical activity with a 'sharp peak' in the field work and a 'broader plateau' in the subsequent processing. The preliminary planning of a census takes time. Well before the 1971 Census was completely processed, thought was being given to the (later cancelled) 1976 Census and then to the 1981 Census. Consultation took place with public and private bodies to find out their needs for census statistics. Voluntary tests were made in a sample of areas both to improve field procedures and to find out about public response to different questions and wording. Parliament and the public at large had to be given sufficient time to discuss the census proposals and the organization and machinery for processing the census results had to be set up in working order to receive the completed forms from the field.

Throughout the planning of the 1981 Census, and its execution, two requirements were for respect of individual privacy and protection of confidentiality. The questions in the census had to be seen by the public as relevant and proper for inclusion in a compulsory enquiry, and the answers could be made available outside the Census Offices *only in statistical form*. Field procedures were devised accordingly, data on census forms and magnetic tape made secure and steps taken to reduce to a minimum the possibility of the statistical output revealing information about identifiable individuals. The success of the census depended on public confidence, and privacy and confidentiality being seen to be properly safeguarded: it seems that the 1981 Census succeeded in this respect.

The legal basis of the census was described in Chapter 1. But, to recap, the statutory authority for the Census of Population in Britain is the *Census Act* of 1920. It lays down that the Registrar-General, under the direction of the Secretary of State for Social Services, takes the census in England and Wales; the Registrar-General for Scotland takes the census there under the direction of the Secretary of State for Scotland. Under the Act, major new legislation is not required for each census, but the approval of Parliament is required and the first Parliamentary step in taking a census is an Order in Council which specifies the topics on which questions are to be asked in the census. The Act authorizes the census to include certain topics which the Act specifies, but other topics are subject to affirmative resolution by both Houses of Parliament.

In addition, a European Community directive (73/403/EEC) required member states to make a general population count between 1 March and 31 May 1981, and directed the European Commission, in collaboration with member states, to design statistical tables of the results. Underlying this directive was the recognition that a fully harmonized Community census, with identical questionnaires and enumeration techniques, is not practicable. In fact, only some of the states took a census in 1981. France obtained an agreement to postpone until 1982 and others had no definite plans at the time of writing.

2.2.2 CONSTRAINTS ON CENSUS-TAKING

An important first step in planning the 1981 Census was to consult census users about their needs, both on topics to be included and on the form of the resulting statistics. The shape of the census obviously depended on users' needs (see Chapter 3), but it also depended heavily on the answers to three questions:

i what topics was it feasible to include in a compulsory self-enumerated census questionnaire – and here the public acceptability both of individual questions and of the questionnaire as a whole had to be taken into account;

ii how much money could be spent in taking a census; and

iii could any of the users' needs be met from other sources either more cheaply or more acceptably or more fully?

Taking the questions in turn:

i the Census Offices judged topics for questions by a number of standards: questions should be factual and easy to answer; only those questions that can be reliably answered should be included; questions that could be represented as an intrusion into people's private affairs should be avoided; and the total set of questions should not be seen as an unreasonable burden on the public;

ii the need for economy in such an expensive operation is obvious. The field cost – of placing an enumerator on every doorstep, first to list his or her points of delivery, then to deliver the questionnaires and later to collect them – is a large and relatively inelastic overhead. But processing costs are more elastic and depend on the depth of analysis and the speed with which results are to be produced. The faster a given set of results is produced, the more costly it can be, because, for example, halving the time can require more than twice the number of clerical staff when allowance is made for learning time;

iii the census is the only means of taking complete stock of the number of people and in the past it was almost the only means of measuring the condition of the people. It is complemented by figures of registrations of births and deaths; these help in carrying forward numbers from the date of the most recent census and also provide information in some depth on two important components of change – fertility and mortality – but rather little on the third – migration. It is also complemented by sample surveys and might in future be complemented by local annual headcounts by extending the annual canvass for the electoral register, but, for the time being, the Government has decided against this (Manners and Rauta 1981, OPCS 1981a).

Since the 1940s, there has been increasing use of voluntary interview surveys addressed to samples of the population as a means of obtaining national statistics. Such surveys can cover more detailed and sensitive matters than the census and can be repeated at different points of time or can be carried out continuously as is the General Household Survey. But even a very large survey, like the Labour Force Survey (OPCS 1982a) carried out on behalf of the European Community in which some 100,000 households are approached in the course of a month, cannot provide reliable statistics for areas smaller than regions. Because statistics are required for local authority districts or for even smaller areas (as on housing and economic activity) or for quite small groups of the population (as on highly qualified manpower), the opportunity to offload census topics to sample surveys is limited. Nevertheless, voluntary sample surveys complement the census in the topics they can handle and in their timing. However, at the time of writing, the Government is considering economies in social surveys, particularly in reducing *ad hoc* surveys.

2.2.3 TOPIC CONTENT OF THE 1981 CENSUS

In 1978, the Census Offices proposed that the questionnaire for 1981 should be the same for all households. A number of the questions were to be asked as multiple choices (with tick boxes provided) to ease the job of form filling. Proposals included the following topics: basic population information (age, sex and marital condition); migration (address one year before census); country of birth, nationality, and, in England and Wales at least, ethnic group; economic activity (including details of occupation, place of work and mode of travel to work); and educational and professional qualifications. The composition of families and households would be covered, as would the accommodation occupied by households (tenure, number of rooms, amenities and sharing with other households). Nearly all these proposals materialized in the final census.

The major exception was a direct question on each person's ethnic group, which would have replaced the 1971 question on the countries of birth of each person's parents. Questions tested for the 1981 Census asked each person to identify himself or herself with one of a pre-listed set of ethnic groups. This approach was expected to yield a better measure of ethnicity than reliance on information on country of birth and parents' countries of birth, because by 1981 there were many more members of ethnic minorities themselves born in Britain and having parents also born in Britain. In the event, results of test censuses and public opposition led to its removal.

2.2.4 FIELD PLANNING AND TESTS

Recent censuses have been preceded by field tests of various kinds in the years leading up to the census. All these tests are voluntary. For the 1981 Census there were, first, specialized small-scale tests of enumeration procedures to make them more acceptable and less taxing for the public, and to improve efficiency. Second, there were sample surveys in which trained interviewers from Social Survey Division of OPCS delivered census-style forms to households as though in a census enumeration, but asked if they might return for an interview to check the correctness of the answers given on the forms, to discuss difficulties, and to record the respondents' opinions. Such tests are designed to improve the wording of questions, so as to make questions more acceptable to the public and to increase the accuracy of response. Third was a fairly large-scale rehearsal – that is a test conducted among all households over quite a wide area – to test all aspects of the proposed census including the field operations and public reactions; follow-up surveys checked the accuracy of the information collected.

After the census itself was taken, a voluntary interview survey was made of a sample of households to assess the reliability of the answers that they gave on the census form. Checks were also made to see whether households had been missed during the enumeration. Results of these checks will be published, either in 1982 or 1983, but are only significant at a national level and, in some cases, at regional level.

A major task in planning a census is to divide the country into enumeration districts (EDs), each of which is made the responsibility of one enumerator. Local authorities were invited to give their views on the boundaries of EDs to ensure that they corresponded, where practicable, with areas which are significant for local planning. In Scotland, EDs were defined in terms of postcodes, so different arrangements applied there. Section 2.5.4 describes the planning of EDs in more detail.

2.2.5 PLANNING THE PROCESSING OF RESULTS

The volume of statistics produced from the 1971 Census was some three times that from the 1961 Census, and output on the 1981 Census could have been bigger still. Regrettably the timetable promised for the 1971 results was not met, though nearly all the standard published results from the 1971 Census came out earlier than they had from either the 1961 or 1951 Censuses. The main reasons for the delay in 1971 in meeting the requests for tabulations were lateness in agreeing with users what results they wanted and the willingness of the Census Offices to accept greater demands than eventually the system could meet. As a consequence, the planning of processing for the 1981 Census began early. The Census Offices aimed to settle the specification of results early so that they could issue some tables for all counties before the end of 1982 and all the main results within three years of census day. They also aimed to reduce the bulk and complexity of the published output.

It was planned that the main results should consist, as previously, of a set of published reports which would be laid before Parliament and an abbreviated set of statistics for smaller areas down to enumeration districts (the Small Area Statistics described fully in section 2.9). Just as users helped in the design of the Small Area Statistics for previous censuses, in 1978 the Census Offices held a series of well-attended regional meetings for potential users of the 1981 SAS. There was a further round of consultation in 1979 and it was decided to use the SAS as the basis for all local statistics. There is also a continuing aim to issue a number of simple summaries and explanatory guides for a wider public.

The services by which special tables of less general interest can be requested and paid for by users were continued. But, by rearranging the way in which the census data are held and by use of standard programs, the Census Offices have aimed to provide a more flexible and timely service for handling *ad hoc* requests for census statistics. The intention has been to avoid asking customers to specify tables too far ahead because then they might be tempted to ask for every conceivable cross-tabulation that just might prove useful. The 1981 processing system is described more fully in section 2.4.

Thus, the main aims in planning the 1981 Census were to make it straightforward, acceptable to the public and within the capacity of the Census Offices to handle it expeditiously. The results of the census had to be timely if they were to be as useful as they ought to be, and provide the information needed for making informed judgements and for efficient management.

2.3 The census questions

2.3.1 THE POPULATION BASE

People are counted, or enumerated, by the census in their home (or someone else's home) at a fixed time: in 1981 this was at midnight on Sunday 5 April. The household is the unit to which the census form relates. This was defined as

> A household comprises either one person living alone or a group of persons (who may or may not be related) living at the same address with common housekeeping.

The form (see appendix 1) asked for information about each member of the household and anyone else present. But it also sought information concerning the household as a unit and every census in Britain since the very first in 1801 has been essentially a census of population and of housing. People in institutions and communal establishments of one sort or another – schools, hospitals, hotels and hostels, for example – are asked for the same information as household members.

The definition of a household used in the British census implies that more than one household may occupy one structurally separate housing unit, for example, a large house that has not been fully converted into self-contained flats. The existence of three statistical units, hierarchically arranged – the housing unit, the household and the person – complicates the field work of the census in many areas because the enumerator has to make the enquiries necessary to distinguish all the households in a multi-occupied dwelling and has to obtain a return from each. It also impedes the introduction of techniques such as sending out forms by mail and sampling in the field.

There are two ways of making sure everyone is counted. The first is to ask each household to enter on the form everyone who spends census night at the address in question, no matter where a person usually lives; similarly to include everyone present in an establishment. Any person usually resident at the address but absent on census night is omitted. This method has the merit of collecting information about persons, who, by their presence, may be able to give accurate details direct to the form-filler.

Alternatively, each household is asked to enter on the form everyone who usually lives at the address, irrespective of whether present at, or absent from, the address on census night. Thus, a visitor who usually lives elsewhere is omitted unless there is someone else present at his or her address to make a return. In general, there is more interest by census users in the population usually resident in an area (the *de jure* population) than in the population that happens to be there on a particular night (the *de facto* population). Each form records the usual composition of the household and this is likely to present a more realistic picture – for such purposes as housing needs – than a form recording the composition at a chance moment of time (census night). But there may be difficulties: it may not be clear in some cases where a person's 'usual residence' is, and so there may be uncertainty about who to enter on the census form. Indeed, in Britain a person's 'usual residence' is not, as a rule, formally determined.

However, if the householder is asked to enter on the form everyone who spends census night at the address in question and is also asked a question about each person's place of usual residence, it is possible to redistribute the persons entered on the form to their areas of usual residence, and so to compile statistics of the usually resident population of each area. But, whilst it is practicable for statistical purposes to redistribute people to their *areas* of usual residence, it is impracticable to redistribute them to the *individual households* where they usually live in order to compile statistics about the usual composition of households. So, beginning with the 1961 Census (though in 1961 only on the long form issued to one household in ten), Britain has attempted to get the best of both approaches by asking households to enter on the form everyone present at the address on census night plus anyone usually resident there but absent on census night. This approach requires two additional questions on the form: was the person present or absent on census night and what was the person's usual address? It then becomes possible to measure the population usually resident in an area by two alternative methods: first, by transferring the data for visitors back to their home areas; and second, by counting the people recorded on forms as 'usually resident here'. In fact, the two methods do not, even in principle, lead to the same results for some categories of person. For example, a member of a household absent abroad on census night is missed by the transfer method, while a complete household absent from home (whether within Britain or abroad) on census night is missed by the count of people recorded as 'usually resident here'. In 1971 only, an attempt was made to collect a form for persons usually resident at addresses where no one was actually present on census night. This was only partially successful and was not repeated in 1981.

For the 1981 Census in Britain, there are tables referring to the usually resident population which are based on the method of transferring visitors back to their home areas, and the official population estimates for local-authority districts adopt this approach. But the large majority of tables referring to the usually resident population will count those recorded on forms as 'usually resident here': these include all tables on household composition and housing, together with all tables in the county reports, and in the SAS.

2.3.2 THE SCOPE OF THE CENSUS

Section 2.2 looks at what determines the topics appearing on the census form. In summary, the starting points are the demands of the users of census statistics inside and outside government. But census questions must conform to firm criteria: they must be objective and capable of being readily and reliably answered by people in all walks of life; they must be acceptable to the great bulk of the public; and the total set of questions must not be seen by the public as an unreasonable burden or an intrusion of privacy. The whole form and the methods of enumeration must be robust. Cost is another factor constraining the topic content. Though additional simple questions have only a marginal effect on the field costs and can usually be accommodated in the processing system, additional complex questions may give rise to unjustifiable costs.

In the 1981 Census every household was given essentially the same form to complete. The form in England contained sixteen questions about each individual and five about the household as a whole. In Wales, there was an extra question on the Welsh language and in Scotland an extra question on the Gaelic language. (Any question answered by the enumerator, for example about the nature of the accommodation – whether a house, flat or caravan, is omitted from this count.)

Table 2.1 shows how the number of questions has varied from census to census in England over the past fifty years. The table is based on the

Table 2.1 Number of questions answered by the public in England, distinguishing questions relating to the household and questions relating to the individual person: 1931–81

	1931	*1951*	*1961**	*1966***	*1971*	*1981*
Standard or long form:						
Household	1	2	4	5	5	5
Person	11	16	21	23	25	16
Total	12	18	25	28	30	21
Short form:						
Household			4			
Person			10			
Total			14			

* The long form was addressed to 1 in 10 households, the short form to the rest.
** A sample census was taken, addressed to 1 in 10 households.

numbering of the questions on the forms, but sometimes one question has contained several sub-questions and sometimes a separately numbered question in one census may correspond to only a sub-question in another census. Moreover, not every question applies to every person, so that the number of questions on the form may overstate the burden of form-filling. The numbers of questions asked in Britain grew steadily from 1951 to 1971, as new questions were introduced or existing questions elaborated, reflecting a period of widening government activity, particularly the planning of industry, housing, health and education and the period of growth of computer methods to handle and analyse the data. The single question in 1931 referring to the household (a question on the number of rooms) had become five questions by 1971, and the eleven questions in 1931 referring to individual persons had become twenty-five by 1971.

A change in the trend occurred before the 1981 Census. Omission from the census of several topics on which questions were asked previously reduced the number of questions referring to individual persons to sixteen compared with the twenty-five in the 1971 Census. Among topics covered in 1971 but not in 1981 were: address five years ago (five-year migration); occupation one year ago; parents' countries of birth; and the 'fertility' questions that were addressed to married, widowed or divorced women about date of marriage and the date of birth of their children. This diminution in the number of questions in 1981 was the result of changing data needs and the need to design a form that, in terms of both size and topics, had general public acceptability. The cuts in public expenditure required contractions in the census; and the development of sample surveys provided alternative sources for certain topics at a national level (the GHS was first taken in 1970 and the LFS in 1973). The result of this pruning was to give Britain forms which were notably shorter than those of the other countries; the British forms, for instance, contain only about one third of the number of questions in the long form in the 1980 US Census.

2.3.3 THE 1981 QUESTIONS

The great majority of information in the 1981 Census comes from questions answered by the householder. In addition, however, the enumerator in England and Wales categorized the household's accommodation as one of the following: (i) a caravan; (ii) other mobile or temporary structure; (iii) a flat or maisonette in a purpose-built block; or (iv) other permanent building. In case (iv). the enumerator recorded whether the entrance from *outside* the building was shared with another household; and, if it was shared, the householder recorded whether the rooms occupied by the household were enclosed behind their own front door *inside* the building. These answers provided limited information about the occupation of a dwelling by more than one household and about shared accommodation. The enumerator also recorded some information about accommodation where a household was absent and about vacant accommodation.

In Scotland, the enumerator collected some additional facts about permanent housing. Houses were divided into three categories (detached, semi-detached, terraced) and flats were categorized by the number of storeys in the building. In addition, the enumerators in Scotland recorded information on the level of the household's accommodation (for example, 'all of the first or higher floor, entry on first floor') and the means of access ('lift', 'external stair' or 'internal stair'). These additional questions reflected the significant proportion of households in high-rise blocks in Scotland and concern about certain types of people and households living in such accommodation.

The facsimiles of the 1981 census forms reproduced in appendix 1 show how the census topics look as questions on the census forms. Nearly all topics appeared in previous censuses, but the questions were re-designed.

Although every individual question is an important source of statistical information in its own right, they cannot be seen in isolation from other questions. Much information is derived from answers to more than one question; for example, social class is derived from answers on employment status and occupations. Cross-analyses of statistics from several topics will also produce additional information; for example, statistics about the internal migration of people with particular skills and qualifications would be based on the answers to questions 7, 8, 12 and 16.

2.3.3.1 Questions about persons

(Number on census form and short title of question is given in each case)

1 Name and surname

Names were on the census form for the following reasons:

- i to distinguish the persons entered on the form, so helping the householder to complete it accurately;
- ii to enable census staff to apply to the right person when information on the census form is missing; and
- iii to establish whether householders and others have discharged their legal obligation to provide all the information asked for on the census form.

Names and addresses are not entered in the computer records. They remain on the original returns, and are kept under strict security until released for public inspection at the Public Record Office after 100 years: then they may be used for genealogical and historical research.

2 Sex

Very many census statistics are given separately for men and women. Answers to the questions on sex and marital status also provide the means of structuring households and families.

3 Date of birth (day, month and year)

The question asked for date of birth rather than age because tests have shown that the former gives better answers except, perhaps, for the very elderly. Measures of age in the population provide essential benchmarks for central and local administration (see Chapter 3). Figures are used, for example:

- i for resource allocation schemes such as the grants to local authorities and the corresponding scheme for the health services;
- ii for making national and local population projections, on which plans for many of the social services are based;
- iii for estimating the future income and expenditure of the social security system; and
- iv for the construction of national life tables, also used by insurance companies.

4 Marital status

The question asked whether a person fell into one of three non-married categories (single, widowed and divorced) or the married category to which the separate category 're-married' was added in 1981 to measure a growing and important social phenomenon and its implications for family building patterns. The answers provide basic knowledge about the structure of households and families, including the various categories of one-parent families. They also yield figures that contribute to the calculation of rates of marriage, divorce, re-marriage and fertility, and economic activity rates for single and married women.

Questions on *marital and fertility history* first appeared in a British census in 1911 and re-appeared with variations in three post-war censuses – 1951, 1961 and 1971. The questions about births were restricted to births occurring within marriage. All these questions were dropped from the 1981 Census. Monitoring of socioeconomic differentials in fertility will now depend more heavily on voluntary sample surveys such as the GHS and special surveys on family formation, and on the OPCS Longitudinal Study. Analysis of the 1981 Census material on household composition will, however, provide some detail on the fertility of younger women in recent years because young children will usually be recorded on the same census form as their mothers; but this approach will not provide a reliable record of the total fertility of older women (some of whose children may no longer be living with their mothers or children may have died), nor of remarried women (within whose households there may be stepchildren).

5 Relationship in household

The question asked for the relationship of each person to the first person on the form, thus families of various types can be recognized, as can those households containing more than one family and those containing none. Statistics on the numbers of families are used particularly by local social services. Information about the types of family in an area (for example, the frequency of one-parent families) is used in calculating grants to local authorities.

6 Whereabouts on night of 5–6 April 1981
and
7 Usual address

These questions were needed to count the many people who were away from home on census night – on business, on holiday or at school or college. The census form asked for a return of people who were usually resident at the address and were present there on census night, of people usually resident there but absent on census night and also of visitors. For some purposes, statistics of the people actually present in an area on census night are used; many other statistics are based on those usually resident in the area (the different bases have been described in section 2.3.1). The basic population counts used for grants to local government and resource allocation in the Health Service are the numbers usually resident in an area. Some of the other figures used in the calculation of grants for local government (for example, one-parent families, pensioners living alone and persons per room) can only be obtained by considering everyone returned as usually resident at this address (tick-box of question 7) regardless of where they were on census night.

Migration

Answers to the census question on a person's place of birth give information on migration between the countries of the UK and into the UK in terms of the accumulated surviving migrants from various countries. Migration during a *fixed* period of years preceding the census first appeared as a topic in a British census in 1961. This reflected the demand from demographers, geographers and regional and local planners for information on a key component in population change. In the censuses in Britain in 1966 and 1971, questions on each person's usual address one year before the census and on his or her usual address five years before the census were asked, but in 1981 only the question on the usual address one year before was asked.

8 Usual address one year ago

This question provides complete information on the net result of all population movements within the country within the year preceding the census (less any migrants not surviving to the end of the year, or migrating then leaving the country). The census is the only source of such information where social and economic characteristics of the migrants are also known, and the only source of complete migration statistics for local areas such as the inner cities. In a mobile society, local authorities regard information on the numbers and characteristics of migrants as essential for their policies on housing, employment, the elderly and the overseas-born. The statistics are also used by OPCS in the preparation of the annual estimates of population, which in turn are then used for resource allocation and in population projections for local areas.

9 Country of birth

The country of birth question provides statistics on the numbers of people who were born in the various countries of the UK or overseas, and thus identifies areas where there are concentrations of people with particular birthplaces. Certain tables also give the number of people and their characteristics in households headed by people born in the UK or overseas, and this may help to make estimates of the number of people, for example, of New Commonwealth origin.

A question on nationality or citizenship of persons not born in this country appeared in some form in every census from 1851 to 1961. There were, however, particular difficulties in the term 'British citizen' for many persons born in present and former parts of the British Commonwealth and in Ireland. Though the White Paper *1981 Census of Population* (HMSO 1978a) proposed that such a question should be re-introduced in 1981, it was omitted from the census.

In the same White Paper, the Government saw a need for authoritative and reliable information about ethnic minorities in Britain and stated its belief that a question on race or ethnic origin should be asked in the 1981 Census, at least in England and Wales. But a final decision on the question to be asked was deferred until the Registrars-General had reported on the reliability and acceptability of possible forms of a direct question on ethnic origin. A series of tests of questions was made, both before and after the publication of the White Paper, culminating in a major test of the whole census form and census procedures in Haringey in the northern part of inner London in April 1979. In Haringey, both a direct ethnic question and a question on parents' countries of birth (as used in the 1971 Census) were tested. In the event, there was considerable opposition from some members of the ethnic minorities in the test area to both of these questions, as well as to the test questions on nationality and year of entry to the UK. There was also a keen debate among representatives of the ethnic minorities and among experts in the study of minorities as to the way a question should be asked, but no consensus emerged. The Government finally concluded that it was impracticable to devise an ethnic question which would not put at risk the success of the census as a whole and hence decided that the 1981 Census would not contain any questions on ethnic origin, parents' countries of birth, nationality or year of entry to the UK. Information about ethnic minorities will be collected in the 1980s through the LFS and GHS.

Economic activity, industry, occupation and place of work

An analysis of the population in terms of the work in which they are engaged has, from the beginning, been a primary objective of the census. Five questions were asked in the 1981 Census about each person's work or economic activity.

The first sought, by means of a series of tick-boxes, to find out whether 'last week' (the reference period) each person was: in a job, seeking work, permanently sick or disabled, a housewife, retired, at school or a full-time student etc. Then, for those in a job last week, and for some others, there were questions on a person's *occupation* (the kind of work that he or she does), *industry* (the kind of business in which he or she works), *employment status* (that is, whether apprentice, employee, self-employed, etc.) and *place of work*. As an economy measure, a question on hours of work was dropped in 1981, though the distinction between a full-time job and a part-time job was retained by providing separate tick-boxes in the question on economic activity.

10 Whether working, retired, housewife etc. last week

The purpose of this question is to find out how many people of each age are in the working population, how many are potentially available for work and how many are not available because they are, for example, permanently sick or retired. The question asked for all boxes appropriate to the person's activity to be ticked and one or two answers are carried forward into the computer where the 'prime' activity is determined if necessary, but tables based on combinations of answers can also be produced. Comprehensive information about the working population is not available from any other source. The regular employment statistics collected by the Department of Employment do not cover the self-employed, and the regular unemployment statistics exclude people who are seeking work but are not registered as unemployed. Household surveys exclude people who are resident in institutions. The census figures are used by central government, local authorities and the private sector as benchmarks in conjunction with less complete but more frequently available statistics.

11 Name and business of employer
(if self-employed, the name and nature of the person's business)

and

12 Occupation

Question 11 is used to determine the industry in which a person is employed as distinct from his or her occupation (Question 12). Although the regular employment statistics give figures of the total number of employees in each industry, they do not provide any information about occupations; it is the combination of questions on industry (11) and occupation (12) which makes the information obtained from the census unique. The variety of response to these 'write-in' questions is enormous and classifications of the data obtained are complex (HMSO 1980a).

The statistics produced are an essential benchmark for all studies of occupations and hence for the estimates of social classes which are used extensively, for example, in market research and other social surveys. The answers to the question on occupation, in conjunction with answers to the question on industry, show the deployment of skilled workers. In conjunction also with answers to the question on higher qualifications, they show the deployment of highly qualified people.

13 Employment status

This question is the only source for figures of the total number of self-employed persons and so provides a benchmark for the total working population. The Department of Employment's statistics do not cover the self-employed and the Inland Revenue statistics cover only those who are liable to tax. The Department of Employment, for example, needs periodic census information about the self-employed for the analysis of changes in the labour force; this, in turn, helps in understanding changes in the level of unemployment. The question provides the only complete count of apprentices required, for example, by the Manpower Services Commission for assessing the training needs in skilled occupations.

14 Address of place of work

This question provides the 'day-time' workforce population of an area. Statistics can be provided for quite small and flexibly defined geographical areas; section 2.6.8.1 gives more information. The answers to this question, in conjunction with the answers to the question on usual address, also produce data on movements between residence and workplace. These, for example, are used by the Department of Employment to define 'Travel-To-Work-Areas' (TTWAs) – the smallest areas for which unemployment rates issued by the Department of Employment are generally made available. In turn, TTWAs are used by the Department of Industry for designating assisted areas. The Manpower Services Commission uses them both in organizing its services and in giving advice on labour availability to prospective employers. Travel-to-work statistics are extensively used by local authorities and local transport authorities, especially when cross-analysed with the answers to question 15 on method of travel to work.

15 Daily journey to work

A question on means of travel was first asked in Britain in the sample census of 1966, reflecting a need to measure changing demands on urban transport systems as the use of cars grew. The question was repeated in 1971, and extended in 1981, in the case of travel by car or van, to distinguish between travel as a driver, travel as a passenger and travel as a member of a car pool.

The information on mode of travel is used essentially in conjunction with the information on movements produced from question 14. The split between journeys by different modes, and changes in volume and direction, have an obvious impact on the provisions that need to be made. Widespread information is collected by the Department of Transport and local authorities in various travel surveys and traffic 'censuses', but these cannot provide the comprehensive range of associated variables or the synchroneity available from the census nor are the data from surveys necessarily made available. So such surveys provide quick and frequent information whilst the census provides the 'benchmark' information.

Education

Questions on educational attainments were introduced in Britain in 1951. In that year, and again in 1961, the question asked the age at which full-time education ended. In 1961, a second question asked for details of a person's qualifications at university-degree level in science and technology (including graduate or corporate membership of professional institutions). By the time of the sample census in 1966, the question on terminal educational age had been dropped and the question on higher qualifications had been extended to include all degrees, diplomas, associateships or other professional or vocational qualifications obtained after the age of eighteen; it was thus no longer restricted to subjects in science and technology and the minimum level had been lowered to include qualifications such as HNC and HND. This question has been repeated essentially unchanged in 1971 and 1981. In 1971, it was complemented by a question that asked whether the person had obtained specified school-level qualifications (GCE 'A' level, Higher School Certificate, equivalent Scottish qualifications, OND and ONC), but this question was dropped in 1981 as an economy measure.

16 Degrees, professional and vocational qualifications

Question 16, in conjunction with questions on economic activity, measures the country's stock of qualified people and shows the industries and occupations in which they are employed or whether they are not employed. The census is the only source for such statistics. Experience has shown that, to obtain usable information, it is necessary to ask for the qualifications to be shown individually, because of their great range and diversity. The question is an example of the use of the census to measure a dispersed minority population, difficult to survey specifically by other means. Interest is at a national rather than local level, thus the major part of the analyses are at national level, and the subject is not even included in the 1981 County Report tables – the only topic not covered in these Reports – though a limited table on qualifications is included in the SAS.

Language

Questions on languages in British censuses have been confined to a question asked only in Wales on the Welsh language and a question asked only in Scotland on the Gaelic language; such questions have appeared in every decennial census since 1891. The answers to the questions are used to measure current use of – and hence changes in – the languages in different parts of the Principality and in the Scottish highlands and islands.

2.3.3.2 *Questions relating to the household*

The questions addressed to the household as a whole referred to the accommodation it occupied, with the exception of the number of cars and vans available to the household. The number of questions on household amenities was less than in previous censuses, though more types of tenure were identified than previously.

H1 Rooms

In conjunction with the number of persons in a household, a count of rooms gives the number of persons per room and so measures overcrowding and under-occupancy. The measures of overcrowding are used in calculating grants for local authorities, and are also used in defining areas for special action, especially within the inner city.

H2 Tenure

Comparison of figures of tenure from the 1971 and 1981 Censuses will, for example, show national and local trends in owner-occupation and in the amount of furnished and unfurnished accommodation rented from private landlords: this last will throw light on the effects of legislative changes. Tenure is also a key variable in socioeconomic classifications of areas, and in multivariate counts acts as a 'crude' proxy for socioeconomic types.

H3 Amenities

The 1981 question was confined to the key household amenities of a fixed bath or shower, an inside WC and whether a household had exclusive use, shared use or lacked use. The answers to the third part of the question (on outside WCs) – included to ensure better answers to the previous part of the question – will not be used extensively in tabulations. The statistics produced will provide a measure of inadequate housing and show where it is concentrated. The results will be used to identify areas for improvement under Housing Action Area and General Improvement Area powers. They will also be used for grant calculations, and in defining areas for special action.

H4 Nature of accommodation and sharing

Enumerators entered on each census form whether a household's accommodation was in a permanent building, a caravan or any other mobile or temporary structure. If it was a permanent building, the enumerator recorded whether it was a purpose-built flat or maisonette or, if not, whether the entrance to the household's accommodation from outside the building was shared with any other household. (The householder had the opportunity, if he or she wished, of amending the enumerator's entries on the form.) Estimates of numbers of dwellings depend on the information on sharing. Also, sharing of accommodation by two or more households is a pointer to inadequate housing and overcrowding, and hence to potential housing demand.

H5 Cars and vans

The census is the only source of statistics on car availability in households and is a particularly valuable source at small-area level. The uses of the statistics are many, though the question was only finally included in the 1981 Census after amendment to the Census Order was proposed in Parliament after being dropped from the Government's earlier proposals. Among its uses are the definition of areas with low car ownership and hence which have a greater need of public transport. Additionally, answers to the question on car availability, in conjunction with answers to the question on daily journey to work, yield important evidence on how many people who have a car choose other modes of transport for travelling to work. The level of car ownership is also an element in deciding where such services as shops, health and welfare facilities may be sited.

2.4 Producing the results

2.4.1 MEETING USER NEEDS

The 1978 White Paper (HMSO 1978) on the 1981 Census provided the starting point for planning the production of results. It was published nearly three years before census day to allow time for public discussion and because the Government believed that, to plan the census properly, it was important that firm instructions should be given early to the census planners. The Government was determined that delays like those experienced in the processing of output from the 1971 Census should be avoided.

In Section V of the White Paper the Government set out their policy for the results of the census:

> The Government recognize that the longer it takes to publish the results of the census the less useful they are. Owing largely to delays in making decisions about the census and to the unprecedented volume of demand for output, it took longer than expected to complete the publication of the results from the 1971 Census. The Government intend to publish the results of the 1981 Census quicker, so far as resources permit. Procedures will be simplified and automated where practicable. Statistics for some topics which are expensive to process will be produced using only a sample of the answers where this will provide statistically satisfactory results.

The Census Offices planned the quicker and more efficient production of results by revising their approach to the design of output and by changes in the processing system, as well as through earlier planning. In particular, the specification of tables came later in the design process, with more scope for specifying tables at short notice after the census.

As each stage of design proceeded, the Census Offices consulted census users inside and outside central government; documents were circulated to government departments and to the Census Advisory Committees (OPCS 1978/1), and were publicized in the Census Monitors. Users were then able to react, if they wished, before the next stage of planning commenced.

The results of a census fall into two groups defined by Section 4 of the 1920 Census Act. First, under Section 4(1), results are published as printed reports laid before Parliament. These *published* results are available to a general readership at a cost covering printing and distribution. Second, under Section 4(2), the Registrar-General is permitted to prepare, at the request and cost of any local authority or person, *abstracts* containing statistical information not contained in the published reports and which in his opinion it is reasonable for the local authority or person to require. These are sometimes termed the 'unpublished' results, though most of these results are widely available and thus the term is somewhat misleading and is not used here. The latter results are of two types: standard output, such as the SAS, which is requested by a number of users; and special output which, in the first instance, is requested by a single user.

Reports to Parliament are given priority of output. Their content is not set out in census legislation; but clearly the reports must contain a broad range of information of public interest from the topics that Parliament has approved in the Census Order. Their design must secure satisfactory continuity with previous censuses, yet fit the needs of the times (see sections 2.6.1 and 2.6.2).

2.4.2 PROCESSING THE CENSUS FORMS: CREATION OF DATA FILES

Few census users would suggest that their own demands did not have high priority. Nevertheless, as the following paragraphs explain, the processing of some eighteen million census forms can only be done serially. Thus it is important for an understanding of census output to distinguish those results that can begin to be produced soon after the first census forms have been processed from those results that must be drawn later from national files.

Little of the output from the 1981 Census is not produced by the main processing system. The preliminary reports (HMSO 1981a, 1981b) contained, as previously, counts of persons and intercensal comparisons (see section 2.6.1). They were produced from returns made by census field staff. But in 1981 the Census Offices did not produce any estimates based on early small samples or alternative input systems; thus there was no delay to the main processing and no output of conflicting sets of figures.

In the main processing system, census forms are handled in batches, county by county. For each county in England and Wales a validated basic data file on magnetic tape is created; in Scotland these files are created for regions. Some topics are processed on a 10 per cent sample only following the processing of other topics (see list in section 2.6.2). First results are derived from the county/region files and are published and distributed when they become available. For national results all the county/ region files are brought together and, for the production of most output, further files are created selectively.

In processing operations, the time taken to create a fully validated file has two components: first, the system time and, second, the processing time. The forms for an ED and the data from the forms for the ED are always handled together as a batch during processing, and the system time is the time taken by one ED to pass through all of the many stages of processing: a number of coding sections; checking; keying and verification; and data validation and correction cycles. It is thus analogous to the time taken by a single car to pass down an assembly line. Although the system time is affected by the volume of the data that is presented on the census forms, once the design is settled, the system time is essentially constant and is not affected by staffing levels.

In contrast, the processing time is the time taken by all the items being processed (whether 100 per cent or 10 per cent) to pass a single point in the process. It is analogous to the time taken by a batch of cars to pass a single point in an assembly process. The processing time can be varied by increasing or decreasing the clerical, keying, and computing resources, but staff efficiency and computer capacity set practical limits, for example, the computer capacity available for the computer-intensive process of data validation during a two month-long period of peak demand. But, even if the computer capacity could be increased, the additional costs of reducing the processing time would be large.

So, after the first forms are opened, a period corresponding to the system time elapses before the information on them emerges on the first fully validated 100 per cent or the first fully validated 10 per cent files. After the first forms are opened, a period corresponding to the processing time elapses before the last forms are opened, but there is a further lapse of time – the system time – before the information on the last forms becomes part of the 100 per cent and 10 per cent files. In the case of the British census, the 100 per cent file will then contain between one and a half and three thousand million characters stored on forty to eighty reels of magnetic tape, depending on the degree of compression and file structure; and the 10 per cent file will contain between two and seven hundred million characters on five to twenty reels of tape.

2.4.3 VALIDATION OF THE CENSUS RESULTS AND AUTO-EDIT

Users of census statistics require guidance on the range of possible error in the basic count of population and in the counts of subpopulations within the total (for example, males aged five to nine). Errors arise because (inevitably) some people are missed entirely and some are double-counted, and because characteristics such as age and occupation are wrongly recorded, wrongly coded or wrongly key punched. As an example, failure to recognize that the people at an address constitute two households instead of one can, if repeated at all frequently, distort the distribution of household size.

A number of techniques have been developed in an attempt to measure the magnitude of these errors:

- the census processes of listing addresses and the people in them, and also recording their characteristics can be repeated for a sample of the population by an independent field force. This 're-run' must be done very soon after census day. The main drawback with this method is that shortcomings in the original census procedures may be repeated in the re-run. Results from the voluntary Post Enumeration Survey suggest that the 1981 Census under-counted the persons present on census night by 0.4 per cent (OPCS 1982a);
- the results of the census may be compared with statistics from other sources, for example, statistics of births in a period before the census or statistics of school pupils at a date near to census day. The problem in this case is to know how much of the difference between a census figure and a figure from a second source represents an error in the census, how much an error in the second source and how much differences or definitions or of timing between the two sources;
- the census material may be tested for internal consistency. For example, the OPCS Longitudinal Study (Fox and Goldblatt 1982, HMSO forthcoming, OPCS 1973) (which is based on a 1 per cent sample of persons) yielded an estimate of the number of persons counted twice in the 1971 Census in England and Wales;
- if an external source provides a list of named persons in some category, with their addresses, for a date near census day, it may be possible to match the list against the census records to check whether everyone on the list has been accurately recorded in the census. Babies born in the month or so before census day are a group to which this technique can be applied. There are problems in this approach too: failure to find a listed person in the census may arise because of movement or because of discrepancies in names or addresses either in the external list or in the census, and it may not be possible to disentangle these different causes of failure.

Checks by the enumerator, either on the doorstep or later, remedied some of the missing answers on census forms. But inevitably a proportion of census forms reached census headquarters in an unsatisfactory state and at that stage reference back to the householder was usually ruled out. Some of the omissions still remaining were dealt with by the initial clerical editing. Key-punch operator error was detected by edit checks built into the keying: the data being keyed in were continuously checked by a computer against an acceptable range of values and errors were displayed. But the system was also designed to detect omissions and inconsistencies after the data had been fed into the computer. In the 1971 Census a series of checks for validity (that is, completeness and consistency) were applied by the computer to each record, and the computer printed out details of any that failed the checks. After appropriate reference back to the original form completed by the householder, the data were corrected clerically according to empirical rules and the corrections read into the computer. This system of editing was slow and labour-intensive: over two million edit messages were printed out by the computer in respect of topics that were fully processed for all returns (that is, 100 per cent topics).

For the 1981 Census, the computer made a preliminary check on the returns for each ED taken as a whole which, if judged as a failure, was subjected to a clerical scrutiny. But, thereafter, a wholly automatic editing system was employed for some topics with the aim of speeding up the processing. In this auto-edit system an unacceptable (or missing) value of an item in a record was replaced by an acceptable value taken from a recently processed error-free record with similar demographic or other characteristics. An extended programme of testing was needed in designing the auto-edit to ensure that the results were better or not worse than would have been achieved by the 1971 system. The process applies only in the case of topics which were fully processed (i.e. at 100 per cent). In the case of the hard-to-code topics (such as occupation) which are processed only for a 10 per cent sample, computer detection and clerical correction of errors continues as in 1971; this is because of the greater complexity of the data and because, for these topics, the biggest cause of the errors is mistakes made in coding and not, as for the 100 per cent topics, mistakes made by the original form-fillers.

2.4.4 DESIGNING OUTPUT

The basic data files contain, in full, the numerical codes for each question response. Before output can be produced, the files are restructured and further codes are derived and added by computer. All output planned from the 1981 Census to date is in the form of either (rarely) aggregates of data to single counts or (normally) aggregates of data to two or more counts presented as cross-tabulations. The content of the 1981 Census output are best described in terms of the following concepts: universes, distributions, and geographical coverage.

The *universe* defines the population to be counted in a cross-tabulation, for example, 'economically active males'. In order to derive universes, each item in the original input from the census forms is given a unique number; examples would be 'single person' or 'male', since both are single attributes that can be taken directly from the forms. Universes defined in terms of the original input are usually referred to as *primary universes*. *Secondary universes* are derived either by considering successive persons or the interaction of persons and households; they are normally constructed within the computer and are added to a file before output begins. Such universes are defined by algorithms and separate universe numbers are given. Common combinations of primary universes are also given separate universe numbers and are included in the secondary universes. An example would be those 'born in the United Kingdom', that is, persons born in England plus those born in Scotland plus those born in Wales plus those born in Northern Ireland.

A *distribution* is essentially a form of classification of the data into categories or groups. To illustrate this concept, the variable of marital condition can be taken from the 1981 Census. The Census question gave five possible states: single, married (first marriage), re-married, widowed or divorced (any other written-in answers were re-coded to these categories), and these constituted the full distribution for the variable; but, for some output, modified distributions were used, for example, in the 1981 SAS a two-class distribution was used for certain tables – (i) single plus widowed plus divorced and (ii) married. A distribution defines a tabulation in a single dimension. A multi-dimensional table combines two or more distributions. Distributions are defined in terms of the universe to be included in each tabulation cell. Each distribution is identified by mnemonic, a serial number and the number of tabulation categories. The universes and distributions are defined together in a document called the Glossary.

Geographical coverage of output defines the area set for which the data are to be presented and the basis on which data are to be included. The most familiar area sets are the local authority areas from which may be built counties/Scottish regions, standard regions and the three countries of Great Britain. These and other area sets have to be defined as far as possible at an early stage in planning so that the processing units – the Enumeration Districts – can be designed to fit or nest within each area set. Data about a person can be included, for example, in the area:

- where a person is present on census night;
- where a person is usually resident;
- where a person works;
- where a person was usually resident, say, one year before the census.

It is not necessarily possible for data to be sorted on all four bases for every data set.

In summary, output was designed by: defining the universe, defining the distribution(s), and defining the geographic coverage. The Census Offices organized the design of output from the 1981 Census into the following stages:

i definition of primary universes – this involves deciding for each census question the categories to be input to the system;

ii definition of secondary universes;

iii definition of geographical coverage concurrent with the first two stages;

iv specification of those variables required to be cross-analysed – users were asked to define the maximum degree of cross-analysis required and geographical coverage;

v specification of distributions for each variable; and

vi definition of tables in terms of the universes, distributions and geographic coverage.

When stage (iii) was completed, the Census Offices designed a number of restructured national files that contain only the information for particular output. This device speeds up production of output once the files have been created. The files are shortened by the elimination of data that are not pertinent, for example, persons under sixteen from the file on economic activity.

In earlier censuses, users have been asked, more or less from the outset, to state their needs precisely enough for tables to be specified. The 1981 approach focussed at first on the data content, then on the interrelationships between data and, though output will usually be thought of in terms of cross-tabulations, users can identify a data need but leave open to a later stage the precise format for tabulations and table content.

The Census Offices provided users with definitions of the primary universes and of secondary universes as these were defined. Users then had the opportunity to define their own secondary universes, though the number of specially designed secondary universes was kept small. Output was then defined in terms of these fully documentated universes.

2.4.5 PRIORITIES

The processing system for output (other than output produced as the county/region batches are processed) is designed so that the order of production may reflect user needs rather than the technicalities of the system. The 1981 system differs radically from the 1971 system. In the latter, every effort was made to avoid duplication of steps in the creation of subsidiary data files. The system had a branching design in which problems at an early critical point could have adverse effects throughout much of the rest of the system. The 1981 system has parallel lines of processing which may involve duplication, but which operate most efficiently with economically restructured files.

OPCS, in consultation with the Department of the Environment and the Welsh Office, decided the order of processing for counties in England and Wales, and hence the production of county reports and SAS; in Scotland GRO(S) consulted with the Scottish Office. For the remaining output, published tables are generally being given precedence.

2.5 The geography of the census

2.5.1 GENERAL CONSIDERATIONS

The design of the area base is just as important as the design of questions and tabulations for effective interpretation of census results at subnational levels. In this section, we define the general characteristics of the areal bases used for the 1981 Census and explain where further details of these may be found – in particular the differences between Scotland and the rest of Britain.

The information in census tables is determined as much by the choice of the geographical base as by the choice of the characteristics or attributes to be covered in the census and the classes into which the attributes are to be divided. While a great deal of effort has gone into the design of census questions and tables in order to give results that are believed relevant to the needs of a wide range of users, restriction of the results to statutory areas (or aggregates of them) for the geographic base would mean that analysis of phenomena which are independent of this base would be impaired.

It is worth noting three important geographical criteria so far as most users are concerned:

- the geographical resolution which they require must be related to the processes they are studying; hence, studies of inner cities generally require enumeration district (ED) or, possibly, grid-square data. Openshaw and Taylor (1981) and many others have demonstrated that different results occur at different levels of geographical resolution (see Chapters 7 and 8);
- it is essential that users know through maps which area of ground is covered by each of the areas for which they have data. Though apparently self-evident, this is not always appreciated: when a complete set of ED data from the 1971 Census was obtained for academic research, an accompanying set of ED maps was not requested;
- it is also desirable that the handling of the data is within the technical capability of the user: for many users interested in a restricted set of variables, the selection of the geographical resolution has a dramatic effect upon the work involved – to use ward and postcode sector data for an analysis of all of Britain (such as those carried out at local authority, ward and ED levels by Webber and Craig, 1978), rather than those for administrative districts, would, for instance, raise the amount of computation by a factor of about twenty times.

For the obvious reason of inter-censal comparability, it is also desirable that areas for which census statistics are available should be constant through time or, alternatively, be capable of being used as building blocks to produce comparable areas, preferably of consistent size. Changes to the area base are unfortunately characteristic of censuses everywhere; they are, for many users, a further complication to the use of census data.

The geography of the census in Britain is based on some 130,000 small areas specially drawn up for each census and known as enumeration districts (EDs). These build up to the standard administrative divisions of the country, but can also be regrouped to non-standard areas. The following paragraphs briefly describe how the geographical base of the census was first established and is now planned in conjunction with census users. How continuity of census geography between the 1971 and 1981 Censuses is being achieved is also examined (see also Chapter 9).

2.5.2 AREAS FOR CENSUS REPORTS

From the first census in 1801, it has been customary to give results for statutory areas (such as counties) and other areas defined for administrative purposes (Denham 1980). These remain the main geographical base in the published census reports. However, the Census Act, 1920, makes no mention of the areas for which a census is to be reported, and the choice is left to the Registrars-General.

Census results for areas defined for statistical purposes first appeared in the Reports of the 1921 Census which gave tables for six regions; these were aggregates of existing statutory areas. A further development was the definition of five conurbations prior to the 1951 Census. The conurbations too were aggregations of existing statutory areas, the grouping being done in a way which recognized 'functional interrelationships' in large urban agglomerations. Tables of a more complex nature were provided for the large populations of these newly defined areas, but the area base remained essentially inflexible.

Statutory and administrative divisions of the country generally have a hierarchical structure. However, many divisions of the country have been made at different times, often unrelated to one another, so that several sets of areas with overlapping boundaries have been reported in each census. In 1901 and again in 1921, reports were prepared for twenty different kinds of area. Although various traditional areas such as ecclesiastical and court areas have been dropped from recent censuses, the area base for the 1971 Census was the most complex ever (Denham 1980). Some twenty-two different types of areas featured in the geographical framework of the 1971 Census – the country being broken down into several hierarchies of progressively smaller areas, ultimately related together only at the lowest level of EDs. The framework was complicated by coverage both of those areas existing before the 1974 local-government reorganization and for the new areas created by reorganization of local government in 1974 and 1975. The framework for the 1981 Census is somewhat less complex.

2.5.3 SMALL AREAS

For the 1961 Census a fundamental innovation was made in the geographical base of the statistics; simple, standard statistics were made available for wards and civil parishes and, below them, for enumeration districts (Denham 1980). This new development meant that the number of areas for which separate statistics were available increased tenfold (by the provision of wards and parish statistics) and forty to fiftyfold (by the provision of ED statistics). Thus not only were statistics for very local areas provided, but the standard statistics could be aggregated for any combination of the areas – the building brick approach. At first these statistics were known as the Ward Library, but they are now known as Small Area Statistics (SAS). The coverage of the EDs in the 1961 Ward Library was incomplete as statistics for EDs were produced only on demand, but the Ward Library from the 1966 sample Census and the SAS from the 1971 Census covered all wards, civil parishes and EDs. The 1981 SAS are described in section 2.9.

2.5.4 PLANNING ENUMERATION DISTRICTS IN ENGLAND AND WALES

EDs are both the basic area building brick for census statistics and the foundation of census fieldwork. Dividing the country into EDs and marking them on large-scale maps is a major task in planning a census (OPCS 1978/5) – there were, for instance, some 110,000 EDs in England and Wales in the 1981 Census.

Each ED is the responsibility of one enumerator who delivers and collects a form at each household within the defined area of that ED. The totality of the EDs covers the entire country without omission or overlap. Each ED represents a workload that can be performed in the time available, given the circumstances of the area. On average, the population of an ED in urban areas is about 500, the comparable figure for rural areas being about 150. Wherever possible, ED boundaries follow significant physical features such as roads and railways. Each boundary used in any of the standard geographical bases for tables must coincide with ED boundaries. In addition, however, certain other boundaries may be recognized as nearly as possible as special requirements; in the 1981 census results, these include health districts and national parks. The census forms for each ED are given a unique identification number and are handled as a unit throughout field operations and processing, so as to avoid the expense and delays of re-sorting.

Because of the importance to local authorities of the SAS for EDs and for *ad hoc* areas built from them, OPCS worked in close touch with the local authorities – at county and district level – to construct 1981 EDs which recognize areas of special local interest. An initial approach to local authorities in 1977 showed that many had specific requirements and would like to be consulted about ED planning. Most local authorities were also prepared to supply OPCS with details of new housing and of demolition since 1971 and of that expected up to 1981 – information needed to estimate

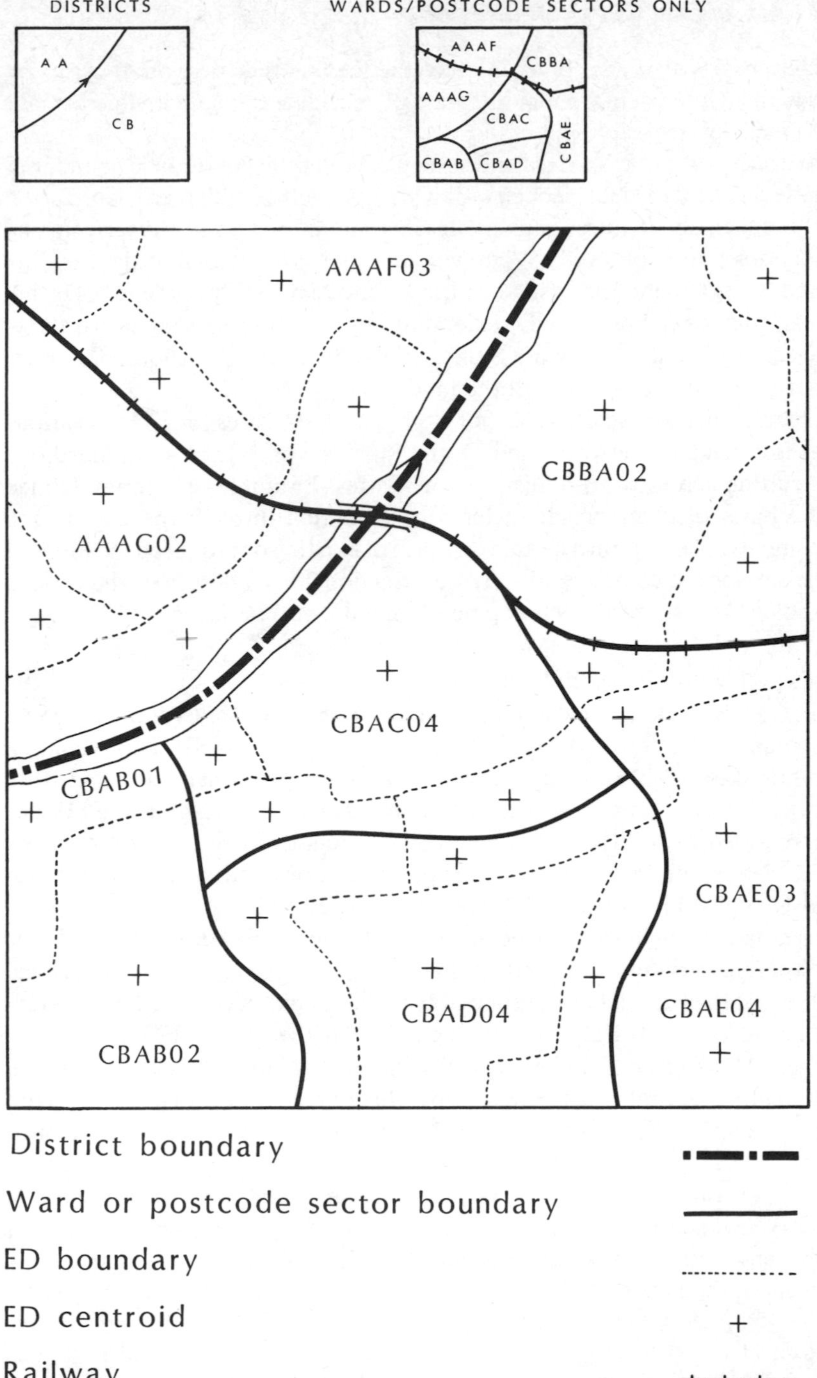

Figure 2.1 Map showing the relationship of EDs, Wards and Districts in a hypothetical area

enumerators' workloads. In addition to the local authorities, other organizations with an interest in the identification of special areas were invited to make their needs known.

Figure 2.1 is a map of EDs and shows the relationship of their boundaries with the physical landscape of an urban area, as well as with ward boundaries. Easily recognized features such as streets (centre lines), railways, rivers and watercourses are followed. Wherever possible, blocks of housing are not divided by ED boundaries and are grouped into reasonably compact EDs, but the map shows examples of EDs extending beyond compact shapes in order to make up sufficient workloads. Some EDs extend over considerable areas, even if unpopulated, so that all the land area is covered.

The map also shows the scope for aggregating statistics for EDs to various zones intermediate between the ED and the ward or district – or indeed to a zone cutting across ward or district boundaries. Examples are zones defined on the basis of common characteristics identified through the census and 'catchment' zones within a certain distance of existing or proposed locations of public services or commercial activities. Section 2.9.10 describes the various maps of EDs and wards that can be obtained from the Census Offices.

2.5.4.1 Continuity of EDs through time

When OPCS wrote to local authorities in England and Wales about the 1981 EDs, many asked for the 1971 EDs to be used again in 1981. This would, of course, make possible a straightforward comparison between 1971 and 1981 statistics for these areas. As far as possible, 1971 EDs in England and Wales were retained for 1981. But, after taking account of revisions to statutory boundaries, shifts in the distribution of population, and users' requests for changes, only 44 per cent of EDs were unchanged from 1971; the proportion varies greatly from locality to locality (see Chapter 9). Where ED boundaries were altered, every effort was made to give 1971–81 comparability at the local level so that the boundary of a group of 1981 EDs coincided with the boundary of a group of 1971 EDs even though, within the group, ED boundaries changed. Unchanged EDs are typically found in relatively stable residential areas, including rural areas. EDs comparable only at group level are found on the developing outskirts of towns, or in areas which have been redeveloped between the two censuses. In some cases, the strictly comparable areas may contain several thousand households. However, some of the slight shifts in statutory boundaries, and consequential shifts in ED boundaries, do not involve any transfer of population. So some EDs comparable only as groups could safely be subdivided on the basis of local knowledge.

2.5.4.2 Census tracts

During 1981 arrangements were made for OPCS to draw up small areas consistent between the 1971 and 1981 Censuses for use by the Department of the Environment and for the results to be made available to other census users. All areas which do not form part of a civil parish (or community in Wales) will be covered. The main work was completed in April 1982. A related exercise has been carried out on the comparability of civil parishes. A different approach operates in Scotland (see section 2.5.5.2).

The comparable areas, known as *census tracts*, are defined in terms of 1971 and 1981 EDs. Each tract comprises one or more EDs from each census. Individual EDs unchanged between the censuses are included as tracts. A tract has a centroid (the grid reference centroid of one 1981 ED within the tract) and a tract identifier (that of one of the 1981 EDs within the tract). This information is recorded on punching documents, and the boundaries of the tracts with their identifiers drawn on transparent overlays of the OS 1:10,000 scale map sheets. A batch of punching documents has been produced for each local government district. These carry 1981 Census county and district codes and district name, as well as, for each tract, the tract identifier, grid reference of the centroid to 100 m resolution, 1981 ED number(s) and 1971 Census District (CD) and ED number(s).

OPCS Census Customer Services can supply copies of the punching documents and copies of the overlays on a transparent medium at the cost of copying, plus an administrative charge and VAT. Prices at the time of writing are about 15p per sheet for the punching documents and about £5 each for the overlays. The constitution of tracts can also be supplied on magnetic tape.

Shapes and sizes of census tracts vary considerably, depending partly on the number and the geographical distribution of EDs changed and unchanged between the 1971 and 1981 Censuses. Some idea of the typical pattern of tracts can be gained from Morgan and Denham (1982). They show that, in a limited number of cases, quite large groups of EDs have to be combined to form tracts and that irregularly shaped tracts may emerge, though there is sometimes scope for breaking down large tracts into approximately comparable areas. However, it is advisable when using tracts in making 1971–81 comparisons *to group together contiguous tracts with small populations in a way suitable for local purposes.*

Where civil parishes (or communities in Wales) exist, these form a suitable areal base for 1971–81 comparisons, with the exception of the 100 or so civil parishes with populations of 10,000 or more where tracts have been specially drawn up. OPCS therefore prepared documents for each local government district listing 1981 parishes by name and SAS identifying number by 1971 SAS identifying number, and also covered the limited number of cases where civil parish boundaries changed between 1971 and 1981.

For those wishing to construct their own census tracts, comparability sheets (also known as 'POD3' sheets) are available from OPCS Census Customer Services. They are extracts from the basic OPCS documentation and show for each 1981 ED the constituent 1971 ED(s), but the parts forming tracts may be scattered over one or more sheets. Comparable extracts of SAS data from the 1971 and 1981 Censuses are also to be made available by OPCS for census tracts, in a separate file (see section 2.9.11). Morgan and Denham (1982) illustrate how a set of comparable small areas can be derived from tracts and parishes – using the district of South Wight as an example – and use the areas for analysis of 1971–81 change in a few key variables from the SAS.

2.5.5 POSTCODES

The local geography of the 1981 Census in Scotland is somewhat different to that in England and Wales in so far as GRO (Scotland) built up 1981 EDs in Scotland from postcode areas, and are using the postcode base more widely in their statistics (de Mellow 1979). Since both Census Offices now make use of postcodes and since this use is a major innovation in Britain, we now consider postcodes in some detail.

Postcodes were originally conceived by the GPO as an aid to the sorting of mail by automated means and are hence defined to meet the requirements of the Post Office's own distribution system which delivers mail to 21½ million addresses; here we are only concerned with their secondary use, namely as a country-wide, detailed and familiar method of describing the geography of the built-up parts of Britain.

Postcodes are a collection of one or more 'letter boxes' on the ground. Each postcode relates to part of a postman's normal delivery; the unit, or most detailed postcode, comprises on average about fourteen houses. The Post Office is not concerned with the whole land surface, but *all* of the space around the mail delivery points in a postcode unit can be partitioned and allocated to the enclosed set of delivery points, the sum of these postcode areas exhausting all the land surface of Britain. However, the system is complicated by the fact that large users of mail, notably businesses receiving over twenty items of mail per day, have their own unique postcodes independent of the 'spatial' organization of other postcodes. Every address in the UK is now postcoded and details of these are available in 114 Post Office Postcode Directories (see appendix 8 for contact addresses).

The postcode is, in essence, a hierarchical reference to nested areas. Thus a full, unit postcode such as DH1 4LA can be broken down as follows:

DH	The postcode area (120 in the UK)
DH1	The postcode district (c.2690)
DH1 4	The postcode sector (c.8880)
DH1 4LA	The complete, unit postcode (c.1.45 million)

There are, however, several formats with different positions and numbers of the alphabetical and numerical elements, though the postcode area (or town) – including the unique central London codes – is always first and the unit postcode element is always last in the standard format. An example of how these exist on the ground is given in figure 2.2. Maps of postcode districts are produced and details can be obtained from the Post Office.

For our purposes, the variations in the populations that the postcodes represent are of some significance. By dividing the 1971 total population of UK (55,350,000) by the number of addresses excluding 'large users' (c.21,200,000), we get a national average of 2.61 people per 'house'; applying this to the published Post Office postcode statistics (Post Office, undated), we obtain the results given in table 2.2:

Table 2.2 Variations in the size of postcode zones

	Areas	*Mean Populations*
Postcode areas	120	461,250
Postcode district	2,690	20,580
Average per area	22.4	
Maximum per area	79	
Minimum per area	3	
Postcode sector	8,880	6,200
Average per district	3.3	
Maximum per district	10	
Minimum per district	1	
Unit postcodes	1,453,000	38
Average per sector	541	
Maximum per sector	4,000	
Minimum per sector	1	

Source: Post Office, *Postcode fact sheet.*

In theory at least, the postcode system provides the smallest 'building block' in the country. Furthermore, it provides three other levels of detail which are comparable with the areal levels already used in census statistics. In principle, the lowest level – the unit postcode – should also be up-dated very frequently since detection of newly built areas is forced upon the Post Office by mail to be delivered. In practice, of course, a number of complications exist, for example, business users may, under certain circumstances, take their postcodes with them when moving within short distances and deletion of postcodes is inevitably a much slower procedure than adding new ones. Postcode areas and districts are often unsuited in shape and position for analytical purposes and rarely approximate to the areas of administrative or other recognized zones; postcode sectors too may be unsatisfactory. While other large zones can be constructed from unit postcodes, the procedure is tedious and may not even be open to some users (where the data they need are confidential at unit postcode

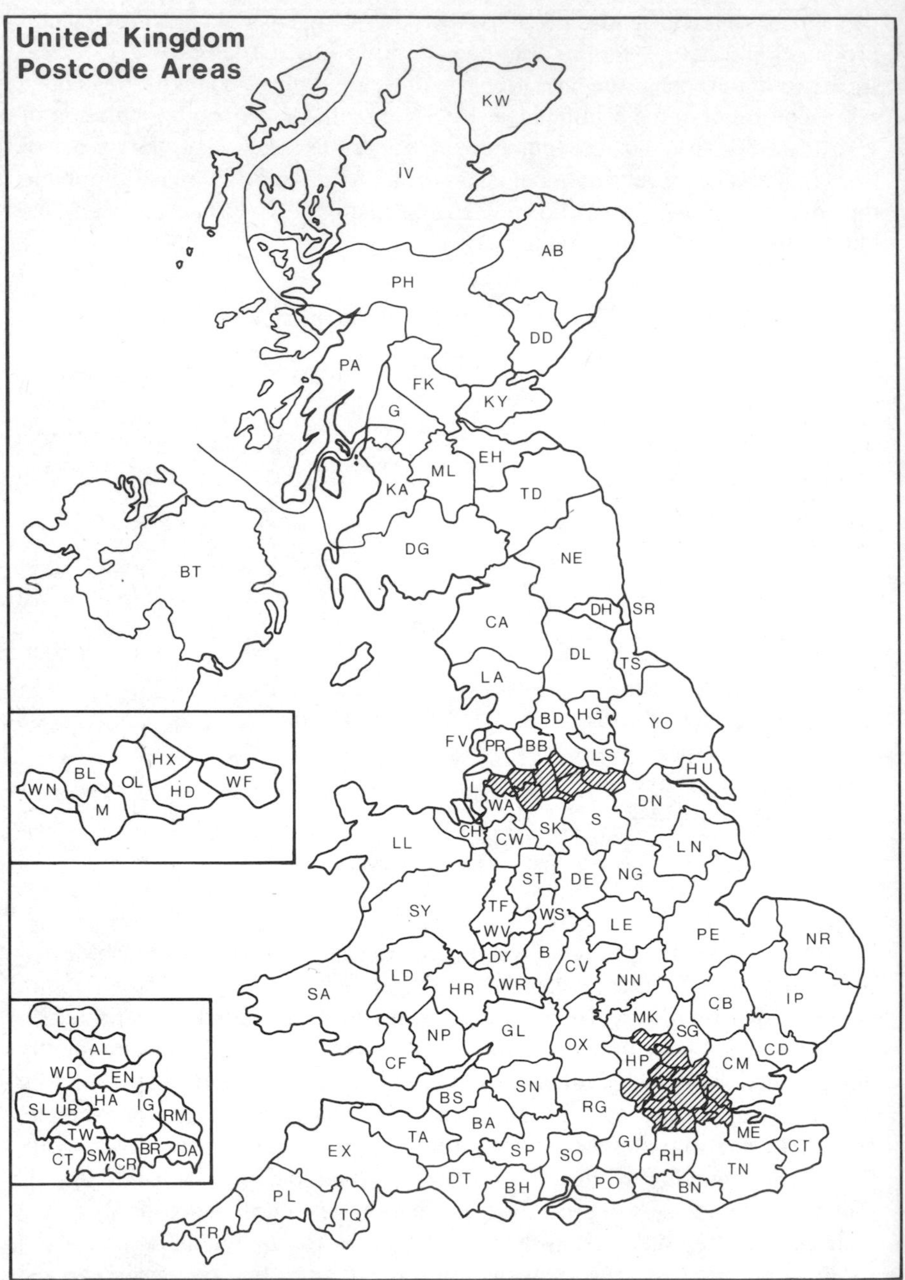

Figure 2.2 Postcode areas in the United Kingdom

Table 2.3 Strengths and weaknesses of three area bases

	Enumeration districts	*Grid squares*	*Postcodes*
Ready availability of maps showing the boundaries	a	Yes	No
Permanence of the boundaries	No	Yes	No
Spatial regularity of the areal base	No	Yes	No
Correspondence with physical features or administrative boundaries	Yes	No	b
Flexibility of *ad hoc* aggregation	c	No	Yes
Code or reference known to many of the respondents	No	No	Yes
Limited variability of population in a unit area	Yes	No	Yes

a Supplied with SAS.
b Approximate correspondence by aggregation of postcodes.
c Areas of special interest recognized in planning.

level). Finally, it is self-evident that the accuracy of aggregate statistics will depend very substantially on the correctness with which data is postcoded. Among area codes used in the census, the postcode is by far the most difficult to check for geographical correctness; a geographically incorrect postcode with a valid format may not be detected at any stage. Table 2.3 summarizes the strengths and weaknesses of postcodes as an area base and compares them with the other main contenders.

Despite these disadvantages, the attractions of the postcode system, maintained for one purpose but useable in practice for many others, are considerable. Recognizing this, a Central Statistical Office Task Force on the Use of Postcodes made important recommendations in 1977: that all statistical directorates in central government take steps to include the postcode as part of the address in their mailing records and postal contacts; that the ward be adopted as the smallest common statistical unit and that postcodes should be the mechanism of aggregating data to wards.

For a variety of reasons, the use of postcodes within the Census Offices has varied in character and extent. Thus we consider England and Wales separately from Scotland.

2.5.5.1 Postcode use in England and Wales

The use of postcodes in OPCS is based on the creation of a directory linking unit postcodes to the ward, district and county in which the postcode wholly or mainly lies. This directory is designed for use in creating aggregate statistics for the analysis of births and deaths by administrative districts – each birth and death record must now include a postcode. It is also in use to code postcoded addresses of workplace and previous residence in the 1981 Census (see section 2.6.8).

In England and Wales, after a feasibility study, it was decided not to use postcodes for 1981 ED planning; their use would have required an increased number of staff. Respondents in the census were asked to give the postcodes (if known) of their addresses one year before the census (where different from present usual residence) and of their workplaces. When not given by respondents, postcodes are being added in processing by reference to postcode directories. Full postcodes are being put onto the computer records and, by the use of the computerized directory specifying the ward to which each postcode belongs, data are being coded to wards of former residence and wards of workplace. This allows OPCS to produce migration and workplace statistics for the wards and other areas defined in terms of postcodes, as well as for local authority areas; there is some asymmetry in that the wards as defined for residence-based statistics (e.g. the SAS) will not necessarily be identical to those created via the postcode approximation.

The computerized postcode directory prepared by OPCS is also for statistical use by other government departments. As well as showing a ward code for each postcode, the directory contains a ten digit 'spot' grid reference, a county and district area code, and an allowance of up to sixteen characters for additional user codes. It is regularly up-dated. Discussions have been taking place between central government and the Post Office to consider how the service might be made available to other organizations.

2.5.5.2 Postcode use in Scotland

After the 1971 Census, a system of continuous planning for areal bases was set up by GRO(S), with the aim of dividing up Scotland into parcels of houses to be used in creating EDs. Gazetteers of grid references were considered but rejected at that time on the grounds of cost. The need for a fundamental re-think of the previous system of providing area-based statistics was increased by the reorganization of Scottish local government in 1975. The complete upheaval of this change meant that easily referenced and aggregated small-area data were necessary both to build to the new local-government areas and to construct data for the old ones, at least until such time as historical series existed for the new ones. Moreover, the very size of the new areas (in particular, the regions) suggested that data for a variety of smaller areas were likely to be needed by users.

For these and other reasons, postcodes were adopted by GRO(S) as the basis of the geography of the 1981 Census in Scotland. The process of ED creation is described in the next section. Perhaps of most interest, however, is that, in a hiatus in processing the 1971 census data, the 1971 enumerators' record books were marked up with postcodes. Using the computer version of this information, it is thus possible to create to a very good level of approximation and detail either 1981 data on a 1971 area base or 1971 data on a 1981 area base, and GRO(S) have stated their intention of providing the latter, subsequent to the general release of the 1981 data. As an interim measure, the 1971 SAS have been aggregated to postcode sectors using an allocation procedure based on whole EDs. This compares with the system of tracts being used in England and Wales (see section 2.5.4.2), though the actual data comparable between 1971 and 1981 will be much the same north and south of the Border.

Overall, then, the 'standard' 1981 census statistics for Scotland relate to rather different areas than those in 1971, notably in the use of postcode sectors in place of wards. Given the unit postcode coding of addresses of enumeration, however, GRO(S) have the ability to produce a very flexible range of areal bases and, at some stage, to produce data which are highly compatible with those of 1971 in terms of the underlying geography.

2.5.6 PLANNING ENUMERATION DISTRICTS IN SCOTLAND

In order to plan roughly equal workloads for enumerators, GRO(S) wished to develop a system for recording changes in the numbers of households and communal establishments in small areal units to provide the building bricks that would allow flexible grouping into EDs. Unit postcodes were selected for this purpose for a number of reasons: they were familiar to both public and to census users; they were maintained on a continuous basis by the Post Office who produce printed and computerized directories of the address content of unit codes at a reasonable cost; their content is relatively stable over time; and because topographical features constrain access by enumerators as well as postmen, they usually group to suitable units for enumeration. The system of updating codes used by the Post Office provides valuable information about new building developments and demolition, although there are delays in recording the latter. In addition to the information obtained from the Post Office, local authorities provided GRO(S) with important information about new developments and other information was derived from the valuation roll where this was available in suitable form.

As a first step towards planning EDs, GRO(S) drew unit postcode boundaries onto 1:10,000 and 1:2500 scale maps covering the whole of Scotland. ED boundaries were then superimposed on these maps to cover the whole surface area of Scotland without overlapping. These EDs were planned to an upper limit of 150 households, with suitable reductions to allow for distance in rural areas, and generally consist of groups of, or single whole unit postcodes. In some cases, such as large blocks of flats, an ED exceeds this limit. Unit codes are only split to recognize region, district, health board area, health district and new town boundaries. In addition, the ED boundaries recognize (to whole unit code approximation) civil parish boundaries, boundaries of localities with 500 or more population in 1971 and, so far as is practical, boundaries of zones specified by individual local authorities where these zones were notified to GRO(S) during the planning stage. These local-authority zones differ between authorities and reflect school catchment areas, travel to work areas and areas based on a variety of other criteria.

2.5.6.1 Postcodes as the base for statistics in Scotland

The computer record for each household in Scotland contains its postcode reference. This allows statistics to be produced for each unit postcode or for aggregates of these units. As in England and Wales, postcodes are added to 'remote' addresses in Scotland and a computerized directory is used for area coding. This directory contains the following range of area codes for each postcode: local-government region, district and islands area codes, health board area and health district codes, a new town code, a civil parish code, a code for the 1981 ED, a local-authority zone code, a locality code, a regional electoral division code, a district ward code, and a classification of the unit code to one of five urban–rural types. In addition, each unit code carries a 'spot' National Grid reference to 10 m resolution. These codes are attributable through this directory to both enumeration and 'remote' addresses on individual records or to statistical tables at unit postcode level. It is also possible to reference the directory from any postcode file: thus GRO(S) also uses this method to area code vital statistics (such as mortality data) for publication.

Even before the 1975 local government reorganization, only a rough distinction between urban and rural areas was possible using administrative areas. Reorganization made a separate definition of urban areas for statistical purposes even more necessary. As a first step, the 1971 EDs in Scotland were classified according to the population size of the continuously built-up areas in which they lay. The classification used was:

over 1 million population
100 thousand to 1 million
10 thousand to 100 thousand
1 thousand to 10 thousand
rural and under 1 thousand

Gaps in the continuity exceeding 1 km were recognized as delineating the limits of the built-up areas. Unit postcodes have since also been classified in this manner and used to classify EDs as lying within population groups of these sizes.

The addition to the directory of a 'spot' or centroid grid reference allows the use of postcodes with computerized mapping facilities. Experiments have shown that in urban areas in Scotland the average distance of households from the spot reference is about 40 m, giving a reference of the same order of precision as allocation to 100 m grid squares. Reasonable approximations of statistics for 1 km squares in built-up areas are possible using such grid-referenced data. However, for comparison of 1 km squares in Scotland over time, approximations should be based on the same unit postcodes, and this can be done through the 1971 postcode link described above. Where a postcode is available for both ends of a migration move or a journey to work, the 'spot' grid reference enables a rough estimate of the distance between the ends to be made. It is planned to include tables of this type in postcode-based workplace and migration statistics for Scotland.

2.5.7 WARDS/POSTCODE SECTORS

Wards are an important geographical unit, partly because of their use for local government elections. Local authorities have produced census statistics comparing wards in terms of overcrowding, demographic profiles and so on to provide information for elected representatives. The number of wards is less than one-tenth of that of EDs, though the proportion varies between parts of the country.

The boundaries of wards are progressively altered by the Boundary Commission. Census data in England and Wales relate to the ward in existence on census day. In some areas these boundaries will have changed after census day but before the census data appear. Definition of the boundaries of the wards on census night is best taken from the OPCS maps described in section 2.9.10. Ordnance Survey maps at 1:10,000 scale also show ward boundaries where this is not the largest scale of survey (i.e. where the area is also covered by 1:1250 or 1:2500 scale maps), but these are liable to be out of date in a significant number of areas.

Digital versions of all the ward boundaries in England and Wales have been created for the Department of the Environment and may be purchased from them in a format suitable for the GIMMS mapping package; details of these may be obtained from the relevant contact addresses given in appendix 8.

In Scotland, the equivalent of the ward, so far as census data are concerned, is the postcode sector; it was not possible to build wards into the ED structure since not all ward boundaries were known at the time of planning (though GRO(S) plan to produce them at a later stage). The postcode sectors are, by contrast, relatively unchanging (as of yet). Maps of postcode sectors are available from the GRO(S). Digital versions of their boundaries have been produced for Scotland and are available via the Scottish Development Department. Digitizing of the boundaries of postcode sectors for England and

Wales was in progress at the time of writing; details may be obtained from the editor of this volume.

2.5.8 LOCAL-AUTHORITY AREAS

Local-authority areas – the district/county duality in England and Wales and the district/region and island authorities in Scotland – were reconstructed by the Local Government Acts of 1974 and 1975 respectively. These differ in many respects from the prior set of local authority areas, but, fortunately, an approximation for their total populations has been produced at near-decennial intervals back to 1901 (see Chapter 9).

The boundaries of the current areas are defined on a variety of map sources, notably Ordnance Survey 1:50,000 scale topographic maps and 1:100,000 scale administrative boundary maps. The Department of the Environment publish a convenient summary map of these boundaries for England and Wales at 1:750,000 scale and also make available digital data describing them (the contact address is given in appendix 8). Baxter (1976a) has produced a cruder but convenient and economical set of boundary data for these areas extending to all of Britain; these have been used in, for instance, some of the maps in Chapter 6. These boundary data now exist on many university computers but are formally available from the Building Research Establishment (see appendix 8).

2.5.9 GRID SQUARES

After the 1971 Census, SAS data almost identical in content to those for EDs were produced for the square areas of grid printed on all OS maps for the whole of Britain (CRU/OPCS/GRO(S) 1980). These data, which have certain advantages – notably consistency of geographical position and ease of definition from *any* Ordnance Survey map – and disadvantages (see Rhind *et al.* 1980) are not being produced for the whole country from the 1981 Census. The reasons for this are essentially cost – users were asked to pay for the grid referencing of the household records and this led to a proposed charge by OPCS of seven and a half times that for data for standard areas, such as EDs. However, it seems likely that the data will be produced for restricted areas of the country, either for 1 km squares or for 1 km squares and 100 m squares.

The data would be compiled in a slightly different fashion to those in 1971. For England and Wales, actual grid references would be given to each one of the 10 per cent sample of households (see section 2.9.4); the remainder would be generated by computer by linear interpolation. Some constraints would be applied, such as that interpolation would only be permitted within EDs and that all non-private establishments would be given individually assigned grid references; in areas of low density of settlement more manual intervention would be necessary (see OPCS 1980a). Some errors would undoubtedly be introduced by this procedure. The magnitude of such errors, as percentages of the true value, reduce rapidly as population density increases and as the size of the grid square increases. Table 2.4 shows the likely standard error expressed as a percentage of the true value ('the coefficient of variation') for various population densities.

Table 2.4 Coefficient of variation for 1981 grid-square data

Number of persons per km^2	*Grid squares of area* 1 km^2	10 km^2
3000	0.7	0.13
1000	1.6	0.3
300*	4.0	0.7

* mean value for Britain in 1971
Source: OPCS 1980a

Certain variables which vary greatly from household to household may have larger errors than these values. Naturally, the errors for 100 m squares would be much larger than the values in table 2.4 and it seems unlikely that such data would be meaningful for single squares. Finally, it should be noted that SAS data for grid squares tend to suffer from 'data suppression' much more frequently than do those for EDs (see section 2.9.6 and CRU/OPCS/GRO(S) 1980); while large numbers of areas are affected, the percentage of the population thus affected is small, nationally amounting – on the basis of 1971 experience – to just over 2 per cent.

In Scotland, grid-square statistics could – on user demand – be made available by use of the grid-referenced postcode directories. GRO(S) have investigated this procedure and have concluded that, though substantial local variations may occur, the overall level of misallocation to 1 km^2 areas would be about 2 per cent in urban areas (compared with 0.5 per cent in 1971). In rural areas, errors would be very much larger since rural unit postcodes are often larger than 1 km^2 in size.

2.5.10 FUNCTIONAL REGIONS

Two general criticisms may be made of the areas for which census data are normally produced. The first is that the larger areas – such as local authorities (viz districts and counties in England and Wales and districts and regions in Scotland) or health authorities – are not related to certain functions going on in the real world, such as journey-to-work patterns. Thus, as areas for which data relating to such functions are available, they are heterogeneous and this inevitably means that the statistical description of that activity is blurred. (For many functions, of course, administrative areas are functional ones, notably in relation to the 'stock' variables such as local authority housing and even the provision of public transport for journeys-to-work.) Trying to establish processes which are going on in society is difficult enough from aggregate data, but is almost impossible if the areas for which data are available do not relate to the operation of the processes. In this respect, Britain can be compared with the United States: since the 1950 Census, data for functional areas (Standard Metropolitan Statistical Areas or SMSAs) have been produced by the Bureau of Census. These have been redefined as cities have grown, on the basis of the latest census data (Berry and Horton 1970). The basis of the American definitions is that of the Daily Urban System (DUS), essentially viewing each city area as an employment core surrounded by a commuting hinterland. Though strictly defined upon trips to work, Berry (1967) and many others have used the DUS concept to describe the set of areal zones in which most of the nation's population carry out the great majority of their daily activities: employment, retail and social. Britain had only limited officially produced data for cities defined upon similar criteria, but the major changes in local government organization in 1974–5 partially created functionally related administrative areas by merging urban districts, county boroughs and rural districts in many places into functionally related urban cores and 'rural' hinterlands. But the process was inconsistent and incomplete.

A number of British geographers have concerned themselves with functional regions, particularly for functional urban regions. The most recent and arguably the most thorough is that study by Coombes *et al.* (1981) working in the Centre for Urban and Regional Development Studies (CURDS) at the University of Newcastle. Their proposals have been prepared for coding into the 1981 Census area master file by OPCS so that users may either obtain SAS by functional regions or, alternatively, construct them from data for 1981 wards (England and Wales) and postcode sectors (Scotland) or smaller areas (Redfern 1981b). Figure 2.3 illustrates the CURDS functional regions.

2.6 Statistics from the census

The results of a census fall in two groups defined by Section 4 of the 1920 Census Act: first, published reports to Parliament and, second, other statistical abstracts. In section 2.2.5 it was explained that serial processing of the census determined the order of the output of statistics. These two factors dominate the nature of output from the census. All results from the census are presented as aggregates of individual data – counts of individuals with a particular characteristic or with a particular combination of two or more characteristics arranged with other combinations in a cross-tabulation – ranging from the basic fact of being present in Britain on census night to complex combinations

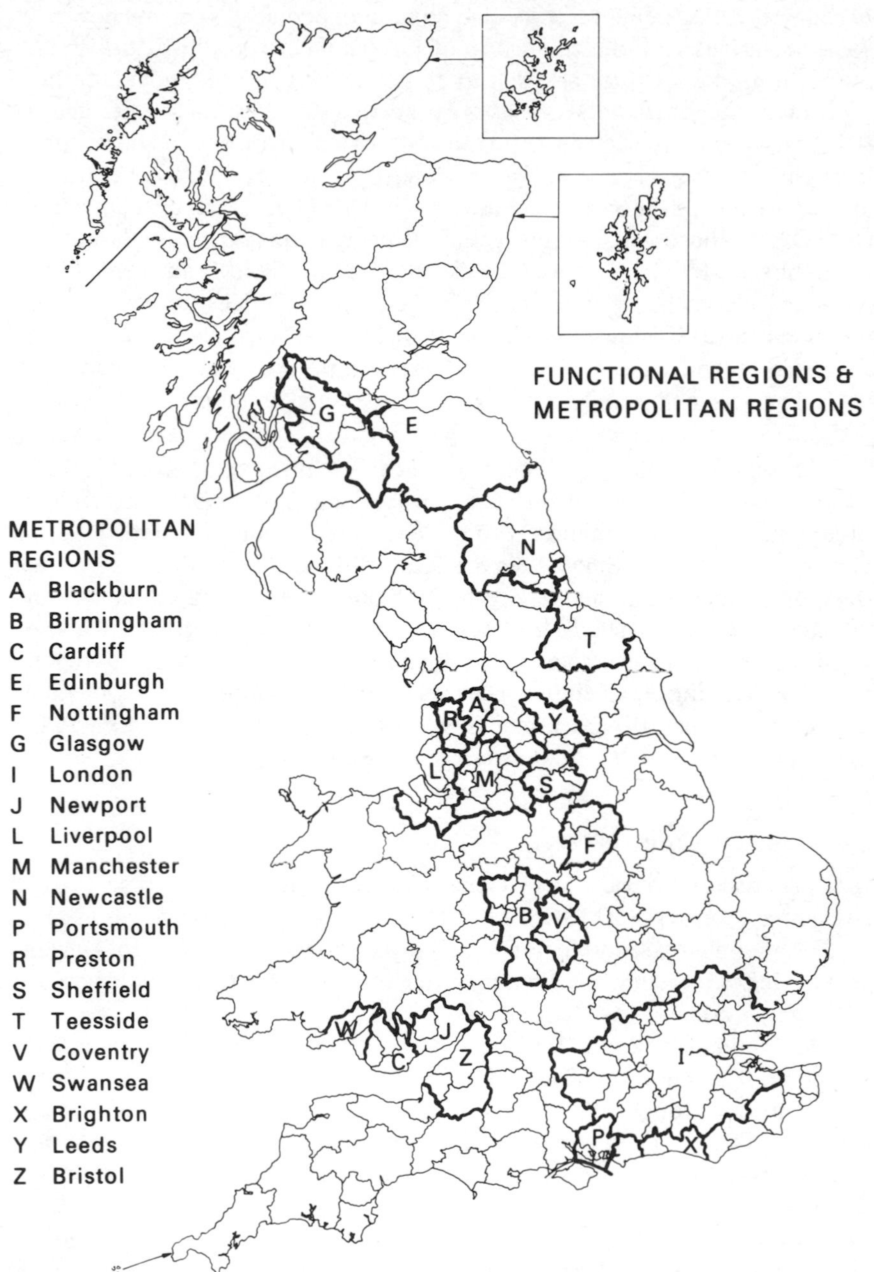

Figure 2.3 Functional regions in Britain, as defined by the Centre for Urban and Regional Development Studies

of characteristics shared by a relative handful of people. There are, however, some variations between the nature of the output designed primarily to be issued in hard-copy form and that to be issued in machine-readable form.

Primary output from the census is obtainable from several sources and, in secondary form, from a wide variety of sources which are beyond the scope of these chapters, but which have been reviewed recently (Hakim 1982). Reports to Parliament are generally published by HMSO and are available from HMSO bookshops, but less substantial results that are laid before Parliament are published by the Census Offices and are available from them. Other statistical abstracts are obtained from the Census Offices through specific orders to Census Customer Services and are then held on microfilm and can be examined at the Census Offices. Other organizations may also be licensed to hold abstracts and supply entire copies, extracts or derived statistics on demand.

This section of the handbook looks at the main outputs from the 1981 Census in the order in which they become available. It therefore starts with the preliminary reports, continues with the integrated set of local statistics – the County Monitors, the Small Area Statistics and the County Reports -- covers the programmes of national reports to Parliament, associated summaries and commentaries and concludes with the variety of special tables that can also be obtained. There are also notes on the documentation which must be used for a full understanding of the output. The treatment here of most of this wide range of output is necessarily brief, but more space is devoted in section 2.9 to the SAS as a major source of data from the 1981 Census.

2.6.1 PRELIMINARY REPORTS

The first results from the 1981 Census were published on 30 June 1981 in preliminary reports (HMSO 1981a, 1981b); later, in November 1981, a further preliminary report for towns and rural areas was published for England and Wales. All preliminary figures were issued either in these printed reports or as paper copies.

The Preliminary Report for England and Wales gave an initial count of the population present on census night in every local-authority district as well as for London boroughs, New Towns and aggregates such as regions and counties. These figures were derived from summary returns from the census field staff and are subject to some revision in later reports, but the general patterns were reliable. Moreover, counts were of *persons present in an area on census night* (see section 2.3.1) and subject to the effect of considerable short-term fluctuations in some types of area, for example, university towns. District-level tables in the Report included comparable figures for 1961 and 1971, the size of the area in hectares and population density. For counties, amounts and rates of change 1951–61, 1961–71 and 1971–81 were shown, and for England and Wales there was a summary of census counts of males and females from 1801–1981 showing intercensal changes and the proportion of females to males at each census. The Report also included census counts from 1841 onwards of persons, males and females in the United Kingdom and its constituent countries, and in the Isle of Man and the Channel Islands. Preliminary 1981 counts were given except for Northern Ireland and the Isle of Man where 1979 estimates and 1976 Census counts respectively were given. In addition, the Report contains an outline of the procedures followed in taking the census and in extracting the preliminary counts. There is also a commentary on the results which uses summary tables and charts to highlight some of the trends and patterns. This commentary looks at 1971–81 trends and compares the preliminary counts with what had been expected on the basis of information previously available.

The Preliminary Report for Scotland contained a wider range of statistics than that for England and Wales and included initial counts for local-authority areas, New Towns, postcode sectors and built-up localities with a population greater than 500. Provisional figures were given for household populations present on census night, household populations usually resident and populations in non-private establishments. Statistics at the region level showed comparable populations for 1961, 1971 and 1981 and tables for Scotland gave populations and intercensal changes from 1801 to 1981. The introduction contains definitions and a summary of results, and an appendix describes more fully the localities mentioned in the tables.

The second set of results for England and Wales from the 1981 Census gave preliminary population figures for towns and rural areas (HMSO 1981c). The report was aimed at a wide audience: businessmen, politicians and administrators and the general readership for whom towns and cities are familiar entities. As in the Preliminary Report, the figures were obtained from summaries prepared by the census field staff, which gave figures of the population present on census night. These provisional results were published because of widespread interest in populations of towns and in the relative proportions of the population living in urban and rural areas. The first section of the report considers the definition of towns and explains the methods adopted. This is followed by an illustrated commentary that examines the distribution of population between urban and rural areas over the last two decades, and the distribution of population between towns of different sizes and types. The main table in the report gives the population present in each town in 1961, 1971 and 1981, intercensal change, area (hectares) and population density in 1981. This information is summarized in a further table as urban and rural populations within each post-1974 county. There is an alphabetical index of the towns included in the report, and a table that ranks, by size, towns with 50,000 or more people in 1981. The first printing of the report for towns sold out by early 1982, and the opportunity has been taken in the second printing to make a number of revisions which came to light as the geographical definition of the towns was checked.

In the report, the term *town* is used in a broad sense to include urban places formerly known as cities, boroughs and urban districts such as Canterbury, King's Lynn or Llandudno, but which may no longer be local-authority districts. Generally, the towns are defined in the same way as in the 1971 Census – that is, as far as practicable, by the pre-1974 boundaries – but have been extended to include areas designated as New Towns. This is an interim measure and a more satisfactory, long-term method of defining urban areas is being sought by OPCS.

In 1981, for the first time after a census, OPCS also made available the preliminary counts for enumeration districts (EDs) as copies of working sheets, and many local authorities took advantage of this to make early updates of local population estimates which had been revised by information from non-census sources since 1971.

2.6.2 MAIN RESULTS

As has been explained in section 2.4, the census questions are divided into those to which the answers are easy to process and those to which the answers are more difficult and expensive to process. In general, this division determines whether the answers are fully processed (100 per cent item) or whether they are processed only for a 10 per cent sample of forms for private households and a 10 per cent sample of persons returned on forms for communal establishments (a 10 per cent item). The division is strongly apparent in the organization of census results, as the remainder of this section will demonstrate.

The division in input is as follows:

100 per cent items	*10 per cent items*
for persons	*for persons*
date of birth (age)	relationship in household (household/family composition)
sex	occupation
marital status	name and business of employer (industry)
whereabouts on census night	address of place of work
usual address	means of daily journey to work
usual address one year ago (migration)	higher qualifications
country of birth	
Welsh language (for forms in Wales)	
activity last week	
employment status	
for households	
nature of accommodation and sharing	
number of rooms	

100 per cent items	*10 per cent items*
tenure	
amenities	
availability of cars and vans	
non-private establishments	
type of establishment	
person's position in the establishment	

2.6.3 LOCAL RESULTS

In the planning of the 1981 Census it was decided to produce an interrelated set of cross-tabulations which would form the basis of the reports to Parliament on local areas and the other abstracts for small areas, and would range across the 100 per cent and 10 per cent items, so that there would be comparability between different areal levels. It was also decided to make summary extracts from the same basic cross-tabulations. The core of the system is the Small Area Statistics (SAS), which are introduced briefly in section 2.6.5 below, but described later in more detail (section 2.9), and the tables based on the SAS published as reports to Parliament in the County Reports. Drawn from the core are the key statistics published early in County Monitors, and various summaries that will be published when the programme of local results is complete.

2.6.4 COUNTY MONITORS

The first of the main results from the 1981 Census – that is 100 per cent items coming from the full computer processing system and superseding the preliminary counts – are being presented county by county in leaflets called *County Monitors* (or *Regional Bulletins* in Scotland). The data in the County Monitors are issued only in printed form. The series began in October 1981 and was complete by the end of 1982. At the end of the programme, national figures will be published, and the series will be rounded off with a review giving a national overview. In addition there are supplements giving figures at ward level in the Special Areas (designated by Inner Urban Areas (Special Areas) Orders) of Liverpool, Newcastle/Gateshead, Birmingham, Manchester/Salford, Hackney/Islington, Lambeth and the London Docklands.

The Monitor for each county contains a summary of key statistics for the county as a whole and for individual local-government districts. These range over the population present on census night, the usually resident population, age distribution, percentages of men and women in employment, out of employment and economically inactive and other selected characteristics of the population, households and housing. There is a brief commentary in each

Monitor – similar in outline for each county – covering such topics as children and the elderly, men and women at work, vacant accommodation and availability of cars. Figures for the population present on census night are given for 1961, 1971 and 1981; other 1981 figures are compared where possible with the nearest 1971 equivalents. *County Monitors* (or *Regional Bulletins*) are available direct from the Census Offices (see list of contact points in appendix 8), and the complete series for England and Wales costs £20.00, though specimen copies are available without charge. The Monitor for each county is also being reproduced in the introductory text of the County Report.

2.6.5 SMALL AREA STATISTICS (SAS) AND COUNTY REPORTS

The SAS are a standard set of statistics for small areas throughout Great Britain, and are produced by the Census Offices under the authority given by Section 4(2) of the Census Act. SAS have been previously produced from the 1961, 1966 and 1971 Censuses. Use has progressively increased and the content of the SAS has been developed with the participation of their users. The 1981 SAS contain around 4400 counts for each area and represent the whole range of 100 per cent and 10 per cent items available from the census. They are supplied by the Census Office on magnetic tape or as microfilm or paper-copy versions, and are available for enumeration districts (EDs), local-government district electoral wards, civil parishes and local-government districts. Detailed information on the SAS is given in section 2.9.

With a few exceptions, the counts in the 1981 SAS appear at county and local-government district level in County Reports published by HMSO in two parts for each county – part I containing the 100 per cent items and part II the 10 per cent items. The 1981 County Reports therefore show substantial changes from those of earlier censuses; the number of pages of tables are reduced, but the range of topics covered is increased. The standard SAS table outlines present statistics for one area, but, for the county reports, most of the tables have been re-designed to present the statistics for the districts within the county together. Certain tables in the county reports have been expanded, for example, a wide range of birthplaces is shown, and further tables give intercensal change and have no equivalent in the SAS. A *User Guide* showing the relationship between the SAS tables and the County Report tables is available from OPCS (see section 2.8). A guide to the content of the tables in Part I of the County Report may be found in the *'Keywords'* section included in each report. This section, which is new to the census publication programme, may be used to locate the tables containing key variables. There is also an index of tables in each part of the reports.

Unlike the county reports of previous censuses, the 1981 reports do not contain any statistics for wards or civil parishes. These statistics will be published by HMSO in separate leaflets. One set of leaflets will be published for each county giving basic statistics for district wards as existing on census day. A second set of leaflets will be published for each county giving basic statistics for civil parishes and successor parishes in England and communities in Wales as defined in 1974; these areas largely exist in what were administrative Rural Districts prior to local government reorganization in 1974. Both series of leaflets are scheduled to be published in 1983. The first County Reports were published in March 1982 and the programme of part I reports is due to be completed in November 1982.

2.6.6 NATIONAL RESULTS

When all the counties have been processed and data from them can be aggregated to national figures, regional and national versions of the tables in the county reports will be published by HMSO. These will be in two parts: the first for 100 per cent topics and the second for 10 per cent topics. The first part is planned for publication in autumn 1982, the second part for publication some four months later. Publication will be during the County Reports (Parts I and II) programmes, since publication of national figures will be given priority as soon as they are computed.

Further reports with summary versions of the SAS/county report tables for local authorities and for towns and the populations of rural areas in England and Wales are planned for publication as soon as possible after the national and regional versions. Summary results for parliamentary constituencies have a high priority – a series of twelve 'regional' Monitors on the lines of those for counties (see section 2.6.4) is scheduled for publication in September 1982; figures will also be published later for redefined constituencies. Since the statistics in this series of reports are, in the main, aggregates of those in the SAS, it will be possible to compare local, regional and national figures.

It is planned to issue commentaries, on the lines of those in the preliminary reports, to accompany some of the general reports to give the less experienced census user an introduction to their contents. Also planned are reviews which will deal with selected topics, such as migration, in greater depth.

As for all British censuses, there will be a series of national results published by HMSO in topic volumes after the completion of the programme of County Reports. The topic volumes are designed in the main to meet the needs of central government. The probable order for publishing topic volumes based on 100 per cent processing is:

- historical tables – giving comparisons of the population with previous censuses;
- sex, age and marital status;
- population in communal establishments;
- birthplaces;

- housing and households (including availability of cars);
- Welsh language (in a bilingual volume);
- persons of pensionable age;
- migration cross-analysed with 100 per cent items.

Further volumes based on 10 per cent processing will be published as follows:

- economic activity (occupation, industry, socioeconomic group);
- household and family composition – household tables;
- household and family composition – family tables;
- qualified manpower;
- workplace and transport;
- migration cross-analysed with 10 per cent items.

There will also be a series of county leaflets providing figures on occupation, industry and socioeconomic groups for residents and for those with workplaces in counties and districts.

The first topic volumes based on 100 per cent processing are planned for publication as soon as possible in 1983 with those based on 10 per cent processing following about six months later. It is planned to complete all publication before the end of 1984.

It is not possible in a brief review to give an idea of the scope of each of the national topic volumes, though more information can be obtained from the Census Offices. However, the tables in the topic volumes generally give statistics for more detailed categories in more complex cross-tabulations than those in the general and local reports. The published national topic tables are also usually presented in no finer areal detail than metropolitan counties and standard regions, though the migration and workplace and transport volumes, for example, will contain statistics down to local-government district level.

2.6.7 FURTHER TABLES

In addition to the published reports and summaries and the SAS, further tables can be obtained direct from the Census Offices at the cost of production, often giving more local detail and sometimes designed to customers' special requirements, if the Offices' resources permit. In particular, tables will be available to order giving migration figures for areas below the size of local-government districts; similarly, local figures on workplaces and journeys to work will be available.

2.6.7.1 Extensions of published tables

To publish all available tables would make census volumes too bulky. Tables, for example, may be produced for more detailed areas at the same time as those to be published. The availability of such tables (sometimes described as 'unpublished versions') is shown in the volumes containing the published equivalents, and they are supplied at the cost of making the copy.

2.6.7.2 Special analyses

These can be produced at customers' request and expense. Briefly, either already designed tables can be produced for a new set of areas (often local areas), or special tables can be designed from concepts already specified in the processing system, or special tables can be designed using specially requested concepts. Costs rise from the first to the third of these options. Details of the service for special analyses are available from the Census Customer Services, who can advise whether a relevant special analysis has already been produced or ordered. Steps have been taken to facilitate the sharing between customers of the costs of special analyses from the 1981 Census (OPCS 1981/2), and it has also been the practice to supply special tables to third parties, after a lapse of time, for the cost of copying.

2.6.8 SPECIAL LOCAL WORKPLACE AND MIGRATION STATISTICS

The workplace and migration statistics to be published as reports to Parliament will relate to local-government districts or to larger areas. Standard sets of statistics will, however, be available for smaller areas which can be defined in terms of wards and, in the case of workplace statistics, postcodes or as co-ordinate-referenced polygons. The special local statistics will be produced on demand at cost to the customer. The statistics will be supplied on magnetic tapes. Special local workplace and migration statistics were similarly available from the 1966 and 1971 Censuses.

At the time of writing, the Census Offices had circulated proposals for local workplace and migration statistics (OPCS 1981b), and had incorporated suggested modifications, but had not issued final prospectuses. However, the workplace statistics will show the characteristics of people with addresses of place of work in each area and counts of the trips made between zones of residence and zones of workplace; most of the statistics on the workforce resident in an area are in the SAS. All local workplace statistics are based on the 10 per cent sample analysis. Migration statistics will relate to the one-year migration period and will give the characteristics of people migrating to, or from each area and, in a separate set of tables, the flows of migrants between areas. Migration statistics will be based on 100 per cent analysis, but some tables will cross-tabulate 10 per cent sample items. More detail is given in the following paragraphs.

2.6.8.1 Local workplace statistics

The method of production of local workplace statistics is that those filling in census forms were asked to give the address, with the postcode if known, of the place of work of each person aged sixteen or over in a job 'last week'. In the Census Office, a 10 per cent sample of the census forms is being taken and, on these forms only, answers to workplace address are being coded as complete postcodes, i.e. including the last two alpha characters which give a precise geographical location. Using a computerized central postcode directory that links postcodes to wards, the postcoded workplace data are referenced to wards (district polling wards) and to the areas used in the published reports. As further options for special workplace statistics, the workplace data can also be referenced to other zones defined in terms of postcodes, or, as the central directory contains a national grid reference for each unit postcode, workplace data can be referenced to zones defined as grid-referenced polygons. The use of postcodes to identify zones of workplace, but not zones of residence, results in some asymmetry in the zones, i.e. zones for data at place of usual residence will be aggregates of enumeration districts (EDs), but aggregates of postcodes for data at workplace.

Local workplace statistics will be in a set of three groups of tables for zones specified by users on the lines of:

(A) for persons aged sixteen or over in a job 'last week' with *workplace* in the zone:

- industry class by sex by employment status (employees/self employed)
- occupation order by sex
- socioeconomic group (SEG) by sex
- social class by sex
- industry class by office/non-office worker by sex
- full time/part time by marital status by sex

(B) for persons aged sixteen or over in a job 'last week' with *usual residence* in the zone:

- occupation order by sex
- industry class by sex

The two tables in group (B) could be supplemented by information derived from the Small Area Statistics.

(C) for trips between usual residence and workplace:

- mode of transport to work by car availability (in households) by sex
- industry by sex.

Tables in group (C) will be for persons resident in zone 'a' and with a workplace in zone 'b' and so on, and will include cases where zone of residence is zone of workplace. Tables will be available for: trips within and into, or trips within and out of, or trips within, into and out of an area.

Zones of origin (residence) would be defined by customers for special workplace statistics as enumeration districts or aggregations of enumeration districts or as district wards, local-government districts, counties, standard statistical regions or remaining parts of Great Britain. Zones of destination (workplace) would be defined by customers as aggregations of postcodes or by co-ordinate references, or as district wards, local-government districts, counties, standard statistical regions or remaining parts of Great Britain. Zones of destination would have to be at least the size of an average enumeration district. If tables were required for all persons with workplaces in an area, zones of residence would have to cover the whole country, and vice versa for tables for all persons with residences in an area, to allow for lengthy trips. Zones outside a customer's special system would normally be made up of wards, local-government districts and other standard areas to avoid the expense of specifying the zones by postcodes or as co-ordinate referenced polygons. Zones distant from a customer's area of interest would normally be large.

2.6.8.2 Local migration statistics

The method of production of local migration statistics is similar to that for local workplace statistics. Those filling in census forms were asked to give the address one year before the census, with the postcode if known, for each person who had changed his or her usual address within the past year. Together with responses to the questions on whereabouts and usual address, this enables migrants over the year preceding the census to be identified. All previous addresses are coded as complete postcodes. Using the computerized central postcode directory that links postcodes to wards, the postcoded migration data are referenced to wards (district polling wards) and to the areas used in the published reports. The use of postcodes to identify areas of previous usual residence, but not areas of current usual residence results (as with local workplace statistics) in some asymmetry, i.e. wards will be exact aggregates of enumeration districts (EDs) for data at current usual residence, but will be approximate aggregates of postcodes for data at previous residence. At ward level, 1 or 2 per cent of addresses are referenced to an incorrect ward by postcode.

Local migration statistics will be in two sets for wards existing at census day. For the first set, certain types of migrant within, to, or from the ward are distinguished and for each type there will be 100 per cent tables on the lines of:

- economic position (8 classes) by sex
- migrants in private households: tenure (3 classes) by economic position (4 classes) by sex
- marital condition (4 classes) by sex
- age (ten year groups up to 80+) by sex

and 10 per cent tables on the lines of:

- occupation order (17 groups)
- socioeconomic groups (SEG) (21 groups, including 'inactive residents in non-private households', 'students and children under sixteen', 'other economically inactive persons').

The second set gives flows of migrants between zones (wards). For each ward for migrants (i) *from* each ward of previous usual residence and (ii) *to* each ward of current usual residence (including moves within the ward) there would be a 100 per cent table for age (ten year groups up to 80+) by sex, and a 10 per cent table for socioeconomic groups (SEG) (twenty-one groups including 'inactive residents in non-private households', 'students and children under sixteen', 'other economically inactive persons'). In the second set, the areas presented would be the ward (moves within ward) and all wards from or to which five or more migrants (100 per cent) had moved, with a remainder. In the 100 per cent tables, to prevent the disclosure of information about identifiable individuals, each cell in all tables would be modified by the addition of +1, 0 or –1; totals in the tables would be the sum of modified cells.

The local workplace and migration statistics are a very substantial source for analysis, but their design is oriented to the local authority user and this, together with the need to present all data as aggregates without disclosure of information about identifiable individuals, introduces a certain lack of flexibility for 'secondary' analysis. This is particularly so in the spatial dimension, where the possibility of aggregating zones to new area sets is restricted.

2.7 Summary of sources by area level

To bring together the information on the geographical base of the census and on the types of statistics available, table 2.5 shows the main 1981 census output by area level (*excluding* any special analyses).

Table 2.5 The geographical basis of census statistics

Area level	*Published reports*	*Abstracts*
ED	–	SAS
Ward (Postcode sector in Scotland)	County Leaflets County Monitor supplements (special areas only)	SAS Local workplace and migration statistics
Civil parish (inc. successor parishes and communities in Wales)	County leaflets	SAS
Local government district	Preliminary report County Monitors SAS-based summary report Certain topic volumes	SAS Extensions of published tables (published at higher area level)

Area level	*Published reports*	*Abstracts*
County (Region in Scotland)	Preliminary reports County Monitors SAS-based summary report Certain topic volumes	Extensions of published tables
Standard statistical regions	Preliminary report County Monitor (regional version) County Report (regional version) Certain topic volumes	Extensions of published tables
Nation (Great Britain, England, Wales, Scotland)	Preliminary reports County Monitor (national version) County Report (national version) Topic volumes	Extensions of published tables
New Town	Preliminary reports New Town volume	SAS (user's aggregates)
Parliamentary constituency	Special 'Monitors'	SAS
Health District		SAS Extensions of published tables
Towns, conurbations, urban and rural areas	Preliminary report SAS-based summary report	SAS (user's aggregates)
'Ad hoc'	–	SAS (user's aggregates) Local workplace statistics

Note: Titles given to published reports and abstracts are abbreviated; they enable cross-reference to fuller descriptions in previous sections, but may not be the final titles. Additions may be made to the programme of reports and abstracts if new information needs arise.

2.8 Documentation for the 1981 Census

It is Government policy to improve the documentary guidance to users of the 1981 Census. Throughout the planning of the census, information was disseminated through the *OPCS Census Monitors* – a series commencing in 1978 and available without charge from OPCS (see appendix 8 for contact point). The Monitors are a link between the census organization and census users, providing information on many aspects of the 1981 Census, including more specialized publications and discussion papers. Following the census, the Monitors form a major source of information on census output. In summary, they are both a newsletter and a 'part-work' introduction to the census for any user of the census.

Documentation specifically concerned with the output from the census is divided, like the output itself, into volumes published by HMSO to accompany the reports to Parliament, and into material issued direct from the Census Offices. It has been traditional practice to publish substantial reports on the conduct and content of each census, but this lapsed with the 1966 Census, and the 1971 general report has been much delayed but is under preparation. The publication of a general report is being resumed for the 1981 Census, but the extent of the matters to be covered is not yet certain. However, the guide to the definitions and terms used in the output from the 1981 Census was published in January 1982.

2.8.1 CENSUS 1981, DEFINITIONS, GREAT BRITAIN

Census 1981, Definitions, Great Britain is a comprehensive guide to the definitions, classifications and the population bases used in the 1981 County Report tables and in the closely associated SAS. It also covers most of the definitions to be used in subsequent national summary and topic reports. The material in the volume will not be duplicated in published reports, nor will it be repeated at any length in the explanatory notes for the SAS. It is therefore an *essential* reference for users of these reports and statistics. The volume contains an introduction to the 1981 Census and sections on population bases, population and household definitions and the definition and classification of communal establishments, followed by notes on all topics in the census. Some reference is made to the major differences between the treatment of topics in the 1971 and 1981 Censuses, but a more comprehensive account of intercensal changes is due to follow in a general report on the 1981 Census.

2.8.2 USER GUIDES

At the time of writing, a variety of other documentation is under production. It covers, for example, tape lay-outs and area constitutions. Availability is announced in the Census Monitors and a catalogue of User Guides is available from Census Customer Services (see appendix 8). Some of the documentation is issued automatically with sales of statistics, for example, the SAS Explanatory Notes; other documentation is available on demand. Further sources of information from the Census Offices are articles and notes that appear in *Population Trends* published quarterly by HMSO and monographs in a series of *Occasional Papers* published by OPCS. OPCS Library issues reading lists on the census and information sheets for the interested lay readership are available from OPCS Information Branch.

2.9 Small Area Statistics (SAS)

2.9.1 INTRODUCTION TO SAS

The SAS are a standard set of census statistics for small areas throughout Great Britain. They have been produced from the 1961, 1966, 1971 and 1981 Censuses. Use has progressively increased and the content of the SAS has been developed with the participation of users. The 1971 SAS – 1571 standard counts and ratios for the population in each of approximately 125,000 areas in Great Britain – were the most widely used set of tables from the 1971 Census. Over 6000 orders for 1971 SAS were supplied, ranging in size from a set of SAS for the whole country to SAS for a single community. There is every indication that there will be a similarly wide use of the 1981 SAS – now expanded to over 4300 counts.

SAS are produced by the Census Offices under the authority given by Section 4 of the 1920 Census Act which permits the Registrar-General to prepare, at the request and cost of any local authority or person, abstracts containing statistical information. The characteristics of SAS have developed in response to demand: the statistics refer to populations smaller than those reported in the published volumes; they range over the whole content of the census; and they are supplied to the order of customers who jointly share the cost of preparing standard SAS from the basic computer files of processed census records – a cost which is low in relation to that of similar information from other sources and in relation to the total cost of a census.

Uses of SAS are too diverse to be adequately represented in a summary and, in any case, are partially dealt with in Chapter 3. Nevertheless, the following examples give some indication of the range of applications. In local authorities, SAS form an important part of the information needed for the planning and management of local services, particularly to study trends and possible future patterns in population and the need for housing. In commerce, SAS are used, for example, to look at the characteristics of populations in catchment areas of retail outlets or to pinpoint localities with market potential. In central government, SAS, analysed on a national scale, have been used to locate areas of multiple deprivation. In schools, students use SAS to study their local communities, while the SAS are the largest body of data on population available for academic research in general. SAS are also an information resource for individuals, local businessmen and local interest groups with questions about their communities.

There was early wide consultation on the 1981 SAS. In May 1978, to initiate discussion, the Census Offices published a background paper (OPCS 1978/2) containing general proposals, and circulated a set of draft SAS tables. Discussion meetings were arranged and many users responded with comment. Revised draft tables were issued in April 1979 and this second round of consultation resulted in a number of further revisions. As soon as the content of the census was finally settled by Parliament in May 1980, planning for the production of SAS went ahead so that the system would be fully operational when data became available in the final months of 1981.

To appreciate the nature and scope of the SAS, it is helpful to be aware of the principles that influenced their design. In putting together proposals for the 1981 SAS, the Census Offices drew, first, in the evidence gained from the discussion of SAS before the 1976 Census was cancelled, second, on continuing liaison with SAS users and, third, on the results of reviews of applications of SAS. It was decided that there should be reasonable continuity between 1971 and 1981 SAS, in table content and area base (see Chapter 9) and there should be comparability between populations and classifications in the 1981 SAS and other 1981 census tables. It was clear that tables in the SAS would have to be abbreviated versions of tables available for larger populations in published census reports. Simple classes would have to be used and the number of dimensions in tables limited. This related to the reliability of census statistics for small populations, where sampling and non-sampling errors may give misleading figures in over-complex tables. But there were nevertheless strong arguments for enlarging the scope and content of the SAS, particularly after the reduction in the number and the redefinition of local-authority areas for which census statistics would appear in published reports. The public would, however, have to have confidence that the individual information collected in the 1981 Census was being kept confidential. The Census Offices had therefore to take steps to ensure that no information about identifiable individuals would be disclosed through SAS. Finally it was decided that there should be considerable improvements in the dissemination of 1981 SAS, including early and comprehensive documentation, and a revision of charging and copyright arrangements. In the four years spent on developing and producing the 1981 SAS, it has proved possible to respect most of these sometimes conflicting principles.

2.9.2 STATISTICAL CONTENT OF THE SAS

Under the Census Act, a wide variety of special local tables may be requested, but the 1966 and 1971 SAS were standard for all areas throughout Great Britain and for all customers, as are the greater part of the 1981 SAS. In opting for standard SAS, as many user needs as possible are met, though inevitably there are compromises. The advantages of standard SAS are readily demonstrated. They enable users' needs to be met quickly, more simply and at a lower price. The customer is able to use standardized means of handling and analysing the data. But perhaps most important is that the complete coverage of the census can be exploited – identical variables being available across the whole population. Re-aggregation of SAS will give comparisons across larger populations up to national level.

2.9.2.1 Format

The 1971 SAS consisted mainly of counts arranged into abbreviated cross-tabulations and, for compactness, a number of basic counts were obtainable only by summing: they also, however, included a number of ratios (variables given as 'per thousand of the population'). All cells in the 1981 SAS are counts but otherwise this general arrangement is repeated in the 1981 SAS, though line and column totals are provided where necessary. The 1981 SAS tables extend across the whole range of census topics, and include certain derived variables such as socioeconomic groups (SEG) and social class.

The 1981 SAS tables are the basis for 1981 County Report tables to be produced at the same time as the SAS; district and county-level versions of virtually all SAS counts will be published in these Reports. Shortly before the end of the County Reports programme, national and regional summaries of the tables will be published. Thus, comparison of statistics for a range of areas from the local to the national will be possible.

Each area in the 1981 SAS is uniquely identified by a number of alphabetic and numeric characters. Hence 'AAAB01' refers to the first ED (01) in the second ward AB within district AA. In addition, areas down to ward level are named in printouts of the SAS data and on computer tape.

2.9.2.2 General statistical aspects

The SAS demonstrate the opposing impacts of demand for local detail and the maintenance of statistical reliability. In designing each SAS table and in designing the whole set of tables for the small populations of EDs, the Census Offices had to consider the accuracy and reliability of the statistics and the need to preserve confidentiality and, therefore, the restriction of detail. Nevertheless, many of the counts in the tables, particularly those based on a 10 per cent sample, are of a degree of detail that would normally be reliable only when counts and/or areas are aggregated. Section 2.9.4 discusses the effect of the sample base.

The Census Offices have made two general changes that will improve the usefulness of 1981 SAS in comparison with previous SAS. First, because respondents in 1981 were required to include all members of their household irrespective of their whereabouts on Census night, data for absent household members is processed as fully as for the present residents, and present residents plus enumerated absent residents form the base population for most 1981 SAS. This provides better information on household characteristics such as one parent families; however, the usually resident population counted in these tables is not a comprehensive count of the population of the area because it excludes members of households in which no-one was present on census night and residents of communal establishments who were absent on census night. Nearly all 1971 SAS tables had base populations of persons present on

Table 2.6 The number of cells in different sections of the 1981 SAS

	Common 100%	*Country – specific 100%*	*Common 10%*	*Country totals*
England	2597	453	1295	4345
Wales	2597	501	1295	4393
Scotland	2597	1124	1295	5016

Source: Derived from appendix 2

census night. Second, data on employment status (self-employed, employee, and so on) and migration, which were processed on a sample basis in 1971, have been taken into the 100 per cent record in 1981, thus increasing the scope of 100 per cent tables in the 1981 SAS.

2.9.3 THE SAS TABLES

The table layouts for 1981 SAS are shown in appendix 2 and a summary of the numbers of cells involved is given in table 2.6. The SAS tables are grouped into three sections:

- i population and household tables on a 100 per cent basis, available for areas throughout Great Britain (pages 1, 2, 3 and 4 covering tables 1 to 32);
- ii population tables on a 10 per cent basis, available throughout Great Britain (pages 5 and 6 covering tables 44 to 53);
- iii tables available for areas in England (pages 7 and 8 covering tables 33 to 38) or these tables and the Welsh language table (39) available for areas in Wales only or tables available for areas in Scotland only (pages 9 and 10 covering tables 40 to 43).

Relatively few of the statistics are one-dimensional counts; most relate two or more characteristics – a great advantage of census data drawn from a series of questions asked at the same time. So that the content of tables is as clear as possible, column and row headings have been made as full as space allows and there are additional footnotes on the pages. More complex aspects are covered in additional *Explanatory Notes* and in the volume of definitions.

There are fifty-three numbered SAS tables (some available only in England and Wales or in Scotland or in Wales), but many of the tables comprise two or more *cross-tabulations*, i.e. a group of cells in which the individual members of the population being counted are counted only once (except for 'TOTALS'), and there are some single cell counts. Cross-tabulations are grouped together to save space on headings and for ease of cross-reference, but some care is necessary to avoid double counting, for example, when aggregating values. Cross-tabulations are normally divided by ruled lines, but there are a few 'interleaved' tables, such as table 10, and others where cross-tabulations have common 'TOTALS', again such as 10.

The individual items (people, households, rooms, cars and so on) counted in each cross-tabulation, i.e. the *population base* (or *universe*), are shown for each table in a banner heading at the top of each table alongside the table number. Two or more population bases are separated in headings by semi-colons. Awareness of the precise population base used is critical to the manipulation of statistics within the SAS and to the interpretation of results generally, also in making comparisons with past SAS or with data from other sources. Other conventions are: all total rows and columns are headed in capitals, otherwise lower case is used; sub-total rows are followed by indented headings, and cells where no statistics will be printed are shown by three crosses. Each cell in the 1981 SAS has a *unique number* for reference in the magnetic tape versions and for other reference purposes, such as specifying cells to be used in a particular calculation. These cell numbers are shown in the table outlines in appendix 2.

The full scope of the SAS is too large to be summarized in a few paragraphs, but some general notes follow:

- the tables on page 1 (standard for all parts of GB) give basic demographic statistics, including age structure, country of birth and migrants, plus economic status figures. Populations in private households and establishments are given separately, as are persons present on census night and usually resident – enabling users to see the effect of using the latter as a population base;
- page 2 (GB) is devoted to housing statistics; including tenure, amenities, density of occupation, availability of cars and second residences. Tenure and car availability are regarded as increasingly important measures of an area's socioeconomic status;
- page 3 (GB) is devoted to statistics about resident households and residents; including household composition, 'earners' in households, and the economic activity of married women and whether they are in households with children;
- page 4 (GB) is also devoted to statistics about resident households and residents, but concentrates on particular groups which may be clients for various social services or may be counted as deprived; including lone 'parent' households, households with pensioners and households with children. These tables in particular are arranged so it can be seen how many households or people share certain characteristics, for example, table 31 shows how many lone 'parent' households lack the key amenity of a bath, and how many children aged nought to four and five to fifteen live in such circumstances;

- page 5 (GB) – based on the 10 per cent sample – gives the socioeconomic profile of the area, broad industry groupings and means used for travel to work;
- page 6 (GB) – based on the 10 per cent sample – adds further information on the socioeconomic profile of an area, including social class. Table 49 is a complex grouping of cross-tabulations including figures on families in households derived from the relationship question in the census;
- there are different versions of the remaining pages for England and Wales and for Scotland. The statistics in the main deal with housing circumstances and different concerns north and south of the Border are reflected; high-rise housing in Scotland, for example, and multi-occupied housing in England and Wales. The England and Wales version also includes two tables (36 and 37) from which the numbers in ethnic minorities may be estimated. Finally, there are statistics on Welsh language in Wales and Gaelic in Scotland.

2.9.4 SAMPLING IN THE SAS

Statistics in Section 2 of the SAS (tables 44 to 53) are based on the 10 per cent sample of private households and the 10 per cent sample of persons in communal establishments; tables 49 and 52 are based on the sample of households alone.

The 10 per cent sample is taken in census processing from the fully validated 100 per cent records of households and persons in establishments, i.e. it is taken from the records from which the 100 per cent statistics are derived. The sample consists of one household selected at random from each stratum of ten consecutively recorded households, and a similar sample of persons in establishments. The sample is taken from blocks of fifty enumeration districts (EDs), the strata running continuously from the first household in the first ED to the last household in the fiftieth ED and from the first person in the first communal establishment to the last person in the last establishment of the fiftieth ED. The sample of persons comprises all persons in the sample households, plus the sample of individuals in establishments. Figures derived from the sample can only provide estimates of the population values. Although many of the cells in the 10 per cent tables will be a good estimate, say within 1 per cent of the actual value, some will also occur at the other extreme where the difference may be of the order of 50 or more per cent. There is no way of establishing whether any particular 10 per cent cell is a good, bad or intermediate estimate.

The ordinary laws of probability demonstrate, however, that, in the case of a random sample of a scale as small as 10 per cent, the range of the possible deviations (the standard error) associated with any sample item is approximately dependent on the square root of the sample value, and that if the deviations are expressed as proportions of the square root and then arranged according to size, they conform to a definite and uniform pattern which is largely independent of the size of the sample item itself. The distribution pattern shows that small deviations are relatively far more numerous than large deviations and that there is an equal likelihood of their being positive or negative. Also, it enables the chance that the error falls within any given percentage limits to be measured, and it is the measurement of this chance which provides the basis for judging whether the sample statistic is sufficiently accurate for use in the particular circumstances.

For any sample item which is a small proportion (say, less than one quarter) of the total sample population (or total sample households) in an area, providing the sample is random, the odds are of the order of:

a 2 to 1 that the error is less than the standard error of the item value
b 20 to 1 that the error is less than twice the standard error.

However, the 10 per cent sample is not, in fact, random. The stratified nature of the household sample tends, in general, to reduce the degree of error, but for counts of persons this is offset by the effects of clustering within the household. An investigation is being made by OPCS to establish empirical sampling errors for the 1981 10 per cent sample as a means of calculating the effects of the stratification and clustering. The results of this exercise will be included in an evaluation of the 10 per cent sample planned for publication in 1983.

Given that only a 'rule of thumb' guide can be provided at present, a table of standard errors for critical values can be produced, and expressed as percentages of the sample value:

Table 2.7 Standard errors in sampled SAS data

Sample value (a)	*Standard error* = $\sqrt{}$ *sample value* (b)	*Percentage error* (b) × 100 ÷ (a)
10,000	100.0	1 per cent
2,500	50.0	2 per cent
1,111	33.3	3 per cent
625	25.0	4 per cent
400	20.0	5 per cent
204	14.3	7 per cent
100	10.0	10 per cent
25	5.0	20 per cent
4	2.0	50 per cent

Source: OPCS

Therefore, roughly, if a cell in one of the tables has a value of twenty-five, the chances are 2 to 1 that the error is less than ±5 (i.e. 20 per cent) and 20 to 1 that it is less than ±10 (i.e. 40 per cent). However, when estimating the 100 per cent population for a cell, it must be remembered that although the percentage errors remain the same, the actual errors become ±50 and ±100 respectively.

Thus, at the ED level, 10 per cent SAS tables are subject to large errors and will generally need to be aggregated to much higher area levels to ensure small variability in the cell values. The statistics are presented at ED level, primarily to allow flexible aggregation.

2.9.5 HOW THE SAS ARE MADE AVAILABLE

The SAS Prospectus, issued as *Census Monitor CEN 80/8* in December 1980, contained full information on how the SAS are made available and how to make orders. A number of revisions were made during 1981 and announced in Census Monitors; revised versions were issued as *User Guides 50 and 52* and contain full information on how the SAS are made available and outlines of the tables (UG 52). The *Explanatory Notes* for the SAS comprise *User Guides 50 (Part I), 51 (Part II)* and 52. The following paragraphs contain an extract of the information in the User Guides.

Each section of the SAS is available on the following *media*:

magnetic tape (ICL 1900 character; ICL 2900 EBCDIC; IBM EBCDIC (unlabelled only))

microfilm (16 mm roll film), as pages of tables – four pages for Section 1, two pages for Section 2, and two pages for Section 3

paper copies of the pages of microfilmed tables (A4 size)

microfiche.

Customers can have any combination of the three sections and, on paper copies, any combination of pages.

The content of SAS, i.e. the counts and cross-tabulations, is identical on microform and paper copies. The magnetic tape version contains some extra figures summing the content of tables. The table outlines in appendix 2 show the design and page lay-out for microform and paper copies.

All sections of the SAS are available on any of the media, for the following *standard areas*:

enumeration districts (EDs)

district electoral wards as existing at Census Day (England and Wales) *or* postcode sectors (Scotland)

local-government districts

Civil parishes, as defined at local-government reorganization in 1974, are either single EDs or two or more EDs. Lists matching EDs to civil parishes are available from OPCS with the SAS for each county (part II of the SAS Explanatory Notes gives further details). Following the completion of the SAS for all counties, SAS will be aggregated to civil parishes and will be available from OPCS in 1983 at the normal charges. SAS for civil parishes are therefore available directly or by summing. SAS for communities in Wales and Successor Parishes in England are available in the same way as those for civil parishes.

2.9.6 CONFIDENTIALITY

As discussed earlier, the public have a right to expect that the confidentiality of their personal details on census forms will be respected. Assurances were given to the public that all the information given will be treated in strict confidence by the Census Offices. In particular, the Census Offices will not pass information about identified persons or households to other government departments or to anyone else outside the census organization. This is carried out by two procedures – modification and suppression of data.

The 1981 statistics, with the exception of tables 1 and 17, are modified by the addition of one of a series of quasi-random permutations (+1, 0, –1) to counts based on 100 per cent processing, thus ensuring that no information can be related with certainty to any identifiable individuals. 'TOTALS' in the tables are the sums of modified cells. The procedure by which modifications are made means that, wherever possible, *ad hoc* areas constructed by amalgamation of smaller areas should be produced from the largest available whole building blocks, i.e. using a mixture of wards and EDs should give more reliable results than using only all the component EDs.

In addition, if an ED or ward has less than twenty-five persons present, tables counting persons in Sections 1 and 3 (with the exception of tables 1 and 17) are not released; also if an ED or ward has less than eight households present, tables counting households in Sections 1 and 3 (with the exception of table 17) are not released. Also, if an ED has fewer than twenty-five residents in private households, tables relating to the population in private households are suppressed. In Section 2, person and household tables, or parts of tables, are suppressed if the person and/or household tables have been suppressed in Sections 1 and 3. The suppressed tables in Section 2 are amalgamated with those of an adjoining area. Suppression will only affect a few EDs (about 800 out of 125,000 in the 1971 SAS). It will affect 1 km grid-square SAS much more severely (see Rhind *et al.* 1977).

2.9.7 CHARGES

The Census Offices are required by Section 4(2) of the Census Act to recover the costs of all abstracts prepared. Where there are likely to be a number of customers for the same abstracts, such as the SAS, costs are divided between customers and copyright rules prevent loss of revenue to the Census Offices. The cost of SAS includes making the customer's copy of the SAS and preparation of the SAS from the basic computer files, to which each customer makes a contribution. A separate charge is made for handling each order. The costs differ between the media used to supply the SAS. A table of current charges is set out in the Prospectus; modest upward revisions of charges may be made.

To help users calculate outlay on SAS, the SAS Prospectus lists the number of wards and EDs in each county. The number of wards and EDs in districts can be obtained on enquiry from Census Customer Services, and estimates of the numbers in any other specified area can also be obtained from Census Customer Services.

2.9.8 COPYRIGHT

The SAS are Crown copyright and may only be supplied by customers to a third party with the agreement of the Census Offices (under delegated authority from the Controller of HMSO). The Offices are prepared to licence customers to share the SAS with others for an extra charge, and are also prepared to enter into an agency agreement by which the customer could disseminate the SAS without restriction on the payment of royalties.

There are, nevertheless, wide 'communities' of use where SAS may be freely disseminated once initial payment has been made to the Census Offices. No licence is required for the dissemination of SAS between local authorities (including water authorities). This permits the free interchange of SAS between counties and between counties and districts. A similar free interchange of SAS is permitted between the various health service authorities. The Social Science Research Council (SSRC) have negotiated a purchase of SAS for all EDs in Great Britain and will make the data available for academic research and teaching in universities and polytechnics, regardless of discipline. The SAS are being mounted at a number of regional university computer centres. Thus these arrangements mean that one part of a local authority can receive the SAS – probably on magnetic tape – and pass them on to other rate-supported activities, such as schools or public libraries, as well as to its various departments and to other local authorities. Most large local authorities will have facilities to make extracts and/or hard-copy versions of the SAS for reference purposes, whilst others will have on-line enquiry points. Similarly, the SAS will be distributed within the health authorities or in the universities. Computer programs to handle the SAS have been created at the instigation of the Local Authorities Management Services and Computer Committee (see appendix 8) and are in widespread use.

Users in commerce may find it more effective to access SAS through agencies – paying when data are wanted, rather than making a relatively large initial capital payment. These agencies may be set up to offer a 'retail' service to all comers, perhaps simplifying the SAS in the process, or they may be consortia of users where business associations may take the lead.

2.9.9 SAS TIMETABLE

Target dates have been set for the production of 1981 census results. These are the earliest practicable dates and, whilst the Census Offices take all possible steps to meet them, unforeseen circumstances during processing may cause delay. The first 100 per cent SAS were produced on time, and Sections 1 and 3 (100 per cent items) of the SAS on magnetic tape are one of the earliest outputs. The sections became available for the first county at the end of 1981 and became available for the last counties in May 1982. Section 2 (10 per cent items) on magnetic tape should be available from October 1982 onwards. Microfilm and microfiche versions will be available about one month later than the magnetic tape version for each county and paper copies shortly after that. Production dates for each county are shown in the SAS Prospectus.

2.9.10 MAPS

Maps are an integral part of the SAS 'package'. A first task is to relate zones of study to the zones for which the SAS data are available. EDs throughout Great Britain are shown only on maps available from the Census Offices, from whom maps of wards are also available. There are small-scale maps of postcode sectors (for Scotland). EDs in England and Wales of course do *not* relate to the geography of the postcode system (as explained in section 2.5); the areas lie haphazardly in relation to one another, and the census files do not carry postcodes for address of enumeration so the data cannot be re-sorted. Thus SAS for postcode sectors or any other area defined by postcodes in England and Wales can only be aggregated on a 'best fit' basis.

Figures 2.4 to 2.6 are examples of the maps produced by OPCS which show the boundaries used in the SAS: a 1:50,000 map showing local-government district and ward boundaries; a 1:10,000 map showing ward and ED boundaries; and a 1:2500 map showing EDs in more detail.

The maps showing local-government district and ward boundaries and names are copies of OPCS index maps, drawn up district by district, each one showing only the wards within a district. Users are likely therefore to wish to transfer the boundary information, say, onto 1:50,000 scale outline maps for easier reference.

The maps showing the boundaries of EDs and wards (as in figure 2.5) are available as paper copies of microfilmed Ordnance Survey 1:10,000 (6 inches to the mile) scale maps or as microfilm copies. The map sheets cover an area of 5 × 5 kilometres, i.e. four sheets for each 10 km National Grid square, and the number of whole or part EDs per sheet will vary. The charge for the maps is per sheet, regardless of the number of EDs covered. The number of sheets required to cover an area for which SAS are being ordered can be estimated by reference to the National Grid on Ordnance Survey maps. A copy of 1:10,000

Local Govt District and Ward Boundaries

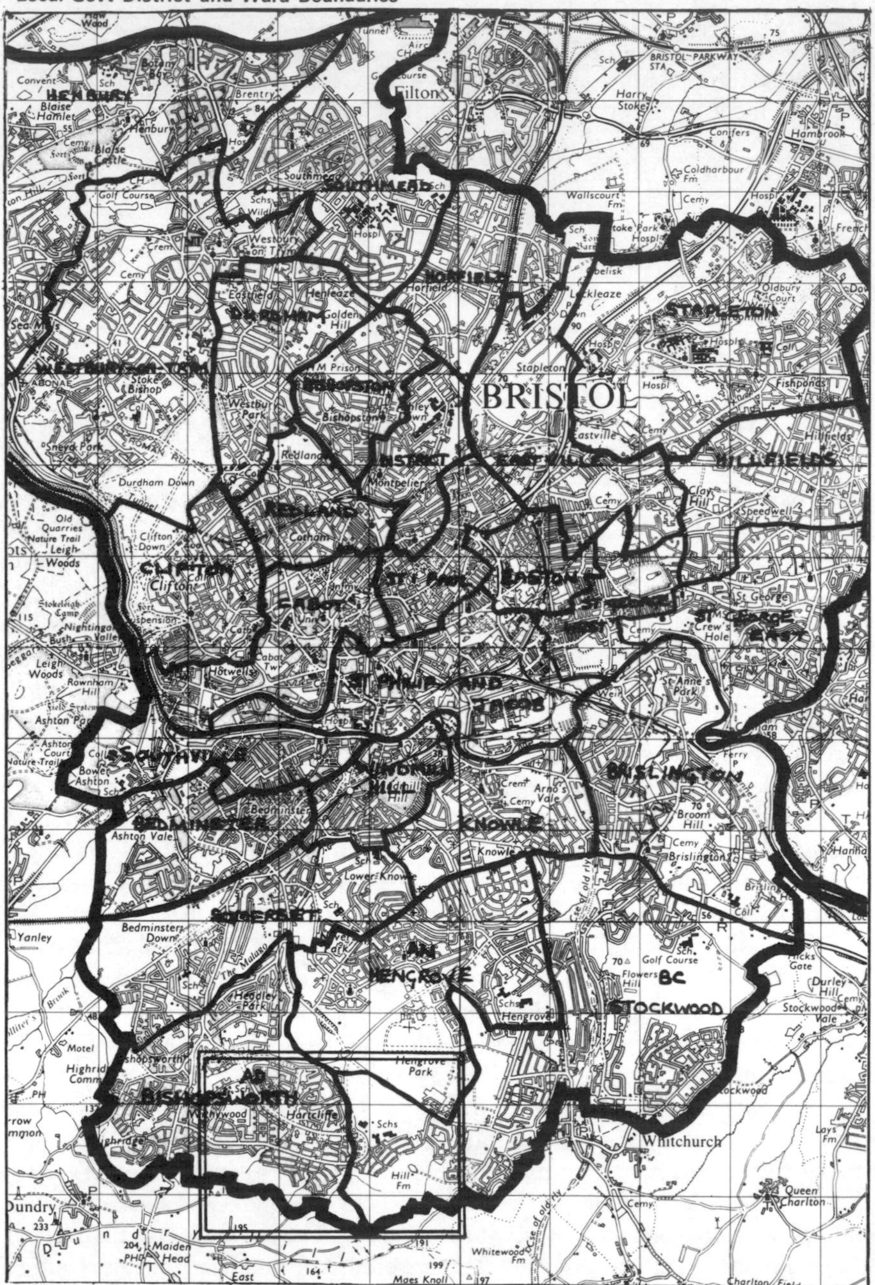

Figure 2.4 Local government district and ward boundaries on an OS map of Bristol

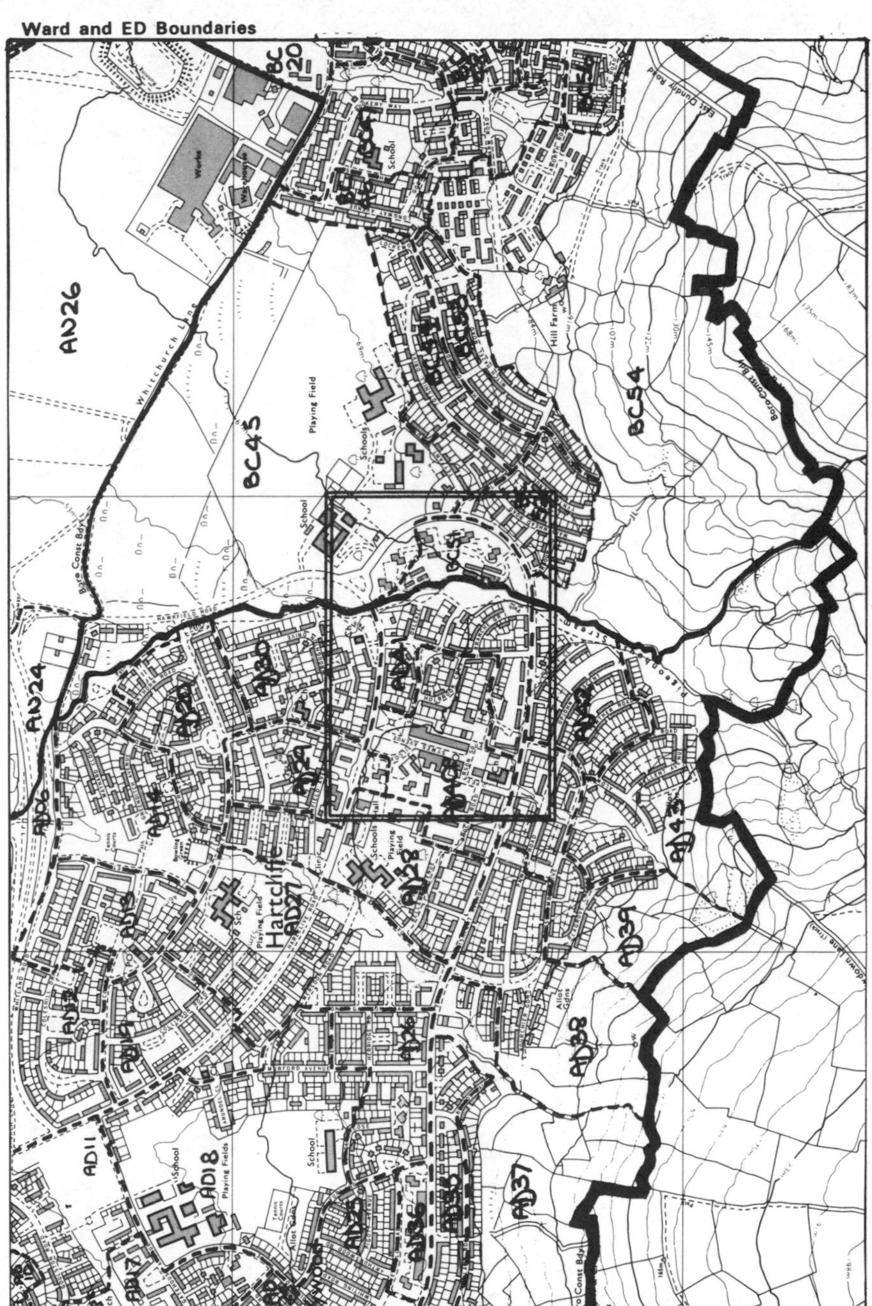

Figure 2.5 Ward and ED boundaries on a larger scale OS map for the area shown as a rectangle on figure 2.4

Enumeration District – detail

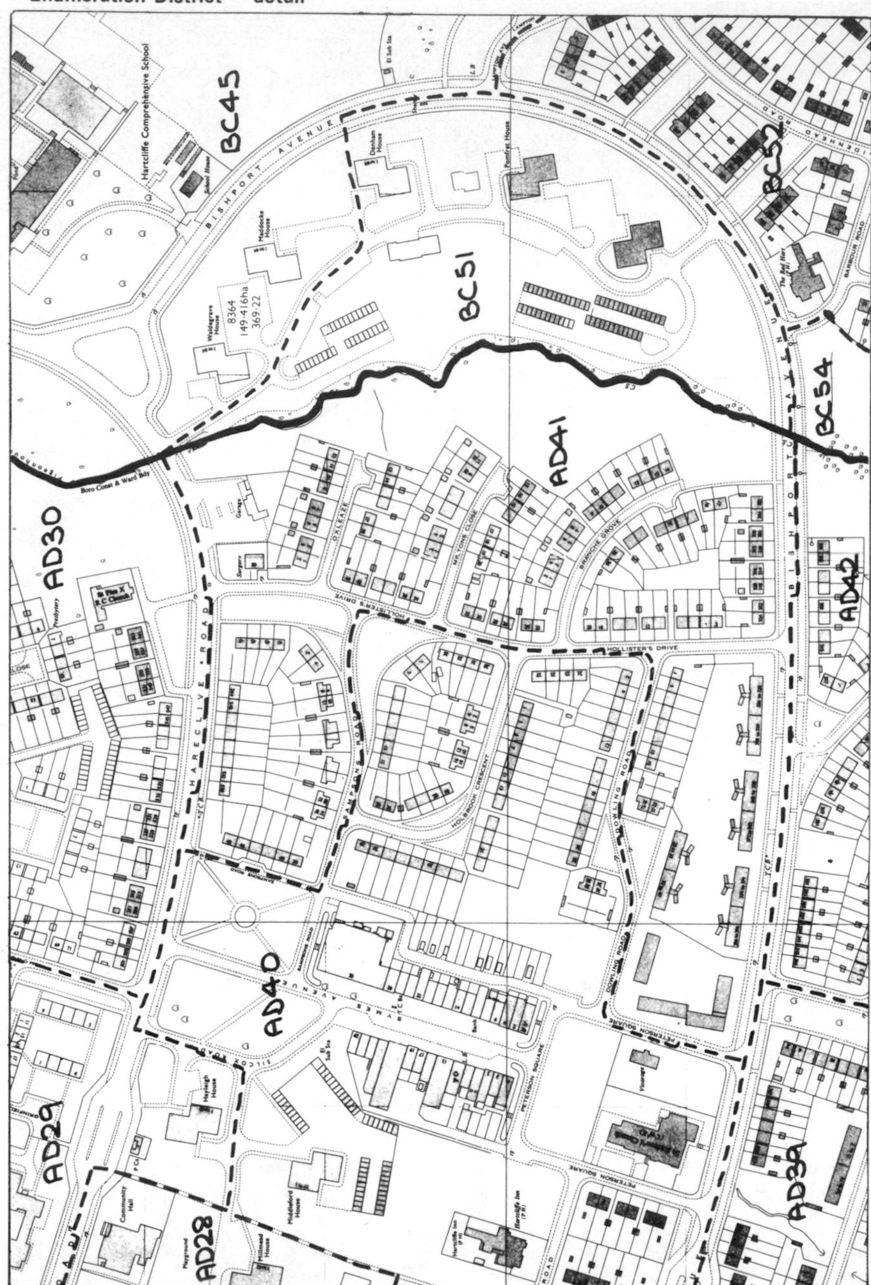

Figure 2.6 Enumeration Districts and the houses therein, shown on a large scale OS map for the rectangular area on figure 2.5

scale ED maps on microfilm for the whole of England and Wales is also available. In England and Wales individual wards can also be identified on the ED maps from the ED numbering system. This is a six character system where the first two characters identify the local-government district, the second two the ward within the district, and the last two the ED within the ward. Thus AA AB 03 in the identification for the third ward in the district AA. A list relating names to district and ward identifications can be obtained.

Copies of *larger scale maps* of ED boundaries (as in figure 2.6) in urban areas can be obtained. The maps are at 1:2500 (25 inches to the mile) or 1:1250 (50 inches to the mile) scale and are available for areas in which this large-scale coverage was essential to ED planning. There is not complete large-scale coverage and in some cases only parts of EDs are at the large scale. At 1:1250 scale, all sheets cover an area of 1 km^2; at 1:1250 all sheets cover an area of 500 × 500 metres, that is four sheets for each 1 kilometre grid square.

The prices of maps supplied for use with SAS are shown in the SAS Prospectus and include an element for the payment of royalty charges to Ordnance Survey when the copies for customers are made by the Census Offices. These charges were reviewed and increased by Ordnance Survey during 1981 and may be reviewed again. The Census Office must therefore reserve the right to revise charges for SAS maps supplied, and these may differ from the charges obtaining at the time of order. Whilst the Census Offices place no restrictions on the copying and reproduction of ED boundaries or zones based on them, the copying of the base maps on which they are drawn requires permission from Ordnance Survey and may involve the payment of royalties; advice should be sought direct from Ordnance Survey (appendix 8).

The spatial position of every ED is also given by a 'centroid' National Grid reference, stored as 100 m units in standard Ordnance Survey form. Thus SZ 123 876 would be the grid reference of Birkbeck College Geography Department to the nearest 100 m. These can be used in the computer for various spatial retrieval processes and in producing maps which plot data at points. A development is to describe the whole boundary of an area in terms of grid references which the computer can store and manipulate – called 'digitized' boundaries – and these are available for wards and civil parishes (from SIA Ltd., acting as agents for the Department of the Environment). Other census users such as the GLC have announced plans to digitize ED boundaries. Certain aspects of this are discussed in sections 2.5.7 and 2.5.8 and in Chapter 6.

2.9.11 COMPARISON OF 1971 AND 1981 SAS

OPCS is offering additional services to help the comparison of 1971–81 statistics for small areas in England and Wales. Comparable small areas comprising one or more 1971 and/or 1981 EDs, known as census tracts, are being drawn up by OPCS (see section 2.5.4.2). Tract constitutions will be available as outlines on transparent overlay maps of OS 1:10,000 sheets or as listings on punching sheets or magnetic tape. Comparable 1971 and 1981 SAS counts for census tracts – a sub-set of the full SAS in each case – will be available together on magnetic tape. Identical data for post-1974 administrative districts will also be available. The content of the 1971–81 SAS has been designed (OPCS 1982), and the file itself was produced in late 1982. There will also be an associated *Guide to Comparability* giving further information and for use, for example, with 1971 and 1981 SAS on hard copy. In Scotland, geographical comparability between 1971 and 1981 is being given in a different way (see section 2.5.5.2) and GRO(S) Customer Services should be contacted for information (see appendix 8 for address).

2.9.12 SAS DOCUMENTATION AND BACK-UP

Customers for SAS are supplied with explanatory notes. These are for use in conjunction with a volume of definitions published by HMSO for use with 1981 census output (see section 2.8.1). Customers for SAS on magnetic tape are supplied with explanatory notes relating to the magnetic tape. A number of other documents relating to the SAS are planned and these will be announced in Census Monitors. The staff of Census Customer Services and at other user enquiry points in the Census Offices are available to SAS customers to answer technical and statistical queries.

3 User needs – an overview

BARBARA BALLARD AND PETER NORRIS

3.1 Introduction

Nearly seventy years ago T.A. Welton (1911) wrote:

> the figures which they (the Registrar-General and the Census Commissioners) supply are like stones in a quarry, of little use unless they are dug out and shaped, and built up in an intelligent manner.

In this chapter, we shall examine how census users are able to shape census statistics to their needs and how far the Census Offices provide statistics which are already shaped to the needs of users. We shall also be concerned with the identification of purposes which the census data do not meet; the intention of this is twofold – to suggest areas in which the census might develop to meet user needs and to save the researcher time spent seeking, from the census, information which it cannot provide.

Our examination of the uses of census output will be preceded by an examination of the different types of census users; some slight overlap between these is inevitable (and intentional). Our information on uses and users draws on published and unpublished research, on statutory uses, on requests for tabulations made to OPCS, and on responses to a questionnaire concerned with academics' plans for using the 1981 Census (Norris 1980).

3.2 The census use study

Since 1974 an index of census use has been compiled by research officers in OPCS Census Division. The study is carried out, with limited resources, to help the design of the census and the improvement of services to users, and to provide a basis for reviews of census usage by representing current practice and trends in the use of census output. Many of the examples of census use mentioned in this chapter are drawn from this index.

The index, however, has its limitations. Although some research using census information becomes known to Census Division through research liaison or through users' links with Census Customer Services, the index is compiled mainly by scanning relevant journals and bibliographies. Intuition

Barbara Ballard is employed in the Census Division of the Office of Population Censuses and Surveys. The views expressed in this chapter are the author's and do not necessarily represent those of OPCS.

plays an important part in this process; at times, references found in bibliographies or books reviewed in journals are judged to merit further examination not because the census is specifically mentioned as a source of information but because either the topic, the area level, or the period of time covered by the research are unique (or almost so) to the census data sets. Additionally, despite special efforts by researchers to keep track of innovative development in census use, the practice of scanning only what are considered to be *relevant* journals and bibliographies will inevitably militate against the discovery of new uses. A particular handicap, affecting the study of both established and innovative use, is that it has been found extremely difficult to investigate the extent of use of published census volumes held in libraries or the use of selections from these volumes published in secondary sources. Recent technological developments enabling dissemination under licence of 'unpublished' statistics via outlets other than OPCS – for example, by libraries and census 'agencies' – only serve to exacerbate this problem.

Indeed, for some types of census use the index is selective. Only a proportion of the many examples of the use of census statistics for validating a sample are included. Any sample survey which claims to be representative of the population being studied is likely to require census statistics or estimates interpolated from census statistics for validation, as long as the population being studied is counted in the census. This extremely common use of the census is often overlooked in debates about the necessity for censuses of the whole population; survey researchers are not only provided with 'benchmark' statistics of the whole population classified by age, sex, marital status, and so on, but they are also provided with statistics for particular geographical areas and for subsets of the population such as the self-employed, the elderly living alone, the highly qualified, and local authority tenants.

One of the main sources of information for this examination of the uses and users of census output is therefore biased. It favours census use in academic research – because academics are more likely to publish and publicize their work than other types of user; it may not cover some innovative uses of census output; and it may not give very comprehensive information about the use of published volumes or the use of statistics disseminated via secondary outlets. To some extent, the index also favours examples of census use where the census data are central to the research; instances of census data being the only data set used or one of only two data sets are in the majority. Such distortions in our knowledge of census usage will inevitably influence our impressions of different types of census user and our understanding of the problems encountered in using census statistics. Finally, it almost goes without saying that we know very little about the needs of those who could have used the census but who, for one reason or another, were deterred.

3.3 Central government as a census user

The Census Act of 1920, which provides statutory authority for the Census of Population in Great Britain, charges the Registrar-General with a duty to prepare census reports and lay them before both Houses of Parliament. Further, if the Registrar-General thinks fit and if the request is judged by him to be reasonable, he is empowered to prepare abstracts containing statistical information other than that contained in the reports *at the request and cost of any local authority or person.* By specifying the Registrar-General's responsibility to Parliament, and by making the right to request other tabulations open to all users, the Act embodies the principle that access to census statistics should be available to all.

During the consultation period before the 1981 Census, OPCS Census Division identified four main user-groups. These were central government, local government, research and academic interests, and a large group comprising industry and commerce (including nationalized industries), pressure groups, and community groups. These were useful categories for setting up formal consultation machinery for liaison with likely users of 1981 Census results, but informal liaison with census users and examination of examples of census use have highlighted the potential complexity of any rigid classification of users. For the purposes of this section, we will not attempt to be comprehensive and will concentrate on users within central government – the main commissioner and paymaster for the census. Users in local government and in academic communities will be described in passing in section 3.4 and elsewhere in the book. Comparatively little commercial use was made of detailed 1971 census data, but this seems likely to differ so far as 1981 data are concerned (see the appendices for contact addresses).

Central government departments use statistics from the census in a number of different ways: as indicators for resource allocation; as the basis for population estimates and population projections; for estimating the future income and expenditure of the Social Security system and the National Insurance system; for the construction of National Life Tables; as input to policy-making decisions; as a basis for further research; and (particularly the Central Statistical Office and the Department of the Environment) as input to statistical information services.

3.3.1 RESOURCE ALLOCATION

One of the Census Topic sheets made available to the public at the time of the 1981 Census looked at each census question in turn and gave the main uses of the statistics derived from that question (OPCS 1980b). It was clear from this summary that the census provided important input to the complex formulae used by the Government in resource allocation schemes such as the Rate

Support Grant (RSG) and the corresponding scheme for the health services from the Resource Allocation Working Party (RAWP). For 1981/2 £9025 million was transferred from central government to local government in England and Wales by the RSG; for the same period the RAWP allocation from central government to local health authorities in England was £7900 million.

Starting from the financial year 1981/2, the calculation of the RSG for local authorities in England and Wales has been modified as a result of the Local Government, Planning and Land Act of 1980. The new RSG calculation introduces a single element grant – known as Block Grant – to replace the needs and resources elements of the former system. The effect of the introduction of Block Grant has been to place increased emphasis on numerical indicators which are reliable at district level and comparable across England and Wales. The importance of centrally-collected large data sets such as the census in providing such measures is clear. Indeed, OPCS was committed to make all 100 per cent Small Area Statistics (SAS) available by May 1982 – giving SAS priority over other output – so that 1981 census figures could be introduced into the 1983/4 Block Grant calculation. The availability of 1981 census data will iron out some of the uncertainties existing in the calculations prior to those for 1983/84, especially since one of the sources used to update 1971 census information, the National Dwelling and Housing Survey (NDHS), was not designed to give reliable information at the area levels for which it was being used.

The distribution of Block Grant is, at the time of writing, governed by an assessment of spending needs known as Grant Related Expenditure (GRE). In a radical departure from the methods used in the previous system, it was determined that assessments would need to be made separately for *each* individual authority, not just for shire counties, metropolitan districts and London boroughs as before (for an account of reasons for this change see Bramley and Evans 1981a). Hence, in England alone, over 400 assessments are now made (including assessments for higher-tier authorities) compared with the 108 assessments required for the needs and resources elements of the RSG – the vast majority of these new assessments being the ones at shire district level. For those numerical indicators derived from statistical sources (rather than administrative sources), the census is the only nationally available source which can reliably meet demand for shire district statistics. Furthermore, because responsibilities are split differently between different tiers of local government, a knock-on effect of individual assessments of spending need for each authority has necessitated separate GRE formulae for individual services; some major services are split into sub-components, each with a formula. Over fifty separate GRE formulae have been determined – for example, for housing, environmental health, education, refuse collection, and parks – which, after calculation, are aggregated in the appropriate combinations for each type of authority to arrive at a composite GRE assessment.

The number of numerical indicators required for GRE assessments for each local authority is about ninety – a figure which includes the separate elements of several composite indicators and which should be compared with the fifteen indicators previously required for the needs elements (these figures and the subsequent description of the indicators are taken from an analysis of the GRE formula in paper 2 of Bramley and Evans 1981b). About half of the ninety or so indicators appear to require at least some census information for their calculation; many of these census-related indicators are multivariate counts or inputs to composite indicators which have been devised to measure special educational needs and the effects of poor housing and social conditions and adverse economic situations. Much of the detailed census data required for GRE calculations is concentrated in the formulae for personal social services, primary and secondary schools, other educational expenditure (school meals, libraries and so on), refuse handling and environmental health, and housing. However, nearly all service formulae appear to require basic indicators of resident or daytime population and, of particular interest to the study of census use, there is an indicator used in a wide range of service formulae which is designed to be sensitive to settlement patterns *within* local authority boundaries. Hence population figures right down to ward/parish level are required and will rely heavily on census information.

We have examined use of census data for RSG allocation at some length because the new system represents a major change in the importance of the census, both in the number of variables used and the areas for which the data are required.

3.3.2 POPULATION ESTIMATES

Population estimates for England and Wales are prepared annually by the Population Statistics Division of OPCS and are initiated from data from the preceding census. For any year, the first estimates to be made are the national estimates; these are then followed by local authority estimates to district level and NHS administrative area estimates to health district level. At national, regional and county level, and for London boroughs and Metropolitan districts, estimates of the numbers of males and females and age distribution are provided; for shire districts (non-metropolitan and Welsh districts) estimates show only the numbers of males and females.

Census data are updated from a wide variety of sources to take account of births, deaths, civilian migration, changes in institutional populations and so on. Most of the statistics used are derived from data collected for other purposes; only a few statistics, such as those from the International Passenger Survey, are specially collected. Changes in the availability and reliability of these sources, and the introduction of completely new ones, require that the methodology for population estimates is constantly under review. In 1978, for example, as a result of the availability of new sources, the cancellation of the

1976 Census, and the methodological changes made possible by local government reorganization, the 1971–7 estimates were re-calculated to a revised formula which is still in use. A full account of the current methodology for local authority population estimates, giving both general principles and a detailed outline, has recently been published by OPCS (1980c). The results of the 1981 Census are likely to lead to further improvements in methodology.

The census provides more than basic age, sex and population data for the estimates. In Great Britain, internal migration is one of the most difficult elements of population change to measure. Statistics from the 1981 Census question on 'usual address one year ago' will provide a comprehensive set of migration data for estimates early in the decade and will underpin information from other sources until the next set of census data becomes available.

As well as being the base for population estimates until the next census, each census also provides a check on the accuracy of the estimates made since the last census (OPCS 1981c). The paper *The revised mid-1971 population estimates for local authorities compared with the original estimates* describes a comparison, at district level, of the estimates for mid-1971 which were carried forward from the 1961 Census with the revised estimates for mid-1971 which used 1971 census statistics as a base. A similar study will be carried out to assess the accuracy of mid-1981 estimates.

We have already alluded to the importance of local authority population estimates to resource allocation; the interest in retrospective examinations of the accuracy of estimates, in order to assess current methodology, may be understood partly as a reflection of this. Within a month of the availability of the 1981 Census preliminary figures they had been compared, at district level, with the estimates that would have been expected on the basis of information previously available (HMSO 1981a, 1981b).

3.3.3 POPULATION PROJECTIONS

Projections of the population of the United Kingdom and of its constituent countries by sex and age have been made by the Government Actuary's Department, in consultation with the Registrars-General, since the 1920s. One of the main uses of the earlier projections was in connection with long-term financial estimates under the Contributory Pensions Acts and other schemes of social insurance. Although projections made since the Second World War have been increasingly used in all areas of government planning, departments estimating the future income and expenditure of the social security system and the national insurance system are still major users of population projections. Between 1955 and 1979, new national projections were made every year. The current series, which from time to time includes projections subdivided by marital status as well as by age and sex, contains projections for a forty-year period, and is revised biennially.

In the mid-1960s, when the Government drew up the National Plan, sub-national population projections were required as input to the formulation of regional planning policies. The first set of projections by age and sex, for each of the regions of England and Wales, appeared in an Appendix to the National Plan and were also published separately by the Registrar-General (HMSO 1965a, 1965b). From 1974 onwards, projections for counties and metropolitan districts, as well as for regions, have been produced in response to increasing emphasis on planning below the regional level as a result of local government and National Health Service reorganization. The mid-1977 based projections for 1977–1991, published in 1980, for the first time also included projections for each of the London boroughs (HMSO 1980b).

The projections are made by the *demographic component method* which makes assumptions of the future number of births, deaths and migrants and builds these onto the base population (for further details of this methodology see HMSO 1981d). The census is important for the calculation of all four of these elements. The base populations for both national and sub-national projections are the appropriate population estimates – though, at a regional and sub-regional level, interpolations for single years of age have to be made for the projections. Age distribution is an important input to the calculation of the future numbers of births and deaths in each local area; national age-specific birth and death rates, modified to take account of local variations in fertility and mortality, are applied to the numbers of males and females in each age group of the local population.

Migration, however, is usually the main determinant of population change in sub-national areas; it is the most difficult element to predict because there are few sources of comprehensive statistics to show past trends and the current situation, especially in respect of internal migration. At the national level, OPCS, in consultation with other Departments, makes estimates of the future numbers of people entering or leaving the country, but the task of making assumptions of net migration for sub-national areas has been undertaken by the DoE in consultation with each local planning authority (a fuller description of local authority involvement in migration assumptions is given in Morrey 1980). Until migration data from the 1981 Census becomes available, the most comprehensive source of migration statistics is still the 1971 Census, although data from the National Health Service Central Register (NHSCR) also provide a useful indication of migration trends (see below). Some local planning authorities are able to supplement these sources with locally available statistics in making their estimates of future net migration. Ultimately, however, the final decisions on local migration assumptions for authorities in England have rested with the DoE, because the predicted net migration flows for each area must balance to zero for movements within the country as a whole.

A fairly recent development in the use of the census within central government is reported in a migration study carried out by the Building Research Establishment (BRE) of the Department of the Environment (Ogilvy 1980). The BRE study is an appraisal of alternative sources of migration statistics which might be used to assist planners and demographers – at least in the estimation of *inter-regional* migration – during the inter-censal period. The National Health Service Central Register (NHSCR) and the Labour Force Surveys (LFS) are the two sources studied. Regional-level statistics from both sources are compared with regional migration data from the 1971 Census; in both cases the statistics under scrutiny are for the time period closest to the period covered in the census migration data (1970–1). The analysis shows a generally high degree of consistency between the two alternative sources and the census, suggesting that the NHSCR and the LFS might be useful alternative sources of regional statistics for periods not covered by the census. The LFS was considered the better source for estimating levels of migration, the NHSCR better for continuous monitoring of trends.

This study is of interest because it shows how census statistics are used not only as input to population projection models but also as a yardstick to calibrate or test possible developments in methodology. The use of the census to compare present and past methodology for population estimates is a similar example.

3.3.4 RESEARCH

Census-based population estimates and projections are used in all areas of government planning but departments also use census results in a more comprehensive way, to meet a variety of statistical needs. For this section, we shall examine what we *know* about the use of census for government research and discuss the importance of the census as one of a number of data sets available to the researcher in government.

First, the topics in the census, the wording of the questions and the answer categories provided therein should all be regarded as important clues to the departmental requirements for statistics. All users are invited to submit to OPCS their views on the information that should be obtained from the census, and the 1920 Census Act requires that census plans should be approved by Parliament. However, because of the need to justify to Ministers and to Parliament the expense of the census and its burden on the public, judgements of the suitability of topics for inclusion in the plans presented to Parliament by government put considerable weight on departmental use of the statistics (see OPCS 1980/1, published in March 1980 to coincide with the publication of the Census Order 1980 which was debated by both Houses of Parliament). This does not imply that all departmental requirements are satisfied; the progress of 1981 census plans –from the White Paper published in 1978 up to the 1980 Census Order finally presented to Parliament – illustrates how reviews of expenditure and concern about public reaction to the census can influence the topic content, despite departmental needs for the statistics.

For each topic, the way the questions are asked and the answer categories provided – as well as the preparation of coding frames – are normally less open to influence from non-departmental users, unless the topic itself is extremely controversial. Census Division statisticians, in consultation with statisticians from 'client' departments, are responsible for the detailed specification of the census forms, taking into account the often conflicting demands for comparability with previous censuses, and relevance to current conditions. Suitability for use on a self-completion form, performance in previous censuses and processing considerations must also be taken into account.

Unlike other users, government researchers have the opportunity to influence the content of the published volumes, especially the topic volumes supplying statistics at the national and regional level which – in some senses – might be regarded as departmental handbooks. Clearly, published tabulations in the topic volumes (and the 'standard unpublished' tables supplementary to them) can only meet statistical needs known at the time the tables are prepared, and there is a limit to the size and complexity of these tabulations. For complex tables, and to meet new statistical needs, departments make requests for special tabulations. After the 1971 Census there was criticism of the delays in the provision of special tabulations – especially the ones required by departments – and as a result, for 1981 census output, a quota system has been imposed by OPCS which will restrict each department to a specified volume of work. Departmental tabulations will be derived from specially-created sub-files, some containing a 1 per cent sample, and an interactive programming facility will enable the tabulations to be programmed by the user requesting them (OPCS Report annexed to H.M. Government 1981).

The evidence we have of the sales of 1971 SAS shows that by June 1977 central government users had spent more than other users on the purchase of SAS (about 47 per cent of the total), and had, on average, spent much more per purchase than other users – the most likely explanation of this being that 'small area' research carried out by central government tends to cover a larger number of areas than the research carried out by other users (Hakim 1978a).

Many of the examples of SAS use within government bear this out. OPCS' Population Statistics Division, in a joint project with the Planning Research Applications Group (PRAG) of the Centre for Environmental Studies (CES), developed a cluster analysis technique to classify national sets of 1971 SAS at ED, ward/parish and local authority district level. A number of papers by Webber and Craig – (1978) for example – describe the techniques used and the results obtained. DoE used indicators drawn from SAS to study social deprivation in urban areas on behalf of the Home Office (Holtermann 1975a and 1975b) and, after the introduction of the 1974 Housing Act, recommended the use of SAS indicators together with other official data in the selection of potential housing action areas, priority neighbourhoods and general improvement areas (DoE 1975a; see also O'Dell and Parker 1977). Similarly, DoE, at the request of the National and Local Government Statistical Liaison Committee, commissioned a research project for developing a method of estimating the average income per household using data from the census and the General Household Survey (Rothman 1977). At DHSS, the 108 health authorities in England with responsibility for the personal social services were classified using multivariate techniques on twenty-three SAS-derived indicators (Imber 1977). A study carried out by the Scottish Office Central Research Unit yielded a range of socioeconomic indicators from the 1971 Census and other sources for rural areas in Scotland. The purpose was to provide a set of comparative data to local authorities faced with the assessment of rural problems and the identification of the appropriate policy response. Indicators relating to demography, economic activity and housing/household characteristics were provided for 28 districts/islands areas and 644 parishes. A second stage of the study produced a typology of rural areas using multivariate techniques (Burbridge and Robertson 1978a and 1978b).

Studies such as the ones mentioned above take advantage of the fact that SAS are available as a national set of comparable statistics. Government studies, however, also benefit from other research possibilities offered by SAS. In a study to see what could be deduced about crime amongst ethnic minority groups, the Home Office Research Unit needed statistics to define the social characteristics of areas covered by police force divisions in each of the six metropolitan counties and Greater London. Since police force areas do not match areas for which census statistics are routinely produced, the solution was to aggregate 1971 SAS areas, at a variety of levels, to create the *ad hoc* areas required and hence arrive at 1971 census statistics for these areas. For each division, correlations between crime rates and proportion of ethnic minority settlement were then made. A similar study of arrest rates carried out in London aggregated ward-level SAS to Metropolitan Police Department divisions (Stevens and Willis 1979).

The Department of Employment (DE) and the Manpower Services Commission (MSC) are major users of census statistics, particularly those relating to economic activity, occupation, industry and higher qualifications (for example, DE 1975, 1977). Of particular importance to the operational work of MSC is the census information on the unemployed. DE's own regular statistics on unemployment are derived from the administration of the unemployment benefit system and do not include the unregistered unemployed; this particularly affects the measurement of unemployment amongst women. The census is also one of the few detailed sources of information on the self-employed and because it contains such a wide range of information, can provide cross-tabulations of information not otherwise simultaneously available within the same data set. The internal migration of people with particular skills and qualifications – cross-tabulating four questions on the census form – provides important information on labour mobility, and the deployment of people with particular skills and qualifications can be determined by cross-tabulating qualifications with details of employment. The Finniston Report, for example, recommended that the census should be used to obtain information about the stock and deployment of engineers (DI 1980).

The census asks respondents currently in a job to provide the address of their place of work. This information, when analysed in conjunction with the address of usual residence, provides statistics which show patterns of travel between home and work. DE uses these statistics to define a set of labour market areas with a high level of 'self-containment' – that is, each area provides work for most of its residents and fills most of its jobs from workers who live in its area. These 'travel-to-work areas' (TTWAs) are the smallest areas for which unemployment rates are calculated; they are currently used by the Department of Industry in consideration of assisted areas policy, and by the MSC in the organization of its services. The TTWA(s) will be revised when work-trip information from the 1981 Census becomes available. It should be noted that unemployment statistics have been provided for aggregations of postcode sector areas only as from some time in 1982.

The availability of both home and workplace addresses on each census form enables OPCS to compile SAS *workplace-based* statistics and some others. This has major implications for manpower planning, not least since where people presently work rather than where they live is often of prime interest to potential employers. A pilot study of the differences between workplace and residence-based census employment statistics was carried out on 1971 data in a project sponsored by MSC (Owen *et al.* 1981). Plans exist for a much more extensive study based on 1981 census data.

The Government Statistical Service provides a wide range of resources to the government researcher embarking on an empirical study. For those whose main data source is one of the national continuous sample surveys of individuals or households, the census provides both a framework for validating the sample and a reference point for evaluating statistics derived from the survey. Examples of the use of the 1971 Census to examine non-response bias in continuous surveys can be found in studies carried out by the Social Survey Division of OPCS (Kemsley 1975, 1976; Barnes and Birch 1975). In many respects the census and the national sample surveys also have complementary functions. The census provides information for subgroups of the population and for areas below regional level where sample survey results would not be reliable, but sample surveys are more flexible and can be taken more frequently, thus updating the national and regional census results during the inter-censal period. (Barber 1980, for example, summarizes some of the findings of the 1977–8 National Dwelling and Housing Survey and compares them with data from the 1971 Census.)

Since the census is able to provide statistics of subgroups of the population, any *ad hoc* survey, whether national or local, of a subgroup counted in the census can use census statistics for sample validation. However, one of the particular advantages of the census to government researchers is that 'follow-up' surveys from the census – using the census as a sampling frame – are a possibility, though, for confidentiality reasons, the surveys have to be conducted by the Census Offices. These are voluntary surveys carried out among individuals or households whose names and addresses have been picked out from the census forms. The 1971 follow-up survey of qualified manpower, for example, was carried out amongst a sample of people specifying qualifications above A-level on the form. A similar survey of qualified manpower was carried out after the 1966 Census (DES 1971). After the 1981 Census the only follow-up survey carried out in England and Wales was the post-enumeration coverage check in a sample of just over 1000 enumeration districts, and a quality check of the answers given by about 5000 households within the same enumeration districts (OPCS 1982/3). Any other surveys would have had to have been notified to Parliament and approved, prior to the census being taken. In Scotland similar quality and coverage checks were conducted, but there were two other follow-up surveys as well: one obtained further information about vacant or owner-absent property; the other was carried out amongst a sample of people with teaching qualifications but not teaching at the time of the census.

Within the Census Offices it is also possible to use the census as an input to a longitudinal study, in which data collected over a period of time are linked together so that the relationship of a variety of events occurring at different times can be studied. The current OPCS Longitudinal Study was started with a 1 per cent sample from the 1971 Census which has since been updated and supplemented with data derived from other records handled within OPCS. The methods used in creating and maintaining the study, and those used for ensuring confidentiality are described in a paper by OPCS (1973); it also discusses the importance of this type of study to medical research. The first major report of the study concerns mortality occurring in the sample between Census Day 1971 and the end of 1975. Differences in mortality according to characteristics recorded in the 1971 Census are described and analysed (Fox and Goldblatt 1982). A similar project which updated until 1978 a sample drawn from the 1961 Census has provided important evidence about cancer risk to hairdressers. Observed and expected mortality among a sample of nearly 2000 male hairdressers was examined, with particular attention to five malignancies reported to have increased amongst hairdressers (Alderson 1980).

1971 census data has also been linked, within OPCS, to data derived from a 1970–1 study of morbidity in general practice. This has allowed cross-tabulation of the survey data with census data and has greatly extended the range of the original study (RCGP/OPCS/DHSS 1982).

3.3.5 INPUT TO STATISTICAL INFORMATION SERVICES

Nearly all Government departments generate statistical information derived from their own administrative records, and some departments also conduct or commission surveys to yield statistics specifically for research alone. In one sense, therefore, all departments provide a statistical information service and indeed the Business Statistics Office and all statistical divisions of OPCS except Registration Division exist mainly as collectors and disseminators of statistics. In this section, however, we shall look at two departments whose role as disseminators of statistics extends to statistics which were not generated from within their own departments.

The Central Statistical Office (CSO) is a small department with responsibility for the co-ordination of the Government Statistical Service (GSS) and for the overall process of disseminating the products of the GSS to the public. The task of setting up the framework for dissemination is tackled in four ways: by providing publicity for the GSS as a whole by means of touring displays, explanatory leaflets, advertising and so on, and acting as a clearing house for enquiries from the public; by preparing user guides – the most comprehensive being the *Guide to Official Statistics*; by producing a range of statistical digests, for example, *Monthly Digest of Statistics, Social Trends* (annual), *Regional Trends* (annual) and the Penguin reference book *Facts in Focus* (revised periodically); and by publishing a quarterly journal *Statistical News* in which the latest developments in the collection and dissemination of official statistics are discussed. The statistical digests, in particular *Social Trends*, serve as important secondary sources of national and regional census statistics.

The Department of the Environment also disseminates census-based statistics, but in this case the statistical information service is directed at local authorities rather than at the general public. Since many local authorities are looking for statistics which describe their own administrative areas or parts of them and wish to contrast these with equivalent statistics for other authorities, many of the DoE initiatives have extended and facilitated the use of *small area* census data, in contrast with the service provided by CSO.

3.4 The use of the census by topic

A major attraction of the census is that it involves the simultaneous collection of data on a range of characteristics of individuals and households, and the production of statistics for small areas. Our major purpose in this section is to examine the adequacy of the 1981 Census in dealing with different topics, though most sections are illustrated with examples of important recent work based on earlier census data. The topics covered in the last two censuses are classified under eight headings.

3.4.1 THE DEMOGRAPHIC TOPICS

The 1981 Census asked questions on name, sex, marital status, date of birth, position in household, whereabouts on census night and usual address (see Chapter 2). These can be considered as the basic variables against which other variables are often measured – cross-tabulations by age, sex and marital status are frequent in SAS tables. Statistics on the elderly (married or single), on one-parent families and on age structure are frequently used in assessing need and in planning services by central and local government, and as indicators in area profiles.

Because these topics are so fundamental, criticism of their provision is generally directed against the failure to exploit fully the data available to OPCS. For example, the 1971 Census was criticized because it was not possible to calculate from SAS how many children under five were in one-parent families, even though it was possible to calculate the number of one-parent families containing children aged under five (Hakim 1978a). The grouping of ages (usually into quinquennial groups) has also provoked criticism, in that it removes from the user the opportunity to aggregate age groups as desired. Ambiguity about the marital status of cohabiting couples has caused problems and led to the probable over-estimation of the number of one-parent families in 1971 (Leete 1978). Recent evidence concerning the prevalence of pre-marital cohabitation (Kiernan 1980) suggests that a case could be made for a 'cohabiting' category in response to the marital status question. However, such a category would probably be deemed an intrusion on privacy.

The change from a *de facto* to a *de jure* population base is discussed at length elsewhere (section 2.3.1). While the change poses considerable problems for studies of change over time, the old *de facto* base posed occasional problems for planners. Obviously it makes more sense to plan for usual residents rather than a mixture of usual and temporary residents: the 1971 population statistics for Nairn, a small town of some 8000 people, were dramatically inflated by the presence of about 2000 sailors on *HMS Ark Royal* then anchored off the coast.

3.4.2 MIGRATION

Migration, rather than births or deaths, is primarily responsible for the redistribution of population within Great Britain. The 1971 Census recorded 17.5 million people moving between 1966 and 1971. In the absence of any register of moves, the census remains the major source of information on internal migration in Great Britain. Though the National Health Service Central Register is a possible source of information on moves (Goldblatt and Fox 1978), it misses an unknown number of moves where movers fail to register with a new doctor, or to notify a change of address when they stay with the same doctor. The census attempts only to detect whether or not an individual has moved within a certain time period – five years and one year before the 1971 Census, one year before the 1981 Census.

Census migration data fall into two types – stock of recent in-migrants and flow. In the 1981 SAS tables, the stock of in-migrants moving in the year before the census is given, cross-tabulated against housing amenities (100 per cent) and socioeconomic group of head of household (10 per cent sample), and analysed by age and sex. In 1971, SAS in-migrants were also categorized according to whether they had come from within the local authority area and, of course, data were also available on those who had moved within the last five years rather than just in the last year.

Migration is one of two topics (journey-to-work is the other) for which census data relating to flows from one place to another are given. Data have been provided for various area levels of origin and destination since a question on place of previous residence was first asked in 1961, but never below the local authority district level. Flows were available for 1971 at the district level classified by sex, and the total number of in-migrants and out-migrants for each district was broken down by age group. Flow data by age group were available for sub-planning regions, and by socioeconomic group of family head for eighteen conurbations and regional remainders. Flow data broken down by tenure were also available for conurbations and remainders. Flow data from the 1961 and 1966 censuses tend to be for rather coarser area levels, as Johnston (1969) noted in his study of migration in the London boroughs in 1960–1. Kennett (1978) has dealt with the shortcomings of census migration data thoroughly: we summarize these briefly here, and recommend that readers wishing to undertake migration analysis refer to his paper and to Willis (1974). Kennett identifies four general shortcomings of the data: movements missed; lack of data on emigration; problems of under-enumeration; and problems in comparisons of patterns between censuses. Movements missed include those where the mover dies during the period under study, or where the mover is aged below one or five years, multiple moves (where the mover has had one or more address in addition to present address and that given on the census form as place of previous residence) and return moves (where the mover lived at the present address one or five years previously, but has moved away and back in the interim). More arcane sources of under-enumeration of migrants could stem from the respondents writing 'SAME' in response to the question on previous address, intending the same as the head of household's previous address but actually being construed as the same as present address.

Problems in comparison of migration over time stem largely from the changes in area levels for which data are provided, as well as from changes in area boundaries and in definitions used. Sampling error could also cause problems: in 1971 and before, migration data was taken on a 10 per cent sample, but most 1981 SAS migration figures are 100 per cent. An obvious criticism of SAS figures is that they refer only to in-migrants, whereas information on out-migrants might be more valuable for some tasks; it is possible to order special migration flow analyses from the 1981 Census defining, for any destination, areas of origin in terms of postcode areas, and so gain information on out-migrants. Some important work has been carried out with such special tabulations, as by Dugmore (1975), who obtained socio-economic groupings of migrants at the London borough level and constructed a full matrix of flows, and Lamont (1979), who studied intra-urban movements in Glasgow. Champion (1976) and Law and Warnes (1976) have carried out interesting studies at coarser levels, but researchers wishing to study migration at finer levels have often resorted to other sources: Johnston (1967) and Short (1978b) have used electoral registers, and Walter (1980) and Short (1978a) have used questionnaires. While Ford (1979) has drawn attention to the shortcomings of the electoral register (see also section 10.2.4), researchers wishing to study migration to and (especially) from small areas should consider these sources in addition to the census.

3.4.3 RACE

A question on place or country of birth or nationality has been asked in every census since 1841 (until 1891 respondents were asked simply to indicate whether or not they were British subjects rather than to give nationality). However, since 1961 the framing of a question on nationality has been a more delicate and time-consuming task than has the framing of any other question. In 1971, no question on nationality was asked, but respondents were asked to give their own place of birth, parents' country of birth and, where relevant, year of entry into the UK. In 1981, respondents were asked simply to state their own place and country of birth. The lack of more searching questions on race in this census should not be taken as any lack of need: Sillitoe (1978) has explained in detail OPCS' efforts to find a question on ethnic origin which would yield accurate information and also gain public acceptance. Questions on nationality, year of entry to the UK, parents' country of birth and ethnic origin were considered, and the last two appeared on the form for the Test Census carried out in 1979 in Haringey, a multi-ethnic area of North London. Public opposition to both questions was considerable, and, in the light of this, OPCS recommended to the government that neither question should be asked in the 1981 Census. The government accepted the recommendation, although a motion from Mr Alex Lyon MP, calling for the inclusion of a question on ethnic origins, forced the first division on the Census Order ever taken in Parliament.

Mr Lyon's desire for a question on ethnic origins was matched by those of a number of umbrella bodies representing ethnic minority groups, such as the

Commission for Racial Equality and the Runnymede Trust, and of many census users. Broadly, their reasoning is that if ethnic minorities are disadvantaged if they live in areas suffering deprivation, then it is necessary to understand the nature, spatial distribution and seriousness (compared with deprivation suffered by other groups) of this deprivation if satisfactory steps are to be taken to alleviate it.

Opposition to the ethnic questions has come chiefly from members of ethnic minorities, and is centred around two main points. First, there is the fear that statistics would be used within government for purposes very much less humanitarian than those outlined above.

The second reason for opposition to the ethnic question was that many foreign-born parents objected to having their British-born children classified as anything but British. Lomas (1974) has criticized the official notion of colour – that anyone with one parent of Asian, African or West Indian origin should be counted as coloured. Thus OPCS were faced with an impasse: in order to gather statistics to define any differences in levels of living amongst different racial groups and possibly to lead to revised policies, they had to define categories which cleaved society into sharply bounded groups and the character of these groups offended certain individual respondents. As a consequence of all this, the 1981 data on country of birth do not permit direct identification of second generation black communities: given this, it is impossible to tell whether segregation is increasing or decreasing. With only country of birth data, it is impossible to tell how many of High Wycombe's Asian-born are Sikhs working in the furniture factories and how many are retired colonels or sons of white British army officers, returned to what they would consider the family home. However, OPCS has announced plans to use the results of the 1981 Labour Force Survey to try to produce factors showing the relationship between classifications of country of birth and those relating to ethnic origin, and to show how such relationships vary between areas so that factors can then be applied to census data to give improved estimates of the numbers and demographic characteristics of ethnic minority populations for areas below the national level (OPCS 1982c).

Further shortcomings exist in census data relating to ethnicity. Dissimilar birthplace groups are frequently aggregated into a single category: for example, all those born in the American New Commonwealth (chiefly the Caribbean) are usually grouped together in the published statistics. More seriously, several cross-tabulations in both 1971 and 1981 SAS group all New Commonwealth-born together. Prandy (1980) has demonstrated that the 'social distance' between Asian and West Indian groups living in Britain can be as great as that between either of these groups and the British-born.

Another shortcoming of the data is the lack of cross-tabulation in SAS tables with country of birth as one variable. In 1971, there were no cross-tabulations of it against housing amenities, car ownership or unemployment:

this meant that deprivation of ethnic groups could only be implied through correlation – if areas with a high percentage of residents apparently coming from a particular ethnic group were also areas of overcrowding, of poor housing amenities or of high unemployment. Correlation, of course, does not equal causality and such inference frequently leads to an ecological fallacy (see Chapter 7).

Although ethnicity has been used as one variable in many studies of deprivation, the nature of the data has limited the scope for the study of deprivation of ethnic groups. Considerable attention has been given to studies of segregation, such as those by Jones and McEvoy (1978), Peach (1979), Lee (1978) and Prandy (1980). In passing, we might cast an envious eye at the US census, which includes questions on person's ancestry, Hispanic/Spanish descent, naturalization, year of entry, languages spoken and ability to speak English. However – and possibly due in part to the quest for such detail – the proportion of minority groups such as black males aged eighteen to thirty which was missed by the 1970 US Census would probably blunt the researcher's enthusiasm !

3.4.4 EDUCATION

Respondents were asked two questions on education in 1971 – whether they had degree-level or equivalent qualifications and whether they had A-level or equivalent qualifications. The latter question was not asked in 1981. The value of data on qualifications lies first in defining the geographical distribution of examined skills amongst the workforce and secondly as a social indicator. An obvious drawback of the questions as asked is that they measure attainment of paper qualifications rather than of acquired skills and, in their orientation toward mental rather than manual skills, they perpetuate the image of what may well be an anachronistic division – that between white-collar workers and blue-collar workers. Moreover, a relatively small proportion of the population of Britain hold A-levels and their equivalent, and even fewer hold degrees or their equivalent. In a period of high youth unemployment it is arguable that some information on O-level and CSE qualifications might be of more use. The argument is countered by OPCS and the Department of Education and Science who insist that such data on educational qualifications are publicly available at local-authority district level from other sources. While it would, in principle, be possible for those central government agencies concerned with education, careers or unemployment who have access to individual records to relate these to data for the relevant ED, they would still forgo the possibility of cross-tabulating information on education with information on other topics in the census. Indeed, the paucity of cross-tabulations using education as one variable in 1971 and 1981 SAS suggests that the possibilities for examining relationships with other topics have not been fully explored. The map of educational qualifications in *People in Britain* (CRU/OPCS/GRO(S) 1980) gave what was described as a 'particularly distinctive pattern'.

3.4.5 HOUSING

Census data on housing can be divided into four sections: tenure, amenities, number of rooms and sharing – the last two often being combined to provide indices of overcrowding. Seven of the twenty-eight tables in 1971 SAS were wholly or partly concerned with housing topics: sixteen of the forty-nine tables in 1981 SAS (including tables produced only for England and Wales) involve housing topics. Housing is obviously a central topic in the British census, even though this is not so explicitly stated as in Australia, where the census is described as being of 'Population and Housing'.

Information on housing is used directly in drawing up housing policies: in determining the need for new housing, in selecting areas for improvement, and in illustrating trends in the owner-occupied and private rented sectors. Local government, central government and community groups have all used census data in this way.

Housing amenity, tenure and overcrowding have also been used heavily in studies of deprivation or social well-being. In the absence of any question on income, the standard and means of tenure of one's accommodation is an important censal indicator of wealth. The importance of housing data to such studies is best illustrated with two studies which used very few indicators: Davidson (1976) used four indicators in his study of deprivation in Hull, two of which were overcrowding and lack of an inside WC. Of the five criteria used by Prandy (1980) to interpret the 'social distance' between birthplace groups, two are housing quality and council housing.

Only since 1951 has the census asked questions on housing amenity, tenure and sharing, as well as a question on the number of rooms. Thus before 1951, the only housing data available concerned number of rooms and hence persons per room. While the amount of information available has greatly increased since then, the later data are not without drawbacks. Definitions can be a problem: the question on number of rooms was found to be the least accurately answered of all questions in the 1966 Census (Gray and Gee 1972), and the definition of an outside or inside WC has changed through time. The number of tenure categories has increased in 1981, for the 1971 categories (owner-occupied, rented from council, privately rented furnished, privately rented unfurnished) were rather limited. No count of dwellings was undertaken in 1981: useful though a dwelling count can be, definitional problems occur and the count is prone to error. In 1971, SAS housing variables tended to be cross-tabulated against other housing variables only: this has been remedied in 1981 SAS.

Questions on availability of stove, hot water supply and sink, which were used between 1951 and 1971, have now been omitted, since virtually all households have use of these. While this seems a sensible omission, the opportunity to introduce questions on other amenities – refrigerators, telephones or television, for example – has not been taken. While it is true that data on such amenities are available from voluntary sample surveys such as the General Household Survey, the data are not available for small areas: and while it might be claimed that the amenities mentioned above are indicative of lifestyle rather than of living standard, questions on presence of refrigerator and a telephone are asked in the US census (Kaplan and van Valey 1980), along with questions on fuel used for domestic heating, average monthly cost of gas, electricity, water and oil used and monthly rent. The Australian census asks how much monthly mortgage payments are, and who holds the mortgage, in addition to most of the questions asked in the US census (Australian Bureau of Statistics 1977). Set against these, the restriction of the housing questions in the British census is apparent.

3.4.6 MARRIAGE AND FERTILITY

Although a question on marital status has been asked in every census since 1851, questions on the date of marriage and on fertility have been asked only since 1951 (though isolated questions on duration of marriage and number of children born alive in marriage were asked in 1911). No question on fertility or on date or duration of marriage was asked in the 1981 Census.

Cope and Baum (1979) have discussed the reasons for, and the effects of, omitting questions on fertility from the 1981 Census. We summarize their main points here.

The questions asked in 1971 (on month of birth of children born alive in marriage, and on year and month of first marriage and of its dissolution if ended) were considered by some respondents to intrude on privacy, since it was feared that the data could be used along with data on household composition to reveal illegitimacy and cohabitation. Having experienced this criticism, OPCS were concerned lest public opposition to certain questions put the whole of the 1981 Census at risk, and so potentially offensive questions, including those of marriage, fertility and parents' country of birth, were omitted.

Some initial findings from the 1971 Census quality check (Blunden 1975) indicated that the quality of fertility data was less than that of other census topics – possibly a reflection of public opposition to the questions. Only 89 per cent of women entered the correct number of live-born children, for example. (These response rates to 1971 fertility questions were not, however, appreciably worse than responses to similar questions in previous censuses or surveys.) A further reason for dropping the fertility questions was that little use had been made of the 1971 data. While some of this lack of use could be ascribed to the delay in publication of the fertility report – which had not taken place by 1979 – prepublication tables were available. A more likely reason for the lack of use is that other sources – the National Family Formation Survey, the General Household Survey and the National Dwelling and Household Survey – offer more information on such matters as fertility intentions and attitudes and contraceptive usage. Finally, Cope and Baum (1979) point to the limited significance of detailed areal information in fertility analyses. They mention the resilience of regional differences in fertility through time in support of this assertion.

3.4.7 CARS, VANS AND TRAVEL-TO-WORK

In 1971 a question on the number of cars and vans available to each household was asked for the first time. OPCS had planned not to repeat the questions in 1981 after the Department of Transport had expressed the opinion that its omission would not pose it serious problems. However, pressure from local authorities and researchers resulted in the question being reinstated when the Census Order was debated in Parliament.

The question can be used in two main fields: transport studies and area profiles. Information on the proportion of persons and households in an area with use of a car gives some assistance towards planning public transport services and road systems (Lambeth Borough Department of Town Planning 1980). The responses to this question could also have wider implications for planning, since car ownership implies mobility: a settlement twenty miles from the nearest major source of employment and services might appear hopelessly remote if few of the inhabitants are car owners yet, if many of them are, it could function as a dormitory village. It could be argued that this use of the question could be fulfilled from other sources. Vehicle Licence records are postcoded, but these records are not generally available. Traffic censuses can indicate the use of particular roads, but will not necessarily separate out local and 'foreign' traffic or regular and occasional traffic. It could also be argued that the census question on method of travel to work obviates the need for a further question on car ownership – but use of a means of transport other than a car to get to work does not imply non-ownership of a car. Indeed, the 1981 SAS cross-tabulation of means of travel to work and car ownership could be most revealing.

Even if the alternative sources listed were accurate enough for transport planning, they could not fulfil the second use of the car and van question: area profiles. Car ownership can and has been used as a surrogate of wealth or social status. Several cross-tabulations in 1981 SAS facilitate its use in this manner: many cross-tabulations of household types against housing amenity include car availability as an extra amenity, and car availability is also tabulated against socioeconomic group, New Commonwealth household heads and migrant households.

The question on means of travel to work yields a distinctive national pattern (see maps 22 to 25 in *People in Britain*), and the range of answer categories in 1981 was extended to include underground, car passenger and car pool. In the SAS tables, however, means of travel to work is only tabulated against socioeconomic group and car availability, and then only on a 10 per cent sample. At ED level, therefore, with a small base population and many categories, many small values will occur causing problems of statistical reliability. At a coarser level, the information on means of travel to work will be combined with information on destination to derive traffic flows as given in data available later. However, it is obvious that journeys to work constitute only a proportion of regular journeys undertaken; journeys to shops, to school and those undertaken at work are others. The journey to work question does not, therefore, give a complete picture of traffic flows. It does, however, allow the construction of Travel-To-Work-Areas and hence, to some extent, of labour markets (Smart 1974).

3.4.8 EMPLOYMENT, OCCUPATION AND INDUSTRY

The census has been described in a recent survey of employment statistics (Buxton and Mackay 1977) as the most comprehensive source available. The statistics can be divided into three types: those published in the economic activity tables, mostly at national and regional level; those published in county leaflets (to district level); and those included in SAS. The published statistics give a detailed breakdown of the economically active population (employees in employment, employers, self-employed, unemployed and HM Forces) by detailed occupational headings, industry, age, sex, marital status, socio-economic group and social class. At a national scale, the statistics collected by the Department of Employment are becoming increasingly useful for man-power planning, but the census remains an important source, partly as a benchmark against which the Department's figures can be checked, partly as a universal survey which covers every individual in the country and thus includes the unemployed who are not registered, and partly as a means of identifying long-term trends. While there are breaks in comparability caused by changes in the definitions of the employed or in the occupational classifications used, the census does give a much clearer impression of the working population than do other sources. Before 1948, for example, the Ministry of Labour records referred to the insured population only. Lee (1979) has exploited the possibilities of comparing occupational census data through time, and Buxton and Mackay (1977) have discussed the possibilities and problems involved in so doing. In Chapter 9 we discuss some of the problems of comparability.

The central position of the census in the gathering of employment statistics is illustrated by the fact that, until 1972, it was the classification of occupations prepared by OPCS (chiefly for census purposes) which was used in all government departments. This is no longer the case, since the Department of Employment has now published CODOT (the Classification of Occupation and Dictionary of Occupational Titles), which is to be used as the basis for the classification of 1981 census data (see Chapter 2).

The published national volumes of employment by occupation and industry are of obvious interest to central government, large companies and pressure groups, Showler's (1974) examination of employment and retirement for Age Concern providing an example of the latter. These employment data also provide the bases for the definition of social class and (more recently) socioeconomic groupings used in the census. Whether occupation is an adequate basis for such groupings is debatable – Allt (1979) has argued that social and socioeconomic classifications would be improved if some measure of income were to be employed in their construction.

The census is unique in providing detailed employment data for small areas, by residence and workplace. The Department of Employment does not publish statistics below the Travel-To-Work-Area level (some 60,000–80,000 people), although unpublished data are available to central and local government bodies for Employment Office Areas (10,000–30,000). Census employment data are available at the ED level – indeed, employment (in various classifications) is one of the major variables in SAS. Sixteen of the forty-two tables in SAS produced for all of England, Wales and Scotland include an employment variable, whether it be employment status (employee, self-employed, apprentice, etc.), economic position (economically active or inactive and sub-categories of these), whether employed or not, whether working full- or part-time, industry, social class or socioeconomic group. The range of information about the employed population of small areas is thus considerable and has been used extensively (Lambeth London Borough 1974).

SAS employment data are not, however, without their problems. Eight of the tables concerned with employment are based on a 10 per cent sample of the data, which means that some very small numbers – giving rise to problems of statistical reliability – occur in certain cells when the tables are presented for small areas. The table cross-tabulating industry against socioeconomic group, for example, contains 126 cells, yet in an average ED the 10 per cent sample of residents aged over sixteen in employment would involve some twenty-five to forty individuals; hence the great majority of the cells would be zero and many others could only contain one or two individuals. Such problems could be alleviated by coding the data 100 per cent but, for the present, it would appear safer to study that particular table at the ward rather than at ED level or to aggregate categories together to give less detail by way of employment 'type', etc.

Having already complained of one problem posed by a multiplicity of cells, it might seem unfair to complain that some of the industrial categories are too broad for some uses ! For example, the category 'energy and water', which includes miners, quarrymen and workers in various public utilities, is too broad to allow the identification of the number of coal miners in a particular settlement. In contrast, the 'mining and quarrying' category in 1971 SAS allowed a close approximation to such a group. As a consequence of the change, we are unable to trace the decline in the number of miners in individual pit villages.

It is particularly apposite that we should end this section with these two criticisms of small area employment data from the census, for OPCS' experience of having data criticized for diametrically opposed reasons illustrates the impossibility of pleasing all users. One of the most important criteria used in judging the census is its accuracy, and we should conclude this section with the observation that the post-censal quality check of 1966 found that in 10.7 per cent of cases occupation was incorrectly classified. On the 1981 Census form, however, respondents were asked not only to name their occupation but to describe the work done: therefore by manual checking it should be possible to achieve a higher level of accuracy than was possible from earlier censuses. The great majority of other census data is, of course, of much greater accuracy than is that on occupation.

3.5 Conclusion

We have examined the adequacy with which each topic is covered in the British census. Lack of space prevents a thorough investigation of other aspects of the census, for instance the adequacy of the output available, the area levels for which data are made available, accuracy and cost. It is appropriate that we should conclude this chapter with brief reference to each of these aspects.

While the number of questions asked, and the topics covered, in the British census are fewer than in the censuses of several other countries (Australia, France and the United States, for example) the cross-tabulations of British census data stand up well in such comparisons. Moreover, the forty-eight tables, totalling some 4300 cells that make up 1981 SAS were designed in consultation with potential users. The same can be said of the area levels for which data are made available. Certainly few other countries provide data for areas as small as the ED (the related but separate issue of microdata is treated at greater length in Chapter 11), and the range of administrative areas for which published and unpublished data are provided is helpful to the user, though the lack of grid-square data from the 1981 Census at a cost comparable to the standard SAS, i.e. as standard unpublished output (for reasons of economy) will be regretted by some. The accuracy of the British census also compares favourably with other censuses (Gray and Gee 1972; Kaplan and van Valey 1980), and the relatively narrow range of topics covered in the

British census can be explained partly as a reluctance to ask questions which will not be answered accurately.

The adequacy of the census is partly determined by the resources put into it. Some of the suggestions made in this chapter (the 100 per cent coding of occupations, for example) would require more resources. The cost of the 1981 Census was rather less than £1.00 per head of population, and a small part of that cost will be recouped by the sale of data. The decision on how much to spend on a census is essentially a political one, but it is a decision which can be influenced by what census users say and, perhaps more importantly, what they achieve with the aid of census data.

4 Univariate analysis: presenting and summarizing single variables

IAN S. EVANS

4.1 Introduction: describing variability

Suppose we wish to concentrate on one variable that is of particular interest, for example, 'the percentage of people who are of retirement age'. This is calculated for each small part of the study area – such as for each enumeration district or grid square – which is treated as a 'place' or fundamental unit. Each place is necessarily treated as an homogeneous spatial aggregate, since we usually have no statistical data on variations within it. Variation between these places or units may be studied by the techniques of 'univariate analysis'.

Univariate techniques are quite straightforward and, with the widespread availability of powerful computing facilities in the last two decades, many census users have largely ignored univariate analysis and been seduced by the greater sophistication of bivariate and multivariate analyses (Chapters 7 and 8). Unfortunately, these users have often overlooked important characteristics of their data which could have been revealed by simpler analyses. Here we attempt to redress the balance by demonstrating that univariate analysis is an essential preliminary phase in the analysis or mapping of census data. Even when a group of variables is of interest, each should be studied individually before multivariate techniques are applied.

In this chapter we deal first with graphical, then with numerical procedures in univariate analysis. Examples are taken from 1971 and 1981 census data for counties and for grid squares, plus 1981 unemployment data for counties. Though these are aggregate data related to places located in space, they are analysed here as statistical frequency distributions without reference to the geographical position of each place.

Sometimes, such frequency distributions are summarized by a single number, such as a mean (obtained by adding the values together and dividing by the number of values) or a median (obtained by ranking values in order of magnitude and taking the middle value). One number alone, however, rarely suffices, since the distribution of values around the mean or median can be very different from one variable to another. Indeed, if variation *around* the mean or median were not important, the variable would be of little interest.

Variation can be summarized by a second number such as the standard deviation (defined below), the range or the interquartile range. The need for this is apparent when we compare two variables with nearly identical national average values; 'percentage of males' (48.53 per cent in 1971), and 'percentage of owner occupiers' (48.30 per cent). For 1 km grid squares (weighted by population), their standard deviations were 3.66 per cent and 27.00 per cent respectively. Clearly the degree of owner occupation varies between grid squares very much more than does the sex ratio.

Even two numbers tell us nothing about the *shape* of a frequency distribution, or its asymmetry. Nor do they highlight aberrant values, arising perhaps from a Special (institutional) Enumeration District. For a fuller picture, we need the frequency of values for each of a series of classes of constant width, as in table 4.1. These provide a generalized view of the original values, but the degree of generalization is limited and controlled; information on middle value, variability, shape of the distribution, extreme and aberrant values is still present.

Table 4.1 Frequency distribution of 'county' unemployment rates, 1981

lower inclusive class limit (%)	*frequency (no. of counties)*	*downward cumulated frequency*	*percentage frequency*	*downward cumulated % frequency*
5	1	65	1.5	99.8*
6	2	64	3.1	98.2
7	3	62	4.6	95.2
8	8	59	12.3	90.6
9	6	51	9.2	78.3
10	8	45	12.3	69.1
11	7	37	10.8	56.8
12	3	30	4.6	46.0
13	11	27	16.9	41.4
14	3	16	4.6	24.5
15	5	13	7.7	19.9
16	3	8	4.6	12.2
17	2	5	3.1	7.6
18	1	3	1.5	4.5
19	1	2	1.5	3.0
20	1	1	1.5	1.5

Source: *Employment Gazette*, September 1981

* Difference from 100% is a rounding error

Unemployment rates on 13 August 1981, male and female numbers combined, expressed as percentages of 'employees in employment plus the unemployed' from the then latest available estimate (mid-1977). The areal divisions used as 'individuals' in this distribution are approximations to counties formed by combining 'Travel-To-Work-Areas'; no rate is given for Warwickshire because of difficulties in implementing this definition.

4.2 Histograms

If the distribution of frequencies tabulated in table 4.1 is portrayed graphically as in figure 4.1, we have a histogram, a plot of number of values (vertical scale) for each class of magnitude (horizontal scale). This is a 'vertical' histogram; when a computer line printer is used, the scales are usually interchanged, giving a 'horizontal' histogram which is more convenient to print and equally valid. Good programs producing such histograms are found in the BMDP79 and MIDAS packages.

A histogram gives a visual impression of the 'typical' or 'central' value, of the variability around this (so long as we notice how stretched or squeezed the horizontal scale is, and whether zero is shown), and of the shape of the frequency distribution. Important aspects of the shape are whether it is symmetrical or skewed, whether it is peaked, flat topped or with several distinct peaks, and whether it ends abruptly or has 'tails' of values much different to the others. All of these should be apparent from a glance at a histogram. Note that each bar of a histogram has a definite width; when drawn on a graph plotter, each bar has a flat end or top. Such a presentation is more realistic than the alternative 'frequency polygon', where points representing the end of each bar are joined up by slanting lines; although slightly simpler, this can be misleading unless there are very many classes.

4.2.1 CLASS WIDTH AND NUMBER

Whether presentation is in tabular or graphic form, the main decision involved is the number of classes, or the class limits (once one of these has been chosen, the other follows). If there are too many classes, the detail reduces the prominence of the general shape of the distribution; if there are too few (especially if there are less than six classes), too much information on the shape is lost. Clearly the number of classes that are appropriate varies with the number of values grouped: for twenty values, eight classes give a detailed picture; while, for 10,000 values, eight give an extremely generalized picture. Various rules have been proposed (Gardiner and Gardiner 1978), but most suggest too few classes for large numbers of observations. The only rule which seems to work over a broad range is that the number of classes should equal the square root of the number of values, and this should be rounded up. In figure 4.1, then, the nine-class representation would be preferable to the sixteen-class one.

I have found that for 10,000 values, 100 classes give very informative histograms which portray the overall shape of the frequency distribution very well. Ten classes might suffice for 100 values, while five classes would be justifiable for twenty-five values, below which drawing a histogram is hardly worthwhile. There is no need, however, for a slavish adherence to this or any

UNEMPLOYMENT RATES
13 August, 1981; male and female combined by 'COUNTY' (from table 4.1)
The class limits are lower inclusive limits

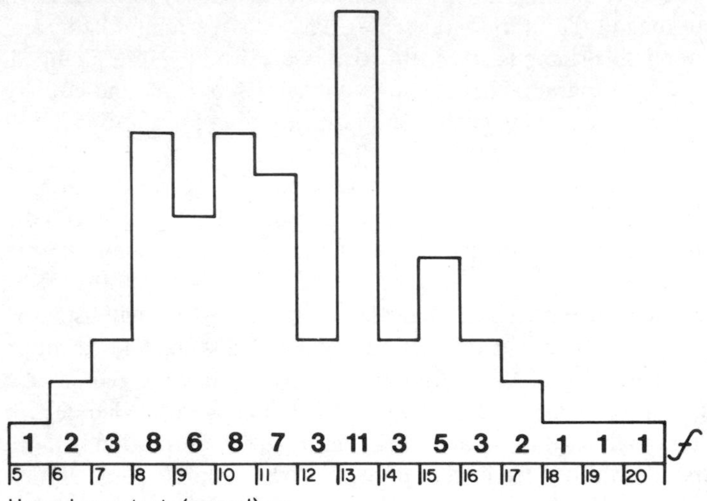

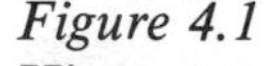

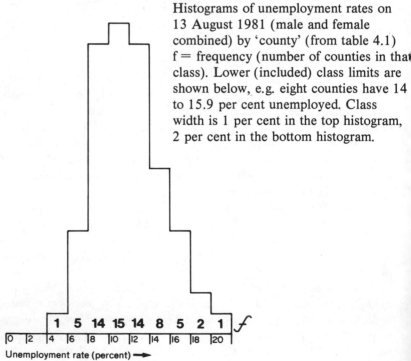

Figure 4.1
Histograms of unemployment rates on 13 August 1981 (male and female combined) by 'county' (from table 4.1) f = frequency (number of counties in that class). Lower (included) class limits are shown below, e.g. eight counties have 14 to 15.9 per cent unemployed. Class width is 1 per cent in the top histogram, 2 per cent in the bottom histogram.

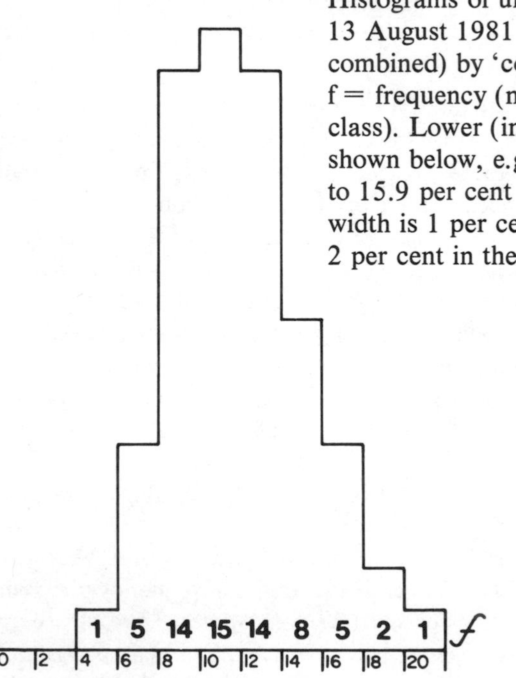

other rule. For some purposes a very generalized distribution might be appropriate, while for detection of aberrant values (outliers), for the calculation of, for example, median, quartiles, etc. by interpolation, and for detection of data bias such as rounding off to certain values, very detailed histograms are of greatest value.

4.2.2. 'NICE NUMBERS'

It is common to specify the number of classes, m, in a histogram to be produced by a computer program. The program then generally goes on to divide the range from maximum to minimum into m equal classes. This is unfortunate, as the computed class width is likely to be an irregular number, with several places of decimals interfering with the readability of the scale of magnitude. Programs can be written to round this class width up or down to the nearest nice, round number (1, 2, 5, 10, 20, 50, 100, 200, 500, 1000, etc.); Lewart (1973) provided such an algorithm. The same result can be achieved if the class width is specified, rather than the number of classes; this is simple if the data range only between two limiting values such as 0 and 100 per cent, or if the extreme values are known approximately beforehand.

For a given m, restriction of class width to the significant digits 1, 2 or 5 is likely to reduce the number of occupied classes (compared with widths of 0.6, 1.1 or 2.3) and may even halve the number. If so, the number of classes should be increased (e.g. by using a width of 10 instead of 20). Alternatively, the roundness requirement may be relaxed: any number with a single significant digit (e.g. 700, 40 or 0.003) may be accepted as a class width. The following expression

$$\text{class width} = \text{trunc}\ (\text{range}/m)$$

where 'trunc' means ignore digits after the first significant one, gives rather more than m classes. For example, a range of 257 and a proposal for $m = 8$ classes gives class width $=$ trunc (32.125) $=$ 30, requiring 9 classes to cover the range. A range of 0.0572 and $m = 9$ gives class width $=$ trunc(0.00635) $=$ 0.006, requiring 10 classes.

The greatest rounding effect now comes with the jump from a class width of 1 to that of 2. For example, if the range is 1.593, a proposal of $m = 8$ gives a class width of trunc (0.199) $=$ 0.1 and hence 16 classes, whereas $m = 7$ gives trunc (0.227) $=$ 0.2 and hence only 8 classes. Nevertheless, rather than accepting fewer classes than proposed, it is preferable to propose the minimum acceptable number of classes, and accept the next larger number which permits rounded class widths. *Excessive detail is more acceptable than excessive generalization*, since the information is still present and generalization can easily be increased by combining pairs of classes. (Note that if the minimum value is not zero, part of the lowest class may be 'wasted', and hence one more class than indicated above may be required.) An alternative algorithm requiring specification of the set of numbers regarded as rounded ('nice') is given by Velleman and Hoaglin (1981, 296 and 316).

4.2.3 CLASS LIMITS

Not only class widths but also class limits should be rounded: a series of values such as 1.995, 2.995, 3.995 ... are irritating and scarcely conducive to easy communication. In any case, such limits are often meaningless: where the data are expressed as integer values (whole numbers), or a ratio is calculated from small integer values (e.g. for EDs), it is absurd to imply greater detail than is present. It is highly desirable that all class limits should be simplified and specified as inclusive limits, i.e. values 25, 35, 45 as the upper bounds of classes mean that all values up to and including 25 lie in the lowest class, values greater than 25 and up to 35 lie in the next and so on. Other methods of labelling class limits are either clumsy (such as 1.00 to 1.99, 2.00 to 2.99, etc.) or ambiguous (such as 1 to 2, 2 to 3, etc.), as are class midpoints (such as 1.5, 2.5, etc.). The statement that 1, 2, 3, etc. are inclusive class limits is both visually tidier and much more readily grasped; we should also be told whether the resolution is 0.1, 0.02 or whatever. The histogram header must specify whether these are upper or lower inclusive class limits, i.e. whether 1.00 is in the first or second class. Class limits should have *fewer* significant digits than the data values: in the latter example, each row (of a horizontal line-printer histogram) can be labelled by one character, i.e. 1, instead of the nine characters of 1.00 – 1.99. The resultant saving of space is even more necessary for a vertical histogram.

The lowest class limit is the next lower rounded value below the data minimum. For census data, this will often be zero. However, even if the lowest data value is a few class widths away from zero, it is still worth extending the magnitude scale to zero to provide a firm 'anchor' to the histogram. If the gap is intolerably large, a zigzag in the axis is the conventional way of emphasizing that zero is not reached, on both histograms and scatter plots.

4.3 Other graphical presentations

4.3.1 SUBDIVIDED HISTOGRAMS AND STEM-AND-LEAF PLOTS

The bars of histograms can be subdivided by filling parts of them with different shading. For example, in a histogram for Great Britain, values for Wales and Scotland may be distinguished; metropolitan areas may be distinguished from others; or several classes of population density may be distinguished to portray differences in distributions along the urban–rural continuum. This approach is useful if the subsets are too small to merit separate histograms, but it is not the most useful way of making comparisons; central values and spreads are more apparent and more readily comparable if separate histograms are drawn suitably adjacent to each other.

Bertin (1981) provided a stimulating and well-exemplified discussion of the graphic and semi-graphic representation of tabular data, including examples of what should *not* be done. Ehrenberg (1975) gave advice on the production of simplified, ordered tables for communication of information; he also indicated some limits to the value of graphics, but these limitations do not affect the uses advocated here.

The stem-and-leaf plot of Tukey (1977) is a sort of subdivided histogram, the divisions being the next digit (sometimes 'half-digit') within each class (figure 4.2). This is appropriate for small data sets, but the extra information it

Stem	Leaf	
20	8	W. Isles
19	0	Cleveland
18	3	Merseyside
17	2 5	
16	1 2 5	
15	2 4 5 9 9	
14	3 4 6	
13	0 4 5 5 5 5 6 6 7 8 8	
12	3 3 5	
11	0 3 4 5 6 6 8	
10	3 3 4 4 5 5 7 8	
9	1 1 3 3 3 5	
8	1 4 4 4 6 7 7 7 9	
7	1 6 8	
6	7 9	Surrey, W. Sussex
5	1	Shetlands

Figure 4.2 Stem-and-leaf plot of unemployment rates

Ordered stem-and-leaf plot of the 13 August 1981 unemployment rates by 'county', for Great Britain (from the source for table 4.1). The left-hand column (stem) gives each whole percentage; the right-hand digits (leaf) give the first decimal point for each of the sixty-five counties. The six extreme values are named.

Upper quartile 13.9 per cent; median 11.6 per cent; lower quartile 9.25 per cent. The median is the 33rd value ($33 = (n/2) + ½$); the upper quartile is located at rank $(n/4) + ½ = 16¾$, counting downward and the lower quartile is located at rank $(3n/4) + ½ = 49¼$. Note that the median is well determined, whereas the upper quartile is interpolated within a 0.5 per cent gap (13.8 to 14.3) and would thus be affected by the loss of a single data value. These results are specific to counties: unemployment values for the median District and the median Employment Office Area could be rather different.

contains can be presented just as well (indeed, more immediately) in a histogram with ten (or five) times as many classes. There is no need to avoid large histograms with many blank classes – after all, a double-page spread of line printer paper usually has about 120 rows – and the use of many classes is highly desirable for large data sets. For smaller data sets, a detailed histogram (permitting a check on bias toward particular increments and on subgroupings) might need to be supplemented by a more generalized one with the number of classes originally proposed.

The further claim by Erickson and Nosanchuk (1977, 30) that stem-and-leaf plots are 'quicker to do' than histograms is untrue: if tallies of frequency are made directly onto graph paper, a histogram has been created as soon as the last value is tallied. A stem-and-leaf plot must take slightly longer (for the same number of classes/leaves) because digits are being distinguished, and its additional information is not apparent until the digits have been ordered within each 'leaf'. The main advantage of ordered stem-and-leaf plots is that they facilitate exact determination of the median and quartiles (figure 4.2).

4.3.2 CUMULATIVE PLOTS

A further and rather different portrayal of a frequency distribution is in *cumulative* terms. The frequency per class is translated into a percentage of the total frequency, and the results are cumulated (added together) in a consistent direction, *either* upward *or* downward (table 4.1). If cumulated percentage is plotted against magnitude, the frequency distribution is represented by a curve that is monotonic: its slope varies but is always consistently in one direction. Since varying frequency in each class is represented by variations in the slope of this plot, the cumulative plot is a less sensitive one than the histogram, where frequency is represented by length of bar (if class widths are equal); the eye can compare differences in length of adjacent bars more readily than changes in gradient of a continuous line. Hence the histogram is best for showing details, complexities of the class-to-class distribution, and outliers. On the other hand, the cumulative plot emphasizes the overall shape, spread and level of the distribution, and has the advantage that, because of its simplicity, plots of different variables or for the same variable in different regions can be superimposed (figure 4.3) with less confusion than with histograms. Cumulative plots are commonly used for grain-size distributions in sedimentology and for biometric distributions; for no obvious reason, they are rarely used in the social sciences.

Cumulative plots are at their most sensitive, and most readily comparable, when their slopes average 45°. With this, or more gentle gradients, it is easy to read off the median, quartiles or other percentiles (on graph paper) by taking the intersection of the plot with the appropriate percentile line, which is horizontal, and dropping a vertical line from this to the magnitude axis. For

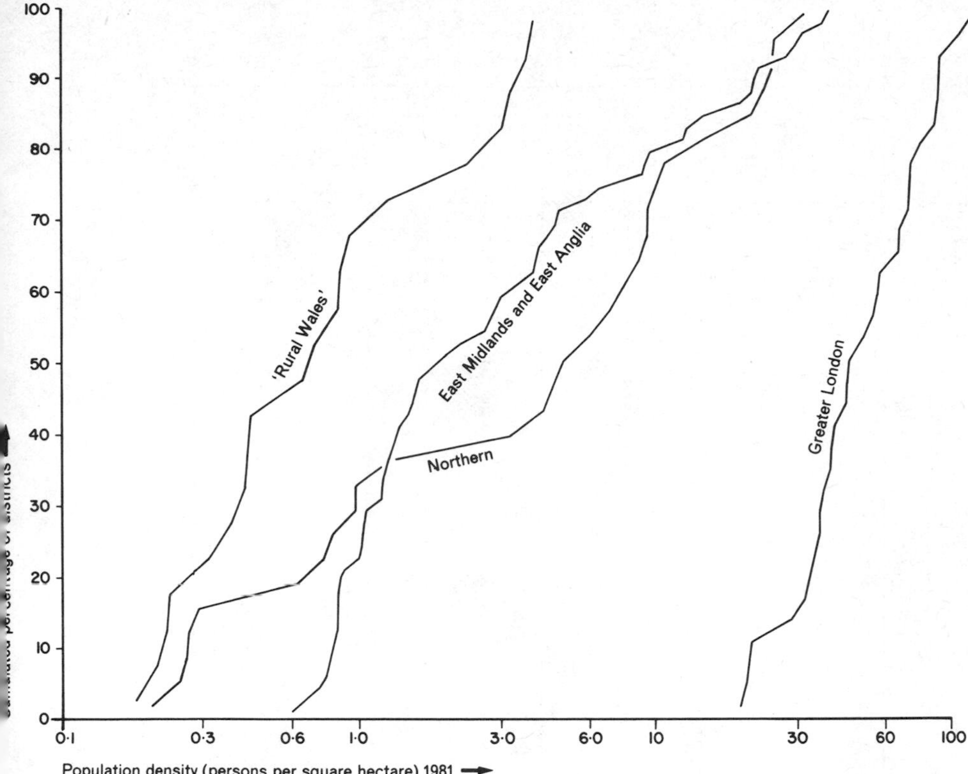

Figure 4.3
Cumulated plots of population density per administrative district, 1981 Census preliminary results. The horizontal scale is logarithmic; its use is justified in section 4.7. The percentage of districts is cumulated upward, i.e. in order of increasing population density. For any density, the vertical scale gives the percentage of districts with a lower population density, e.g. 63 per cent of London districts have less than sixty people/ha (6000 people/km^2).

Most cumulated plots are based on grouped data, but for these small data sets the density of each individual district has been plotted in the middle of the $(100/N)$ per cent of the vertical scale which it represents (the total N districts sum to 100 per cent). This is achieved by plotting the lowest district against $(100/2N)$ per cent, the second lowest against $(300/2N)$ per cent, the third against $(500/2N)$ per cent and so on. Separate plots are produced for each of four 'regions': 'Rural' Wales includes Clwyd, Gwynedd, Dyfed and Powys, i.e. all but Glamorgan and Gwent. 'Rural' Wales and (at the opposite extreme) Greater London are relatively homogeneous in population density, whereas the districts of Northern Region are more varied.

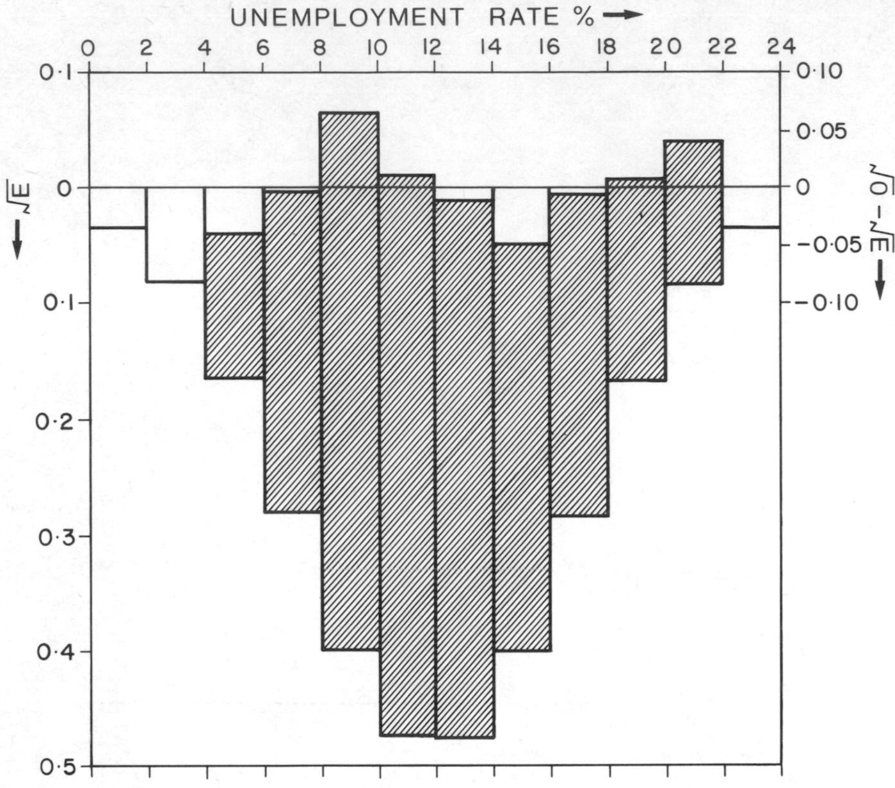

Figure 4.4 'Suspended rootogram'
The lower histogram of figure 4.1 is here compared with a Gaussian frequency distribution having the same mean (unemployment = 11.97 per cent) and standard deviation (3.333 per cent).

The proportionate frequency per class, E, expected from the Gaussian model is calculated by converting class limits (0.05 per cent below the lower inclusive limits given above the graph) to standard deviates and using tables of the area up to each such value. Classes in the tails are pooled, and the square root of this proportion is plotted downwards from a horizontal line. Square roots of O, the observed proportionate frequency, are represented by the shaded bars, so that positive deviations ($\sqrt{O} - \sqrt{E}$) show above the horizontal line, negative ones below. The square root scale gives an appropriate impression of deviations from expectation, and deviations from a horizontal line are visually clearer than deviations from a curve. The comparison shows that the actual frequency distribution is shorter in both tails than is the Gaussian, and there is a slight positive skew in the middle of the distribution.

example, in figure 4.3, the median of 'Rural Wales' is 0.69 people/ha and its upper quartile is 1.7.

4.3.3 SUSPENDED ROOTOGRAMS

Another way of comparing two distributions is by a 'suspended rootogram' (Tukey 1970; Velleman and Hoaglin 1981). A vertical histogram is plotted upside down (suspended). The second histogram, equal to it in total area (e.g. by plotting with percentages instead of frequencies in both histograms), is plotted in the same way, with the bottom of each column coincident (figure 4.4). Differences are then apparent in deviations of the tops of the columns, representing the second distribution, from the straight line representing the 'top' of the first distribution. This is an extremely sensitive display, showing subtleties of the differences, and hence it is especially useful for comparing observed frequencies with those predicted by a fitted distribution conforming to a statistical model. The term 'rootogram' is used instead of histogram when frequencies or percentages are replaced by their square-roots, since (as Tukey demonstrates) such deviations are best assessed on a square-root scale.

4.4 A comparison of graphics using population density data

Given all the above discussion, we can now evaluate the relative strengths and weaknesses of the various graphical procedures; for this, we use information on population density gleaned from the 1981 Census provisional data.

Population density data for both districts and counties are similarly skewed, and the two dispersion diagrams (univariate scatter plots) in figure 4.5 show the effect of logarithmic transformation (see section 4.6) for counties (regions in Scotland). That on the left gives population density per hectare (multiply by 100 to obtain population per km^2), while that on the right plots the same values on a logarithmic scale. The order of counties, from London (42.4/ha) to Highland (0.08/ha) is the same, but the logarithmic scale stretches apart the lower values and squeezes together the higher ones. This is very necessary, since on the arithmetic scale the high values are widely spaced while the lower ones are so close together that it is difficult to plot each value separately, and an extra two columns must be used simply for the overflow. On the logarithmic scale there is a concentration of values in the middle, thinning out symmetrically at either end; clearly this is the better scale for further analysis.

The same figure gives corresponding 'skeletal box plots' (Tukey 1977; Velleman and Hoaglin 1981). The median is represented by an asterisk, the upper and lower quartiles by a box, and the maximum and minimum by crosses. Hence half of the observations fall within the box (one-quarter above and one-quarter below the median), one-quarter fall above the box, and one-quarter below. This illustrates well the symmetry of population density on a

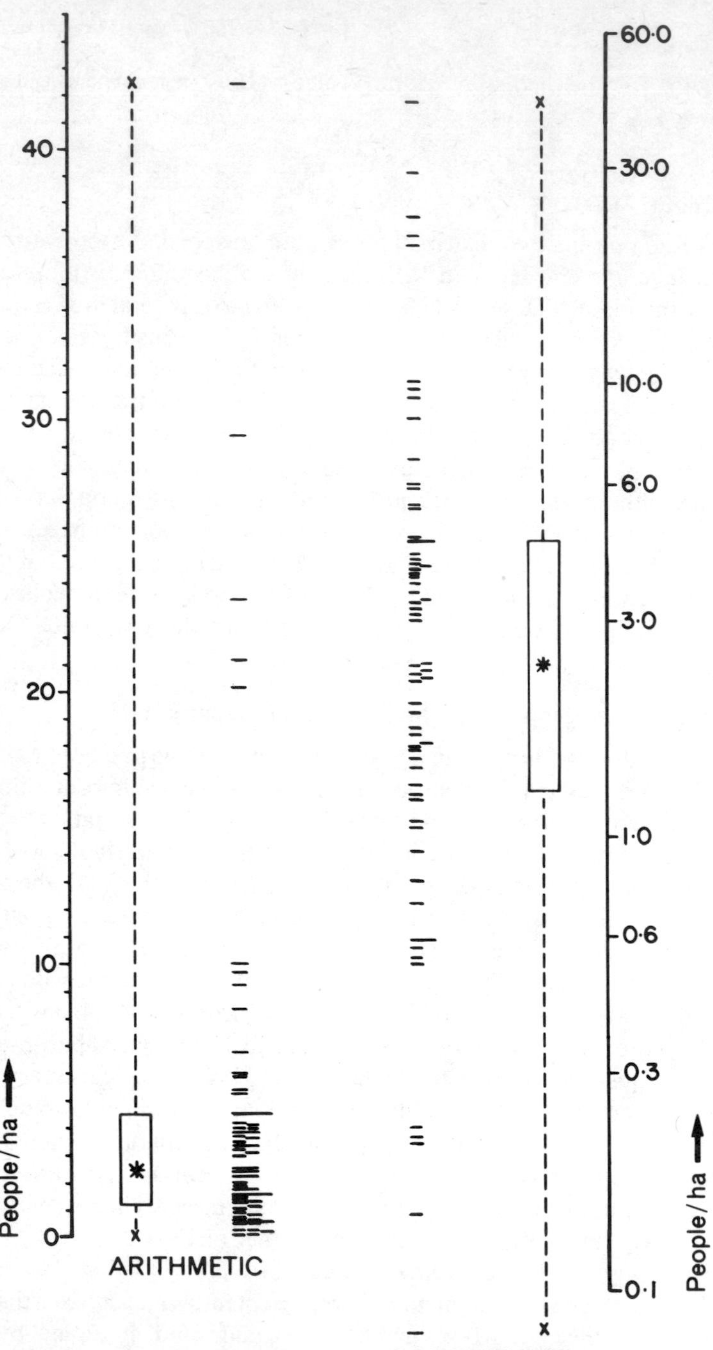

Figure 4.5
Dispersion diagrams and box plots of 1981 population densities for the sixty-four counties of Great Britain (including the Regions of Scotland), showing the effect of logarithmic transformation in removing skew.

logarithmic scale, but the arithmetic box plot implies that the great skew on an arithmetic scale might be due to the maximum being an outlier. The dispersion diagrams show clearly that this is not the case, for the other metropolitan counties fill the gap between Greater London and the main body of the distribution.

In detail, there are two groups: West Midlands, Greater Manchester, Merseyside and Tyne and Wear have between twenty and thirty people/ha, while the other two metropolitan counties, West and South Yorkshire, have between eight and ten, like Cleveland (Teesside) and South Glamorgan (Cardiff). County boundaries in the first group are drawn tightly around the built-up area of a conurbation, while those of the Yorkshire conurbations are much more liberally drawn. The two-fold difference between the bottom of the first group and the top of the second is more remarkable than Greater London's density being 1.4 times that of West Midlands. Other counties have less than seven people/ha, and the rural counties of Wales and Scotland have fewer than 0.6. Of the seven most lightly populated 'counties', six are in Scotland and one (Powys) in Wales.

Clearly the box plots are summaries which lose most of the information present in dispersion diagrams. They are useful, however, in comparing a number of distributions side by side. Figure 4.6 does this for population density per district in four different regions, again on a logarithmic scale. Since the transformation has practically eliminated skew, the box plots essentially give comparisons of overall level and of spread (dispersion).

The dispersion diagrams do suggest groupings of the individual values. Although these form only minor deviations from the smooth overall distribution, if the districts are named (or labelled for groups) as they are plotted, the groupings of adjacent values are of interest. For Northern England, for example, five of the six highest values are in Tyne and Wear; the main body (twelve) of those districts which have densities of three to eleven people/ha are in Cleveland county (a small conurbation) or on the Durham–Northumberland coalfield. The next group, of six districts, covers rural areas and small towns, while the five districts with less than 0.3 people/ha incorporate areas of uninhabited moorland or forest.

Comparison of these three modes of display shows that dispersion diagrams are most complete, permitting identification of groups and of individual values, while box plots are most generalized, providing little information individually but facilitating comparison of medians, spreads and extremes when plots for many distributions are placed side by side with the same scale. As we shall see in section 4.7, numerical summaries involving two or three numbers are slightly more generalized still.

Histograms are, in general, intermediate in degree of generalization and information loss, but they cover the whole range of detail depending on the number of classes in relation to the number of values classified (figure 4.7). A

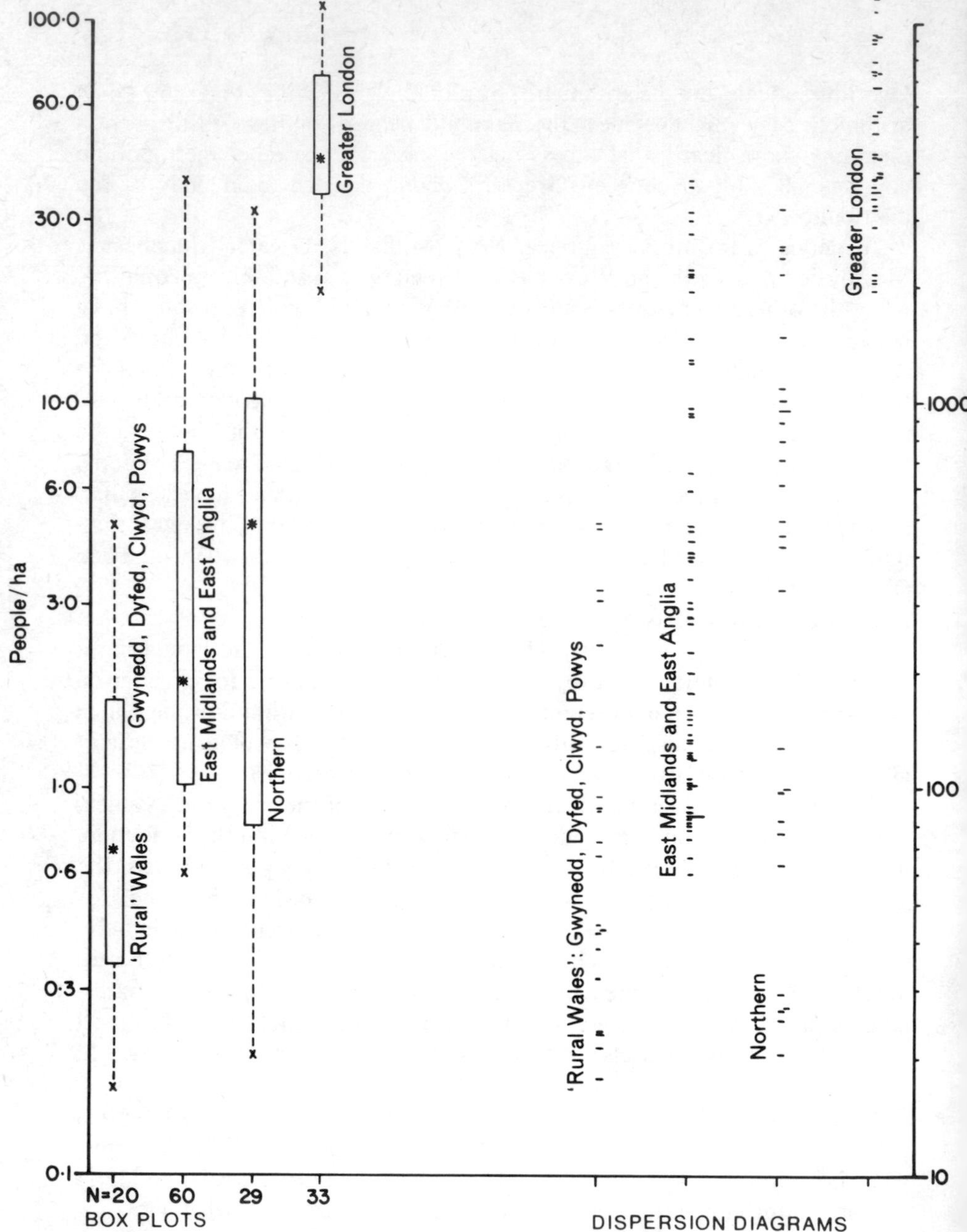

Figure 4.6
Dispersion diagrams and box plots of 1981 population densities of administrative districts in various regions; from left to right, 'Rural' Wales (Gwynedd, Dyfed, Clwyd, Powys), East Midlands and East Anglia, Northern Region and Greater London. The box plots show the relative levels and the greater variability of Northern Region, but the scatter plots also show any tendencies toward grouping, and whether the extreme points are outliers.

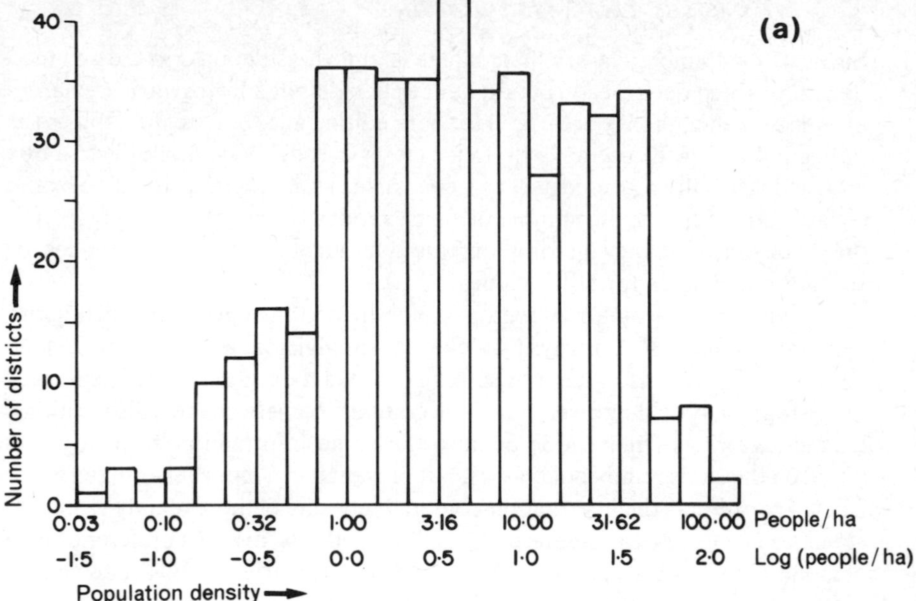

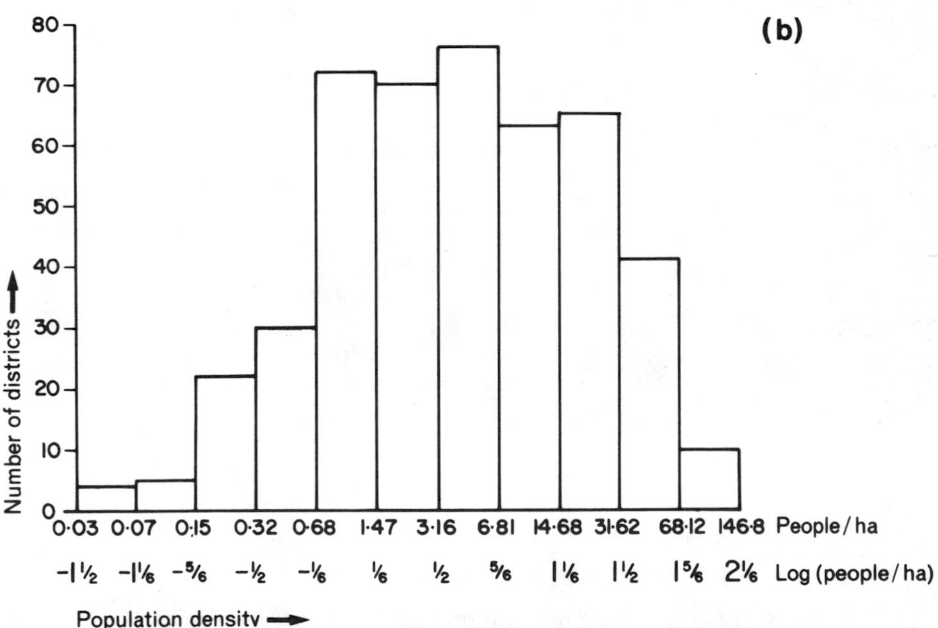

Figure 4.7
Histograms of 1981 population densities of the 458 administrative districts in Great Britain. To reduce skewness, equal class widths on a logarithmic scale are used. Class widths on a logarithmic (base 10) scale are 1/6 for (a), giving seventeen classes (close to the twenty-two suggested by the square root (N) 'rule'), and 1/3 for (b), giving a highly generalized view but still showing the flat-peaked nature of the distribution.

histogram with more classes than values is almost as detailed as a dispersion diagram, which does the job better; hence such detailed histograms are hardly ever drawn, though they are useful for data editing and for revealing spikes (as in figure 4.11). A histogram with four classes is roughly comparable to a box plot, and is usually regarded as over-generalized. A histogram classified by the square-root rule, with the number of classes rounded up, is best for portraying the shape of a frequency distribution; this gives eight classes for fifty values, or seventy-one classes for 5000 values.

A stem-and-leaf plot, regarded as a subdivided histogram or a histogram which simultaneously portrays two levels of subdivision, is placed towards the detailed end of the histogram range. A suspended rootogram is a refinement of the histogram, providing a very sensitive comparison between two distributions. Cumulative plots (figure 4.3) contain the same information as histograms based on the same number of classes, but present it in a more generalized form. Table 4.2 presents the information-content hierarchy of these mainly graphical summaries. Despite the plethora of possible methods, my own preference is to combine detailed histograms with numerical summaries. If bivariate scatter plots are to be produced (Chapter 7), dispersion diagrams have little to add.

Table 4.2 The hierarchy of summarization

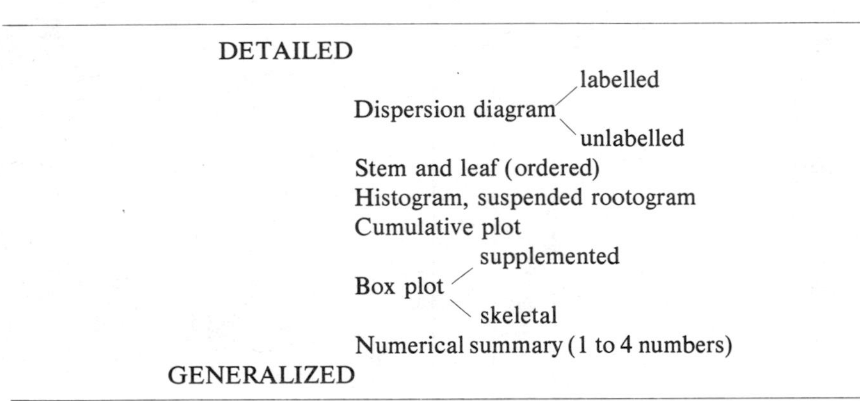

DETAILED

Dispersion diagram — labelled / unlabelled

Stem and leaf (ordered)

Histogram, suspended rootogram

Cumulative plot

Box plot — supplemented / skeletal

Numerical summary (1 to 4 numbers)

GENERALIZED

4.5 Frequency distributions

4.5.1 SHAPES OF FREQUENCY DISTRIBUTIONS

Each of the graphical presentations described above rapidly provides an impression of the shape of a frequency distribution. A wide variety of shapes is possible and in fact does occur in British census data. All the following examples, portrayed by simple histograms, are taken from commonly used 'indicator' variables, created by Rhind *et al.* (1977) from the 1 km grid square

cum. f	f	lower limit
3704	3704	0
3718	14	100
3772	54	200
3877	105	300
4074	197	400
4417	343	500
4813	396	600
5403	590	700
5950	547	800
6558	608	900
7376	818	1000
8361	985	1100
9226	865	1200
9976	750	1300
10962	986	1400
11977	1015	1500
13273	1296	1600
14108	835	1700
15493	1385	1800
16243	750	1900
18038	1795	2000
19251	1213	2100
20852	1601	2200
22277	1425	2300
23088	811	2400
25313	2225	2500
26658	1345	2600
28239	1581	2700
29833	1594	2800
30956	1123	2900
32839	1883	3000
34174	1335	3100
35261	1087	3200
37530	2269	3300
38570	1040	3400
39940	1370	3500
41323	1383	3600
42774	1451	3700
44029	1255	3800
44902	873	3900
46458	1556	4000
47631	1173	4100
48954	1323	4200
49774	820	4300
50954	1180	4400
51955	1001	4500
52868	913	4600
53659	791	4700
54345	686	4800
54821	476	4900
56471	1650	5000
57039	568	5100
57674	635	5200
58348	674	5300
58956	608	5400
59671	715	5500
60195	524	5600
60859	664	5700
61385	526	5800
61825	440	5900
62477	652	6000
62934	457	6100
63459	525	6200
63871	412	6300
64228	357	6400
64557	329	6500
65091	534	6600
65350	259	6700
65634	284	6800
65925	291	6900
66221	296	7000
66490	269	7100
66695	205	7200
66860	165	7300
66985	125	7400
67224	239	7500
67353	129	7600
67496	143	7700
67592	96	7800
67668	76	7900
67777	109	8000
67847	70	8100
67902	55	8200
67995	93	8300
68029	34	8400
68096	67	8500
68110	14	8600
68150	40	8700
68182	32	8800
68194	12	8900
68219	25	9000
68231	12	9100
68249	18	9200
68258	9	9300
68260	2	9400
68262	2	9500
68263	1	9600
68263	0	9700
68263	0	9800
68263	0	9900
68422	159	10000

AND TOTAL CF CASES= 68422

CH STAR REPRESENTS 37 CASES

100x%Owning no car

Figure 4.8
Histograms of proportion of households owning *no car* in 1971, for 1 km grid squares

The length of each horizontal bar is proportional to the frequency (f), i.e. the number of 1 km grid squares, falling into that class. Each class is 1 per cent wide: its lower (included) limit is given next to the bar as 100 × percentage. Hence the bar labelled 300 represents the 105 grid squares with 3.00 to 3.99 per cent of households car-less. The number on the left is the frequency cumulated upward. Data are included for all 68,422 grid squares in Great Britain with 8 or more private households: each star represents 37 squares. The 'spikes' are due to bias toward fractions such as 2/8, 4/8, 3/9, 5/10 etc. Most of these, and squares with 0 or 100 per cent, probably have small numbers of households.

data for the 1971 Census. In general terms, grid-square data *usually* give more varied frequency distributions than do data for EDs, wards, etc.; thus here we are dealing with what is *usually* the worst case.

Our reference point for distributions of continuous variables is the Gaussian model – symmetrical, unimodal and bell shaped (the commonly used label 'normal distribution' is a propaganda term, and is avoided here). The central peak of the frequency distribution is convex up, terminated at plus and minus one standard deviation by inflections, beyond which the upper and lower limbs are concave up. These concave sections are asymptotic (i.e. tend at the limit) to zero frequency, so that however far out we go in the tails there is a finite possibility of that value being observed. Because these tails extend to plus and minus infinity, the Gaussian model cannot exactly fit any ratio-scale variables or, indeed, any of the SAS cell values (since negative values for these are impossible).

However, some census variables come sufficiently close to this model that many of the more sophisticated techniques based on the Gaussian distribution (see Chapters 7 and 8) can be applied without worry. Such variables include large age groups, such as 'numbers of people aged forty-five to sixty-four as a percentage of total population' (these vary too little for the limiting value of zero to have much effect), and the 'proportion of households which do not own cars' (figure 4.8) – the national average in 1971 was 49 per cent, so the upper and lower limits of 100 per cent and 0 per cent are remote and have balanced effects.

Most variables, especially minority groups, have a positively skewed distribution, i.e. there are many low values and a thin tail of higher values, so that the maximum is much further from the mean or median than is the minimum. 'Employers and managers' (figure 4.9), with a national average of 9.8 per cent in 1971 of civilians gainfully employed, is moderately skewed in this way; smaller groups such as 'unemployed males' (4.25 per cent of males seeking employment in 1971 on the census definition), 'students' (3 per cent) and 'shared households' (3.4 per cent of private households) are considerably more skewed. Conversely, majority variables such as 'the proportion of adult males working' (91.5 per cent), 'the proportion of households with no children' (63.5 per cent), or 'the proportion of households with exclusive use of a bath, hot water and inside toilet' (83 per cent) are negatively skewed; most observations are near the maximum (100 per cent cannot be exceeded), and there is a tail of lower values toward zero, so that histograms for these variables may represent a 'mirror image' of the minority variables.

Some minorities are strongly concentrated in limited geographical areas. These include 'very overcrowded households', 'privately rented unfurnished households', 'New Commonwealth immigrants', 'defence employees', 'miners', 'those travelling to work by motor-cycle' and 'people not in private households'. Their frequency distributions are so skewed that most 1 km grid squares (or

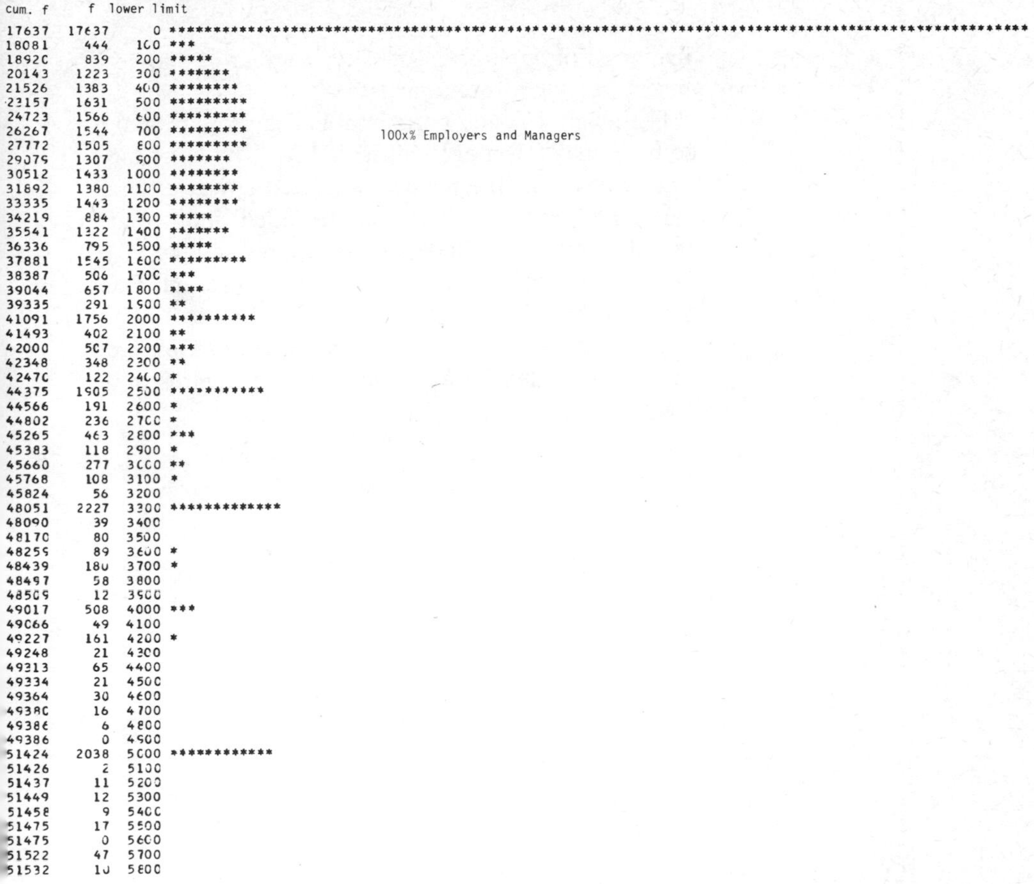

HISTOGRAM FOR VARIABLE 71
LEFT COLUMN = CUMULATED FREQUENCY, NEXT COLUMN = FREQUENCY, THEN LOWER INCLUSIVE LIMIT OF CLASS

cum. f	f	lower limit	
17637	17637	0	**
18081	444	100	***
18920	839	200	*****
20143	1223	300	*******
21526	1383	400	********
23157	1631	500	*********
24723	1566	600	*********
26267	1544	700	*********
27772	1505	800	*********
29079	1307	900	*******
30512	1433	1000	********
31892	1380	1100	********
33335	1443	1200	********
34219	884	1300	*****
35541	1322	1400	*******
36336	795	1500	*****
37881	1545	1600	*********
38387	506	1700	***
39044	657	1800	****
39335	291	1900	**
41091	1756	2000	**********
41493	402	2100	**
42000	507	2200	***
42348	348	2300	**
42470	122	2400	*
44375	1905	2500	***********
44566	191	2600	*
44802	236	2700	*
45265	463	2800	***
45383	118	2900	*
45660	277	3000	**
45768	108	3100	*
45824	56	3200	
48051	2227	3300	*************
48090	39	3400	
48170	80	3500	
48259	89	3600	*
48439	180	3700	*
48497	58	3800	
48509	12	3900	
49017	508	4000	***
49066	49	4100	
49227	161	4200	*
49248	21	4300	
49313	65	4400	
49334	21	4500	
49364	30	4600	
49380	16	4700	
49386	6	4800	
49386	0	4900	
51424	2038	5000	************
51426	2	5100	
51437	11	5200	
51449	12	5300	
51458	9	5400	
51475	17	5500	
51475	0	5600	
51522	47	5700	
51532	10	5800	

100x% Employers and Managers

Figure 4.9
Histogram of proportion of those in stated civilian employment who were employers and *managers* (socioeconomic groups 1, 2 and 13) in 1971, for 1 km grid squares; numbers and classes as for figure 4.8

Each star represents 176 cases. Data are included for all 53,308 grid squares in Great Britain with 2 or more households in the 10 per cent sample census and with someone in stated civilian employment: hence 'spikes' are more apparent because of the fractions such as 0/2, 1/2, 1/3, 2/3, etc. Of the 1884 squares with over 50.99 per cent, 466 are in the class 66.00–66.99 per cent, and 942 are 100 per cent.

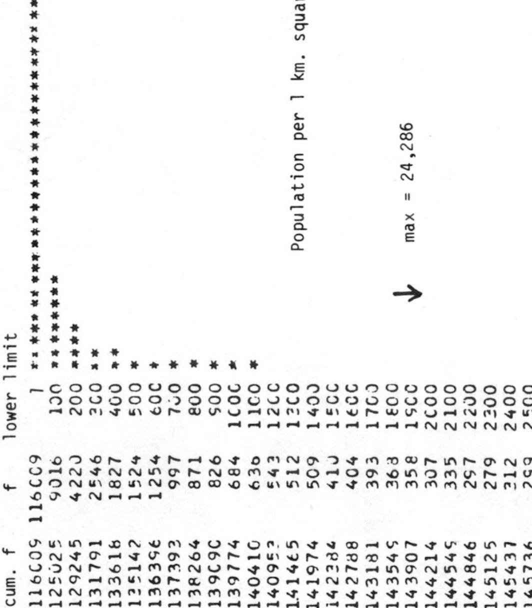

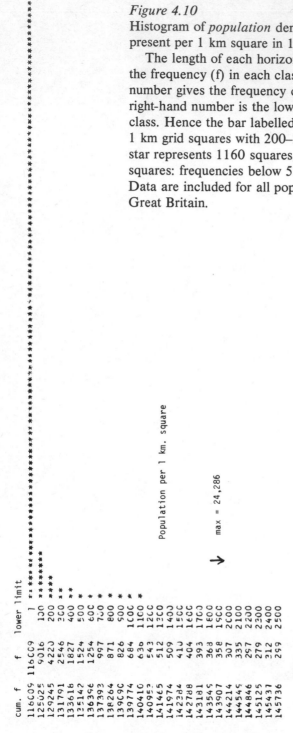

Figure 4.10
Histogram of *population* density: number of people present per 1 km square in 1971

The length of each horizontal bar is proportional to the frequency (f) in each class of 100. The left-hand number gives the frequency cumulated upward: the right-hand number is the lower (included) limit of each class. Hence the bar labelled 200 represents the 9016 1 km grid squares with 200–299 people present. Each star represents 1160 squares, i.e. from 581 to 1740 squares: frequencies below 581 are therefore left blank. Data are included for all populated grid squares in Great Britain.

EDs) have near-zero values, yet there is a very thin 'tail' of higher values. The term 'J-shaped' (or even 'L-shaped') is sometimes applied to such extremely skewed distributions. The application of conventional (least squares) statistical techniques to such variables is fraught with dangers. All distributions of absolute numbers for grid squares, including total numbers of people or of households per square, take this form (figure 4.10); distributions of absolute numbers for non-minority variables in EDs are rather less skewed.

Skewness can have severely practical as well as statistical effects. Taylor and Johnston (1979) have demonstrated the importance of shape of frequency distributions in 'first-past-the-post' elections. For parties with a mean vote of near 50 per cent, positive skew of share of vote per constituency produces many lost seats (in a two-party contest) and 'wastage' of votes in a few very safe constituencies, whereas negative skew can produce a landslide victory. For minority parties, variability and skew (as for nationalist parties concentrated in certain regions) can produce a few seats, while a uniform share of the vote produces none. The shape of a frequency distribution is also important in selecting class intervals for a map (section 6.3.1.5; Evans 1977).

All skewed frequency distributions are non-Gaussian, but so are some symmetrical distributions. Compared with the 'bell-shaped' model, they may be either more peaked and with longer tails on both sides, or flatter with broad shoulders and sometimes without tails. The two main tenure variables, 'owner occupied' (figure 4.11) and 'council rented', vary greatly within their 0 and 100 per cent limits, hence their tails are truncated and their peaks flattened, especially if attention is confined to more populated grid squares (many low-population squares have values of 100 per cent or, more commonly, zero). As yet, sharp-peaked, long-tailed symmetrical distributions are not known from British census data.

The histogram for 'proportion council rented' in 1 km grid squares with over 5000 people does have a weak tendency to bimodality (two peaks of high frequency): its main peak is near zero, and there is a weak second peak at 98 per cent, with a broad minimum from 44 to 93 per cent. This is probably because many council estates cover 1 km^2 or more. Use of smaller squares would exaggerate this bimodality, while larger ones would reduce it: the same effect should be observable in EDs and in wards. *Thus the shapes of frequency distributions are highly related to the areal divisions which are being used* (see Chapter 7). Equally, 'proportion born in England' (figure 4.12) is truly bimodal when the whole of Great Britain is included; if England were treated separately, this would be unimodal. The shape of a frequency distribution, then, is highly related not only to the level of geographical detail in the study but also *to the geographical extent of the study area.*

100x% Owner-occupied

cum. f	f	lower limit
3531	3531	0
3813	282	100
4088	275	200
4382	294	300
4654	272	400
4994	340	500
5331	337	600
5705	374	700
6065	360	800
6435	370	900
6866	431	1000
7303	437	1100
7728	425	1200
8052	324	1300
8472	420	1400
8861	389	1500
9360	499	1600
9645	285	1700
10132	487	1800
10417	285	1900
11065	648	2000
11473	408	2100
12030	557	2200
12519	489	2300
12749	230	2400
13567	818	2500
14006	439	2600
14575	569	2700
15154	579	2800
15536	382	2900
16244	708	3000
16718	474	3100
17081	363	3200
18112	1031	3300
18516	404	3400
19153	637	3500
19785	632	3600
20483	698	3700
21145	662	3800
21529	384	3900
22446	917	4000
23182	736	4100
24008	826	4200
24536	528	4300
25330	794	4400
26164	834	4500
26925	761	4600
27656	731	4700
28271	615	4800
28625	354	4900
30427	1802	5000
30986	559	5100
31795	809	5200
32606	811	5300
33455	849	5400
34419	964	5500
35122	703	5600
36129	1007	5700
37023	894	5800
37591	568	5900
38767	1176	6000
39644	877	6100
40546	902	6200
41481	935	6300
42274	793	6400
42979	705	6500
44381	1402	6600
44929	548	6700
45685	756	6800
46426	741	6900
47370	944	7000
48222	852	7100
49174	952	7200
49970	796	7300
50458	488	7400
51644	1186	7500
52513	869	7600
53393	880	7700
54139	746	7800
54590	451	7900
55614	1024	8000
56458	844	8100
57089	631	8200
57911	822	8300
58584	673	8400
59379	795	8500
59931	552	8600
60697	766	8700
61495	798	8800
61930	435	8900
62698	768	9000
63202	504	9100
63748	546	9200
64223	475	9300
64655	432	9400
65058	403	9500
65376	318	9600
65599	223	9700
65729	130	9800
65760	31	9900
68422	2662	10000

GRAND TOTAL OF CASES= 68422

EACH STAR REPRESENTS 35 CASES

4.5.2 OUTLIERS, SPIKES AND WEIGHTING

Two further features are detectable with graphical procedures, notably with histograms. One is the presence of outliers – values which are widely separated from the bulk of the distribution. A wider definition provided by Barnett and Lewis (1980, 3) is (one or more) 'observations which appear to be inconsistent with the remainder of that set of data'. For small-area data, outliers may be due to institutions such as prisons or colleges, which distort the age or sex structure of a neighbourhood; it is best to study these separately, and conduct the main analysis in terms of private households. Outliers due to clerical or key-punching errors should have been eliminated by OPCS editing procedures (section 2.4.3), so the histograms presented here contain no outliers. It is nevertheless desirable to check that ratios which, by definition, cannot fall outside the range 0 to 100 per cent do in fact obey this restriction; and to check that ratios created by users from OPCS data do not contain outliers. Outliers in data for large areas, on the other hand, may represent truly anomalous areas; when considering counties in an analysis of Britain, Greater London is an outlier for many census variables. Such outliers should be 'set aside' and accounted for separately, but not discarded.

The second feature is that variables are quite commonly biased toward rounded values or certain common ratios. As an extreme case, numbers in Canadian census data are rounded to the nearest five, a procedure intended to preserve confidentiality. We frequently wish to create ratios from SAS count values, such as 'percentage of old people' (see Chapter 5); ratios consist of a numerator (top) and denominator (bottom), both of which in census data analysis are usually integers. If both these are small integers, as is common in EDs and 1 km grid squares, only a small number of fractional values are possible. For a closed ratio with a denominator of three, only four values are possible; 0, ⅓, ⅔, and 1. Hence the theoretically continuous ratio variable is 'discretized'.

This does not occur for large populations, which provide large and variable denominators so that millions of values are possible. But full, unsuppressed census SAS (adjusted as discussed in section 2.9.6) are given for populations as low as twenty-five, or households as few as eight: denominators can be much

---

Figure 4.11
Histogram of proportion of private households *owner-occupied* in 1971: each star represents 35 1 km grid squares

Numbers and classes are as for figure 4.8. Data are included for all 68,422 grid squares in Great Britain with 8 or more households. 0 and 100 per cent are particularly frequent (also 50 per cent, 60 per cent, 66 per cent, etc.), and the full range of possible values is represented.

100x% Born in England

```
 cum. f      f  lower limit
  1842    1842      0 ********************************
  2384     542    100 **********
  3212     828    200 ***************
  4076     864    300 ***************
  4817     741    400 *************
  5509     692    500 ************
  6180     671    600 ************
  6747     567    700 **********
  7254     507    800 *********
  7654     400    900 *******
  8041     387   1000 *******
  8382     341   1100 ******
  8732     350   1200 ******
  9023     291   1300 *****
  9266     243   1400 ****
  9505     239   1500 ****
  9762     257   1600 *****
  9959     197   1700 ***
 10145     186   1800 ***
 10265     120   1900 **
 10477     212   2000 ****
 10618     141   2100 **
 10743     125   2200 **
 10871     128   2300 **
 10974     103   2400 **
 11124     150   2500 ***
 11249     125   2600 **
 11349     100   2700 **
 11443      94   2800 **
 11514      71   2900 *
 11602      88   3000 **
 11666      64   3100 *
 11736      70   3200 *
 11810      74   3300 *
 11870      60   3400 *
 11927      57   3500 *
 11985      58   3600 *
 12027      42   3700 *
 12074      47   3800 *
 12115      41   3900 *
 12168      53   4000 *
 12202      34   4100 *
 12243      41   4200 *
 12289      46   4300 *
 12329      40   4400 *
 12351      22   4500
 12378      27   4600
 12410      32   4700 *
 12443      33   4800 *
 12457      14   4900
 12506      49   5000 *
 12536      30   5100 *
 12577      41   5200 *
 12610      33   5300 *
 12644      34   5400 *
 12675      31   5500 *
 12709      34   5600 *
 12753      44   5700 *
 12793      40   5800 *
 12828      35   5900 *
 12878      50   6000 *
 12929      51   6100 *
 12985      56   6200 *
 13032      47   6300 *
 13089      57   6400 *
 13154      65   6500 *
 13225      71   6600 *
 13294      69   6700 *
 13394     100   6800 **
 13501     107   6900 **
 13618     117   7000 **
 13725     107   7100 **
 13873     148   7200 ***
 13994     121   7300 **
 14144     150   7400 ***
 14353     209   7500 ****
 14583     230   7600 ****
 14838     255   7700 ****
 15130     292   7800 *****
 15418     288   7900 *****
 15843     425   8000 *******
 16229     386   8100 *******
 16766     537   8200 *********
 17384     618   8300 ***********
 18132     748   8400 *************
 19071     939   8500 ****************
 20225    1154   8600 ********************
 21513    1288   8700 ***********************
 23314    1801   8800 ********************************
 25301    1987   8900 ***********************************
 27977    2676   9000 ***********************************************
 31161    3184   9100 ********************************************************
 35136    3975   9200 **********************************************************************
 39727    4591   9300 *********************************************************************************
 44265    4538   9400 ********************************************************************************
 49033    4768   9500 ************************************************************************************
 54723    5690   9600 ****************************************************************************************************
 59129    4406   9700 *****************************************************************************
 61710    2581   9800 *********************************************
 62221     511   9900 *********
 67543    5322  10000 *********************************************************************************************
GRAND TOTAL OF CASES=    67543

EACH STAR REPRESENTS     57 CASES
```

lower since they may be confined to 'women aged fifteen to twenty-nine' or 'number of people employed', hence discretization is common. Since low-population grid squares (and EDs) are much more frequent than are populous ones, discretization has a great effect on histograms, in which each ratio value is given equal weight; hence there is a need for further histograms confined to populous EDs or grid squares or to 'population slices', such as for all grid squares with between 480 and 520 people per square kilometre.

The '10 per cent sample variables' in the SAS (i.e. those on OPCS pages 5 and 6 in appendix 2) are particularly severely affected by this discretization, but in all those variables with means below 10 per cent the effect shows mainly as a great 'spike' of zero values in the histogram. For variables such as 'semi-skilled workers', with a mean of 20 per cent, there are further spikes at one-quarter, one-half, two-thirds, etc. (see also figure 4.11). The effect of this discretization is reduced in further analyses by *weighting each area by its population;* this greatly reduces the prominence of the numerous areas with low populations, data for which just escaped suppression on the OPCS confidentiality criteria. *This procedure is desirable even for district or county data, but is essential for grid squares and for EDs, both of which vary considerably in population (e.g. the 1981 populations in EDs in Avon County vary between 0 and over 1300).* Most standard statistics packages such as SPSS readily permit population-based weighting.

4.6 Data transformations

4.6.1 THE NEED FOR TRANSFORMATION

Statistics such as standard deviations, regression coefficients and product-moment correlation coefficients that are based on least-squares analyses (see Chapter 7) work best for data that follow the Gaussian frequency-distribution model. They are robust to small deviations from this, but frequency distributions should be near symmetrical, with a clear mode, and without long tails or outliers. Important deviations from this are clearly visible in a good histogram, so it seems unnecessary to devote considerable effort to testing the significance of deviation from the Gaussian model, as do Gardiner and Gardiner (1978). Indeed, such tests often fail to detect any significant difference because of the small size of the data set; this is hardly a reassuring basis for further analysis.

Figure 4.12
Histogram of proportion of people born in *England* in 1971: each star represents 57 1 km grid squares

Numbers and classes are as for figure 4.8. Data are included for all 67,543 grid squares in Great Britain with 25 or more people present. Squares with less than 50 per cent are mainly in Scotland and Wales, forming a separate statistical population for this variable.

Conversely, small but significant deviations from the Gaussian are inevitable for very large samples, and do not distort further analyses.

Nevertheless, it is clear that *strongly skewed distributions require transformation prior to application of least-squares-based techniques*, i.e. the measured value for each area is replaced by a value related to it in a mathematically consistent fashion (e.g. its square root). This is mainly because near-Gaussian distributions are associated with simplification of bivariate and multivariate models. Such transformation usually improves the linearity of relationships, the independence of variance from mean, and the absence of interaction effects so that simple effects are additive (Dunlap and Duffy 1974). Compared with these, approximation to the Gaussian model so that least-squares statistics are optimal estimators is a minor goal.

Some researchers (e.g. Gould 1970) seem to regard transformation of variables as unnatural, a perversion of the purity of their data. Such squeamishness does not afflict workers in better established sciences such as physics, chemistry and biology; statisticians (Gnanadesikan 1977; Mosteller and Tukey 1977) take it for granted that transformation is one of their standard tools, necessary to make techniques and data mutually compatible. What is unnatural about a reciprocal transformation of 'persons per room', a variable that could easily have been defined in the first place as 'rooms per person'? We should use whichever mode of expression is best suited to the analysis and presentation of the data.

Another natural transformation is to take logarithms. Equal intervals on a logarithmic scale represent multiplication of values by a constant factor; this is just as natural as equal intervals on an arithmetic scale, representing addition of a constant factor. Logarithmic transformation is appropriate for distributions with strong positive skew, such as those of absolute numbers (of people or of households of some type) per grid square. Figure 4.5 demonstrates the need for such transformation. Kruskal (1968, 1978) provided the best simple accounts of the choice and use of transformations, making the distinctions used below.

4.6.2 TRANSFORMATIONS FOR ABSOLUTE NUMBERS AND OPEN RATIOS

Although very useful for counts and for measurements of magnitude (Gardiner 1973), the logarithmic transformation is of limited value for the ratio variables commonly used by planners, human geographers and sociologists. For the 102 variables defined by Rhind *et al.* (1977), logarithms are appropriate only for two variables giving density per unit area (as above), and even then only if weighting for population is not applied. *Weighted* distributions of population and household density are initially less positively skewed (more weight is given to the few high-population grid squares), and are made roughly symmetrical when the square-root transformation is used. Taking square roots has the same

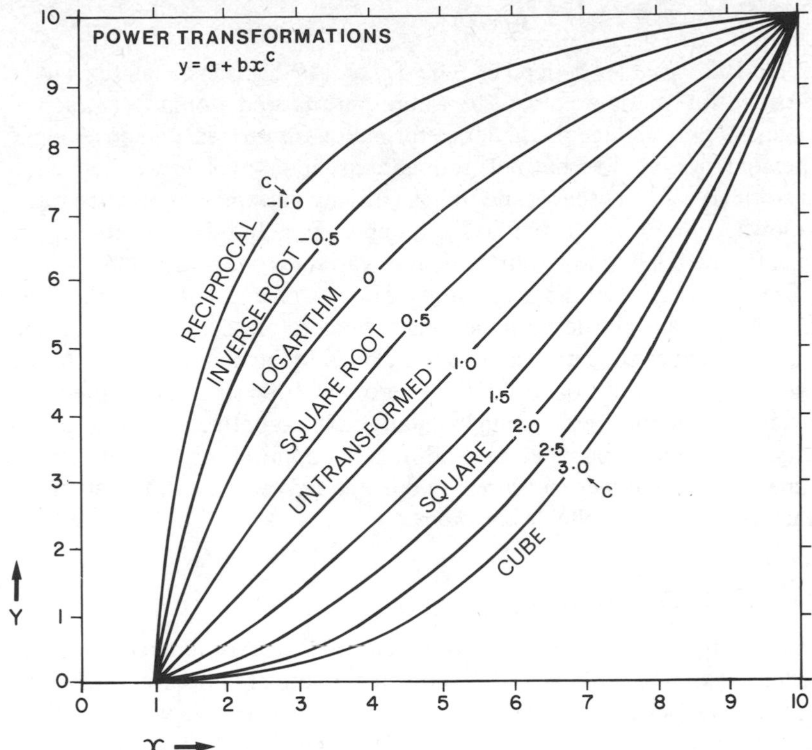

Figure 4.13
The 'ladder' of power transformations

Curves concave-up here rectify negative skews; curves convex-up rectify positive skew. The strongest transformations are represented by the greatest curvatures. The curves are specified by $y = a + bx^c$ with a and b varied so that curves coincide at (1, 0) and (10, 10). For $c = 0$, $y = a + b \log x$.

effect as taking logarithms but the transformation is gentler, i.e. suited to less skewed distributions. The effects of a cube root transformation are intermediate between those of square roots and logarithms, while the reciprocal transformation is more severe even than the logarithmic in bringing high values close together and spacing low values further apart in the frequency distribution.

All of these transformations reduce positive skew, but they provide an obvious clue as to how *negative* skew may be ameliorated. If raising values to the powers one-third (cube root) or one-half (square root) effects the former, raising values to the power two or three must weaken negative skew by spreading out the high values and squeezing together the low ones. This provides Tukey's 'ladder of transformations' (Mosteller and Tukey 1977, 79; Erickson and Nosanchuk 1977). Figure 4.13 shows the close relationships between these power transformations, including the logarithmic transformation.

For the 102 variables defined by Rhind *et al.* (1977) transformations were found useful for 'numbers of children born per married woman' (in each of three age groups), while reciprocal transformations improved 'persons/rooms' and 'persons/households' but not 'rooms/households' which was better left untransformed. Each of these (and the two density variables) is an open ratio, with a lower limit of 0 or 1, but no fixed upper limit. In this respect they are atypical, for the other ninety-four 'indicator' variables on the CRU list (Rhind *et al.* 1977), and most of those in many other sets of indicator variables (see Hakim 1978a), are closed variables; their numerators cannot exceed their denominators, since the numerators are included in the denominators. As we have seen above, the absolute limits of zero and 100 per cent do affect the frequency distributions, preventing long tails either at both ends or (for strong majority or minority groups) at one end. It is not appropriate to treat these in the same way as variables measured on open-ended scales; a different family of transformations is available for them.

4.6.3 TRANSFORMATIONS FOR 'CLOSED' RATIOS

For closed ratios, such as most of those measured on a percentage basis, the difference between 1 per cent and 2 per cent is relatively important, whereas that between 48 per cent and 49 per cent is much less so (we will ignore the political importance of differences between 49 per cent and 50 per cent!). Yet the difference between 98 per cent and 99 per cent is no less important: in many ways it is just as important as the difference between the complements, 2 per cent and 1 per cent. Remember that many variables can be expressed either way round: *either* 'proportion with a car', *or* 'proportion without a car'. Hence we need transformations which treat the two extremes in the same way, but have less effect around 50 per cent. This is achieved by 'two-bend' (S-shaped) transformations, of which three examples are shown in figure 4.14: the angular, the probit and the logit.

Between 10 per cent and 90 per cent, these transformations have very little effect – they are nearly linear – but towards either limit they increase the spacing of values. The logit (the 'folded log' of Tukey 1977) has the strongest effect, and in theory cannot represent the limiting 0 and 100 per cent values. These must be replaced by arbitrarily less extreme values (as for zero values in reciprocal and log transforms: see Mosteller and Tukey 1977, 112). The logit transform of the proportion p is proportional to

$$\log [p/(1-p)] \text{ which equals } \log [p] - \log [1-p].$$

For variables concentrated near the low end of the scale, this transformation has an effect very similar to the logarithmic one, since for $p \leq 0.1$, $(1-p)$ varies only between 0.9 and 1.0, making the second term near constant. But values of p approaching 1.0 are stretched out by the logit transform, whereas they would be squeezed together by the log.

The angular transform replaces each proportion by that angle whose sine is the square root of the proportion (the 'arc-sine square root'). This equalizes the variability of proportions based on binomial distributions, and is widely used in biology. It works very well for census proportions for age groups and sizes of household, which are distributed throughout the country with only small tendencies to segregate. Except in so far as adjacent 1 km squares are not independent of each other, the binomial model seems to apply to these groups. It also applies to 'socioeconomic groups' such as 'proportions of workers skilled' or 'unskilled' (see appendix 4), and occupations such as manufacturing and construction, which were almost ubiquitous in Britain in 1971; but it does *not* apply to small and segregated minorities such as 'defence employees', 'farmers (etc.)' and 'miners': the frequently zero but occasionally large proportions of these violate the binomial model, so that an angular transformation is too gentle and leaves a sizeable positive skew. These variables require the stronger logit transformation. The same procedure should be applied to those proportions noted above as having J-shaped frequency distributions, also 'visitors', 'shared households', 'privately-rented furnished households' and all birthplace variables. (Even 'born in England' is rather less skewed after logit transformation.)

It is satisfying when whole sets of closed proportions can be transformed in the same way, but unfortunately not all sets permit a clear-cut choice between angular and logit. Among the four tenure types recognized in our 1971 census-based list, the two majority ones, 'owner occupied' and 'council rented', are suitable for angular transform; for the national data sets, this reduces the moderate skew of the latter while imparting a slight negative skew to the former. But the angular transformation under-transforms 'furnished' and 'unfurnished privately rented accommodation', which are much more localized and require the logit transform. Likewise, most travel-to-work variables require use of the logit transform, but 'travel by bus' and 'by foot and no travel' would be over-transformed by its use; they require the angular transform.

In several other cases, certainly when dealing with 1 km grid squares, transformation has different effects on weighted and unweighted variables. In unweighted analyses, the logit transformation is suitable for 'proportions unemployed (male or female)' or 'sick', and for 'households without exclusive use of bath, hot water or inside WC', although it does produce a weak negative skew in each. But with population weighting, the negative skew becomes excessive and the angular transform should be used instead of the logit, especially for 'unemployed' and 'sick'. In marginal cases, the weaker (angular) transformation is preferred. Altogether, sixty-nine of our ninety-three closed ratio variables (Rhind *et al.* 1977) require angular transformation in weighted analyses of the grid squares, and twenty-four require use of the logit – but there are some eight marginal cases.

It is clear from all this that the *common use of log transforms instead of logit or angular, for 'closed' census variables, should be discontinued: it distorts relationships, often leading to correlations being overstated.* In regression analyses, impossible predictions (below 0 or above 100 per cent) may be made for closed-ratio dependent variables, unless 'two-bend' transformations are applied.

At present, computer packages such as SPSS (Chapter 5) facilitate, for example, log and square root transforms, but rarely provide the angular transformation (GENSTAT and BMDP79 are exceptions), and the logit must be composed from two log transforms. For those without access to convenient routines, FORTRAN code written for both transformations is available from the author.

This section has concentrated on reduction of skewness, not as an end in itself, but because this is associated with the other improvements of simplifying relationships and in fitting models, as discussed above. Even in a multivariate analysis, it is desirable to choose provisional transformations on the basis of univariate evidence, so as to have only one transformation for a variable in a set of different relationships. Nevertheless, the performance of the chosen transformation should then be checked by reference at least to the scatter plot of each bivariate distribution (Chapter 7). In general terms, aggregate data such as those from the census are 'messier' than individual data and rarely fit simple statistical models well; it seems inevitable that for different areal divisions (see Chapter 7), or for different regions, some of the variables will have distributions so different as to require different transformations.

4.7 Numerical summaries: moments and percentiles

Until the last two decades, there were two rival systems for summarizing frequency distributions in a few numbers: these were based on powers of deviations, and on percentiles of ordered data. The former included the mean (about which deviations sum to zero), the standard deviation (the square root of the mean squared deviation from the mean), and moment measures of skewness and kurtosis (based on cubed- and fourth-power deviations respectively). A 'percentile' is a level which divides a frequency distribution so that the specified percentage of the observations is lower, e.g. 25th percentile is the value below which 25 per cent of all observations occur. Percentile measures include the median and the interquartile range, and are unaffected by changes in magnitude of values except for changes past the median, the upper and lower quartiles, or whatever critical percentiles had been chosen.

The recent development of Exploratory Data Analysis (Tukey 1977; Erickson and Nosanchuk 1977; Velleman and Hoaglin 1981; Cox and Jones 1981) has provided many further statistics which compromise between these two systems, using less information than moment-based statistics, but more

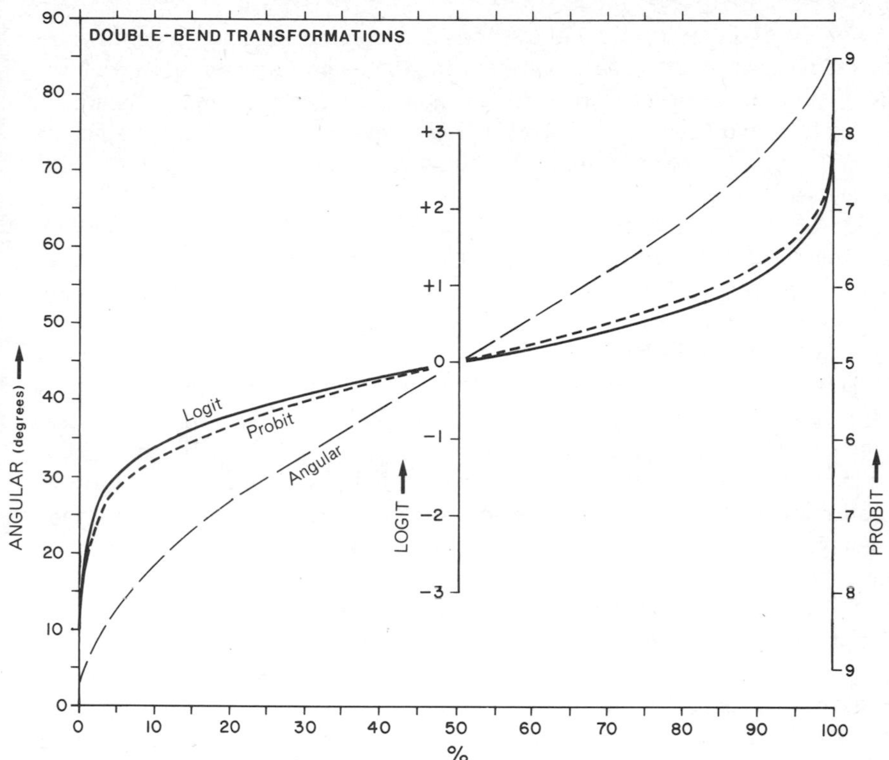

Figure 4.14
Three 'double-bend' transformations for closed percentages ($x = 100p$, where p is a closed proportion)

The angular transformation is most gentle, and is specified by $y =$ arcsine $\sqrt{p}$: here it is given in degrees, but many programs give radians. The 'probit' is given by 5 + Gaussian deviate, the latter being the z value in a table of cumulated proportions (p) in the Gaussian ('normal') frequency distribution model. The 'logit' is the strongest of the three, suitable for more skewed distributions: it is given by 0.5 $\log_e (p/(1-p))$. Note that the relationship between the three scales plotted here is arbitrary.

than the percentile-based ones. These statistics are intentionally more resistant than the former, but less resistant (insensitive to unusual values and strange shapes of distribution) than the latter.

For example, the 'q per cent-trimmed mean' ignores the q per cent highest and the q per cent lowest values, since these may contain outliers: $q = 50$ gives the 'interquartile mean' or 'midmean'. The (Erickson and Nosanchuk 1977) 'trimean' = (2 × median + upper quartile + lower quartile)/4 modifies the median by taking asymmetry of the body of a distribution into account, while excluding asymmetry of the tails (which can influence the mean considerably). Equivalent resistant measures are available for dispersion and (Chapter 7) correlation and regression. Tukey's 'biweight' estimators are resistant in several ways, but require iterative estimation (chapter 10 in Mosteller and Tukey 1977).

In the graphical approach to data exploration which we have already examined, outliers are identified from histograms (on a transformed scale where appropriate) and set aside for separate explanation. Since transformation should have produced a nearly symmetrical frequency distribution, it is likely that the median will be very close to the mean and that, over a series of frequency distributions, the interquartile ranges and the standard deviations (or mean deviations, or other measures of spread) will have the same rank order. In this case, compromise measures will essentially be redundant; moment measures may safely be used, and the way is open for further, confirmatory analyses. (Unlike exploratory analyses, confirmatory analyses employ a particular model: they involve either parameter estimation or significance testing.)

The four moment measures are defined in table 4.3. Mean and standard deviation are in the same unit of expression, measuring location and spread on the original measurement scale or its transformation. The standard deviation is based on the second moment, i.e. on squared deviations from the mean, and converted into the same units as the mean by taking a square root; squaring gives considerable weight to values in both high and low tails. The formula for estimating population standard deviation from a sample has the denominator $(n-1)$ instead of n because deviations measured around the sample mean total less than would those around the unknown, true population mean: one 'degree of freedom' has been lost in estimating the mean from the sample. The difference is slight for large values of n (the number of areal divisions), both for standard deviations and (despite the complexity of the formulae) for skewness and kurtosis. The SPSS (see Chapter 5) program package switched from the first (sample) to the second (estimate) basis between version 7 and version 8.

Skewness and kurtosis extend the moments principle by using the third and fourth moments respectively. Unlike the mean and standard deviation, they are used to express the *shape* of a frequency distribution, hence they are rendered dimensionless through division by an appropriate power of the standard deviation. The third power of deviations is positive for the upper tail, but negative for the lower one; hence skewness weighs the extent of one against the other and measures the asymmetry of distribution, being zero for any perfectly symmetric distribution (such as the Gaussian), positive for those with an extensive upper tail, and negative for those with an extensive lower tail. Obviously extreme values produce extreme deviations which, once cubed, are extremely influential in determining skewness.

Table 4.3 Definitions of moment measures (after Fisher; see Bliss 1970) for n values of x

Summation is over all cases in the sample.

Mean:	$\bar{x} = \Sigma x/n$	
Standard deviation:	$s = [\Sigma(x - \bar{x})^2/n]^{1/2}$	(sample)
	$\hat{s} = [\Sigma(x - \bar{x})^2/(n - 1)]^{1/2}$	(estimate of population)
Skewness:	$\sqrt{b_1} = \Sigma(x - \bar{x})^3/s^3 n$	(sample)
	$g_1 = n\Sigma(x - \bar{x})^3/\hat{s}^3(n - 1)(n - 2)$	(estimate of population)
Crude Kurtosis:	$b_2 = \Sigma(x - \bar{x})^4/s^4 n$	(sample)
	$g_2 = [n(n + 1)\Sigma(x - \bar{x})^4 - 3(\Sigma(x - \bar{x})^2)^2(n - 1)]/\hat{s}^4(n - 1)(n - 2)(n - 3)$	(estimate of population)

Kurtosis, like standard deviation, is based on an even power of deviations, so values in either tail work together in increasing its value. It is very low for a rectangular distribution, 3.0 for the Gaussian, and high for distributions with longer tails, including skewed distributions. To facilitate reference to the Gaussian 'standard', kurtosis is usually obtained by subtracting 3.0 from what is here termed 'crude kurtosis' – but it will be necessary to check whether or not a particular program does this; remember that crude kurtosis involves only even powers of deviations, and hence cannot be negative. For census data, the salient feature of kurtosis is that it increases with the degree of (positive or negative) skewness. Most census variables, as defined here, are affected by lower limits of 0 or 1, and hence symmetrical, long-tailed distributions do not occur. Nor do truly rectangular ones; the bimodal variables English-born, Scots-born and Welsh-born are special cases.

Clearly these measures are not 'resistant' to extreme values – they are not intended to be – and thus they require that data have been properly edited and transformed. Skewness is indeed a major guide to a useful transformation. In some applications (not census data of the present type), kurtosis is considered jointly with skewness, but is rarely valuable independently of skewness.

It is useful to check that analyses based on percentile measures give results compatible with those from moment measures, to reassure ourselves that results are not artefacts dependent upon the choice of method. The median (fiftieth percentile) will approximate the mean for symmetric distributions, while the interquartile range (difference between twenty-fifth and seventy-fifth percentiles) will generally exceed the standard deviation (which, in a Gaussian distribution, approximately equals the difference between fiftieth and eighty-fourth *or* sixteenth percentiles). *The range between maximum and minimum should not be used alone as a summary of dispersion.*

Various percentile-based measures of skewness and kurtosis (Gardiner and Gardiner 1978) are in use in sedimentology, where the percentiles are read by interpolation on cumulative curves. For example, the difference in separation of upper and lower quartiles (or any other complementary percentiles) from the median, divided by the interquartile range, provides a measure of skewness (note, though, that some definitions of percentile skewness invert the conventional positive and negative signs). Kurtosis – the relative extent of the tails – is measured by relating the spread between two complementary outer percentiles, and two complementary inner percentiles, e.g. (95th–5th)/(75th–25th). Such measures are considerably more resistant than moment measures, but there is little experience as yet of their use with census data. Since they are based on limited information, results from small data sets should be viewed with suspicion.

The advantage of moment measures is that they are well established and lead on to further statistical techniques. Mean, standard deviation and moment-based skewness have been found very useful descriptions in the analysis of census variables, and skewness has guided the choice of appropriate transformation (see section 4.6). Means and variances (or rather, *sums* of squared deviations) are additive and can be combined, which can be very useful in further analysis. Medians, interquartile ranges, etc., are not additive, but percentiles have the useful property that, for monotonic transformations such as those discussed here

transform of percentile of raw data = percentile of transform of raw data

This commutative property can also be useful in choosing a transformation.

4.8 Conclusions

4.8.1 EXPLORATION AND RESISTANCE

In summary, the approach to data analysis advocated here is essentially exploratory, emphasizing 'getting a feel for the data' rather than a 'cook-book' yes/no answer to a significance test. It differs from Tukey's *Exploratory Data Analysis* (1977) in advocating even greater use of graphics, combined with use of traditional percentile-based and especially moment-based statistics in preference to newer, resistant statistics which can be regarded as compromises between these. I find that the objectives of data exploration are better achieved by scrutiny of graphical displays than by the numerical techniques proposed thus far. Graphics are also advantageous for published display of data (and of some analytical results), for which purpose they should be very carefully designed for effective communication (e.g. see Bertin 1973).

If transformation to a near-Gaussian distribution is successful, the wide range of linear model techniques becomes available for more sophisticated analysis (Chapters 7 and 8), and is still highly attractive. Selection of a good transformation improves our understanding of the measurement scale involved, whereas use of percentile-based or other resistant techniques may 'sweep this under the carpet'. These issues are contentious, but there can be broader agreement that moment-based techniques should not be used without graphical analyses and the use of appropriate transformations.

4.8.2 RECOMMENDATIONS

Before mapping or carrying out multivariate statistical analysis, *always* examine each of the variables of interest using univariate procedures.

The recommended procedure is:

i compute moment-based descriptive statistics for each variable;
ii plot histograms of each variable;
iii select provisional transformations to reduce skewness;
iv repeat (i) and (ii); also (iii) and (iv) if the results are unsatisfactory;
v on the transformed scale, check for tendencies to divide into several groups.

The transformation for a variable should be chosen with a view to its being useful in several different study areas, not optimized for a single data set. If possible, similar variables should be transformed in the same way. If the transformation is successful, analyses using moment-based, percentile-based and 'robust' statistics should all give compatible results.

5 Creating new variables and new areas from the census data

DAVID RHIND

5.1 Introduction

For many purposes, the extremely detailed information available from the census is not enough: we have already seen that five year migration data are not available from the 1981 Census, and it will become clear in Chapter 9 that making some comparisons through time are not feasible simply because different classifications (or groupings) of census questionnaire responses have been made in different censuses. Sometimes the smallest areas for which data are available are too large for a particular purpose. Nothing whatever can be done about the first and third of these situations and risky palliatives are the only 'solution' to the second.

Quite often, however, the converse is the case: that aggregation of census areas (such as EDs) or of census variables (such as to give numbers of all children under sixteen years old) – or of both – is required. This chapter discusses the methods by which such aggregations are best carried out. We assume that a computer is to be used for such calculations but the principles are unchanged even if they are carried out by hand.

5.2 Computing derived variables

5.2.1 RATIOS AND COUNTS

At the time of writing, all of the data to be produced from the 1981 Census are counts. This greatly simplifies arithmetic manipulations. Indeed, if such manipulations are to be carried out on ratio data, it is vital that these are transformed into counts prior to aggregation *unless all the ratios have the same denominator and are not overlapping.* (Such an obvious comment is necessary because examples have been seen by the author in which ratios with different denominators have been added together !)

Consider the figures 10 per cent, 15 per cent, 20 per cent, 16 per cent and 39 per cent which are taken to represent the percentage of the population in an area in the age groups 0–5, 6–15, 16–25, 26–65, and 66 and over; it is perfectly feasible and sensible to add together several of these figures, say, to get the percentage of the population between nought and fifteen years old (25 per cent). If the same figures represent densities of different subgroups of the population in that area, e.g. density of people per km^2 in socioeconomic groups 1, 2, 3, 4, and 5.1 (see appendix 4), then it is still perfectly permissible to sum the figures or apply other algebraic operations to them. It is *not,* however, permissible to sum the ratios where each denominator differs, such as in the case of age-specific masculinity ratios. (We use masculinity ratio, rather than sex ratio as customarily defined, for statistical reasons described in Evans (1979).) Table 5.1 contains hypothetical data previously derived from cells in table 21 of the 1981 SAS.

Table 5.1 Hypothetical partial age distribution and masculinity (= males/(males + females))

Age	*Male*	*Female*	*Masculinity*
0–4	150	100	0.6
5–15	200	200	0.5
16–24	200	300	0.4
	550	600	

Clearly, in no sense is the masculinity of the 0–24 age group equal to 1.5, or even 0.5 (dividing the sum into three equal parts) ! The answer (0.48) is obtained by summing up all the males and all the females and recomputing the formula.

5.2.2 THE ALGEBRAIC PROCEDURES

Two types of operation are commonly carried out on census variables:

i to add, subtract, multiply or divide involving other variables and/or constant terms, e.g.

$$\text{NEWVAR} = \text{C36} - \text{C43}$$

would give the difference between the *de facto* and the *de jure* populations (section 2.3.1) for the given area in 1981, where C is an array – best considered as a sequence of numbered 'pigeon holes' – and the succeeding numbers are the OPCS cell or 'pigeon hole' numbers (appendix 2) in which the values are stored. C36 therefore implies the contents of that particular 'pigeon hole'.

ii to carry out transformations on the data once the overall characteristics are known from calculating descriptive statistics (see Chapter 4). Hence, it may be sensible to take the square root of all the values for cell number 36 for a set of areas (say, all EDs in a county) so that the data may then conform to the assumptions made in more sophisticated statistical analysis (Chapter 7).

Most commonly available statistical computer programs readily permit the user to create new variables from combinations of others and/or transformations. The capabilities available to the user are dependent both on what package exists locally and on the computer in which it sits. Rowe and Scheer (1976) and Rowe (1980a and 1980b) have described all the known statistical packages in common use in Britain. We discuss these technical points in more detail in appendix 7 but, for illustrative purposes, give examples here using statements provided by the user to the package in most common use – the Statistical Package for the Social Sciences or SPSS (Nie *et al.* 1975). We also use only SAS-type data as examples; dealing with what we have called flow or interaction data, including some of the journey-to-work and the migration data, is more difficult in such packages than is handling 'stocks'. In SPSS, the calculation of NEWVAR given above would be carried out by the statement:

```
COMPUTE   NEWVAR=C36 – C43
```

There are – as in any widely available tool – a number of pitfalls for the unwary. Perhaps the most obvious but significant one is that the sequence in which the arithmetic operations are carried out on a computer may well be significant. In computing overall masculinity ratios the two statements below – each acceptable to SPSS – would give different results.

```
COMPUTE   NEWVAR=C45/C45 + C46
COMPUTE   NEWVAR=C45/(C45 + C46)
```

This is because a fixed priority generally exists in which the different operations are performed. Expressions within brackets – such as (C45 + C46) – are evaluated first; brackets may be nested, i.e. expressions may exist within other expressions. Exponentiation is followed by multiplication and division, with addition and subtraction the last two in the sequence of evaluations. Hence, if there are 500 males and 500 females in this area, the first statement above would produce the value of 501 (absurd!) and the second the value of 0.5 (correct). The more complex the expression, the more simple it is for such errors to be made: in computing their indicator variables from the 1971 SAS, Rhind, Evans and Dewdney (1977, appendix 5a) often used thirty or forty cell values. The only sensible procedure is to use brackets around every expression and not to rely upon the implicit order in which calculations are carried out. It is also important to note that, throughout this chapter, we assume the use of census data held in the computer as floating point (or decimal, e.g. 5.0) form, rather than as integers (e.g. 5): integer division, say, of 9 by 5 will give the answer 1 (!).

Constants are readily entered into modern statistics packages. Thus we could calculate the difference between the national average percentage of retired people and that in each and every ED, ward, district or other area by using the following SPSS-like command and statistics from table 32 (see appendix 2)in the 1981 SAS:

COMPUTE DIFF=(C2571/C2570) * 100.0 – 16.0

where 16.0 could be the national average percentage of retired people and is obtained from some previous analysis.

One of the most important uses of constants in working with census data is that, when using data from both the 100 per cent and the 10 per cent sections, all the counts from the 10 per cent section of the record (OPCS pages 5 and 6, cell numbers 4223 to 5517; see appendix 2) must be multiplied by ten to make them comparable with the other counts.

Current statistical and, particularly, database packages normally also contain a set of functions which can be used in transforming variables. Thus:

COMPUTE TRANSF=SQRT (NEWVAR)

will, in SPSS terms, create a new 'pigeon hole' called TRANSF and put in this the square root of the value in the 'pigeon hole' called NEWVAR.

Subsequently, the results of the computation(s) may be printed out, sent to a computer file for later use, or used immediately in further statistical analysis. Again in SPSS terms,

WRITE CASES (4F8.2) NEWVAR, NEWVAL, DIFF, TRANSF

would send all of the above results into a file, with eight columns allowed for each of the four numbers.

5.2.3 COPING WITH DATA SUPPRESSION

In certain circumstances (see sections 1.7 and 2.9.6) not all the census data may be provided for an area. Generally this occurs when very few people are present and there is therefore a risk of disclosing identifiable information about individuals in detailed cross-tabulations.

Standard statistical packages can normally only cope with rectangular sets of data, i.e. for each and every area (ED or whatever) there is the same number of cells or variables. This is, of course, inefficient of storage if much more than half of the data are suppressed. In practice, there are various strategies which can be used to analyse data which include suppressed elements. The simplest strategy, in SPSS terms, merely includes only the areas for which all data are present by saying

SELECT IF (SUP EQ 0)

where SUP is a variable in the OPCS data which is set as zero if the data are unsuppressed.

Since this action excludes even the data which are always available in the SAS (section 2.9.6), a better but still simple solution is to have all the suppressed data cells set to a number which can be regarded as missing data.

Since the standard SAS are all counts, any negative number will suffice as a missing data flag (e.g. –1) and the appropriate SPSS line to exclude all of these suppressed values would be

MISSING VALUES C1 TO C500 (–1)

if only the first 500 cells in the SAS were being considered. Such action, it should be stressed, is only necessary in general purpose computer packages: packages such as SASPAC (appendix 7) which have built into them considerable knowledge of the characteristics of the data are rather easier to use. Failure to set the 'missing data flag' appropriately may lead to catastrophic but sometimes not readily visible results: OPCS insert full records for every area, even when data are suppressed, and fill out suppressed fields with blanks which are read as zeros by unsophisticated programs on some computer systems. Zero can thus be considered to have two meanings in OPCS data: either a true value of zero or, alternatively, 'missing data' when the record has been suppressed. A number of early analyses of 1971 census data did not apparently take this into account and, as a consequence, too many zero values were included in the analyses! A consequence of all this is, of course, that the results for different variables will inevitably be based on different numbers of areas: no new variable can be computed for any area in which any one component of the numerator or denominator (if it is a ratio) is missing, or if the denominator is zero. Table 5.2 illustrates this for the extreme case: the effect is unlikely to occur on district level data and above.

Table 5.2 Different numbers of 1 km grid-square areas for which selected 1971 SAS statistics were available for all of Britain

Variable	*Number of areas*	*% of population included*
Total population	147685	100.0
Sex composition	147685	100.0
Household amenities	68422	98.7
Born in Scotland	67546	96.7
Persons over retirement age	65021	95.4
Miners	54153	99.2
Educational qualifications	53277	not known

Source: CRU/OPCS/GRO(S) (1980), tables 1 and 2, Rhind, Evans and Dewdney (1977)

5.2.4 COPING WITH 'ADJUSTMENT' (OR 'BLURRING') OF THE DATA

Adjustment is the process of adding small random numbers by OPCS to maintain confidentiality of the 100 per cent SAS data (section 2.9.6).

In many senses coping with this is more difficult than coping with data suppression, since its effects can be serious for small areas. However, for variables which use a table total as the denominator, such as 'per cent of the residents who were born in Scotland', no problems of any significance should be discernible – though the figures may not be *correct* owing to the adjustment procedure. In passing, we would produce this variable in SPSS by:

```
COMPUTE   SCOTS = (C327 + C328)/(C321 + C322) * 100.0
```

In other situations, though,more problems arise. Consider the situation where the new variable 'New Commonwealth-born residents as a percentage of Old Commonwealth-born residents' is being derived for the unsuppressed EDs in the 1981 SAS data. We would derive the data from SAS table 4 and would compute it, in SPSS terms, as follows:

```
COMPUTE   NEWOLD = (C342 + C343)/(C339 + C340) * 100.0
```

For the great majority of EDs in Britain, these figures would be very small or zero. In this example, four separate cell values have been adjusted – those for male and female New and Old Commonwealth-born residents. None of these is a total or a sub-total and hence the three possible additions to each value are +1, 0 or –1 (see section 2.9.6). Table 5.3 gives the minimum and maximum values of the ratio which might occur for different total populations of those two groups but which have a truly constant ratio of 1.0 between them: the maximum value occurs when both the numerator terms – New Commonwealth-born residents – are incremented by +1 and the two denominator terms are incremented by –1; the minimum value occurs when the situation is reversed. Twenty-five possible permutations of the values exist in this case but many of these give the same ratio.

Table 5.3 Possible ratio values between two variables (see text) based upon adjustment by OPCS of originally equal numbers for each variable

Number of both Old and New Commonwealth-born residents equally split between male and female	*Maximum ratio*	*Minimum ratio*
2	infinite	zero
4	3.00	0.333
6	2.00	0.500
20	1.22	0.820
50	1.08	0.920
200	1.02	0.980

It is important to note that *these effects are dependent not upon the total population of the area but upon the total numbers in the categories in the numerator and in the denominator.* In passing, the example given above does not indicate good practice: it is much better statistical practice to compute 'New Commonwealth-born residents as a percentage of *all* Commonwealth-born residents', i.e. to ensure that all such ratios have a minimum of 0 and a maximum of 100 per cent, rather than a theoretical maximum of infinity.

In the 1981 census data, the totals and subtotals are the sum of the individual, previously adjusted cells in that table. It follows that – unlike the situation in the 1971 data and unlike the situation where areas are being added together (below) – new variables created from individual cells will be no less accurate than those constructed from totals (though use of totals is generally more convenient wherever possible).

Where cells which are used to create new variables are taken from different tables, the probability of adjustment effects being significant rises. Consider, for instance, the calculation of male employment in manufacturing industry as derived from the 10 per cent sample SAS data. This would be defined as: total male residents economically active and formerly employed in manufacturing but not in employment (table 53) divided by the total male residents economically active in manufacturing (table 51) plus the total male residents economically active and formerly employed in manufacturing but not in employment (table 53). The result would normally be multiplied by 100 to convert to a percentage unemployment rate. Hence, in SPSS-like terms, this becomes:

```
COMPUTE  UNEMPL = C5499/(C5330 + C5499) * 100.0
```

In passing, users should note that this is a hypothetical example: we have pointed out in section 2.9.6 that calculations based on 10 per cent statistics *at ED level* are liable to be significantly in error. In at least two circumstances, then, it is possible for the resulting percentage figure to exceed 100 per cent. This is nonsensical in such a 'closed' ratio, even if it is entirely likely in others like that of 'children per married female'. Evidence of such absurd values due to adjustment have been detected as high as ward level in 1971 SAS data. Such nonsensical values are important because the presence of non-feasible and undetected values can have enormous effects upon statistical procedures such as regression. Such extremes have very disproportionate effects upon the results, hence it is important to obviate such spurious values. Because of the nature of the adjustment procedure (no –1 values are added to a cell if that would thereby make the stored value negative) no illogical negative values of ratios can occur except by user mis-specification. Rhind *et al.* (1977) have argued that a similar trimming procedure should be applied to the top end of ratios where there is a logical limit, i.e. percentage values calculated from census data should always be checked and trimmed back to 100 per cent wherever necessary. This procedure was followed by Rhind *et al.* (1977) in creating a set of 102 indicator variables from the 1971 1 km grid square SAS data and a total of 26,734 values were trimmed out of a total of the approximately 6.8 million values calculated. Though only about 0.4 per cent of the total, some 15,000 of these occurred in two of the 102 variables. These were the 'percentage of working males' and 'percentage of households with exclusive use of all amenities'. It is no coincidence that these were also the two percentage variables in the set of 102 with the highest national values: *the nearer is the national average to 100 per cent, the more likely is an illogical value and the more vital is the need for trimming.* Despite the fact that in applying trimming we are improving the data, we should be well aware that this is by an unknown amount and an amount which will vary between different variables.

Trimming may often be carried out by use of a standard statistical package. In SPSS, for example, it can be achieved by the statement:

```
COMPUTE    NEWVAR = as in previous examples
RECODE     NEWVAR (100.0 THRU HIGHEST = 100.0)
```

Such procedures are, however, clumsy if many but not all variables are subject to trimming and, without extra effort, do not provide useful information, such as how many trimmings have been made. There is therefore something to be said for creating one computer program to calculate a set of indicator variables and to produce all the relevant descriptions: one such program is listed by Rhind *et al.* (1977) though much of its complexity is now unnecessary because of the simpler organization of the 1981 SAS.

5.2.5 COPING WITH SMALL POPULATIONS

Many users require the most detailed census statistics available, usually for EDs or for 100 m or 1 km grid squares: the national average population of 1981 EDs and wards in Britain are, respectively, about 400 and 5500, while the average population of populated 1 km grid squares in 1971 was 365. Without this detail, the populations in any one area under consideration may be so heterogeneous that no generalized relationships of any value can be defined, whether these are between variables (see Chapter 7) or between different areas (see Chapter 8). Indeed, a good case can be made out for the supply of even more detailed data than is presently available (see Chapter 11).

The use of such detailed data does, however, bring us disadvantages; these are largely of meaningfulness. We have already seen that the effects of adjustment (section 2.9.6) are likely to be greater in small populations and in Chapter 6 we will argue that many, perhaps most, maps yet published based on ED data are liable to be highly misleading because of the small numbers of people involved. Clearly, the chances of getting twenty people out of a population of thirty as being over the age of sixty-five are much greater than getting 2000 people out of 3000 yet the percentages of retired people will be the same and give no clue as to whether this is a statistical accident or not. Enormous variations in base population are typical of grid squares but also occur in EDs (see the Avon county example quoted in section 4.5.2). How can we at least minimize such effects of small population bases?

A small number of approaches to this have been made in recent years. That devised at Durham University specifically for census data – the calculation of a signed chi-squared measure, rather than a ratio – has much to commend it and has successfully been used in much mapping (CRU/OPCS/GRO(S) 1980) and statistical analysis. This statistic is a compromise measure taking into account both the absolute deviation (in number of persons, households, etc.) from the national average, and the relative deviation (effectively the proportionate difference from expectation). It is computed as:

$$X^2 = \Sigma\left((O - E)^2/E\right)$$

where O is the observed number of individuals, E is the expected number based upon the national average, and X^2 is the chi-square value, summed over two classes. It is then given a negative sign if the expected number (derived by multiplying the national average by the base population of the area) is greater than the observed number.

The effect of this computation is that a high-population area will obtain a larger chi-square statistic than will a low-population area which has the same percentage difference from the national average. In other words, a weighting is applied such that small population areas must be very unusual indeed before they are given a high chi-square value. Figure 5.1 illustrates the way in which variations in base population and in the proportion of interest interact in calculation of the chi-square statistic and, subsequently, in assignation of map class and colour in the *People in Britain* atlas.

It is important to note that, like all such schemes, this one contains certain arbitrary elements. The conventional squaring of (O – E), for example, homogenizes the variance for binomial variables only. The justification for using the method is that it certainly steers a middle course between emphasizing high or low population areas, and it does not lead to undue loss of information. That the results are usually more readily interpretable than those of either ratio or absolute-number based maps is, of course, a further benefit!

5.3 Aggregating areas

5.3.1 DEFINING WHICH AREAS TO AGGREGATE

In arithmetical terms, operations carried out on areas are more restricted than those carried out between variables or cell values – we only add or subtract the values for the same variable as measured in different areas! Most frequently we aggregate areas and therefore add their respective counts together. For

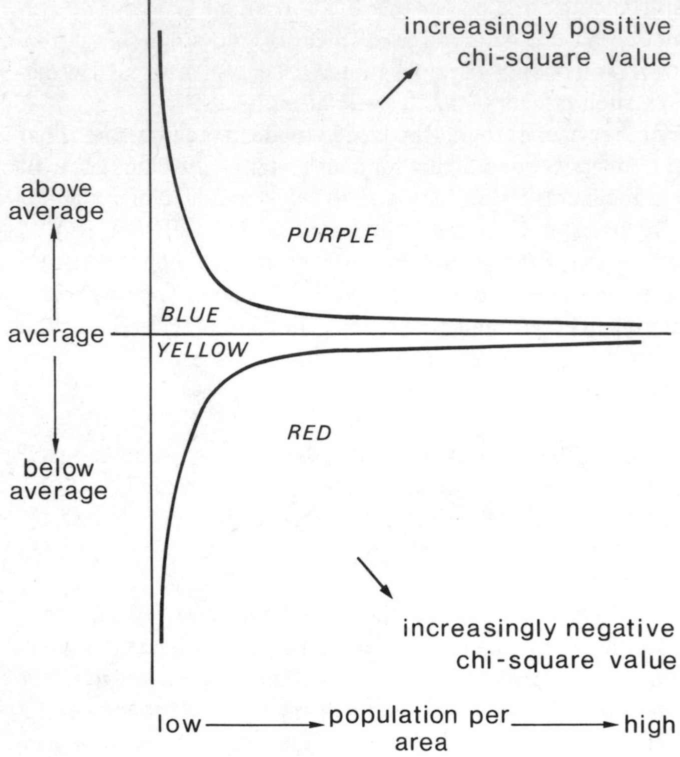

Figure 5.1
Distribution of the X^2 statistic, as used in the *People in Britain* atlas

The colours used to show areas change in relation to deviation from the national average and the number of people in the area. 'Unusual' areas are thus shown as purple or red.

different purposes, however, we tend to define the areas to be aggregated in one of three different ways.

5.3.1.1 Area lists

Ad hoc areas such as traffic zones are often defined by the user providing a set of names of the areas grouped together. Hence, we might say (in SASPAC 2.5 but not in SPSS – see appendix 7):

```
NEW ZONE     LABEL=ZONE1     AAAA01+AAAA02+AAAA05*0.3
NEW ZONE     LABEL=ZONE2     AAAA03+AAAA04
NEW ZONE     LABEL=ZONE3     AAAA05*0.7
```

where ZONE1, ZONE2, and ZONE3 are the names and AAAA01, etc. are the names of EDs from which they are built. The decimal fractions indicate that only that fraction of the ED's population is to be added to the totals for the new area.

It is also possible to carry out aggregations using the names embedded in the census data: since the codes describe a hierarchy of areas (section 2.9.2.1), all EDs within each ward can be aggregated together in SPSS by holding the various parts of the ED identifier as two numbers, e.g. AAAA01, referred to respectively by the names WARDS and EDS and making the command:

```
SORT CASES     WARDS(A)
AGGREGATE GROUPVARS = WARDS
            VARIABLES = VAR001 TO VAR100
             AGGSTATS = SUM
```

Note that the preliminary sort to ensure that all records for EDs within the same ward are next to each other is an SPSS requirement for aggregation. It is not wise to sort such alphanumeric fields (see section 11.8 in Nie *et al.* (1975) but this procedure should work on most computer systems). Equally, all EDs or wards can be aggregated to districts and, in Scotland, all postcode sector data can be readily aggregated to the postcode districts in which they lie (section 2.5.5) and to the postcode area. This is, however, bad practice. Since 1981 (and 1971) census data were adjusted *after* aggregation from census forms to cross-tabulations at the level requested by the user, data obtained from OPCS at one particular level will be less affected by adjustment than will the data previously obtained at a more detailed level and subsequently aggregated.

5.3.1.2 Spatial search

All SAS records contain an Ordnance Survey grid reference – a co-ordinate pair which defines the geographical position of the centroid of that area to the nearest 100 metres within Great Britain. It has become quite common in recent years to use these unique grid references in the selection of, say, all EDs within a stipulated zone (General Improvement Area, traffic zone, Travel-To-

Work-Area and so on). The principle is to test whether each one of these centroids falls within a polygon and, if so, add the area identifier (e.g. ED number) to a list which makes up that zone. In practice there is a trivial difficulty because OPCS follow Ordnance Survey practice in quoting their grid references using letters to define the 100 km square within which the point lies and 'normal' (x, y) co-ordinates to define position within the 100 km square. We describe this in more detail in section 6.3.2.3; for simplicity, the examples below are constrained to lie entirely within one 100 km square (TQ in the OS terminology).

The simplest form of selection by polygon is probably the 'box search' and is readily carried out on a standard statistical package. With the easting and northing grid references held in 'pigeon holes' or variables called X and Y, the SPSS statement

```
SELECT IF (X GE 260.0 AND X LE 340.0 AND Y GE
                    750.0 AND Y LE 840.0)
```

would select all SAS data within a 9 by 10 km rectangle enclosing Central London.

A simple extension of this gives us the facility for radial search, i.e. selecting all areas whose centroids fall within a stipulated radius of a defined point. Thus the SPSS statements

```
COMPUTE   DIST = (X-303.0) ** 2 + (Y-796.0) ** 2
COMPUTE   DIST = SQRT (DIST)
SELECT IF (DIST LE 200.0)
```

would select all areas with centroids less than or equal to a distance of 20 km from the Palace of Westminster. Alternatively, the version below is marginally more efficient.

```
COMPUTE   DIST = (X-303.0) ** 2 + (Y-796.0) ** 2
SELECT IF (DIST LE 40000.0)
```

In many circumstances, however, it is important to aggregate together those census areas which make up larger but irregularly shaped zones. Figure 5.2 illustrates this principle and also one method by which the principle can be implemented on a computer: if any line from the centroid intersects the boundary of the zone an odd number of times then the centroid is within the polygon. In practice, a variety of methods are used; details of a simple program for such a 'Point in Polygon' (PIP) procedure is given in Baxter (1976b), while DoE (1975) have published a much more sophisticated and complex program. At least one computer mapping package – GIMMS 4 (see appendix 7) – contains very sophisticated facilities for such spatial selection, including the ability to stipulate 'all points (centroids) within (say) 1 km of a given motorway' and to handle multiple polygons.

It is critical, however, to remember that in all this spatial selection for

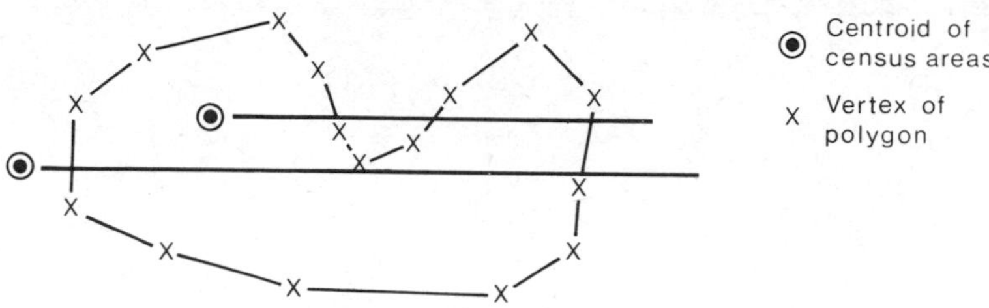

Figure 5.2
A method of determining whether an ED centroid lies within an area
If a line from the centroid cuts the boundaries an even number of times, the point is outside of the area.

irregularly sized and shaped areas the centroid is taken to represent *the whole of the area*. Thus areas are always either inside or outside the new, larger zone. It is possible to use a more realistic description of the geography of the areas, particularly with data for grid squares but also for polygons, using a technique known as 'polygon overlay' and an assumption that the population is spread evenly throughout the areas represented by centroids: such sophistications are, however, immensely more difficult to organize and costly to run. As a 'rule of thumb', therefore, the areas to be aggregated should be small (and therefore numerous) in relation to the large zones: an overall ratio of ten small areas to be 'PIPped' on the basis of centroids to each large one is probably the lowest reasonably safe criterion. Figure 5.3 illustrates a plot of all the 7000 or so centroids of 1971 SAS EDs in the Northern Region superimposed on the 70 Employment Office Areas in mid-1979: here the PIP process was working on a ratio of 100 to 1. For most practical purposes, wards are the largest census areas to which spatial search can be meaningfully applied.

5.3.1.3 Topology

On some occasions,it is the areas surrounding one or more ED or ward or district (etc.) which are of interest. One rather novel example of this comes from the study by Helen Mounsey (see Chapter 9) which produced data for present local government areas at each census date since 1901. It was decided to send the results for comment to local planning officers who, in many cases, made helpful comments based on local experience. Rather than send the data for 458 areas to all planning officers, however, a trivial computer program was written to print out the total populations in the planner's area and also for the other local government areas contiguous with it: the method of allocation of pre-1971 census data to new local government areas meant that any mis-allocations were most likely to be nearby areas.

To produce a list of, say, all districts with more than 15 per cent unemployment and all those districts adjacent to them cannot be done solely on the basis

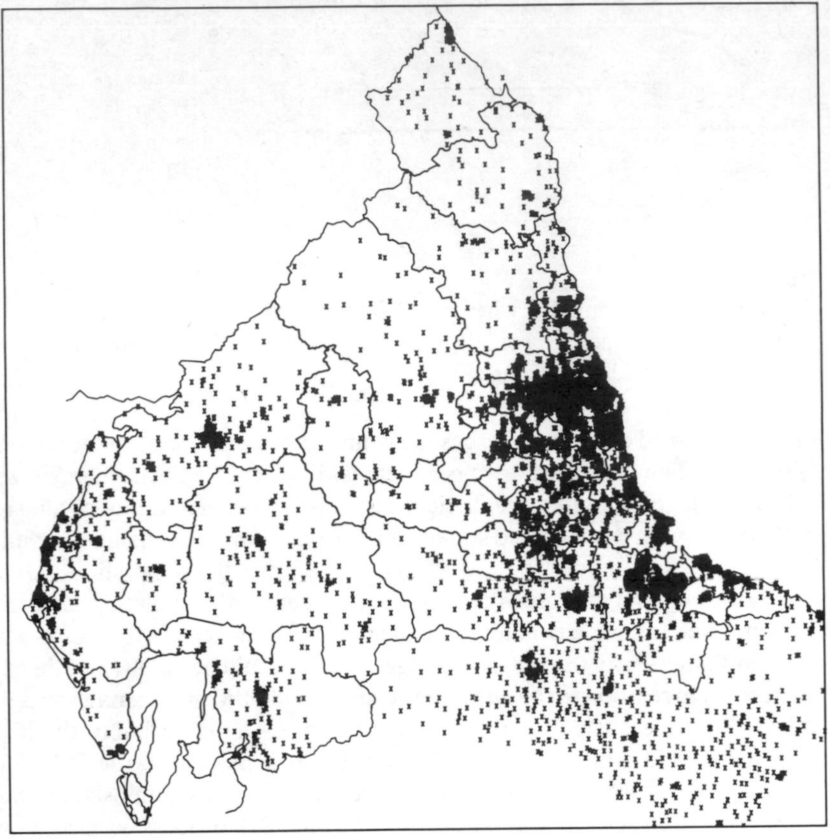

Figure 5.3
The boundaries of Employment Office Areas in the Northern Region and the centroids of EDs

All EDs within each area were added together to produce census data for the EOA.

of the information embedded in the SAS tables (though conceivably it could from the journey-to-work data). In essence, we need to produce a contiguity table, i.e. a matrix as shown in table 5.4. From this, we can readily select all areas contiguous to, say, Derwentside if that district were selected on the unemployment criterion. The contiguity table can be constructed by hand but is much more easily constructed by machine from suitable map data; the Mounsey study, for instance, used the left hand and right hand codes on boundaries in the Baxter (1976a) data to build up the contiguity table.

Table 5.4 Contiguity table for all local government districts within Durham, Tyne and Wear and Cleveland (all outside areas ignored)

	District																
	1	*2*	*3*	*4*	*5*	*6*	*7*	*8*	*9*	*10*	*11*	*12*	*13*	*14*	*15*	*16*	*17*
1	-	0	1	1	0	0	0	0	1	0	0	0	1	0	0	0	0
2	0	-	0	0	0	1	1	0	0	0	0	0	0	0	0	0	1
3	1	0	-	1	0	0	0	1	1	0	0	0	0	0	0	0	0
4	1	0	1	-	1	1	0	1	0	0	0	0	1	0	0	0	0
5	0	0	0	1	-	1	0	0	0	0	0	0	1	1	0	0	0
6	0	1	0	1	1	-	1	1	0	0	0	0	0	0	0	0	1
7	0	1	0	0	0	1	-	1	0	0	0	0	0	0	0	0	0
8	0	0	1	1	0	1	1	-	0	0	0	0	0	0	0	0	0
9	1	0	1	0	0	0	0	0	-	1	0	1	1	0	0	0	0
10	0	0	0	0	0	0	0	0	1	-	1	1	0	0	0	0	0
11	0	0	0	0	0	0	0	0	0	1	-	1	0	0	0	0	0
12	0	0	0	0	0	0	0	0	1	1	1	-	1	0	0	0	0
13	1	0	0	1	1	0	0	0	1	0	0	1	-	0	0	0	0
14	0	0	0	0	1	1	0	0	0	0	0	0	0	-	1	0	1
15	0	0	0	0	0	0	0	0	0	0	0	0	0	1	-	1	1
16	0	0	0	0	0	0	0	0	0	0	0	0	0	0	1	-	1
17	0	1	0	0	0	1	0	0	0	0	0	0	0	1	1	1	-

Key to districts

Durham

1 Chester le Street
2 Darlington
3 Derwentside
4 Durham
5 Easington
6 Sedgefield
7 Teesdale
8 Wear Valley

Tyne and Wear

9 Gateshead
10 Newcastle upon Tyne
11 North Tyneside
12 South Tyneside
13 Sunderland

Cleveland

14 Hartlepool
15 Langbaurgh
16 Middlesbrough
17 Stockton on Tees

5.3.2 ADDING THE DATA TOGETHER

5.3.2.1 'Stock' data

'Stock' data are those relating to one area (such as an ED) rather than the interactions between specified locations (which are defined by 'flow' data). Accumulating the stock data pertaining to several areas is therefore easy in concept and easy in practice – if done by hand. Figure 5.4 illustrates the principle and the results for SAS.

MAP

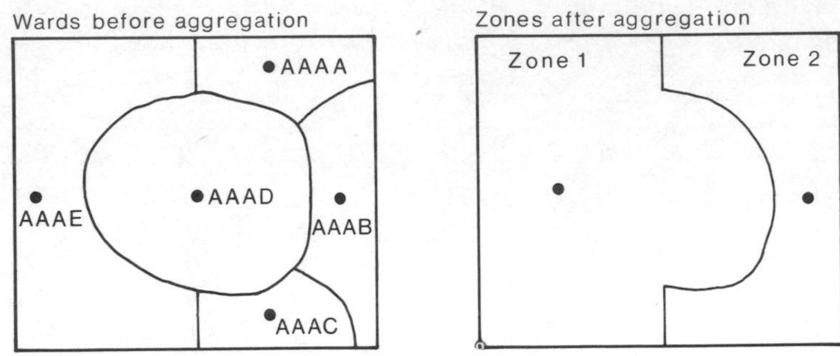

DATA areas before aggregation

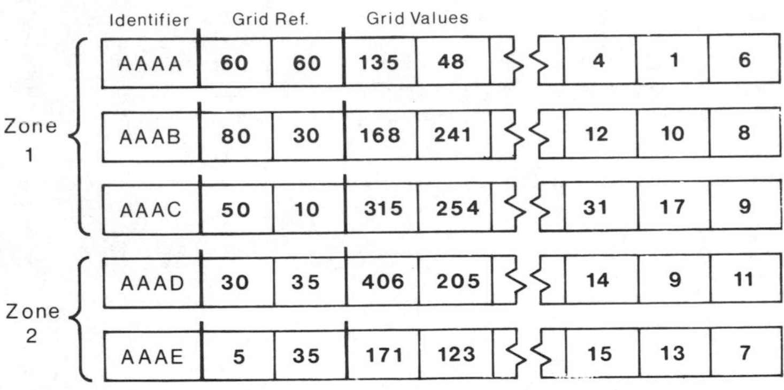

Zone	Identifier	Grid Ref.		Grid Values				
Zone 1	AAAA	60	60	135	48	4	1	6
	AAAB	80	30	168	241	12	10	8
	AAAC	50	10	315	254	31	17	9
Zone 2	AAAD	30	35	406	205	14	9	11
	AAAE	5	35	171	123	15	13	7

DATA zones after aggregation

Zone 1	60·3	26·4	618	543	47	28	23
Zone 2	22·6	35·0	577	328	29	22	18

Figure 5.4
Adding together areas and the SAS or similar 'stock' data for these areas
Shown by maps and data values before and after the aggregation.

Note, however, that such addition is only logical and correct if carried out on counts or upon ratios with a common, global denominator – adding together the percentage of the national total of people under 5 in one district (A) with those in another district (B) is thus entirely reasonable. Adding together the percentage of people under 5 in district A with those under 5 in district B is, however, meaningless because different base populations are used as denominators. Similarly, adding together population densities in, say, five districts and dividing by five to get a mean density is nonsensical, though adding together the absolute populations and dividing by five will give a correct arithmetic mean value of absolute populations (whether this is a useful description is discussed in Chapter 4). In aggregating areas, it is good practice to calculate a new centroid weighted by the population in each of the component areas – if one area has only 20 per cent of the population of another, it should only have 20 per cent of the other's influence on the location of the centroid.

Using standard statistical computer packages, aggregating data for different areas is easy if the aggregation is based on part of a data hierarchy, e.g. all EDs within wards, all wards within districts and so on. The generally available facilities to aggregate specified areas into larger zones is more troublesome to use – in SPSS, for example, it would involve many recoding operations.

Fortunately, some other more specialist packages (such as SASPAC – see appendix 7) provide convenient facilities for such an operation, generally working from a list of the areas which contribute to the zones (see section 5.3.1.1).

In some instances, such specialist packages improve the quality of the results, largely as a consequence of the nature of most census data and the package's ability to handle data at different levels in the hierarchy of EDs, wards, etc. *Ad hoc* zones should always be built up from the largest census areas possible: this minimizes the effects of adjustment (or 'blurring' – see section 2.9.6). The ability to combine a mixture of districts, wards, EDs or fractions of them is not normally available in statistics packages – but is present in SASPAC. Furthermore, and for the same reasons, it may be desirable to create a new zone by subtracting one or more EDs from a larger one – the fewer areas used in aggregations to create a given new zone, the better.

Finally, the calculation of inter-censal change can – from a technical viewpoint – be treated simply as a form of aggregation. Thus if 1971 census data were arranged in exactly the same form as the 1981 data except that all the values were negative, then aggregation would produce the inter-censal differences. In practice, though, such a simplistic approach is not feasible (see Chapters 2 and 9): comparatively few EDs and wards have remained the same in England and Wales as ten years ago and virtually no EDs and postcode sectors in Scotland are directly comparable; the number of directly comparable cells is quite small and, finally, the codes for even the constant areas have themselves changed. Defining inter-censal change then – especially for small areas – is a major theoretical and practical task and the user is recommended to obtain the 1971–81 'change files' (see sections 2.5.4.2 and 2.5.5.2).

MAP

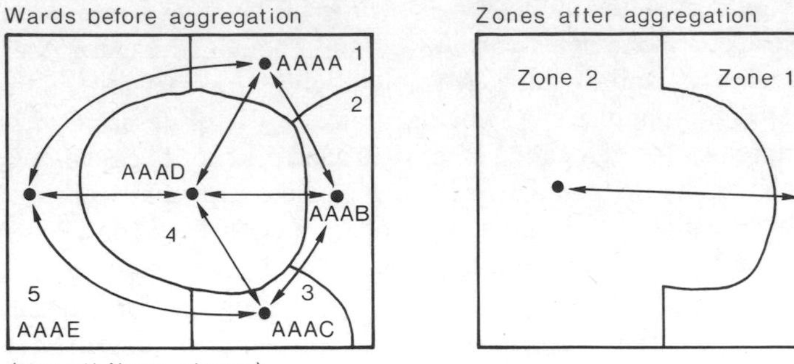

DATA areas before aggregation (area names as in fig. 5·4)

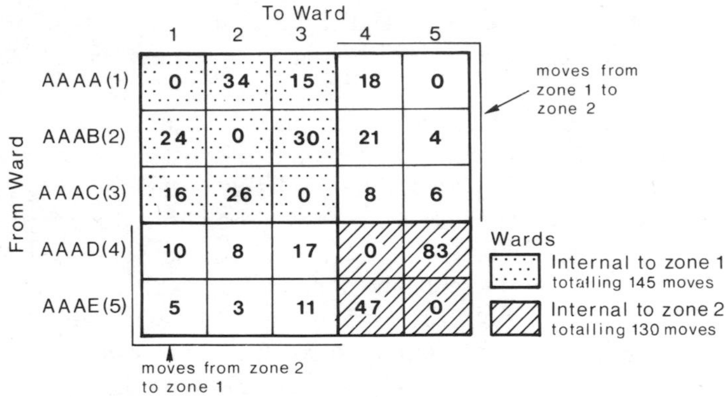

From Ward \ To Ward	1	2	3	4	5
AAAA(1)	0	34	15	18	0
AAAB(2)	24	0	30	21	4
AAAC(3)	16	26	0	8	6
AAAD(4)	10	8	17	0	83
AAAE(5)	5	3	11	47	0

DATA zones after aggregation

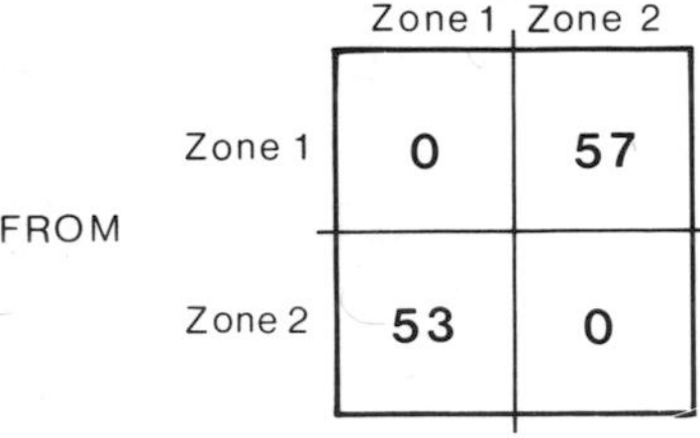

FROM \ TO	Zone 1	Zone 2
Zone 1	0	57
Zone 2	53	0

Figure 5.5
Adding together areas and 'flow' data, such as migration statistics, for each area

5.3.2.2 'Flow' data

Many of the comments from the previous section apply also to aggregation of flow data. Two other considerations, though, are important. The first of these is that very few standard statistics packages have the ability to handle such data in any meaningful or simple way.

The second consideration is that adding up 'flows' is slightly more complex than adding up 'stocks'. Figure 5.5 illustrates the principles and practice involved. All moves within each of the new zones (see shaded areas) are set as zero; all other moves are summed up as shown.

5.4 Summary

In calculating new, derived variables by aggregation of cells in the census data (see appendices 2 and 3), it is relatively easy to specify which of the OPCS cells must be added together. It is critical, however, that the following points be considered:

- i is the new variable meaningful in any conceptual sense?
- ii do the definitions of the cells used overlap, i.e. are you counting some of the same people twice?
- iii the manner and sequence in which the computations are specified;
- iv is the denominator used a global one (for ratio variables)?
- v are the effects of adjustment likely to be significant and, if so, how is the palliative of data trimming best carried out?

In general, existing statistics computer packages such as SPSS are good at performing such calculations and storing or using the results.

In aggregating areas together to give new zones similar considerations apply (but see the detail in previous sections):

- i is the new zone meaningful in any sense or will it be so internally varied as to be meaningless?
- ii does each new zone consist of the minimum number of EDs, wards, districts, etc.?
- iii is the denominator used a truly global one (for ratio variables only)?
- iv is the centroid an adequate description of the size and shape of the area, at least as compared with the size and shape of the zone (Point in Polygon processing only)?
- v the zone centroids should be calculated on a population-weighted basis.

In general, standard statistics packages cannot, or are very clumsy at, simultaneously handling data for different areas, especially in aggregating data from different levels in a hierarchy such as EDs/wards/districts or in dealing with 'flow' data.

6 Mapping census data

DAVID RHIND

6.1 Introduction

Mapping census data is potentially an extremely effective way of communicating information for tens, hundreds or even thousands of different areas through the medium of one (sometimes small) piece of paper. The extreme example of census mapping is probably the national maps in *People in Britain,* the census atlas based on 1971 grid-square data: these maps contained between 50,000 and 150,000 areas on each A4 size page. It is important to emphasize at the outset, however, that all such 'statistical' maps are a complement to, rather than a substitute for, statistical tables. Moreover, as we shall see, there are many different ways of mapping census data, some of which give misleading results. Mapping, then, can be extremely informative but it can also mislead.

The mapping, indeed the graphic portrayal, of British census data has always been a decentralized and in many respects an *ad hoc* affair. After the superb maps produced by Petermann from the 1841 and 1851 Censuses – partly at the instigation of the then government – little 'official' mapping was done until that carried out after the 1951, 1961 and 1971 Censuses by what is now the Department of the Environment: much of their later work was carried out for internal purposes and was not widely disseminated. In the 1950s and 1960s, a tradition grew up that individual geographers mapped those elements of the census in which they were interested and in 1968 one of the Transactions of the Institute of British Geographers (Hunt 1968) consisted of a set of twelve maps of variables from the 1961 Census. The most comprehensive and widely available mapping of the 1971 census data was that carried out by the Census Research Unit (CRU) at Durham University, in conjunction with OPCS and with GRO(S). This collaboration led to a large wall chart circulated to all secondary schools in the country, the national census atlas (CRU/OPCS/GRO(S) 1980), an atlas of Durham County (Dewdney and Rhind 1975) and many other maps produced for a variety of purposes.

Most of the remarks made in this chapter are relevant to maps made by either humans or computer. Census mapping by computer is, however, very much on the increase around the world, notably in the United States and in

Canada (Broome and Witiuk 1980), Britain (CRU/OPCS/GRO(S) 1980; Rhind, Evans and Visvalingam 1980), Australia and in most countries of Europe. The reasons for this are self-evident: with the increasing availability of census data in computer form, it makes little economic sense to convert the data into human form for mapping. In addition, computer-based mapping provides a considerable increase in flexibility of map style and symbolism (see Rhind 1977).

The aim of this chapter is a severely practical one: to suggest how to make effective maps from census data. Relatively little account is taken of the often abstruse theoretical formulations of some academic cartographers (see Rhind 1980) though some of these are, of course, of some significance. For those wishing to investigate mapping further, English language text books by Keates (1973), Muehrcke (1978), Robinson, Sale and Morrison (1978), Taylor (1980) and Monkhouse and Wilkinson (1971) all contain some interesting and relevant material.

6.2 A cartographer's view of census data

If we are doing our mapping by hand, we need base maps showing the boundaries of the areas under consideration. If we are making our maps by computer, the fundamental need is for explicit co-ordinates describing the location of the centre and (possibly) of the outline of each and every one of the areas for which census data are available. Postcodes in themselves are not useful as a mapping tool (though we could make crude maps with them if we knew which ones were adjacent to others). In essence, then, we need National Grid or similar type co-ordinates describing the centre points of areas or a series of such points describing the peripheries of the areas. Figure 6.1 illustrates the boundaries of areas digitized by Baxter (1976a). (Extremely useful information is also given by Baxter (1976b) on the necessary computing background, computer programing for mapping, the best organization of boundary data and other relevant topics.) SAS data for 1971 and 1981 contain 100 metre resolution centroids of the areas to which they relate, though those for the earlier date may not be unique in some urban areas. The boundaries of census areas must be obtained from other sources (see section 6.3.2.3).

The form our mapping takes is, or should be, conditioned by the type of data we have. For this purpose, we can best consider census data under the following headings:

1. 'stocks' (e.g. SAS data) or 'flows' (journey-to-work and some migration data);
2. instantaneous (e.g. for 5 April 1981) or change through time (e.g. between 1971 and 1981) data;
3. quantitative or qualitative data (e.g. the results of classifications of areas, as in Chapter 8). If quantitative, are these data counts (e.g.

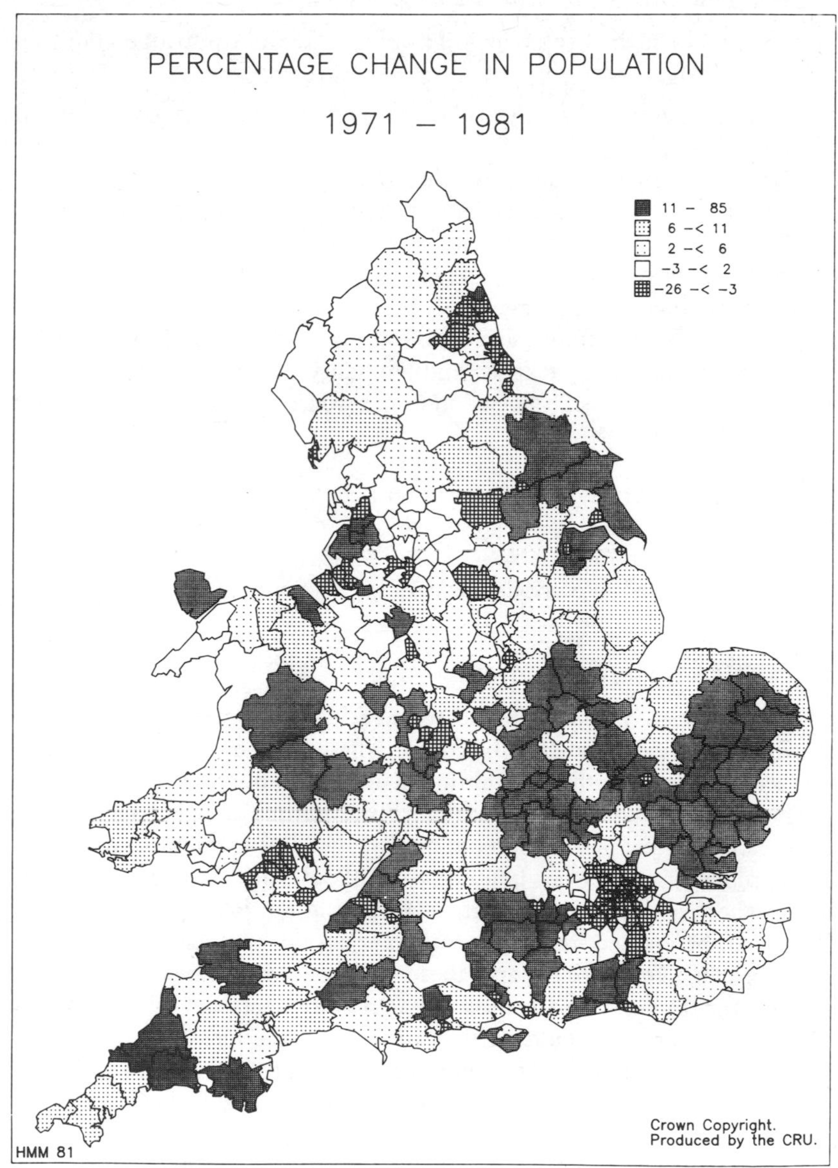

Figure 6.1 Choropleth map of percentage population change in England and Wales, 1971–81, based upon provisional 1981 figures for existing districts

'numbers of people who are over retirement age') or proportions (e.g. 'percentage of people who are over retirement age')?

Other matters which have or should have considerable impact on the way we map census data are:

1 the type of areal units (e.g. grid squares or irregularly sized and shaped areas);
2 the geographical resolution of the data;
3 the 'uncertainty' introduced by data suppression and by adjustment or 'blurring' (see section 2.9.6);
4 the symbolism available to us – such as choropleth, point symbol, contour or block diagram mapping;
5 the technical capabilities available to us in computer form, such as computer mapping packages and boundary data;
6 the reproduction technology and cash resources (e.g. to pay for colour printing).

Many of these interact, of course, but for simplicity we shall now consider each of the headings in turn, dealing first with the constraints imposed on mapping by the nature of the source data and then (section 6.3) with the opportunities afforded by various cartographic methods.

6.2.1 CHOOSING THE VARIABLES

The traditional method of selecting census variables for mapping is to utilize those which have been used in the past – where inter-censal comparability exists (see Chapter 9) – thus permitting historical comparisons, to use those which have broad substantive interest for the particular user (such as the dominance of old people in the community), or those which have specific policy implications (such as households without basic amenities). In the situation where about 4400 cells are available in the SAS and many more variables can be created from them (Chapter 5), the number of maps which could be drawn, even if we observe these traditional guidelines, is very large indeed. Fortunate indeed is the user whose requirements can only be met by one variable: he or she should pass on to the next section.

One study which attempted to minimize the number of maps produced and yet meet a multiplicity of objectives was that described by Rhind, Evans and Visvalingam (1980). Following the definition and construction of 121 counts and 102 ratio variables on the criteria given above, two further criteria were used to reduce the numbers to a meaningful level for the final mapping. These were:

i to construct a correlation analysis of the data (see Evans 1979 and Chapter 7). As a result of this, large numbers of the variables were eliminated since they were highly correlated: there was little point, for instance, in producing maps of population density and of household density since, for Britain as a whole and with the specific geographical resolution of the available data (see section 6.2.5), the Pearson product-moment correlation coefficient between them was +0.99;

ii to prepare 'rough maps' and to select only those in which the mapped patterns were significantly different from those in other maps.

On the basis of the success of this procedure both in Britain and elsewhere, we then recommend the following shorthand for picking variables:

i define any variable which might reasonably be relevant to your study, in the light of the available data;
ii construct these variables from the census data (see Chapter 5);
iii produce descriptive statistics for each variable and use this both to check for errors in the computational logic and to see what transformations need to be applied to the data (Chapters 4 and 7);
iv carry out a correlation analysis after transforming the data appropriately;
v on the results of (iv), weed out one of any pair of variables with high positive or negative correlations;
vi produce a 'rough plot' of the remaining variables and select the final set to be mapped from these, on the basis of detectable patterns and relevance to the study objectives.

It is obvious from the above that we see mapping and statistical analysis to be intertwined activities, just as we see maps and statistics as complementary.

6.2.2 DEALING WITH QUANTITATIVE DATA

By quantitative data we mean those on ordinal, interval or ratio measurement scales (see Rhind and Hudson (1980) or Unwin (1981) for definitions). Confusingly with this terminology, all OPCS count data are on ratio measurement scales! – i.e. they have a true zero base and strict multiplicability exists throughout the range of numbers – hence 200 people are twice as many as 100. Thus, apart from the effects engendered by small populations, OPCS data meet the most demanding of statistical requirements so far as measurement scale is concerned.

6.2.2.1 'Stock' data

Most of the data from the 1981 Census and certainly most of those mapped from previous censuses have been 'stocks', in the sense that these are attributes of each area. Hence 'total resident population' (cell 43), 'number of self-employed married women with employees' (cell 632) and 'number of residents aged one or over with a usual address one year before the census different from present usual address' (cell 642, i.e. recent migrants) are 'stocks'.

The conventional cartographic solution to mapping stocks is twofold:

i map using a choropleth technique after standardization (usually by conversion to a percentage, e.g. of the total population in that area);
ii map using point symbols proportional in area to the counts.

Examples of both methods are given in figures 6.1 and 6.2, based upon data from the Preliminary Report of the 1981 Census. Both methods have theoretical and practical limitations (see sections 6.3.1.1 and 6.3.1.2) but both are readily produced using existing mapping software (section 6.3.2.2).

6.2.2.2 'Flow' data

'Flow' data is that formed from the interaction between pairs of areas, notably in terms of journey-to-work statistics and some of the proposed migration statistics (see section 2.6.8). In general terms, the data usually exist as an asymmetric matrix in which the values on the principal diagonal are either ignored or are used for standardizing the other values. One example would be of journey-to-work flows by one mode of transport between different areas. Such a matrix or table includes no explicit geographical information and to map the flows some geography must be added – normally the co-ordinates of the areas involved. Programing the mapping of anything other than the most crude versions of such flow maps is not trivial, not least because large flows tend to occur between areas close together on the ground and numerous lines occur if all flows are mapped. Most frequently, they are mapped by arrows whose width is proportional to the flow involved. Figure 6.3 illustrates the flows from one of the local authority areas in Durham in 1971 – to show all (35 × 34) flows proved quite impossible. Depiction of all the flows in a given area is only possible if one population centre totally dominates the flow pattern or if radial inflows to two or more near-equally-spaced centres of population occur. In short, it is unlikely that more than thirty flows can be shown successfully on one map and planning the design of a flow map is singularly difficult – 'try it and see' is an essential element of such map creation.

6.2.2.3 Change through time

Very little cartography of change through time has been carried out – maps are traditionally viewed as snapshots of 'stocks'. In recent years, however, 'moving maps' of topography have been installed in both military and civilian aircraft and, more prosaically, dynamically changing weather maps have appeared on our television screens. Massey (1979) has produced crude cine film maps of agricultural and climatic change in Australia. Mounsey (1982) has reviewed the cartographic attempts to depict the change over time of geographical patterns in census and related data. Furthermore, she has developed quite sophisticated methods for making colour cine films directly by computer and has produced films showing the development of urban areas (on a population density criterion) and of deviations from the national norm in population increase (using a signed chi squared statistic – section 6.2.6), all

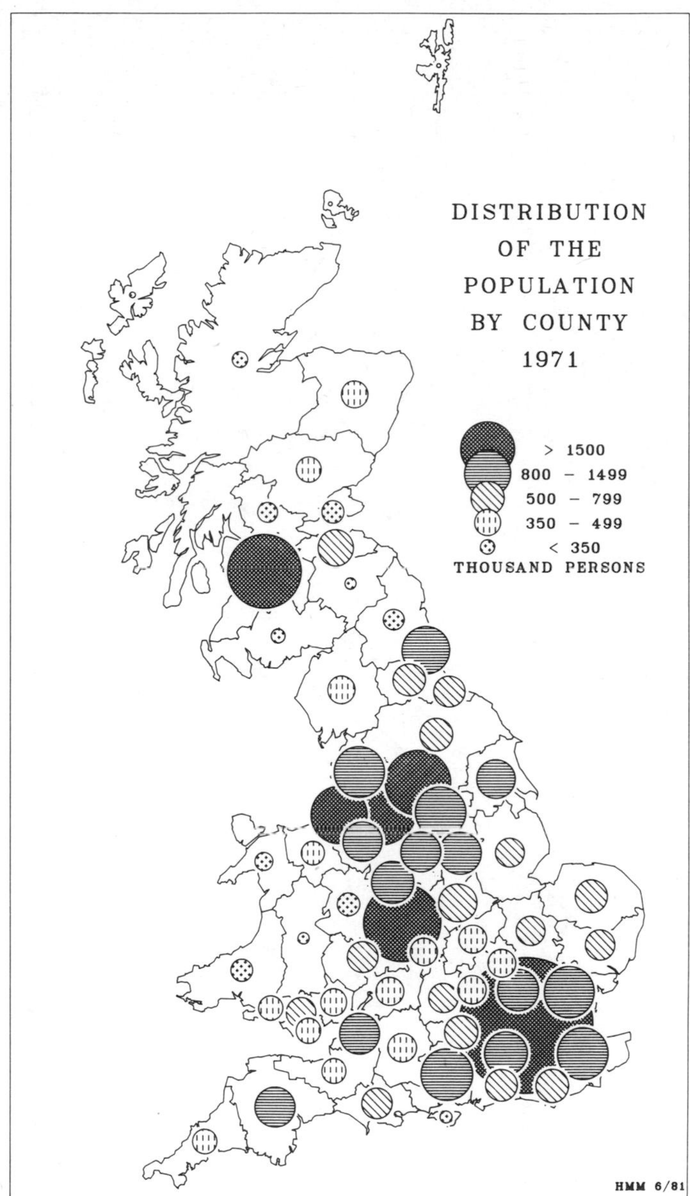

Figure 6.2 Point symbol map showing absolute population by counties, based upon 1981 provisional figures: the area of each symbol is proportional to the population it represents

TOTAL JOURNEYS TO WORK IN DARLINGTON

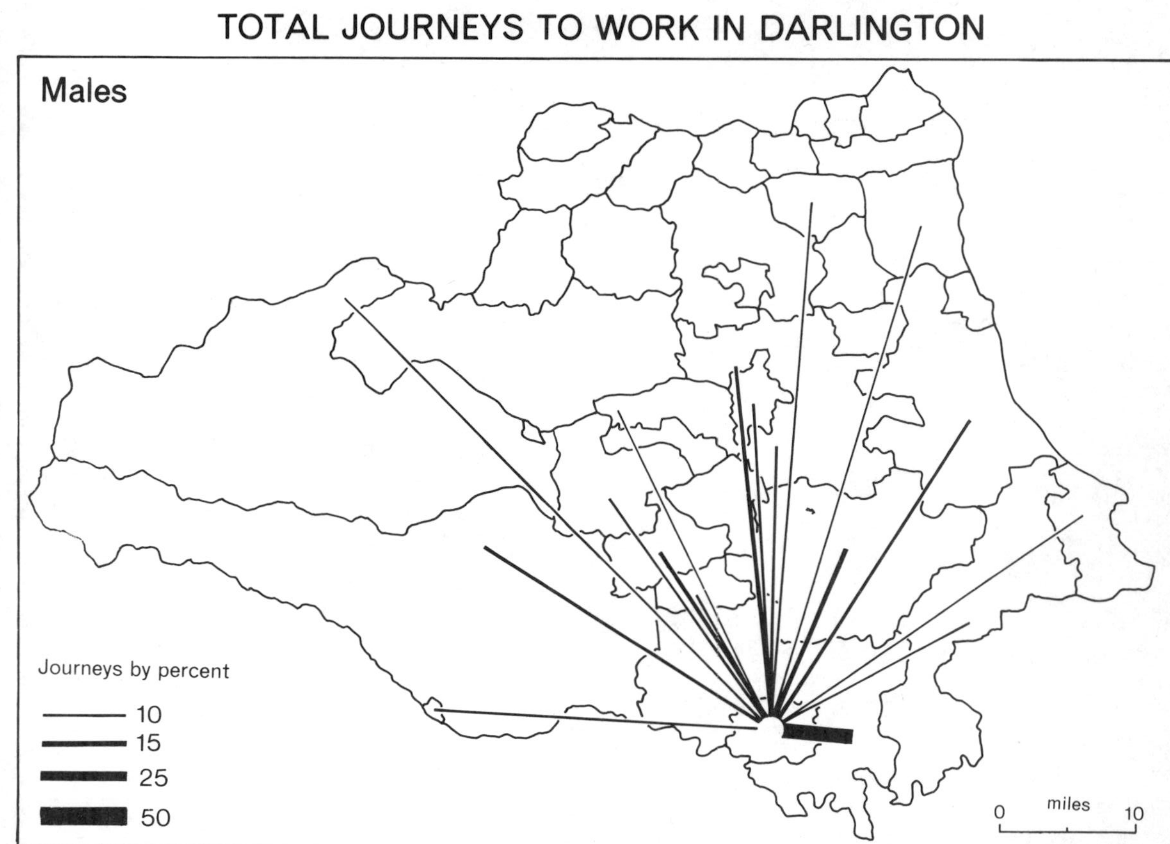

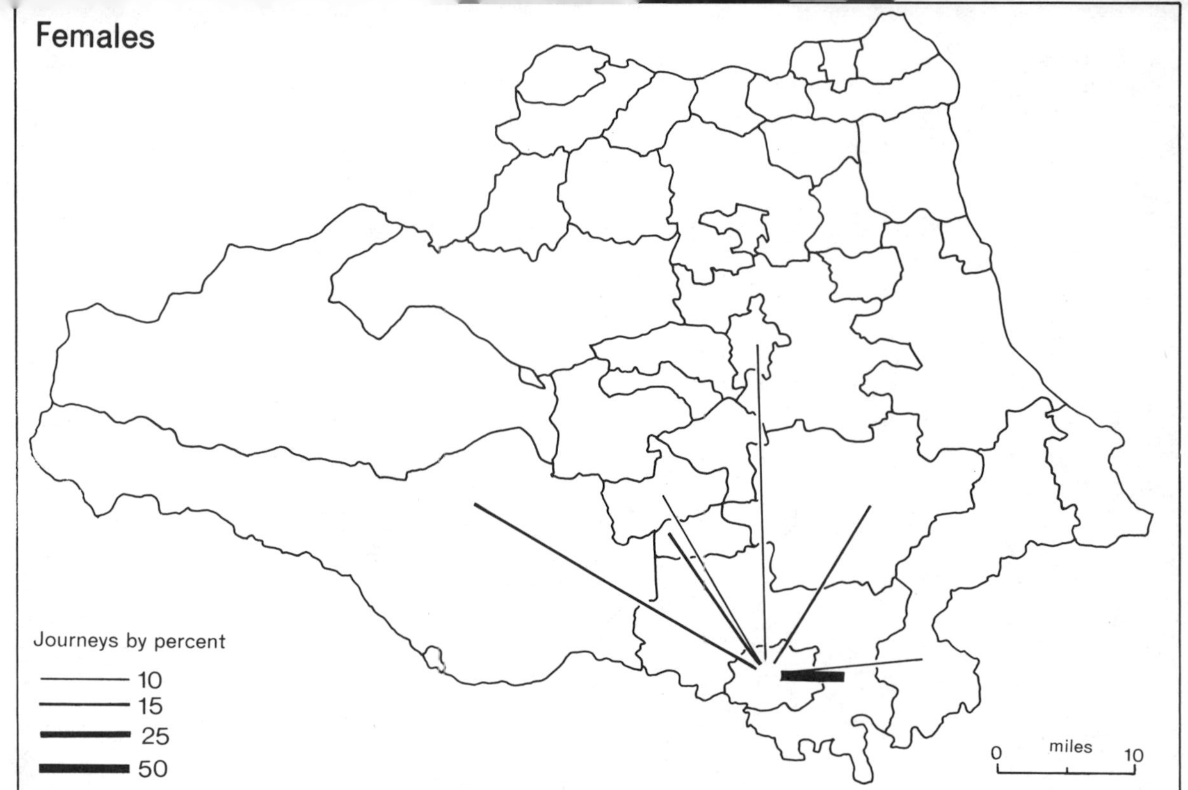

Figure 6.3 Journey-to-work flows from Darlington to other pre-1974 local authorities in County Durham for males and females, each flow shown as a percentage of the total flow (courtesy of Eric Berthoud)

based on data for the period 1901-71 and relating to all the current local authority districts in Britain. Appendix 5 sets out these data.

The statistics which could be mapped to illustrate change are numerous – 'absolute change in population between two census dates', 'change as a percentage of the earlier population', 'change in relation to the national average change' are obvious measures. Choropleth or point symbol maps are best used for percentage (ratio) and for count data respectively (sections 6.3.1.1 and 6.3.1.2). Where these maps are based upon inter-censal change, the picture is essentially the difference between two snapshots and problems of change of definition can be very serious in distorting the pattern: Mounsey (1982), for instance, has pointed to the serious effects on the *de facto* population of seaside towns which appear in the 1921 Census (see appendix 5), simply because the census was taken not in April but in June of that year. Assessing trends based upon two points in time is clearly a hazardous procedure !

Some other data emanating from OPCS does, however, give the possibility of improved time-series mapping, at least for total population and when corrected by whatever census figures are available – the mid-year estimates. Using these for the 1970s, Mounsey and Clarke (1981) have been able to map not only the change in population (i.e. the first derivative with respect to time) but also the rate of change (i.e. the acceleration in population increase or decrease, strictly the second derivative of population with respect to time).

It is reasonable to conclude from all this that mapping population change is rarely done and is not easy to do successfully – partly because of the paucity of comparable data over time (see Chapter 9) and partly because comparatively little thought has been given to it. Mapping of change would, of course, be facilitated by the use of grid-square data: at least one variable (the geographical areas) would remain constant ! In any event, practical experience thus far suggests the need to keep mapping of change as simple as possible: when making cine films of change, the upper limit to successful depiction seems to be about fifty geographical areas, or about the county/Scottish region level for all of Britain. Certainly to map in more detail more than the 458 local authorities in this fashion would be very difficult.

6.2.3 DEALING WITH QUALITATIVE DATA

Qualitative data are those which are qualitatively different – even if the different states are represented by numbers. Hence different land uses such as water, woods, arable crops and built-up areas are essentially different in kind, even if, inside a computer, they are represented by the numbers 1, 2, 3, and 4. No sensible arithmetic operations can be carried out on such data, other than to count how many areas labelled 1, etc. there are within the zone of interest to the user.

The most common appearance of qualitative-type data when dealing with the census occurs when areas are classified (see Chapter 8). Webber and Craig (1978) and Webber (1978a), for instance, produced classifications of all local authorities and of all EDs in Britain, such that areas were grouped on their similarity (though we are somewhat unhappy with their grouping methods – see Chapter 8) and subsequently mapped (e.g. see Bickmore *et al.* 1980). Such groups cannot be said to be 'greater' or 'less than' other groups (except in terms of the mean values of the important variables) – they are qualitatively different. Such qualitative data are usually represented by area-filling symbolism which is not on a density scale, unlike normal choropleth mapping (section 6.3.1.1). The symbolism may be in monochrome or colour: if the latter, progressive changes in hue, chroma and brightness (Keates 1973) are avoided.

6.2.4 THE TYPE OF AREAL UNITS

Mapping grid squares or, indeed, any regularly shaped areas is intrinsically easier than mapping irregularly sized and shaped areas. Two reasons account for this: the maximum size of any area is known once the map scale is fixed and the location of *all* map boundaries are known even though only one co-ordinate pair needs to be stored in a computer to represent the area. Hence it is easy to ensure that no symbol overlaps others, provided there is enough space in which to draw such a symbol. It is also convenient that, for grid-square count data, mapping of absolute numbers also produces maps of density per km^2 (or whatever other measurements are being used). In the early days of computer mapping, maps of grid-square-type data were much easier to produce than maps of irregular areas because each square area could be readily approximated by one or a phalanx of typewriter-like symbols on the computer line printer. Unhappily, most computer line printers – the standard form of producing lists and tabulations – used characters which were rectangular rather than square; in some cases, this led to the production of maps whose vertical scale was three-fifths of the horizontal one ! Interim solutions to this were the use of special character sets (see Coppock 1975) but the increasing availability of electrostatic and other similar plotters has diminished the problem. Finally, so far as grid-square data are concerned, we should again note two other important consequences of their use for mapping: at 1 km^2 and smaller, they – unlike all other data – only show populated areas and, as a corollary, they show the unpopulated areas. Hence, the maps in *People in Britain* (CRU/OPCS/GRO(S) 1980) are the first reliable maps of unpopulated areas in Britain! The second consequence is that related to data suppression: because of their fixed size, many more grid squares than EDs are suppressed (section 2.9.6) in census data and as a consequence mapping of the grid-square data is not possible for a large percentage of the rural areas of the country.

Successful mapping of irregular areas is essentially a matter of skill, luck and perseverance. In manually-based mapping, the first two of these are generally critical since it is rarely possible to redraw anything other than the most ghastly errors. The prime determinant of the map scale and symbolism is likely to be the smallest important area. In choropleth maps (section 6.3.1.1) its size on the map must be sufficient to permit every one of the different forms of shading used to be distinguished; in point-symbol maps the edges of the symbol may safely be allowed to overlap the edges of the area to which it relates – provided it does not thereby obscure symbols for surrounding areas in a way which makes it impossible to read them. A good 'rule of thumb' in planning such mapping is that if anything can be complex, it will be. One such example arises in mapping absolute numbers: highly populated administrative areas in Britain are generally the smaller ones, notably the metropolitan counties and districts.

Another complication which exists in all mapping but is particularly significant in choropleth mapping of irregular areas is the 'figure/ground' phenomenon. Put simply, this is the title of a common experience: colours and grey tones differ in their apparent value or density depending on what other colours or tones surround them. Hence, while logically reasonable density scales – perhaps relating to a proposed linear perception scale of increasing greyness with increasing value of the variable being mapped (such as population density) – may be followed, the acceptability of the resulting map is partly determined by the shapes and contiguities of the census areas and by the values of the variable being mapped for those areas.

Where only one co-ordinate pair, say of a centroid, is given for each irregular area (as on the SAS data), no very useful knowledge of the boundaries of these areas can be inferred and planning of the map must be based solely on the data values. It is generally unsatisfactory to use small, fixed-size symbols for such mapping, so proportional symbols (possibly shaded) are often used. Here luck also plays a critical role – to get such a computer map satisfactory on the first run is to be extremely fortunate. Iterations must therefore be expected – figure 6.2 illustrates an example from a second iteration in which certain of the centre points of areas were edited to minimize symbol overlaps. Of course, the human cartographer is much better than the computer in planning the map production, but to draw such a map manually would take very much longer than the twenty seconds which it took to compute and even the twenty minutes it took to draw.

6.2.5 GEOGRAPHICAL RESOLUTION OF THE DATA

We will see elsewhere (e.g. in Chapters 7 and 8) that the geographical resolution of the data – whether they are for EDs, for wards or postcode sectors or for some other sets of areas – influences, sometimes strongly, the end results. Until recently, it has been easy to demonstrate this statistically, as statisticians did from the 1930s onwards (Yule and Kendall 1950) and geographers rediscovered in the 1960s and 1970s (Openshaw and Taylor 1981). However, because of the human labour involved and the difficulties of visually interrelating data at different sets of areas, few mapping demonstrations of this phenomenon have been made. Clarke and Mounsey (1981) demonstrated the effect of mapping population per km^2 on the basis of data for districts, counties/Scottish regions and standard regions.

It is also obvious that mapping at high geographical resolution maximizes the chance of encountering small groups of people in each area: indeed, this is the rationale for high resolution, since in dealing with census data we are interested in people rather than in areas. With small groups of people, however, percentages which are not based on land area ('percentage of the population which is male' c.f. 'density' of the population per km^2) are frequently very unstable: the highest and lowest values, and consequently the most visually striking areas, on a map may therefore commonly be based upon very few people. Most mapping of detailed census data has ignored this effect which is rampant in use of ED and 1 km^2 grid-square data. Indeed, many authors have been even more misleading: where the population is small and also clustered in one part or another of the area being mapped, they have none the less shaded the whole of that area and greatly extended the misleading effect of small populations. Thus, ISER (1977) shaded the whole of central Newfoundland (one of the data areas in the Canadian census) even though almost all of the population lives around the coast. The correct solution to this is to follow Rhind and Trewman (1975) and Taylor *et al.* (1976) – 'mask out' the areas such as lakes, forests, etc. in which no significant number of residents occur.

Even given these complications, it is essential, in general terms, to use the most detailed data available for mapping, consistent with the resources available and the particular purpose of the mapping. In principle, the appropriate resolution varies with the particular census variable chosen, since some variables are much more locally variable, or less spatially autocorrelated, than are others. Maps 3 and 4, of population density at 1 km^2 and 10 km^2 resolution respectively, in the *People in Britain* atlas (CRU/OPCS/GRO(S) 1980) clearly demonstrate the quite different results from mapping at appropriate and inappropriate geographical resolutions. To map the percentage of retired people on a county basis for all of Britain would patently be absurd since a very large percentage of such people live by the coast and county values are therefore partly related to the length of the county coastline divided by the area of the county! Only a few clear guidelines can be defined and the most obvious of these is that to map census data for standard regions in Britain (or to quote their statistics) is almost a complete waste of time since the internal variation within these larger areas is so much greater than the variation between them. In general, then, mapping should be carried out for functioning areas, i.e. at the resolution at which processes are proceeding or at which areas of concern exist. Sensible mapping of 'deprivation' therefore necessitates use of ED data or 1 km (or smaller) grid squares. Alternatively, there is some logic in mapping areas which are functional in another sense – they are areas of administrative responsibility. Hence a map of the percentage of population over the age of seventy by health districts would have practical utility in displaying which districts were likely to be faced with disproportionate percentages of their populations needing medical facilities and whether this was a geographically isolated occurrence or part of a sub-regional (or even national) situation ... and so on.

6.2.6 DEALING WITH UNCERTAINTY

Measurement error is associated with all data but census data include both measurement error and deliberately induced error. Section 2.9.6 discussed the deliberate introduction by OPCS and GRO(S) of 'adjustment' or 'blurring' of certain census data values (notably most of the SAS) in order to preserve confidentiality. This is achieved by adding −1, 0 or +1 to all the cells in the 1981 SAS data which go to make up the tables of statistics; the totals are sums of the adjusted cells. In addition, many variables are suppressed (not provided) where there are so few people in an area that an observer might be able to work out characteristics of one individual from the detailed aggregate figures. Ideal mapping of census data therefore differs from mapping of much other data in that it should take account of such uncertainty wherever it occurs – to ignore it may give the map reader a misleading picture of the data.

Coping with suppression is easiest and is simply a matter of ensuring that the symbolism for areas for which no statistics are available is discernibly different to any other symbolism employed. It is not sensible, for instance, in a choropleth map to show areas at the bottom of the data range as unshaded and also to show areas of missing data as unshaded with some symbol (such as an 'M') in the middle. The symbolism employed should be qualitatively different, e.g. unshaded for areas with missing data and line shaded for all areas for which data exist. Hence in most of the maps in *People in Britain* all areas of the country for which there were less than twenty-five people per km^2 or eight households per km^2 were shown as white and all other areas as colours (compare maps 1 and 2 of populated and of 'unsuppressed' squares).

Coping with adjustment or blurring is rather more difficult. The effects of adjustment are most severe in small population areas, in ratio variables and in variables whose mean value taken over the whole country is low. Hence the effects are generally worst in EDs and in small grid squares but almost always insignificant at local-authority district level; ratios created by the user are liable to suffer more than counts from the 1981 Census because adjustment of the numerator and denominator will have been carried out independently and an addition of +1 to a value of 5 has a much greater proportionate effect than it does when added to a value of 5000. It is the contention of this author that many, many of the census maps for small areas of Britain (such as EDs) are highly misleading because the ratios used (e.g. percentage values) are based upon small denominators and have been variably influenced by adjustment. Even without adjustment, percentages based on small populations often reach extreme values and, when mapped, these may dominate the map.

At least two approaches are obviously possible to the solution of this problem, apart from ignoring it. The first is to calculate the absolute outer limits of the induced error and relate it to the value for that area. It is perfectly possible to devise symbols – such as bars with a portion shaded – to indicate the maximum error or divided pie charts (Monkhouse and Wilkinson 1971) in which the overall size of the symbol provides population and a shaded sector the magnitude of the maximum error. Giving graphic expression to the uncertainty in choropleth maps is rather more difficult and it is best to compute a new statistic to map which takes this into account.

One candidate for such a new statistic is the signed chi-squared measure described in section 5.2.5. This takes into account both absolute and relative (e.g. percentage) deviations from some stipulated average figure such as the national average. The only census maps known to have been published in this form are those in *People in Britain* (CRU/OPCS/GRO(S) 1980, see also Rhind *et al.* 1980), though other workers have used it for medical data. Choropleth mapping with this statistic is then simply a matter of depicting data on a scale whose mid-value is the national or some other appropriate average. To be included in the outermost categories, the area must be of a low population but have an enormous proportionate deviation from the nominated mean value or, alternatively, have a large population but a much smaller proportionate deviation from the mean: thus to be in an outer class signifies that the area is distinctly unusual and needs further, detailed examination. The choice of class intervals is, as for all other maps, one which contains a certain degree of arbitrariness and probably necessitates examination of the frequency distribution of the signed chi-squared values (see Rhind *et al.* 1980).

6.3 Mapping techniques and their applications

6.3.1 MAP SYMBOLISM

Cartographers have devised many different classifications of the types of maps used. Here – as we have done implicitly in all the preceding sections – we shall use a very simple scheme in which we consider only:

choropleth mapping - where areas are shaded with a density in relation to the mapped value (e.g. figure 6.1).

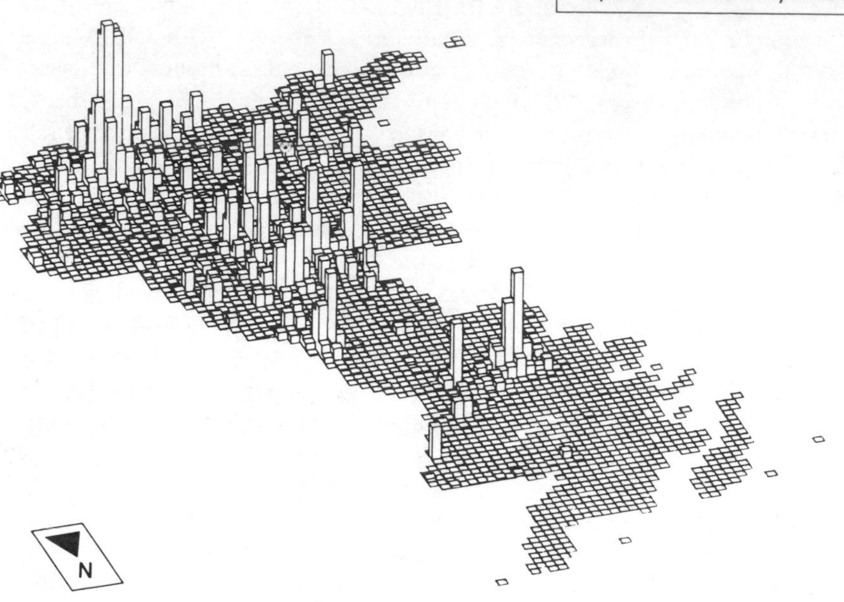

Figure 6.4 Block diagram of the population per 10 km² in 1971, the height of each column being proportional to the population contained

point symbol mapping - where the mapped value is shown by the size, area or simulated volume of a single symbol located at a central point in each area (e.g. figure 6.2), or by a spread of constant sized symbols throughout the area, their number indicating the value mapped (often referred to as dot mapping, see figure 6.6).

surface mapping - where the mapped value is considered to be part of a continuous smooth or, alternatively, a stepped surface. Various ways of portraying the surface are available, notably by contouring or by block diagrams (see figure 6.4).

flow mapping - where some symbol, usually an arrow or a band, indicates the strength of the interaction between pairs of areas by width, symbol or colour (see figure 6.3).

In all of these types of mapping, a key to the values and the meaning of the symbolism must be shown.

6.3.1.1 Choropleth mapping

This is essentially a tedious process by hand but a trivial one to automate. There are, nonetheless, several important ground-rules which should be observed in producing maps of this type, irrespective of whether they are done by hand or machine:

i a full range of densities from black to white should be used in each map unless white is used to indicate missing (e.g. suppressed) data;

ii the map boundaries should never be suppressed even if the two areas have the same shading. Without these, the user has no idea of whether the results arise from one large area over which all the figures are averaged or whether they arise from several adjacent but similar areas;

iii absolute numbers should never be mapped by this means when using a standard set of boundaries. To do so is grossly misleading since large areas will automatically tend to be black. Two solutions exist:
   - to standardize the data, most commonly by converting the variable to a percentage or other ratio form;
   - to transform the map base, such that the basic areas are enlarged or reduced in size so as to represent the total numbers of people therein, then to map, say, absolute numbers of retired people on this new base map (see figure 6.5);

iv wherever possible, the map should be based upon a ratio whose denominator is the land area, i.e. producing a map of the density of retired people (retired people per km^2), rather than a ratio such as percentage of retired people in the population. Mapping the latter type of ratio is liable to be misleading since large rural areas often contain few people yet the values in these areas can appear to dominate the map. In practice, this may be an unavoidable difficulty since density maps of many variables will look very similar. An alternative solution in these circumstances is to use point symbols (see below).

6.3.1.2 Point symbol mapping

Point symbol mapping is also tedious by hand. Though trivial by machine, most computer programs (such as GIMMS) do not make allowance for overlapping symbols and blithely superimpose them, regardless of whether they can be perceived (but see the results from the Rase (1980) software in figure 6.2). Point symbol mapping is ideal for mapping absolute numbers though it can also be used for depicting proportions. It is critical that the single point symbol is well positioned at or near the centre of gravity of the area to which it relates, assuming this point does not lie outside the area (as for 'horse shoe' shapes).

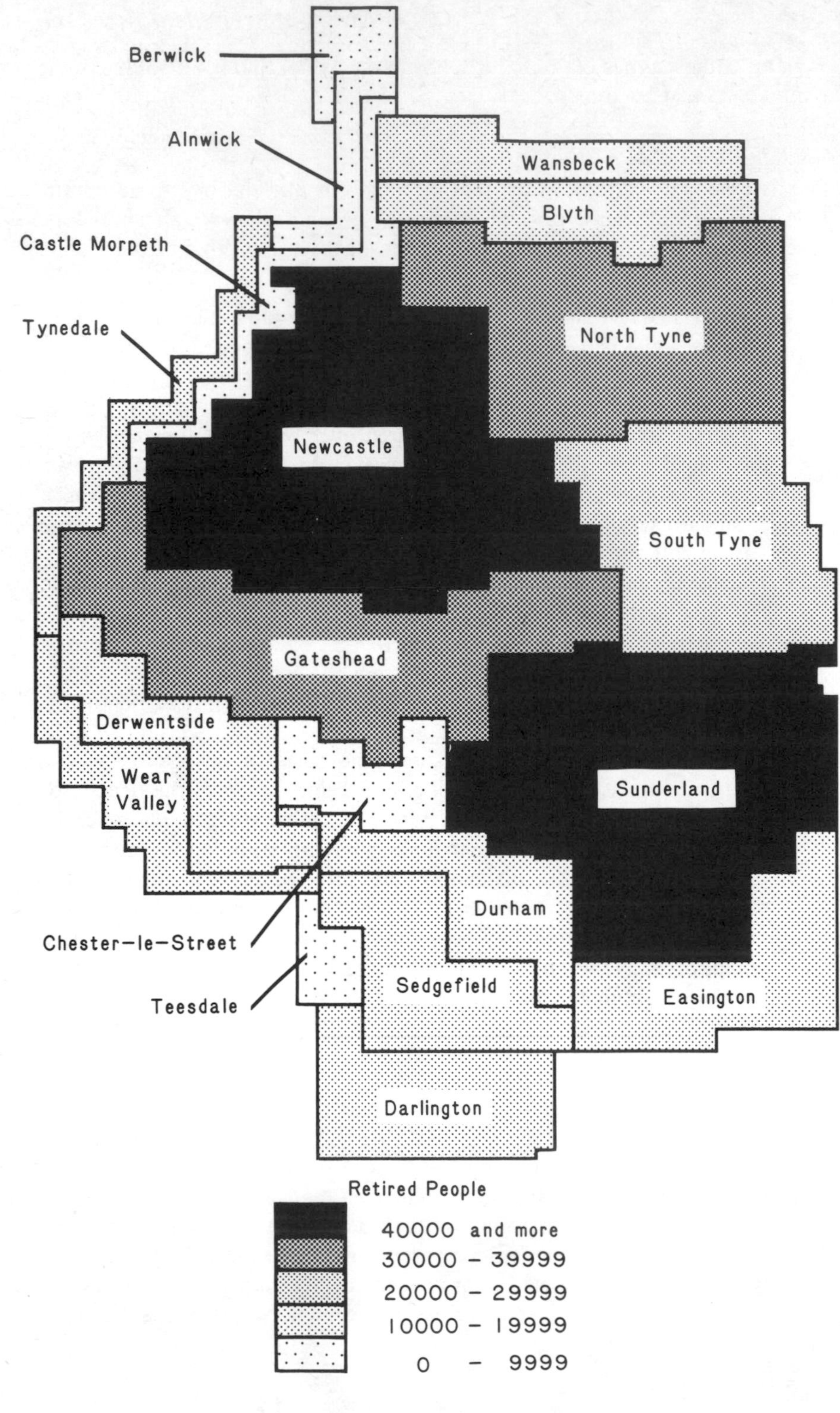
Berwick
Alnwick
Wansbeck
Blyth
Castle Morpeth
Tynedale
North Tyne
Newcastle
South Tyne
Gateshead
Derwentside
Wear Valley
Sunderland
Durham
Chester-le-Street
Sedgefield
Teesdale
Easington
Darlington
Retired People
40000 and more
30000 - 39999
20000 - 29999
10000 - 19999
0 - 9999

Figure 6.5 Cartogram to show absolute numbers of retired people in 1981 in the districts of Northumberland and Durham: the area of each district has been adjusted to be proportional to the total population

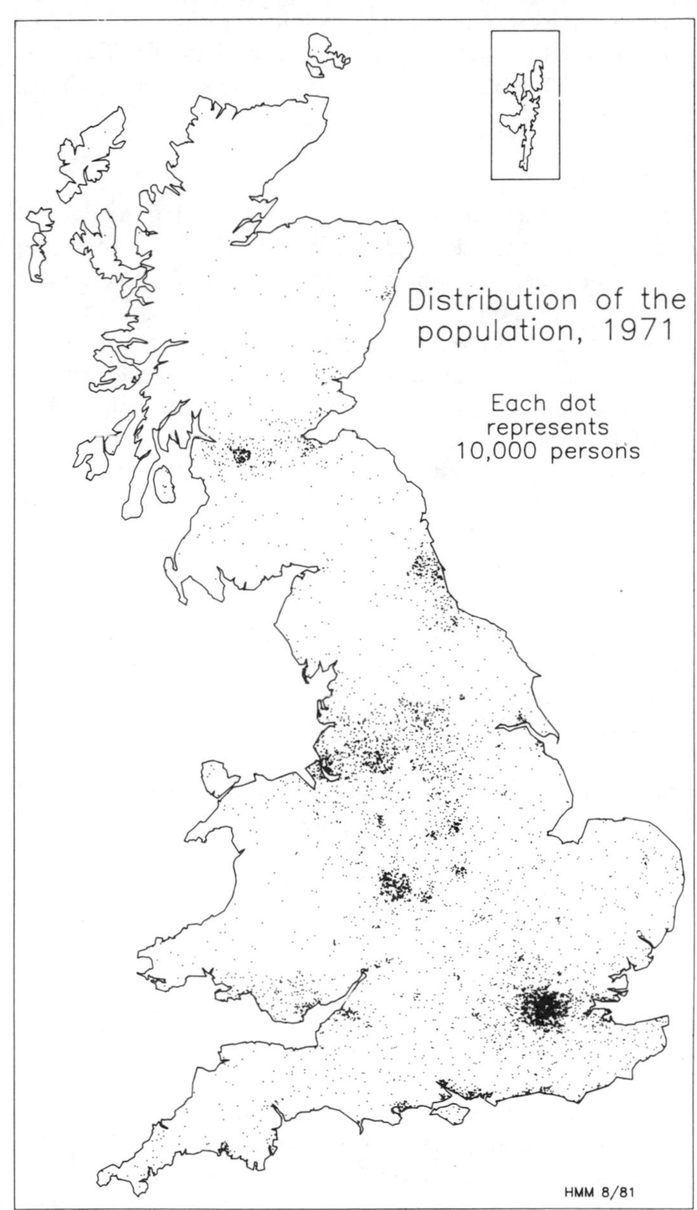

Figure 6.6 Dot map of 1971 population in Britain

Dot mapping can often be highly expressive although it is well known that the choice of the number of people (or households or whatever is being mapped) per dot greatly affects the appearance of the final map. At its best, dot mapping can give some hint of clustering of people within certain parts of each data area and suffers less from disassociation of the whole area from the symbol representing it than does 'single point' mapping. It is easily produced by hand and can be produced by some computer packages, including GIMMS 4 (figure 6.6), but such mapping often has ruinous effects upon simple mechanical vector plotters!

6.3.1.3 Surface mapping

Some mapping of census data has been carried out by regarding the data as being part of a continuous surface – Rosing and Wood (1971), for instance, produced contour maps of census variables for parts of the West Midlands, based upon ward data from the 1966 Census, each centroid being considered a data point for interpolation. Unless the number of areas is very large in relation to the map area and the variations between adjacent areas is small, such a procedure is most misleading – particularly if each centroid is not weighted by the total population of the area which it 'describes'. In practice – and however tempting the converse is because computer programs are available – it is extremely wise to avoid contour-type mapping of census data. Only where some suitable smoothing or transformation has been made of the data can it sensibly be contoured. Figure 6.7 is one such example: it shows population potential (see Clarke 1972) for the whole of Britain, based on 1971 data for 8 × 8 km grid squares. For each square, the potential was calculated considering all other squares. This thus gives a measure of accessibility – the nearer a town or the larger a nearby town to a square, the greater will be the latter's potential. The resulting statistics were automatically contoured using the Calcomp GPCP package.

Alternatively, 'raw' census statistics can be treated as a stepped surface. If the areas are grid squares, then a variety of computer programs can be used to produce 'bird's eye views' from any chosen orientation and altitude, with the computer suppressing all hidden lines. Figure 6.4 is one such example, created using the Harvard SYMVU program. Another Harvard program, PRISM, can produce similar block diagrams for irregularly shaped areas. Though attractive, there is some doubt amongst cartographers as to whether these are really useful.

6.3.1.4 Flow mapping

Few computer programs exist for flow mapping, although it is easy to create simple ones which do not take account of overlapping symbolism. For the reasons given in section 6.2.2.2, conventional flow mapping is best restricted to a small number of flows and carried out by hand; Tobler (pers. comm. 1981)

Figure 6.7 Population potential in Britain, based upon 1971 data for 8 × 8 km grid squares

has devised very different flow mapping techniques which might be capable of mapping a 5000 by 5000 flow matrix!

6.3.1.5 Class intervals

Although Tobler (1973) has argued that it is not necessary or desirable to have data shown on maps divided into classes, most cartographers still believe this to be desirable and the use of certain computer equipment may necessitate it. The user is, then, often faced with deciding how to divide his data into groups or classes, most commonly in making choropleth maps. Evans (1977) has considered this in detail. For our present purposes, the following possibilities exist:

- i choose the class intervals in relation to important thresholds (e.g. at specified levels of 'deprivation' or of population density). This will show which areas are 'good' or 'bad' on these criteria;
- ii choose them at breaks or troughs in a histogram of the data (see section 4.2). This *ideographic* approach is not recommended;
- iii choose them on the basis of an arithmetic scale in which *the width* of the classes is constant, e.g. having class limits of 50, 100, 150, 200, etc. per km^2. Alternatively, if the data are skewed (section 4.5.1) use a geometric scale of class widths, e.g. 20, 60, 140, 300, etc. people per km^2. Arithmetic scales are most easily understood;
- iv choose class intervals centred upon the mean value for that variable and based upon its standard deviation. This greatly facilitates comparison of maps of different variables.

In practice, different class intervals can make two maps of the same data almost unrecognizably different. Users should pick the class interval scheme appropriate to their specific task; a labelled key to the classes used must be shown.

6.3.1.6 The base map

The extent to which topography – the presence of named towns, of roads, rivers and other 'locating' features – is necessary on a map clearly differs with the user and with the purpose of the map. In some cases, the framework given by the area boundaries is sufficient to provide orientation, particularly if these are well known, such as county boundaries. For final presentation purposes, however, it is usually necessary to have some names and other identifiers and not all of these can be arranged along the coastline! Thus the symbolism used in such maps must, at least in critical areas, have some degree of transparency. Beyond that, the design of a good base map, particularly one which is good for a whole series of variables, is a matter of manual cartographic skill. Frequently the base map is best prepared by hand on one piece of material and photographically combined with the map overlays, especially if these are produced by computer.

6.3.2 AUTOMATED VS MANUAL MAPPING

If you have a computer mapping facility yet are mapping only ten areas and perhaps three variables, do it by hand. If you have no computer mapping facility, do not attempt to get one unless you wish to map more than, say, fifty areas for each of ten variables. Beyond these rough and ready guidelines, you would be unwise to map by hand unless you are without access to a suitable computer and reasonably intelligent human beings to run it. Even for non-owners of computers, such access is quite easily arranged (see appendices 7 and 8).

The differences between mapping by hand and by machine are exactly paralleled by those between travelling by foot and by underground railway. Travelling by foot pre-dated travel by underground railway and it may well be faster if you are only going short distances (producing few maps); it also has the attribute that you can see where you have reached at all stages! Travelling by underground railway requires more skills – finding a station (computer system and program), knowing or finding out what is the nearest station to your desired destination (what is the most suitable map form which can be produced), knowing how to obtain the ticket to travel (the parameters) and navigating the system, often without a glimpse of the real world until you reach what you hope is your desired destination. Nonetheless, once understood, underground railways offer a vital and convenient method of communication even though different systems in different places have different methods of organization: mapping systems offer the same benefits. In practice, a judicious combination of manual and automated methods is as wise as travel by foot and underground railway.

In short, for a few 'one-off' maps covering a limited area, automated mapping systems have little to offer. For series map production, such as of one hundred maps of the demographic, housing and socioeconomic characteristics of a city, they are invaluable. For the in-between situation, the decision to map by computer will depend upon what facilities are already available and the number of maps and extent of geographical coverage.

6.3.2.1 Equipment needs

Maps are made by two means: filling areas or drawing lines. In manual mapping, both are often carried out by use of pen and ink, though area filling might be produced by Letraset stick-down film (Lawrence 1979). In computer terms, two different kinds of equipment – computer peripherals – exist which are naturally suited to each one of these two types of procedure, though both can also perform the other one. The two types of peripherals are known as raster and vector plotters. A good example of a raster plotter is the standard computer line printer, which prints out alphabetic and numeric symbols. The computer can be arranged to over-print one symbol on top of another, giving different densities of shading. Such maps are cheap to produce. Though they were once widely used for research purposes (see Coppock 1975), they have become rather unpopular in Britain because they are coarse-grained (unless photographically reduced) and rather difficult to overlay on topographic maps to determine the local geography. Of course, much more refined raster maps can now be produced by more sophisticated plotters and the electrostatic plotters now becoming commonplace in some computer centres have printing positions much, much smaller than the 1/6 × 1/10 inch of the standard line printer character. Perhaps the most detailed census raster maps yet produced are the national maps in *People in Britain* (CRU/OPCS/GRO(S) 1980), all of which are based upon 2 × 2 groups of dots produced by a laser beam, each of the dots being 1/200 inch (c. 0.125 mm) across. The smaller the size of the printing position, the more precisely can the plotter mimic irregularly shaped areas, but the more computing effort is involved. Access to sophisticated plotters is often best achieved through a commercial bureau: to plot the 150,000 areas on one map in *People in Britain* in three colours cost about £6 (see Rhind, Evans and Visvalingam 1980).

The vector plotter mimics the human draughtsman – one or more pens or a beam of light being steered over a sheet of paper or film, in response to instructions from the computer. The computer program will convert, say, boundaries stored in National Grid co-ordinates into millimetres on the paper and compute where horizontal and vertical lines used for shading start and stop at each boundary they intersect. Such plotters are now commonplace and cost upwards of £1000.

In addition to the machine drawing the maps, a computer is of course needed to control the process. Computer mapping is carried out on all sizes of computer from the very smallest, such as an Apple micro-computer, to the very largest. Generally, however, sophisticated mapping programs such as GIMMS require at least a mini-computer, currently costing about £30,000 (which would, naturally, be used for many other tasks simultaneously). By the mid-1980s, it is likely that the very same programs will fit into the so-called micro-computers costing perhaps £1000.

6.3.2.2 Software needs

'Naked' computers and even sophisticated peripherals will not produce computer maps – computer programs or 'software' are also needed. Almost anyone can learn to write a simple, one-off mapping program on a computer – it is, indeed, an entertaining intellectual puzzle. Some authors have provided computer programs for readers which are quite useful (e.g. MacDougall 1976; Baxter 1976b), but to obtain a program which produces good quality maps, annotated with readable text, and which also offers a variety of options, it is wise to obtain a mapping package from a reputable source.

Only three such programs will be described: their sources are set out in appendix 8. We will ignore the software used for creating the much-quoted *People in Britain* atlas since this was essentially special-purpose and designed to be highly efficient in one computer system. Our three computer packages represent current practice and have run successfully in different parts of the world.

The oldest of the computer mapping packages is SYMAP. It is raster-based, dating originally from the mid-1960s and Harvard University. This produces maps using the standard computer line printer and one of the earliest census atlases (Rosing and Wood 1971) was produced using the program. Thus the map is built up from filling in areas with symbols of different density – lines are produced by leaving areas white or by approximating them by adjacent print positions. SYMAP can produce choropleth, contour (see section 6.3.1.3) and Thiessen polygon maps (in which all parts of the map are shaded in relation to the nearest data point such as an ED centroid). By juggling with the shading used – an easy task – the whole map area can be made white and fixed size symbols produced at each centroid. Though cheap to run and quite easy to use once it is understood, SYMAP is highly limited by comparison with newer packages, especially in its graphic quality.

The best general-purpose mapping package available at the present time is GIMMS 4 (Waugh 1980). Unlike SYMAP, this uses vector plotting methods. Like SYMAP, it requires a medium-sized computer and is written in the FORTRAN language. Some skills are needed to extract the best from GIMMS: putting it up on a computer is also not entirely a trivial task. Despite all this, it provides an unrivalled set of choices for the user: maps may be based on choropleth, point symbol or flow mapping symbolism, and infinite permutations of these are possible. Data may be manipulated within the package, e.g. to create new variables and, on suitable computer systems, the positions of title, key, etc. and the general map layout may be composed directly on the computer terminal screen. It can produce graphs and a variety of other output as well as maps and, at an earlier stage, can prepare and check the boundary information which it needs to shade areas. Finally – and unlike many home-grown mapping packages – GIMMS comes with quite extensive documentation on how to use it. Proof of its success can be seen from its long list of customers. These include the Department of the Environment, the Greater London Council and many other local authorities, many British universities and Statistics Canada.

Our final piece of software is again raster-orientated and is really at the other end of the market, being designed to work on the widely used Apple II micro-computer. Produced by Carl Youngman and available from Morgan Fairchild Graphics quite cheaply (appendix 8), it is easy to use, very cheap to purchase and run and produces output on a colour TV-like screen: 'hard copy' or paper output necessitates a printer and most such printers only produce black and white results. Inevitably, this is rather more restricted than is GIMMS but performs well on small to medium-sized data sets.

6.3.2.3 Data needs

We have already pointed out that to make any recognizable form of map, some knowledge of the location of the census areas – be they grid squares or irregular areas such as EDs – is essential. For manually-based mapping, the boundaries of census areas are available in a variety of map sources, each of which is described in section 2.9.10.

For computer-based mapping, however, we need X and Y (e.g. National Grid Easting and Northing) co-ordinates of either the centre of each area or, alternatively, many such co-ordinates which define the boundaries of the areas. SAS data already contain the centroids of the areas to which they relate and, for some purposes, these are entirely satisfactory – notably for plotting point symbols in the middle of large areas. When specifying a map, it is worth remembering that these are stored to 100 m resolution and also use the Ordnance Survey notation. As an example, the Geography Department of Birkbeck College in the University of London is located just off Tottenham Court Road: its 100 m National Grid reference is TQ 297 815, i.e. it is 529.7 km east and 181.5 km north of the origin of the National Grid (south-west of the Scilly Isles). Few standard computer packages except SASPAC (appendix 7) will readily cope with such grid references, especially when the area of interest crosses the boundary between adjacent 100 km squares and hence the preceding letters change. Thus to produce a map of the area within 10 km of Heathrow airport would be impossible with many programs since the junction of squares SU and TQ occurs near there. Fortunately, these co-ordinates are easily changed to the standard X and Y co-ordinate form.

For more sophisticated mapping, we need digital versions of the boundaries of the areas. These boundaries should preferably be held as segments, i.e. lines between adjacent pairs of areas, rather than as a closed polygon defining each area. Segments are preferred since they minimize the amount of data collected and stored and ensure that some boundaries are not drawn twice, diminishing the quality of the results. Packages such as GIMMS assemble segments into polygons when required.

Several sources of segment data relating to census areas exist. SIA Ltd and Geoplan (UK) Ltd are the major sources (see appendix 8). Users should be warned that, depending on whether the 'donor' and the 'recipient' computers are compatible, the use of these data may not be simple. In general, however, it is advisable to use existing boundary data since the effort of collecting, checking and editing new data is usually very considerable. For those users who require the boundaries of areas not already available in computer form, a number of bureaux exist at the time of writing which have a successful track record of digitizing these from maps (appendix 8).

6.3.3 WHAT PRICE QUALITY ?

In discussing maps thus far, we have scarcely mentioned quality. Indeed, what is quality so far as maps are concerned ? For most people, map quality has something to do with the amount of detail and the clarity with which this is shown. So far as computer-produced maps are concerned, their quality seems to be enhanced (as far as users are concerned) if they resemble those made by hand. Good cartographic design, a high level of legible detail in a traditional presentation and a base map clear enough to show main towns and routeways is what we might postulate as making up a high quality census map.

Such quality is strictly unnecessary for many research purposes. Nonetheless, if we aspire to produce quality maps – which are certainly more convincing than tatty versions produced, say, on a line printer – then we usually need to enhance the text produced by computers and we need at least to consider the use of colour. A few computer mapping packages currently contain good quality text – GIMMS, for example, has many different alphabets available to the user derived from the work of an American called Hershey. Since good quality text involves many more vectors (lines) than does simple text, it is sometimes the case that the plotting of text can dominate the cost of plotting a census map on a vector plotter.

The decision to use colour is often a difficult one, though in atlases such as *People in Britain* it was unavoidable (Rhind, Evans and Visvalingam 1980) because of the enormous number of areas to be shown on each page. The use of colour adds an extra level of planning and cost since only through considerable experience and/or from a colour proof can the appearance of the final map be predicted safely. Though colour printing material is readily produced by the simplest computer programs (see Rhind's (1975) colour maps from SYMAP), printing costs generally double and sometimes quadruple, depending on the number of colours used, and the photo-mechanical side of reproduction becomes much more complex if several separations, one or more for each colour, need to be handled. Colour, then, can be a great boon but can also be a grave nuisance and expense – use it carefully !

Finally, quality is also related to the method of reproduction chosen. The range of methods available is considerable, though some – such as dye line prints – constrain the type of map which can be produced (dye line prints are generally made from transmitted light, thus the original must be transparent).

6.4 Recommendations

Maps, whatever statisticians might say (and they do), are extremely helpful in summarizing a mass of data, in particular how or whether the mapped statistic varies *systematically* across the country from area to area. But maps must always be used in conjunction with the basic statistics and a significant amount of prior planning is needed to produce good maps. Computer mapping procedures are very suitable indeed for series map production, particularly where the census data and the area boundaries are already in computer form. It is, however, extremely easy to generate the most misleading maps, especially by computer. Potential cartographers should study a good standard text on cartography and previous and successful maps before embarking on what will normally be a lengthier exercise than was anticipated.

Specifically, users should:

- i decide which variables to use;
- ii decide the geographical resolution to use;
- iii decide what symbolism is best suited to the task in hand;
- iv decide whether it is worth using computerized mapping and, if so, make the necessary arrangements to obtain use of equipment, programs, data and skilled staff (or go to a bureau);
- v be prepared to experiment;
- vi re-read this chapter before committing themselves.

7 Bivariate and multivariate analysis: relationships between census variables

IAN S. EVANS

7.1 Why study relationships between variables?

Many users of census data are interested in how characteristics vary together over space. Are the same areas extreme in terms of housing quality, unemployment, occupational structure and age structure, or is the association between these characteristics very loose? Questions such as these are usually formulated in rather vague terms, and often it is hoped that calculation of a correlation coefficient between a pair of variables will provide enlightenment in itself. Irrespective of how the association is calculated, such a coefficient is rarely sufficient; it will be demonstrated here that careful inspection of a scatter plot is essential, together with deeper consideration of the spatial basis of the relationship. In this chapter, then, we develop the emphasis on use of graphical displays already espoused in Chapter 4.

This chapter is concerned only with relationships over geographical space, and thus with aggregates of individual people and households. The alternative of studying associations between different characteristics of individuals is not considered here. Associations between the demographic or socioeconomic characteristics of places are usually based upon numbers or proportions of individuals in each place, or ratios between these.

The first stage in any study of relationships between variables is to sit down quietly and think: *why* are these relationships important to my work? Will their magnitude affect policy – the allocation of grants, the construction (or closing) of service facilities, the improvement of roads, the type of housing to be built? The answers to even a brief meditation of this sort may have an important effect on how the relationship is studied. Assuming the variables have been carefully selected and defined (see Chapters 2 to 5; Evans 1980; Rhind, Evans and Dewdney 1977), we face two further important decisions:

i what definition of 'a place' is appropriate? Should enumeration districts (EDs), wards, 200 m grid squares or 1 km grid squares be used? Since all subsequent analysis will treat 'a place' as a homogeneous aggregate, this decision is very important. The definition should be appropriate to the motivation for the analysis: if the unavailability of data on an appropriate basis necessitates use of coarser or less well-delimited data, the effects of this should be investigated. Indeed, it is good practice to perform analyses at several different scales or levels of geographical resolution (Evans 1980), or for grid-square data as well as ward or ED data, to check whether the results are robust or are sensitive to these changes in spatial basis. There may be good reasons for such sensitivity: if not, divergences between results are a cause for concern and further investigation. If places are to be given equal weight in analysis, we are concerned that they should be near-equal in some respect, probably in total population: it is unreasonable to include areas with a million people and those with 5000 within the same analysis. Thus some amalgamation of the areas may be necessary (see Chapter 5). Alternatively, differences in size may form the basis for subdivision of the analysis (e.g. production of scatter plots for several subsets), or for a weighting scheme in regression or correlation (Evans 1979);

ii how is the total study area to be defined? Sometimes this may be pre-ordained as the whole of a local authority or a group of authorities but, wherever possible, it should be delimited carefully as a *functionally coherent* region, or as the domain to which generalizations about relationships may safely be applied. Either way we must remember that correlations between variables may vary considerably, for example between a study of a large city, of a whole conurbation, or of a metropolitan region (Coulter 1978): in fact, these differences may be greater than those between levels of geographical resolution (Evans 1979).

Differences between broadly and narrowly defined areas may arise because some study areas lack certain types of place. Conurbation core areas may lack modern low-rise housing estates with youthful age structures; hence some of the differences between analyses of enumeration districts in Birmingham and of wards in the West Midlands conurbation by Rosing and Wood (1971). Counties such as Dyfed and Cumbria may lack really densely settled inner-city areas. In these cases, results based on more broadly defined areas encompassing a more complete spectrum of variation are more interesting, but comparison of results based on several definitions of study area is likely to be even more enlightening. Clearly it is even more vital that a study relating to journey-to-work should encompass a whole catchment (functional region), or set of overlapping catchments, and not be truncated at administrative boundaries across which there are large flows, such as the northern and southern boundaries of County Durham.

Census data deal with numbers, proportions or ratios of individual people or households within an areal division. Census variables may be associated at the level of individual households, for example unskilled workers are more likely to be unemployed – this can be established from cross-classifications such as table 23 of the 1971 Small Area Statistics (appendix 3). But if we know only that there are a larger proportion unemployed in areas where more workers are unskilled, this is a geographic association which may or may not apply at the individual level. If we assume that it must apply, we are making what sociologists call the 'ecological fallacy', which is but one type of scale-transference fallacy (Alker 1969). Only if more than 50 per cent of individuals in an area fall into the one category, and more than 50 per cent into the other, can we know even that some individuals must fall into both categories. In Britain, many of the highest values for 'lone-parent families' are in areas with relatively high values of 'one-person households': since these categories are mutually exclusive, the relationship is purely one of spatial association and logically cannot apply at the individual household level.

7.2 Correlation

7.2.1 PRODUCT-MOMENT CORRELATION

Since we are interested in how closely or loosely two variables (x and y) reflect each other, or are predictable from each other, we usually start with the statistician's classic tool for measuring this: the product-moment correlation coefficient of Karl Pearson. This coefficient, r, varies between +1 and −1. A correlation of zero means that neither variable can be predicted from the other by a straight-line relationship (there may of course be nonlinear relationships, but r does not measure these). Correlation is positive if x and y decrease together, and negative if x increases as y decreases.

Correlations of +1 and −1 mean that there is a perfect linear relationship, so that once x is known, y can be predicted exactly, and vice versa. This 'ideal' is approached mainly when we measure the same phenomenon in two different ways: correlations between number of people and number of households in a grid square or ED may exceed +0.99, since variation in population size is much greater than variation in the average number of people per household. The strongest correlations, then, are not necessarily of the greatest interest. If we want a set of variables each of which provides distinct information, we look for variables which have low correlations with each other. If two variables are strongly correlated, it is unnecessary to produce maps of each (see section 6.2.1).

The product-moment correlation coefficient is so named because it is calculated from the cross-products of x and y. However, the calculation is made a little more complicated because the coefficient must be independent of the units of x and y: we should get the same answer whether the data are in metres or feet, in percent or parts per thousand, in months or years. We just want a coefficient which measures how closely x and y vary together in the study area; it should be dimensionless, and not reflect the variability of x and y.

This can be achieved by converting x and y to 'standard units', by subtracting the mean value ($\bar{x}$ or $\bar{y}$, respectively) and dividing by the standard deviation, SD (a measure of variability, see section 4.6). Hence:

$$x' = (x - \bar{x}) / (\text{SD of } x);$$
$$y' = (y - \bar{y}) / (\text{SD of } y)$$

where x' and y' are in standard units; their averages are 0.0 and their standard deviations are 1.0. r is simply the average value of (x' multiplied by y'), that is, the average cross-product of x and y after they have been transformed to standard units. Hence, r is the sum of $[(x-\bar{x}) / (\text{SD of } x)]\,[(y-\bar{y}) / (\text{SD of } y)]$, divided by N, the number of observations of (x, y). For computation,

$$r = [\text{the sum of } (x - \bar{x})(y - \bar{y})] \;/\; N(\text{SD of } x)(\text{SD of } y).$$

How is it that these standardized cross-products provide an appropriate quantitative measure for our intuitive notion of the 'strength of association' between two variables? Since x' and y' have means of zero, there will be a fair number of negative values as well as positive values. If both x' and y' are positive, their cross-product is positive; if both are negative, the cross-product is still positive. If either x' or y' is negative, but not both, the cross-product will be negative. The four possible combinations of signs relate to the four quadrants of the plot of x' against y'.

If an equal number of points plot in each quadrant, and the scatter from the central point (0, 0 ; i.e. $\bar{x}$, $\bar{y}$) is roughly uniform in all directions (i.e. x and y are unrelated), the positive cross-products will cancel out the negative ones and the average cross-product will approximate 0. If the points fall on a rising straight line through (0, 0), there will be no negative cross-products and, in standard units, the average cross-product (r) must be +1. If the points all fall on a declining straight line through (0, 0), there will be no positive cross-products, and the average cross-product must be –1. Moderately strong relationships will give a majority of points in either the positive or the negative quadrants, and hence a value of r between 0 and +1 or –1 respectively, depending upon whether the elongated scatter of points slopes upward or downward with increasing x.

Disregarding the sign of r, it measures the degree of scatter about a straight line (section 7.4) which reflects the elongation of the cluster of points plotted. With $r = \pm 1$ there is no scatter: ± 0.7 implies considerable scatter, ± 0.5 implies great scatter, and ± 0.3 implies such scatter that the relationship is of little value for predicting y from x or vice versa.

A correlation of ± 0.9 seems extremely strong, and it is surprising that there is considerable scatter in such a relationship. Actually, the strength of a relationship is better viewed in relation to r^2, which would be 0.81 in this case: this means that the residual variance about a best-fit line (section 7.4.1) is 0.19 of the total variance in y. Ehrenberg (1975, 237) pointed out that if we are concerned with the *standard deviation* of the residuals about the best-fit line, these are 100 $\sqrt{(1-r^2)}$ per cent of the standard deviation of y:

$\pm r$	.3	.5	.7	.8	.9	.95	.98	.99	.999	.9999
$100\sqrt{(1-r^2)}$	95	87	71	60	44	31	20	14	4.5	1.4

Thus, even with a correlation of ± 0.9, taking account of the relation with x reduces the standard deviation of (predictions of) y only to 44 per cent of the original ($\sqrt{0.19} = 0.44$); hence the visual impression of high scatter. Perhaps it is this $\sqrt{(1-r^2)}$ scale which accords best with our intuitive view of scatter.

The actual SD of residuals, in the original units of y and without standardization for SD (y), may be even more important. Because r has been 'standardized' for means and standard deviations, it can be a little misleading. Although r is an appropriate number for expressing the degree of scatter, its interpretation usually requires knowledge of $\bar{x}$, $\bar{y}$, SD of x and SD of y to make it more tangible and to prevent distorted interpretation, that is, bivariate analysis should be preceded by univariate analysis (Chapter 4). Also we do of course need to know N, to suggest how strong is the basis for our calculations. In total, then, six numbers are the minimum required to summarize x, y and their interrelation; and six is not enough for some of the more complex relationships presented towards the end of section 7.3.

In the simple application of correlation, each observation is given equal weight. Where census data relate to areas which vary considerably in population, imposition of such spurious equality would fail to make proper use of the data; that for more populous regions is both more reliable and more important. It is appropriate, in terms of statistical theory, to weight each observation by the population on which it is based; when correlating unemployment rate with rate of overcrowding, we would give a ward with 10,000 people the same weight as ten wards with 1000 people; fuller justification for this approach is given in Evans (1979). Such weighting is easily applied in most program packages, and *is the basis for all correlations between ratios quoted here.* Of course, weighting is *not* required when we correlate absolute numbers.

7.2.2 RANK CORRELATION

Several alternative measures of correlation are based solely on the rank order (from smallest to largest) of observations along the x scale and along the y scale. Since actual magnitudes are not used, rank correlation coefficients are insensitive to outliers. Also they are unaffected by curvilinearity, so long as the relationship is monotonic, that is, either positive throughout or negative throughout, with no reversals.

For example, Spearman's rank correlation coefficient:

$$r_S = 1 - [6.\text{sum of } (d^2)/N(N^2-1)]$$

where d is defined for each observation, and is the difference between the rank of its x value and that of its y value. When calculating this, the sum of d is also calculated, as a check; it should equal zero. The meaning of r_S is suspect if many ties in rank occur. Like a product-moment coefficient, Spearman's and other rank coefficients vary between +1 and −1; however, their magnitudes are not identical, $r_S = 0.5$ is not equivalent to $r = 0.5$ and different significance tables are used. The relationship between Spearman's and Pearson's coefficients, on certain assumptions, is curvilinear (Kendall 1949).

Before the availability of computers, r_S was often used as a substitute for r, because it was easier to calculate by hand (but only for small data sets). Now that even hand-held calculators can be programmed for r (or have a special button) this motivation no longer applies; r_S is best reserved for data which originate in rank form or where, as in psychology, uncertainty about the scale of measurement makes use of ranks prudent. Since all data in the population census are provided on a ratio scale of measurement (mainly as counts or proportions), *rank correlation is unnecessary* so long as data are properly edited and scatter plots are checked for outliers and curvilinearity.

7.2.3 DISSIMILARITY INDICES

Duncan and Duncan's (1955) dissimilarity index, D, provides a much more distinct (and valuable) alternative to r, since it measures association in a different way. It compares absolute numbers after scaling for totals over the study area. For example, x may be the number of skilled workers and y may be the number of managerial workers in each grid square or ED; the dissimilarity of their distributions between these areal divisions is

$$D = \tfrac{1}{2}[\text{Sum of differences between } (x/\text{sum of } x) \text{ and } (y/\text{sum of } y)]$$

and the sign of the differences is ignored. Summation is over all the areal divisions in the study area.

Unlike r and r_S, D varies from 0 (all x are in a different set of areal divisions to all y) to 1 (the x/y ratio is identical in all areal divisions). D has a tangible interpretation as the minimum proportion of *one* variable which would have to be moved between areal divisions to make its distribution identical to that of the other variable. Nevertheless, D is just as *aspatial* a measure as r and r_S; none of these coefficients takes account of the relative position of areal divisions in space.

Note that D is based on proportions of a study-area total for a given variable, not on proportions of the total of several variables in an areal division. Hence it is unaffected by the closure problem (see section 7.3.3), and is especially useful for variables within a single, mutually exclusive classification. This is where it has been used most widely, especially in studies of segregation of minority groups, for example by Jones and McEvoy (1978) and Peach

(1975). It is, of course, extremely sensitive to the size and definition of areal divisions (Woods 1976): two distributions can easily be mixed at borough or district level, but strongly segregated at street or ward level (see section 11.4.3). Different study areas should be compared only if their areal divisions are very similar, but comparisons of changing segregation over time are safe if areal divisions are constant.

There seems no reason to confine *D* to variables which are mutually exclusive; Evans (1979, 176-81) extended *D* to measure associations between a large range of variables and made comparisons with correlation coefficients (for absolute numbers). Calculation of both *r* and *D* permits sounder interpretation of associations between distributions. It would seem that *r* has been over-used by census analysts, whereas *D* has scope for broader application.

7.2.4 'SIGNIFICANCE'

With small data sets, there is a possibility that a weak (or even a moderate) correlation coefficient may be '*insignificant*'. In conventional statistics, this means that a correlation is based on a random sample from a population in which the correlation between the two variables might be zero. Although such a hypothetical population – and, indeed, random sampling – might seem far removed from studies based on 100 per cent census data for a set of contiguous places, one way of applying the notion of significance is to appeal to the arbitrary way in which these 'places' are defined (Taylor 1977, 215). There are an almost infinite number of ways in which the boundaries of EDs may be defined, and the same applies to grid squares (through translation and/or rotation). Hence the question is whether a correlation of similar sign might be found, if the boundaries were redrawn in a different but equally arbitrary way.

If we have only two observations, *r* must be +1 or –1, so the question of significance – or rather, of correlation – is meaningless. If a random sample of ten provides $r = +0.5$, there is a 95 per cent probability that the population from which it was drawn has a correlation between – 0.18 and +0.84: this is still not very informative. But if, with a data set of twenty or more grid squares, we observe a correlation stronger than ± 0.5, we need not worry about the possibility that a different incidence of grid squares would yield a correlation of opposite sign; likewise with fifty or more squares and a correlation stronger than ± 0.3. (Of course, the correlation may still mean very little, especially if there is similarity between residuals for adjacent squares; see Silk (1979, chapter 9) on such 'autocorrelation'.)

It is necessary to be more sceptical about correlations based on EDs, since their definition is not truly arbitrary and may be relevant to the relationship considered. Significance testing has been over-enthusiastically applied to census and other geographical data, and used often as a replacement for

Scotland
Wales
England - North
England - South,east
Midland England
Bivariate median

Islands
Highland
Powys
Buckinghamshire
Cheshire
Warwickshire
Oxfordshire
Cumbria
Dumfries - Galloway
Borders
Tayside
Strathclyde
London

Population change, 100 (1981 - 1971)/1971

1971 Population density, Persons/ha (log. scale)

common sense when it should have been but a minor support. Relationships near the threshold of 'significance' are unlikely to be of much interest in reaching substantive conclusions: we need a data set of reasonable size, and then the strength and nature of relationships can be emphasized, instead of their statistical significance. 'Confidence intervals are not used as often as they should be, while tests of significance are perhaps overused' (Moore 1979, 292).

7.3 Scatter plots

7.3.1 AN EXAMPLE: POPULATION DENSITY AND CHANGE

Either before or after calculating a correlation coefficient, a crucial step in exploring the relationship between two variables is to plot the magnitude of one against the magnitude of the other in a graph known as a (bivariate) scatter plot (figure 7.1). Each point plotted here represents one 'place'; it has been abstracted from its geographical or spatial location and plotted in terms of its characteristics. Here population change is plotted on the vertical ('y') axis, and population density (P) on the horizontal ('x') axis. Each point is plotted in a position fixed by its values for x and y: for example, Islands region (top left) has $x = 0.121$ people/ha, $y = 20.36$ per cent.

'The scatter plot is the workhorse of statistical graphics ... the essential tool for displaying results' (Chambers 1977). A scatter plot implicitly provides the information given by histograms for the two variables separately, but it shows much more information because the distribution of each variable at any particular level of the other variable can be seen. The impatient researcher may make use of these properties to skip the univariate stage of investigation (Chapter 4) and go directly to production of a set of scatter plots. This may be appropriate if he already has a clear idea of what transformations are necessary, but otherwise the haste may prove a false economy. If twenty variables are involved, it is easier to detect (most) outliers and to choose trans-

---

Figure 7.1
Population change and density

Scatter plot relating 1971–81 population change (vertical axis, y, as percentage of 1971 population) to 1971 population density (horizontal axis, x, in persons per hectare), by counties (regions in Scotland). Major regions are distinguished by different symbols: England is divided into North (including Northwest and Yorkshire), Midlands (East and West), and 'South and East' (Southwest, Southeast, and East Anglia). Warwickshire ($x = 2.3$ people/ha, $y = 4$ per cent) is very close to the bivariate median (intersection of median x with median y).

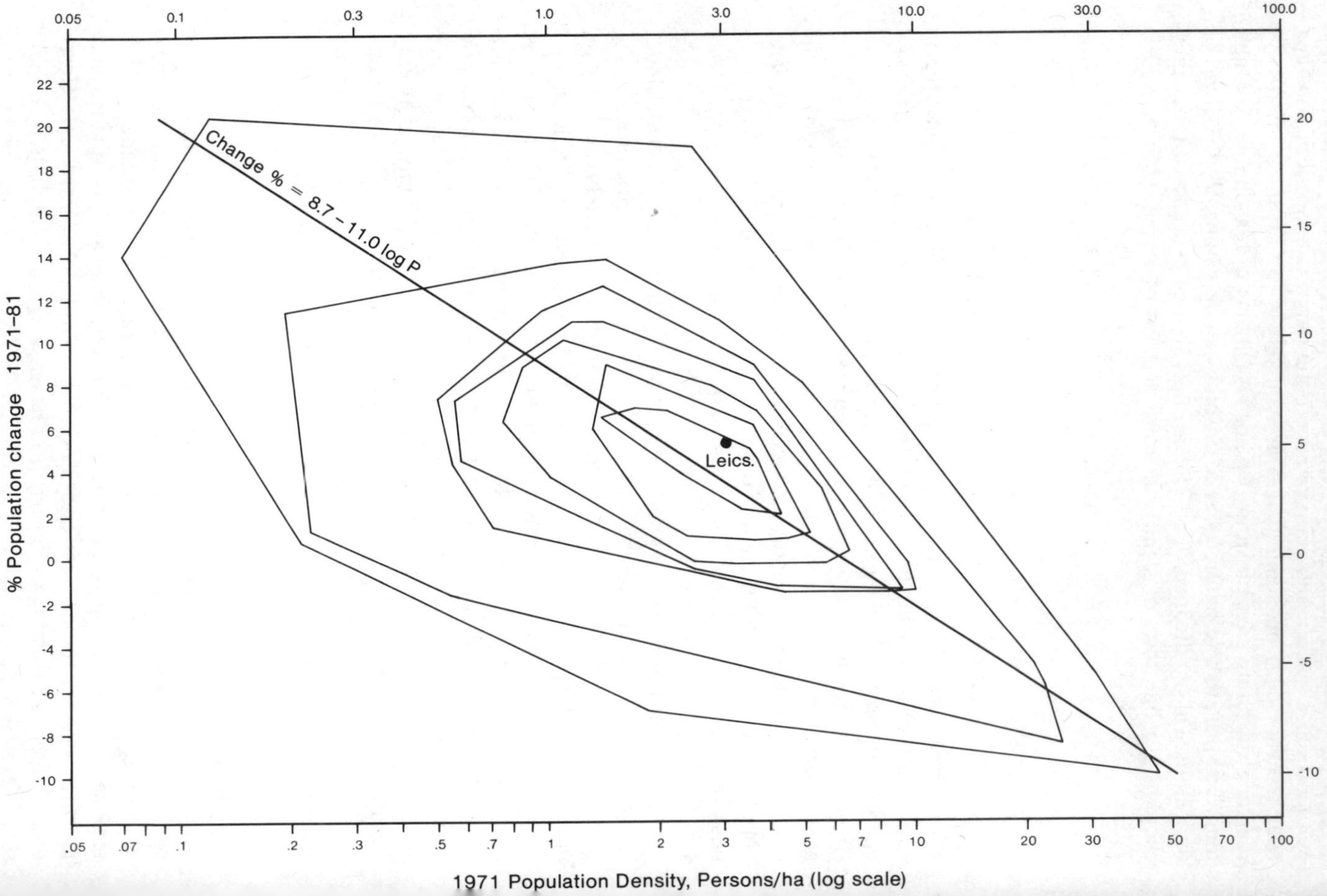

Change % = 8.7 – 11.0 log P
Leics.
% Population change 1971–81
1971 Population Density, Persons/ha (log scale)
0.05
0.1
0.3
1.0
3.0
10.0
30.0
100.0
22
20
18
16
14
12
10
8
6
4
2
0
-2
-4
-6
-8
-10
20
15
10
5
0
-5
-10
.05
.07
.1
.2
.3
.5
.7
1
2
3
5
7
10
20
30
50
70
100

formations on the basis of twenty histograms than of 190 scatter plots (i.e. $k(k-1)/2$ plots where k is the number of variables). Indeed, the latter may need to be repeated with better transformations (see section 4.6).

In Chapter 4 we noted the necessity of logarithmic transformation of population density, at least for county or district data; hence the x axis in figure 7.1 is logarithmic. Most counties fall into a central cluster with between 0.5 and 10 people/ha, and population changes between −2 and +14 per cent. The five English 'conurbation counties' form a second cluster, with greater population declines and higher densities. Scottish regions plot well to the left, with a broad range of population changes. Buckinghamshire plots noticeably above the main cluster. It might be considered an outlier, due to development of the Milton Keynes 'new city'. On the other hand, it is closer to the main cluster than are the low-density regions and Powys county.

No points plot in the bottom left or top right, so the points as a whole suggest a negative relationship – high rates of increase for low-density populations, population decrease for high densities. This is supported by elongation of the scatter of points within each of the clusters noted – it is not due simply to the contrast between 'conurbation counties' and 'others'. Nevertheless, the scatter of points shows considerable variation in rate of change for a given population density, especially for moderate densities.

7.3.2 CONVEX AND CONCAVE HULLS

Scatter plots may be 'enhanced' in several ways; commonly this is done by hand, but these procedures can be automated. Given a small number of points, drawing 'convex hulls' (Bebbington 1978; Barnett 1976, 324) around them aids interpretation of the scatter, and is particularly valuable for relationships which are weak or irregular. Imagine an elastic band thrown around the scatter of points: this will touch the three or more 'most peripheral' points, which are joined up by straight pencil lines to form the 'convex hull' of the bivariate

---

Figure 7.2
Convex hulls for population change and density

The technique described in section 7.3.2 has been applied to the data of figure 7.1, so that each data point falls on one (and only one) convex hull. Seven hulls are required, with Leicestershire (x = 3.13 people/ha, y = 5.37 per cent) remaining as the 'most internal' and therefore most typical county in these terms (though it is above the bivariate median). The gradient of the line describing the relationship between x and y is determined (visually) by elongation of the convex hulls; it is positioned to pass through the bivariate median. The line is discussed in section 7.4.3.

M Overall bivariate median
* Bivariate medians of each x - half of the data
m Bivariate medians of each x - third of the data
Scotland
Wales
North
Midland
South, East
% Population change 1971 – 1981
1971 Population Density, Persons/ha (log scale)
0.05
0.1
0.3
1.0
3.0
10.0
30.0
100.0
22
20
18
16
14
12
10
8
6
4
2
0
-2
-4
-6
-8
-10
.05
.07
.1
.2
.3
.5
.7
1
2
3
5
7
10
20
30
50
70
100
20
15
10
5
0
-5
-10

distribution (convex because there are no re-entrant angles, all internal angles of the polygon being less than 180°). The procedure is repeated disregarding the points on this outer 'hull', and so on until all points are accounted for by a series of nested convex polygons (figure 7.2). These reveal any tendencies for elongation in the scatter plot – better than would a 'naked eye' inspection of the points alone. Elongation is not noteworthy unless several convex hulls are involved, showing that it is defined by the body of the scatter of points and not by the accidental location of a few points.

For those who are reluctant to trust visual evidence, the sixty-three line segments forming the convex hulls may be divided into those with negative and those with positive gradients. For the seven hulls in turn, starting with the outermost, the negative:positive segment counts are 6:1, 9:2, 6:4, 6:2, 7:4, 5:3 and 7:1. Hence each hull shows definite negative elongation, and the overall count is forty-six negative and seventeen positive line segments.

In figure 7.3, outer convex hulls are drawn separately for five major regions. The ratio of negatively to positively sloping segments increases to 22:7 (plus 23:10 for inner hulls). Since the negative segments are longer than the positive ones, elongation of these hulls is rather greater than in figure 7.2. This suggests that the relationship within each major region is at least as strong as the overall relationship.

My interpretation is that the dominant process of change in population distribution in Britain in the 1970s was diffusion from more densely to less densely populated regions. This applied at both national and regional scale, and further evidence suggests the importance of diffusion at urban scales. The further implication is that population distribution was still adjusting to cheap petrol and low transport costs – even though that era ended in 1973.

If distributions are strongly curvilinear or complex (see section 7.3.5), some line segments on the convex hulls will be considerably longer than others, and will enclose empty space. These may be replaced by shorter lines between points, defining a re-entrant in the scatter. Such a 'concave hull' technique is objective if the maximum chord length is specified, re-entrants being permitted only to avoid chords longer than this distance.

A second modification is appropriate when plots involve many points, as do most of the illustrations in this chapter. Line-printer scatter plots then use various digits to represent point density, and convex (or concave) hulls can be

---

Figure 7.3
Convex hulls for each major region

On the population change versus density plot, single convex hulls are drawn separately for each major region. Elongation is more marked than for the overall convex hulls, suggesting that the relationship between change and density is stronger within each region than overall.

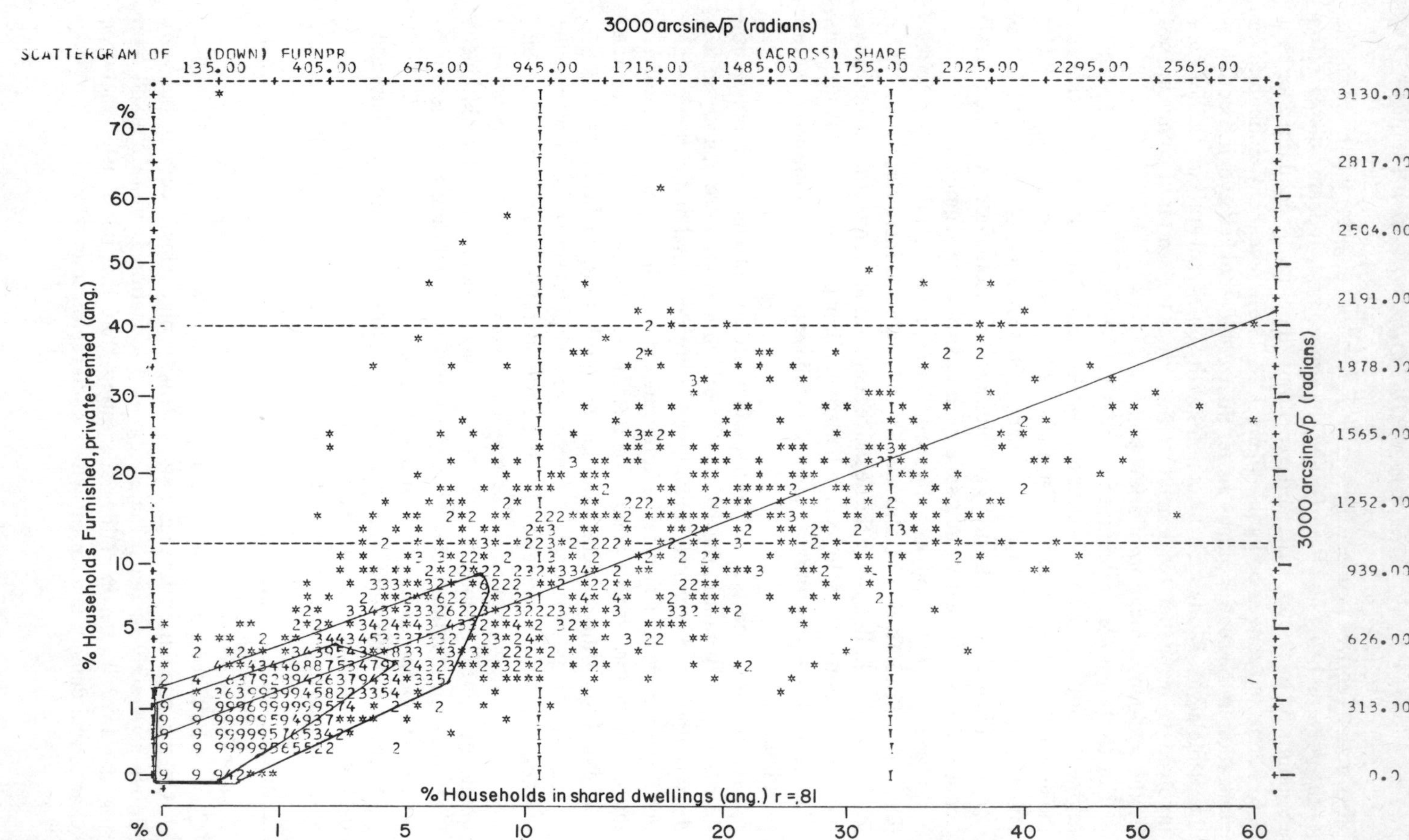
3000 arcsine√p (radians)
SCATTERGRAM OF (DOWN) FURNPR (ACROSS) SHARE
135.00 405.00 675.00 945.00 1215.00 1485.00 1755.00 2025.00 2295.00 2565.00
3130.00 2817.00 2504.00 2191.00 1878.00 1565.00 1252.00 939.00 626.00 313.00 0.0
3000 arcsine√p (radians)
% Households Furnished, private-rented (ang.)
% 70 60 50 40 30 20 10 5 1 0
% Households in shared dwellings (ang.) r =.81
% 0 1 5 10 20 30 40 50 60

drawn around each digit. (This approach can be dangerous if data rounding, etc. causes concentration of points into stripes or lines, separated by empty space, as in figure 7.8; the digits do not then give a good indication of density.) A combination of these two modifications of the 'convex hull' technique has been applied to figure 7.6.

A different enhancement, useful when one variable is dependent on the other, is the plotting of 'running medians' (Hartwig and Dearing 1979). Here the median y value is plotted for a series of overlapping bands of x. Bands may be defined either in equal units of x, or by taking a given number of points each time. Moving quartiles can also be added, but this is best done by computer program rather than manually. Cleveland and Kleiner (1975) programmed the smoothing and plotting of running midmeans and semi-midmeans, which serve a similar purpose. Each of these techniques, however, treats y as a response to x, whereas in census data x and y are often simply interdependent (section 7.4); convex or concave hulls are then more appropriate.

7.3.3 EXAMPLES OF STRONG RELATIONSHIPS

If the scatter is 'bivariate Gaussian', i.e. symmetrical and elliptical, with a slow decline in density of points toward the edges, the scatter plot serves chiefly as a visual representation of the degree of scatter versus the strength of the relationship, which is well summarized by the product-moment correlation coefficient r. A more common – but relatively well-behaved – situation is portrayed in figure 7.4. This shows the strong positive association ($r = +0.81$) between 'households in shared accommodation' (x) and 'furnished private-rented accommodation' (y), both expressed as proportions of private households for each grid square. Both variables are undertransformed, since the angular transformation applied here has proved too weak, reducing the positive skew without eliminating it. Undertransformation may exaggerate such a correlation: if most points are concentrated in one cluster, the correlation may be controlled by one or two outlying points. Clearly, the 'effective' sample size for significance testing is then much less than the total number of points. In the present example many points are involved and, though overstated, the correlation is real. Both types of household are strongly

---

Figure 7.4
Shared and privately rented furnished accommodation

Both variables are expressed as proportions of private households, in each 1 km grid square, 1971, and angular transformations have been applied. As in the other figures, 7.4 to 7.10, axes are labelled for transformed (top and right) and original percentage (bottom and left) scales.

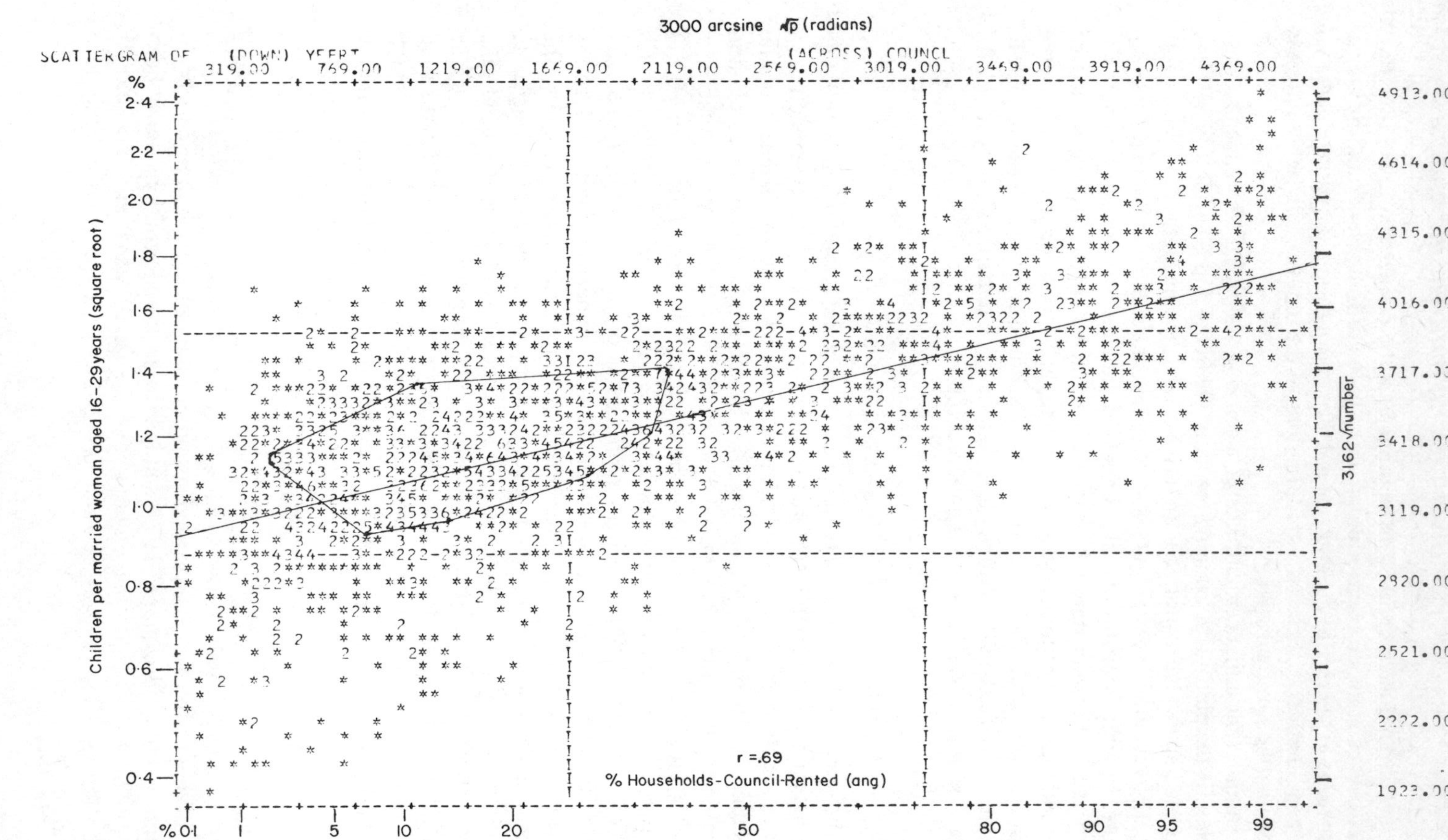
3000 arcsine √p (radians)
SCATTERGRAM OF (DOWN) YEERT (ACROSS) COUNCL
319.00 769.00 1219.00 1669.00 2119.00 2569.00 3019.00 3469.00 3919.00 4369.00
%
2·4
2·2
2·0
1·8
1·6
1·4
1·2
1·0
0·8
0·6
0·4
Children per married woman aged 16–29years (square root)
4913.00
4614.00
4315.00
4016.00
3717.00
3418.00
3119.00
2820.00
2521.00
2222.00
1923.00
3162√number
r =.69
% Households-Council-Rented (ang)
%0·1
1
5
10
20
50
80
90
95
99

concentrated in the inner areas of large cities. The relationship between 'unemployment' and 'overcrowding', with $r = +0.62$, provides a similar plot.

This and the succeeding scatter plots are for 1 km grid-square data for all of Britain from the 1971 Census. To reduce the number of squares (places) to about 2000 and hence to be manageable for plotting on one sheet of paper, only squares with over 5000 people are plotted: these are densely built-up areas, found only in large towns. The plots are produced by the SPSS program SCATTERGRAM (Nie *et al.* 1975): each asterisk represents a single square. To permit plotting on a line-printer, printer positions into which several grid squares fall are shown by an appropriate digit, '2', '3', '4', etc. This approach is not really suitable for plotting large numbers of data points, since many positions then have nine or more points and are represented by '9': a different program with a series of density classes, with shading intensity related to number of places in that category and shown by overprinting of line-printer characters, is then desirable.

Figure 7.5 shows how the 'fertility of young women' (y; square root transform) is greater in areas with greater proportions of 'council-rented housing' (x; angular transform). Although the frequency distribution of x is 'skewed rectangular' rather than Gaussian, the correlation ($r = +0.69$) is well supported by the scatter plot and a regression of y on x (though not of x on y: see section 7.4.1) is acceptable since it runs through the median of the scatter of y values, for any value of x. The relationship is partly due to social class differences in mother's age at conception, and partly because number of children is a factor in whether a family is allocated a council house.

7.3.4 RELATIONSHIPS AFFECTED BY CLOSURE

The next example illustrates the effects of 'closure' (Evans and Jones 1981). These arise when several variables are expressed as proportions of a given total, as is common in use of census data. For example, numbers in each age group may be expressed as proportions of total number of people; numbers of each tenure type may be expressed as proportions of the total numbers of households; or, for the example illustrated here, numbers in each occupational group are expressed as proportions of the total number of workers. In each

---

Figure 7.5
Fertility and council housing

This is *not* a direct cause–effect relationship, but there is a definite association. The square root of 'number of children ever born, per 1000 married women aged 16–29 years, in private households' (y) is plotted against the angular transform of 'proportion of households rented from local authorities and new town corporations'.

case, the sum is always 100 per cent or 1.0 and, if one group is larger, the other groups together must be smaller. Thus, if 40 per cent of workers in a particular place are in manufacturing and 35 per cent in service industries, no more than 25 per cent can be in any other occupational group.

This 'closure effect' imposes a tendency toward negative correlation when the proportion of one group is correlated with the proportion of another, mutually exclusive, group. The larger the overall proportions (p_i) of each group, the more negative the correlation is likely to be – simply because of the way the variables are defined, without there being any interaction between the groups. A simple model to account for this has been presented by Mosimann (1962). Instead of the 'null expectation' of the product-moment correlation coefficient being zero, it is given as a function of the overall proportions (p) of the two variables, i and j, which are being correlated:

$$\text{closure } r = -\sqrt{[\,p_i\, p_j \,/\, (1 - p_i)\,(1 - p_j)\,]}.$$

Table 7.1 permits comparison of observed correlations between transformed variables (for all 54,000 1 km grid squares unsuppressed for this 10 per cent record in the 1971 Census) with the Mosimann null expectations.

The results show the danger of taking such correlations at face value. (Rank correlations would be affected in the same way, though no 'null model' is available for them.) The strongest correlation observed, that of –0.575 between service and manufacturing workers, is accounted for entirely by the closure effect: large proportions in manufacturing make large proportions in services less likely, and vice versa, but there is no preferential effect of

Table 7.1 Matrix of correlations between proportions of occupational groups, 1971, for 1 km grid squares in Great Britain; (a) observed *r*; (b) closure *r*, after Mosimann

1–pi	*pi*	*variable*							
.983	.017	FARMRS							
.982	.018	MINERS	(a)	–.028					
			(b)	–.018					
.652	.348	MANUF	(a)	–.192	+.065				
			(b)	–.096	–.099				
.928	.072	CONSTR	(a)	–.064	+.080	+.156			
			(b)	–.037	–.038	–.203			
.918	.082	TRPTUT	(a)	–.132	+.030	+.162	+.384		
			(b)	–.039	–.040	–.218	–.083		
.604	.396	SERVIC	(a)	–.047	–.195	–.575	–.098	–.021	
			(b)	–.106	–.110	–.592	–.226	–.242	
.933	.067	GOVDEF	(a)	–.103	–.013	–.009	+.280	+.351	+.014
			(b)	–.035	–.036	–.196	–.075	–.080	–.217
6.000	1.000			FARMRS	MINERS	MANUF	CONSTR	TRPTUT	SERVIC

manufacturing and services avoiding each other; the proportions vary independently, apart from the in built negative tendency due to the closure effect.

Despite the closure effect, three groups have positive intercorrelations greater than 0.25: these are construction, transport and utilities, and government and defence employees. Each of these has less than 9 per cent of overall employment in Britain, and closure effects are therefore much smaller than for the two large groups, manufacturing and services. Indeed, after allowing for the larger negative tendencies affecting its correlations, manufacturing should be added to the group despite its negligible observed correlations with government and defence. Services also associate with the latter and with transport and utilities, while miners have some spatial associations with manufacturing and construction.

There is a real negative association between miners and services, and farmers have no clear positive associations, but (not surprisingly) are segregated from manufacturing and transport and utilities employment. Since the incidence of closure effects is variable, this interpretation is quite different to one naively based on the observed correlations. Evans and Jones (1981) gave a further example, for age-structure variables, and discussed other types of inbuilt correlation between ratios. They demonstrated that the results of factor analysis of such sets of closed variables can be very misleading.

This interpretation is quite informal; only recently has a formal approach been provided for testing association between proportions, one which opens up the possibility of further statistical investigation once the absence of independence has been demonstrated. This is Aitchison's (1981) application of a log-ratio transformation.

Closure necessitates that the proportions of x and y sum to 1.0 or less. Because of the '$x + y = 1$' limit, scatter plots of relationships affected by closure are commonly triangular; this is modified but slightly by angular transformation. For example, the two main tenure variables are 'owner-occupied' and 'council-rented', which correlate – 0.78 compared with a null expectation of – 0.65; on their scatter plot, many points lie just below the line $x + y = 100$ per cent. The relationship between 'owner-occupied' and a minority tenure variable, 'unfurnished private renting', is much more complex (figure 7.6). The scatter is approximately L-shaped (actually, an asymmetric T) with a positive trend where proportions of both are low, but a negative trend over most of the plot as the line $x + y = 100$ per cent is approached. This is not an ordinary curvilinear relationship, but a conflict between (a) the tendency of 'privately-rented' to mix with 'owner-occupied' rather than with 'council-rented housing', and (b) the closure effect which prevents both from taking high values together. The resulting correlation of +0.14, and the regression lines to which it relates, are meaningless. The correlation for Great Britain (including less populous squares) is – 0.08, compared with a Mosimann (1962) null value of – 0.41.

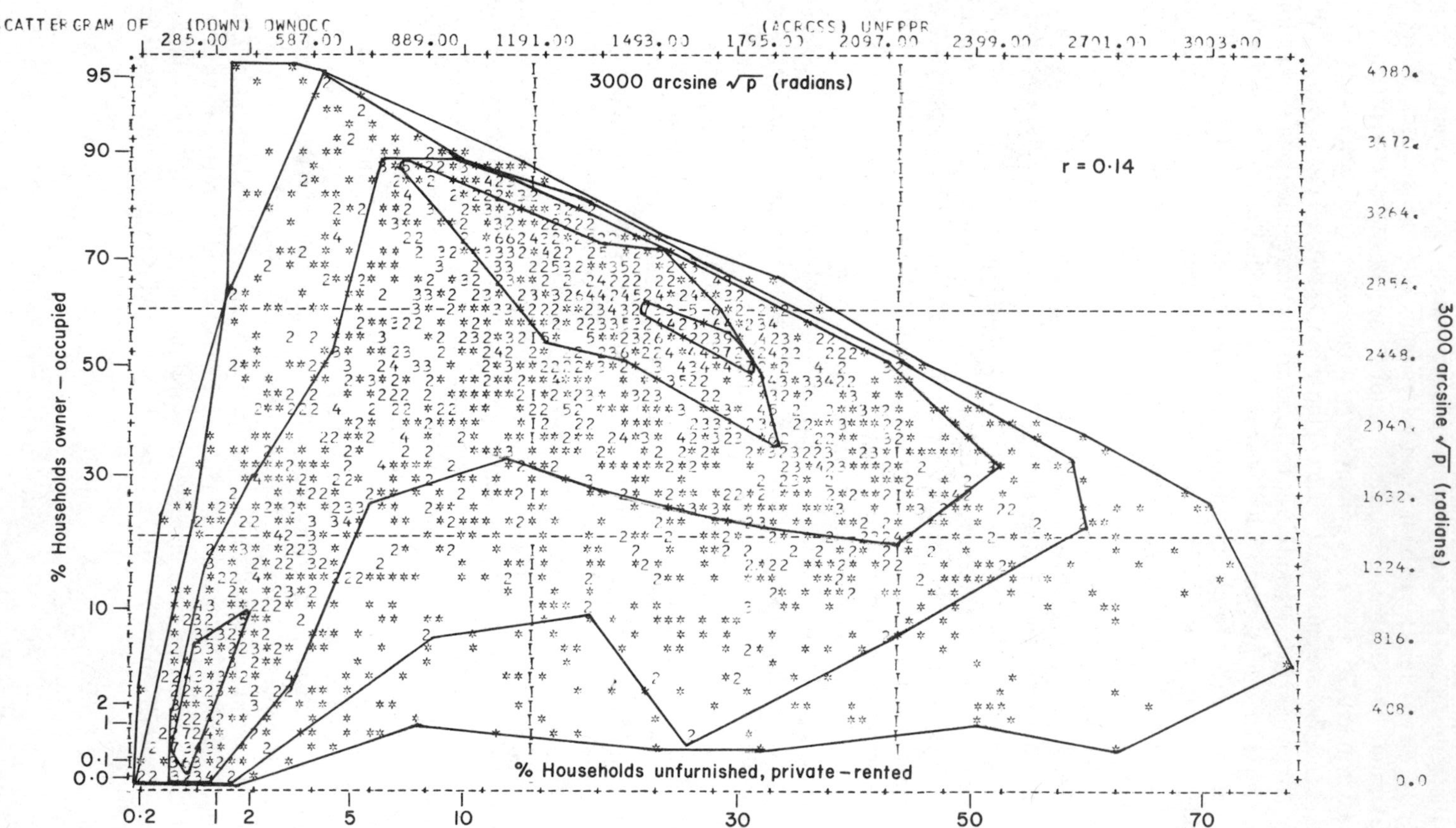

SCATTERGRAM OF (DOWN) OWNOCC (ACROSS) UNFPPR
285.00 587.00 889.00 1191.00 1493.00 1795.00 2097.00 2399.00 2701.00 3003.00
3000 arcsine √p (radians)
r = 0·14
95 90 70 50 30 10 2 1 0·1 0·0
% Households owner – occupied
4080. 3672. 3264. 2856. 2448. 2040. 1632. 1224. 816. 408. 0.0
3000 arcsine √p (radians)
% Households unfurnished, private – rented
0·2 1 2 5 10 30 50 70

7.3.5 CURVILINEAR AND COMPLEX RELATIONSHIPS

Triangular relationships seen on scatter plots are not necessarily due to closure. Figure 7.7 shows that, though no combination of the two variables is ruled out beforehand, in practice high rates of 'car ownership' are not combined with 'lack of household amenities'. (ALAMEX = exclusive use of the three basic amenities: an inside toilet, a fixed bath, and running hot water.) The concentration of points near the top of the plot, contrary to the general negative trend, may reflect council estates which were constructed or updated to Parker-Morris standards and hence have the basic amenities, but variable rates of car ownership. Even so, despite the triangular scatter, the correlation is −0.51.

In figure 7.8, the variance of y (angular transform of 'proportion of households with two or more cars') is greater for higher values of x (reciprocal of 'persons/rooms'), but the distribution of y here is symmetrical for each value of x, so it is difficult to see how further transformation of y would help. The scatter plot reveals a minor problem of a different type; discretization of x giving vertical stripes. This is due to x being calculated to too few decimal places. The correlation is +0.48, which may be a reasonable description of the relationship despite the shape of the scatter plot.

Curvilinear relationships are rare among this large set of scatter plots based on transformed variables. There are no true outliers (completely isolated points) because the national data set is well-edited and large enough to give a scattering of points toward the extremes, rather than gaps isolating one or two points. In fact, outliers are unlikely in data for small areas. Nevertheless, *the detection of curvilinearity and/or outliers is an important motivation for the construction of scatter plots,* especially as part of the data-editing process for variables which are unfamiliar. Numerical techniques for identifying several outliers together are clumsy, even in two dimensions (Gnanadesikan 1977; Barnett and Lewis 1978). If correlations with and without the possible outliers (Devlin *et al.* 1975) differ radically, the 'outliers' must be studied very carefully.

The correlation between 'household amenities' and the 'proportion of old people' is −0.43. These variables are related, however, only in areas with high

---

Figure 7.6
Owner-occupation and unfurnished private renting

The proportion of private households 'owner-occupied' (y) is plotted against the proportion 'rented privately, unfurnished' (x); both scales have undergone angular transformation. The plot is 'contoured' by 'concave hulls' for the density digits 1, 2, 3, 5 and 7; see section 7.3.2.

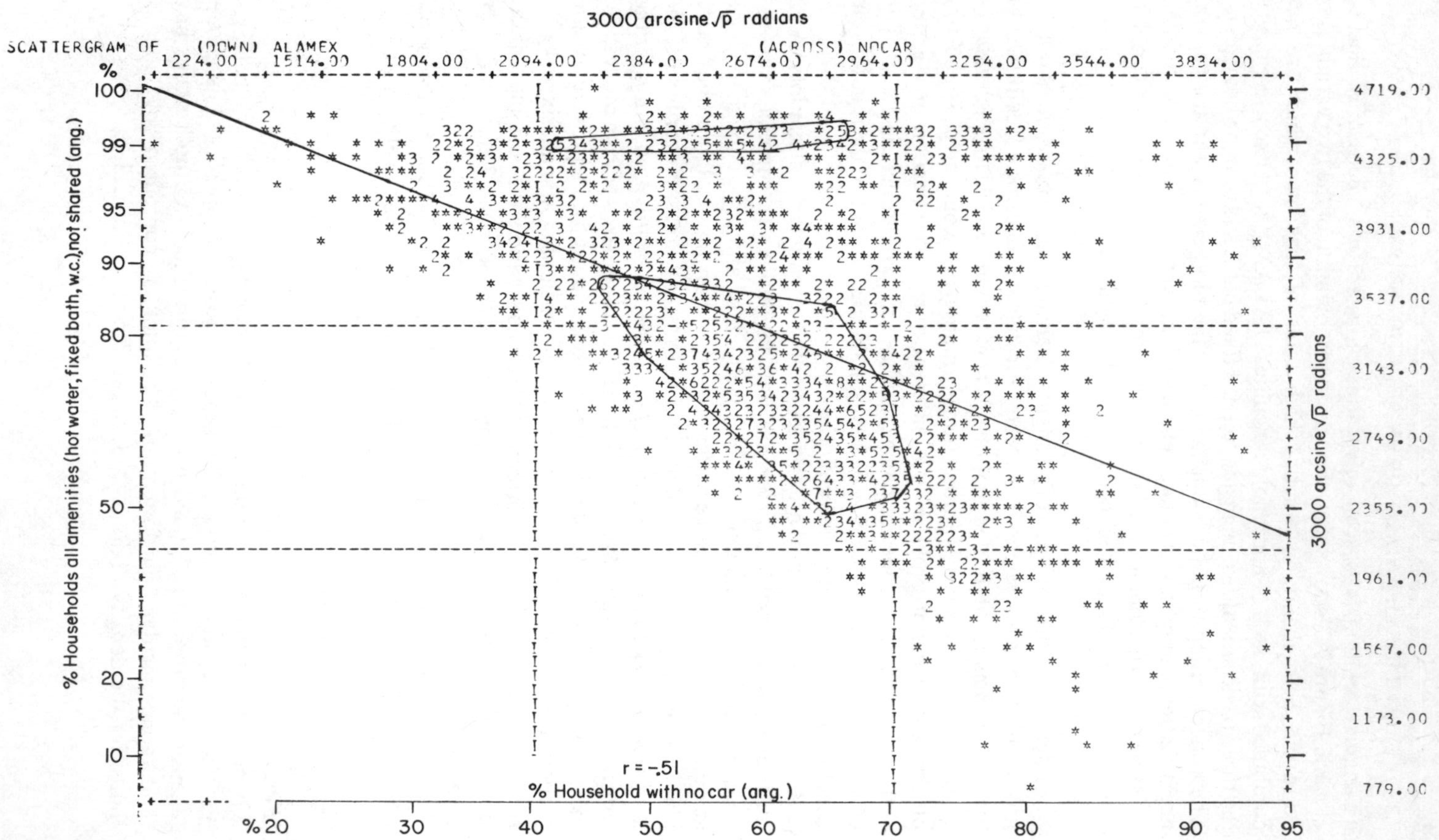
3000 arcsine √p radians
SCATTERGRAM OF (DOWN) ALAMEX (ACROSS) NOCAR
1224.00
1514.00
1804.00
2094.00
2384.00
2674.00
2964.00
3254.00
3544.00
3834.00
4719.00
4325.00
3931.00
3537.00
3143.00
2749.00
2355.00
1961.00
1567.00
1173.00
779.00
% Households all amenities (hot water, fixed bath, w.c.), not shared (ang.)
%
100
99
95
90
80
50
20
10
r = -.51
% Household with no car (ang.)
%20
30
40
50
60
70
80
90
95

rates of basic amenities, giving a peculiar type of curvilinear relationship which is displayed most clearly on the scatter plot (figure 7.9). This implies that, in cities, old people are fewer where housing standards are best – in new housing areas. But in areas of poor and mediocre housing, the proportion of old people shows only random variation.

More serious non-linearity is shown by figure 7.10. The definite and obvious relationship between these two variables is completely hidden by the correlation coefficient, +0.08. Rank correlation would hardly do any better, since the relationship is not consistent throughout the range of proportion of foreign-born. It seems that varying degrees of overcrowding are found where there are few 'foreign-born' (the more overcrowded areas here may largely be in Scotland); otherwise, the proportion of overcrowded households increases with the proportion of foreign-born households per grid square.

These scatter plots do not illustrate all possible irregularities – skewness has already been greatly reduced by transformation, there are no truly parabolic relationships and no outliers, and zero values have only a minor effect – but they do illustrate some situations which cannot be cured by rank-order correlation, separation of outliers, or even by improved transformation. The later examples show that correlations of ±0.4 or 0.5, which some authors regard as 'moderate', can be obtained for relationships which scatter plots show to be very strange indeed. And in examples involving closure, even very strong negative correlations may mean very little.

7.4 Lines through data

If a scatter plot or correlation coefficient suggests an interesting relationship between two variables, it is reasonable to attempt to summarize the relationship. Such summarization necessarily involves a line, straight or curved, which 'goes through' the scatter of data points and can be described by an equation, preferably a simple one. An equation complements the correlation coefficient, r (see section 7.2), which expresses the degree of scatter about an appropriate straight line. The purpose of an equation is to suggest which values of x and y

---

Figure 7.7
Car ownership and household amenities

Areas where few households lack a car have even fewer households without exclusive use of all three basic amenities (hot water, fixed bath and inside WC). Areas where few households own cars are much more varied in the provision of household amenities. Overall, however, the relationship between amenities and lack of a car is negative. Both variables are angular-transformed.

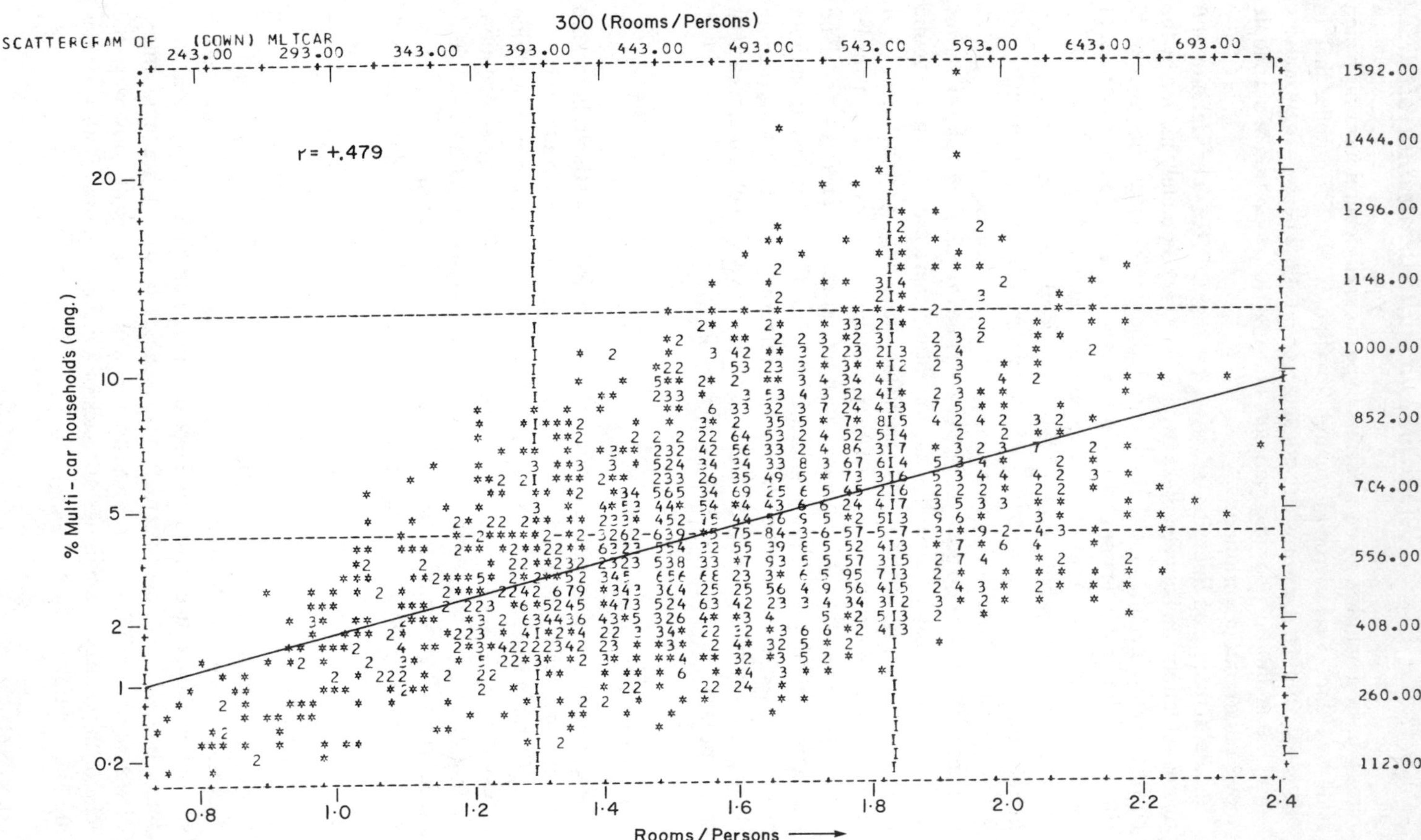
SCATTERGRAM OF (DOWN) MLTCAR
300 (Rooms / Persons)
243.00
293.00
343.00
393.00
443.00
493.00
543.00
593.00
643.00
693.00
1592.00
1444.00
1296.00
1148.00
1000.00
852.00
704.00
556.00
408.00
260.00
112.00
r = +.479
% Multi - car households (ang.)
20
10
5
2
1
0·2
0·8
1·0
1·2
1·4
1·6
1·8
2·0
2·2
2·4
Rooms / Persons

'go together', and how y can be predicted from x, or vice versa. The equation for a straight line gives us the rate of change of y with x (the change in y associated with a given change in x) and the value of y when $x =$ zero (or vice versa).

Although there are various ways in which such lines may be calculated, any line through data – straight or curved, regression or 'neutral' – is meaningful only if

- i there are points around the line throughout the range over which it is to be applied;
- ii there are no isolated points unduly influencing the line;
- iii the scatter of points around the line is comparable throughout its length, unlike figure 7.8;
- iv the line is in the middle of the scatter of points; middle is defined differently for the different types of line.

7.4.1 REGRESSION LINES

Ask any student who has taken an introductory course in statistics or its application, 'how do we fit a line relating y and x?', and he is likely to answer, 'by fitting a regression line to minimize the sum of squared residuals of y'. A regression line is indeed the most widely applied answer to this question, but it is not the only answer, and it is often not the appropriate answer (Till 1973; Mark and Peucker 1978). It is appropriate only where there is a definite distinction between cause and effect, or where the equation will be used to predict an unknown variable from a known one – not where x and y are on equal footing. But cause–effect situations are of great interest, and so regression and its extensions are the most widely and fruitfully applied of all statistical techniques.

We may wish to summarize, for example, the relationship between the proportion of (potential) workers unskilled and the proportion unemployed. Lack of skill is presumably a factor contributing to unemployment, and most of us would regard an individual's lack of skill as 'cause' (x) and his unemployment

---

Figure 7.8
Roomy and multiple-car households

Areas with more households with two or more cars (y) also have more rooms in relation to the number of people (x). The correlation is only moderate, and a peculiar vertical 'striping' effect (increasing to the right) is caused by x being the reciprocal of a variable stored in terms of three digits.

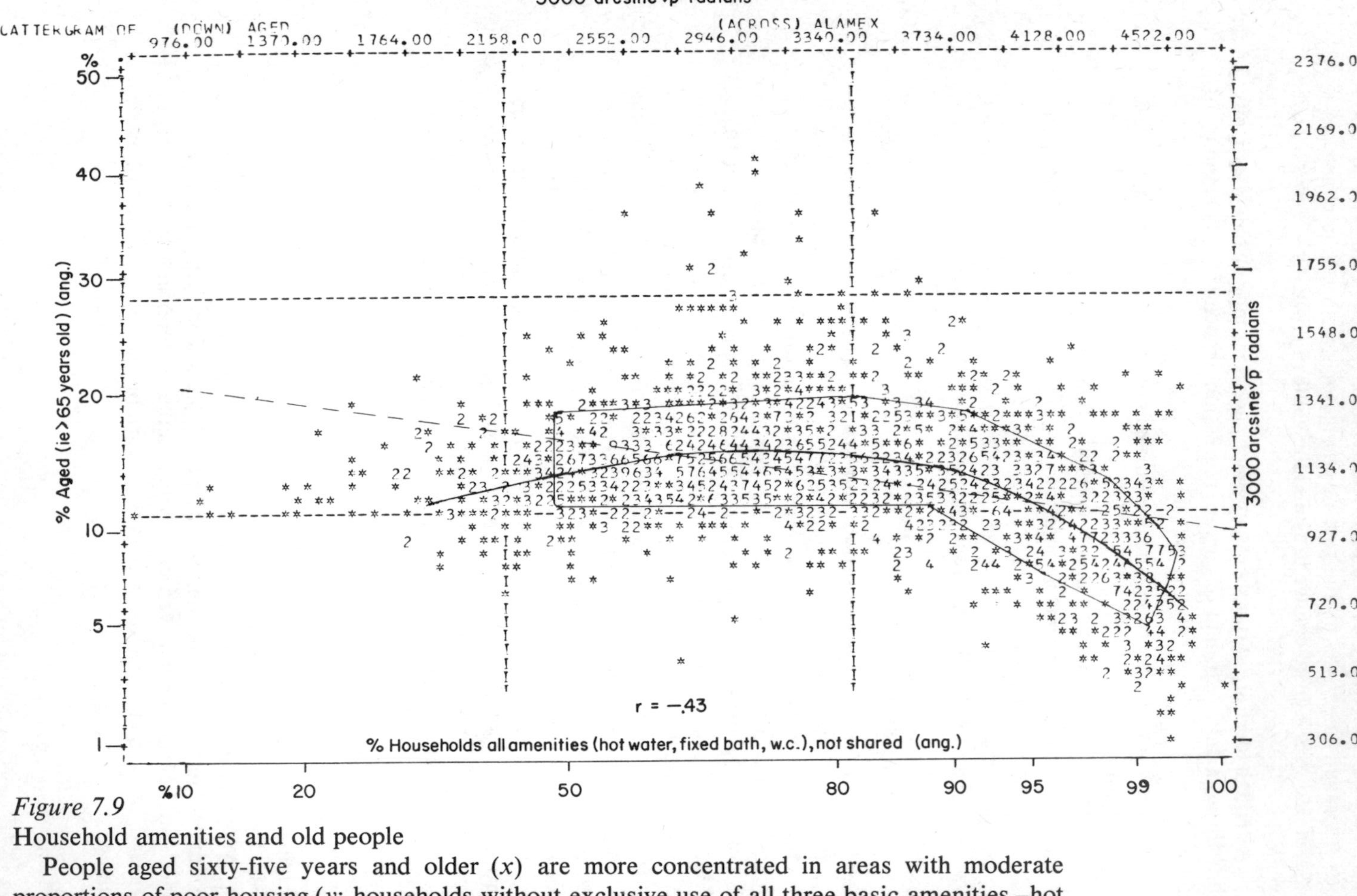

Figure 7.9
Household amenities and old people

People aged sixty-five years and older (x) are more concentrated in areas with moderate proportions of poor housing (y: households without exclusive use of all three basic amenities –hot water, fixed bath and inside WC). Much smaller proportions are in areas of mainly good as 'effect' (y). Even this example is open to some discussion (because of feed-back effects) and, because our census data relate to areas and not individuals, we must beware of the 'ecological fallacy' (see section 7.1); nevertheless, it is reasonable to apply regression here.

Regression is a natural extension, to two dimensions, of the 'mean', which we applied in one dimension in section 4.7. Instead of taking all observations of y, take only those for a particular class of x, and calculate their mean. Do this for each class of x, and plot the series of means of y against x on the scatter plot. This is a plot of the value of y expected for a given class of x; hence it is appropriate to the prediction of y from x. Since these 'conditional means' of y given x will show a certain amount of scatter, especially for the classes of x with few observations, they are generalized by a straight line – the 'linear regression of y on x'. This will go near most of the conditional means, but greater weight is of course given to those based on more observations. (The line is in fact fitted so as to minimize the average squared residual – a residual is the difference between an observed and a predicted value.)

This regression line permits us to predict y for any value of x, not just for the midpoints of classes. Any temptation to predict y for values of x higher or lower than those in our data should, however, be resisted; this would be extrapolation and the extrapolation of empirical relationships is extremely dangerous and very rarely justifiable.

In standardized units (see section 7.2), the equation of the linear regression line is simply

$$y' = rx'.$$

In the original units, means and standard deviations have to enter the equation, which becomes

$$(y - \bar{y}) = r\,(x - \bar{x})\,(\text{SD of } y) \,/\, (\text{SD of } x).$$

Note that when $x = \bar{x}, y = \bar{y}$: like all other empirical straight lines relating x and y, the regression line must pass through the 'bivariate mean', $(\bar{x}, \bar{y})$. Usually this is simplified to

$$y = a + bx.$$

Where $b = r(\text{SD of } y) / (\text{SD of } x)$, b is the gradient, the change in y for a given change in x, expressed in (units of y) / (units of x), and

$$a = \bar{y} - b\bar{x} = \bar{y} - \bar{x}.r\,(\text{SD of } y) \,/\, (\text{SD of } x)$$

is the value of y expected when x equals zero, and is of course expressed in units of y.

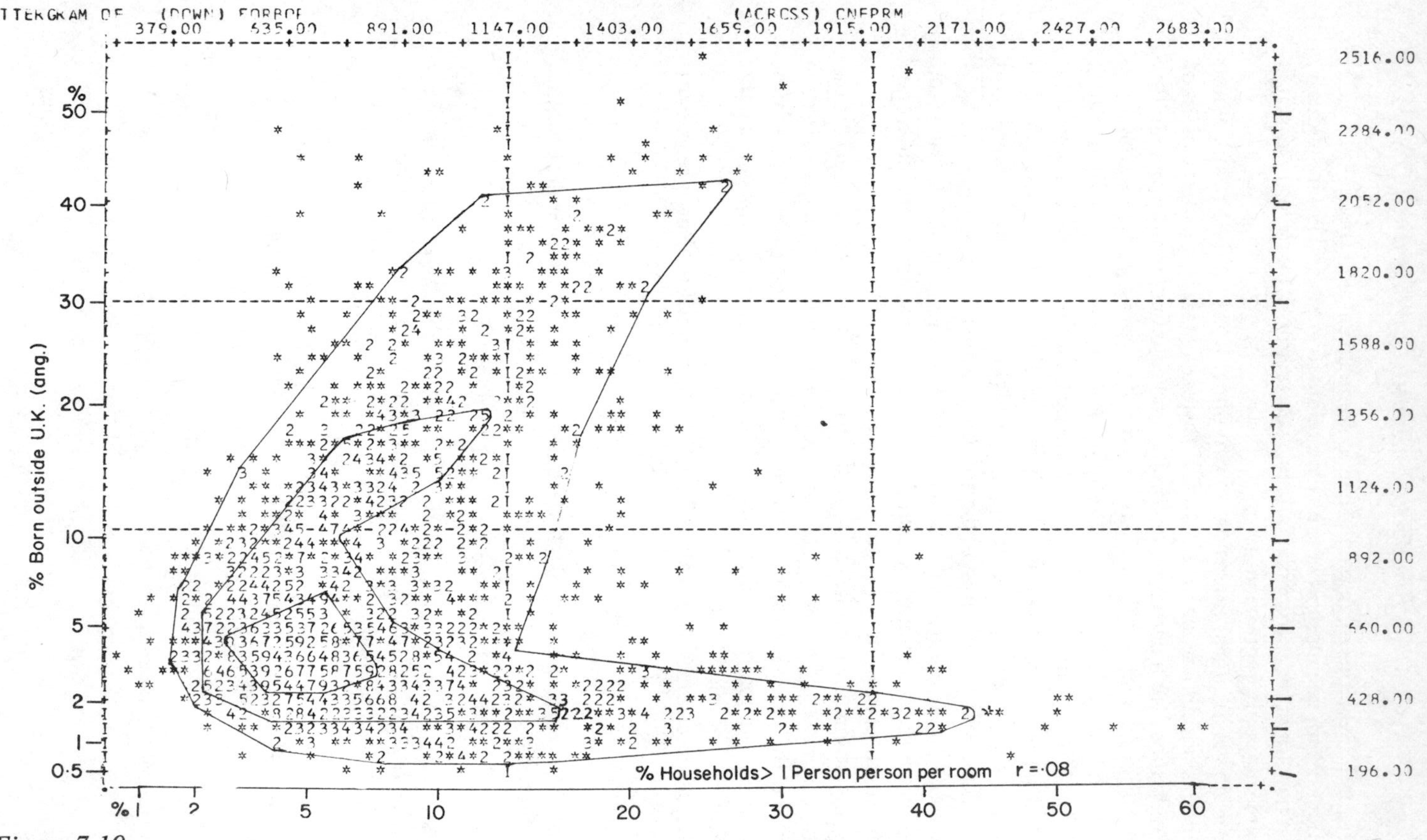

Figure 7.10

Foreign born and overcrowding

The relationship between (angular transforms of) proportions from outside the UK (x), and households with more than one person per room, is compound.

7.4.2 CURVILINEAR REGRESSION

In most cases we are able to transform variables (see section 4.6) until a linear relationship with even scatter about the line is produced. The transformations take care of any non-linearity. Occasionally, however (figures 7.7–7.10), transformations may not entirely succeed: a plot with even scatter may have a curved trend, and a plot with a linear trend may have uneven scatter, with greater variation around the regression line at one end of the x-scale than at the other.

The problems should be apparent from the scatter plot; numerical screening is also possible. Some of them may be solved by applying curvilinear regression, on the scales of x and y which provide even scatter (Bliss 1970). Equations such as $y = ae^{bx}$, $y = a + bx^c$, $y = a \arcsin (bx)$, $y = a + bx + cx^2$ may be applied, and it is possible to test whether the improvement of fit justifies the extra complexity of the model. A sufficiently complex polynomial equation can fit any scatter of points exactly, but we are concerned that there should be some possible theoretical justification for a curve of the form fitted and so we prefer a fairly simple equation. 'Usually a number of different curves or mathematical functions can approximate any particular set of data, especially when the range of variation is limited ...' the decision as to which to try is based upon theory and previous work (Ehrenberg 1975, 128).

7.4.3 LINEAR REGRESSIONS BOTH WAYS

So far, we have stated firmly that a regression line predicts a value of y from a given value of x. What if we know y and wish to predict x ? The same line should not be used; obviously if r is near zero, the regression of y on x has a very gentle gradient, and only near average values of y can be related to x within the range of values observed. The whole procedure must be inverted; we may plot the average values of x for each class of y and generalize this to form a quite different line, the regression of x on y. If there is any scatter at all in the data, this will differ from the regression of y on x; they will cross at the bivariate mean $(\bar{x}, \bar{y})$.

If y is still plotted on the vertical axis, the regression of x on y is the steeper line; its gradient is (SD of y) / r (SD of x), that is, it is *inversely* related to the correlation coefficient. If r is zero, the gradient is infinite, i.e. the line is vertical at x. This simply means that if x is unrelated to y, our expectation of x is $\bar{x}$, whatever the value of y. As correlation strengthens, the two regression lines draw closer, until they coincide when $r = +1$ or -1. (Note that since x is *not* controlled in census data, this discussion is in terms of a 'random x' model – which requires a bivariate Gaussian distribution – rather than a linear regression, 'fixed x' model.)

For the county data of figure 7.1, the two regressions are:

$$\text{Change (\%)} = 6.77 - 6.871 \log(\text{Density}) \quad \text{and}$$
$$\log(\text{Density}) = 0.59 - 0.05446 \text{ Change (\%)}$$

(The second equation is included for demonstration only.) The reciprocal gradient of the latter is –18.36, which is expressed in per cent population change per unit log (Density) and can be compared directly with the –6.871 gradient of the first regression. That is, the regression of x on y is 2.7 times as steep as that of y on x, in this example of moderate correlation. The two lines cross at the 'bivariate mean', ($\bar{x}$ = log density = 0.3518, Density = 2.25/ha, Change = 4.35 per cent); $r = -0.611$ and the standard deviation of y-residuals is 5.01 (compared with 6.28 for y regardless of x), while that of the x-residuals is 0.447 (compared with 0.56 for x).

To emphasize the importance of the scale of areal divisions used, similar regressions for 1971–81 population change and 1971 population density were performed for the 458 districts in Great Britain: r fell to –0.488, suggesting that diffusion of population was less marked at the district scale. The means of log (Density), and of Change were (0.578, 4.86 per cent) and standard deviations (0.73, 11.14 per cent). The main regression is slightly steeper than for counties, because variability in y (population change) has increased more than that in x:

$$\text{Change \%} = 9.18 - 7.463 \log (\text{Density}).$$

The other regression (included only for comparison) is:

$$\log(\text{Density}) = 0.734 - 0.03188 \text{ Change (\%)}.$$

This too is steeper, viewed in terms of the rate of change of population change with density.

All these regressions are unweighted, hence the means of x and y differ between counties and districts. They were produced by the MIDAS package. I am grateful to Helen Mounsey for providing the two data sets.

The non-coincidence of the predictions of x given y and of y given x is an inevitable result of the uncertainty produced by scatter in the data. It can be avoided only if we have another 'anchor point' through which the regression must pass, in adition to ($\bar{x}$, $\bar{y}$). For example, when relating height, length or weight, we often know that any relationship must also pass through the origin (0, 0); this fixes the regression line with the values $a = 0$ and $b = (\bar{y}/\bar{x})$. Of course, b is no longer a least-squares estimate, but in view of our knowledge of the situation this line must be an improvement over the least-squares fit.

Unfortunately, such supplementary knowledge is usually absent for census data, and we are left with two different regression lines. But this only serves to reinforce the point we have made throughout this section, that *regression is appropriate only if x and y differ in status;* one is a controlling variable (a 'cause', sometimes called a 'predictor', 'regressor' or an 'independent' variable) and the other is a dependent variable (an 'effect' or 'response'). If we cannot make such a distinction, we must use a different type of line to summarize the relationship between x and y.

7.4.4 'NEUTRAL LINES'

Suppose that x and y are related, but we do *not* consider one a 'cause' and one an 'effect'. For example, the 'proportion of old people' and the 'proportion of one-parent families' are spatially associated (especially within conurbations), but there is no obvious causal link either way. Many such situations occur in the geographical analysis of census data, and if we wish to summarize the general trend of the relationship in a *single* line some alternative to regression is required.

Obviously some compromise between the regression of y on x and that of x on y is appropriate. Since the gradient of the former involves r, and of the latter, $(1/r)$, a simple possibility is to remove r from the formula and take a line whose gradient is $\pm$(SD of y) / (SD of x), and which passes through $(\bar{x}, \bar{y})$; the gradient has the same sign as r. This is known as the *reduced major axis* (Kermack and Haldane 1950), and on the standardized plot of y' against x' its gradient is simply ± 1.0, regardless of the degree of scatter. This line is approximately the 'principal axis' of the standardized data, assuming that the scatter of points is roughly elliptical. A very clear account of this line was given by Freedman, Pisani and Purves (1978) in their introduction to the topic of regression: they called it 'the SD line'. More advanced points are discussed by Mark and Church (1977) and Jones (1979).

The reduced major axis is close to the line we would draw if asked to fit a line visually to the data – even though, viewed with the x-axis horizontal, the scatter of points places more points below the line at high values of x, and more above at low values of x. The same applies with the y-axis horizontal, as between high and low values of y: these two tendencies are balanced, so that any attempt to mitigate one imbalance will worsen the other. The reduced major axis minimizes residuals neither in y' nor in x', but it minimizes residuals at right angles to the fitted line – it is a neutral line, optimized for predicting neither y' from x' nor x' from y'. Clearly it is the most appropriate summary line if x and y have equal status as variables, if cause and effect cannot be distinguished and the relationship should be viewed as bilateral or symmetrical. Hence *it is the appropriate summary line for most relationships between census variables for geographical areas.*

7.4.5 'ROBUST' LINES

In common with regression lines, the reduced major axis is based upon squared deviations (these are involved in calculating standard deviations). Both are thus sensitive to outlying points, and require that the scatter of points be well-behaved, even and balanced around the line throughout its length. If the univariate distributions have been transformed to minimize skewness, and scatter plots have been inspected for isolated points, curvilinearity, and other problems discussed in section 7.3, then it may well be appropriate to apply sensitive techniques; they make the best use of all the information available. Otherwise, or if there are lingering doubts on any of these points, it is useful to apply rougher and more robust techniques as advocated by the Exploratory Data Analysis school (see section 4.7).

Attention has focused on techniques of regression (and correlation) which are robust to unusual data points. Some involve discarding points extreme in either x or y, but it is doubtful whether all of these are outliers; even more so, if all the points on the outer convex hull are in question. Alternatively, all points may be retained but less weight given to the larger deviations from a fitted line, by minimizing the sum not of their squares (power 2) but of some smaller power of the deviations, such as 1.5 or even 1.0 (Hogg 1974).

More recent robust methods start with a trial line (possibly the least-squares one) and then recalculate the line giving points a weight which initially increases with their deviation from the trial line, then flattens out, and finally perhaps declines to zero. This is discussed in several mathematical papers in Launer and Wilkinson (1979). Such iterative techniques have been very successful in detecting unreliable data, but they are fairly complex.

One very easily applied technique for robust regression is to split the data into three parts along the x-axis and calculate measures of central tendency in x and y for each part. These could be medians, mid-means or tri-means (see section 4.7). If the middle point of the three so defined is far from the line defined by the other two, a curvilinear relationship is suspected. Otherwise, a line with a gradient determined by the two outer points may be plotted, displaced one-third of the way to the middle point. Alternatively, a line with this gradient may be plotted to pass through an overall central point, determined by the same robust measures.

From the preceding discussion, however, we are more concerned with robust alternatives to the reduced major axis. These can be found simply by replacing the means and standard deviations by more robust versions; medians and interquartile ranges, or mid-means and mean absolute deviations. Many other possibilities exist based on use of the 'tool kit' of robust methods described in Chapter 4, but note that even 'robust' line-fitting is not safe unless accompanied by the inspection of scatter plots. For the data of figure 7.1, robust 'major axes' based on convex hulls gave gradients of –11.0 and –9.4. Regressions based on bivariate median points for thirds or halves gave –8.1 and –10.0. These compare with –11.235 for the reduced major axis, and –6.872 and –18.37 for the two regression lines.

A study of 'robustness' reveals that it is better to have a range of possible answers than a single, possibly wrong, answer – tempting though a single answer may seem. This is certainly relevant to applied work, since users are likely to place excessive faith in predictions from a single, precise equation; the uncertainties which statistics cannot eliminate must be emphasized.

7.4.6 RESIDUALS

It is common for residuals from the regression of *y* on *x* to be plotted against *x* (or against the prediction of *y*, which amounts to the same thing); any pattern, or unevenness of scatter, is thus made more evident (Mosteller and Tukey 1977). Unless scatter is very slight, the gain involved in such magnification and skewing of the scatter of points is rather small. For the degree of scatter found in most census data relationships, we can rest content with scatter plots; for multiple regressions (see section 7.5), however, residual plots are much more important in presenting the result of a many-dimensional relationship in two dimensions.

A spatial element can usefully be reinjected to the analysis by mapping the residuals from an aspatial relationship. Any non-randomness (especially clustering) in the spatial distribution of residuals suggests model inadequacy, and may prompt hypotheses concerning further variables to be incorporated, as discussed in most texts on quantitative geography (Taylor 1977, 204). Thomas (1968) gave the most thorough appraisal. The residual maps of most value are likely to be those from *multiple* regression. The next step is to plot these residuals on a graph, against the new predictors suggested from the maps. If there is any consistent trend, the predictors are included in a new multiple regression equation. Residuals from this are then plotted against each included variable in turn, and must have approximately the same scatter (variance) and zero mean at any value of a given predictor variable. The latter implies that the residuals show no trend – they must be unrelated, both linearly and curvilinearly, to each predictor variable included.

Finally we note, with Ferguson (1978, 31–2), that the error of any prediction made from a regression involves *more* than this residual scatter from the fitted line. Scatter is inherent, but our regression equation is only an estimate of the true relationship; it contains error in its *intercept* and error in its *gradient*, which makes extrapolation especially uncertain. To these we should add possible error due to our data set being *unrepresentative* of areas concerning which predictions are desired. Further errors in data for small populations arise from 10 per cent sampling, and from the addition of ± 1 or 0 to counts to increase the 'confidentiality' of data (see Chapter 2).

7.5 Multivariate analysis

Although it is necessary and convenient to consider bivariate relationships first, most of the more interesting and important relationships in census data are multivariate – they involve more than two variables, and are thus more difficult to represent graphically. Preliminary inspection of all relevant bivariate scatter plots permits us to avoid some errors in multivariate relationships yet, with many dimensions in the data, some outliers, nonlinearities, or variabilities in scatter may escape the most thorough set of bivariate scrutinies. This makes examination of residuals from any fitted model all the more important (Gnanadesikan 1977; Mosteller and Tukey 1977).

7.5.1 MULTIPLE REGRESSION

Regression is readily extended to include more than one predictor ('controlling' or 'explanatory' variable; the term 'independent' variable is avoided here because these variables are never independent of each other, in census or other observational data). Ferguson (1978) provided a fine introduction to multiple regression and the assumptions on which it is based, while Kendall (1975) and Mosteller and Tukey (1977) have given fuller but still practical accounts. In the two-predictor regression for 1971–81 county data

$$\text{Change (\%)} = 26.96 + 5.00 \log(\text{Area}) - 8.616 \log(\text{Population})$$

the first constant is the intercept, as before, the value of change when both logarithms are zero (that is, a population of one on an area of one hectare). The other two numbers are *partial regression coefficients*, meaning the effect of one predictor when the other is held constant (or more realistically, the effect of one predictor averaged over all observed values of the other predictor).

Note that it remains necessary in multiple regression to select one variable which differs logically from the others, and is treated as dependent upon them; all regression relations are directed, not symmetrical. Multiple regression has all the problems of simple regression (for example, in comparing results between data sets with different overall means), plus a few more. The conventional least-squares estimators are appropriate and accurate only if:

a the effects of predictor variables are additive; that is, their effects on the dependent variable are independent of each other. For example, the effect of a unit increase in log (Population) should be the same whatever the value of Area – as the equation above implies. (These effects would certainly *not* be additive had a logarithmic transformation not been applied.) Otherwise, the required prediction surface would be curved, and the plane described by our equation would be just a rough approximation to it;

b the predictor variables are mutually uncorrelated. Although we must expect some degree of intercorrelation, the greater this is, the greater the error margin on each partial regression coefficient (Ferguson 1978, 32); the effect of one predictor is easily traded off against that of a correlated predictor. Hence we always inspect the matrix of correlations between all variables in a multiple regression;

c all variables with important effects on the dependent variable are included. If an omitted variable is correlated with any of the predictors, their partial regression coefficients will be changed to incorporate part of its hidden effect, giving a 'specification error';

d each predictor covers much of its range for various different values of each of the others – otherwise, we are extrapolating. In any case, the standard error of the partial regression coefficient is inversely proportional to the standard deviation of the predictor involved.

These conditions are additional to the need for:

e linearity in the relationships;

f homogeneous residual scatter; and

g independence of residuals from each other

as noted above for the bivariate case.

Since, for census data, we are not *controlling* the predictor variables, these are viewed as random variables and application of multiple regression depends on their distribution being multivariate Gaussian. We still rely upon the univariate methods of transforming each variable individually (Chapter 4), and on scrutiny of numerous scatter plots; but as noted above, this may not suffice. It is difficult even to check whether the multivariate Gaussian has been approximated. This reduces confidence in any model which does not fit the data very closely. 'In practice, a single overall multivariate analysis of data is seldom sufficient or adequate by itself, and almost always it needs to be augmented by analyses of subsets of the responses, including univariate analyses of each of the original variables' (Gnanadesikan 1977, 162-3).

Often we have many possible predictors, and wish to choose a manageable subset which gives the 'best' predictions for a given number of variables. This is easy if the predictors are nearly independent of each other, but quite different equations can give the same degree of fit if the predictors are moderately intercorrelated. The statistical problems are grossly oversimplified in textbooks for geographers and earth scientists, except in Mather (1976). Recently Thompson (1978) has provided a rigidly statistical view of the selection of predictors, while Hocking (1976) took an approach more oriented toward applications. 'Ridge regression', advocated by Mather and Hocking but not by Thompson, demonstrates the instability of partial regression coefficients in this situation, and may suggest a suitable compromise set of coefficients. Although the ridge regression technique is 'messy', it seems appropriate to the 'messiness' of real data.

The application of least squares can produce some very poor results, especially when two intercorrelated predictors have strong positive and negative effects on the dependent variable. It is desirable also that the combination of variables selected should be causally interpretable, and not contain logical overlaps. (Hence we did *not* add log (Population) as a second predictor in the regression of population change on population density.) This rules out any purely statistical optimization procedure (except for exploration).

Large and heterogeneous sets of variables should not be submitted to stepwise regression programs; more initial thought is required. Subsets of variables should then be chosen carefully. Some package programs (such as MIDAS) permit classification of variables into a mandatory set, included in all regressions, and an optional set, to be included or excluded on statistical grounds.

As in the application of curvilinear regression, addition of further terms to an equation cannot *reduce* its degree of fit: we are concerned with whether the improvement in fit is sufficient to justify the more complicated regression model. Usually this is judged in terms of R^2, the square of the correlation between observed values of the dependent variable and those predicted by the regression equation. Both Hocking (1976) and Thompson (1978) prefer to incorporate the number of predictors (p) in the given equation, the overall number of candidate predictor variables considered (k), and the number of cases (or, in census data, areal divisions) observed (n), in the criterion

$$C_p = [(n-k-1)(1-R^2_p)/(1-R^2_k)] + 2p - n$$

which is to be minimized. This usually leads to more variables being included than when the flattening of a plot R^2_p against p is taken as the guide. The difference will be slight if the number of cases, n, *greatly* exceeds the number of variables, k – which is in any case highly desirable.

Note that most significance tests (e.g. the variance ratio test) which have been applied in multiple regression are biased, through their failure to take account of the large number of combinations of predictors which are being assessed, and of the sequential and non-independent nature of most predictor selection procedures. As in the case of simple regression, R^2 has been over-emphasized as a measure of equation value or success. The standard deviation of the residuals should always be given, so that the accuracy of prediction can be assessed in units of y and not just in relative terms.

7.5.2 PRINCIPAL COMPONENT ANALYSIS

It follows from the discussion in sections 7.4.3 and 7.4.4 that *multiple regression will only rarely be truly applicable to census data*, because of the conceptual difficulty of identifying a dependent variable – quite apart from the technical difficulties just noted. Interdependence of sets of variables requires different techniques. It also makes procedures for condensing many, correlated dimensions into few, uncorrelated dimensions highly attractive. If the data are quantitative, and *can be transformed to approximate the multivariate Gaussian distribution*, principal components analysis (PCA) is outstanding among the techniques available. Compared to the alternatives, it is also much more efficient in computation.

Principal components analysis can be viewed as the extension to many dimensions of the two-dimensional reduced major axis technique. It provides a set of linear combinations of the original variables. These are known as components; the first component encompasses as much variation as possible, by following the principal axis of the multivariate data distribution. It provides a new scale, exactly specified as a linear combination of the scales of the original variables; by taking account of the intercorrelation of these variables, it expresses as much of the information contained in the original data as any single dimension possibly can. The second component encompasses as much of the remaining variation as possible; and so on, subject to the constraint that all axes are at right angles to each other.

Principal components analysis is a straightforward mathematical technique, involving subjective decisions only about definition of places, study area and the set of variables to be analysed – these decisions are inevitable – plus a choice between standardized analysis (based, in effect, on the correlation matrix) and unstandardized analysis in which the units and variances of the original variables are retained, by analysing the covariance matrix. Applications of the latter have been the more successful (e.g. in paleoecology and in climatology), but applicable only if each variable is in the same units: hence analyses of standardized variables have been much more frequent (Chatfield and Collins 1980).

The first principal component is readily interpretable as the common element in a set of intercorrelated variables. Second and subsequent components are leftovers whose interpretation is less natural, hence principal component analysis works best for sets of variables which have only one major component. The analysis should be repeated, excluding variables which are not strongly related to this dominant component.

Space prevents consideration here of techniques, such as principal coordinate analysis, which may be regarded as 'more robust' alternatives to principal component analysis. Kruskal and Wish (1978) have provided a good introduction to 'multidimensional scaling' which defines a given number of dimensions so as to portray as accurately as possible the proximities of a set of cases. This may be regarded as the most general solution to the portrayal of multivariate data sets in fewer dimensions, because the proximities (dissimilarities) of the cases may be defined in many different ways. Mather (1976) has made a useful comparison of this and related techniques.

7.5.3 FACTOR ANALYSIS

When several dimensions are important for the expression of their data, many census analysts, geographers and sociologists have succumbed to the temptation of using a controversial technique known as factor analysis. Its popularity (see summaries in Taylor 1977, chapter 5; Johnston 1978) stems from its appearance of compressing a large body of data into relatively few dimensions, by the application of sophisticated mathematics. Two basic differences from principal component analysis are that factor analysis

i presupposes knowledge of the number of dimensions required; and
ii explicitly recognizes the presence of error, so that the basic dimensions cannot incorporate all the variability observed.

Factor analysis is therefore a *statistical* technique, whereas PCA is a purely mathematical one. One consequence is that the relation between the observations and the basic dimensions can only be estimated, and the 'factor scores' which express this are poorly determined; indeed, they fail to fulfil the basic function of making each dimension linearly uncorrelated with the others.

Factor analysis cannot be recommended because its model is underdetermined. It leaves open an infinite number of solutions (Ehrenberg 1975) from which an investigator can subjectively choose that which best suits his preconceptions. Hence it is unpopular with statisticians, who need 'to know about the method if only to advise against its use in inappropriate situations' (Chatfield and Collins 1980, 53).

7.5.4 CORRELATION STRUCTURES

As applied to census data, factor analysis is a subjective but quantitative technique, used to express the groupings of variables in terms of their correlations. That is, it supposedly simplifies correlation structures. The technical and conceptual difficulties involved can be avoided by resort to a graphical technique which attempts to portray correlation by proximity and linkage in a two-dimensional diagram. Each variable is represented by a circle or box positioned close to those variables with which it is most strongly correlated, positively or negatively (figures 7.11 and 7.12). With more than three variables, proximity cannot be exactly related to correlation (more than two dimensions would be required), so compromises are involved: this is subjective, but the subjectivity (and its effects) are more clearly evident than with factor analysis. Since the two-dimensional space will thus be distorted, a second graphical technique is employed to show correlations, rather broadly grouped; thickness of line is varied with strength of correlation.

Figures 7.11 and 7.12 show the relationships between thirty-one selected variables (ratios) for 1 km and 64 km squares respectively, for the whole of Great Britain in 1971. The positioning takes some account of correlations 0.1 weaker than those actually shown. Both diagrams show groupings for:

1 Household *space* and major tenures (that this is the strongest grouping in both cases is due in part to overlapping definitions and the closure effect);
2 *Deprivation* – 'unskilled', 'unemployed', 'sick', 'lacking a car' and 'travelling to work by bus';

3 *Immigrants*;
4 *Age* and household size.

It is particularly striking that housing problems, age and crowding do not relate to the main deprivation variables at either scale, and nor do immigrants.

The main differences are:

i the general level of correlation is stronger at 64 km; the scale of class limits for r has been shifted by 0.1 to allow for this. The numerous 1 km squares show different relations in urban and rural areas, and in different regions, and correlations are probably weakened by mixing these together;

ii at 64 km (regional) scale, there is a group (5) of *Industry*, since 'manufacturing', 'foremen and skilled workers', and (lack of) 'managers' intercorrelate much more strongly than at local scale. 'Furnished private-rented accommodation' correlates with these rather than with Immigrants, and sex ratio correlates with these more than with Age. 'Miners' also is close to this group;

iii population density correlates with Deprivation at 1 km scale, but only with Immigrants at 64 km scale. It is indeed logical to think of crude density as crowding and hence deprivation at local scale, whereas at regional scale it simply implies the congestion of metropolitan areas, associated with a broader range of services and job opportunities;

iv the Age and household size variables, contrary to the general trend, are somewhat less intercorrelated at 64 km scale. Age and family stage segregation is characteristically between different parts of an urban area, rather than between regions;

v poor housing (lack of 'exclusive use of all amenities') is more strongly associated with unfurnished private renting and with one-person households at the 1 km level. As in (*iv*), these associations are found within cities, rather than between cities;

vi council-rented accommodation is associated with deprived regions rather than deprived neighbourhoods.

I maintain that this graphical portrayal of all strong correlations is more revealing than any correlation-based factor analysis, partly because it remains closer to the data. The clarity of definition and isolation of groupings of variables is more evident, and variables outside these groupings can nevertheless be placed so as to show their main relationships. Correlations between groupings are not obscured or 'swept under the carpet', and variables can be positioned on the side of a group which is appropriate to their correlations beyond the group: in particular, variables which are intermediate between groups can be clearly portrayed (for example, SHARE and MANAG at 64 km, NOCAR at 1 km). Production of such diagrams requires several iterations and some hours of thought about the relative positions of variables, at the end of which a researcher has perforce considerable familiarity with the correlation structure in all its rich detail. This is indeed a graphical alternative

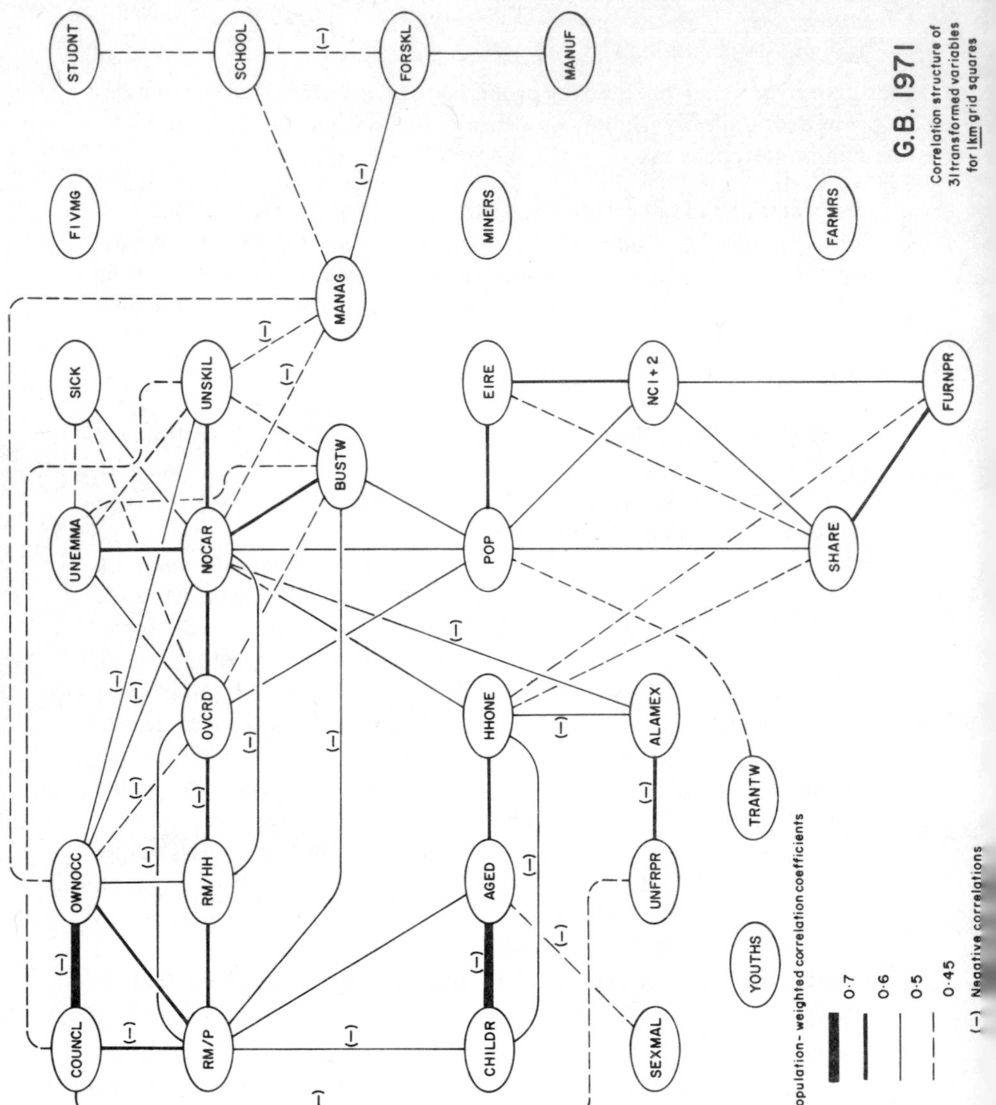

Figure 7.11
Correlation structure diagram (1 km)

The strengths of population-weighted correlations between thirty-one transformed variables are represented by thicknesses of lines and, as far as possible, by relative proximity. The data, for 1 km squares of the National Grid, come from the 1971 population census and all squares in Great Britain are included, except those for which data are not released because of the small numbers of people or households. The variables are defined in table 7.2.

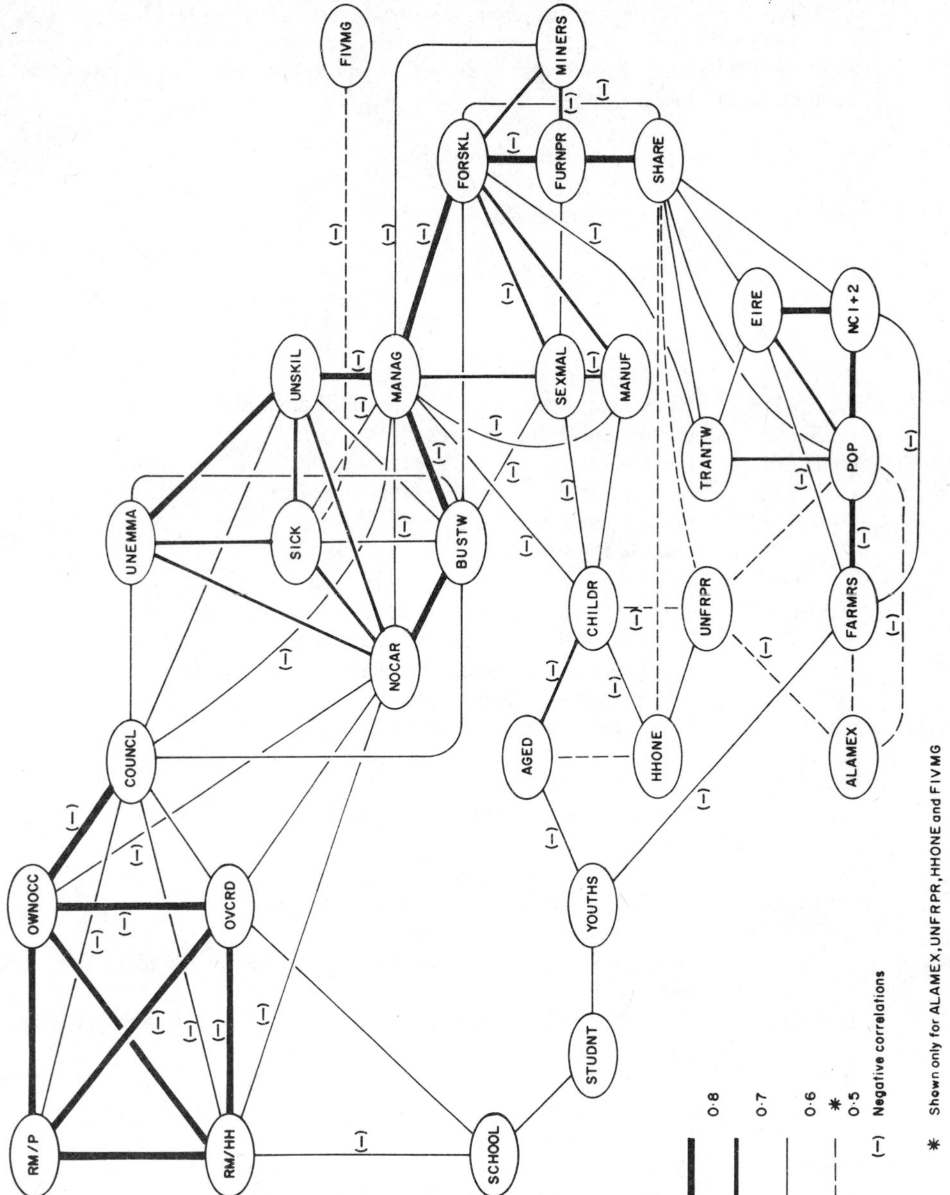

Figure 7.12

Correlation structure diagram (64 km)

As for figure 7.11, except for 64 × 64 km squares covering all of Great Britain, again excluding data suppressed for confidentiality.

Table 7.2 Definition of abbreviations used in figures 7.11 and 7.12

POP, RM/HH and RM/P are open ratios: all others are closed ratios, with denominators as follows:

*	as % of total population present
×	as % of present residents
+	as % of private households
□	as % of those employed
◊	as % of those in stated civilian employment

AGED	Persons aged 65 and over *
ALAMEX	Households with exclusive use of all amenities +
BUSTW	Persons travelling to work by bus □
CHILDR	Persons aged 0–14 years inclusive *
COUNCL	Households in accommodation rented from local authorities and new town corporations +
EIRE	Born in the Republic of Ireland ×
FARMRS	Employed in agriculture, forestry and fishing □
FIVMG	Persons having changed address in last five years *
FORSKL	Foremen and skilled manual workers (SEG 8 and 9) ◊
FURNPR	Households in furnished, privately-rented accommodation +
HHONE	One-person households +
MANAG	Employers and managers (SEG 1, 2 and 13) ◊
MANUF	Workers employed in manufacturing □
MINERS	Workers employed in mining □
NC1+2	Both parents, or one parent and self born in the New Commonwealth ×
NOCAR	Households with no car +
OVCRD	Households with over 1.5 persons per room +
OWNOCC	Owner-occupied households +
POP	Total population present (in the grid square; i.e. population density, except for coastal effects)
RM/HH	(Number of rooms in private households)/(Number of private households)
RM/P	(Number of rooms)/(Number of persons), both in private households
SCHOOL	Employed persons with ONC, HSC or 'A' level □
SEXMAL	Sex ratio: Number of males *
SHARE	Households in shared dwellings +
SICK	Number of sick, as % of economically active persons
STUDNT	Students aged 15 or over, as % of persons in private households
TRANTW	Persons travelling to work by train □
UNEMMA	Unemployed males (seeking work), as % of economically active males
UNFRPR	Households in unfurnished, privately-rented accommodation +
UNSKIL	Unskilled manual workers (SEG 11) ◊
YOUTHS	Persons aged 15 to 24 years inclusive *

to factor analysis as it has been applied to census data, yet it is conceptually simpler, easier to communicate, and no more subjective.

Further interpretation of such structures can be in terms of partial correlations; these too have advantages over factor analysis, as Meyer (1971) has shown. Pringle (1980) has provided a recent summary of the Simon-Blalock approach which, in favourable circumstances, may permit cause and effect inferences to be made on the basis of correlations; at least, it can distinguish between direct and indirect associations. The ambitious can proceed to the development of structural equation models (Duncan 1975). These are not without assumptions and pitfalls, but they do promise more fruitful interpretations than does factor analysis. We are still left with a basic problem in interpreting relations between census variables for geographic areas; that of distinguishing the individual from the spatial contributions to an observed association.

7.6 Conclusion and recommendations

7.6.1 CONCLUSION

Census data for geographic areas are far removed from measurements in laboratory experiments, and the analytical techniques which they require are different. *Scatter plots* are essential for assessment of the complexity anticipated. Even after transformation, *regression* techniques are inappropriate unless a 'dependent' variable can be clearly distinguished from one or more 'controlling' (predictor) variables: neutral lines describing *functional relationships* may then be more relevant to geographic hypotheses. *Correlation structure diagrams* are fundamental to multivariate analyses; factor and principal component analyses essentially manipulate these structures so as to replace correlated variables with a smaller number of uncorrelated dimensions, interpreted as compounds of the original variables. Yet the use of these analyses is fraught with danger and usually complicates rather than simplifies the interpretation of relationships.

The availability of package programs has tempted many to use sophisticated multivariate techniques to which neither their data, their experience, nor sometimes even their hypotheses were appropriate. Non-technical users of interpretations based on factor or principal component analyses are well advised to regard the results with considerable suspicion: that they are intuitively reasonable is no necessary guide to whether they are correct or meaningful. A variety of technical considerations and subjective choices may influence the results. Extremely important and useful results can be obtained from the study of relationships between census variables, but future work needs to have more respect for the data and to be based on a scientifically more open-minded attitude, so that it no longer simply 'proves' the obvious (or whatever the researcher set out to prove). Progress may be made slowly but steadily by the cautious and critical use of a range of techniques, starting with simple univariate analyses and keeping in touch with the data by extensive use of graphics.

7.6.2 RECOMMENDATIONS

Complexities of data and of method and the many (often unperceived) choices involved dictate that the census user must exercise considerable care when analysing multiple relationships. It is recommended that he or she should:

- i define the boundary of the study area, to be relevant to the problems under investigation;
- ii obtain data for the smallest possible areal divisions (e.g. EDs);
- iii aggregate these to a well-balanced set of divisions, either arbitrary (and numerous), or meaningful to the problems under investigation;
- iv choose variables of substantive interest, and write down a justification for this;
- v edit the data thoroughly;
- vi on the basis of univariate analyses (Chapter 4) choose transformations which provide scales convenient for further analysis;
- vii check scatter plots for all pairs of transformed variables;
- viii summarize relationships by least-squares regression only *if* one variable is clearly dependent; otherwise, by reduced major axes;
- ix weight by population per areal division when calculating Pearson product-moment correlation coefficients, r, for percentage and ratio variables;
- x measure error not by $(1 - r)$, but by the residual SD in y;
- xi consider the use of D for counted data in place of r, especially for closed data sets;
- xii present the important relationships (measured by r or D) of a set of variables in terms of a correlation structure diagram;
- xiii proceed *very* cautiously into multivariate analysis and use only techniques whose assumptions you thoroughly understand;
- xiv do not use factor analysis unless you have explored all alternatives and are ready to defend the subjectively-produced results against the many fierce critics of this technique;
- xv use principal component analysis only if you (a) are interested only in reducing the number of dimensions handled in further analysis or presentation, or (b) use only the *first* principal component of each grouping of variables, having defined the latter by exploratory analysis such as (xii). Relate compound dimensions to the original variables as simply as possible;
- xvi consider the applicability of partial correlation and causal modelling.

8 Multivariate analysis of census data: the classification of areas

STAN OPENSHAW

8.1 Too much data?

It is obvious from Chapter 2 that the census provides details of a very large number of socioeconomic and demographic variables which are reported for a number of standard areas. For example, the 1981 Small Area Statistics (SAS) provide for Tyne and Wear County details of approximately 4300 variables for each of 2529 enumeration districts (EDs), an unknown number of populated 100 m squares (if available), about 865 populated 1 km squares, 120 district electoral wards, and 5 local-government districts. This reflects the multi-purpose nature of the census with the consequent need for large numbers of variables and a range of geographic units in order to provide adequate coverage of the important features of households and people. In practice, though, it also means that census analysis invariably becomes an exercise in applied multivariate analysis (see Chapter 7). Quite simply there is far too much information to allow policy-makers, planners, geographers, politicians, schoolchildren, and others interested in census data for a particular area to be able to identify easily patterns of characteristics or features of interest from SAS data without processing and condensing it in some way.

Particular difficulties are caused by the large number of geographic units that are often involved when census data are studied at the ED or 100 metre level for even a single local-authority district. This problem can be reduced by studying data only for the larger geographic units, for example, wards or 1 km squares. However, for many purposes these units are too large and of too great a mixture of characteristics to be useful for intra-area studies of, say, a city. Indeed, it is often localized spatial variations in census variables that are of most interest and these are most clearly identified by studying data for the smallest possible census areas. As a result, many studies of census SAS will start with a large number of variables for a large number of areas. We have seen in Chapter 7 how a large number of variables can sometimes be reduced without great loss of information. Here we seek methods of compressing the data by reducing an initially large number of areas through identifying a number of different types of areas.

Another reason for wishing to reduce the initial number of census areas within a study region is to identify 'new' and hopefully more meaningful areas for purposes of comparative study. As was pointed out in section 2.5, there is nothing sacred, inevitable or (sometimes) even meaningful about the areas used by OPCS to report census data. Moreover, the standard areas are not comparable units except in the narrowest sense; for example, EDs have population totals within a specified but broad range, while 1 km squares are all of 1 km^2 in area. Certainly, none of the standard census areas such as wards are homogeneous in terms of socioeconomic and demographic variables. In addition, some of the smaller areas are not even consistently defined across the country: this applies to postcode sectors and particularly to EDs where there was a variable degree of local government participation in their planning. So, if the purpose of analysing census data is to compare how a standard set of census areas score on a particular variable such as some indicator of deprivation, then it should be appreciated that the results depend on the areas being used. EDs are not comparable entities because their degree of internal homogeneity varies tremendously and this affects the results. Hence, before applying sophisticated techniques to census data, it would be advisable to consider carefully the meaningfulness of the geographic units being studied, the definitions of which are arbitrary and modifiable – and yet on which depend the results (see Openshaw 1977, 1978a, 1978b). The problem of what effects such areal units have on analysis is not easy to define (Openshaw and Taylor 1979, 1981; and Openshaw 1981). One possibility is to decide what constitutes a meaningful set of units (Coombes *et al.* 1978). Another approach would be to consider using EDs as building blocks by aggregating the ED data for a particular study area in order to obtain a new set of geographic units which are comparable because they possess a similar degree of homogeneity in terms of a selection of variables. In the absence of data for areas smaller than EDs, this implies that no such user-defined, aggregate, 'comparable areas' can be smaller than, on average, two or three EDs in size.

8.2 A solution: cluster analysis

A family of computer techniques known as cluster analysis can be used both to meet the need for data compression and in an attempt to solve the comparable area problems. Such methods have already been used to analyse the 1971 census statistics. The large number of applications of the four 1971 national census classifications (Webber and Craig 1976, 1978; Webber, 1977, 1978a, 1978b) demonstrate the success of these methods as a means of simplifying multivariate census data by presenting the results in a simple form that non-technical people can readily understand. These classifications provide a summary of 1971 census data for the entire country. For example, the ED classification reduces the 120,000 or so 1971 EDs to sixty groups. These groups have been assigned 'names' based on their census characteristics and have been used for a variety of purposes, such as the definition of urban problem areas and of marketing areas. The classification has been 'updated' to relate to 1978 and is now being marketed commercially (*Computer Talk*, 9 July 1980).

Despite the success of the national classifications and the tremendous potential offered by cluster analysis techniques, it is important to appreciate that there is nothing magic about classification methods. They provide a tool which can be used or misused with ease. There is ample evidence in the past to indicate that it is easier to misuse it than to use it sensibly. The national classifications have themselves been grossly misused by all manner of people (such as Sotto and Donnison 1980). In addition, they have been criticized on technical grounds (Openshaw *et al.* 1980; Webber 1980). This unhappy situation may arise because there are few available sources of practical advice on how best to use cluster analysis, or even which methods to use. The standard texts, such as those by Sokal and Sneath (1973) and Everitt (1974) are surprisingly vague on practical advice whilst the interested user is faced with a large number of different methods which could be used to classify census data. For example, the most widely available program package for cluster analysis is Clustan 1C: this offers the user a choice of no less that seventy-four different methods. The advice generally offered to the uninitiated is basically to try several methods and to compare the results: if they are consistent, all should be well! At first sight this appears plausible, until it is realized that the comparison of different classifications of the same data is not straightforward; Openshaw (1980) has, however, provided details of one algorithm to make such comparisons.

There is also a danger that the apparent objectivity of a numerical classification method performed on a computer may give the results a degree of implicit validity they do not deserve, especially to non-scientists. What is meant by objectivity in the scientific sense is merely that the results can be replicated if *exactly* the same method is used on *exactly* the same data and *exactly* the same operational decisions are made during its application. Openshaw and Gillard (1978) have demonstrated the highly sensitive nature of some classifications of census data when slight changes are made in the application of a particular method. Replication *is* a useful quality but computers can replicate 'poor' classifications just as easily as 'good' classifications. *A classification can only be deemed 'good' or 'poor' when it has been evaluated in terms of the specific purpose for which it is required; there is no magic universal statistical test that can be applied nor is there any possibility of deriving a classification suitable for all purposes.* Evaluation is thus a subjective intuitive process but it should always be attempted. The fact that results appear plausible is, in itself, insufficient to validate a classification.

The aim of this chapter is to describe how to apply classification methods, specifically cluster analysis, to census data, in particular, to the Small Area

Statistics (see section 2.9). It attempts to provide the kind of practical advice that is otherwise lacking and describes a method for classifying census data for any set of areas like the counties or districts in England and Wales or the regions and districts in Scotland or all of the EDs within a county or district. Finally, an attempt is made to dispel some of the mystique that surrounds cluster analysis in order to expose both its weaknesses and its strengths.

8.3 What is cluster analysis?

The general aim of cluster analysis is to reduce a large number of census areas (EDs, wards, squares) to a far smaller number of groups or clusters, each being composed of one or more of the original areas. Areas are included in the same group because their characteristics are judged to be similar. For example, a data set consisting of 2529 EDs in Tyne and Wear County with forty variables calculated from SAS might be reduced to a set of thirty-four groups – a seventy-four-fold reduction in the number of areas. The user would then try to conjure up a name or label for each group to summarize the common characteristics of its members. A map of these groups could then be used to provide an easily understood summary of the SAS data for Tyne and Wear County. Areas with similar characteristics would be mapped in the same colour or with the same symbol (Chapter 6). Of course, in practice, it is unlikely that the members of any group would have identical characteristics but they could reasonably be expected to have broad similarities in terms of the variables being used.

8.4 Constraints imposed by the data

At this point it is necessary to digress a little and consider some aspects of SAS data that have a particularly important effect on the results of a cluster analysis. Our aim is to identify homogeneous groups but this is strictly impossible with census data because the census areas are not in any case homogeneous, the degree of heterogeneity reflecting the type of area, size, and the variables being studied. This causes some special problems to the interpretation of cluster analysis of census data.

The mixed characteristics of many census areas are an inevitable result of OPCS aggregating data for individuals to arbitrary geographic units in order to preserve confidentiality. The characteristics of these census areas depend on the spatial association of the characteristics of individual people and households and thus on the precise location of the geographical boundaries. Data aggregation has the effect of mixing up data patterns which are separate at the individual level. Consider, as an illustration, a simple hypothetical but not unrealistic example. Figure 8.1 shows the distribution of tenure types in a study region. If this region were divided into two parts (say EDs) along the line

Figure 8.1 An example of census area heterogeneity

```
                         d

      c  c  c  c  c  c  c  c  c  c
      c  c  o  o  c  c  c  c  c  c
b                                          b
      o  o  o  o  o  o  o  o  o  o
      o  o  o  o  o  o  o  o  o  o

                         d
```

Notes: c stands for council house
o stands for owner occupier
the horizontal line b to b and the vertical line d to d represent alternative ways of dividing up the area with vastly different results

b–b, then one zone would be 100 per cent council tenants and the other 0 per cent. On the other hand, if the division d–d were used, then both the right hand and the left hand zones would be 50 per cent council tenants. For different variables, clearly these two divisions would yield quite different results.

As a result, the patterns which exist in census data are of two types. Some exist at the individual level and have to some extent survived the aggregation process. Others do not exist at the individual level but have been created by the aggregation process. Both types exist in SAS data. If cluster analysis is to be useful, then, it must be able to penetrate this fog, ignore weak patterns, and amplify strong ones. One important example of artefacts of the aggregation process is the so-called ecological fallacy problem. This can best be described by an example: table 8.1 lists some hypothetical individual census data or microdata of the type that OPCS do not yet release (see Chapter 11). After aggregation to one ED, the resulting data suggest that the resulting ED is characterized by high unemployment, few cars, few baths, and unfurnished rented accommodation – yet no one household experiences all these characteristics. It is important to note, therefore, that a classification of places or areas – inevitable with existing census data – need not necessarily adequately represent the characteristics of the *people* who actually live there (Openshaw and Cullingford 1979). Sadly, with present British census data there is at the moment no way of knowing whether a classification of the same data at the individual level would produce broadly the same results. It is possible, indeed likely, that *some* groups in both classifications will be very different.

More generally, these problems of heterogeneous geographic units and the prospect of massive ecological fallacies are common to much census analysis. It is obvious that they may be reduced – but not eliminated – by concentrating on the analysis of EDs. The basic procedure of cluster analysis is purposefully

Table 8.1 Hypothetical data for households within an ED

household number	*unemployed head*	*own a car*	*own a bath*	*accommodation unfurnished*
1	no	no	no	yes
2	no	no	no	yes
3	no	no	yes	no
4	no	no	no	yes
5	no	no	yes	yes
6	yes	yes	yes	yes
7	yes	no	no	no
8	yes	yes	no	yes
9	yes	no	no	yes
10	yes	no	yes	yes
	50%	20%	30%	80%

to reaggregate data which have already been aggregated at least once before. As such, it may therefore increase the significance of both these problems.

8.5 Which method?

Two important factors influence the choice of a method for classifying census data for areas. The first concerns the nature of the groups that are required – do all the members of a group have to be geographically contiguous or not? The second concerns the computational and taxonomic efficiency of alternative clustering methods.

If the purpose is to identify groups composed of contiguous geographic units so that they form a zoning system, say of EDs to form traffic zones, then it is necessary to incorporate a contiguity restriction into the clustering process. That is, the members of each group must be both relatively similar to each other *and* adjacent when displayed on a map. Geographers call this type of classification a regionalization. Such an approach has certain computational and practical advantages. The former relate to the tremendously increased efficiency of a standard agglomerative clustering algorithm once a contiguity constraint is introduced, provided the program makes full use of this restriction. An efficient program for classifying non-interaction ('flow') data is described in Openshaw (1974), and a version for interaction data is listed in Dixon and Openshaw (1979). The practical advantages relate mainly to the ability of such a regionalization program to handle several thousand geographic units; also to the utility of the resulting regions for certain planning purposes: for instance, the member areas of a region are all next to each other on a map, so that the resulting policy zone is extremely convenient. It is noted that the necessary contiguity lists can be generated by computer as a by-product of a Thiessen polygon program (Green and Sibson 1978) or, even simpler, from area boundaries coded with left- and right-hand codes.

The disadvantages of a regionalization approach relate mainly to the taxonomic inefficiency resulting from the operation of the contiguity constraint. Furthermore, it is usually necessary to operate a two-stage classification process: first to identify a set of regions with a contiguity constraint in operation and, second, to classify the regions into groups without a contiguity constraint. The second stage is needed to identify groups of regions which have similar characteristics but are not contiguous (Openshaw 1976).

The alternative approach is simply the reverse of this two-stage regionalization-classification strategy, i.e. start with the classification without the contiguity constraint, and then convert the preferred classification into a set of contiguous regions. The latter stage is, of course, optional and may even be unnecessary for many purposes. Nevertheless, this use of a non-contiguity constrained method has the advantage of yielding a better classification, albeit at the cost of more computer time if a standard agglomerative method (starting from individual areas and building these up into groups (see Everitt 1974) is used. Indeed, this may not be possible except for the smallest of districts since the computer time required by an agglomerative method usually increases with the square of the number of areas being classified. Thus the cost of classifying 100 areas is four times that of fifty areas. Specifically, with the Clustan 1C program, the error sum of squares method becomes very expensive, even on a powerful computer, for more than about 300 cases. An alternative possibility is to use a fast single linkage method which can cope with large data sets, such as that of Sibson (1973). This method has some attractive theoretical properties; in particular, it does not impose a pre-determined structure on the data. Unfortunately, the results are often useless due to a problem known as chaining.

Perhaps the safest strategy to use with large data sets (between 300 and 10,000 areas) is some kind of iterative relocation procedure. In the Clustan 1C package the method RELOCATE could be used to improve iteratively a classification with a fixed number of groups. A starting classification could be generated by randomly assigning cases to a fixed number of groups. The iterative algorithm would then seek to change the classification so as to optimize approximately some function, for example, the error sum of squares or within-group sum of squares. With this method, computer run times are a linear function of the number of cases, the number of variables, and the number of iterations needed before there is convergence and a stable classification obtained and, as such, is a considerable computational and taxonomic improvement over the conventional agglomerative methods. A version of this method capable of classifying several thousand cases is described later; the equivalent method in Clustan 1C has a limit of 999 cases.

An iterative relocation classification strategy is recommended for census data because of the practical requirement to classify up to about 10,000 cases; for example, all the EDs in London or in the Northern Region. However, the use of an iterative relocation approach means that no dendrograms are produced. We take this as a positive advantage, partly because the hierarchical data structure displayed via a dendrogram is likely to be spurious due to the well-known inefficiencies of the agglomerative methods that produce it, and partly because dendrograms for large data sets are often unmanageable. In general terms, all our experience suggests that an iterative relocation procedure is more likely to provide 'better results' than standard, aggregative methods.

8.6 A standard recipe for classifying areas

Experience also suggests that a standard formula for classifying areas can be defined, although we emphasize again that classification is by no means a fully automatic process – you cannot simply put census data in at one end, turn a handle, and expect to gather results which are both reasonable and meaningful at the other. The human mind is still far better than the computer at deciding which patterns exist in census data that are sensible and which ones are absurd, although of course humans cannot rival the computer's ability to identify and produce plausible patterns for evaluation. The following 'rule of thumb' recipe is presented as a guide for those embarking on the classification of census areas.

8.6.1 STEP 1: WHAT IS THE PURPOSE OF THE CLASSIFICATION?

This is always a difficult question to answer in sufficient detail to guide the subsequent classification process. If the purpose is that of data description, then this will determine the choice of variables in step 2. If the purpose is more specific and, say, is to identify poor housing areas, then again this will determine the variables that would be required. However, in both cases there is obviously no unique and 'correct' single set of variables to use. Different people will use different variables for the same purpose, based upon experience of local conditions and/or intuition.

It is frankly doubtful whether satisfactory general purpose classifications can be devised. Whilst it is possible that a classification exercise concerned with data description *could* identify areas of poor housing, the precision and the clarity of the definitions would almost certainly be far poorer than if a specific 'poor housing' classification had been carried out. Clearly, 'purpose' is also important during the evaluation stage.

As far as policy-related work is concerned, cluster analysis is very much a preliminary data analysis stage which precedes policy formulation. Policy requirements would, or should, determine the choice of variables and condition the interpretation of the results. Cluster analysis is an exploratory technique best suited to data description; yet the results may themselves suggest policies or be useful for testing alternatives. In practice, definition of policy requirements, analysis and policy formulation tend to be interacting and the whole process to be iterative, so it is important not to overlook the unique data-summarizing potential. After all, to be able to show politicians and members of the public a single map, suitably coloured, that summarizes the general 'state' of a county or district or town at the time of the last census is itself a remarkable achievement. It amounts to no more than pure description but, for a while at least, could provide a basis for policy formulation and resource allocation in the broadest sense.

8.6.2 STEP 2: CHOOSE VARIABLES AND CENSUS AREAS

Obviously the choice of variables and of census areas reflects the purpose of the classification. In deciding which areas to classify, you should also bear in mind the previous discussion about data heterogeneity. For many purposes, ED-level analysis will be best. The variables used will normally be formulated as indicators of various socioeconomic conditions and will probably be expressed as rates, ratios, or percentages. It is best not to mix measurement scales and to be careful about possible closed number set problems with ratio data (see Chapter 7). If in doubt about how to define useful indicator variables, then look at those used in previous studies, such as Webber (1977), Rhind *et al.* (1977) and Hakim (1978a), and select an appropriate subset. Generally, the fewer the variables the better. Avoid large numbers of highly interrelated variables and try to obtain a representative selection that satisfy a given specific purpose.

The results depend on the decisions made here. It is not at all satisfactory to 'bung in any old set of data'. However, you should be prepared to revise the initial choice of variables once a preliminary classification has been interpreted. It is also good practice to check the data before proceeding any further: a simple scan for bad data values is required. It may lead to the exclusion of areas with small populations – EDs with less than, say, fifty persons or including ships, prisons, and institutions should be excluded. Cases with missing values (arising perhaps from data suppression) should certainly be deleted.

Some thought may also be given to the possibilities of a data transformation to ensure that the frequency distributions of values for each variable are nearly normal (see Chapters 4, 5 and 7). It can be argued, however, that there is little to be gained by data transformations, bearing in mind the exploratory nature of cluster analysis and the difficulties it may cause during interpretation. Nevertheless, variables which have very peculiar distributions, either highly skewed or very kurtose, should be examined. Such peculiarities may indicate bad data, perhaps from mis-specification of variables derived from arithmetic performed on the SAS data or from adjustment effects (section 2.9.6). They may also indicate outliers in the data which require removal. If transformations *are* applied, then it may be worth examining several and then selecting the one that minimizes skewness (section 4.6).

8.6.3 STEP 3: ORTHOGONALIZE THE DATA

Since many of the variables will be highly inter-correlated, it is good practice to transform the original data from scores on an initial set of variables to scores on a new set of 'derived' variables which have the property that each new 'variable' is uncorrelated with any other and represents as much as possible of the common inter-correlations found in the original data. That is to say, the raw data are orthogonalized and are replaced by principal component scores. The m original variables can be replaced by m new variables or principal components without any loss of information. Normally, you would accept rather fewer components than there were original variables. A rule of thumb is that you would seek to retain at least 90 per cent of the total variance of the correlations found between the original variables.

In practice, we might expect that the number of principal components required might be between one-half and three-quarters the number of original variables. The principal component stage is used here only as a data transformation and no attempt is made to interpret the components (see Chapter 7). Furthermore, it is desirable that the component scores are weighted by the size of the associated eigenvalues. For this reason it would be unwise to use factor scores where the variance of each set of factor scores is the same, since this will distort the multi-dimensional space in which the classification is performed.

8.6.4 STEP 4: CLASSIFY THE DATA

In the Clustan 1C program, both steps 3 and 4 could be done in the same run, by specifying FILES followed by either RELOCATE or CORREL and HIERAR. The preferred method which is described in the next section is broadly equivalent to the RELOCATE option in Clustan. It should be appreciated that different clustering methods *do* produce different results. Sometimes the differences are slight; on other occasions they may be large. There is no single best method since there are no universally accepted definitions of the criteria by which to measure the 'best'. The ultimate criterion of acceptability is whether the results make sense and satisfy the initial purpose, and perhaps whether the classification method has any obvious technical weaknesses.

The inherent weakness of this 'plausibility criterion' should be recognized.

The onus rests with the user to demonstrate that a classification is reasonable and to identify any weaknesses. *It should not and cannot be assumed that the results are automatically of a high quality simply because of the method being employed.*

8.6.5 STEP 5: INTERPRETATION AND EVALUATION

Once a classification has been obtained, it is necessary to try to name the groups for intelligibility purposes. This is inevitably a highly subjective process that may or may not be coloured by preconceived ideas about which groups should be present. Once the groups have been named, it is necessary to decide whether they make sense – perhaps too few or too many clusters have been specified for the operational purpose. Perhaps, indeed, some suspicious data values have resulted in strange results; outliers (Chapters 4 and 7) will often form highly distinctive clusters.

The task of naming groups is based upon the importance of key variables in these groups and can be helped by the provision of diagnostic aids. Statistics such as the mean and standard deviation of each variable for each group give some guide. For example, in trying to name a group you would look for variables with group means which are substantially higher or lower than the global (i.e. for all the data areas considered together) means and with smaller standard deviations. Clustan 1C computes pseudo t and F statistics to help assess the strength of these differences, but in practice this is not always helpful as the statistical tests are frequently invalid. Another way of doing the same thing is to identify as key diagnostic variables those with group means that differ by 1, 2, and 3 standard deviations from the global means. All these diagnostics should be calculated from the raw, untransformed data.

Such use of these statistics is rarely problem-free: the effects of both small group sizes (viz. few cases in a group) and non-normal distributions can invalidate the use of means and standard deviations. An alternative approach is to follow the philosophy of Tukey (1977) and utilize more robust measures. Tukey defines a set of median-based measures – 'far out', 'outer fence', 'inner fence' – which can be used instead of means and standard deviations as classification diagnostics. Thus, a key diagnostic variable may be one which has a high proportion of the members of a group in either the far out, outer fence, or inner fence categories. A distinction can also be made as to whether these categories are above or below the global medians of the variables concerned.

Another useful analysis at this stage is to calculate for each variable the 'within-group' sum of squares, as a guide to the statistical efficiency of the classification. Use is made of the fact that the total sum of squares for a variable can be partitioned into 'between-group' and 'within-group' components. In practical terms, if every area being classified is placed in a separate group, then the within-group sum of squares would be zero since each group is completely homogeneous. Alternatively, if all the areas are assigned to the same group then the 'between-group' sum of squares would be zero. Any real classification will lie between these two extremes. The percentage 'within-group' sum of squares for each variable measures the amount of information 'lost' by a classification of *n* areas into *m* groups. This, of course, assumes that the total sum of squares represents the totality of 'information'.

This measure provides a guide to whether more or less groups are required. However, it is only a crude guide since there is no way of knowing at what point the loss of information becomes critical to a given purpose. Moreover, the results vary from one variable to another and they depend on the nature of the areas being classified. For example, an ED-level classification for Tyne and Wear County recorded an overall information loss of 36 per cent (Openshaw *et al.* 1980), while a classification of Italian EDs for Florence averaged 48 per cent (Bianchi *et al.* 1980). In both cases, the classifications were considered useful. The sum of squares lost by a classification is area- and variable-specific. Nevertheless, it is useful for helping to determine a suitable number of groups; it is particularly useful when the same data variables for the same type of areas are classified in different places, such as different cities.

Other numerical measures can also be used to help summarize the properties of different classifications. For instance, the proportion of cases (such as EDs) with their nearest neighbours (calculated from distances measured in the multi-dimensional Euclidean space defined by the principal component scores) in different groups will provide some indication of 'edge' effects. Other statistics can be used to summarize the distribution of distances to cluster centroids. Such measures can be calculated separately for each group or for all the groups together.

From an applied perspective, a more useful approach is to identify poorly classified cases. The simplest way of doing this is to list those cases which are further away from their cluster centroid than is 'normal' either for the members of the group concerned or based on an analysis of all the groups in the classification. The critical distances again can only be determined by the 'rule of thumb', for example, if the distance to the group centroid exceeds the average distances plus three standard deviations. Tukey's median-based measures can also be used to identify 'outer fence' and 'far out' cases. We make the assumption that such cases are poorly classified and that the user needs to know this when interpreting a classification. If more groups are used, of course, then the proportion of poorly classified cases may well decrease.

Another useful device is to rank the members of each group in terms of their distance from the cluster centroid. An examination of the label assigned to the group and the data values for cases which are the 'closest' and 'furthest' away, may well help with both the interpretation and evaluation processes.

Of course, all numerical diagnostics are only an aid to naming and evaluating the groups. Mapping the location of areas in each group may also be very helpful in suggesting names of group 'types'. However, the subjectiveness of this process should not be overlooked during the application of the results.

The principal aim of the evaluation stage is to develop by empirical study an understanding of both the strengths and weaknesses of a classification. This process is neither easy, nor always quick, but it is nevertheless essential if an overly naive approach to census data classifications is to be avoided. It is noteworthy that this process is very often missing from classification exercises, probably because taxonomists have not bothered to spend much time discovering how best to use the results of the classification methods they have invented ! As a result, the users of the standard classification package programs are simply left to their own devices once their classifications are produced.

8.7 An efficient classification method

(The reader who is not interested in technicalities can skip this section)

The classification method described here has been developed over a number of years and has been extensively tested on a largc number of data sets. We cannot claim with certainty that it is the best method available but, on an empirical basis, it is likely to be one of the best. The basic algorithm is derived from the RELOCATE procedure in Clustan 1A (Wishart 1969), is the same as that in Clustan 1C, and has been extended by the incorporation of various heuristics for improving the quality of the classifications obtained.

The basic algorithm is as follows:

Step 1: Generate an initial classification by randomly assigning the n original areas to one of m groups, the value for m being a guess at how many groups are needed (if in doubt, try twenty !).

Step 2: Apply an iterative relocation process. This is equivalent to the RELOCATE option in Clustan 1C with coefficient 24 specified; that is

- i for any area i, try moving it from the group p it is currently in to another group q;
- ii calculate the error sum of squares (within group sum of squares) for group q with area i assigned to it;
- iii consider all possible groups to which i could be assigned;
- iv move area i into whichever group has the smallest error sum of squares;
- v process all n cases in a similar fashion;
- vi if one or more moves occur then return to (i) and start again.

At this point a preliminary classification has been obtained.

Step 3: Examine the classification, compute statistical diagnostics and the within-group sum of squares. If more groups are thought necessary then return to step 1 and increase *m* or go to step 4; if there are too many groups, then either return to step 1 and reduce *m* or go to step 5; if satisfactory, go to step 6.

Step 4: Identify a fixed percentage of areas ranked by the size of their contribution to the error sum of squares of the groups in which they are located. Assign these cases to a new group, increment *m*, and return to step 2. This is obviously a good way of increasing *m* and of improving the classification. Another way would be to split a specific group into two parts.

Step 5: Join either the two most similar groups or a pair of specified groups, reduce *m*, and return to step 2.

Step 6: Either stop, or consider how stable the classification is to minor changes to it resulting from exchanging a small percentage of the members of each group into other groups, then return to step 2.

This strategy is by no means a 'one-shot' process. The classification part in step 2 is fully automatic, but the other steps all involve a degree of thought and human action. This 'to-and-fro' procedure is a deliberate attempt to combine a computer approach with human intelligence. This iterative procedure is necessary because the number of groups specified in step 1 cannot be determined with any precision prior to the analysis – it is still in part an arbitrary decision. Indeed, the number of groups must also reflect the purpose of the exercise, so that purely statistical rules for when to stop grouping – as some people advocate – are in practice both irrelevant and useless. The basic decision for the analyst is, first, how many groups are thought necessary? Obviously prior knowledge can be useful here, as are constraints such as the maximum number of different symbols that can later be used for mapping the individual groups. Once a firm idea is established of how many groups are necessary, the user can pass on to the exploration and evaluation of different classifications with this number of groups, perhaps by the systematic generation of a number of different classifications with groups in the desired range. Interpretation of the groups in these classifications will then determine whatever constitutes the most plausible set of results.

Once this has been achieved the next stage in the process is to explore the quality of the classifications.

Step 7: Identify poorly classified cases.

Step 8: Assess the sensitivity of the classification to various operational decisions; for example, the number of component scores (try increasing the number used), the use of different random starting classifications, and the effects of re-running step 2 with minor changes being made to the best classification.

There is, of course, always a possibility that either no reasonably stable classification exists with the desired number of groups or that the results are nonsensical or otherwise unsatisfactory. It may be that experience will suggest a different set of variables, or that more groups are required, or that the original data are suspect – in which case, try again from the beginning. Remember that *classification is inevitably an exploratory process*: you will never make best use of the technique unless you are willing to use it in an appropriately exploratory fashion. In essence, you are groping your way almost blind through an unimaginably complex hyper-dimensional space towards (you hope) a set of usable results.

The computer time required by the classification process is not large even with several hundred or a few thousand cases. Furthermore, the basic approach can be applied to very large data sets (over 10,000 cases) either by modifying the programs to handle more cases or by using a revised classification strategy; for example:

- i select a random sample of the areas and classify them;
- ii allocate the unclassified areas to whichever group they are most similar to in this sample classification;
- iii re-run steps 2 through 6.

If the size of the data is such that step (iii) requires large amounts of computing time, then either set up the program to be restartable or consider restricting the relocation only to the most poorly classified areas. It is, however, not sensible to stop after step (ii) because sampling errors in the initial classification will have an unpredictable effect on the results.

8.8 An application

The methods described above were applied to 1971 census ED data for the North Tyneside district of Tyne and Wear County. The annex to this chapter contains a brief description of the computer programs used.

For this study, the forty variables used by Webber (1977) were adopted. The raw data are input into a principal component score program. As table 8.2 shows, eighteen components were needed to account for 90 per cent of the variance of the correlations found in the original data. If a factor analysis had been performed, then the conventional eigenvalue of 1 'rule' would have indicated ten components. However, since the aim here was to orthogonalize the data to avoid giving undue emphasis to the most highly interrelated variables, it was more appropriate to seek to preserve over 90 per cent of the variance. In fact thirty components were used in this instance – it looked a nice round number (the consequences of this decision would of course be investigated in the evaluation stage)! The effect was to reduce the initial 421 ED by forty variable data matrix to a 421 ED by thirty component scores matrix.

The scores were then input into the classification program with twenty groups being specified: the choice of twenty groups is completely arbitrary and it was expected that it would be refined once an initial classification had been obtained and interpreted. Table 8.3 summarizes the results obtained from the

Table 8.2 Component score results: size of eigenvalues and variance retained

rank of component	*Eigenvalue*	*cumulative variance %*
1	10.4	26
2	5.5	39
3	3.8	49
4	2.6	56
5	1.8	60
6	1.5	64
7	1.2	67
8	1.1	70
9	1.0	73
10	1.0	76
15	0.66	86
20	0.42	92
25	0.24	96
30	0.15	98

iterative relocation procedure. By the ninth iteration, no further improvements could be made to the classification. It is possible that a better classification could have been obtained by using some of the heuristics described in the previous section but, for current purposes, it is appropriate to keep procedures as simple as possible.

Table 8.3 Results of the iterative classification program

iteration number	*number of moves*
1	384
2	163
3	84
4	50
5	45
6	42
7	17
8	5
9	0*

* convergence

Table 8.4 Numbers of EDs assigned to each group

group number	*number of EDs*
1	6
2	5
3	11
4	6
5	35
6	13
7	21
8	23
9	35
10	47
11	9
12	12
13	24
14	29
15	20
16	32
17	36
18	16
19	22
20	19

The initial result, then, was a set of twenty groups. Table 8.4 shows the numbers of EDs assigned to each group. The next task was to try to interpret the groups and assign to each a name to summarize its characteristics. Table 8.5 shows the type of result produced by the diagnostic program; in this example, the results relate only to group 6. Even a glance at table 8.5 indicates that the members of this group have high proportions of 'no bath', '1–2 rooms', 'no inside WC', 'overcrowded', 'unfurnished', 'unskilled head of households', 'unemployed people', 'walk to work', etc. In other words, this is a classic inner city deprivation type of group and can readily be named (but remember the discussion in section 8.4 about ecological fallacies and ED heterogeneity if the results are to apply to people rather than places !). It is also necessary to check whether any members of this group are poorly classified and whether any have substantially different characteristics from the label assigned to the group.

On this occasion, some other groups also had general inner-city problem area characteristics. This suggested that perhaps fewer than twenty groups would be required if the purpose is that of a parsimonious general description of the North Tyneside census data.

Finally, it is noted that this twenty-group classification for one district

Table 8.5 Diagnostics for group 6

Variables less than global median values	
far out	
9 : 76%	agriculture
17 : 61%	new commonwealth born
36 : 69%	shared dwelling
inner fence	
3 : 84%	students
4 : 69%	cars per household
5 : 84%	two or more cars
11 : 53%	professional head of household
12 : 61%	non-manual head of household
19 : 61%	aged 5–14
26 : 76%	household size
28 : 100%	dwelling size
32 : 61%	furnished accommodation
39 : 61%	seven or more rooms
Variables greater than global median values	
far out	
**38 : 76%	no bath
outer fence	
**37 : 61%	no inside WC
**40 : 53%	one to two rooms
inner fence	
* 1 : 61%	unemployed
* 6 : 61%	walk to work
*15 : 69%	unskilled
*18 : 69%	aged 0–4
20 : 53%	aged 15–44
*25 : 61%	single non-pensioner household
31 : 100%	unfurnished renting accommodation
34 : 69%	overcrowded

Notes: * group mean greater than one standard deviation from overall mean
** group mean greater than two standard deviations from overall mean
% of cases within group 6 in a particular category for the specified variable

retains about 35 per cent of the original sum of squares, about the same as the Tyne and Wear ED-based classification referred to earlier; clearly, restricting the size of the 'world' considered does not necessarily give more homogeneity! Table 8.6 shows the CPU times for this exercise. Even on a small local authority computer the computer times would not be excessive.

Table 8.6 Computer run times

program description	*CPU times IBM 370/168 (seconds)*
calculate principal component scores	15.6
generate a random classification of twenty groups	0.1
classification program	12.0
calculate diagnostics	9.7
sum of squares analysis	3.6

Notes: CPU stands for central processor or mill time. Approximate cost at commercial rates for this run is £25.

8.9 Discussion

There is no statistical theory to support this form of cluster analysis: indeed, cluster analysis is not a statistical technique. The classification process is arbitrary. Decisions made are based on experience and 'rule of thumb'. There are few hard and fast rules and no guarantee of success, instant or otherwise. It is up to the user to decide whether the results obtained are reasonable and the assessment stage must be as rigorous as is humanly possible. As far as census data are concerned, the assessment problem is not too difficult because most people have a good idea of what results to expect and, for better or worse, it is often possible to manipulate the process to obtain them.

Some researchers put considerable emphasis on natural classifications. They point out that cluster analysis methods will quite happily detect groups in purely random data, although of course such a classification would fail the test of interpretation. Nevertheless, classification methods do force a degree of structure onto data regardless of whether they possess any and regardless of whatever structure may have been present. The method used here attempts to find tight spherical clusters in a multi-dimensional space. If the data structure consisted of rectangles or triangles of overlapping clusters, then it would not be correctly identified. The problem is a 'Catch 22' one in that no one really knows how to determine what structure is present without first carrying out a cluster analysis! It would be ideal if a method could be devised to adjust automatically to whatever type of structure data happened to exist. However, at present such methods do not exist and the so-called natural clustering method known as mode analysis comes nowhere near to reaching this goal. It is now generally considered that the only way a natural classification is going to emerge is by prolonged use. If many different users agree that a given classification is sensible and useful, then it could come to be deemed a natural classification. It is perhaps ironic that the best candidate for this accolade at present is the national 1971 ED classification and this is known to possess grave deficiencies.

At present the safest approach is to view cluster analysis as a numerical technique capable of providing efficient reductions in the size of data matrices. Critics often argue against the use of such pragmatic methods on the grounds that: (i) they lack a theoretical basis, (ii) in the hands of a novice they can be dangerous, (iii) they are arbitrary subjective processes, and (iv) that different methods produce different results. Such criticisms can be easily countered. That there is no theoretical basis to cluster analysis is not necessarily a disadvantage: even if such a framework existed, there is no guarantee that better classifications would be produced. The three other criticisms apply equally well to all methods of multivariate analysis applied to almost all data sets. At least with cluster analysis a novice can, by trial and error, discover how to use it and how to interpret the results: the standard texts also give good introductions to what is actually going on inside the methods. Provided the limitations of each method and of the SAS data are understood, then far more harm may be caused by not making the best use of the available data and analytical procedures than by trying and failing.

It is thus unreasonable to seek for, or expect, a perfect automatic clustering method that unerringly always produces the best results for any data – specifically for SAS data which relate to arbitrary areas and have had either pseudo random numbers added or certain variables suppressed.

It seems very likely that classification methods will be one of the most widely used methods of analysing the 1981 Census. Cluster analysis, in particular, is not a difficult technique to apply. If the necessary expertise is not available, then it can readily be developed. With a little patience, and perhaps some luck, useful results can be obtained surprisingly easily. The method of cluster analysis described here is believed to be at least as good, if not better, than any other that is currently available but the final choice of method and approach is up to the user. You may decide to wait one, two, or perhaps fifty years for better methods to be developed – and these will become available. Alternatively, you can try and make do with the best of what is available now and with a clear understanding of the subjective elements of classification procedures, in order to shake some useful structure out of the 1981 SAS data whilst these are still relevant to contemporary problems rather than being a historical curiosity.

ANNEX: COMPUTER PROGRAMS FOR THE CLASSIFICATION OF CENSUS DATA

A suite of portable programs has been written in ANSI FORTRAN IV to implement the classification methods described in this chapter. Separate programs cover:

- the calculation of principal component scores;
- classification by iterative relocation and including various heuristics for improving a classification;
- the calculation of various diagnostics to help name the groups;
- the calculation of the classification's sum of squares and other statistical measures;
- the conversion of a classification into a regionalization;
- the generation of random starting classifications.

These programs should run on virtually any computer that supports a FORTRAN IV compiler with either no, or very little, modification. Full user manuals, program source and test data are available on magnetic tape. They are available at a nominal charge from the author, from whom further details can be obtained.

9 Analysing change through time

PETER NORRIS and HELEN M. MOUNSEY

9.1 Introduction

The nineteen censuses taken in Britain span 180 years, and are therefore potentially valuable in studying change through time. Researchers have indicated their interest in using the census in this way both by past practice and present intentions (Norris 1980). Our purpose in this chapter is not so much to illustrate uses of the census in studying change through time, but rather to identify the problems inherent in making such studies and to suggest possible solutions. We concentrate on four problems: changes in the questions asked and the definitions and classifications used; changes in tabulations (with special reference to 1971 and 1981 Small Area Statistics); changes in the areas for which published data are provided; and changes in the boundaries of the smaller areas for which mostly unpublished census data have been provided since 1961. We conclude with some general points concerning the problems of providing census data that are amenable to both studying change through time and other uses of the census.

9.2 Questions asked and definitions and classifications used

Table 9.1 gives an outline of the topics covered in the census since 1801. It is apparent that there was relatively little change in topic content between 1851 and 1931 compared with the expansion in coverage which occurred between 1951 and 1971. The 1911 Census was probably the most innovative of those between 1861 and 1931, with questions introduced relating to industry, duration of marriage (never repeated) and children born, alive or dead, in marriage. The introduction of the question on usual residence in 1931 is important since it made possible the construction of tables on a *de jure* population base (see section 9.3). However, the ability of the General Register Office (subsequently OPCS) to handle large data sets improved from 1951 and, particularly, from 1961 when a computer was first used in processing. The census offices were therefore better equipped to meet user demand for a wider topic content, and questions were introduced on housing amenities (1951 onwards), housing

Table 9.1 Census topics, 1801–1981

GB = Great Britain = England, Wales, and Scotland E = England W = Wales S = Scotland

Subject	1801	1811	1821	1831	1841	1851	1861	1871	1881	1891
Names	-	-	-	-	GB	GB	GB	GB	GB	GB
Sex	GB	GB	GB	GB	GB	GB	GB	GB	GB	GB
Age										
quinquennial age groups	-	-	GB	-	GB	-	-	-	-	-
in years	-	-	-	-	-	GB	GB	GB	GB	GB
in years and months	-	-	-	-	-	-	-	-	-	-
Date of birth day, month and year	-	-	-	-	-	-	-	-	-	-
Marital status	-	-	-	-	-	GB	GB	GB	GB	GB
Position in household relationship to head of household	-	-	-	-	-	GB	GB	GB	GB	GB
Whereabouts on census night	-	-	-	-	-	-	-	-	-	-
Usual address	-	-	-	-	-	-	-	-	-	-
Migration										
address one year ago	-	-	-	-	-	-	-	-	-	-
address five years ago	-	-	-	-	-	-	-	-	-	-
Country of birth/birthplace	-	-	-	-	GB	GB	GB	GB	GB	GB
Year of entry to UK	-	-	-	-	-	-	-	-	-	-
Parents' countries of birth	-	-	-	-	-	-	-	-	-	-
Nationality[1]	-	-	-	-	GB	GB	GB	GB	GB	GB
Education										
whether scholar or student	-	-	-	-	-	GB	GB	GB	GB	S
age at which full-time education ceased	-	-	-	-	-	-	-	-	-	-
school level qualifications	-	-	-	-	-	-	-	-	-	-
scientific and technical qualifications	-	-	-	-	-	-	-	-	-	-
higher qualifications	-	-	-	-	-	-	-	-	-	-
Employment										
Activity: whether in job, unemployed, retired, etc	-	-	-	-	-	GB	GB	GB	GB	GB
Students of working age	-	-	-	-	-	-	-	-	-	-
Working full-time or part-time	-	-	-	-	-	-	-	-	-	-
Weekly hours worked	-	-	-	-	-	-	-	-	-	-
Employment status whether employee, self-employed etc	-	-	-	-	-	GB[4]	GB[4]	GB[4]	GB[4]	GB
Apprentice or trainee	-	-	-	-	-	-	-	-	-	-
Name and nature of business of employer ('industry')	-	-	-	-	-	-	-	-	-	-
Address of business	-	-	-	-	-	-	-	-	-	-
Occupation	GB[5]	-	-	GB[5]	GB	GB	GB	GB	GB	GB
Family occupation[6]	-	GB	GB	GB	-	-	-	-	-	-
Occupation one year ago	-	-	-	-	-	-	-	-	-	-
Workplace	-	-	-	-	-	-	-	-	-	-
Transport to work	-	-	-	-	-	-	-	-	-	-
Marriage and fertility										
year and month of birth of children born alive in marriage	-	-	-	-	-	-	-	-	-	-
number of children born alive in marriage	-	-	-	-	-	-	-	-	-	-
whether live born child in last 12 months	-	-	-	-	-	-	-	-	-	-
year and month of first marriage and of end, if ended	-	-	-	-	-	-	-	-	-	-
year and month of present marriage	-	-	-	-	-	-	-	-	-	-
duration of marriage	-	-	-	-	-	-	-	-	-	-
Social conditions										
religion (separate voluntary enquiry)	-	-	-	-	-	GB	-	-	-	-
dependency: number and ages of children under 16	-	-	-	-	-	-	-	-	-	-
orphanhood: father, mother or both parents dead	-	-	-	-	-	-	-	-	-	-
infirmity: deaf, dumb, blind etc	-	-	-	-	-	GB	GB	GB	GB	GB
eligibility to medical benefit	-	-	-	-	-	-	-	-	-	-
Language spoken										
Welsh	-	-	-	-	-	-	-	-	-	W
Gaelic	-	-	-	-	-	-	-	-	S	S
Absent persons whole or part returns	-	-	-	-	-	-	-	-	-	-
Households										
Number of rooms[10]	-	-	-	-	-	-	-	-	-	E,W
Number of **rooms** with one or more windows	-	-	-	-	-	-	S	S	S	S
Sharing accommodation	-	-	-	-	-	-	-	-	-	-
Tenure of accommodation	-	-	-	-	-	-	-	-	-	-
Amenities whether exclusive use, shared use, or lacking										
cooking stove	-	-	-	-	-	-	-	-	-	-
kitchen sink	-	-	-	-	-	-	-	-	-	-
piped water supply	-	-	-	-	-	-	-	-	-	-
hot water supply	-	-	-	-	-	-	-	-	-	-
fixed bath or shower	-	-	-	-	-	-	-	-	-	-
inside WC	-	-	-	-	-	-	-	-	-	-
outside WC	-	-	-	-	-	-	-	-	-	-
Cars or vans	-	-	-	-	-	-	-	-	-	-
Principal returns made by enumerators										
Number of houses	GB	GB	GB	GB	GB	GB	GB	GB	GB	GB
Families per house	GB	GB	GB	GB	-	-	-	-	-	-
Vacant houses or household spaces	GB	GB	GB	GB	GB	GB	GB	GB	GB	GB
House or household spaces otherwise unoccupied		GB	GB	GB	GB	GB	GB	GB	GB	GB
Shared access to accommodation	-	-	-	-	-	-	-	-	-	-
Non-permanent structures	-	-	-	-	-	-	-	-	-	-

[1]1841: only for persons born in Scotland or Ireland; 1851-91: whether British subject or not
[2]also whether full-time or part-time.
[3]asked of part-time workers only.
[4]asked of farmers and tradesmen only.
[5]only distinguishing (a) agriculture, (b) trade, manufacture or handicraft, (c) others.
[6]1811-31: only distinguishing (a) agriculture, (b) trade, manufacture, or handicraft, (c) others.

Table 9.1 Census topics, 1801–1981

GB = Great Britain = England, Wales, and Scotland   E = England   W = Wales   S = Scotland

1901	1911	1921	1931	1951	1961	1971	1981	Subject
GB	GB	GB	GB	GB	GB	GB	GB	**Names**
GB	GB	GB	GB	GB	GB	GB	GB	**Sex**
								Age
–	–	–	–	–	–	–	–	quinquennial age groups
GB	GB	–	–	–	–	–	–	in years
–	–	GB	GB	GB	GB	–	–	in years and months
–	–	–	–	–	–	GB	GB	**Date of birth** day, month and year
GB	GB	GB	GB	GB	GB	GB	GB	**Marital status**
GB	GB	GB	GB	GB	GB	GB	GB	**Position in household** relationship to head of household
–	–	–	–	–	GB	GB	GB	**Whereabouts** on census night
–	–	–	GB	GB	GB	GB	GB	**Usual address**
								Migration
–	–	–	–	–	GB	GB	GB	address one year ago
–	–	–	–	–	–	GB	–	address five years ago
GB	GB	GB	GB	GB	GB	GB	GB	**Country of birth/birthplace**
–	–	–	–	–	–	GB	–	**Year of entry to UK**
–	–	–	–	–	–	GB	–	**Parents' countries of birth**
GB	GB	GB	GB	GB	GB	–	–	**Nationality**[1]
								Education
S	GB[2]	GB[2]	–	GB[2]	–	–	–	whether scholar or student
–	–	–	–	GB	GB	–	–	age at which full-time education ceased
–	–	–	–	–	–	GB	–	school level qualifications
–	–	–	–	–	GB }	GB	GB [	scientific and technical qualifications
–	–	–	–	–	– }		[	higher qualifications
								Employment
GB	GB	GB	GB	GB	GB	GB }	GB [	**Activity**: whether in job, unemployed, retired, etc
–	–	–	GB	GB	GB	GB }	[	**Students of working age**
–	–	–	–	GB	GB	–	[	**Working full-time or part-time**
–	–	–	–	–	GB[3]	GB	–	**Weekly hours worked**
GB	GB	GB	GB	GB	GB	GB }	GB [	**Employment status** whether employee, self-employed etc
–	–	–	–	GB	GB	GB }	[	**Apprentice or trainee**
–	GB	GB	GB	GB	GB	GB	GB	**Name and nature of business of employer ('industry')**
–	–	–	GB	–	–	–	–	**Address of business**
GB	GB	GB	GB	GB	GB	GB	GB	**Occupation**
–	–	–	–	–	–	–	–	**Family occupation**[6]
–	–	–	–	–	–	GB	–	**Occupation one year ago**
GB[7]	GB[7]	E,W	–	GB	GB	GB	GB	**Workplace**
–	–	–	–	–	–	GB	GB	**Transport to work**
								Marriage and fertility
–	–	–	–	–	–	GB	–	year and month of birth of children born alive in marriage
–	GB[8]	–	–	GB	GB	–	–	number of children born alive in marriage
–	–	–	–	GB	GB	–	–	whether live born child in last 12 months
–	–	–	–	GB[9]	GB	GB	–	year and month of first marriage and of end, if ended
–	–	–	–	GB	GB	–	–	year and month of present marriage
–	GB	–	–	–	–	–	–	duration of marriage
								Social conditions
–	–	–	–	–	–	–	–	religion (separate voluntary enquiry)
–	–	GB	–	–	–	–	–	dependency: number and ages of children under 16
–	–	GB	–	–	–	–	–	orphanhood: father, mother or both parents dead
GB	GB	–	–	–	–	–	–	infirmity: deaf, dumb, blind etc
–	–	S	S	–	–	–	–	eligibility to medical benefit
								Language spoken
W	W	W	W	W	W	W	W	Welsh
S	S	S	S	S	S	S	S	Gaelic
–	–	–	–	–	GB	GB	GB	**Absent persons** whole or part returns
								Households
E,W	E,W	E,W	E,W	GB	GB	GB	GB	Number of **rooms**[10]
S	S	S	S	–	–	–	–	Number of **rooms** with one or more windows
–	–	–	–	–	–	GB	GB	**Sharing** accommodation
–	–	–	–	–	GB	GB	GB	**Tenure** of accommodation
								Amenities whether exclusive use, shared use, or lacking
–	–	–	–	GB }	GB {	GB	–	cooking stove
–	–	–	–	GB }	{	GB	–	kitchen sink
–	–	–	–	GB	GB	–	–	piped water supply
–	–	–	–	–	GB	GB	–	hot water supply
–	–	–	–	GB	GB	GB	GB	fixed bath or shower
–	–	–	– }	GB	GB {	GB	GB	inside WC
–	–	–	– }		{	GB	GB	outside WC
–	–	–	–	–	–	GB	GB	**Cars** or vans
								Principal returns made by enumerators
GB	GB	GB	GB	GB	GB	–	–	**Number of houses**
–	GB	GB	GB	GB	GB	–	–	**Families per house**
GB	GB	GB	GB	GB	GB	GB	GB	**Vacant houses or household spaces**
GB	GB	GB	–	–	–	GB	GB	House or household spaces otherwise unoccupied
–	–	–	–	–	–	GB	GB	**Shared access** to accommodation
–	–	–	–	–	GB	GB	GB	**Non-permanent** structures

[7] 1901–1911: restricted to whether those carrying on trade or industry worked at home.
[8] also number living and number dead.
[9] date first marriage ended not asked.

[10] 1891–1901: only required if under 5 rooms; 1921–1961: returned by the enumerator.
[11] 1811–1921: houses uninhabited.
[12] 1811–1921: houses being built.

Source: OPCS

tenure (1961), migration (1961), car ownership (1971) and the sharing of accommodation (1971). In addition, the number of questions on education, marriage and fertility was increased during this period. Topic coverage in 1981 is notably narrower than in 1971 (see sections 2.2 and 2.3).

Table 9.1 can be used to indicate whether comparisons through time of a particular census topic might be possible. However, the presence of questions on a particular topic in two censuses does not guarantee comparable statistics. Questions might be framed differently, variables might be defined differently and classifications might change. In 1951, for example, 'occupation' was to be considered as the usual employment by which one's living was earned: in 1961, 'occupation' was defined as employment in the week before the census (Pickett 1974). In addition, the classifications used for defining occupation varied between 1951 and 1961: the former was based on the 1951 Classification of Occupations and the latter on the 1958 International Standard Classification of Occupations. Boston (1980) compared the classification used in 1971 and that used for the 1981 Census. He noted that:

> Up to 1972, the classification of occupations prepared by OPCS primarily for Census purposes was the sole list used within government for the statistical analysis of occupations .... In 1972 the Department of Employment published CODOT, 'The Classification of Occupations and Dictionary of Occupational Titles'.

The 5000 occupational headings in CODOT have been formed into 549 smaller groups with the aim of preserving comparability with the 1971 census classification. CODOT was adopted as the basis for the classification of occupations used for the 1981 Census because of its detail and in the light of miscodings using previous occupational classifications: Gray and Gee (1972) reported that the post-censal quality check in 1966 found 10.7 per cent of individuals wrongly classified. A 1 per cent sample of the 1971 census returns has been recoded using the 1981 classification. Boston stated that:

> Early results suggest that 23 of the 27 Occupational Orders in the (Department of Employment) 1970 classification could be reconstructed from the categories in the 1980 classification to within ± 10%.

It is apparent, then, that changes of this order in the proportion of the population in different occupational orders between 1971 and 1981 could be due to classificatory rather than actual change. Because social-class and socio-economic-group categories used in the census (such as in tables 49, 50 and 52 in appendix 2) are both based on occupation, changes in occupational classification also affect these classifications. First results from the recoding of the 1 per cent sample suggest that 4 per cent of cases would be recoded into a different social class: Boston noted that this effect would vary according to age group and 1971 social class.

Since 1921 the census has classified people according to the industry in which they work as well as the occupations which they follow. Again, problems of comparability occur, as the 1951, 1961 and 1971 Censuses were based on Standard Industrial Classifications drawn up in 1948, 1958 and 1968. However, a comparable post-war time series covering the 1951–71 Censuses has been drawn up by Buxton and Mackay (1977). The same authors have examined the comparability of occupational statistics, as has Bellamy (1978) who concentrated on nineteenth-century censuses, and Lee (1978) who attempted to cover the period 1841 to 1971. While these works are useful starting points for anyone interested in studying changes in occupational and industrial structure through time, none cover the 1981 Census. OPCS Customer Services (see appendix 8 for address) can provide definitions of all variables used, and also have further details of the 1 per cent sample recoding of occupations cited by Boston.

One reason for change in industrial and occupational classifications is that they need to take account of the appearance of new occupations and the disappearance of others. This is one of many ways in which census definitions and classifications change to reflect changes in society. Another manifestation of these changes is that many categories in SAS tables which used, say, a fifteen-to-nineteen or fifteen-to-twenty-four age group or referred to students aged fifteen and above in the 1971 Census refer to sixteen-to-nineteen or sixteen-to-twenty-four age groups and students aged sixteen and above in 1981. This is to take account of the raising of the school leaving age in 1972. However, in several tables in 1981 SAS the fifteen-year-olds are separated out so that the user can decide whether he or she wishes to compare, for example, those aged fifteen-to-nineteen in 1971 and 1981 or that part of the group above school-leaving age – the fifteen-to-nineteen-year-olds and sixteen-to-nineteen-year-olds respectively.

A further reason for changing definitions or classifications is that inaccuracies may have been noted in responses to questions in previous censuses. The accuracy of response varies with topic: it is generally higher when the question is unambiguous (e.g. date of birth) than when it is dependent on the definition of a particular term (e.g. number of rooms). The census user who wishes to study change through time would be interested in knowing how the accuracy of data on particular topics varied through time. Unfortunately, results of quality checks have not been published for every census. However, the 1966 quality check (Gray and Gee 1972) indicated the topics for which the responses were least accurate and for which, by implication, there was most room for accuracy to vary through time. Tillott (1972) has written a comprehensive survey of the sources of error in nineteenth-century censuses.

Definitions also change in order that the data produced may be more useful. One illustration here will indicate how data incompatibility can occur even when the topic covered appears to be unambiguous. In 1951, a WC to which a household had sole or shared access could be located anywhere so far as the census was concerned. In 1961, the WC could have an indoor or outdoor entrance but had to be physically attached to the house to be counted (Pickett 1974). In 1971, inside and outside WCs were differentiated in all tabulations. In 1981, though respondents were asked to state the presence of inside and outside WCs on the census form, reference is only made to inside WCs in SAS tabulations. It is apparent, then, that an effort to study the proportion of households with these amenities in a given area would be hampered by changing definitions.

Finally, it should be stressed that the possibility of comparing data through time is also dependent on the area level at which the study is carried out, since it is a general rule – at least in the past – that the coarser the area studied, the more detailed the tabulations provided. This can be illustrated by contrasting Buxton and Mackay's production of a compatible post-war series of industrial classifications at the national level with the extreme difficulty – perhaps even impossibility – of comparing industrial structures at ward or ED level by using 1971 and 1981 SAS. Only seven industrial categories are used in the 1981 census SAS tables: agriculture, energy and water, manufacturing, construction, distribution and catering, transport, and other services. The seven categories used in 1971 SAS were agriculture, mining, manufacturing, construction, utilities and transport, distribution and services, and national and local government and defence. Even without examining the contents of these categories, it is obvious that their comparability is limited. It is not possible, for example, to determine how many miners there are in EDs or wards from 1981 SAS though this was possible using 1971 SAS. The comparability of 1971 and 1981 SAS as a whole is examined in the next section.

9.3 Comparability of tabulations at fine area levels

Straightforward data on a particular topic (e.g. the number of children aged nought to four or the number of agricultural workers in an area) are often not sufficient to meet census users' needs. The cross-tabulation of one variable against another (e.g. number of rooms against housing tenure) or indicators

---

Notes:
* Some cells in the 1981 table are not in the 1971 table
† Some cells in the 1971 table are not in the 1981 table
‡ The 1971 values are ratios and not counts

The 1981 table numbers refer to the tables published in *Census Monitor* CEN80/8.

This comparison is on a table-to-table basis: therefore, where it is stated that no 1971 tables are comparable to a 1981 table, this does not deny the possibility that some cells in the 1981 table can be matched to cells in the 1971 SAS.

Table 9.2 Comparability of 1971 and 1981 SAS tables provided for England, Wales and Scotland

1981 SAS	*1971 SAS*
1	1
2	7*
3	2
4	8
5	6†, 7†
6	4*, 6*, 7*, 11‡
7	None
8	22*†
9	5*, 24*
10	21
11	16†, 17*
12	15, 18*
13	19†
14	19†
15	None
16	None
17	19†
18	20*
19	24*
20	7*
21	7*, 4*
22	25*
23	24†, 5
24	None
25	4
26	7*
27	None
28	None
29	None
30	None
31	20*
32	None
44	28*
45	None
46	None
47	27*
48	23†
49	23*
50	23†
51	None
52	None
53	None

derived by the manipulation of data (e.g. percentage of residents with both parents born in the New Commonwealth who are children aged nought to four) are often of greater interest. SAS offer such cross-tabulations, and in this section we examine the extent to which the SAS tables for 1971 and 1981 are comparable, and how far it is possible to replicate some of the most commonly used indicators derived from 1971 SAS with 1981 SAS.

The 1981 SAS tables for each country within Britain contain well over 4000 cells, compared with the 1571 cells in the 1971 SAS. While there were 28 tables produced in 1971 SAS, in 1981 there were 42 tables for the whole of Great Britain, along with 6 for England and Wales only, 4 for Scotland only and 1 for Wales only. In 1971 some of the cells in SAS were ratios rather than counts; all 1981 SAS tables are composed of counts.

Table 9.2 offers a comparison of 1971 and 1981 SAS tables. The purposes of this list are, first, to give an idea of the extent to which 1971 SAS can be compared with 1981 SAS, and second to save the user time in searching through the two sets for comparable tables. However, it must be stressed that the comparisons noted are at table level, and certainly do not mean that each cell in the 1971 table can be matched in the comparable 1981 table. Moreover, the table seeks to find 1971 tables which are comparable to 1981 tables, rather than 1981 matches for every 1971 table: there are three 1971 tables – 3, 9 and 26 – for which there are no 1981 matches, as well as tables 10 to 14, which are composed of ratios.

The 1971 tables which cannot be replicated in 1981 are concerned with persons with New Commonwealth-born parents, five-year migrants, and persons who entered the UK between 1960 and 1971. The 1981 tables which have no match in 1971 are concerned with employment status, households with no usually resident persons, the cross-tabulation of housing tenure by household size, a breakdown of sixteen to twenty-four-year-olds by marital status and economic activity, one-parent families, shared accommodation, the cross-tabulation of household structure by tenure, the housing amenity characteristics of households with migrant heads, the housing amenities of pensioner households, the cross-tabulation of age of the economically active by industry, of employment status by industry and of marital status by former industry, and the cross-tabulation of persons by sex and in various age and employment categories by the social class of household heads.

Although table 9.2 gives an initial idea of comparability, an index linking cells in 1971 and 1981 SAS is needed to facilitate comparisons. Appendices 2 and 3 provide the raw data from which such an index could be created, but OPCS have produced a more comprehensive index (contact Census Customer Services at the address given in appendix 8). The index itemizes about 400 comparable variables or cells. Moreover, OPCS have made available these comparable variables in magnetic tape form for both districts and for census tracts (see section 2.5.4.2). It should be stressed that census tracts rarely have any geographic meaning as entities and may vary considerably in their internal characteristics: they are simply the smallest grouping of 1981 EDs which have external boundaries coincident with those of a group of 1971 EDs. Since almost 50 per cent of the EDs in England and Wales were unchanged in 1981, nearly half of the census tracts thus comprise one ED each, the remainder being formed by two or more EDs. As a consequence, the populations in census tracts might be expected to be bimodal in character (Chapter 4). Census tracts are best considered as time-invariant building blocks, useful for creating areas of ward-type size.

Obviously users are more likely to wish to compare certain variables through time than others. Hakim's (1978a) 260 variables and the 102 CRU indicators (Rhind *et al.* 1977) cover most of those variables from the 1971 Census which were heavily used. Table 9.3 shows how far the Hakim variables can be replicated using 1981 data, ignoring for the moment the comparability problems caused by the change in population base. Only 27 per cent of Hakim's indicators cannot be repeated (mostly those relating to migration and country of birth), and only 10 per cent of the CRU indicators cannot be compared.

Table 9.3 Hakim indicators

Description of indicator	*Number*	*Number comparable 1971–81*	*% comparable*
Demographic	25	19	76
Housing	73	64	88
Household and family	36	30	83
Employment	72	58	81
Country of birth	37	18	49
Migration	17	2	12
Total	260	191	73

Source: Hakim (1978a)

Of the 102 CRU indicators, it is possible to ensure an *exact* 1971–81 comparison for only 22. This is because of a fundamental change in the population base used for SAS (see section 2.3.1). In 1971 and before, SAS and most other census tables were drawn up on a *de facto* base, but in 1981 a *de jure* base is used. A *de facto* population includes those within a particular area at the time of enumeration: a *de jure* population includes those usually resident in an area, whether or not present at the time of enumeration. Only four tables in 1981 SAS use a *de facto* base. OPCS table 1 gives total population figures on both the 1971 and 1981 base. OPCS table 3 gives a breakdown of persons

Table 9.4 Availability of some census variables at selected levels of geographical detail

	Area	*Population (M/F)*	*Age (1) (single years)*	*Age (quinquennial)*	*Marriage* Total no.	*Marriage* by age (quinquennial)	*Place of birth*	*Education – no. students*	*Economically active?*
Administrative counties	0123567	0123567	0123567	013567	0123567	0123567	012567	2567	012567
County boroughs	0123567	0123567	0123567	013567	0123567	0123567	012567	2567	012567
Municipal boroughs	0123567	0123567	0123567	013567	0a*123567	0a*1a*235 67	0*1*2* 5*6*7*	25*6*7*	0a*1a*2a*56*7*
Urban districts	0123567	0123567	0123567	013567	0a*123567	0a*1a*235 67	0*1*2* 5*6*7	2a5*6*7*	0a*1a*2a*5*6*7
Rural districts	0123567	0123567	0123567	013567	0a123567	0a1a2345 67		2a	0a1a2a
Civil parishes	0123567	0123567		5‡*	5*				
Wards	123567	0123567							
Conurbations	567	567	567	567	567	567	57	57	567
Conurbation centres	67	67	67	67	67	67		67	67
New Towns	67	67	67	67	67	67	6	6	67
Parliamentary divisions	01235	01235							
Petty Sessional Divisions, County Court circuits and Commissions of Peace	01235	01235							
Registration districts and subdistricts	012	012	01	012‡	1				
Registration counties	012	012	01	012‡	1	1			
Poor Law Unions	2	2		2‡					
Ancient counties	0	0					0		
Ecclesiastical parishes		0135e							
London boroughs	67	67	67	67	67	67	7	7	7
Post-1974 districts	7	7	7	7	7	7	7	7	7
Scotland									
Counties	123567	0123567	0123567	012567	0123567	0123567	0123567	67	567
Cities	123567	0123567	0123567	012567	0123567	0123567	0123567	67	367
Large Burghs	23567	0123567	3567	567	567	567	3567	67	567
Small Burghs	23567	0123567	67	567	567	567	6*7	6*	6*
Landward areas	3567	0123567	67	567	567	567	7		
Scottish DCs	3567	23567	67	567	567	567	7		
Scottish wards	67	3567	67	567	567	567			
Scottish CCEDs	67	3567							
Inhabited islands		3567							
Post-1975 districts	7	7		7	7	7	7	7	7

Notes:

1 Single year data only available to a certain limit (some years 21, others 25). Exceptions:
   i) 1921, e, s, and w;
   ii) 1951, s counties and cities; single years from 0 to 100+;
   iii) 1931, s large burghs, counties and cities.

2 Termed families in the Scottish censuses of 1901 and 1911, and separate occupiers for the Scottish censuses of 1921 and 1931.

3 There are no data on the number of occupied rooms in the Scottish censuses of 1911 and 1921. Data for Rooms with Windows are substituted as it is assumed the two are approximately compatable.

1931 refers to part I of the census volumes for that year. Part II (representing areas as reconstructed under the 1928 Local Government Act) contains limited data on population and households only.

Where the symbols * and a appear together, interpret as figures for some areas over a certain lower population limit, and aggregates for that type of administrative area as a whole.

Whilst every effort has been made to ensure the accuracy of this table, the authors had very limited access to Scottish census volumes pre-1951, and thus this section of the table may possibly be incomplete.

Occupation (extended SIC)	Status	Dependency, infirmity or orphan	Migrant (1)	Migrant (5)	Language	No. house-holds (2)	No. occupied rooms (3)	Persons/ room	No. rooms/ size family	Tenure	Access to amenities
12567	567	012	6	67	0w1w2w3w5w6w7w	123567	23567	123567	0123567	67	567
12567	567	02	6	67	0w1w2w3w5w6w7w	123567	23567	123567	0123567	67	567
a*1a*2a*56*	56*7*	2	6	67*	0w1w2w3w5w6w7w	123567	23567	1a*23567	012356*7*	67	567
*											
a*1a*2a*5*6*	5*6*7*	2	6	67*	0w1w2w3w5w6w7w	123567	23567	1a*23567	012356*7*	67	567
*											
a1a2a		2			0w1w2w3w5w6w7w	123567	23567	1*23567	0135	67	567
					2w3w5w6w7w	123567	23567	23567			5*
					6w7w	123567	23567	3567			
67	567		67+	67	7s	567	567	567	567	67	567
7	67		6	6		67	67	67	67	67	67
7	67		67	67	6s,w7s,w	67	67	67	67	67	67
						1					
						1					
						01					
						01					
	7		7	7		67	67	67	67	67	67
			7	7		7	7	7	7	7	7
123567	01567		6	67	0s1s2s3s5s6s7s	0123567	0123567	0123567	123567	67	567
123567	01567		6	67	0s1s2s3s5s6s7s	0123567	0123567	0123567	123567	67	567
a*1x23567	0a*1x567		6	67	0s2*3*6s7s	0123567	0123567	01*23567	23*5*67	67	567
a*1x26*	0a*1x6*		6	6	0s6a*s7s	0123567	0123567	01*23567	23*5*6	67	567
			6	6	6s7s	23567	23567	23567	256	67	567
*			6	6	6xs7s	567	23567	2567	26	67	
					6s	1567	567	567	6	67	567
					6xs7xs	67	67				
					7xs	7	7	7	7	7	7

– England
– Scotland
– Wales
– lower population limit as criterion for publication
– data otherwise only published to sub-division of region (=groups of counties) (e,w) or planning sub-region (s)
– not all
– limited and more than quinquennial
– aggregates

present not in private households by the type of establishment. OPCS table 6 breaks down persons present by age; and OPCS table 17 gives household size on the 1971 and 1981 bases. There is no satisfactory method of determining how any differences indicated in table 1 are distributed according to, say, socioeconomic group, occupational group or country of birth. *Therefore it is not possible, in many comparisons, to determine how far change between 1971 and 1981 is genuine and how far it is a result of the changed population base.* Although the closer the figures given in table 1 for *de jure* and *de facto* populations, the more comparable the data should be, it is still possible that a *de jure* population could be composed of a set of individuals considerably different from the *de facto* population even if the totals are identical: 'present usual residents' would be common to both, but 'present non-residents' would only be included in the *de facto* population while absent residents would only be included in the *de jure* population. The effect of the changed population base is as yet unquantifiable, but will obviously be higher in certain areas, for example, holiday resorts, in which 'present usual residents' make up a smaller proportion of the total population than elsewhere. While its effect on the comparability of some variables concerning the attributes of individuals (e.g. employment, country of birth and socioeconomic group) might be serious, its effect on housing attributes (e.g. tenure, amenities) is likely to be less serious.

Finally, some specific areas in which differences in the treatment of 1971 and 1981 data hamper SAS comparisons should be mentioned. There have been changes in the definition of a household and of a room: boarding houses were enumerated differently: information on one-year migrants is in the 100 per cent file rather than the 10 per cent file. Perhaps most fundamentally, the 1981 Census was taken on the night of 5 April (before Easter and out of term for higher education institutions) and the 1971 Census was taken on 25 April (after Easter and in term for higher education institutions). In towns where the number of holiday-makers and students cause seasonal fluctuations in the size of the population, this three-week difference is likely to have some impact on the results obtained.

9.4 The availability of published data by topic and area

The presence of a particular question in more than one census still does not guarantee that data derived from that question will be published for the same area levels in all the censuses in which the question was asked. Table 9.4 cross-tabulates selected variables from the census against selected area levels. The fact that both variables and areas are selected must be stressed: tabulations have been produced for other areas and other variables, but those shown in the table have been selected for their importance as indicators of demographic and socioeconomic conditions and as areas for which data are available from sufficient censuses to make the construction of a time series worthwhile. Table

9.4 relates to censuses in this century, but a similar table relating to nineteenth-century censuses has been produced by Drake (1972): in fact, certain variables have been included in table 9.4 with the specific purpose of extending Drake's table.

9.5 The comparability of small area bases

9.5.1 INTRODUCTION

All the areas discussed in section 9.4 owe their existence to administrative functions other than the census. Their boundaries are not necessarily constant and are amended according to the area's administrative function. Parliamentary constituency boundaries, for example, are periodically reviewed and amended with the aim of equalizing the number of electors in each constituency as far as is possible without dividing settlements or neighbourhoods.

In this section we shall be concerned with five area bases used in the census, two (local authority district and ward) that are administrative/political in nature, one (the ED) set up for census purposes and two (the postcode unit and grid square areas based on the Ordnance Survey National Grid) which allow the unique identification of a building or small group of buildings.

The local-authority area or district is the coarsest of the areas discussed here. It is discussed at some length, however, since it is the smallest area for which data on most topics have been available during this century. A few data are available at ward level before 1961, but most of the provision of data at this level and at ED, grid square and postcode levels is for censuses of 1961 and thereafter.

9.5.2 COMPARABILITY AT DISTRICT LEVEL

The provision of data for local-government areas to be used in local administration has always been an important function of the census. The rapid urbanization during the nineteenth-century produced a multiplicity of local-government areas as the previously existing parish system proved inadequate for the government of growing towns and cities. The local-government areas for which census data were tabulated in the nineteenth century are indicated in table 9.5. Further details on these areas, and also on the parliamentary, ecclesiastical and legal entities for which nineteenth-century census data are provided, are given by Wrigley (1972) and Jackson (1976).

By the end of the nineteenth century, local-government areas had stabilized into the system of metropolitan boroughs, municipal boroughs, county boroughs, urban districts and rural districts which existed until 1974. The stability of the *type* of area does not mean that any individual area is constant:

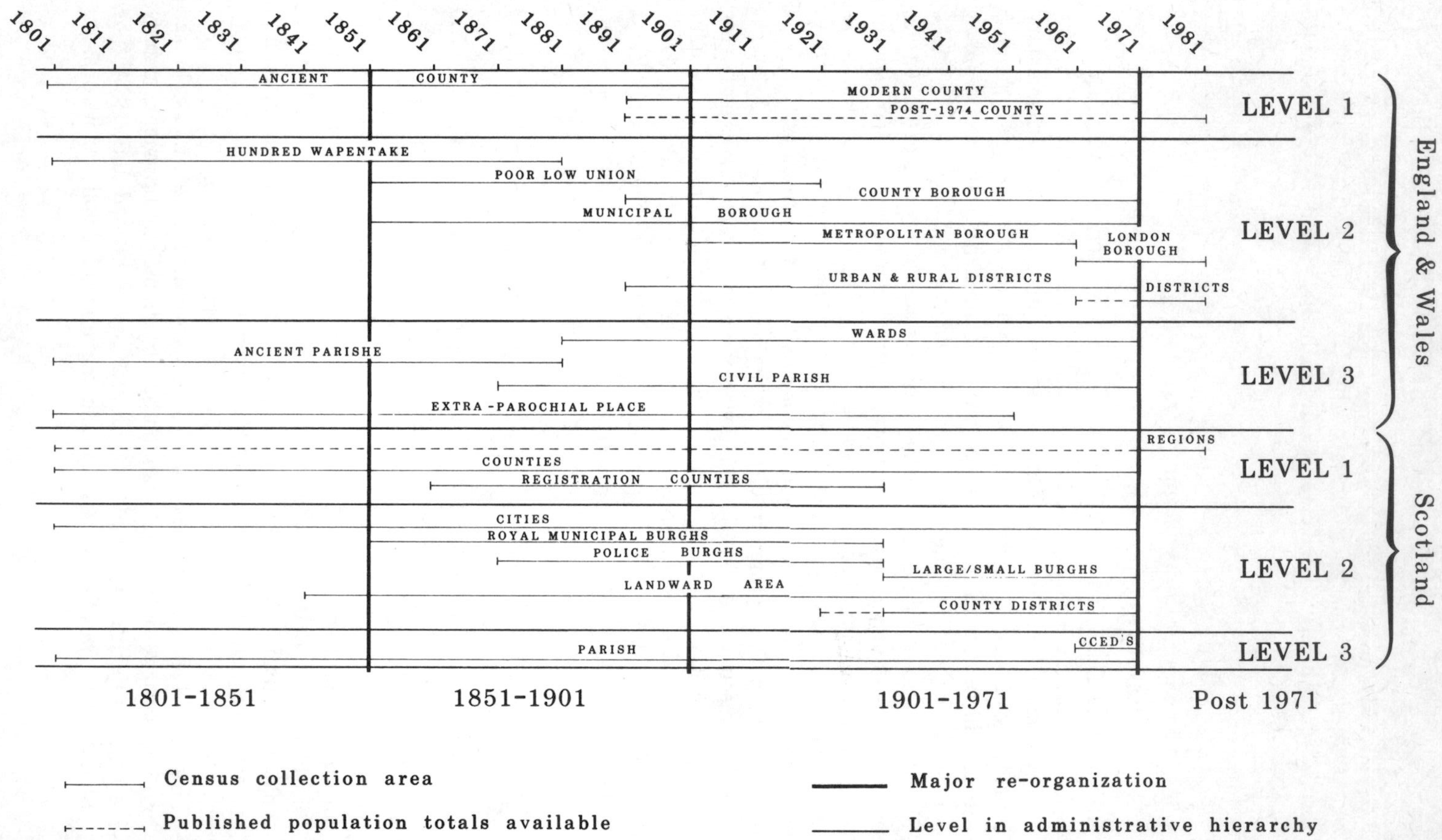

1801
1811
1821
1831
1841
1851
1861
1871
1881
1891
1901
1911
1921
1931
1941
1951
1961
1971
1981
ANCIENT COUNTY
MODERN COUNTY
POST-1974 COUNTY
LEVEL 1
HUNDRED WAPENTAKE
POOR LOW UNION
COUNTY BOROUGH
MUNICIPAL BOROUGH
METROPOLITAN BOROUGH
LONDON BOROUGH
LEVEL 2
URBAN & RURAL DISTRICTS
DISTRICTS
WARDS
ANCIENT PARISHE
CIVIL PARISH
LEVEL 3
EXTRA-PAROCHIAL PLACE
England & Wales
REGIONS
COUNTIES
LEVEL 1
REGISTRATION COUNTIES
CITIES
ROYAL MUNICIPAL BURGHS
POLICE BURGHS
LARGE/SMALL BURGHS
LEVEL 2
LANDWARD AREA
COUNTY DISTRICTS
CCED'S
PARISH
LEVEL 3
Scotland
1801-1851
1851-1901
1901-1971
Post 1971
Census collection area
Published population totals available
Major re-organization
Level in administrative hierarchy

boundary changes occurred throughout the period 1894 to 1974, but especially in the 1930s and 1960s. The changes during the 1930s were in response to the *Local Government Act* of 1929, which required county councils to make decennial reviews of their internal boundaries. These reviews were completed between 1932 and 1937 and, after each county completed its review, a census volume was published for that county sorting population and household data from the 1931 Census to the new boundaries. The general trend was one of reduction in the number of local authorities. While this was sometimes accomplished by the straight amalgamation of existing entities, it was more frequently done by splitting existing areas and then amalgamating parts from adjacent areas. The latter procedure poses problems in making comparisons of those data not included in the volumes of reworked 1931 data. However, since there were relatively few boundary changes between 1937 and 1951, the data which do occur in the volumes of reworked 1931 data are usually on the same areal base as are 1951 data.

The changes during the 1960s followed from the 1953 *Local Government Act* and the setting up of the Boundary Commission. The most important changes were the creation of the county boroughs of Teesside and Torbay and extensive boundary changes in Shropshire, Staffordshire and Warwickshire. The last two counties had also been subject to some of the greatest changes which occurred before 1930. In both periods, the expansion of the West Midlands conurbation was the principal cause of boundary changes. The extensive boundary changes in West Yorkshire in the 1920s and 1930s can be attributed to the expansion of the Leeds-Bradford conurbation.

Revision of local-government areas in London in 1965 can be attributed to the same cause. Suburban expansion meant that the area covered by the London administrative county prior to 1965 was considerably smaller than the continuously built-up area. The revision created thirty-two new London boroughs. The new inner London boroughs were mostly amalgamations of old metropolitan boroughs of the London administrative county. As these old metropolitan boroughs had experienced few boundary changes since 1899, comparison through time for these boroughs is thus relatively easy. However, the outer London boroughs were made up of areas previously in Kent, Essex, Surrey, Hertfordshire and Middlesex. While they were, in many cases, simple amalgamations of entire districts and boroughs existing prior to 1965, these districts and boroughs had been subject to much change in the 1930s. It is, therefore, rather more difficult to construct a series of data going back to 1901 for the outer London boroughs.

Table 9.5 Local government areas for which nineteenth- and twentieth-century census data are available

The most fundamental overall change in local-authority boundaries in the twentieth century took place in 1974 in England and Wales, following the *Local Government Act* of 1972. The 1366 districts and boroughs existing outside Greater London prior to 1974 were replaced by 369 new districts, and considerable reorganization of counties occurred, notably in the creation of six new metropolitan counties. The correspondence of new districts to old areas is shown in table 9.6.

Table 9.6 Correspondence of old and new administrative areas

	Cases
One new district = one old district or borough	49
One new district = 2 or more old districts or boroughs	169
Two or more new districts = 2 or more old districts or boroughs	151

OPCS reaggregated much of the 1971 census data, including SAS, to the new district boundaries and made these generally available. In the 218 cases where new districts are either exact matches or straight amalgamations of old areas, a simple addition process can be used to obtain data for the new districts for the censuses prior to 1971. For the remaining 151 areas, however, comparable data can only be obtained from the 1961 and 1966 Censuses by aggregating data for smaller areas (wards and, where available, EDs); even then, old wards will not necessarily build to new districts. For the period before 1961, when data for areas finer than the district are scant, figures for these 151 new districts are even harder to obtain. Mounsey (1982) has constructed a set of 1901 to 1971 *de facto* population figures for all new districts in Britain by applying a consistent set of assumptions and procedures to local-authority data from the census. The figures were discussed with the appropriate planning officers and, where local knowledge was available, were adjusted through appropriate corrections at county level. These figures, and the 1981 provisional population totals, are set out in appendix 5.

The development of local-government areas in Scotland, and the possibilities of making comparisons through time in that country, are rather different. At the start of the century, the local-government system in Scotland consisted of counties divided into burghs and extra burghal county or landward areas. The third level in the hierarchy was the civil parish: this has remained very stable over the last eighty years. In 1929, the landward (i.e. rural) areas were divided into districts of counties (which were groups of complete civil parishes): by the same Act, the cities of Edinburgh, Glasgow, Aberdeen and Dundee were made counties of cities, and divided into wards. Other burghs were reclassified as large and small burghs, but in these cases there were few boundary changes.

The major change of boundaries in Scotland this century came in 1975, as a result of the 1973 *Local Government (Scotland) Act*. The 399 existing local-authority areas were reduced to 56, of which only 1 exactly matches one old district, and 12 are simple amalgamations of old districts. This would pose serious comparability problems but for two facts: the constancy of the civil parish and the postcoding of the 1971 Census. Unfortunately, the usefulness of the civil parish is limited because relatively few census data are available at this level, especially for earlier periods. Fortunately, though, Scottish 1971 census data have been tagged with postcodes; since the basis for 1981 EDs was the unit postcode and 1981 census data is also available for the postcode sector (e.g. DH1 3), it should be possible to obtain census data for 1981 areas which match 1971 administrative areas very closely, and vice versa, for Scotland (see sections 2.5.5 and 2.5.6). The extent to which such tabulations will be available only by special request, and their cost, had not been settled at the time of writing.

9.5.3 COMPARABILITY AT WARD LEVEL

As an illustration of the problems which attend 1971–81 comparisons for smaller areas, the wards in County Durham for which 1981 census data are provided are compared in table 9.7 with the wards and civil parishes for which 1971 census data were provided. The table indicates that less than one-quarter of 1981 wards exactly match 1971 wards, and that 36 per cent of the new wards must be aggregated, in groups of three or more, before an areal match

Table 9.7 Areal comparability of new (1981 Census) wards and old (1971 Census) wards in the Districts of County Durham

	Wear Valley	*Teesdale*	*Darlington*	*Easington*	*Sedgefield*	*City of Durham*	*Chester-le-Street*	*Derwentside*	*County Durham*	*Percentage*
One new ward matches one old ward	4	2	1	4	4	11	7	8	41	23.0
One new ward matches more than one old ward	7	13	4	2	6	8	2	3	45	25.3
Two new wards match one or more old wards	4	4		8	4	2	4	2	28	15.7
Three or more new wards have to be aggregated to match aggregated old wards	6		20	13	8	3	4	10	64	36.0

Note: Cell numbers refer to the number of wards in each category.

can be found using 1971 data. It is possible to find 1981 comparisons for 1971 civil parishes, since OPCS have decided to make SAS available in 1981 for civil parishes, which are mostly unchanged since 1971. However, in Durham, ward boundary changes have been most frequent in urban areas, which were not covered by the civil parish system.

Where a 1981 ward does not match a 1971 ward, it might be possible to make a comparison on a common areal base if the 1981 ward is equal to the 1971 ward plus or minus a number of whole 1971 EDs. However, the tables produced by OPCS showing the composition of 1974 wards in County Durham in terms of 1971 wards, civil parishes and EDs indicate that there are several instances where 1971 EDs are split. Moreover, the 1974 wards are not those for which 1981 census data are provided in County Durham since there has been a further, intervening, revision of ward boundaries which began in 1979. Clearly detailed comparisons necessitate the use of maps of 1971 and 1981 EDs; these are available from OPCS Customer Services (see appendix 8).

9.5.4 COMPARABILITY AT ED LEVEL

The enumeration district (ED) is the only areal unit whose basic function is censal, being the district within which census forms are delivered and collected by one enumerator. In urban areas, the ED usually contains between 130 and 170 households; rural EDs are often somewhat smaller, since each civil parish is made up of one or more EDs. Although OPCS stated their aim to be of matching 1971 and 1981 EDs wherever possible (OPCS 1978/2), it appears likely that this was not achieved for 1981 EDs. Table 9.8 illustrates how the degree of matching between 1971 and 1981 EDs varied across the country. The reasons for the failure to keep exact matches include the need to ensure that EDs build to wards and the desire to keep workloads roughly the same for each enumerator. The latter factor explains why ED boundaries tend to change in areas of new building and demolition in particular.

ED boundary changes also result from the submissions made by local authorities when given the opportunity to comment on EDs within their areas. One suggested amendment is illustrated in figure 9.1. In this instance, Wear Valley District Council recommended the amendments because the 1971 EDs cut through settlements, thus making it impossible to obtain data for those settlements alone (pers. comm. T. Miller 1980). In Stockton-on-Tees, the Borough Council replied that they would like all EDs to be directly comparable for 1971 and 1981; if it were possible only to have *some* 1981 EDs directly comparable to 1971 EDs, the Council said they would prefer to have 1981 EDs capable of aggregation to Standard Zones, which were developed by Cleveland County Council for their own General Household Survey in 1976 (pers. comm. S. Kitching 1980).

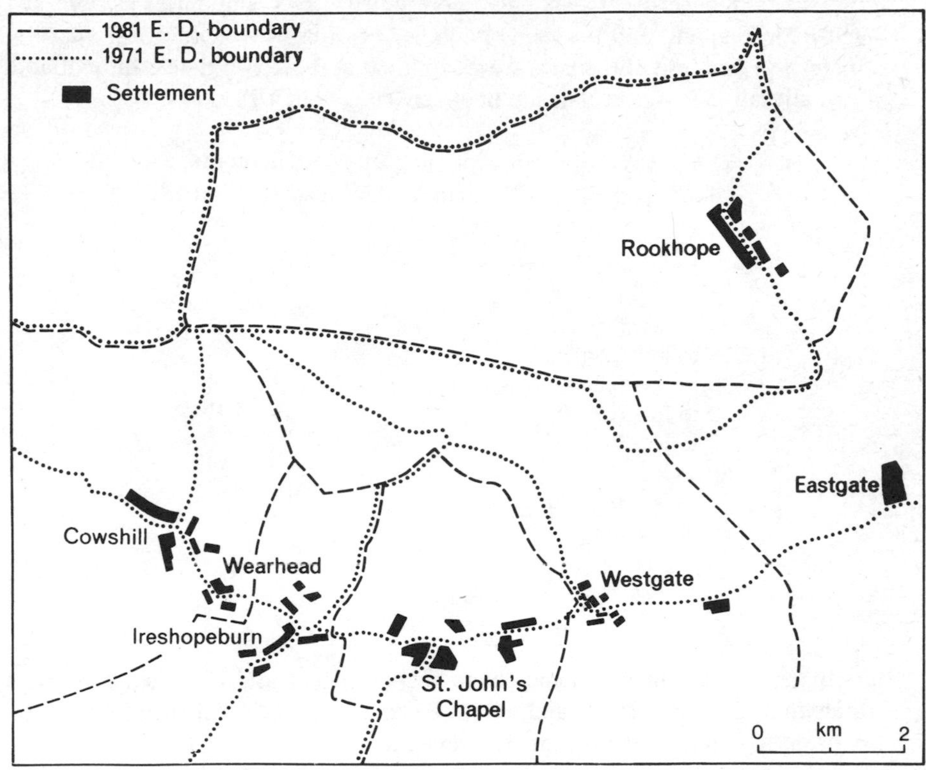

Figure 9.1 1971 EDs and proposed 1981 EDs in Upper Weardale, Co. Durham

Table 9.8 describes the extent of continuity in ED boundaries in 1971 and 1981 for England and Wales as a whole. For these two countries, approximately 44 per cent of the EDs were identical at these two dates. In Scotland, virtually all EDs were changed between 1971 and 1981.

Table 9.8 Number of districts and percentage of unchanged EDs in England and Wales, 1971 to 1981

Percentage unchanged	*Number of districts*
less than 25	45
25 to less than 30	34
30 to less than 40	94
40 to less than 50	101
50 to less than 60	75
60 to less than 70	37
70 to less than 80	16
80 and more	1
	403

In general, the lack of coincidence between 1971 and 1981 is less marked than that between 1961 and 1971 EDs, since 1961 EDs tended to be considerably larger on average. However, since 1961 ED data were available only for special requests, they are now available for limited areas only. Thus the incongruity of 1961 and 1971 EDs is likely to be less of a stumbling block than is the non-availability of 1961 ED data in many areas.

The only solution is then to group EDs into larger units unchanged through time, as Denham (1980) demonstrated for one area. Work by the Department of the Environment (pers. comm. B. Rose 1981) in Cleveland suggested that, on average, three or four EDs would need to be grouped together to be directly comparable for 1971 and 1981. OPCS christened these consistent areas *census tracts* and have now produced a set of comparable variables (see sections 2.5.4.2 and 9.3) for these tracts as well as for districts.

9.5.5 COMPARABILITY USING GRID REFERENCES AND POSTCODES

Ordnance Survey grid squares have disadvantages as geographical units for which census data can be provided; the most obvious is their lack of correspondence with physical and settlement features on the ground, since grid-square boundaries will dissect settlements and even buildings. However, a major factor behind the introduction of SAS census data in 1971 for the grid square at 1 km level (and, in urban areas, at 100 m level) was that the unchanging nature of the grid would be a constant areal base for the comparison of data through time. SAS grid-square data will not be made available in 1981 for the whole country as it was in 1971. Nonetheless, even in those areas in which grid-square data are available, the 1971 and 1981 variants are not exactly comparable. Apart from the *de facto/de jure* difference, this non-comparability arises from the different methods of allocation of grid references to the individual household census forms. The implications of this are described in section 2.5.9.

The Scottish approach to the longitudinal comparability of small-area data has been rather different (see section 2.5.5.2). GRO (S) abandoned any idea of trying to keep 1981 EDs identical to 1971 EDs, and decided instead to draw up 1981 EDs on the basis of postcode units. Moreover, GRO(S) marked up the 1971 enumerators' records with postcodes, thus linking postcodes to household reference numbers. This link was run against the 1971 datafile, thus postcoding the 1971 Census for Scotland. Those 1981 SAS tables for which 1971 data are available will be produced at a later stage using the 1971 data and the 1981 EDs, thus providing a set of geographically comparable data. This might not provide a perfect match on every occasion, but the correspondence is very close. Moreover, the linkage of postcodes to 1971 areas – districts, wards and civil parishes, for example – facilitates the continuation of historical series by the provision of 1981 data for 1971 areas (de Mellow 1979).

In short, 1971–81 comparability of data for very small areas is better for England and Wales than Scotland so far as the standard unit – the ED – is concerned. Much closer comparability is, however, theoretically possible for any unit in Scotland by means of the coding of records with the unit postcode which describes a unit of between one and about thirty houses (see section 2.5.5). For some users interested in cross-national studies, this dichotomy of approach may be a problem since its effects on data comparability are as yet unknown.

The potential of such referencing extends beyond the matching of census data through time; the methods could equally be applied to link census and non-census data (see Chapter 10). A postcode directory has been drawn up by OPCS linking postcodes to wards, districts and coarser units (Brown 1980) and the commercial firm CACI (Consolidated Analysis Centers, Inc.) provides a service linking EDs and postcodes by identifying centroids of each (OPCS 1979).

9.5.6 MICRODATA

Thus far, we have pointed out some of the problems in comparing data through time for aggregates of individuals. Most of these problems would not arise if data were made available from the census pertaining to individuals – either for all variables or for the same set of individuals for two censuses. Such data, referred to in this book as microdata, are not available from contemporary censuses for reasons discussed in Chapter 11. However, microdata are available from the censuses of 1841–81, the confidentiality of which are deemed to have expired after one hundred years. The problems and possibilities of comparing data through time which are specific to the nineteenth-century censuses are also discussed in Chapter 11.

9.6 Conclusion

We have assumed throughout this chapter that the need for census data which are comparable through time is proven both by past use (often in the face of adversity) and present intentions. Our purpose in pointing out the limitations – which are often considerable – is certainly not to dissuade users from attempting comparisons. Rather, we hope that users will be able to undertake comparative work with greater confidence through knowledge of the most likely areas of incompatibility. Finally, we should stress that we have been concerned throughout this chapter with the comparability of published or standard unpublished data (SAS is an example of the latter). Those readers who are interested in obtaining a particular tabulation which is not available in these forms can request a special tabulation from OPCS. Such tables are often costly and OPCS are not obliged to meet all feasible requests, but the availability of this service should not be ignored. The address of OPCS Customer Services is given in appendix 8.

10 Linking census and other data

DAVID RHIND and ERIC TANNENBAUM

10.1 What is linkage and why is it necessary?

By 'linking' we mean associating data from two different sources (such as the Population Census and unemployment or medical data) in such a way that incorporated detail from both sources is available for each 'individual' or 'case' – where census data are concerned, an area of ground such as an enumeration district (ED). Nowadays, such linkage is most commonly carried out by computer. There are two good reasons why this operation is frequently essential:

i to improve the thematic or temporal coverage of data;
ii to standardize non-census data sets.

We shall consider both of these in turn. We begin with an examination which relates to (i) above; why has the community of social scientists made comparatively little use of census data in Britain? Such a question has ramifications far beyond social science research; it helps us to understand the need for frequent sample surveys.

10.2 Improving data coverage

10.2.1 SOME SHORTCOMINGS OF CENSUS DATA

We have already seen (Chapter 3) that census data are used for a variety of purposes, often simply as a matter of report: thus areal profiles based on variables such as 'percentage of old people', 'percentage of households without all amenities' and so on are commonplace. Yet rather less use has been made of data from the 1971 and earlier censuses by social scientists than might be expected. Hakim's (1979b) bibliography of research applications of British census data suggests that, in the main, such data are primarily of interest to geographers, planners and demographers. To these authors at least, the relative disregard of census data by other social science disciplines reflects both their commitment to other techniques of data generation and their acceptance of a set of beliefs about the weaknesses inherent in census data.

Many social scientists in Britain remain less numerate than their counterparts in North America. This apart, there are at least five important reasons why the existence of census data is neglected when research is carried out on problems relating to the interaction of individuals both with each other and with their social environment. These are:

i *Data cost.* A very significant factor in the past, this has been much diminished by the purchase of a complete set of SAS by the Social Science Research Council; these are available in computer form to all *bona fide* research workers and teachers in universities and polytechnics (see appendix 7);

ii *Data age.* It is useful to consider that all data – like radio-active material – have a 'half life', i.e. that period at the end of which the data are only half as valuable as at the beginning. We might consider that census data halve in value about every two or three years. The 1971 Census SAS were not generally available to academics until 1977/8 but the 1981 SAS were available to the same group – and to most others – in 1982. Thus this problem is now also much diminished.

A more general point arises here, however: are the social phenomena which can be studied with census data more dynamic than is the census collection schedule? For example, does urban decay or replenishment occur more rapidly than can be described with data collected on a 'snapshot' basis every ten years? There are good grounds to believe that such infrequent data collection may give rise to aliasing in the data series (see Rhind and Hudson 1980, 32) and, as a consequence, to erroneous deductions on trends. Clearly, then, census data are to be regarded at best as a framework, rather than as an ideal monitor of social and environmental change;

iii *The fear of the ecological fallacy.* We have already described the spurious inferences which may arise from being forced to use data derived from groups of people, rather than from individuals (Chapters 7 and 8; see also Chapter 11). As we have argued elsewhere, there is at present no solution to this problem (the magnitude of which varies greatly) but the effects can be minimized by use of the most disaggregated data available and by constant vigilance. Langbein and Lichtman (1980) have reviewed research work which is based upon grouped data yet produces inferences at the individual level;

iv *The effects of the chosen geography.* We now know (e.g. Openshaw 1977) that using different sets of areal units can produce very different answers in analysis of grouped data – that is, the definition of the size, shape, position and number of the EDs may greatly influence the results of analyses (Chapter 7). Yet, apart from its constraint to include a geographically congruent set of households, the ED may well have no sociological, political or administrative significance and its geography is volatile (Chapter 9);

v *Restricted thematic coverage.* Despite the 4400 or more variables or 'cells' available for each area in each country in Britain from the 1981 SAS, the coverage of themes is rather restricted by comparison with many censuses overseas; for instance, we ask no questions about income (unlike the 1980 US and the 1976 Australian censuses). The population numbers, household structure, amenity provision, economic activity and geographical mobility characteristics of British censuses *are* of interest to social scientists, but often because the researcher wishes to measure an individual's reaction to them.

As a consequence of all these perceived shortcomings (some of which are no longer valid), social researchers have developed the individually-designed and individually-orientated social survey to the point where it is their dominant data collection technique. In most social sciences, the questionnaire-based survey not only allows data to be collected directly at the individual level but also permits some evaluative coverage (see (v) above). The advantages of such surveys include:

- within the range of ethical constraint, broad coverage of variables;
- individuals can be related to their attributes without the likelihood of committing the ecological fallacy;
- since people are universal, they are natural 'units' on which to observe attributes (c.f. areas of ground) and, furthermore, cross-time and cross-national comparisons can be drawn;
- survey-generated data are as new as they can be within the limits of available funding;
- survey techniques permit access to mental processes and so allow assessment of subjective reactions to 'objective' conditions.

On the other hand:

- most survey-based analyses 'atomize' individuals. That is, the 'average' survey gathers data about the individual with little regard for the wider social context. Lazarsfeld and Menzel (1965) have developed this argument more fully, claiming that there are four types or levels of individual data which have to be considered if a comprehensive view of social relations is to be provided. These are the 'absolute' properties unique to an individual, such as income; relational properties, such as marital status; comparative properties, such as occupational hierarchy; and contextual properties, such as the individual's neighbourhood. Most social surveys concentrate on the first and third of these, though the common stratified random selection from a sequential sampling frame (e.g. the electoral register) diminishes the possibility of studying geographical effects in both the third and fourth aspects;
- almost all social surveys are sample surveys and, as a consequence, have associated with them a larger possibility of error than a census-

type operation. This has important geographical complications: unless the sample is a large one, characteristics of the properties of communities within an area of ground can only be done for large areas.

In passing, though, we should note that many social scientists promptly aggregate the individual (micro-) data (see Chapter 11) arising from their surveys into groups. These groups are rarely geographically defined; rather they are defined to be homogeneous in such characteristics as identification with a particular political party (e.g. Butler and Stokes 1969) or with subjective identification with a particular social class (e.g. Nordlinger 1967). In each case, the group's characteristics are obtained by averaging those of the individual members.

10.2.2 USING CENSUS DATA TO SUPPLEMENT SURVEY DATA

Although it is technically feasible to collect data from a statistically sufficient number of respondents in close spatial contiguity to each other by using a tightly-clustered sampling design (see, for example, Fields, 1970/1), this will be extremely expensive if the research design calls for a nationally representative sample. A more feasible approach is to merge data from sources like the census with those collected by the survey phase of study. While, as Linz (1974) notes, this will yield a measure of 'abstract structural effects' rather than a direct measure of context, the researcher can treat these 'structural' effects as a surrogate of the socioeconomic milieu in which the respondent conducts his or her life. As such, this tactic offers promise for the survey researcher who fears that he/she is neglecting the fourth level of individual data that Lazarsfeld and Menzel described (see above). This suggestion is not new and has been implemented in several survey-based studies. As these differ in subject and approach, five will be cited and briefly reviewed.

10.2.2.1 Applications of merging census-type and individual data

In Finland in the 1960s, Valkonen (1969) examined the effect of community-level variables (specifically the age and educational qualifications of the population – both census variables) in his study of the 'contagious effect' of politicization. He reasoned that, as the better educated are more politicized, there should be a reinforcement of the impact of individual-level variables on individual politicization in areas with high concentrations of people with the preferred characteristics. That is, all things being equal, the city dweller with high socioeconomic status should be more politicized than the rural resident of similar status.

In Wisconsin, in the mid-1950s, Sewell and Armer (1966) tested the hypothesis that the socioeconomic status of the high school district – since it presumably reflects the shared norms and aspirations of its members – would have an important effect on the educational aspirations of its youth over and above that of family socioeconomic status or individual ability. They used variables from 188 Milwaukee census tracts which offered information on the characteristics of housing and population.

Rutter and his colleagues (1980), in their *15,000 Hours*, examined, among other things, whether differences found in school outcomes (e.g. delinquency rates) were largely accounted for by differences in the home neighbourhoods from which the children came. These investigators used census data aggregated to the ward level and an areal classification scheme based on forty variables contained in the 1971 Census in their analysis.

Studler (1977) was interested in the genesis of attitudes toward immigrants to the United Kingdom. He merged data from the 1966 Census which were aggregated to the parliamentary constituency level with survey data from the Butler-Stokes (1969) three-wave panel election study to determine whether context, as measured by age structure, social class composition, material possessions, immigration and job competition, had an impact on opinions about immigrants.

Hoinville (1980) provides the fifth example of the use of census data to complement survey-generated data by offering an indicator of contextual effect. She was interested in the differential impact that these effects (as indicated by population, employment activity, age, etc.) aggregated to the parliamentary-constituency level, had on the response rates on nine national surveys that her firm (Social and Community Planning Research), had carried out.

It will not have gone unnoticed that this brief review of projects in which census data were merged with survey data avoided any mention of the results of the integration. Frankly, at first glance the results are unimpressive. Nevertheless, there are at least six reasons why researchers should consider the merger of census data into individual-level files generated by the survey technique. All demand some reflection on what successful research implies.

As mentioned earlier in this chapter, social researchers have been sensitized to the problem of making fallacious inferences about individual attributes from aggregated data. However, while they justifiably fear committing an ecological fallacy, they show less sensitivity to the 'contextual fallacy' (Alker 1974) which stems from the assumption that individual functions take the same form in all areas, or, put another way, that there is no interaction between a set of individual-level variables and a particular set of contextual attributes (which vary among locales). Looked at in this sense, the studies reviewed have in fact successfully circumvented – at least for the phenomena that they were interested in – any such contextual error.

These studies can also be considered in a second sense which is not entirely unrelated to the first. Scheuch (1974) notes that in all forms of secondary analysis (i.e. the analysis of data not generated by the researcher) the 'most crucial problem is to what extent the statistical units used are theoretically relevant as contexts of individuals'. He argues that if those that have been used are theoretically defensible, 'non-findings', such as those that have been reviewed, are significant findings, for they help put to rest otherwise potentially interesting hypotheses.

It is also arguable that small increments to the explanation of relationships such as the 1.8 per cent initially reported by Sewell and Armer is a meaningful addition. Granted, the social scientist is trained to look for much larger correlations, but in many instances in social sciences the extremely large correlations which are deemed desirable are either spurious or tautological (see Chapter 7).

However, even if the 1.8 per cent variation in student aspiration that Sewell and Armer attributed to contextual factors is still considered too small to be of interest or to warrant the additional labour that merging the second source of data can entail, it should be remembered that Sewell and Orenstein (1965) had somewhat greater success in similar work. In particular, they demonstrated the presence of interaction effects that would not have been teased out of the data without the inclusion of census-based indicators in their study.

Merging census data with individual-level survey data permits the specification of forms of relationships at different levels of analysis. Hannan (1971) noted that we cannot assume that a relationship between two phenomena, simply because it assumes a particular form when observed at one level of aggregation, will retain the same functional form at another level. Consequently, he urges that we examine the consistency between micro-models which pertain to individual level variables, and macro-models which reflect the phenomena at an aggregated level. This would entail including in questionnaires items designed to obtain data at the individual level similar to those provided by the census. Of course, where individual census returns are available, as they are in the public-use samples of census data that are released by some census authorities, this is not necessary (see Chapter 11). However, in those countries which do not have such data sets, replication of census-type questions in local questionnaires is almost the only way in which correspondences can be established. In fact, since many of the census items are similar to the 'fact-sheet' questions included by survey researchers in their questionnaires, this is not a particularly costly exercise. All that it would require is the merger of census data from the survey respondent's immediate locality.

The final reason for incorporating census data into survey-based data collections has more to do with posterity than with the researcher's own immediate objective. Increasingly, quantitative social data are lodged with national social data archives so that they may be re-analysed either in the form collected or after combination with other data sets by researchers other than the primary investigator. While the form that such secondary analyses take is still developing, several fairly powerful techniques have taken root. One of these, that exemplified by the simulation of the American electorate reported by Pool, Abelson and Popkin (1965), seems a particularly strong contender for future adoption in different fields. Basically, Pool and his colleagues used data from over 100,000 respondents in sixty-five opinion polls which measured the same demographic characteristics to create over four hundred 'voter types' to whom sets of social and political attitude profiles could be ascribed. These 'groups', in conjunction with their putative socio-political evaluative frameworks, provided a powerful base for the analysis of American presidential voting.

The accretion of survey-based data sets to which have been appended data from other levels of aggregation will create, at quite a low cost, an immensely valuable stock of data for future generations of researchers. These researchers will not only have the capability of looking at new problems with these enriched data but they will also be able to re-examine the propositions originally investigated with the aid of this material. Clearly, the latter capability is logically outside the possibilities available to the initial investigator.

We believe there are substantial research benefits to be gained by linking survey and census data. What has not been emphasized in all of the above is the commercial advantage of linking individual and aggregate data or the possibility of bridging time. We consider these related items next.

10.2.3 THE COMMERCIAL ASPECTS

Consider the situation where, on the basis of a national sample, we know how many tins of beans, cans of beer and indigestion tablets are purchased by families or individuals of specified social class and other attributes. Assuming that all families or individuals of the same type consume approximately the same amount and, moreover, purchase from within their own neighbourhood, success in marketing these staple commodities will be greatly enhanced if the vendor locates his shop near the most prolific consumers of his goods. A firm known as CACI (building upon the work of Webber) has pioneered the use of census data to identify the EDs in Britain which have, for example, such high bean-buying propensities.

In essence, the work is based upon two foundations (Bickmore, Shaw and Tulloch 1980). The first of these is ACORN – A Classification of Residential Neighbourhoods – carried out by Richard Webber whilst employed at the Centre for Environmental Studies, in association with OPCS (see Webber and Craig 1978, Webber 1977). The actual procedure used in commercial work was based upon a grouping of the 16,714 wards and civil parishes in Britain in 1971 which had more than fifty people. The grouping was based upon forty variables describing age structure, household composition, etc. and was carried out by cluster analysis (see Chapter 8). On this basis, thirty-six clusters or residential types were identified; for simplicity, these were further grouped into seven neighbourhood types. Each ward or parish was then allocated to a residential area type and a neighbourhood type.

The second foundation is the Target Group Index (TGI) of the British Market Research Board. This is a consumption survey, collecting information from 24,000 adults annually. The 'informants' live in 200 parliamentary constituencies nationwide and supply information by postal questionnaire on 2500 brands in 200 'fast-moving' consumer product fields. It extends to consumer durables, financial services, recreation, leisure and travel. The TGI information for 1978 was coded by 1971 census ward or parish; as a consequence, it was a trivial operation to match together ACORN and TGI.

National analyses of the individual TGI responses indicate, for instance, that bingo players are concentrated in council estates, older terraced neighbourhoods and tenement areas. Some complications occur – wine drinking, it appears, is a habit in both high status areas and in low status, multi-occupied ones! In principle, then, it is a simple matter to find those parts of Britain which have certain consumption characteristics. Since TGI includes information on which newspapers are read and which radio and TV stations are heard and seen by the respondents, targeting advertising is also comparatively easy.

The whole procedure is an ingenious exploitation of two different data sources which, when linked, offer much more than either does independently so far as marketing is concerned. It would, however, be intellectually remiss if we did not point out three difficulties in the approach:

- i the area classification technique used has been fiercely criticized by Openshaw (see Chapter 8) who has demonstrated many different – equally good and interpretable, but very different – classifications from their data;
- ii the problems of making valid inferences from a mixture of aggregate (census) and individual (TGI) data are staggering, as we have hinted at in section 10.2.2.1;
- iii no reasonable evidence to show that the approach works consistently (or even occasionally) 'on the ground' is known to these authors.

Nonetheless, the practical importance of such classifications has fired academics such as Openshaw and firms such as Geoplan (see appendix 8) to provide improved methods based on SAS data from the 1981 Census.

10.2.4 BRIDGING TIME

Given their usual decennial frequency, much can happen between censuses and, for certain purposes, it is essential to obtain as up-to-date demographic, housing or socioeconomic information as is possible. One obvious example is in the allocation of the Block Grant (see section 3.3.1) from central to local government. Part of the input to this computation comes from OPCS in the form of the published mid-year population estimates. Such estimates are, of course, calibrated on the basis of the latest available census figures: after the

1971 Census, it was found that the worst discrepancy between the mid-year estimates and the 'correct' value given by the census was no less than 8 per cent. The method by which these estimates are calculated has been described in OPCS (1980c).

The mid-year estimates, however, are only available down to the local-government district level and their accuracy, particularly for their age break-downs, has been criticized. For smaller areas, such as wards and EDs, other solutions are necessary and a number of solutions which involved using individual level data – either on a sampled basis or, alternatively, collected through normal administrative processes – to up-date the census aggregate statistics have been investigated. Much the most common approach in Britain is to use a data source which relates to individuals, is up-dated frequently and yet is publicly available: the Electoral Register.

Considerable interest had arisen over the possible use of the electoral register to supplement census data as long ago as 1976 when, in the wake of the cancellation of the 1976 Census, a Steering Committee was set up to examine the feasibility of such a scheme.

Obtaining local information on births and deaths is not a problem, since such individual data are registered and are freely available. In contrast, adequate data on the final component influencing net population in an area – net migration – is much less available. This has to be estimated from some proxy or surrogate, of which change in the number of people on the Electoral Register is the most obvious one. The limitations of the Register for this purpose are well known (Masters and Shortridge 1981) and include:

- it provides only partial coverage; it excludes those too young to vote, service voters and aliens;
- it does not relate to a single point in time but rather to a period of two weeks or more – some multiple registrations therefore occur;
- canvass methods vary between areas and over time;
- it provides very little information on age structure.

Proposals for extending the electoral canvass to collect improved population estimates were made by the Steering Committee and duly rejected by the Government in June 1980 (see Manners and Rauta 1981; OPCS 1981a). The reasons given were the increased burden on the public, the extra cost (estimated at £5 million each time), the difficulty of reconciling the traditional independence of electoral register officers with the need for some central oversight of canvass methods and the basic incompatibilities between the electoral registration process and the collection of accurate population statistics.

Masters and Shortridge (1981) have argued both that the Government was wrong to make this decision and that the Committee placed too much emphasis on developing a survey methodology which would produce results of census quality, rather than results which would be a significant improvement on those currently available. Based upon their own experience in Shropshire in 1976 and 1979, they claim that response rates to a county-wide population survey in conjunction with the electoral canvass were between 87 and 89 per cent and, furthermore, the whole process was inexpensive because it 'piggy-backed' the register. The results, in so far as they can be assessed by comparison with other sources, are claimed to be at least as good as the mid-year estimate for the county as a whole and provide, of course, geographical detail not otherwise available. It is worth adding, however, that Brazier and Hayward (1981) – while supporting the value of electoral register-based population surveys – stressed the much greater difficulties in carrying these out in more urban areas. In inner city areas, their response rates went down to 50 per cent compared with response rates of over 90 per cent in the rural hinterland. They have argued that such variable response rates ensure that the figures could not be grossed up reliably to provide a headcount. The debate continues!

We have used the electoral register as an (important) example of methods of bridging between decennial census data. There are, of course, many others which could be used either singly or as a 'battery'. Some are indeed only available to the general public as areal aggregates: the *Statistics of Trade Act* forbids dissemination of very detailed statistics from the Census of Employment (carried out every year from 1971 to 1978 and, in the future, probably on a three-yearly basis) to the general public but data for employment office areas – from henceforth to be based on postcode sectors (see section 2.5.5) – are normally available. Other data which might give, even in aggregate form, some indication of net migration are the time series of car registrations for postcode sectors created by the Driver and Vehicle Licensing Centre.

10.3 Standardizing non-census data

Quite apart from the role of the census in providing a fixed end or 'anchor' point for the mid-year estimates (OPCS 1980c), enabling re-calibration of the projections after each census, the data from the population census have a vital standardization role. Consider the situation where information is available or collected on only a sample of the population, but an involuntary sample which is of unknown representativeness. Such samples are commonplace: perhaps the most common being in the medical field where examples include mortality, morbidity and congenital malformation statistics. It is, for instance, of little analytical significance to know that 1000 of the people between forty and fifty years of age in a given area died in one year; the significance of this statistic is only clear after it has been related to the number of people living in the area who are in the same age group. Such standardization as that involved in creating standardized mortality ratios (see, for instance, Clarke 1972 and Howe 1970) necessitates census or census-type population data. Another similar example is crime statistics.

In a slightly different but related category are global figures for a given area which are not samples. Examples of these are expenditures on education (which Coates *et al.* 1977, 208-10) have shown to vary considerably and, to some extent, systematically between different local authorities in Britain). Unless standardized by the numbers of pupils of school age, etc., it is extremely difficult to compare area with area on a like-with-like basis. In general terms, almost all the annual financial statistics produced by the Chartered Institute of Public Finance and Accountancy (e.g. see CIPFA 1982) need to be standardized in some fashion on the basis of census data – by total population, population in certain age groups, or whatever is appropriate.

All such standardization is straightforward for areas as heavily populated as local government districts. As finer and finer geographical resolution is approached, i.e. towards EDs or small grid squares, a number of complications can appear. Indeed, for a small number of 1 km grid squares in County Durham, one of the authors (DR) found that, over a seven-year period, more people in specified age groups died per annum than – according to the 1971 Census – lived there! A variety of factors were responsible for this, one of the most important being that census figures were not typical of the whole seven-year period. As we have indicated in other places (e.g. Chapter 6), any operation involving the calculation of ratios – as standardization does – becomes more fraught the smaller are the aggregate populations in the areas under consideration.

10.4 How to do it

At its simplest, the merger of census and other information poses no technical problems; at its most complex, the problems are such as to pose real doubts about the utility of the results. We consider this range of possibilities below.

10.4.1 THE SIMPLEST SITUATION

This arises when both data sets pertain to the same areas of ground and have the same identifiers, i.e. area 1 in the first data set is also called area 1 in the second. It is a trivial job to match up the records using standard packages such as SPSS or OSIRIS. Slight complications may occur when:

- i not all areas are present in one data set;
- ii some of the names are spelled differently in the two data sets (necessitating editing or probability-based matching);
- iii though the areas are the same, the names given to them differ (e.g. the identifiers used by OPCS and by Baxter (1976a) for the same districts are different). This necessitates creating a 'look-up table' to translate one set of identifiers to the other set.

Such a simple situation is common in dealing totally with post-1974 English and Welsh districts and with post-1975 Scottish districts and regions. It may well be the situation in the future for much more detailed data as the use of postcode sector data increases (see section 2.5.5).

10.4.2 A LESS SIMPLE BUT EASY SITUATION

This arises when matching aggregate (e.g. census) data with individual (e.g. social survey) data. In all such cases, the procedure is to aggregate the geographically detailed data to fit the less detailed. Provided that each individual's record has an identifier showing which area that person resides in, the procedure is simple – computer packages such as SPSS will permit all individuals with the same identifier to be aggregated into groups. Thereafter, the matching process is identical to that described in section 10.4.1. Without such 'geographical identifiers' matching is, of course, virtually impossible.

A variant on this is where the individual's records contain only a grid reference (such as of their home address). These can then be aggregated together into data for census areas, provided that the boundaries of the areas are in computer form and appropriate software is available (as in SASPAC and GIMMS 4: appendix 7). The necessary Point-In-Polygon procedure is described in section 5.3.1.2.

10.4.3 DIFFICULT SITUATIONS

These arise in a number of circumstances where changes in the areal units (such as of EDs or local authority areas) have occurred over time, or where two data sets are collected over different areal bases (such as English 1981 SAS data and pre-1982 unemployment statistics). Two solutions exist to such problems:

- i aggregate both sets of areas into larger geographical groups until these are compatible. This may mean considerable loss of resolution: DoE, for instance (see Chapter 9), have found that it requires an average of between three and four EDs to be added together to make comparable 1971 and 1981 SAS data, at least on geographical grounds;
- ii select one data set as the 'master one', 'overlay' the other set of areas on the master one and allocate fractions of the numbers of people, etc., in each of the areas in the 'minor data set' to the areas in the master data set. The procedure is essentially that followed by Mounsey in producing a time series of census data from 1901 for the post 1974/5 district level (see Chapter 9).

The situation is eased somewhat if one set of areas (the 'minor set') is, on average, much smaller than the other – under these circumstances many whole areas and parts of others will be used to construct data for each major area.

Complications proliferate when numerous changes occur in both data sets at different moments in time.

Computer software exists (e.g. in the Harvard University Laboratory for Computer Graphics' Odyssey package) to carry out such 'overlay' purely on the basis of the geographical boundaries of the two sets of areas. This is an extremely dangerous and 'blunderbuss' approach: it necessitates some simplifying assumption such as that the population ('total resident population', 'number of unemployed males', etc.) is spread evenly within each of the areas. Nonetheless, this may be the only solution available in some cases. Unhappily, we have no means of measuring how reliable are the end results.

10.5 Recommendations

Users wishing to carry out data linkage between two sets of data should proceed as follows:

- i identify – on paper – the various area types for which each of the data sets are available, plus the time of collection of these data
- ii if the purpose is not to 'bridge time' (section 10.2.4) yet the time of collection differs, make a decision – based on as much local evidence as is available – on whether it is worth proceeding with the data linkage
- iii if both sets of data are not available on the same area basis, study the degree of difference on maps. If no maps are available, do not carry out the linkage. Decide at which level of geographical detail the two data sets may reasonably be linked;
- iv if one set of areas nests totally within the other (e.g. unit postcodes within postcode sectors) proceed from (v) below. If not, find out whether an index already exists and relates to the time of data collection (e.g. the OPCS postcode to ward directory); using it, rename all of the areas to give a common set of names
- v recompute the data, converting any ratio variables such as percentages into count variables
- vi aggregate all of the data within one data set for new, larger areas; repeat this for the second data set
- vii combine the two data sets using one of the few standard statistics packages which permit multiple input files.

11 Microdata from the British Census

PETER NORRIS

11.1 What are microdata?

Microdata are defined in this book as census data pertaining to unaggregated individuals or households. A chapter on such data might appear out of place in a book whose prime purpose is to guide the intending user through the products currently available from the British census, since microdata are not, at the time of writing, available to the public from any British census since 1881. However, there are three reasons for discussing microdata here. The first is that two recent White Papers suggest that OPCS and the Government are not implacably opposed to the release of microdata. Second, the Registrar-General has recently requested submissions from potential users of microdata regarding the form which the data might take if released (HM Government 1981). Third, microdata are much more flexible than are area aggregates such as data for EDs: not only can they be aggregated to area aggregates but their use in raw form minimizes certain methodological problems, as we shall see. Thus the purpose of this chapter is, essentially, identical to the purpose of the book except that it serves as a guide to data which might and should be produced whereas other chapters are, of course, guides to data which are already produced. However, an important secondary purpose of this chapter is to make readers aware that the release of microdata is partly dependent on submissions from users.

We review below the arguments for and against the release of microdata, and then examine the current position regarding such a release from the British census. Before making some concluding remarks we examine some uses of microdata – from the US Census, from pre-1881 British censuses and work undertaken within OPCS using 1971 British census data.

Microdata can take several different forms. Moore (1979) identifies eleven different types of microdata (1979), but we shall be concerned with four types, as listed in descending order of information given:

- type 1: data relating to every individual or household within an area;
- type 2: data relating to every individual or household within an area, with no identifiers attached;

type 3: data relating to a sample of identified individuals;
type 4: data relating to a sample of unidentified individuals.

In the next section, we shall consider which of the above types of microdata would meet user needs.

11.2 Cases for and against the release of microdata from the British Census

11.2.1 CASES FOR THE RELEASE OF MICRODATA

Perhaps the most basic argument in favour of the release of microdata is that it would allow the user to analyse the information according to his or her specific needs. Although the amount of data now available from the census is much greater than that from pre-1961 censuses, especially for small areas, the user still has to deal with categories into which OPCS classifies data. Although age categories, industrial categories, and so on are determined after consultation with census users (and ED boundaries are determined in consultation with local authorities), these categories inevitably cannot meet the needs of every user. Standard SAS, for example, give no information on occupational groups (as opposed to socioeconomic groups), on the employment status of the foreign-born, or on female activity rates by educational standard. By providing all the data pertaining to a sample of unidentified individuals (type 4 data), OPCS would permit studies of the sort mentioned above and many others. Such data would also be valuable for studies of subgroups of the population. Hakim states:

> As a sociologist, I am most aware of the limitations imposed on social research in Britain by the non-availability of microdata, for example in the study of social groups such as children, the elderly, one-parent families, or ethnic minorities (Hakim 1978c).

Such studies might require only a coarse area identification – district, county or even national level data might suffice.

OPCS also limits the flexibility of census data by prescribing the areas for which they are available. A user who wishes to study a particular housing estate or general improvement area has to take the chance that his or her area of interest coincides with one or more EDs. If type 2 data were released, then the user would be able to aggregate the individuals within the area of interest. In practice, providing microdata would be an infinitely flexible but, for many users, a clumsy way of meeting the needs of such a study: if the user is interested in the characteristics of the community as a whole rather than the characteristics of individuals, then he or she derives no benefit from obtaining data on each individual but rather is faced with the tedious task of aggregating individual data to the level of the community being studied. Moreover, the release of such data would be criticized on the grounds of breaching confidentiality, especially as very precise geographical identifiers on each household return would be needed to enable users to aggregate to the desired geographical area, and such geographical identifiers might be used to identify the individuals to whom data pertain (so that the data are, in effect, of type 1). An alternative solution to such requirements would be a service by which users could specify areas in terms of very precise geographical codes, for example postcode units or 10 m grid references, and the census office would provide aggregate data relating to all individuals within the specified area. At present, OPCS will provide special tabulations to order for areas composed of specified EDs or larger areas.

There are, however, uses of microdata which would specifically require the release of at least type 2 data with precise geographical identifiers. One such use is the study of aggregation effects. The areas for which the census offices provide data are a small selection from a very large number of possible areas which could be used. While it might be claimed that census areas tend to be meaningful in respect of physical and social homogeneity, it has already been demonstrated that the results obtained from aggregating individual data can vary greatly as the boundaries of the areas used are altered (Openshaw 1977, Openshaw and Taylor 1981). The effect of aggregation into one area rather than another is one of a number of problems concerning the reliability of aggregate statistical descriptions of individuals. A check on reliability of classification into area is currently being carried out using 1971 Italian census data for Tuscany (Bianchi *et al.* 1980): household and population data have been classified at the ED and at the individual level, and preliminary results indicate that in some areas these classifications are entirely different (Openshaw 1981, pers. comm.). Individual and aggregate data will exactly match only when the characteristics of the aggregated individuals are identical. Clearly this is generally unlikely: when an area is made up of individuals identical in one respect, e.g. employment status, they need not be identical in respect of, say, educational attainment. To design census areas homogeneous in respect of every attribute on which data are collected would probably be impossible and certainly cannot be done without the detailed household returns. For future census planning purposes at least, it would be instructive to know which attributes are most likely to be areally homogeneous and whether areal homogeneity tends to be greater in some parts of Britain than others. Type 1 or type 2 data would be necessary for such analyses.

The problems of drawing inferences regarding individuals from aggregated data is encapsulated in the ecological fallacy, propounded by Robinson in 1950, although work indicating the fallacy had been done earlier (Yule and Kendall 1950). In brief, it states that it is fallacious that a correlation at one level of aggregation will apply at another level, and is often applied to assert that a correlation at any level of aggregation will not necessarily apply at the individual level. Thus an area might contain a large number of old people and a large number of economically active unemployed: it would not follow that one could expect to find a large number of unemployed old people within such an area. Moreover, correlation of aggregate data does not imply causality: one cannot infer from the facts that there are low percentages of retired people and unemployed in Area A, and high percentages of retired people and unemployment in Area B, that an elderly population causes unemployment or vice-versa. Although most researchers who have worked with census SAS are aware of the ecological fallacy (see Chapter 10), the fact that SAS for EDs and wards have been available and microdata have not, has inevitably resulted in a large number of studies using aggregate data and, more importantly, a number of social policies based upon them. Area-based positive discrimination policies developed, such as the setting up of housing action areas and general improvement areas (Edwards 1975), based on the belief that deprivation was and is spatially concentrated. Fears about the adequacy of this approach are apparent in the Home Office's request for special counts from a sample of 1971 EDs which could be used to assess the extent to which deprivation is area- or household-based (Hakim 1978b). However, a more thorough investigation of the suitability of area-based policies would require type 2 or type 4 microdata. The latter could be used to determine the extent to which correlations of aggregated data do exist at the individual level – whether, for example, a correlation between the number of one-parent families and the unskilled in a number of areas really is reflected in a large number of parents in one-parent families appearing as unskilled in microdata. Type 2 data could be used to determine whether, in a particular area, a correlation at the area level holds for the individuals within that area.

The dangers of being restricted to a set of conceptual and methodological tramlines in using aggregate data has been summarized by Moore, who has commented that

> In (the) overall process of generating an understanding of human behaviour, the activities of theory construction, data collection and use are intimately related. Each step in the evolution of theory both guides the types of data sought and is influenced by the types of data available (Moore 1979).

His statement suggests that both theory and practice would evolve further if microdata were to be released – a common situation when new data or techniques become available. Thus we cannot expect to outline all possible applications of microdata here: some will not be apparent until or if the data are released. To some extent, the uses of microdata are dependent on the technology available. Fortunately, methods of analyses capable of handling categorical data are available now whereas they were not ten years ago, and so the handling of large individual data sets is now practical. Further methodological developments can confidently be expected.

Not all socioeconomic data of relevance to local and central government staff and researchers generally are collected in the census: indeed there are many fields where census data are merely used to calibrate figures derived from other sources (see section 10.3). One such example is in medical studies, where the percentage of people of specified age and sex in a given area who contract a disease or who die is compared with the corresponding national or regional figure to establish 'bad risk' areas. Such an aggregate approach is very unsatisfactory since, quite apart from the ecological fallacy, the decennial 'snapshot' nature of the census means that a very non-random sample of the population might be at risk (e.g. recent in-migrants) and not be detected. The simplest solution is to merge individual census data with corresponding medical and other statistics; subsequently, those of like experience – rather than all those in a small geographical area – may be aggregated together. To carry out such file merging or data linkage (see Chapter 10) requires identified individuals, i.e. type 1 or type 3 data. Such research has already been carried out within OPCS in its Longitudinal Study: this is discussed at some length in the next section.

11.2.2 CASES AGAINST THE RELEASE OF MICRODATA

This is an appropriate point at which to turn to the arguments put forward against the release of microdata, since the major argument is that the release of data pertaining to individuals, and in particular to identifiable individuals, would breach the confidentiality of the census. Although the census is compulsory, with non-completion of the form punishable at law, a successful census depends on the consent of the people, for it would be impracticable to fine, say, 500,000 people for non-completion of their census forms. Consent is most likely to be forthcoming if the public does not find the questions asked in the census unduly intrusive and if assurances regarding the confidentiality of the data are given. Against a background of public and pressure-group concern regarding the privacy and confidentiality aspects of the 1971 Census – a concern which has been voiced in relation to governmental and non-governmental databanks over the last ten years – OPCS has stressed their respect for the need for privacy and confidentiality in taking the 1981 Census. Most of the questions criticized as intrusive in the 1971 Census were omitted from the 1981 Census (see Chapter 2). The British Computer Society has examined the security arrangements for the storage and production of census data, and reported in a White Paper (HM Government 1981b). OPCS have given assurances that the data collected will be used for statistical purposes only, and that no data relating to named individuals will be released from the census offices to other government departments or to any other person (Hakim 1978b). Such assurances thus appear to preclude the release of type 1 and type 3 microdata. Moreover, a leaflet issued with the 1971 census form stated that no information on identifiable individuals would be revealed through statistical tables. If this is an aim which OPCS would still espouse, it might rule out type 2 microdata (since fine areal identification might make personal identification a possibility) and casts doubt on the possibility of releasing type 4 microdata. Hakim (1979a, 145) notes that

> It is considered that in Britain, unlike the United States with a much larger population, the release of microdata on a sample basis does not adequately prevent the disclosure of information about identifiable individuals unless additional censoring techniques are applied to the data.

The validity of her argument is questionable, for although the United States does have a population four times that of Great Britain, censored microdata are released from the US Census for neighbourhoods, and samples containing full information on the selected individuals and households are released for counties of population 250,000 upwards. Clearly, then, the fact that the USA has a larger total population does not justify non-release of a microdata sample for Great Britain (population 54 million). It might (perhaps) be argued that OPCS are over-cautious in not releasing microdata samples because of the fear that this will be seen as a breach of confidentiality which will lead to a lowering in the quality of response to subsequent censuses and a reduction in the highly-valued accuracy of the British Census (Redfern 1981a).

The confidentiality issue is of great complexity, and is dealt with at greater length by Bulmer (1980) and Flaherty (1979). It is readily apparent that the release of microdata of types 1 and 3 would be politically impossible and perhaps in the long run self-defeating, if such a release were to create public hostility towards subsequent censuses. Hakim's comment above suggests that type 2 and type 4 microdata might also be considered to breach confidentiality constraints, but we are far from convinced that this stricter interpretation is a legitimate one. In the first place, microdata are not alone amongst census data in providing the possibility of the identification of data pertaining to an individual. Despite precautions taken by OPCS (see Chapters 1 and 2), it is still possible that somebody with local knowledge studying SAS tables for a small ED might be able to relate some data – though (thanks to the adjustment procedure) not with great certainty – to a particular individual. Indeed, the outlandish possibility exists that data in a 0.1 per cent national microdata sample could be recognized as relating to a particular individual but microdata of type 4 need be no greater a threat to confidentiality than data already released by OPCS.

All our discussion thus far presupposes the release of what are essentially the full household returns, with or without full identification or, alternatively, a sample of them. The breach of confidentiality might, however, be minimized by censoring techniques. For example, data obtained from more delicate questions might be omitted, or responses might be coded into broad categories.

Spatial labelling of each return at ED level might not in itself be sufficient to prevent the identification of individuals but, combined with the censoring mentioned above, it might be acceptable – all the more so for 1971 data. The risks to confidentiality of censored data from the 1971 Census labelled at ED level cannot be great – yet such data would be sufficient – even now – for some of the purposes mentioned in the first part of this section.

However, even if OPCS were to be convinced of the research value and safety of releasing certain forms of microdata, legal obstacles to such a release would have to be overcome. The 1920 Census Act allows for the Registrar-General to release statistical abstracts from the census. It is unclear whether microdata could be so defined. In any case, it is unlikely that the release of microdata would be sanctioned before some form of public debate.

A public debate, as well as indicating whether or not the public would be prepared to accept the release of certain types of microdata, might also serve to show the level of general demand which exists for microdata. Lack of demand is a further argument advanced against the release of microdata, for the 1920 Census Act obliges the Registrar-General to recoup the cost of producing statistical abstracts. While this obligation is open to criticism (is it fair that the public, having co-operated in the gathering of the data, should be charged for the finished product?), it underpins the census office's charging policy for all unpublished data and, if challenged, it should be challenged in relation to all data and not only microdata. Given the constraint imposed by the Census Act, it is understandable that OPCS should be reluctant to commit time and other resources to the production of microdata unless sure that a market for the data exists. However, there are indications that a market does exist. The Home Office's concern to achieve a suitable balance between area-based and household-based programmes has already been mentioned: indeed, central and local government have much to gain from studies which will show whether or not data at ED or ward level are adequately indicative of the characteristics of individuals and therefore suitable for the development of social policy. Central government can be seen as a suitable market for microdata (local government's interest will depend on the area levels for which microdata are released: a district is unlikely to be interested if data are available only for the region and coarse units). The academic world has shown interest in microdata: in a recent questionnaire on uses of the census by academics, 41 per cent of respondents (149 individuals) indicated that they would be interested in using microdata (Norris 1980). Finally, as has already been suggested, many potential uses (and hence potential users) of microdata will not be apparent until the data have been released – though this is scarcely a cost-justifiable basis for production of microdata! Some risk is always involved in putting any new product onto the market: however, the cost of releasing microdata is unlikely to be as great as the cost of preparing complete cross-tabulations, since the requirement (type 3 and 4 data) is for a sample of cases drawn from existing records. Precise costing will depend on the types of microdata released (censoring would increase cost, for example) and on whether the census offices decide to produce standard microdata tapes along the lines of the US Public Use Sample Tapes, or to announce their willingness to meet *ad hoc* requests for microdata of a certain type. In either case, it is probably fair comment that the census offices regard the possible loss of public confidence as a greater cost of the release of microdata than the expenditure of time and resources in their preparation.

It would be inappropriate to end this assessment of the arguments for and against the release of microdata before considering the present position regarding such a release from the British Census. Some recent developments are therefore considered in the next section.

11.3 The present position in Britain

The present position regarding microdata from the British Census is that none have been released to the public from contemporary censuses, although the confidentiality of census data is deemed to have lapsed after 100 years and enumerators' books containing type 1 data are publicly available for the censuses of 1841–81. Contemporary microdata are used in studies within the census offices, notably in the Longitudinal Study discussed in the next section.

Microdata have not been available because of the reasons listed in the previous section, namely confidentiality, the need for statutory authority, and the lack of sufficient demand. However, two White Papers published in 1981 indicate that the release of some types of microdata is looked on favourably by some government advisers.

In *1981 Census of Population: Confidentiality and Computing* the British Computer Society reported on the safeguards used in the computing operations for the census. The report notes that census data are at present available only in aggregated form, and recommends that

> ... consideration be given to the provision of raw, but unidentified, data in machine-readable form drawn from the census records on a sample basis (HM Government 1981, 2.45).

The government reply noted the availability of public use sample tapes from censuses in North America and recognized that their release enabled users to make their own statistical analyses without placing extra demands on the census authorities' computing facilities. While mentioning the three arguments against the release of microdata, and pointing out that these would preclude the release of some types, the reply invited interested bodies and persons to make proposals on the type of public use tape (i.e. microdata) which would meet a range of user needs while maintaining confidentiality (HM Government 1981, 3.14).

It is encouraging that microdata should find support in a report whose prime concern is with means of ensuring the confidentiality of the census. It is also encouraging that the second White Paper to offer support for microdata is chiefly concerned with the cost-effectiveness of government statistical services. This paper is based on Sir Derek Rayner's report to the Prime Minister, and is entitled *Government Statistical Services* (HM Government 1981). In the section on OPCS the following observation was made

> ... less costly (to government) and more flexible means of enabling the public, in the form of interested bodies, researchers, historians and so on to have access to figures held in government should be exploited. I have in mind here the use of camera-ready copy, public use tapes, computer printouts, microfiche and so on (HM Government 1981, 17.5).

Like the British Computer Society report, this White Paper recommends that a code of practice relating to the use of data for statistical purposes be published, and explicitly states that this should enable more statistical research to be undertaken in universities and other academic institutes rather than in the civil service.

These two reports open the way for the discussion of the release of type 4 and possibly type 2 microdata. Some suggestions are put forward in the conclusion; in the next section we examine three practical examples of uses of different types of microdata – the US Public Use Sample Tapes, the OPCS Longitudinal Study and enumerators' books from the 1871 British Census.

11.4 Practical uses of microdata

11.4.1 US PUBLIC USE SAMPLE TAPES

The first US census from which microdata were made available was that of 1960, when 1 per cent and 0.1 per cent Public Use Sample Tapes (PUSTs) were released. In 1970 six PUSTs were released, each comprising 1 per cent samples of the population drawn from the responses to the two long questionnaires administered to one in five and one in twenty households and made available at three levels – state, standard metropolitan statistical area (SMSA) and neighbourhood. The neighbourhood tapes, known as neighbourhood characteristics files, are censored. Since steps are taken to ensure that no individual appears in more than one file, 1970 microdata are available on 6 per cent of America's population, or approximately twelve million people. Most users, however, work with subsamples of one or two files, as is the case in the two studies cited here.

Oppenheimer (1974) has drawn subsamples from both the 1960 and the 1970 Censuses in order to study the relationship between male occupational life cycles and family life cycles, with the particular purpose of assessing the extent to which income meets the financial needs of the family at different stages in the cycles. In the article discussed here only the 1960 subsample has been used. To classify family structures, Oppenheimer calculated the typical number and ages of children according to the age of the father. To assess income, occupations were classified into major groupings and, within each grouping, occupations were sorted according to maximum income achieved. Having thus classified occupations, the median 1959 earnings in each classification were calculated according to age. The study showed that lower-paid sales workers, craftsmen, operatives, service and clerical workers and labourers reached their peak incomes between the ages of thirty-five and forty-four, whereas the financial needs of their families peaked when the father was in his later forties and early fifties. Oppenheimer suggested that the economic disadvantage of these lower-paid males in the later stages of the family lifecycle created pressure for their wives to work.

Women's employment and family size was the subject of an article by Weller (1977), drawing on over 90,000 records from both the 1960 and 1970 Censuses. The purposes of the study were to determine the nature and extent of the negative relationship between the employment of wives and cumulative family size, to examine how far this relationship varied amongst different age, educational and racial groups, and how it changed through time. With 'children ever born' as the dependent variable, a multiple classification analysis was applied, involving such variables as duration of marriage, race, years of education, husband's income and wife's income, the presence of relatives in the household, occupation and weeks worked in the year preceding the census. The results confirmed that the negative relationship between wife's employment and cumulative family size is stronger amongst whites than non-whites, amongst women with more than twelve years' education, amongst those who have been married less than ten years and amongst families with no relatives living with them.

As the British census covers a narrower range of topics than does the US census, it would not be possible to duplicate either of these studies exactly even if microdata were available, but the central theme of Weller's study – the relationship between wife's employment and cumulative family size – could be followed using British microdata, with a range of variables which might act on this relationship brought into consideration. Using 1981 SAS, such a study could only get as far as identifying for each area (EDs, etc.) the proportion of married women, with children aged 0–4 or 5–15, who are in employment – which is clearly very much less satisfactory.

11.4.2 THE OPCS LONGITUDINAL STUDY

The US Public Use Sample Tapes are an example of type 4 microdata: the data incorporated in OPCS's Longitudinal Study are of type 3. It is necessary for OPCS to identify individuals to whom data relate because data from other sources are merged with census data. The study is based on a 1 per cent sample of individuals counted in the 1971 Census as resident in England and Wales, and is supplemented by 1 per cent of those born in, or migrating to, England and Wales after 1971. By using the National Health Service Central Register, subsequent events pertaining to those people in the sample can be recorded. These include death, births, death of spouse, emigration, internal migration and cancer registration. Some of these records contain further information – birth and death records, for example, carry occupational classifications which have been used to compare social class with that recorded in the 1971 Census, which will permit the examination, as families and individuals move through the life cycle, of changes in medical, demographic, social and economic aspects. The study has already been used to calculate standardized mortality ratios for household types differentiated by tenure, amenity and housing density. Each of these has been further examined in relation to cause of death (Goldblatt and Fox 1978). The researchers working on the study are at pains to point out the safeguards taken to ensure confidentiality: indeed, the researchers do not know who the individuals in the study are, since the matching of data is done by others within OPCS and identifiers are then removed. They emphasize that

> Strict measures are taken to safeguard the confidentiality of information supplied by the public. The results of ... analyses will be presented ... in the form of statistical tables and diagrams which do not reveal information about any identifiable individual. At the same time no information relating to identifiable individuals will be used for administrative purposes (Goldblatt and Fox 1978, 21).

11.4.3 HISTORICAL MICRODATA

Information on identifiable individuals (type 1 data) is available from the British censuses of 1841–81, since confidentiality is deemed to lapse after 100 years (in the USA the period is 72 years). A transcription of some pages from an 1871 enumerator's book for Tow Law, County Durham, is given in figure 11.1, to indicate the information available: the 1851, 1861 and 1881 censuses carried the same information, and 1841 rather less. Though only a few items of information are given for each person, the number of questions which can be answered is large. What is the mean household size? Does it vary according to occupation? How many households have servants, and how are they distributed according to the occupation of the household head? What is the ratio of children to women of child-bearing age? Does it vary according to parents' birthplace, or according to the occupation of the household head, or from one part of the community to another? Does occupation vary with birthplace? Can we calculate an index of social status from occupation, number of servants and family size? Are immigrants to the community of higher or lower status? Do

```
79107DC JOHN          HEWITT     BDR U23 MINER                    DUR   BEECHBURN
79107DC OWEN          KEEGHAN    BDR M35 COLLY LAB                IRE
79108DC JOHN          BURNS      H   M50 COLLY LAB                IRE
79108DC ROSE          BURNS      W   M40                          IRE
79108DC CATHERINE     BURNS      D    14 SCHOLAR                  DUR   WOLS
79108DC ANN           BURNS      D    11 SCHOLAR                  DUR   WOLS
79108DC MARGT         BURNS      D     9 SCHOLAR                  DUR   WOLS
79108DC MICHAEL       BURNS      S     6 SCHOLAR                  DUR   WOLS
79108DC ROSE          BURNS      D     4 SCHOLAR                  DUR   WOLS
79108DC PATRICK       BURNS      S     2                          DUR   WOLS
79108DC THOS          MCMAHON    BDR U30 COLLY LAB                IRE
79108DC JAMES         HARDY      BDR U60 COLLY LAB                IRE
79108DC MICHAEL       TRAYNOR    BDR U32 COLLY LAB                IRE
79108DC PETER         WARD       BDR U47 LAB IRON FURNACES        IRE
79109DC JOHN          WAGGOT     H   M23 CHARGER AT IRONFURNACEDUR  STANHOPE
80109DC ANN           WAGGOT     W   M21                          DUR   STANHOPE
80109DC JOHN   G      WAGGOT     S    M8                          DUR   WOLS
80109DC THOS          EGGLESTON  COUSU19 COLLY LAB                DUR   CROOK
80110DC THOS          JACKSON    H   M23 IRON FURNACE LAB         NHUMBGRAFTON
80110DC ANN           JACKSON    W   M25                          DUR   WOLS
80111DC ANN           PAINE      H   U74                          DUR   STANHOPE
80112DC ABRAHAM       DYSTON     H   M20 JOINER JOURN             DUR   WOODIFIELD
80112DC LOUISA        DYSTON     W   M18                          DUR   JOBSHILL
80112DC JANE A        DYSTON     D     1                          DUR   CROOK
80113DC JOSEPH        ELLISON    H   M53 QUARRYMAN LAB            NHUMBHEALEY
80113DC ELIZ          ELLISON    W   M51                          DUR   STANHOPE
80113DC JOHN          ELLISON    S    19 IRON FOUNDER JOURN       DUR   WOLS
80113DC JANE   A      ELLISON    D    14                          DUR   WOLS
80114DC HENRY         O'BRIAN    H   M56 COLLY LAB                IRE
80114DC MARY          O'BRIAN    W   M42                          DUR   STANHOPE
80114DC SAMUEL        BUCKLEY    BDR U50 COLLY LAB                DERBYGLOSSOP
80115DC WM            BELL       H   M42 JOINER JOURN             DUR   SATLEY
80115DC ANN           BELL       W   M47 MILLINER                 DUR   STANHOPE
80115DC JOSEPH        BELL       S   U19 GROCERS SHOPMAN          DUR   WOLS
80115DC JANE   A      BELL       D   U18 MILLINER                 DUR   WOLS
80115DC MARY          BELL       D    15 SCHOLAR                  DUR   WOLS
80115DC ELIZ          BELL       D    13 SCHOLAR                  DUR   WOLS
80116DC WM            TATE       H   M27 MINER                    NHUMBOVINGTON
80116DC MARY          TATE       W   M24                          DUR   DARLINGTON
80116DC SAMUEL        TATE       S     4                          NHUMBMICKLEY
```

Figure 11.1

A transcription from the census enumerator's book covering part of Tow Law, Co. Durham, in 1871

The first set of characters (e.g. 79107DC) contains the transcriber's page reference (79), the number of the census schedule (107) and the street in which the house is situated (DC = Dan's Castle).

After the name, the next columns give relationship to household head (boarder, head, wife, daughter, son and cousin are given in this example).

Next comes marital status (U or blank = unmarried, M = married, W = widowed), then age in years (M8 = 8 months).

Occupation is given next (Lab = labourer and Journ = journeyman), and finally county and place birthplaces of children indicate that families move frequently? How many unmarried women are there, and how many widows? Can different parts of the community be differentiated according to occupation, birthplace, family size, number of servants, number of boarders and the proportion of households sharing accommodation? At what age are more children at work than at school? How many of the people present in a community at one census are still there ten years later? It is clear that most of these questions can be answered without the need for the individuals to be identified by name. The last is an exception, though an important one. By tracing individuals from one census to another, not only can we assess the stability of the community, but also build up life-cycle histories. Names can also be used to link census and non-census data: Welford (1980) has, for example, linked data from the 1851–71 censuses for two villages near Hartlepool with parish register data. Indeed, the microfilms of nineteenth-century censuses are amongst the most heavily used materials held by county record offices, and the heaviest users are genealogists and family historians tracing the family history of their own or other families.

A specific and simple illustration of some of the advantages of microdata can be given by considering the distribution of the Irish-born in Tow Law, County Durham in 1871. They constituted some 10 per cent of the town's population, distributed amongst the five EDs as shown in table 11.1. While this table reveals some concentration in ED9 and an under-representation in ED10, it does not suggest that the Irish in Tow Law are heavily segregated. However, if we consider the proportion of Irish living in each street, a different pattern emerges, as table 11.2 shows. While this table should be interpreted with caution (for example, highest and lowest percentages are more likely to occur in streets with fewest inhabitants), it is apparent that segregation at street level is more marked than it is at ED level. Several streets contain no Irish inhabitants, while in others – notably Baring Street and The Hutts – the Irish make up more than one-third of the population. The impression of segregation is increased by an arbitrary division of the population into blocks of 120 people

Table 11.1 Irish-born as a proportion of the population of each ED, Tow Law, Co. Durham, 1871

Area	*Total population*	*Irish-born population*	*Irish-born as a percentage of total population*
ED 7	948	83	8.75
ED 8	994	119	12.00
ED 9	942	133	14.12
ED 10	1017	76	7.47
ED 11	932	86	9.23
Total	4833	497	10.28

Table 11.2 The proportions of Irish-born living in each street in Tow Law, Co. Durham, 1871

Street	*Households*	*Persons*	*Irish-born*	*Irish-born as percentage of inhabitants*
Wolsingham Road	67	358	35	9.78
Thornley Road	30	158	10	6.33
Harrison Street	25	135	17	12.59
Bridge Street	22	98	12	12.24
Park Terrace, Thornley Pit, Gas Works & Deerness House	31	199	9	4.52
Wesley Street & Back Wesley Street	19	100	12	12.00
Campbell Street	37	172	32	18.60
Back Campbell Street	20	106	12	11.32
Back Railway Terrace & Battery Cottages	8	49	15	30.61
Bridge Street	16	93	2	2.15
Back Bridge Street	6	32	–	–
St. Albans Street	13	58	8	13.79
Back High Street	25	133	17	12.78
High Street	52	251	21	8.37
Baring Street	38	242	94	38.84
High Street	68	415	38	9.16
Castle Bank	27	143	–	–
Grove Road	15	95	–	–
Railway Cottages, Ironworks Road, Stable House & Furnace Shed	8	47	1	2.13
Pease's Row	7	28	2	7.14
Smith's Cottages	3	18	6	33.33
Dan's Castle Inn & Dan's Castle	122	588	52	8.84
Hopwood's Yard	9	54	13	24.07
Dan's Castle	19	100	1	1.00
Private Road	7	29	–	–
Thornley Terrace	9	47	1	2.13
Tow Law House, Back of Offices & Keeper's Row	18	102	–	–
The Vicarage & Alma Cottages	5	35	–	–
Dan's Castle	3	13	1	7.69
Cornsay Road	1	3	–	–
Inkerman Cottages	74	323	22	6.81
Blackfield & Blackfield Gate	3	14	–	–
Hutts	14	66	32	48.48
North Cottages	52	282	26	9.22
Ridley's Houses	10	67	4	5.97
Black Prince Row	36	180	2	1.11

Table 11.3 The proportion of Irish-born in equal population divisions of Tow Law, Co. Durham, 1871

Area	*Population*	*Irish-born population*	*Irish-born as % of area population*
A	120	9	7.50
B	120	21	17.50
C	120	5	4.17
D	120	9	7.50
E	120	14	11.67
F	119	11	9.24
G	120	6	5.00
H	120	8	6.67
I	120	21	17.50
J	120	20	16.67
K	120	14	11.67
L	120	18	15.00
M	120	8	6.67
N	120	11	9.24
O	120	15	12.50
P	120	8	6.67
Q	120	40	33.33
R	120	57	47.50
S	120	8	6.67
T	120	14	11.67
U	120	9	7.50
V	120	8	6.67
W	120	–	–
X	120	–	–
Y	120	11	9.24
Z	120	7	5.83
AA	120	15	12.50
BB	120	1	0.83
CC	119	10	8.33
DD	120	30	25.00
EE	120	2	1.67
FF	120	–	–
GG	120	3	2.50
HH	120	6	5.00
II	120	13	10.83
JJ	120	35	29.17
KK	120	9	7.50
LL	120	15	12.50
MM	120	4	3.33
NN	120	2	1.67
OO	35	–	–

each (table 11.3). There are four blocks in which the Irish constitute more than one quarter of the population – two in Baring Street (47 per cent and 33 per cent), one in The Hutts/North Cottage area (29 per cent) and one in Dan's Castle/Harles Yard (25 per cent): in another four blocks there are one or no Irish-born – in Castle Bank, Grove Road, Dan's Castle and Temperance Terrace/ Keepers Row.

Two points should be stressed. First, the street and 'block' level studies indicate that at ED level the segregation of the Irish-born is understated because EDs are composed of areas which are unlike in the proportion of Irish-born which they contain. This is most striking in ED9 which contains one of the most Irish areas of Tow Law – Baring Street – and two of the least Irish areas – Castle Bank and Grove Road. In this respect, then, ED9 is lacking in internal homogeneity and is, in fact, extremely heterogeneous.

Secondly, if 1981 SAS – the most comprehensive cross-tabulations ever produced from the British census at ED level – were reproduced using 1871 returns, they would not offer cross-tabulation of birthplace against occupation, age or relationship to head of household. Microdata, on the other hand, shows that the Irish-born in Tow Law in 1871 were over-represented amongst the lower-status coke oven labourers and iron-workers and under-represented amongst the higher-status miners, were over-represented amongst the twenty to twenty-nine-year-olds and that many of them lived as boarders or lodgers. Moreover, microdata afford the opportunity to repeat the analysis classifying as Irish those children born in Durham but with one or both parents Irish-born. Against this flexibility, possible use of ED data can seem rigid (Microfilm M18/23, Durham County Record Office).

Those readers interested in studying nineteenth century censuses will find Wrigley (1972), Lawton (1978) and Rogers (1972) most valuable in suggesting areas for study, problems and possible solutions. Smith (1977) and Patterson (1977) provide examples of work done with the 1851 Census in adult education classes. Two seminal studies concerned with larger settlements should also be consulted – Anderson on Preston (1971) and Armstrong on York (1974).

11.5 Conclusion

The evidence of the two White Papers cited in section 11.3 suggests that the release of microdata from the British census is a distinct possibility. In this chapter we have attempted to suggest some of the uses to which different types of microdata might be put, and some of the problems involved in releasing microdata. Three sorts of use of microdata can be defined:

i to permit greater flexibility in the analysis of census data than is possible using published or unpublished standard census output; such flexibility being particularly useful in the study of characteristics of subgroups, e.g. one-parent families, agricultural workers, car owners;

ii to permit an analysis of the reliability of ED and other aggregate data as descriptions of the individuals who are aggregated;

iii to permit the matching of census to non-census data pertaining to the same individual.

The basic problem concerning the release of microdata is the confidentiality of the census: it is from this that other problems stem, and in this concluding section we shall examine each of the three sorts of uses of microdata in the light of the confidentiality problem.

The matching of census to non-census data requires type 1 or type 3 microdata because of the need for an individual identifier (name and address are not the only possible unique identifiers, but are the easiest to use). Although much of the information gathered at the census would seem to be innocuous, the census offices have given the assurance that no data on identifiable individuals will be released and so such a release would damage the confidence in the census of some of the public. While the value of linking census and non-census data can be considerable, as is shown by the results of the Longitudinal Study, the work is only safely done within OPCS. The prompt release of the results of such studies would be of great interest to researchers and to statutory bodies. In practice, it could be advantageous for 'external' researchers to commission OPCS to carry out such research for them – an inversion of the usual relationship between researchers and central government!

The use of microdata for more flexible analysis can largely be met by the release of type 4 data, i.e. data which are anonymized and sampled. The chances of identifying an individual from an anonymized sample would vary with the areal identification attached, but if a sample were identified as being drawn from the records of a particular county or district, the likelihood of individual identification would be very small indeed. It should be stressed that, while we cannot say that identification would be absolutely impossible, the same statement is also true of SAS data: there is always the remote possibility that an unlikely combination of characteristics could be attributed to a particular individual. Research on the relative risks to confidentiality posed by different types of data, including microdata, might be considered by the census offices as a prerequisite for the release of microdata. Type 4 data carry the least threat to confidentiality, and it is worth noting that such data are already released by OPCS from the General Household Survey (GHS), if at a very coarse geographical resolution. Users are required to submit details of their plans for using the GHS microdata to OPCS and, on receiving OPCS' approval, they agree to use the data only for the purpose specified. Finally, OPCS request that they should see and approve the draft of any report before it is made (SSRC Survey Archive 1981). The most remarkable aspect of this arrangement is not so much that restrictions are applied, but that type 4 data are already released by OPCS, albeit from a voluntary survey, without being considered a breach of confidentiality. Taking this together with the release of type 4 data from foreign censuses, a strong case can be made for such a release from the British census. It is the responsibility of the census offices and potential users to decide on the form that such a release should take. Matters to be determined include the smallest geographical area to which data might be coded, the method of release, whether standard tapes should be prepared or whether the census offices should indicate their willingness to fulfil *ad hoc* requests meeting certain criteria, pricing, and whether any of the safeguards mentioned below and pertaining to type 2 data, should be applied to type 4 data.

Type 2 data (anonymous 100 per cent records) do not breach confidentiality in the obvious way that types 1 and 3 do, but the risks of individual identification are greater than they are for type 4 data. Type 2 data is needed for an analysis of the reliability of ED data in view of the problems posed by the ecological fallacy and aggregation effects. It might be claimed that such studies could be carried out using nineteenth-century census data which are no longer confidential. While it is evident from section 11.4 that some work along these lines could be done using these data, some problems could not be dealt with adequately, and the manual collection of a data set pertaining to a contiguous settlement containing, say, 30,000 people would be time-consuming. Nineteenth-century data would also be inappropriate if a local authority wished to test the extent to which data for particular EDs reflected the characteristics of individuals, or if a researcher wished to discover which personal or household attributes for which census data are available tend to be spatially clustered. Furthermore, since 1981 EDs are planned according to different criteria than were nineteenth-century EDs, it might be unfair to assess the adequacy with which the former describe the characteristics of the individuals contained by reference to the adequacy of the latter. Yet it is clear that if contemporary 100 per cent records are released with a precise spatial identifier, it would be possible to infer to which individual or household a particular record pertained.

Despite these difficulties, however, the reliability of SAS data at ED level as a basis for social policy needs to be tested if resources are to be allocated and programmes set up using these data. Similar data are currently being tested in other European countries (Openshaw 1981), and it is possible that the results of these tests could cast doubt on the utility of British SAS data. In order to forestall this eventuality, OPCS should either undertake a programme of research into aggregation effects and the ecological fallacy themselves (and this might be hard to achieve in view of recent recommendations regarding staffing levels (HM Government 1981), or they should make available the microdata with which such studies could be carried out. If necessary, the following safeguards might be applied to the data

i information on more contentious items could be removed;
ii responses could be classified into broad categories;

iii spatial identification could be limited to the ED or 100 m resolution (though this would hamper studies of alternative zoning);

iv 1971 microdata could be used (the data would probably be of little embarrassment even if assignable to named individuals).

Because type 2 and type 4 data meet different needs, the cases for them should be argued separately, with the release or non-release of one independent of that of the other. In conclusion, while agreeing with Hakim that

> the non-availability of microdata constitutes a significant limitation on the type of census analysis which can be carried out in Britain (Hakim 1978c)

we have reason to hope for the removal of this 'significant limitation'. The speed with which it is removed depends, in part, on the demand for microdata expressed by users.

Appendix 1

Census questionnaire forms

The following pages contain photographically reduced versions of:

i the 1981 census questionnaire form for England (pp. 321–5);

ii the Welsh question section of the 1981 census questionnaire form for Wales (the rest of the Welsh form is identical to that for England) (p. 326);

iii the 1981 census questionnaire form for Scotland (pp. 327–31).

Note: Only one side of the census forms is shown, the other side being identical and used for other members in the household.

In strict confidence

1981 Census England

H Form for Private Households

A household comprises **either** *one person living alone* **or** *a group of persons (who may or may not be related) living at the same address with common housekeeping. Persons staying temporarily with the household are included.*

To the Head or Joint Heads or members of the Household

Please complete this census form and have it ready to be collected by the census enumerator for your area. He or she will call for the form on **Monday 6 April 1981** or soon after. If you are not sure how to complete any of the entries on the form, the enumerator will be glad to help you when he calls. He will also need to check that you have filled in all the entries.

This census is being held in accordance with a decision made by Parliament. The leaflet headed 'Census 1981' describes why it is necessary and how the information will be used. Completion of this form is compulsory under the Census Act 1920. If you refuse to complete it, or if you give false information, you may have to pay a fine of up to £50.

Your replies will be treated in STRICT CONFIDENCE. They will be used to produce statistics but your name and address will NOT be fed into the census computer. After the census, the forms will be locked away for 100 years before they are passed to the Public Record Office.

If any member of the household who is age 16 or over does not wish you or other members of the household to see his or her personal information, then please ask the enumerator for an extra form and an envelope. The enumerator will then explain how to proceed.

When you have completed the form, please sign the declaration in Panel C on the last page.

A R THATCHER
Registrar General

Office of Population Censuses and Surveys
PO Box 200 Portsmouth PO2 8HH
Telephone 0329-42511

Please answer questions H1 - H5 about your household's accommodation, check the answer in Panel A, answer questions 1-16 overleaf and Panel B on the back page. Where boxes are provided please answer by putting a tick against the answer which applies. For example, if the answer to the marital status question is 'Single', tick box 1 thus:

1 ☑ Single

Please use ink or ballpoint pen.

To be completed by the Enumerator

Census District	Enumeration District	Form Number

Name ....

Address ....

....

.... Postcode ☐☐☐☐☐☐☐☐

Panel A
To be completed by the Enumerator and amended, if necessary, by the person(s) signing this form.

This household's accommodation is:

- In a caravan ☐ 20
- In any other mobile or temporary structure ☐ 30
- In a purpose-built block of flats or maisonettes ☐ 12
- In any other permanent building in which the entrance from **outside** the building is:
  - NOT SHARED with another household ☐ 10
  - SHARED with another household ☐ 11

H1 Rooms

Please count the rooms in your household's accommodation.

Do not count:

small kitchens, that is those under 2 metres (6ft 6ins) wide, bathrooms, WCs.

Number of rooms ....

Note
Rooms divided by curtains or portable screens count as one; those divided by a fixed or sliding partition count as two.

Rooms used solely for business, professional or trade purposes should be excluded.

H2 Tenure

How do you and your household occupy your accommodation? Please tick the appropriate box.

As an owner occupier (including purchase by mortgage):

1 ☐ of freehold property
2 ☐ of leasehold property

By renting, rent free or by lease:

3 ☐ from a local authority (council or New Town)
4 ☐ with a job, shop, farm or other business
5 ☐ from a housing association or charitable trust
6 ☐ furnished from a private landlord, company or other organisation
7 ☐ unfurnished from a private landlord, company or other organisation

In some other way:

☐ Please give details

....

Note

a If the accommodation is occupied by lease originally granted for, or since extended to, more than 21 years, tick box 2.

b If a share in the property is being bought under an arrangement with a local authority, New Town corporation or housing association, *for example, shared ownership (equity sharing), a co-ownership scheme,* tick box 1 or 2 as appropriate.

H3 Amenities

Has your household the use of the following amenities on these premises? Please tick the appropriate boxes.

- A fixed bath or shower permanently connected to a water supply and a waste pipe

1 ☐ YES – for use only by this household
2 ☐ YES – for use also by another household
3 ☐ NO fixed bath or shower

- A flush toilet (WC) with entrance inside the building

1 ☐ YES – for use only by this household
2 ☐ YES – for use also by another household
3 ☐ NO inside flush toilet (WC)

- A flush toilet (WC) with entrance outside the building

1 ☐ YES – for use only by this household
2 ☐ YES – for use also by another household
3 ☐ NO outside flush toilet (WC)

H4

Please answer this question if box 11 in Panel A is ticked.

Are your rooms (not counting a bathroom or WC) enclosed behind your own front door **inside** the building?

1 ☐ YES 2 ☐ NO

If your household has only one room (not including a bathroom or WC) please answer 'YES'.

H5 Cars and vans

Please tick the appropriate box to indicate the number of cars and vans normally available for use by you or members of your household (other than visitors).

0 ☐ None
1 ☐ One
2 ☐ Two
3 ☐ Three or more

Include any car or van provided by employers if normally available for use by you or members of your household but **exclude** vans used solely for the carriage of goods.

PLEASE TURN OVER →

Where boxes are provided please tick the appropriate box (Please use ink or ballpoint pen)

1-3 Include on your census form:

- all the persons who spend Census night 5-6 April 1981 in this household (including anyone visiting overnight and anyone who arrives here on the Monday and who has not been included as present on another census form).
- any persons who usually live with your household but who are absent on census night.
  For example, on holiday, in hospital, at school or college. Include them even if you know they are being put on another census form elsewhere.

Write the names in the top row, starting with the head or a joint head of household (BLOCK CAPITALS please)

Include any newly born baby even if still in hospital. If not yet given a name write 'BABY' and the surname.

1st person	2nd person
Name and surname	Name and surname
Sex ☐ Male ☐ Female	**Sex** ☐ Male ☐ Female
Date of birth Day .... Month .... Year	**Date of birth** Day .... Month .... Year ....

4 Marital status

Please tick the box showing the present marital status.

If separated but not divorced please tick *'Married (1st marriage)'* or *'Re-married'* as appropriate.

1st person	2nd person
Marital status 1 ☐ Single 2 ☐ Married (1st marriage) 3 ☐ Re-married 4 ☐ Divorced 5 ☐ Widowed	**Marital status** 1 ☐ Single 2 ☐ Married (1st marriage) 3 ☐ Re-married 4 ☐ Divorced 5 ☐ Widowed

5 Relationship in household

Please tick the box which indicates the relationship of each person to the person entered in the first column.

Please write in relationship of *'Other relative'* – for example, father, daughter-in-law, brother-in-law, niece, uncle, cousin, grandchild.

Please write in position in household of *'Unrelated person'* – for example, boarder, housekeeper, friend, flatmate, foster child.

1st person	2nd person
	Relationship to 1st person 01 ☐ Husband or wife 02 ☐ Son or daughter ☐ Other relative, please specify .... ☐ Unrelated, please specify ....

6 Whereabouts on night of 5-6 April 1981

Please tick the appropriate box to indicate where the person was on the night of 5-6 April 1981.

1st person	2nd person
1 ☐ At this address, out on night work or travelling to this address 2 ☐ Elsewhere in England, Wales or Scotland 3 ☐ Outside Great Britain	1 ☐ At this address, out on night work or travelling to this address 2 ☐ Elsewhere in England, Wales or Scotland 3 ☐ Outside Great Britain

7 Usual address

If the person usually lives here please tick *'This address'*. If not, tick *'Elsewhere'* and write in the person's usual address.

The home address should be taken as the usual address for a head of household who lives away from home for part of the week.

For students and children away from home during term time, the home address should be taken as the usual address.

Boarders should be asked what they consider to be their usual address.

1st person	2nd person
☐ This address ☐ Elsewhere – write the person's usual address and postcode Address (BLOCK CAPITALS please) .... including Postcode ☐☐☐☐☐☐☐	☐ This address ☐ Elsewhere – write the person's usual address and postcode Address (BLOCK CAPITALS please) .... including Postcode ☐☐☐☐☐☐☐

8 Usual address one year ago

If the person's usual address one year ago, on 5 April 1980, was the same as that given in answer to question 7 please tick *'Same'*. If not, please tick *'Different'* and write in the usual address.

If everyone on the form has moved from the same address, please write the address in full for the first person and indicate with an arrow that this applies to the other people on the form.

For a child born since 5 April 1980 write 'UNDER ONE'.

1st person	2nd person
☐ Same as at Question 7 ☐ Different – write the person's address and postcode on 5 April 1980 Address (BLOCK CAPITALS please) .... including Postcode ☐☐☐☐☐☐☐	☐ Same as at Question 7 ☐ Different – write the person's address and postcode on 5 April 1980 Address (BLOCK CAPITALS please) .... including Postcode ☐☐☐☐☐☐☐

9 Country of birth

Please tick the appropriate box.

If box 6 is ticked please write in the present name of the country in which the birthplace is now situated.

1st person	2nd person
Country of birth 1 ☐ England 2 ☐ Wales 3 ☐ Scotland 4 ☐ Northern Ireland 5 ☐ Irish Republic 6 ☐ Elsewhere. Please write the present name of the country.	**Country of birth** 1 ☐ England 2 ☐ Wales 3 ☐ Scotland 4 ☐ Northern Ireland 5 ☐ Irish Republic 6 ☐ Elsewhere. Please write the present name of the country. ....

Where boxes are provided please tick the appropriate box (Please use ink or ballpoint pen)

1-3 Include on your census form:

- all the persons who spend Census night 5-6 April 1981 in this household (including anyone visiting overnight and anyone who arrives here on the Monday and who has not been included as present on another census form).
- any persons who usually live with your household but who are absent on census night.
  For example, on holiday, in hospital, at school or college. Include them even if you know they are being put on another census form elsewhere.

Write the names in the top row, starting with the head or a joint head of household (BLOCK CAPITALS please)

Include any newly born baby even if still in hospital. If not yet given a name write 'BABY' and the surname.

1st person	**2nd person**
Name and surname	Name and surname
Sex ☐ Male ☐ Female	**Sex** ☐ Male ☐ Female
Date of birth Day Month Year	**Date of birth** Day Month Year

Answers to remaining questions are not required for persons under 16 years of age (born after 5 April 1965)

10 Whether working, retired, housewife, etc last week

Please tick all boxes appropriate to the person's activity last week.

A **job** (box 1 and box 2) means any type of work for pay or profit but not unpaid work. It includes:

casual or temporary work
work on a person's own account
work in a family business
part-time work even if only for a few hours

A **part-time** job (box 2) is a job in which the hours worked, excluding any overtime, are usually 30 hours or less per week.

Tick box 1 or box 2, as appropriate, if the person had a job but was not at work for all or part of the week because he or she was:

on holiday
temporarily laid off
on strike
sick

For a full-time student tick box 9 as well as any other appropriate boxes.

Do not count as a full-time student a person in a paid occupation in which training is also given, such as a student nurse, an apprentice or a management trainee.

1st person	2nd person
1 ☐ In a full-time job at any time last week	1 ☐ In a full-time job at any time last week
2 ☐ In a part-time job at any time last week	2 ☐ In a part-time job at any time last week
3 ☐ Waiting to take up a job already accepted	3 ☐ Waiting to take up a job already accepted
4 ☐ Seeking work	4 ☐ Seeking work
5 ☐ Prevented by temporary sickness from seeking work	5 ☐ Prevented by temporary sickness from seeking work
6 ☐ Permanently sick or disabled	6 ☐ Permanently sick or disabled
7 ☐ Housewife	7 ☐ Housewife
8 ☐ Wholly retired from employment	8 ☐ Wholly retired from employment
9 ☐ At school or a full-time student at an educational establishment not provided by an employer	9 ☐ At school or a full-time student at an educational establishment not provided by an employer
0 ☐ Other, please specify	0 ☐ Other, please specify ....

Questions about present or previous employment

For persons in a job last week —**please answer questions 11-15 in respect of the main job during the week**

For persons wholly retired
For persons out of work last week
For persons prevented from working because of permanent sickness or disablement —**please answer questions 11-13 in respect of the most recent full-time job, if any.**

For other persons including those with no previous job—please write 'Not applicable' at question 11 and leave questions 12-15 blank.

11 Name and business of employer (if self-employed the name and nature of the person's business)

a Please give the name of the person's employer. Give the trading name if one is used and avoid using abbreviations or initials.

For members of the Armed Forces, civil servants and local government officers see notes on back page before answering questions 11-15.

b Please describe clearly what the employer (or the person if self-employed) makes or does.

For a person employed in private domestic service write 'Domestic Service'.

1st person	2nd person
a Name of employer	**a** Name of employer
b Nature of business	**b** Nature of business

12 Occupation

a Please give full and precise details of the person's occupation.

If a person's job is known in the trade or industry by a special name, use that name. Precise terms should be used, for example, 'radio-mechanic', 'jig and tool fitter', 'tool room foreman' rather than general terms such as 'mechanic', 'fitter', 'foreman'.

b Please describe the actual work done.

1st person	2nd person
a Occupation	**a** Occupation
b Description of work	**b** Description of work

Question 16 should be answered for all persons aged 18 or over

Where boxes are provided please tick the appropriate box (Please use ink or ballpoint pen)

1-3 Include on your census form:

- all the persons who spend Census night 5-6 April 1981 in this household (including anyone visiting overnight and anyone who arrives here on the Monday and who has not been included as present on another census form).
- any persons who usually live with your household but who are absent on census night.
  For example, on holiday, in hospital, at school or college. Include them even if you know they are being put on another census form elsewhere.

Write the names in the top row, starting with the head or a joint head of household (BLOCK CAPITALS please)

Include any newly born baby even if still in hospital. If not yet given a name write 'BABY' and the surname.

1st person	2nd person
Name and surname	Name and surname
Sex ☐ Male ☐ Female	**Sex** ☐ Male ☐ Female
Date of birth Day Month Year	**Date of birth** Day Month Year

13 Employment status

Please tick the appropriate box.

Box 3 should be ticked for a person having management or supervisory responsibility for other employees. For a person employed as a quality control inspector and concerned only with the technical quality of a product tick box 2.

1st person	2nd person
1 ☐ Apprentice or articled trainee	1 ☐ Apprentice or articled trainee
2 ☐ Employee not supervising other employees	2 ☐ Employee not supervising other employees
3 ☐ Employee supervising other employees	3 ☐ Employee supervising other employees
4 ☐ Self-employed not employing others	4 ☐ Self-employed not employing others
5 ☐ Self-employed employing others	5 ☐ Self-employed employing others

14 Address of place of work

Please give the full address of the person's place of work.

For a person employed on a site for a long period give the address of the site.

For a person not working regularly at one place who reports daily to a depot or other fixed address, give that address.

For a person not reporting daily to a fixed address tick box 1.

For a person working mainly at home tick box 2.

1st person	2nd person
Full address and postcode of workplace Address (BLOCK CAPITALS please)	Full address and postcode of workplace Address (BLOCK CAPITALS please)
....	....
....	....
including Postcode	including Postcode
1 ☐ No fixed place	1 ☐ No fixed place
2 ☐ Mainly at home	2 ☐ Mainly at home

15 Daily journey to work

Please tick the appropriate box to show how the longest part, by distance, of the person's daily journey to work is normally made.

For a person using different means of transport on different days show the means most often used.

Car or van includes three-wheeled cars and motor caravans.

1st person	2nd person
1 ☐ British Rail train	1 ☐ British Rail train
2 ☐ Underground, tube, metro, etc	2 ☐ Underground, tube, metro, etc
3 ☐ Bus, minibus or coach (public or private)	3 ☐ Bus, minibus or coach (public or private)
4 ☐ Motor cycle, scooter, moped	4 ☐ Motor cycle, scooter, moped
5 ☐ Car or van — pool, sharing driving	5 ☐ Car or van — pool, sharing driving
6 ☐ Car or van — driver	6 ☐ Car or van — driver
7 ☐ Car or van — passenger	7 ☐ Car or van — passenger
8 ☐ Pedal cycle	8 ☐ Pedal cycle
9 ☐ On foot	9 ☐ On foot
0 ☐ Other (please specify)	0 ☐ Other (please specify)
....	....
0 ☐ Works mainly at home	0 ☐ Works mainly at home

16 Degrees, professional and vocational qualifications

Has the person obtained any qualifications after the age of 18 such as:

Degrees, Diplomas, HNC, HND,
Nursing qualifications, Teaching qualifications,
Graduate or corporate membership of professional institutions,
Other professional, educational or vocational qualifications?

Exclude qualifications normally obtained at school such as GCE, CSE and School Certificates.

If box 2 is ticked write in all qualifications even if they are not relevant to the person's present job or if the person is not working.

Please list the qualifications in the order in which they were obtained.

Write for each qualification:

the title
the major subject or subjects
the year obtained and
the awarding institution

If more than three, please enter in a spare column and link with an arrow.

1st person	2nd person
1 ☐ NO — none of these	1 ☐ NO — none of these
2 ☐ YES — give details	2 ☐ YES — give details
Title	Title ....
Subject(s)	Subject(s) ....
Year	Year ....
Institution	Institution ....
Title	Title ....
Subject(s)	Subject(s) ....
Year	Year ....
Institution	Institution ....
Title	Title ....
Subject(s)	Subject(s) ....
Year	Year ....
Institution	Institution ....

Notes

Armed Forces

For members of the Armed Forces – write 'ARMED FORCES' at **11a**; for a member of the Armed Forces of a country other than the UK – add the name of the country.

At **12a** give the rank or rating only.

Questions **11b, 12b** and **13** should not be answered.

Civil servants

For civil servants – give the name of their Department at **11a**, write 'GOVERNMENT DEPARTMENT' at **11b** and 'CIVIL SERVANT' at **12a**.

At **12b** for a non-industrial civil servant – give the rank or grade only.

At **12b** for an industrial civil servant – give the job title only, which should be in precise terms, for example, 'radio mechanic', 'jig and tool fitter', 'tool room foreman' rather than general terms such as 'mechanic', 'fitter', 'foreman'.

Local government officers

For local government officers and other public officials – give the name of the local authority or public body at **11a** and the branch in which they are employed at **11b**.

At **12a** give rank or grade and complete **12b**.

PLEASE COMPLETE PANELS BELOW

Panel B

Is there anyone else you have not included (such as a visitor) because there was no room on the form?

☐ YES ☐ NO

Please ask the Enumerator for another form.

Have you left anyone out because you were not sure whether they should be included? If so, please give their name(s) and reason why you were not sure about including them.

Name ____________________

Reason ____________________

Name ____________________

Reason ____________________

Name ____________________

Reason ____________________

Name ____________________

Reason ____________________

May the Enumerator telephone you if we have a query on your form? If so, please write your telephone number here.

____

SPECIMEN

Before you sign the form will you please check:

- **that all relevant questions have been answered**
- **that you have included everyone who spent the night 5-6 April in your household**
- **that you have included anyone who usually lives here but was away from home on the night of 5-6 April**
- **that no visitors, boarders or children including newly born infants, have been missed.**

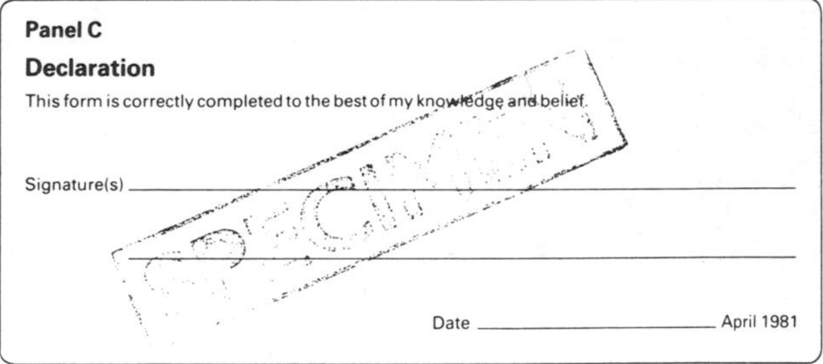

Panel C

Declaration

This form is correctly completed to the best of my knowledge and belief.

Signature(s) ____________________

____

Date ____________________ April 1981

SPECIMEN

Where boxes are provided please tick the appropriate box (Please use ink or ballpoint pen)

1-3 Include on your census form:

- all the persons who spend Census night 5-6 April 1981 in this household (including anyone visiting overnight and anyone who arrives here on the Monday and who has not been included as present on another census form).
- any persons who usually live with your household but who are absent on census night.
  For example, on holiday, in hospital, at school or college. Include them even if you know they are being put on another census form elsewhere.

Write the names in the top row, starting with the head or a joint head of household (BLOCK CAPITALS please)

Include any newly born baby even if still in hospital. If not yet given a name write 'BABY' and the surname.

1st person	**2nd person**
Name and surname	Name and surname
Sex ☐ Male ☐ Female	**Sex** ☐ Male ☐ Female
Date of birth Day .... Month .... Year	**Date of birth** Day .... Month .... Year ....

W Welsh language

For all persons aged 3 or over (born before 6 April 1978).

a Does the person speak Welsh? Please tick the appropriate box.

b If the person speaks Welsh, does he or she also:

Speak English?
Read Welsh?
Write Welsh?

1st person	2nd person
a Speaks Welsh	**a** Speaks Welsh
1 ☐ YES 0 ☐ NO	1 ☐ YES 0 ☐ NO
b if YES	**b** if YES
1 ☐ Speaks English	1 ☐ Speaks English
2 ☐ Reads Welsh	2 ☐ Reads Welsh
4 ☐ Writes Welsh	4 ☐ Writes Welsh

Answers to remaining questions are not required for persons under 16 years of age (born after 5 April 1965)

10 Whether working, retired, housewife, etc last week

Please tick all boxes appropriate to the person's activity last week.

A **job** (box 1 and box 2) means any type of work for pay or profit but not unpaid work. It includes:

casual or temporary work
work on a person's own account
work in a family business
part-time work even if only for a few hours

A **part-time** job (box 2) is a job in which the hours worked, excluding any overtime, are usually 30 hours or less per week.

Tick box 1 or box 2, as appropriate, if the person had a job but was not at work for all or part of the week because he or she was:

on holiday
temporarily laid off
on strike
sick

For a full-time student tick box 9 as well as any other appropriate boxes.

Do not count as a full-time student a person in a paid occupation in which training is also given, such as a student nurse, an apprentice or a management trainee.

1st person	2nd person
1 ☐ In a full-time job at any time last week	1 ☐ In a full-time job at any time last week
2 ☐ In a part-time job at any time last week	2 ☐ In a part-time job at any time last week
3 ☐ Waiting to take up a job already accepted	3 ☐ Waiting to take up a job already accepted
4 ☐ Seeking work	4 ☐ Seeking work
5 ☐ Prevented by temporary sickness from seeking work	5 ☐ Prevented by temporary sickness from seeking work
6 ☐ Permanently sick or disabled	6 ☐ Permanently sick or disabled
7 ☐ Housewife	7 ☐ Housewife
8 ☐ Wholly retired from employment	8 ☐ Wholly retired from employment
9 ☐ At school or a full-time student at an educational establishment not provided by an employer	9 ☐ At school or a full-time student at an educational establishment not provided by an employer
0 ☐ Other, please specify	0 ☐ Other, please specify ....

Questions about present or previous employment

For persons in a job last week **—please answer questions 11-15 in respect of the main job during the week**

For persons wholly retired
For persons out of work last week
For persons prevented from working because of permanent sickness or disablement
—please answer questions 11-13 in respect of the most recent full-time job,

For other persons including those with no previous job—please write 'Not applicable' at question 11 and leave questions 12-15 bla

11 Name and business of employer (if self-employed the name and nature of the person's business)

a Please give the name of the person's employer. Give the trading name if one is used and avoid using abbreviations or initials.

For members of the Armed Forces, civil servants and local government officers see notes on back page before answering questions 11-15.

b Please describe clearly what the employer (or the person if self-employed) makes or does.

For a person employed in private domestic service write 'Domestic Service'.

1st person	2nd person
a Name of employer	**a** Name of employer
b Nature of business	**b** Nature of business

12 Occupation

a Please give full and precise details of the person's occupation.

If a person's job is known in the trade or industry by a special name, use that name. Precise terms should be used, for example, 'radio-mechanic', 'jig and tool fitter', 'tool room foreman' rather than general terms such as 'mechanic', 'fitter', 'foreman'.

b Please describe the actual work done.

1st person	2nd person
a Occupation	**a** Occupation
b Description of work	**b** Description of work

Question 16 should be answered for all persons aged 18 or over

IN STRICT CONFIDENCE

Form H
for private households

1981 Census
Scotland

To the Head, Joint Heads or Acting Head of the Household

Please complete this form and have it ready for collection by the enumerator who will call on Monday, 6 April or soon after that day. If you need help in answering any of the questions, do not hesitate to ask the enumerator or to use the "Freefone" service mentioned below. The enumerator has to ensure that you have completed the form and you should give him any further information he may need for this purpose.

The form is used only for compiling statistics and when you have completed it in accordance with the instructions, it will be treated as CONFIDENTIAL and no information about named individuals will be passed by the Census Office to any other Government Department or any other authority or person. If anyone employed in taking the Census improperly discloses information you provide, he will be liable to prosecution. Similarly, you must not disclose information which anyone (for example, a visitor or boarder) gives you to enable you to complete the form.

The legal obligation to fill in the whole form rests on YOU, but each person who has to be included is required to give you the information you need. However, if anyone aged 16 or over does not wish to give you his or her personal information, the enumerator or local Census Officer should be asked for an individual form and official envelope in which to return it. Then you need answer only questions 1a, 3 and 4 for that person. If the person leaves his completed form with you for collection, pass the envelope unopened to the enumerator.

Completion of this form is compulsory under the Census Act 1920 and there are penalties of up to £50 for failing to comply with the requirements described above or for giving false information.

When you have completed the form, please sign the declaration at the foot of the last page.

Census Headquarters
Ladywell Road
EDINBURGH
EH12 7TF

V C STEWART
Registrar General

SPECIMEN

Please note

Household definition A household comprises either one person living alone or a group of persons (who may or may not be related) living at the same address with common housekeeping. Persons staying temporarily with the household are included.

Answers Please answer questions where boxes are provided by putting a tick in the box against the answer which applies. For example the answer for a female member of your household at question 1b would be:

1 ☐ Male 2 ☑ Female

Lines are provided where a written answer is required.

Additional information If you are in doubt about a question, and the notes given in this form and the Information Leaflet do not clarify the situation, please ask the enumerator for an explanation when he calls again or ask the telephone operator for Freefone 8485 and speak to a member of the Census Headquarters staff. Freefone is available from 8.30 am to 8 pm, Monday to Friday, between 30 March and 10 April and between 2 and 8 pm on Sunday 5 April.

Extra forms If the forms provided are insufficient for the number of persons in your household, additional forms may be obtained from your enumerator or by contacting Census Headquarters by Freefone.

Households without a head If there is no recognised head or acting head of the household the legal obligation to complete the form rests with each member of the household aged 16 or over, any one of whom may complete the form.

To be completed by the enumerator and amended, if necessary, by the person(s) signing this form

(a) ED No ☐☐☐☐☐☐

Form No ☐☐☐

Continuation form reference no. ☐☐/☐☐

(b) Name

____

(c) Address

____

Postcode ☐☐☐☐☐☐☐

(d) Type of building in which household's accommodation is situated – tick only one box

House that is:

1 ☐ Detached
2 ☐ Semi-detached
3 ☐ Terraced (including end of terrace)

Flat or rooms in a building with:

4 ☐ 2 storeys
5 ☐ 3 or 4 storeys
6 ☐ 5 storeys or over
7 ☐ A single flat with a shop, office or other business

Non-permanent structure:

8 ☐ Caravan
9 ☐ Other non-permanent structure

(e) Level of household's accommodation – tick only one box

a ☐ All on ground or on ground and other floors
b ☐ All in basement
c ☐ All on first or higher floor

☐☐ State actual floor of entry to household's accommodation if box c is ticked

(f) Means of access to household's accommodation – either tick box 1 or any of boxes 2-4 that apply

1 ☐ No lift; no external or internal stair (with 6 or more steps) for access
2 ☐ External stair or outside steps (with 6 or more steps) for access
3 ☐ Internal stair (with 6 or more steps) for access
4 ☐ Lift

PLEASE USE INK OR BALLPOINT PEN TO COMPLETE THIS FORM

Include on this form:
- **each person who spends the night of 5-6 April in this household,**
- **each person who usually lives in this household but spends the n**
  during term time and persons on holiday or in hospital even if yo
- **each person who arrives in this household on Monday 6 April wh**

Question	1st person	2nd person
1 Name, sex and date of birth a Write surname and forename(s) in full. b Please tick the appropriate box. c Enter the person's date of birth. *Include any newly born baby even if still in hospital. If not yet given a name write 'BABY' and the surname.*	a Surname Forenames b 1 ☐ Male 2 ☐ Female c Day / Month / Year	a Surname Forenames b 1 ☐ Male 2 ☐ Female c Day / Month / Year
2 Marital status Please tick the box showing the present status. *If separated but not divorced tick box 2 'Married'.*	1 ☐ Single 3 ☐ Divorced 2 ☐ Married 4 ☐ Widowed	1 ☐ Single 3 ☐ Divorced 2 ☐ Married 4 ☐ Widowed
3 Relationship in the household Please tick the box which indicates the relationship of each person to the person entered in the first column. *Please write in relationship of other relatives – for example father, daughter-in-law, brother-in-law, niece, uncle, cousin, grandchild.* *Please write in position in household of unrelated persons – for example boarder, friend, housekeeper, flatmate, foster child etc.* *Step children and adopted children should be returned as son or daughter of their step or adoptive parents.*		Relationship to first person 1 ☐ Husband or wife 2 ☐ Son or daughter ☐ Other relative, please specify ☐ Unrelated, please specify
4 Whereabouts on the night of 5-6 April 1981 Please tick the appropriate box to indicate where the person was on the night of 5-6 April 1981.	1 ☐ At this address, out on night work or travelling to this address 2 ☐ Elsewhere in Scotland, England or Wales 3 ☐ Outside Great Britain	1 ☐ At this address, out on night work or travelling to this address 2 ☐ Elsewhere in Scotland, England or Wales 3 ☐ Outside Great Britain
5 Usual address If the person usually lives here, please tick box 1 'This address'. If not, tick box 2 'Elsewhere' and write in the person's usual address. *The home address should be taken as the usual address for a household head who lives away from home for part of the week.* *For students and children away from home during term time, the home address should be regarded as the usual address.* *Boarders should be asked what they consider to be their usual address.*	1 ☐ This address 2 ☐ Elsewhere – write the person's usual address and postcode Address *(Block capitals please)* including Postcode	1 ☐ This address 2 ☐ Elsewhere – write the person's usual address and postcode Address *(Block capitals please)* including Postcode
6 Usual address one year ago If the person's usual address one year ago, on 5 April 1980, was the same as that given in answer to question 5, please tick box 1 'Same'. If not, please tick box 2 'Different' and write in the usual address. If everyone on the form has moved from the same address, please write the address in full for the first person and indicate with an arrow that this applies to the other people on the form. *For a child born since 5 April 1980 write 'UNDER ONE'.*	1 ☐ Same as at Question 5 2 ☐ Different – write the person's address and postcode on 5 April 1980 Address *(Block capitals please)* including Postcode	1 ☐ Same as at Question 5 2 ☐ Different – write the person's address and postcode on 5 April 1980 Address *(Block capitals please)* including Postcode
7 Country of birth Please tick the appropriate box. If box 6 'Elsewhere' is ticked, please write in the present name of the country in which the birthplace is now situated.	1 ☐ Scotland 2 ☐ England 3 ☐ Wales 4 ☐ Northern Ireland 5 ☐ Irish Republic 6 ☐ Elsewhere. Please write the present name of the country	1 ☐ Scotland 2 ☐ England 3 ☐ Wales 4 ☐ Northern Ireland 5 ☐ Irish Republic 6 ☐ Elsewhere. Please write the present name of the country

Question 8 is for all persons aged 3 or over (born before 6 April 1978).

Question	1st person	2nd person
8 Scottish Gaelic Can the person speak, read or write Scottish Gaelic? Please tick the appropriate box(es).	1 ☐ Can speak Gaelic 2 ☐ Can read Gaelic 3 ☐ Can write Gaelic 4 ☐ Does not know Gaelic	1 ☐ Can speak Gaelic 2 ☐ Can read Gaelic 3 ☐ Can write Gaelic 4 ☐ Does not know Gaelic

PLEASE USE INK OR BALLPOINT PEN TO COMPLETE THIS FORM

Include on this form:
- **each person who spends the night of 5-6 April in this household,**
- **each person who usually lives in this household but spends the n during term time and persons on holiday or in hospital even if yo**
- **each person who arrives in this household on Monday 6 April wh**

Question	**1st person**	**2nd person**
1 Name, sex and date of birth a Write surname and forename(s) in full. b Please tick the appropriate box. c Enter the person's date of birth. *Include any newly born baby even if still in hospital. If not yet given a name write 'BABY' and the surname.*	a Surname Forenames b 1 ☐ Male 2 ☐ Female c Day / Month / Year	a Surname Forenames b 1 ☐ Male 2 ☐ Female c Day / Month / Year

Questions 9-12 are for all persons aged 16 or over (born before 6 April 1965).

	1st person	2nd person
9 Whether working, retired, housewife etc. last week Please tick all the boxes appropriate to the person's activity last week. A job (box 1 and box 2) means any type of work for pay or profit but **not** unpaid work. It includes: casual or temporary work work on a person's own account work in a family business part-time work, even if only for a few hours A part-time job (box 2) is a job in which the hours worked, excluding any overtime, are usually 30 hours or less per week. Tick box 1 or box 2, as appropriate, if the person had a job but was not at work for all or part of the week because he or she was: on holiday temporarily laid off on strike sick Tick box 1 if the job was normally full-time but was interrupted for any reason during the week. *Do not count as a full-time student a person in a paid occupation in which training is also given, such as a student nurse, an apprentice or a management trainee.* *For a full-time student tick box 9 as well as any other appropriate boxes.*	1 ☐ In a full-time job at any time last week 2 ☐ In a part-time job at any time last week 3 ☐ Waiting to take up a job already accepted 4 ☐ Seeking work 5 ☐ Prevented by temporary sickness from seeking work 6 ☐ Permanently sick or disabled 7 ☐ Housewife 8 ☐ Wholly retired from employment 9 ☐ At school or a full-time student at an educational establishment not provided by an employer 10 ☐ Other, please specify	1 ☐ In a full-time job at any time last week 2 ☐ In a part-time job at any time last week 3 ☐ Waiting to take up a job already accepted 4 ☐ Seeking work 5 ☐ Prevented by temporary sickness from seeking work 6 ☐ Permanently sick or disabled 7 ☐ Housewife 8 ☐ Wholly retired from employment 9 ☐ At school or a full-time student at an educational establishment not provided by an employer 10 ☐ Other, please specify

Questions about present or previous employment

For persons in a job last week (boxes 1 or 2 at Question 9 ticked)
For wholly retired persons (box 8 at Question 9 ticked) or persons out of work (boxes 3, 4 or 5 ticked)
For persons who are permanently sick or disabled (box 6 ticked)
For others, including those with no previous job

	1st person	2nd person
10 Name and nature of business of employer (or self-employed person's business) a Please give the name of the person's employer *For members of the Armed Forces, civil servants and local government officials see the notes at the foot of this page before answering questions 10-12.* *For a person employed in private domestic service write 'DOMESTIC SERVICE'.* b Please describe clearly what the employer (or the person if self-employed) makes or does. *General terms such as 'manufacturer', 'merchant', 'agent', 'dealer', 'engineering' are not enough and further details should be given.*	a Name of employer b Nature of business	a Name of employer b Nature of business
11 Occupation a Please give full and precise details of the person's occupation. *If a person's job is known in the trade or industry by a special name, use that name.* *Precise terms should be used, for example, 'radio mechanic', 'chartered electrical engineer', 'jig and tool fitter' or 'toolroom foreman', rather than general terms such as 'mechanic', 'engineer', 'fitter' or 'foreman'.* b Please describe the actual work done.	a Occupation b Description of work	a Occupation b Description of work
12 Employment status Please tick the appropriate box. *Box 3 should be ticked for a person having management or supervisory responsibility for other employees.* *Persons employed as quality control inspectors and concerned only with the technical quality of a product should tick box 2.*	1 ☐ Apprentice or articled trainee 2 ☐ Employee not supervising other employees 3 ☐ Employee supervising other employees 4 ☐ Self-employed not employing others 5 ☐ Self-employed employing others	1 ☐ Apprentice or articled trainee 2 ☐ Employee not supervising other employees 3 ☐ Employee supervising other employees 4 ☐ Self-employed not employing others 5 ☐ Self-employed employing others

Notes: Armed Forces

For members of the Armed Forces write 'ARMED FORCES' in 10a; for a member of the armed forces of a country other than the UK add the name of the country.

At 11a give the rank or rating only.

Questions 10b, 11b and 12 should not be answered.

Local Government and other public officials

For local government officers and other public officials give the name of the local authority or public body at 10a and the branch in which they are employed at 10b.

At 11a give rank or grade and complete 11b and 12.

PLEASE USE INK OR BALLPOINT PEN TO COMPLETE THIS FORM

Include on this form:
- each person who spends the night of 5-6 April in this househ
- each person who usually lives in this household but spends during term time and persons on holiday or in hospital even
- each person who arrives in this household on Monday 6 Apr

Question	1st person	2nd person
1 Name, sex and date of birth a Write surname and forename(s) in full. b Please tick the appropriate box. c Enter the person's date of birth. *Include any newly born baby even if still in hospital. If not yet given a name write 'BABY' and the surname.*	a Surname Forenames b 1 ☐ Male 2 ☐ Female c Day / Month / Year	a Surname Forenames b 1 ☐ Male 2 ☐ Female c Day / Month / Year

Questions 13 and 14 are for all persons aged 16 or over (born before 6 April 1965) who were in a job last week. Give details for the main employment.

Question	1st person	2nd person
13 Address of place of work Please give the full address of the person's place of work. *For a person employed on a site for a long period give the address of the site.* *For a person not working regularly at one place who reports daily to a depot or other fixed address, give that address.* *For a person not reporting daily to a fixed address, tick box 1.* *For a person working mainly at home, tick box 2.*	Full address and postcode of workplace Address *(Block capitals please)* including Postcode 1 ☐ No fixed place 2 ☐ Mainly at home	Full address and postcode of workplace Address *(Block capitals please)* including Postcode 1 ☐ No fixed place 2 ☐ Mainly at home
14 Daily journey to work Please tick the appropriate box to show how the longest part, by distance, of the person's daily journey to work is normally made. *For a person using different means of transport on different days give the means most often used.* *Car or van includes three-wheeled cars and motor caravans.*	Main means of transport to work 1 ☐ British Rail train 2 ☐ Underground, tube, metro etc 3 ☐ Bus, minibus or coach (public or private) 4 ☐ Motor cycle, moped or scooter 5 ☐ Car or van – pool, sharing driving 6 ☐ Car or van – driver 7 ☐ Car or van – passenger 8 ☐ Pedal cycle 9 ☐ On foot 10 ☐ Other, please specify 11 ☐ Works mainly at home	Main means of transport to work 1 ☐ British Rail train 2 ☐ Underground, tube, metro etc 3 ☐ Bus, minibus or coach (public or private) 4 ☐ Motor cycle, moped or scooter 5 ☐ Car or van – pool, sharing driving 6 ☐ Car or van – driver 7 ☐ Car or van – passenger 8 ☐ Pedal cycle 9 ☐ On foot 10 ☐ Other, please specify 11 ☐ Works mainly at home

Question 15 is for all persons aged 18 or over (born before 6 April 1963).

Question	1st person	2nd person
15 Degrees, professional and vocational qualifications Has the person obtained any qualifications after the age of 18, such as: Degrees, Diplomas, HNC, HND, Nursing qualifications, Teaching qualifications, Graduate or corporate membership of professional institutions, Other professional, educational or vocational qualifications? Exclude all qualifications normally obtained at school such as SCE, GCE or School Leaving Certificates. If box 2 is ticked enter all qualifications even if they are not relevant to the person's present job or if the person is not working. Please list the qualifications in the order in which they were obtained Write for each qualification: the title, the major subject or subjects, the year obtained and the awarding institution. *If more than three, please enter in a spare column and link with an arrow*	1 ☐ No – none of these 2 ☐ Yes – give details Title Subject Year Institution Title Subject Year Institution Title Subject Year Institution	1 ☐ No – none of these 2 ☐ Yes – give details Title Subject Year Institution Title Subject Year Institution Title Subject Year Institution

6

Please answer the following questions which relate to your household's accommodation.

16 Tenure

How do you and your household occupy your accommodation?

Please tick the appropriate box.

1 ☐ As an owner-occupier (including purchase by mortgage)

By renting, rent free or by lease

2 ☐ from a local authority (council or New Town) or from the Scottish Special Housing Association (SSHA)

3 ☐ from a housing association other than the SSHA or from a charitable trust

4 ☐ with a job, shop, farm or other business

5 ☐ furnished from a private landlord, company or other organisation

6 ☐ unfurnished from a private landlord, company or other organisation

in some other way:

☐ Please give details

____

If the accommodation is occupied by lease originally granted for 20 years or more, tick box 1 'As owner occupiers'.

If the accommodation is a tied house, or other accommodation provided in connection with the employment of a member of your household on the condition that its tenure is to be given up on leaving the employment, tick box 4 whether rent is paid or not. In the case of a tenancy originally granted by virtue of employment, but extended although the employment has now ceased, tick box 4 if no rent is paid (by yourself or anyone else) but tick box 5 or 6 if rent is paid.

17 Rooms

a How many rooms in your household's accommodation are dining rooms, living rooms or bedrooms? Count spare rooms if they could be used for these purposes. ________ room(s)

b Is cooking generally done in one of the rooms entered in 'a' above? ☐ Yes ☐ No

c Have you any room used for cooking but not included in 'a' above? 1 ☐ Yes 2 ☐ No

Rooms divided by curtains or portable screens count as one, those divided by a fixed or sliding partition count as two.

Rooms used solely for business, professional or trade purposes should be excluded.

18 Household amenities

Has your household the use of the following amenities on these premises?

Please tick the appropriate boxes.

a A fixed bath or shower permanently connected to a water supply and a waste pipe

1 ☐ Yes – for use only by this household

2 ☐ Yes – for use also by another household

3 ☐ No fixed bath or shower

b a flush toilet (WC) with entrance inside the dwelling (exclude any on common stair or landing)

1 ☐ Yes – for use only by this household

2 ☐ Yes – for use also by another household

3 ☐ No inside flush toilet (WC)

c a flush toilet (WC) with entrance outside the dwelling (include any on common stair or landing)

1 ☐ Yes – for use only by this household

2 ☐ Yes – for use also by another household

3 ☐ No outside flush toilet (WC)

19 Shared access

Does your household share the use of any hall, passage, landing or staircase with any other household?

1 ☐ Does not share

2 ☐ Shares only for entry to own household's accommodation

3 ☐ Shares for movement between the rooms of the household's accommodation, that is dining rooms, living rooms and bedrooms shown at question 17a.

20 Cars and vans

Please tick the appropriate box to indicate the number of cars and vans normally available for use by you or members of your household (other than visitors).

0 ☐ None 2 ☐ Two

1 ☐ One 3 ☐ Three or more

Include any car or van provided by employers if normally available for use by you or members of your household, but exclude vans used solely for the carriage of goods.

Before you sign the form will you please check –

- **that all relevant questions have been answered**
- **that you have included everyone who spent the night of 5-6 April in your household**
- **that you have included anyone who usually lives here but was away from home on the night of 5-6 April**
- **that no visitors, boarders, children or newly born infants have been missed**

Declaration:

This form is correctly completed to the best of my knowledge and belief.

Signature(s) ________________________ Date ____ April 1981.

T&T 53-2593 10/80 Dd. 8051876

Appendix 2

The standard layout of the OPCS 1981 SAS tables and the 1981 cell numbers

The following ten pages display the OPCS-designed layout of all 53 of the standard tables from the 1981 SAS. The numbers shown within each table are the cell numbers. Thus 'all present male and female residents in private and non-private households' is referred to as cell (or 'variable') number 1 and the value for each ED, ward, postcode sector, etc. would be printed in this position in computer-produced output from OPCS or from the SASPAC computer package using the COM option (see appendix 7).

Extra information is given in the OPCS header at the top left of each page on area name (e.g. Isle of Wight), ED number, National-Grid reference for area centroid, whether the ED is identical in position on the ground to 1971 or whether this is a special ED, is given in printed output – these would differ for each area.

For areas in Wales, only pages 1 to 8 are available. For areas in England, the identical pages are available with the exception that table 39 on page 8 is not produced. For Scotland, pages 1 to 6, 9 and 10 are available.

Since these pages are generally at least 160 characters wide, few computer line printers can produce such complete pages except by printing left and right halves separately. As a consequence, the SASPAC project team produced 're-jigged pages' by adjusting the pages on which the standard tables are printed: the results can fit on all 'normal' line printers with a carriage width of 131 or more characters. Details of these 're-jigged pages' are given to all computer centres using SASPAC.

CENSUS 1981 SMALL AREA STATISTICS

PAGE 1 — 100%

ED No

Map Reference

Note: $ = ED same as in 1971
$$ = Special Enumeration District

 | Frame No:

Separate explanatory notes are available

1 All persons present; plus absent residents * in private households

	TOTAL PERSONS	In private households: Males	In private households: Fmles	Not in private households: Males	Not in private households: Fmles
1 All present res	1	3	4	6	7
2 All absent res	8	10	11	xxx	xxx
3 All visitors	15	17	18	20	21
Res in UK	22	24	25	27	28
Res outside UK	29	31	32	34	35
ALL PRESENT 1981 1971 BASE (1-3)	36	38	39	41	42
ALL RESIDENT 1981 1981 BASE (1-2)	43	45	46	48	49

2 All residents

Age	TOTAL PERSONS	Males SWD	Males Mrr'd	Females SWD	Females Mrr'd	Ret'd Males
TOTAL	50	52	53	55	56	190
0-4	57	59	xxx	62	xxx	xxx
5-9	64	66	xxx	69	xxx	xxx
10-14	71	73	xxx	76	xxx	xxx
15	78	80	xxx	83	xxx	xxx
16-19	85	87	88	90	91	xxx
20-24	92	94	95	97	98	xxx
25-29	99	101	102	104	105	xxx
30-34	106	108	109	111	112	xxx
35-39	113	115	116	118	119	199
40-44	120	122	123	125	126	200
45-49	127	129	130	132	133	201
50-54	134	136	137	139	140	202
55-59	141	143	144	146	147	203
60-64	148	150	151	153	154	204
65-69	155	157	158	160	161	205
70-74	162	164	165	167	168	206
75-79	169	171	172	174	175	207
80-84	176	178	179	181	182	208
85+	183	185	186	188	189	209

3 Persons present not in private households

Establishments	TOTAL PERS	Males (M)	Fmles (F)	Not usually resident M	Not usually resident F	Residents Staff ## M	Residents Staff ## F	Residents Other M	Residents Other F
TOTAL #	210	211	212	214	215	217	218	219	220
Hotels/boarding houses	221	222	223	225	226	228	229	230	231
Children's homes	232	233	234	236	237	239	240	241	242
Old people's homes	243	244	245	247	248	250	251	252	253
Psychiatric hospitals	254	255	256	258	259	261	262	263	264
Other hospitals	265	266	267	269	270	272	273	274	275
Schools and colleges	276	277	278	280	281	283	284	285	286
Prison dept estabs	287	288	289	291	292	294	295	296	297
Hostels/lodging houses	298	299	300	302	303	305	306	307	308
Other establishments	309	310	311	313	314	316	317	318	319

4 All residents

Country of birth	Males	Fmles
TOTAL	321	322
England	324	325
Scotland	327	328
Wales	330	331
Rest of UK	333	334
Irish Rep	336	337
Old Comm'th	339	340
New Comm'th	342	343
East Africa	345	346
Africa Rem	348	349
Caribbean	351	352
India	354	355
Bangladesh	357	358
Far East	360	361
Mediterr	363	364
Remainder	366	367
Pakistan	369	370
Other E.C.	372	373
Other Europe	375	376
Rest of World	378	379

5 All residents aged 16 or over

Economic Position	TOTAL PERS	Males SWD	Males Mrr'd	Females SWD	Females Mrr'd
ALL PERSONS 16+	380	382	383	385	386
Total econ active	387	389	390	392	393
Working	394	396	397	399	400
Seeking work	401	403	404	406	407
Temp sick	408	410	411	413	414
Total econ inact	415	417	418	420	421
Perm sick	422	424	425	427	428
Retired	429	431	432	434	435
Student	436	438	439	441	442
Other inactive	443	445	446	448	449

NOTES

* Persons returned as usually resident but absent on census night in private households with one or more other person(s) present (Table 1)

\# Includes campers vagrants etc (Table 3)

\## Includes relatives of staff (Tables 3 and 6)

6 All persons present

Age	TOTAL PERSONS	In private households M	In private households F	Not in private households: All present M	All present F	Residents Staff ## M	Residents Staff ## F	Residents Other M	Residents Other F
TOTAL	450	452	453	455	456	457	458	459	460
0-4	461	463	464	466	467	468	469	470	471
5-15	472	474	475	477	478	479	480	481	482
16-24	483	485	486	488	489	490	491	492	493
25-34	494	496	497	499	500	501	502	503	504
35-44	505	507	508	510	511	512	513	514	515
45-54	516	518	519	521	522	523	524	525	526
55-59	527	529	530	532	533	534	535	536	537
60-64	538	540	541	543	544	545	546	547	548
65-69	549	551	552	554	555	556	557	558	559
70-74	560	562	563	565	566	567	568	569	570
75+	571	573	574	576	577	578	579	580	581
Single	582	584	585	587	588	589	590	591	592
Married	593	595	596	598	599	600	601	602	603
Students aged 16 or over	604	606	607	609	610	611	612	613	614

7 All residents aged 16 or over in employment

Employment status	Males	Females SWD	Females Mrr'd
ALL IN EMPLOYMENT	615	616	617
Apprentices and trainees	618	619	620
Employees supervising others	621	622	623
Other employees	624	625	626
Self-empl without employees	627	628	629
Self-empl with employees	630	631	632
ALL EMPLOYEES	633	634	635
Working full-time	636	637	638
Working part-time	639	640	641

8 All residents aged 1 or over with a usual address 1 year before census different from present usual address

Age	TOTAL PERS	Males SWD	Males Mrr'd	Females SWD	Females Mrr'd
TOTAL	642	644	645	647	648
1-4	649	651	xxx	654	xxx
5-15	656	658	xxx	661	xxx
16-24	663	665	666	668	669
25-34	670	672	673	675	676
35-44	677	679	680	682	683
45-59	684	686	687	689	690
60-64	691	693	694	696	697
65+	698	700	701	703	704

9 All Economically Active (EA) residents

Age	TOTAL PERSONS EA	Males EA	Females EA SWD	Females EA Mrr'd	In emp working f/t Males	In emp working f/t Females SWD	In emp working f/t Females Mrr'd	Not in employment Males	Not in employment Females SWD	Not in employment Females Mrr'd	Self empl pers
TOTAL	719	720	722	723	790	792	793	860	862	863	705
16-19	724	725	727	728	795	797	798	865	867	868	706
20-24	729	730	732	733	800	802	803	870	872	873	707
25-29	734	735	737	738	805	807	808	875	877	878	708
30-34	739	740	742	743	810	812	813	880	882	883	709
35-39	744	745	747	748	815	817	818	885	887	888	710
40-44	749	750	752	753	820	822	823	890	892	893	711
45-49	754	755	757	758	825	827	828	895	897	898	712
50-54	759	760	762	763	830	832	833	900	902	903	713
55-59	764	765	767	768	835	837	838	905	907	908	714
60-64	769	770	772	773	840	842	843	910	912	913	715
65-69	774	775	777	778	845	847	848	915	917	918	716
70-74	779	780	782	783	850	852	853	920	922	923	717
75+	784	785	787	788	855	857	858	925	927	928	718

CENSUS 1981 SMALL AREA STATISTICS

PAGE 2 100%

ED No

Map Reference

Note: $ = ED same as in 1971
$$ = Special Enumeration District

 | Frame No:

Separate explanatory notes are available

10 Private households (H) with residents; residents (P)

Tenure		TOTALS	Bath and inside WC present: Both excl	Bath and inside WC present: One/both shared	Lack bath or inside WC	Neither bath nor inside WC	Lack bath	Lack inside WC	Share inside WC	Persons per room: >1.5	Persons per room: >1-1.5	No car
ALL HOUSEHOLDS	H	929	930	931	932	933	934	935	936	945	946	949
	P	937	938	939	940	941	942	943	944	947	948	950
All permanent	H	951	952	953	954	955	956	957	958	1079	1080	1111
	P	959	960	961	962	963	964	965	966	1081	1082	1112
Owner occupied	H	967	968	969	970	971	972	973	974	1083	1084	1113
	P	975	976	977	978	979	980	981	982	1085	1086	1114
Council etc	H	983	984	985	986	987	988	989	990	1087	1088	1115
	P	991	992	993	994	995	996	997	998	1089	1090	1116
Housing association	H	999	1000	1001	1002	1003	1004	1005	1006	1091	1092	1117
	P	1007	1008	1009	1010	1011	1012	1013	1014	1093	1094	1118
Rented with business	H	1015	1016	1017	1018	1019	1020	1021	1022	1095	1096	1119
	P	1023	1024	1025	1026	1027	1028	1029	1030	1097	1098	1120
By virtue of employment	H	1031	1032	1033	1034	1035	1036	1037	1038	1099	1100	1121
	P	1039	1040	1041	1042	1043	1044	1045	1046	1101	1102	1122
Other rented unfurnished	H	1047	1048	1049	1050	1051	1052	1053	1054	1103	1104	1123
	P	1055	1056	1057	1058	1059	1060	1061	1062	1105	1106	1124
Other rented furnished	H	1063	1064	1065	1066	1067	1068	1069	1070	1107	1108	1125
	P	1071	1072	1073	1074	1075	1076	1077	1078	1109	1110	1126
Non-permanent	H	1127	1128	1129	1130	1131	1132	1133	1134	1143	1144	1147
	P	1135	1136	1137	1138	1139	1140	1141	1142	1145	1146	1148

11 Household spaces; rooms in household spaces; rooms in hotels and boarding houses

Occupancy type	TOTAL H/HOLD SPACES	TOTAL ROOMS
ALL TYPES OF OCCUPANCY	1149	1159
H/hold enum with usual resident(s)	1150	1160
Absent household	1151	1161
H/hold enum with no usual resident(s)		
Owner occupied	1152	1162
not owner occupied	1153	1163
Second residence (unoccupied at Census)	1154	1164
Holiday accomm (unoccupied at Census)	1155	1165
Vacant (new, never occupied)	1156	1166
Vacant (under improvement)	1157	1167
Vacant (other)	1158	1168
Hotels and boarding houses	xxx	1169

12 Private households with residents; residents; cars in households

	TOTALS	No car	1 car	2 cars	3 or more cars	TOTAL CARS*
Households	1170	1171	1172	1173	1174	1175
Persons in households	1176	1177	1178	1179	1180	xxx

* H/hlds with 3 or more cars are counted as having 3 cars

13 Private households (H) with residents; residents (P); rooms in household spaces

Tenure		Households with the following rooms: 1	2	3	4	5	6	7+	TOTALS	TOTAL ROOMS
All permanent	H	1182	1183	1184	1185	1186	1187	1188	1189	1190
	P	1191	1192	1193	1194	1195	1196	1197	1198	xxx
Owner occupied	H	1200	1201	1202	1203	1204	1205	1206	1207	1208
	P	1209	1210	1211	1212	1213	1214	1215	1216	xxx
Council etc	H	1218	1219	1220	1221	1222	1223	1224	1225	1226
	P	1227	1228	1229	1230	1231	1232	1233	1234	xxx
Housing association	H	1236	1237	1238	1239	1240	1241	1242	1243	1244
	P	1245	1246	1247	1248	1249	1250	1251	1252	xxx
Rented with business	H	1254	1255	1256	1257	1258	1259	1260	1261	1262
	P	1263	1264	1265	1266	1267	1268	1269	1270	xxx
By virtue of employment	H	1272	1273	1274	1275	1276	1277	1278	1279	1280
	P	1281	1282	1283	1284	1285	1286	1287	1288	xxx
Other rented unfurnished	H	1290	1291	1292	1293	1294	1295	1296	1297	1298
	P	1299	1300	1301	1302	1303	1304	1305	1306	xxx
Other rented furnished	H	1308	1309	1310	1311	1312	1313	1314	1315	1316
	P	1317	1318	1319	1320	1321	1322	1323	1324	xxx
Non-permanent	H	1326	1327	1328	1329	1330	xxx	xxx	1333	1334
	P	1335	1336	1337	1338	1339	xxx	xxx	1342	xxx

14 Private h/holds with residents; residents; rooms in h/hold spaces

H/holds with the following persons	Households with the following rooms: 1	2	3	4	5	6	7+	TOTAL H/HLDS	TOTAL ROOMS
ALL H/HLDS	1344	1345	1346	1347	1348	1349	1350	1351	1352
1	1353	1354	1355	1356	1357	1358	1359	1360	1361
2	1362	1363	1364	1365	1366	1367	1368	1369	1370
3	1371	1372	1373	1374	1375	1376	1377	1378	1379
4	1380	1381	1382	1383	1384	1385	1386	1387	1388
5	1389	1390	1391	1392	1393	1394	1395	1396	1397
6	1398	1399	1400	1401	1402	1403	1404	1405	1406
7+	1407	1408	1409	1410	1411	1412	1413	1414	1415
TOTAL PERS	1416	1417	1418	1419	1420	1421	1422	1423	xxx

15 Private households with residents

H/holds with the following persons	Tenure of households in permanent buildings: All perm-anent	Owner occ	Council etc	House assoc	Rented with business	By virtue of emp	Other rented: Unfurn	Other rented: Furn	House-holds in non-perm accom
ALL H/HOLDS	1425	1426	1427	1428	1429	1430	1431	1432	1489
1	1433	1434	1435	1436	1437	1438	1439	1440	1490
2	1441	1442	1443	1444	1445	1446	1447	1448	1491
3	1449	1450	1451	1452	1453	1454	1455	1456	1492
4	1457	1458	1459	1460	1461	1462	1463	1464	1493
5	1465	1466	1467	1468	1469	1470	1471	1472	1494
6	1473	1474	1475	1476	1477	1478	1479	1480	1495
7+	1481	1482	1483	1484	1485	1486	1487	1488	1496

16 Priv h/holds with pers present but no residents; pers present; rooms and cars in such h/holds

	TOTAL H/HOLDS	Bath + inside wc excl	TOTAL PERS PRES	Stdt aged 16+	TOTAL ROOMS	TOTAL CARS*
H/holds with no usually res persons	1497	1498	1499	1500	1501	1502

17 Line 1: 1981 private h/holds with pers present (1971 pop base); present residents and visitors; rooms
Line 2: 1981 private households* (1981 pop base); present and absent residents; rooms

	H/holds (1981) with the following persons: 0	1	2	3	4	5	6	7+	TOTAL HOUSE-HOLDS	TOTAL PERS (1981)	TOTAL ROOMS (1981)
1: 1971 pop base	xxx	1504	1505	1506	1507	1508	1509	1510	1511	1512	1513
2: 1981 pop base	1514	1515	1516	1517	1518	1519	1520	1521	1522	1523	1524

*Private households with 1 or more usual residents with at least 1 person (a resident or a visitor)

CENSUS 1981 SMALL AREA STATISTICS

PAGE 3 100%

ED No

Map Reference

Note: $ = ED same as in 1971
$$ = Special Enumeration District

 Frame No:

Separate explanatory notes are available

NOTES

* Persons aged 16 or over (Tables 18 and 22)
** Includes households with no persons usually resident aged 16 or over (Table 18)
\#\# Includes a small number of heads aged under 16 counted in the 16-29 row (Table 26)
\# Includes residents in households with heads aged under 16 (Table 26)

18 Private households with residents; residents

Households with the following adults *	Households with no person aged 0-15	Households with person(s) aged 0-15: Households	With one person aged 0-15: Aged 0-4	With one person aged 0-15: Aged 5-15	With two or more aged 0-15: All Aged 0-4	With two or more aged 0-15: All Aged 5-15	With two or more aged 0-15: Others	Persons in households, With no person aged 0-15: TOTAL PERS	With no person aged 0-15: Pers econ act	With person(s) aged 0-15: Pers aged 0-15	With person(s) aged 0-15: Pers aged 16+	With person(s) aged 0-15: Pers econ act
ALL HOUSEHOLDS **	1525	1526	1527	1528	1529	1530	1531	1574	1575	1576	1577	1578
1 Male	1532	1533	1534	1535	1536	1537	1538	1579	1580	1581	1582	1583
1 Female	1539	1540	1541	1542	1543	1544	1545	1584	1585	1586	1587	1588
2 (Married male + married female)	1546	1547	1548	1549	1550	1551	1552	1589	1590	1591	1592	1593
2 (Other)	1553	1554	1555	1556	1557	1558	1559	1594	1595	1596	1597	1598
3+ (Married male(s)+ married female(s) with or without others)	1560	1561	1562	1563	1564	1565	1566	1599	1600	1601	1602	1603
3+ (Other)	1567	1568	1569	1570	1571	1572	1573	1604	1605	1606	1607	1608

19 Married women resident in private households of married male plus one married female with or without others; number of persons aged 0-15 in such households

In households with:	TOTAL MRR'D WOMEN	Mrr'd women econ active	Mrr'd women in employment: TOTAL	Working full-time	Working pt-time
No person aged 0-15	1609	1610	1617	1618	1619
Person(s) aged 0-4 with or without any aged 5-15	1611	1612	1620	1621	1622
Person(s) aged 5-15 only	1613	1614	1623	1624	1625
TOTAL PERSONS AGED 0-15	1615	1616	1626	1627	1628

20 Residents aged 16 or over in private households

Economic position	TOTAL PERS	Males: SWD	Males: Mrr'd	Females: SWD	Females: Mrr'd
ALL PERSONS 16+	1629	1630	1631	1632	1633
Total econ act	1634	1635	1636	1637	1638
Working f/time	1639	1640	1641	1642	1643
Working p/time	1644	1645	1646	1647	1648
Seeking work	1649	1650	1651	1652	1653
Temp sick	1654	1655	1656	1657	1658
Total econ inact	1659	1660	1661	1662	1663
Perm sick	1664	1665	1666	1667	1668
Retired	1669	1670	1671	1672	1673
Student	1674	1675	1676	1677	1678
Other inactive	1679	1680	1681	1682	1683

21 Residents in private households

Age	TOTAL PERSONS	Males: SWD	Males: Mrr'd	Females: SWD	Females: Mrr'd
TOTAL	1684	1686	1687	1689	1690
0-4	1691	1693	xxx	1696	xxx
5-9	1698	1700	xxx	1703	xxx
10-14	1705	1707	xxx	1710	xxx
15	1712	1714	xxx	1717	xxx
16-19	1719	1721	1722	1724	1725
20-24	1726	1728	1729	1731	1732
25-29	1733	1735	1736	1738	1739
30-34	1740	1742	1743	1745	1746
35-39	1747	1749	1750	1752	1753
40-44	1754	1756	1757	1759	1760
45-49	1761	1763	1764	1766	1767
50-54	1768	1770	1771	1773	1774
55-59	1775	1777	1778	1780	1781
60-64	1782	1784	1785	1787	1788
65-69	1789	1791	1792	1794	1795
70-74	1796	1798	1799	1801	1802
75-79	1803	1805	1806	1808	1809
80-84	1810	1812	1813	1815	1816
85+	1817	1819	1820	1822	1823

22 Private households with residents; residents aged 16 or over

Households with the following adults *	Households with the following persons aged 0-15: TOTAL	0	1	2	3	4+
TOTAL HOUSEHOLDS	1824	1825	1826	1827	1828	1829
1 econ inactive	1830	1831	1832	1833	1834	1835
1 econ active	1836	1837	1838	1839	1840	1841
2+, all econ inactive	1842	1843	1844	1845	1846	1847
2+, 1 econ active	1848	1849	1850	1851	1852	1853
2+, 2+ econ active	1854	1855	1856	1857	1858	1859
TOTAL ADULTS*	1860	1861	1862	1863	1864	1865
Persons econ active	1866	1867	1868	1869	1870	1871
Pers econ act out of employmnt (inc above)	1872	1873	1874	1875	1876	1877

23 Married women resident in priv households

Age	TOTAL MARRIED WOMEN	Married women econ active	Married women in empl: TOTAL	Work f/time	Work p/time
TOTAL	1878	1879	1890	1891	1892
16-24	1880	1881	1893	1894	1895
25-34	1882	1883	1896	1897	1898
35-44	1884	1885	1899	1900	1901
45-59	1886	1887	1902	1903	1904
60+	1888	1889	1905	1906	1907

24 Residents aged 16-24 in private households

Age	Persons: Males	Persons: Fmles	Married: Males	Married: Fmles	Student: Males	Student: Fmles	Econ active: Males	Econ active: Fmles	EA out of empl: Males	EA out of empl: Fmles
TOTAL	1908	1909	1928	1929	1948	1949	1968	1969	1988	1989
16	1910	1911	1930	1931	1950	1951	1970	1971	1990	1991
17	1912	1913	1932	1933	1952	1953	1972	1973	1992	1993
18	1914	1915	1934	1935	1954	1955	1974	1975	1994	1995
19	1916	1917	1936	1937	1956	1957	1976	1977	1996	1997
20	1918	1919	1938	1939	1958	1959	1978	1979	1998	1999
21	1920	1921	1940	1941	1960	1961	1980	1981	2000	2001
22	1922	1923	1942	1943	1962	1963	1982	1983	2002	2003
23	1924	1925	1944	1945	1964	1965	1984	1985	2004	2005
24	1926	1927	1946	1947	1966	1967	1986	1987	2006	2007

25 Residents aged 0-15 in private households

Age	Males	Females
TOTAL	2009	2010
0	2012	2013
1	2015	2016
2	2018	2019
3	2021	2022
4	2024	2025
5	2027	2028
6	2030	2031
7	2033	2034
8	2036	2037
9	2039	2040
10	2042	2043
11	2045	2046
12	2048	2049
13	2051	2052
14	2054	2055
15	2057	2058

26 Residents in private households

Age	TOTAL	Males: Mrr'd	Males: S	Males: W/D	Females: Mrr'd	Females: S	Females: W/D
Persons age	PERSONS AGED 16 OR OVER IN PRIVATE HOUSEHOLDS						
ALL 16+	2059	2061	2062	2063	2065	2066	2067
16-29	2068	2070	2071	2072	2074	2075	2076
30-44	2077	2079	2080	2081	2083	2084	2085
45-64/59	2086	2088	2089	2090	2092	2093	2094
Pensioners	2095	2097	2098	2099	2101	2102	2103
Heads age	HEADS IN PRIVATE HOUSEHOLDS ##						
ALL 16+	2104	2106	2107	2108	2110	2111	2112
16-29	2113	2115	2116	2117	2119	2120	2121
30-44	2122	2124	2125	2126	2128	2129	2130
45-64/59	2131	2133	2134	2135	2137	2138	2139
Pensioners	2140	2142	2143	2144	2146	2147	2148
Heads age	ALL PERS IN H/HLDS BY HEADS AGE, SEX, MAR/STAT #						
ALL 16+	2149	2151	2152	2153	2155	2156	2157
16-29	2158	2160	2161	2162	2164	2165	2166
30-44	2167	2169	2170	2171	2173	2174	2175
45-64/59	2176	2178	2179	2180	2182	2183	2184
Pensioners	2185	2187	2188	2189	2191	2192	2193

CENSUS 1981 SMALL AREA STATISTICS

PAGE 4 100%

ED No

Map Reference

Note: $ = ED same as in 1971
$$ = Special Enumeration District

 | Frame No:

Separate explanatory notes are available

NOTES
#Persons aged 16 and over (Tables 27 + 31)
≠Inc households with no persons usually resident aged 16 and over (Table 29)
*Inc renting from LAs, New Town Corporations and Scottish Special Housing Assoc (Table 29)

27 Lone adults # resident in private households of one adult with residents aged 0-15, number of persons aged 0-15 in such households

In households with child(ren):	Male lone 'parents'					Female lone 'parents'				
	TOTAL	Econ active	In employment			TOTAL	Econ active	In employment		
			TOTAL	f/time	p/time			TOTAL	f/time	p/time
Aged 0-4 with or w/out any aged 5-15	2194	2195	2200	2201	2202	2209	2210	2215	2216	2217
Aged 5-15 only	2196	2197	2203	2204	2205	2211	2212	2218	2219	2220
TOTAL PERSONS AGED 0-15	2198	2199	2206	2207	2208	2213	2214	2221	2222	2223

28 Private households with residents not in self-contained accommodation; rooms in such households

Households with the following persons	H/holds not in self-contained accom						
	TOTAL	One or more persons per rm	Bath + inside WC excl	Lack bath	Lack inside WC	No car	TOTAL ROOMS
TOTAL	2224	2228	2232	2233	2234	2248	2244
1 person	2225	2229	2235	2236	2237	2249	2245
2 persons	2226	2230	2238	2239	2240	2250	2246
3+ persons	2227	2231	2241	2242	2243	2251	2247

29 Private h/holds with residents; residents aged 0-15, and aged 60+(Fmles) and 65+ (males)

Household type: Households with persons Aged 16+	Aged 0-15	TOTAL HOUSE-HOLDS	Tenure of households in permanent buildings: TOTAL	Owner occ	Coun-cil etc *	Hous-ing assoc	Rented with bus-iness	Rented by virtue of emp	Other rented: Unfurn	Other rented: Furn	House-holds in non-perm accom
ALL HOUSEHOLDS ≠	Any	2252	2262	2263	2264	2265	2266	2267	2268	2269	2342
1 pensioner	0	2253	2270	2271	2272	2273	2274	2275	2276	2277	2343
1 adult# under pensionable age	0	2254	2278	2279	2280	2281	2282	2283	2284	2285	2344
1 adult any age	1+	2255	2286	2287	2288	2289	2290	2291	2292	2293	2345
Mrr'd male with mrr'd female without others	0	2256	2294	2295	2296	2297	2298	2299	2300	2301	2346
	1+	2257	2302	2303	2304	2305	2306	2307	2308	2309	2347
3+, mrr'd male(s) with mrr'd female(s) with/without others	0	2258	2310	2311	2312	2313	2314	2315	2316	2317	2348
	1+	2259	2318	2319	2320	2321	2322	2323	2324	2325	2349
2+ Others	0	2260	2326	2327	2328	2329	2330	2331	2332	2333	2350
	1+	2261	2334	2335	2336	2337	2338	2339	2340	2341	2351
Households containing pers of pens age only (any number)	0	2352	2353	2354	2355	2356	2357	2358	2359	2360	2361
Persons aged 0-4		2362	2366	2367	2368	2369	2370	2371	2372	2373	2398
Persons aged 5-15		2363	2374	2375	2376	2377	2378	2379	2380	2381	2399
Pers of pensionable age up to and including 74		2364	2382	2383	2384	2385	2386	2387	2388	2389	2400
Persons aged 75+		2365	2390	2391	2392	2393	2394	2395	2396	2397	2401

30 Private h/holds with resident head with different address 1 year before census; residents in such h/holds; all residents in private h/holds with different address 1 yr before census

	Households with migrants						
	TOTAL	One or more pers per rm	Bath + inside WC excl	Lack bath	Lack inside WC	Not self-cont accom	No car
	Households with migrant heads						
Households	2402	2404	2406	2407	2408	2412	2414
Persons	2403	2405	2409	2410	2411	2413	2415
	All households with migrants						
All migrants	2416	2417	2418	2419	2420	2421	2422

31 Private households with dependent children; private households with one or more resident(s) aged 0-15; residents in such households

	Households with child(ren)						
	TOTAL	One or more persons per room	Bath + inside WC excl	Lack bath	Lack inside WC	Not self-cont accom	No car
ALL H/HOLDS WITH DEPENDENT CHILD(REN)	2423	2424	2425	2426	2427	2428	2429
H/holds containing at least one one parent family with dep child(ren)	2430	2431	2432	2433	2434	2435	2436
H/holds with 3 or more dep children	2437	2438	2439	2440	2441	2442	2443
ALL H/HOLDS WITH ONE OR MORE PERSONS AGED 0-15	2444	2453	2462	2463	2464	2489	2498
H/holds of 1 adult# + 1 or more 0-15: Households	2445	2454	2465	2466	2467	2490	2499
Persons 0-4	2446	2455	2468	2469	2470	2491	2500
Persons 5-15	2447	2456	2471	2472	2473	2492	2501
Other h/holds with persons 0-15: Households	2448	2457	2474	2475	2476	2493	2502
Adults#	2449	2458	2477	2478	2479	2494	2503
Persons 0-4	2450	2459	2480	2481	2482	2495	2504
Persons 5-15	2451	2460	2483	2484	2485	2496	2505
H/holds with 3 or more persons 0-15	2452	2461	2486	2487	2488	2497	2506

32 Private households with one or more residents of pensionable age, residents in such households

	Households with pensioners						
	TOTAL	One or more persons per room	Bath + inside WC excl	Lack bath	Lack inside WC	Not self-cont accom	No car
TOTAL H/HOLDS WITH 1 OR MORE PENSIONERS	2507	2516	2525	2526	2527	2552	2561
Lone male 65-74	2508	2517	2528	2529	2530	2553	2562
Lone male 75+	2509	2518	2531	2532	2533	2554	2563
Lone female 60-74	2510	2519	2534	2535	2536	2555	2564
Lone female 75+	2511	2520	2537	2538	2539	2556	2565
2+ all pens >75	2512	2521	2540	2541	2542	2557	2566
2+, all pens, any 75+	2513	2522	2543	2544	2545	2558	2567
1 or more pensioners with 1 non-pensioner	2514	2523	2546	2547	2548	2559	2568
1 or more pens with 2 or more non-pens	2515	2524	2549	2550	2551	2560	2569
TOTAL PERS IN H/HOLDS WITH PENSIONERS	2570	2574	2578	2579	2580	2590	2594
Total pens persons	2571	2575	2581	2582	2583	2591	2595
Total persons 75+	2572	2576	2584	2585	2586	2592	2596
Total persons 85+	2573	2577	2587	2588	2589	2593	2597

CENSUS 1981 SMALL AREA STATISTICS

PAGE 5 10%

ED No

Map Reference

Note: $ = ED same as in 1971
$$ = Special Enumeration District
† = Importing Enumeration District

 | Frame No:

Separate explanatory notes are available

The figures in these tables are a 10% sample of the Census

45 Residents; private households with residents (100% + 10% sample)

	Resident persons			PRIVATE H/HOLDS
	TOTAL	Not in private h/holds	In private h/holds	
100%	4442	4443	4444	4445
10%	4446	4447	4448	4449

44 Residents aged 16 or over in employment (10% sample)

Socio-economic group (SEG)	Industry								Working full time	Working part time	Working outside dist of residence
	Agric	Energy and Water	Manuf	Constr	Distrib and Catering	Trans-port	Other Services	TOTAL IN EMPL			
1	4223	4224	4225	4226	4227	4228	4229	4230	4375	4376	4413
2	4231	4232	4233	4234	4235	4236	4237	4238	4377	4378	4414
3	4239	4240	4241	4242	4243	4244	4245	4246	4379	4380	4415
4	4247	4248	4249	4250	4251	4252	4253	4254	4381	4382	4416
5.1	4255	4256	4257	4258	4259	4260	4261	4262	4383	4384	4417
5.2	4263	4264	4265	4266	4267	4268	4269	4270	4385	4386	4418
6	4271	4272	4273	4274	4275	4276	4277	4278	4387	4388	4419
7	4279	4280	4281	4282	4283	4284	4285	4286	4389	4390	4420
8	4287	4288	4289	4290	4291	4292	4293	4294	4391	4392	4421
9	4295	4296	4297	4298	4299	4300	4301	4302	4393	4394	4422
10	4303	4304	4305	4306	4307	4308	4309	4310	4395	4396	4423
11	4311	4312	4313	4314	4315	4316	4317	4318	4397	4398	4424
12	4319	4320	4321	4322	4323	4324	4325	4326	4399	4400	4425
13	4327	4328	4329	4330	4331	4332	4333	4334	4401	4402	4426
14	4335	4336	4337	4338	4339	4340	4341	4342	4403	4404	4427
15	4343	4344	4345	4346	4347	4348	4349	4350	4405	4406	4428
16	4351	4352	4353	4354	4355	4356	4357	4358	4407	4408	4429
17	4359	4360	4361	4362	4363	4364	4365	4366	4409	4410	4430
TOTAL	4367	4368	4369	4370	4371	4372	4373	4374	4411	4412	4431
Working outside distr of residence	4432	4433	4434	4435	4436	4437	4438	4439	4440	4441	xxx

46 Residents aged 16 or over in employment (10% sample)

Sex and age	TOTAL IN EMPL	Industry						
		Agric	Energy and Water	Manuf	Constr	Distrib and Catering	Trans-port	Other Services
Males 16+	4450	4451	4452	4453	4454	4455	4456	4457
16-29	4458	4459	4460	4461	4462	4463	4464	4465
30-44	4466	4467	4468	4469	4470	4471	4472	4473
45-64	4474	4475	4476	4477	4478	4479	4480	4481
65+	4482	4483	4484	4485	4486	4487	4488	4489
Fmls 16+	4490	4491	4492	4493	4494	4495	4496	4497
16-29	4498	4499	4500	4501	4502	4503	4504	4505
30-44	4506	4507	4508	4509	4510	4511	4512	4513
45-59	4514	4515	4516	4517	4518	4519	4520	4521
60+	4522	4523	4524	4525	4526	4527	4528	4529

47 Residents aged 16 or over in employment (10% sample)

SEG	Means of travel to work										
	Car pool	Car psngr	Car driver	Bus	BR train	Under-ground	Motor-cycle	Pedal-cycle	On foot	Other + n/s	Works at home
1	4530	4531	4532	4533	4534	4535	4536	4537	4538	4539	4540
2	4541	4542	4543	4544	4545	4546	4547	4548	4549	4550	4551
3	4552	4553	4554	4555	4556	4557	4558	4559	4560	4561	4562
4	4563	4564	4565	4566	4567	4568	4569	4570	4571	4572	4573
5.1	4574	4575	4576	4577	4578	4579	4580	4581	4582	4583	4584
5.2	4585	4586	4587	4588	4589	4590	4591	4592	4593	4594	4595
6	4596	4597	4598	4599	4600	4601	4602	4603	4604	4605	4606
7	4607	4608	4609	4610	4611	4612	4613	4614	4615	4616	4617
8	4618	4619	4620	4621	4622	4623	4624	4625	4626	4627	4628
9	4629	4630	4631	4632	4633	4634	4635	4636	4637	4638	4639
10	4640	4641	4642	4643	4644	4645	4646	4647	4648	4649	4650
11	4651	4652	4653	4654	4655	4656	4657	4658	4659	4660	4661
12	4662	4663	4664	4665	4666	4667	4668	4669	4670	4671	4672
13	4673	4674	4675	4676	4677	4678	4679	4680	4681	4682	4683
14	4684	4685	4686	4687	4688	4689	4690	4691	4692	4693	4694
15	4695	4696	4697	4698	4699	4700	4701	4702	4703	4704	4705
16	4706	4707	4708	4709	4710	4711	4712	4713	4714	4715	4716
17	4717	4718	4719	4720	4721	4722	4723	4724	4725	4726	4727
Total pers	4728	4729	4730	4731	4732	4733	4734	4735	4736	4737	4738
Total mls	4739	4740	4741	4742	4743	4744	4745	4746	4747	4748	4749
Total fmls	4750	4751	4752	4753	4754	4755	4756	4757	4758	4759	4760
Persons working o/s distr of resid	4761	4762	4763	4764	4765	4766	4767	4768	4769	4770	xxx
	Persons in employment in private households with:										
No car	4772	4773	4774	4775	4776	4777	4778	4779	4780	4781	4782
1 car	4783	4784	4785	4786	4787	4788	4789	4790	4791	4792	4793
2+ cars	4794	4795	4796	4797	4798	4799	4800	4801	4802	4803	4804

48 Residents aged 18 or over (10% sample)

Age	Persons with degrees, professional and vocational qualifications		
	TOTAL	Males	Females
18-29	4805	4806	4807
30-44	4808	4809	4810
45-64/59	4811	4812	4813
Pensioners	4814	4815	4816
In employment	4817	4818	4819

CENSUS 1981 SMALL AREA STATISTICS

PAGE 6 10%

ED No

Map Reference

Note: $ = ED same as in 1971
$$ = Special Enumeration District
† = Importing Enumeration District

 | Frame No:

Separate explanatory notes are available

The figures in these tables are a 10% sample of the Census

49 Private households with residents; residents; families of resident persons (10% sample)

	Households							Persons			Families by family type	
	Selected tenures of h/hlds in perm blgs			Migrant head of h/hold	No car	Ret head of h/hold	ALL HOUSE-HOLDS	ALL PERS	Pers EA	Dep child-ren		
	Owner occ	Council etc	Unfurn-ished								Mrrd couple	Lone parent
SEG	By SEG of EA or retired (with previous occupation stated) head of household										family	
1	4820	4821	4822	4877	4896	4915	4934	4953	4954	4955	5010	5011
2	4823	4824	4825	4878	4897	4916	4935	4956	4957	4958	5012	5013
3	4826	4827	4828	4879	4898	4917	4936	4959	4960	4961	5014	5015
4	4829	4830	4831	4880	4899	4918	4937	4962	4963	4964	5016	5017
5.1	4832	4833	4834	4881	4900	4919	4938	4965	4966	4967	5018	5019
5.2	4835	4836	4837	4882	4901	4920	4939	4968	4969	4970	5020	5021
6	4838	4839	4840	4883	4902	4921	4940	4971	4972	4973	5022	5023
7	4841	4842	4843	4884	4903	4922	4941	4974	4975	4976	5024	5025
8	4844	4845	4846	4885	4904	4923	4942	4977	4978	4979	5026	5027
9	4847	4848	4849	4886	4905	4924	4943	4980	4981	4982	5028	5029
10	4850	4851	4852	4887	4906	4925	4944	4983	4984	4985	5030	5031
11	4853	4854	4855	4888	4907	4926	4945	4986	4987	4988	5032	5033
12	4856	4857	4858	4889	4908	4927	4946	4989	4990	4991	5034	5035
13	4859	4860	4861	4890	4909	4928	4947	4992	4993	4994	5036	5037
14	4862	4863	4864	4891	4910	4929	4948	4995	4996	4997	5038	5039
15	4865	4866	4867	4892	4911	4930	4949	4998	4999	5000	5040	5041
16	4868	4869	4870	4893	4912	4931	4950	5001	5002	5003	5042	5043
17	4871	4872	4873	4894	4913	4932	4951	5004	5005	5006	5044	5045
Total (inc never act)	4874	4875	4876	4895	4914	4933	4952	5007	5008	5009	5046	5047
Retired 1	5048	5049	5050	5057	5060	5063	5066	5069	5070	5071	5078	5079
Retired 2	5051	5052	5053	5058	5061	5064	5067	5072	5073	5074	5080	5081
Retired 3	5054	5055	5056	5059	5062	5065	5068	5075	xxx	5077	5082	5083
TOTAL PERS	5084	5085	5086	5093	5096	5099	5102	xxx	xxx	xxx	5105	5106
Pers EA	5087	5088	5089	5094	5097	5100	5103	xxx	xxx	xxx	5107	5108
Dep child	5090	5091	5092	5095	5098	5101	5104	xxx	xxx	xxx	5109	5110
					Households with							
No family	5111	5112	5113	5120	5123	5126	5129	5132	5133	xxx	xxx	xxx
1 family	5114	5115	5116	5121	5124	5127	5130	5135	5136	5137	5143	5144
2+ families	5117	5118	5119	5122	5125	5128	5131	5138	5139	5140	5145	5146

50 Residents, economically active or retired (10% sample)

SEG	Economic position								
	All res econ act or retired	EA not in emp			Retd males	Econ active			Econ active mig-rant
		Males	Females			Males	Females		
			SWD	Mrrd			SWD	Mrrd	
1	5147	5166	5167	5168	5223	5242	5243	5244	5299
2	5148	5169	5170	5171	5224	5245	5246	5247	5300
3	5149	5172	5173	5174	5225	5248	5249	5250	5301
4	5150	5175	5176	5177	5226	5251	5252	5253	5302
5.1	5151	5178	5179	5180	5227	5254	5255	5256	5303
5.2	5152	5181	5182	5183	5228	5257	5258	5259	5304
6	5153	5184	5185	5186	5229	5260	5261	5262	5305
7	5154	5187	5188	5189	5230	5263	5264	5265	5306
8	5155	5190	5191	5192	5231	5266	5267	5268	5307
9	5156	5193	5194	5195	5232	5269	5270	5271	5308
10	5157	5196	5197	5198	5233	5272	5273	5274	5309
11	5158	5199	5200	5201	5234	5275	5276	5277	5310
12	5159	5202	5203	5204	5235	5278	5279	5280	5311
13	5160	5205	5206	5207	5236	5281	5282	5283	5312
14	5161	5208	5209	5210	5237	5284	5285	5286	5313
15	5162	5211	5212	5213	5238	5287	5288	5289	5314
16	5163	5214	5215	5216	5239	5290	5291	5292	5315
17	5164	5217	5218	5219	5240	5293	5294	5295	5316
TOTAL	5165	5220	5221	5222	5241	5296	5297	5298	5317

NOTES

Retired 1 = retired [head], previous occupation stated (Tables 49 and 52)

Retired 2 = retired [head] (no previous occupation stated) + never active [head] - in h/hold/family with at least one econ active person (Tables 49 and 52)

Retired 3 = retired [head] (no previous occupation stated) + never active [head] - in household/family without an economically active person (Tables 49 and 52)

51 Residents aged 16 or over in employment (10% sample)

Employment Status	TOTAL IN EMPL	Selected industries						
		Agric (ex forest + fishing)	Forestry and fishing	Manuf	Constr	Distrib and catering	Fin-ance	Pub admin + other services
Males	5318	5328	5329	5330	5331	5332	5333	5334
Self-emp with empl	5319	5335	5336	5337	5338	5339	5340	5341
Self-emp w/o empl	5320	5342	5343	5344	5345	5346	5347	5348
Employees	5321	5349	5350	5351	5352	5353	5354	5355
Females	5322	5356	5357	5358	5359	5360	5361	5362
Self-emp with empl	5323	5363	5364	5365	5366	5367	5368	5369
Self-emp w/o empl	5324	5370	5371	5372	5373	5374	5375	5376
Employees	5325	5377	5378	5379	5380	5381	5382	5383
Working full-time	5326	5384	5385	5386	5387	5388	5389	5390
Working part-time	5327	5391	5392	5393	5394	5395	5396	5397

52 Residents in private households, private households (10% sample)

Social class	H/hlds and Residents in h/hlds					Residents 16+ in h/hlds			
	House-holds	Per-sons	M'rrd fmls	Pers 0-15	Pers 65+	Males	Males 16-64	M'rrd fmls	SWD fmls
	By social class of EA head of household					EA persons social class			
I	5398	5409	5410	5411	5442	5453	5454	5455	5456
II	5399	5412	5413	5414	5443	5457	5458	5459	5460
IIIN	5400	5415	5416	5417	5444	5461	5462	5463	5464
IIIM	5401	5418	5419	5420	5445	5465	5466	5467	5468
IV	5402	5421	5422	5423	5446	5469	5470	5471	5472
V	5403	5424	5425	5426	5447	5473	5474	5475	5476
Armed forces + inad desc	5404	5427	5428	5429	5448	5477	5478	5479	5480
	Households with inactive head					Inactive persons			
Retired 1	5405	5430	5431	5432	5449	5481	5482	5483	5484
Retired 2	5406	5433	5434	5435	5450	5485	5486	5487	5488
Retired 3	5407	5436	5437	5438	5451	5489	5490	5491	5492
TOTAL	5408	5439	5440	5441	5452	5493	5494	5495	5496

53 Residents economically active but not in employment (10% sample)

	Former industry						
	Agric	Energy and water	Manuf	Constr	Distrib and catering	Trans-port	Other Services and NS
Males	5497	5498	5499	5500	5501	5502	5503
SWD females	5504	5505	5506	5507	5508	5509	5510
Married females	5511	5512	5513	5514	5515	5516	5517

CENSUS 1981 SMALL AREA STATISTICS

PAGE 7 100%

ED No

Map Reference

Note: $ = ED same as in 1971
$$ = Special Enumeration District

 | Frame No:

Separate explanatory notes are available

33 Household spaces; permanent buildings; non-permanent accommodation

	Household spaces in permanent buildings with:										Non-perm accom	
	TOTAL H/HOLD SPACES	Self-contained accommodation						Not self-contained accom with shared entrance from o/side the building			Cara vans	Other non-perm
		TOTAL	Purp-ose built flats	Sep entr-ance from o/side bldg	Shared entrance from outside the building			Total	Bed sits	Other		
					2+ rooms bath + inside WC excl	Flat-lets	Other					
TOTAL HOUSEHOLD SPACES	2598	2599	2600	2601	xxx	xxx	xxx	2605	xxx	xxx	2608	2609
Resident household spaces	2610	2611	2612	2613	2614	2615	2616	2617	2618	2619	2620	2621
Other household spaces	2622	2623	2624	2625	xxx	xxx	xxx	2629	xxx	xxx	2632	2633

34 Resident household spaces; rooms; residents in private households

	Household spaces in permanent buildings					Non-perm accom*
	TOTAL	Purp-ose built flats	Sep entr-ance from o/side bldg	Shrd entrance from o/s bldg		
				Self-cont accom	Not self-cont accom	
TOTAL ROOMS	2634	2635	2636	2637	2638	2674
Rooms:						
1	2639	2640	2641	2642	2643	2675
2	2644	2645	2646	2647	2648	2676
3	2649	2650	2651	2652	2653	2677
4	2654	2655	2656	2657	2658	2678
5/6	2659	2660	2661	2662	2663	2679
7/8	2664	2665	2666	2667	2668	xxx
9+	2669	2670	2671	2672	2673	xxx
TOTAL PERSONS	2682	2683	2684	2685	2686	2722
Persons usually resident:						
1	2687	2688	2689	2690	2691	2723
2	2692	2693	2694	2695	2696	2724
3	2697	2698	2699	2700	2701	2725
4	2702	2703	2704	2705	2706	2726
5	2707	2708	2709	2710	2711	2727
6	2712	2713	2714	2715	2716	2728
7+	2717	2718	2719	2720	2721	2729
Persons per room:						
Greater than 1.5	2730	2731	2732	2733	2734	2755
>1 - 1.5	2735	2736	2737	2738	2739	2756
>0.5 - 1	2740	2741	2742	2743	2744	2757
0.5 or under	2745	2746	2747	2748	2749	2758
TOTAL H/HOLD SPACES	2750	2751	2752	2753	2754	2759

* Maximum number of rooms in non-perm accom is five

35 Resident household spaces

	Household spaces in permanent buildings					Non-perm accom
	TOTAL	Purpose built flats	Separate entrance from outside building	Shared entrance from o/s bldg		
				Self-contained accom	Not self-contained accom	
Amenities:						
Exclusive bath with:						
exclusive inside WC	2760	2761	2762	2763	2764	2805
shared inside WC	2765	2766	2767	2768	2769	2806
no inside WC	2770	2771	2772	2773	2774	2807
Shared bath with:						
exclusive inside WC	2775	2776	2777	2778	2779	2808
shared inside WC	2780	2781	2782	2783	2784	2809
no inside WC	2785	2786	2787	2788	2789	2810
No bath with:						
exclusive inside WC	2790	2791	2792	2793	2794	2811
shared inside WC	2795	2796	2797	2798	2799	2812
no inside WC	2800	2801	2802	2803	2804	2813
Tenure:						
ALL TENURES	2814	2815	2816	2817	2818	2859
Owner occupied freehold	2819	2820	2821	2822	2823	2860
Owner occupied leasehold	2824	2825	2826	2827	2828	2861
Council, New Town, etc	2829	2830	2831	2832	2833	2862
Housing association	2834	2835	2836	2837	2838	2863
Rented with business	2839	2840	2841	2842	2843	2864
By virtue of employment	2844	2845	2846	2847	2848	2865
Other rented unfurnished	2849	2850	2851	2852	2853	2866
Other rented furnished	2854	2855	2856	2857	2858	2867

CENSUS 1981 SMALL AREA STATISTICS

PAGE 8 100%

ED No

Map Reference

Note: $ = ED same as in 1971
$$ = Special Enumeration District

 | Frame No:

Separate explanatory notes are available

36 Private households with resident heads born in the New Commonwealth or Pakistan

	New Commonwealth or Pakistani headed households						
	TOTAL	1 or more persons per room	Bath + inside WC excl	Lack bath	Lack inside WC	Not in self-cont accom	No car
Households	2868	2869	2870	2871	2872	2873	2874

37 Residents in private households

Birthplace of household head	TOTAL PERSONS	Age and birthplace of persons														TOTAL HEADS OF HOUSE-HOLDS
		All ages		0-4		5-15		16-29		30-44		45 to pensionable age		Pensionable age and over		
		In UK	Outside UK	In UK	Outside UK	In UK	Outside UK	In UK	Outside UK	In UK	Outside UK	In UK	Outside UK	In UK	Outside UK	
TOTAL	2875	2876	2877	2878	2879	2880	2881	2882	2883	2884	2885	2886	2887	2888	2889	2950
UK	2890	2891	2892	2893	2894	2895	2896	2897	2898	2899	2900	2901	2902	2903	2904	2951
Irish Republic	2905	2906	2907	2908	2909	2910	2911	2912	2913	2914	2915	2916	2917	2918	2919	2952
New Commonwealth and Pakistan	2920	2921	2922	2923	2924	2925	2926	2927	2928	2929	2930	2931	2932	2933	2934	2953
Rest of World	2935	2936	2937	2938	2939	2940	2941	2942	2943	2944	2945	2946	2947	2948	2949	2954

38 Households (H) with residents, rooms and resident persons (P) in owner occupied accommodation in permanent buildings

Tenure	TOTAL HOUSEHOLDS	Households with the following persons						
		1	2	3	4	5	6	7+
Freehold	2955	2956	2957	2958	2959	2960	2961	2962
Leasehold	2963	2964	2965	2966	2967	2968	2969	2970

Tenure		Households with the following rooms							TOTALS	TOTAL ROOMS
		1	2	3	4	5	6	7+		
F/hold	H	2971	2972	2973	2974	2975	2976	2977	2978	2979
	P	2980	2981	2982	2983	2984	2985	2986	2987	xxx
L/hold	H	2989	2990	2991	2992	2993	2994	2995	2996	2997
	P	2998	2999	3000	3001	3002	3003	3004	3005	xxx

Tenure		TOTALS	Bath and inside WC present		Lack inside WC or bath	Neither inside WC nor bath	Lack bath	Lack inside WC	Share inside WC	Persons per room		No car
			Both excl	One/both shared						>1.5	>1-1.5	
F/hold	H	3007	3008	3009	3010	3011	3012	3013	3014	3039	3040	3047
	P	3015	3016	3017	3018	3019	3020	3021	3022	3041	3042	3048
L/hold	H	3023	3024	3025	3026	3027	3028	3029	3030	3043	3044	3049
	P	3031	3032	3033	3034	3035	3036	3037	3038	3045	3046	3050

39 Persons aged 3 or over: Pres & abs h'hold residents

Age	TOTAL PER-SONS	Speaking Welsh				Not Speak-ing Welsh
		Total	Not Speak-ing Eng-lish	Speaking English		
				Reads and writes Welsh	Others	
TOTAL RESIDENTS	3051	3052	3053	3054	3055	3056
3-4	3057	3058	3059	3060	3061	3062
5-15	3063	3064	3065	3066	3067	3068
16-24	3069	3070	3071	3072	3073	3074
25-44	3075	3076	3077	3078	3079	3080
45-64	3081	3082	3083	3084	3085	3086
65+	3087	3088	3089	3090	3091	3092
Present residents and visitors (1981) (1971 Base)	3093	3094	3095	3096	3097	3098

CENSUS 1981 SMALL AREA STATISTICS

PAGE 9 ADDITIONAL TABLES FOR SCOTLAND

ED No

Map Reference

Note: $$ = Special Enumeration District

 | Frame No:

Separate explanatory notes are available

40

Age	Resident population		Speaks, reads or writes Gaelic		Gaelic speakers					
					Read		Read and write		Others	
	Male	Female	Male	Female	Male	Female	Male	Female	Male	Female
0 - 2	3099	3100	xxx	xxx	xxx	xxx	xxx	xxx	xxx	xxx
3 - 4	3109	3110	3111	3112	3113	3114	3115	3116	3117	3118
5 - 9	3119	3120	3121	3122	3123	3124	3125	3126	3127	3128
10 -14	3129	3130	3131	3132	3133	3134	3135	3136	3137	3138
15 -19	3139	3140	3141	3142	3143	3144	3145	3146	3147	3148
20 -24	3149	3150	3151	3152	3153	3154	3155	3156	3157	3158
25 -29	3159	3160	3161	3162	3163	3164	3165	3166	3167	3168
30 -34	3169	3170	3171	3172	3173	3174	3175	3176	3177	3178
35 -39	3179	3180	3181	3182	3183	3184	3185	3186	3187	3188
40 -44	3189	3190	3191	3192	3193	3194	3195	3196	3197	3198
45 -49	3199	3200	3201	3202	3203	3204	3205	3206	3207	3208
50 -54	3209	3210	3211	3212	3213	3214	3215	3216	3217	3218
55 -59	3219	3220	3221	3222	3223	3224	3225	3226	3227	3228
60 -64	3229	3230	3231	3232	3233	3234	3235	3236	3237	3238
65 -69	3239	3240	3241	3242	3243	3244	3245	3246	3247	3248
70 -74	3249	3250	3251	3252	3253	3254	3255	3256	3257	3258
75+	3259	3260	3261	3262	3263	3264	3265	3266	3267	3268
ALL AGES	3269	3270	3271	3272	3273	3274	3275	3276	3277	3278
Aged 16+	3279	3280	3281	3282	3283	3284	3285	3286	3287	3288
Not in pvt h/hlds	3289	3290	3291	3292	3293	3294	3295	3296	3297	3298
Born in Scotland	3299	3300	3301	3302	3303	3304	3305	3306	3307	3308

41

Household type and age of residents	Households in permanent buildings - level and access												
	Basement		Ground		1 or 2			3 or 4		5 or 6		7- 9	10 and over
	All	Any ext stair	All	Any ext stair	All	Ext str only	With lift	All	With lift	All	With lift		
1 pensionable aged under 75 male	3309	3310	3311	3312	3313	3314	3315	3316	3317	3318	3319	3320	3321
female	3322	3323	3324	3325	3326	3327	3328	3329	3330	3331	3332	3333	3334
1 pensionable aged 75 and over male	3335	3336	3337	3338	3339	3340	3341	3342	3343	3344	3345	3346	3347
female	3348	3349	3350	3351	3352	3353	3354	3355	3356	3357	3358	3359	3360
2 pensionable both aged under 75	3361	3362	3363	3364	3365	3366	3367	3368	3369	3370	3371	3372	3373
2 pensionable either aged 75 and over	3374	3375	3376	3377	3378	3379	3380	3381	3382	3383	3384	3385	3386
3 or more pensionable all aged under 75	3387	3388	3389	3390	3391	3392	3393	3394	3395	3396	3397	3398	3399
3 or more pensionable any aged 75 and over	3400	3401	3402	3403	3404	3405	3406	3407	3408	3409	3410	3411	3412
1 pensionable and 1 non-pensionable	3413	3414	3415	3416	3417	3418	3419	3420	3421	3422	3423	3424	3425
1 pensionable and 2 or more non-pensionable	3426	3427	3428	3429	3430	3431	3432	3433	3434	3435	3436	3437	3438
2 or more pensionable and 1 or more non-pensionable	3439	3440	3441	3442	3443	3444	3445	3446	3447	3448	3449	3450	3451
Children in household:													
1 adult with:													
1 or more children all aged 0-4	3452	3453	3454	3455	3456	3457	3458	3459	3460	3461	3462	3463	3464
1 or more children all aged 5-15	3465	3466	3467	3468	3469	3470	3471	3472	3473	3474	3475	3476	3477
2 or more children aged 0-4 and 5-15	3478	3479	3480	3481	3482	3483	3484	3485	3486	3487	3488	3489	3490
2 or more adults with:													
1 or more children all aged 0-4	3491	3492	3493	3494	3495	3496	3497	3498	3499	3500	3501	3502	3503
1 or more children all aged 5-15	3504	3505	3506	3507	3508	3509	3510	3511	3512	3513	3514	3515	3516
2 or more children aged 0-4 and 5-15	3517	3518	3519	3520	3521	3522	3523	3524	3525	3526	3527	3528	3529
TOTAL HOUSEHOLDS	3530	3531	3532	3533	3534	3535	3536	3537	3538	3539	3540	3541	3542
TOTAL PERSONS	3543	3544	3545	3546	3547	3548	3549	3550	3551	3552	3553	3554	3555
0-2	3556	3557	3558	3559	3560	3561	3562	3563	3564	3565	3566	3567	3568
0-4	3569	3570	3571	3572	3573	3574	3575	3576	3577	3578	3579	3580	3581
5-15	3582	3583	3584	3585	3586	3587	3588	3589	3590	3591	3592	3593	3594
65-74 male	3595	3596	3597	3598	3599	3600	3601	3602	3603	3604	3605	3606	3607
60-74 female	3608	3609	3610	3611	3612	3613	3614	3615	3616	3617	3618	3619	3620
75+ male	3621	3622	3623	3624	3625	3626	3627	3628	3629	3630	3631	3632	3633
75+ female	3634	3635	3636	3637	3638	3639	3640	3641	3642	3643	3644	3645	3646
Permanently sick	3647	3648	3649	3650	3651	3652	3653	3654	3655	3656	3657	3658	3659

CENSUS 1981 SMALL AREA STATISTICS
PAGE 10 ADDITIONAL TABLES FOR SCOTLAND

ED No

Map Reference

Note: $$ = Special Enumeration District

 | Frame No:

Separate explanatory notes are available

42 Households in permanent buildings

Rooms	With ancillary kitchen								Without ancillary kitchen								Rooms
	TOTAL	Bath and WC		Bath + / or WC lacking	Exclu -sive WC	Occupancy norm			TOTAL	Bath and WC		Bath + / or WC lacking	Exclu -sive WC	Occupancy norm			
		Both excl	Both other			+	0	-		Both excl	Both other			+	0	-	
1	3660	3661	3662	3663	3664	3665	3666	3667	3724	3725	3726	3727	3728	3729	3730	3731	1
2	3668	3669	3670	3671	3672	3673	3674	3675	3732	3733	3734	3735	3736	3737	3738	3739	2
3	3676	3677	3678	3679	3680	3681	3682	3683	3740	3741	3742	3743	3744	3745	3746	3747	3
4	3684	3685	3686	3687	3688	3689	3690	3691	3748	3749	3750	3751	3752	3753	3754	3755	4
5	3692	3693	3694	3695	3696	3697	3698	3699	3756	3757	3758	3759	3760	3761	3762	3763	5
6	3700	3701	3702	3703	3704	3705	3706	3707	3764	3765	3766	3767	3768	3769	3770	3771	6
7+	3708	3709	3710	3711	3712	3713	3714	3715	3772	3773	3774	3775	3776	3777	3778	3779	7+
TOTAL	3716	3717	3718	3719	3720	3721	3722	3723	3780	3781	3782	3783	3784	3785	3786	3787	TOTAL

43

Households with persons:-		TOTAL	In permanent buildings												In non perm	With migrant head
				House that is			Flat or rooms in				Occupancy norm					
Aged 16 and over	Aged 0-15		Total	Deta-ched	Semi -det	Terr-aced	Two storey	Low rise	High rise	Single with shop	+	0	-1	-2 or more		
* ALL HOUSEHOLDS	Any	4058	4069	4070	4071	4072	4073	4074	4075	4076	4077	4078	4079	4080	4201	4212
1 pensionable	0	4059	4081	4082	4083	4084	4085	4086	4087	4088	4089	4090	4091	4092	4202	4213
1 adult non-pensionable	0	4060	4093	4094	4095	4096	4097	4098	4099	4100	4101	4102	4103	4104	4203	4214
1 adult any age	1+	4061	4105	4106	4107	4108	4109	4110	4111	4112	4113	4114	4115	4116	4204	4215
Married M + married F only	0	4062	4117	4118	4119	4120	4121	4122	4123	4124	4125	4126	4127	4128	4205	4216
Married M + married F only	1+	4063	4129	4130	4131	4132	4133	4134	4135	4136	4137	4138	4139	4140	4206	4217
Marr M(s) + Marr F(s) with or without others	0	4064	4141	4142	4143	4144	4145	4146	4147	4148	4149	4150	4151	4152	4207	4218
Marr M(s) + Marr F(s) with or without others	1+	4065	4153	4154	4155	4156	4157	4158	4159	4160	4161	4162	4163	4164	4208	4219
Other 2 or more adults	0	4066	4165	4166	4167	4168	4169	4170	4171	4172	4173	4174	4175	4176	4209	4220
Other 2 or more adults	1+	4067	4177	4178	4179	4180	4181	4182	4183	4184	4185	4186	4187	4188	4210	4221
All pens only households	0	4068	4189	4190	4191	4192	4193	4194	4195	4196	4197	4198	4199	4200	4211	4222
TENURE																
ALL TENURES		3788	3806	3807	3808	3809	3810	3811	3812	3813	3814	3815	3816	3817	4022	4040
Owner occupier		3789	3818	3819	3820	3821	3822	3823	3824	3825	3826	3827	3828	3829	4023	4041
Council, SSHA and New Town		3790	3830	3831	3832	3833	3834	3835	3836	3837	3838	3839	3840	3841	4024	4042
Housing association		3791	3842	3843	3844	3845	3846	3847	3848	3849	3850	3851	3852	3853	4025	4043
Rent with farm, shop etc		3792	3854	3855	3856	3857	3858	3859	3860	3861	3862	3863	3864	3865	4026	4044
By virtue of employment		3793	3866	3867	3868	3869	3870	3871	3872	3873	3874	3875	3876	3877	4027	4045
Other unfurnished		3794	3878	3879	3880	3881	3882	3883	3884	3885	3886	3887	3888	3889	4028	4046
Other furnished		3795	3890	3891	3892	3893	3894	3895	3896	3897	3898	3899	3900	3901	4029	4047
AMENITIES																
Bath and WC exclusive use		3796	3902	3903	3904	3905	3906	3907	3908	3909	3910	3911	3912	3913	4030	4048
Bath and WC other		3797	3914	3915	3916	3917	3918	3919	3920	3921	3922	3923	3924	3925	4031	4049
Lacking one or both		3798	3926	3927	3928	3929	3930	3931	3932	3933	3934	3935	3936	3937	4032	4050
WC exclusive use		3799	3938	3939	3940	3941	3942	3943	3944	3945	3946	3947	3948	3949	4033	4051
TOTAL ROOMS		3800	3950	3951	3952	3953	3954	3955	3956	3957	3958	3959	3960	3961	4034	4052
TOTAL PERSONS IN HOUSEHOLDS		3801	3962	3963	3964	3965	3966	3967	3968	3969	3970	3971	3972	3973	4035	4053
Persons aged 0-4		3802	3974	3975	3976	3977	3978	3979	3980	3981	3982	3983	3984	3985	4036	4054
5-15		3803	3986	3987	3988	3989	3990	3991	3992	3993	3994	3995	3996	3997	4037	4055
Pensionable aged -74		3804	3998	3999	4000	4001	4002	4003	4004	4005	4006	4007	4008	4009	4038	4056
75+		3805	4010	4011	4012	4013	4014	4015	4016	4017	4018	4019	4020	4021	4039	4057

* Includes households with no persons usually resident aged 16 and over

Appendix 3

The standard layout of the OPCS 1971 SAS tables and the 1971 cell numbers

The following three pages display the OPCS-designed layout of all the standard tables from the 1971 SAS. As in appendix 2, the numbers shown are the cell numbers, i.e. the name or shorthand by which each 'variable' is known: thus 'total population present' is given by the value in the position of cell number 32 (for technical reasons, the 1971 cell numbers start at 32 whereas those for 1981 start at 1).

Again as in appendix 2, information is given in the OPCS header and differs for each and every area.

All three pages were available for England, Scotland and Wales.

SMALL AREA STATISTICS (WARD LIBRARY) — **10% SAMPLE** — **CENSUS 1971**

AREA IDENTIFICATION BOX

22

Age	ONE YEAR MIGRANTS WITHIN L.A. S.W.D. Males	Married Males	S.W.D. Females	Married Females	ONE YEAR MIGRANTS INTO L.A. S.W.D. Males	Married Males	S.W.D. Females	Married Females
1-	32	39	46	53	60	67	74	81
5-	33	40	47	54	61	68	75	82
15-	34	41	48	55	62	69	76	83
25-	35	42	49	56	63	70	77	84
35-	36	43	50	57	64	71	78	85
45-	37	44	51	58	65	72	79	86
65+ 60+	38	45	52	59	66	73	80	87
Total	88	89	90	91	92	93	94	95

Age	FIVE YEAR MIGRANTS WITHIN L.A.				FIVE YEAR MIGRANTS INTO L.A.			
5-	96	102	108	114	120	126	132	138
15-	97	103	109	115	121	127	133	139
25-	98	104	110	116	122	128	134	140
35-	99	105	111	117	123	129	135	141
45-	100	106	112	118	124	130	136	142
65+ 60+	101	107	113	119	125	131	137	143
Total	144	145	146	147	148	149	150	151

24 HOUSE OF WORK OF WOMEN IN EMPLOYMENT

	All women <8hrs	All women 8-30hrs	All women >30hrs	Married women <8hrs	Married women 8-30hrs	Married women >30hrs	Marr. women with children aged under 5 <8hrs	8-30hrs	>30hrs
15-	32	37	42	47	52	57	62	67	72
25-	33	38	43	48	53	58	63	68	73
35-	34	39	44	49	54	59	64	69	74
45-	35	40	45	50	55	60	65	70	75
60+	36	41	46	51	56	61	66	71	76
Wkg in LA	77	78	79	80	81	82	83	84	85
Wkg ex LA	86	87	88	89	90	91	92	93	94

26

S.E.G. of h/hold head	HEAD 5 YEAR MIGRANT WITHIN L.A. H/holds	Persons	HEAD 5 YEAR MIGRANT INTO L.A. H/holds	Persons	TOTAL Cars & Vans
1 2 13	275	283	291	299	307
3 4	276	284	292	300	308
5 6	277	285	293	301	309
8 9 12 14	278	286	294	302	310
7 10 15	279	287	295	303	311
11	280	288	296	304	312
16 17	281	289	297	305	313
Total	282	290	298	306	314

23

S.E.G.	ECONOMICALLY ACTIVE OR RETIRED BY S.E.G. OF HEAD H/holds	/Persons	S.E.G. OF Persons	ECONOMICALLY ACTIVE Males	Females	Married Females	PERSONS IN EMPLOYMENT With O.N. or school cert. or 'A' level	With H.N. or degree	Occupn change in yr.	Wkg ex L.A.	PERSONS ACTIVE BUT NOT IN EMP.	RET'D MALES
1	152	169	186	203	220	237	254	271	288	305	322	339
2	153	170	187	204	221	238	255	272	289	306	323	340
3	154	171	188	205	222	239	256	273	290	307	324	341
4	155	172	189	206	223	240	257	274	291	308	325	342
5	156	173	190	207	224	241	258	275	292	309	326	343
6	157	174	191	208	225	242	259	276	293	310	327	344
7	158	175	192	209	226	243	260	277	294	311	328	345
8	159	176	193	210	227	244	261	278	295	312	329	346
9	160	177	194	211	228	245	262	279	296	313	330	347
10	161	178	195	212	229	246	263	280	297	314	331	348
11	162	179	196	213	230	247	264	281	298	315	332	349
12	163	180	197	214	231	248	265	282	299	316	333	350
13	164	181	198	215	232	249	266	283	300	317	334	351
14	165	182	199	216	233	250	267	284	301	318	335	352
15	166	183	200	217	234	251	268	285	302	319	336	353
16	167	184	201	218	235	252	269	286	303	320	337	354
17	168	185	202	219	236	253	270	287	304	321	338	355
Total	356	357	358	359	360	361	362	363	364	365	366	367
	NEVER ACTIVE			INACTIVE			NOT IN EMP.					
Students	368	371	374	377	380	383	386	389	-	-	-	-
Women <60	369	372	375	378	381	384	387	390	-	-	-	-
Others	370	373	376	379	382	385	388	391	-	-	-	-
Total	392	393	394	395	396	397	398	399	-	-	-	-

25 NUMBER OF FAMILIES WITH NUMBER OF DEPENDENT CHILDREN

	0	1	2	3	4	5+
Lone parent	95	96	97	98	99	100
married couple	101	102	103	104	105	106

27 / **28**

Grouped S.E.G.	TRAVEL TO WORK BY Car	Bus	Train	M.Cycle	P.Cycle	Foot & none	Other not stated	INDUSTRY OF EMPLOYED PERSON Agri.	Mining	Manuf.	Const.	Utilities Transport	Distrib. Services	Nat. and Loc. Govt. and Def.
1 2 13	107	108	109	110	111	112	113	191	192	193	194	195	196	197
3 4	114	115	116	117	118	119	120	198	199	200	201	202	203	204
5	121	122	123	124	125	126	127	205	206	207	208	209	210	211
6	128	129	130	131	132	133	134	212	213	214	215	216	217	218
8 9	135	136	137	138	139	140	141	219	220	221	222	223	224	225
7 10 15	142	143	144	145	146	147	148	226	227	228	229	230	231	232
11	149	150	151	152	153	154	155	233	234	235	236	237	238	239
12 14	156	157	158	159	160	161	162	240	241	242	243	244	245	246
16 17	163	164	165	166	167	168	169	247	248	249	250	251	252	253
Wkg in LA	170	171	172	173	174	175	176	254	255	256	257	258	259	260
Wkg ex LA	177	178	179	180	181	182	183	261	262	263	264	265	266	267
Self emp.	184	185	186	187	188	189	190	268	269	270	271	272	273	274

SMALL AREA STATISTICS
(WARD LIBRARY)

100% HOUSEHOLDS

CENSUS 1971

AREA IDENTIFICATION BOX

15	Present	Absent	With 1 car	2 or more cars
H'holds	32	33	34	35
Persons	36	-	37	38

16	Occupied	Vacant	No hot water	No bath	No inside W.C.	With 3 aments.
Dwellings	39	40	41	42	43	44
Sh'd dwellings	45	-	46	47	48	49

17	Vacant dw'l'g	Absent h'hold	Hotels & boarding houses
Rooms	50	51	52

18

NUMBER PER 1000											
Owner occ.	Council	Unfurn-ished	Furn-ished	Not stated	H'holds in sh'd dw'l'gs	All aments. excl.	Other all aments.	Share or lack hot w.	Share or lack bath	Share inside W.C.	No inside W.C.
53	54	55	56	57	58	59	60	61	62	63	64

PRIVATE HOUSEHOLDS PRESENT												
Persons per room					Rooms		One person H'holds		Two person households			
Over 1½	Over 1 to 1½	Over ½ to 1	½-½	Less than ½	1-3	7+	All h'holds	Pens. pers.	All h'holds	One pension	Two pensions	No car
65	66	67	68	69	70	71	72	73	74	75	76	77

19		PRESENT PRIVATE HOUSEHOLDS WITH FOLLOWING ROOMS						Total households	Total rooms
		1 or 2	3	4	5	6	7 or more		
1 person		78	85	92	99	106	113	120	127
2 persons		79	86	93	100	107	114	121	128
3 "		80	87	94	101	108	115	122	129
4 "		81	88	95	102	109	116	123	130
5 "		82	89	96	103	110	117	124	131
6 "		83	90	97	104	111	118	125	132
7 or more		84	91	98	105	112	119	126	133
Total H/Holds		134	135	136	137	138	139	146	148
Total persons		140	141	142	143	144	145	147	
All in non-perm. bldgs.	(H	149	150	151	152	153	154	245	261
	(P	155	156	157	158	159	160	246	
In perm. bldgs. Owner Occupier	(H	161	162	163	164	165	166	247	262
	(P	167	168	169	170	171	172	248	
Council.New Town. SSHA	(H	173	174	175	176	177	178	249	263
	(P	179	180	181	182	183	184	250	
Private un-furnished	(H	185	186	187	188	189	190	251	264
	(P	191	192	193	194	195	196	252	
Private furnished	(H	197	198	199	200	201	202	253	265
	(P	203	204	205	206	207	208	254	
Not stated	(H	209	210	211	212	213	214	255	266
	(P	215	216	217	218	219	220	256	
All in sh'd dwellings	(H	221	222	223	224	225	226	257	267
	(P	227	228	229	230	231	232	258	
do. without excl. stove and sink	(H	233	234	235	236	237	238	259	268
	(P	239	240	241	242	243	244	260	

20	HOUSEHOLD TYPE							
Adults (Aged 15 or over) in Household	No child	Children aged 0-14 in household: One child 0-4	One child 5-14	Two or more children All 0-4	Two or more children All 5-14	Others	Persons	Persons E.A.
One pensionable (male)	269	270	271	272	273	274	275	276
" " (female)	277	278	279	280	281	282	283	284
One other (male)	285	286	287	288	289	290	291	292
" " (female)	293	294	295	296	297	298	299	300
2+ all pensionable	301	302	303	304	305	306	307	308
2+ none "	309	310	311	312	313	314	315	316
2+ only one not pens.	317	318	319	320	321	322	323	324
Others 2+	325	326	327	328	329	330	331	332
All adult type	333	334	335	336	337	338	339	340

21 All three aments. excl.	Other three aments.	Share or lack hot water	Bath Share	Bath Lack	Inside W.C. Share	Inside W.C. Lack	Persons per room Over 1½	Persons per room Over 1 to 1½	No car
341	351	361	371	381	391	401	411	421	431
342	352	362	372	382	392	402	412	422	432
343	353	363	373	383	393	403	413	423	433
344	354	364	374	384	394	404	414	424	434
345	355	365	375	385	395	405	415	425	435
346	356	366	376	386	396	406	416	426	436
347	357	367	377	387	397	407	417	427	437
348	358	368	378	388	398	408	418	428	438
349	359	369	379	389	399	409	419	429	439
350	360	370	380	390	400	410	420	430	440
441	442	443	444	445	446	447	448	449	450
451	452	453	454	455	456	457	458	459	460
461	462	463	464	465	466	467	468	469	470
471	472	473	474	475	476	477	478	479	480

AREA IDENTIFICATION BOX	SMALL AREA STATISTICS (WARD LIBRARY)	100% POPULATION	CENSUS 1971

1

Total population present	32
Visitors res. in L.A	33
Visitors to L.A. res. in G.B.	34
Visitors to G.B.	35
Total pop. in private H/H	36
Res. at address of enum.	37
Total pop. not in private H/H	38
Res. in the estab.	39

2 PERSONS NOT PRESENT IN PRIVATE HOUSEHOLDS

	All present		Resident staff		Other residents	
	Males	Females	Males	Females	Males	Females
Hotels & B/Houses	40	47	54	61	68	75
Children's homes	41	48	55	62	69	76
Old people's homes	42	49	56	63	70	77
Psychiatric hosps.	43	50	57	64	71	78
Other hospitals	44	51	58	65	72	79
Schools & Colleges	45	52	59	66	73	80
Other non-pvte H/H	46	53	60	67	74	81
Total	82	83	84	85	86	87

3 RESIDENTS WITH NEITHER PARENT BORN IN U.K.

	BOTH PARENTS BORN IN NEW C.				OTHERS			
AGE	SWDM	MM	SWDF	MF	SWDM	MM	SWDF	MF
0-4	88	(96)	104	(112)	120	(128)	136	(144)
5-14	89	(97)	105	(113)	121	(129)	137	(145)
15-24	90	98	106	114	122	130	138	146
25-34	91	99	107	115	123	131	139	147
35-44	92	100	108	116	124	132	140	148
45-54	93	101	109	117	125	133	141	149
55-64	94	102	110	118	126	134	142	150
65+	95	103	111	119	127	135	143	151
Total	152	153	154	155	156	157	158	159
Total E.A.	160	161	162	163	164	165	166	167

4 AGES TO 21 YEARS

	Males	Females
0	168	190
1	169	191
2	170	192
3	171	193
4	172	194
0-4	212	215
5	173	195
6	174	196
7	175	197
8	176	198
9	177	199
5-9	213	216
10	178	200
11	179	201
12	180	202
13	181	203
14	182	204
10-14	214	217
15	183	205
16	184	206
17	185	207
18	186	208
19	187	209
20	188	210
21	189	211

5 AGES OF ALL ECONOMICALLY ACTIVE; **6** PERSONS NOT IN PRIVATE HOUSEHOLDS; **7** PERSONS PRESENT IN PRIVATE HOUSEHOLDS

	5	5 FEMALES		6 MALES		6 FEMALES		7 MALES		7 FEMALES		7 Children ever born to married women
	Males	SWD	Married	SWD	Married	SWD	Married	SWD	Married	SWD	Married	
0-14	-	-	-	359	(373)	387	(401)	269	(283)	297	(311)	-
15-	218	231	244	360	374	388	402	270	284	298	312	494
20-	219	232	245	361	375	389	403	271	285	299	313	495
25-	220	233	246	362	376	390	404	272	286	300	314	496
30-	221	234	247	363	377	391	405	273	287	301	315	497
35-	222	235	248	364	378	392	406	274	288	302	316	498
40-	223	236	249	365	379	393	407	275	289	303	317	499
45-	224	237	250	366	380	394	408	276	290	304	318	500
50-	225	238	251	367	381	395	409	277	291	305	319	501
55-	226	239	252	368	382	396	410	278	292	306	320	502
60-	227	240	253	369	383	397	411	279	293	307	321	-
65-	228	241	254	370	384	398	412	280	294	308	322	-
70-	229	242	255	371	385	399	413	281	295	309	323	-
75-	230	243	256	372	386	400	414	282	296	310	324	-
Total	257	258	259	415	416	417	418	325	326	327	328	-
Working	260	263	266	419	424	429	434	329	334	339	344	-
Seek wk	261	264	267	420	425	430	435	330	335	340	345	-
Sick	262	265	268	421	426	431	436	331	336	341	346	-
Retired	-	-	-	422	427	432	437	332	337	342	347	-
Other	-	-	-	423	428	433	438	333	338	343	348	-

8 BIRTHPLACES OF PRES. RESIDENTS

	Males	Females
England	439	440
Scotland	441	442
Wales	443	444
N.I. etc.	445	446
Irish Rep.	447	448
Old C.	449	450
New C.	469	470
Africa	451	452
America	453	454
Ceylon	455	456
India	457	458
Pakistan	459	460
Far East	461	462
Remainder	463	464
Other Eur.	465	466
O.F. N.S.	467	468

BIRTHPLACE OF THOSE ENTERING U.K. AFTER 1960

	Males	Females
Irish Rep.	349	354
Old C.	350	355
New C.	351	356
Other Eur.	352	357
O.F. N.S.	353	358

10 NUMBER OF E.A. PER 1000 OF:

Age 15 or over	Males age 15 or over	Females age 15 or over	Married Females in pvte h/holds
471	472	473	474

11 NUMBER PER 1000 PERS PRES IN PRIVATE H/HOLDS

Aged 0-4	Aged 5-14	Stds 15 or over	Male 65 or over	Fem 60 or over	Married Females aged 16-29	30-44	45-59
475	476	477	478	479	480	481	482

12 CHILDREN EVER BORN PER 100 MARR FEM IN PVTE H/HOLDS AGED

16-29	30-44	45-59
483	494	485

13 NUMBER PER 1000 PRESENT RESIDENTS

Both parents born N.C.		One Parent N.C.	Person born in		
Born GB	Born NC	Born NC	GB	N Ireland	Irish Rep.
486	487	488	489	490	491

14 NUMBER OF VISITORS PER 1000 PERSONS PRESENT

Res GB	Others
492	493

Appendix 4

Census definitions

These definitions are taken from OPCS (1982d) which gives definitive specifications of a wide range of terms used in relation to the Census.

1 *Present population*: those persons enumerated within a particular area on census night. This was used as the population base for most 1971 census output.

2 *Usually resident population*: those persons normally resident within a particular area, wherever they are enumerated. There are two methods of counting the usually resident population:

a Present/absent method, which counts all those returned as usually living 'at this address', whether or not present on census night.

b Transfer method, by which people are allocated to their usual residence, wherever they were enumerated.

The main difference between the two methods is in their treatment of residents absent from their usual address. Such residents would be counted by the present/absent method unless they formed part of a household wholly absent from place of residence. All absent residents would be counted by the transfer method, unless part of a household wholly absent from Great Britain. While the transfer method was used for some 1971 tables, the present/absent method is predominantly used in 1981 tables.

The census usual resident population differs from that given in the Registrar-General's Annual Estimates in that the former counts students and members of the Armed Services at their home address, whereas the latter counts them at term-time address, camp or barracks.

3 *Household*: one person living alone or a group of people (who may or may not be related) living or staying at the same address, with common housekeeping (which could be manifested by the sharing of at least one meal per day or shared use of a sitting room).

4 *Head of household*: the first person entered on the household's form, aged 16 or over and usually resident at that address. As a last resort persons aged under 16 are accepted as heads of household, but no heads were identified in households consisting entirely of visitors.

5 *Housewife*: the first usually resident female aged 16 or over in a household, or the male head of household if there is no female aged over 16.

6 *Family*: a married couple with or without their never married child(ren), or a father or mother together with his or her never married child(ren) or grandparent(s) with grandchild(ren) if there are no apparent parents of the grandchild(ren) usually resident in the household.

7 *Child*: if never married, a person still living with one or both parents will be considered a child whatever their age. A dependent child has to be either aged under 16 or (for one SAS table) under 25, never married and a student.

8 *Permanent building*: a building which satisfies at least one of the following criteria:

a The walls are of brick, stone and mortar, concrete, breeze block or similar material.
b The roof is of tiles, slate, thatch, shingle or concrete.
c The length of the shortest wall is at least 15 feet.

9 *Migrant*: a person who gave the answer 'This address' as usual residence, and an answer of 'Different' to the question on usual address one year ago.

10 *Economically active*: in a paid job, working full or part time, waiting to start a job already accepted, seeking work or prevented from seeking work by temporary sickness.

11 *Economically inactive*: permanently sick or disabled, wholly retired, housewife or at school or a full-time educational establishment.

12 *Social class*: a broad categorization of economically active, retired and permanently sick persons in the following categories according to their present or former occupations:

I Professional etc. occupations
II Intermediate occupations
III N Skilled occupations – non-manual
III M Skilled occupations – manual
IV Partly skilled occupations
V Unskilled occupations
VI Armed forces and inadequately described

13 *Socioeconomic group*: applied to the economically active, sick and permanently sick, the following classification is designed to group people with jobs of similar social and economic status:

1 Employers and managers in central and local government, industry, commerce, etc. – large establishments
2 Employers and managers in industry, commerce, etc. – small establishments
3 Professional workers – self employed
4 Professional workers – employees
5 Intermediate non-manual workers
6 Junior non-manual workers
7 Personal service workers
8 Foremen and supervisors – manual
9 Skilled manual workers
10 Semi-skilled manual workers
11 Unskilled manual workers
12 Own account workers (other than professionals)
13 Farmers – employers and managers
14 Farmers – own account
15 Agricultural workers
16 Members of the armed forces
17 Inadequately described or non-stated occupations.

It should be noted that social classes are *not* composed of aggregations of socioeconomic groups.

Appendix 5

Population totals 1901–81 for post-1974 counties and districts in England and Wales and for post-1975 regions, island authorities and districts in Scotland

These figures are approximations, the method by which they were produced being described in Mounsey (1982). All figures relate to the total population present on census night (see appendix 4 and Chapter 2). The 1981 figures are the provisional population totals published by OPCS late in 1981.

LOCAL AUTH. NAME	1901	1911	1921	1931	1951	1961	1971	1981
Cambridge	50535	55889	61468	69910	81500	95527	98840	90440
East Cambridge	39243	40774	38964	40532	44925	45124	49109	53629
Fenland	45401	50394	53911	56211	61998	62790	64682	67215
Huntingdon	47725	48842	48632	48157	59824	68218	96986	123450
Peterborough	49523	53644	56635	63405	77484	90957	105637	132464
South Cambridgeshire	50828	52723	48975	50698	65161	73939	90413	107979
Cambridgeshire	283256	302267	308583	328913	390892	436555	505667	575177
Breckland	58536	59493	56257	54450	62851	61895	76417	96444
Broadland	33856	35152	35072	39273	55304	65919	86532	98323
Great Yarmouth	63615	69034	74362	70953	68985	72591	75763	80820
North Norfolk	64152	67033	69646	66190	77358	73855	74238	82037
Norwich	114392	121908	121157	127154	122368	120953	122094	122270
South Norfolk	57675	57551	55527	56358	62958	64690	80706	92842
West Norfolk	83791	87835	91830	90627	101695	106009	110043	120754
Norfolk	476020	498008	503853	505005	551518	565915	625792	693490
Babergh	48342	49377	47851	45493	47618	47132	63249	73697
Forest Heath	23353	23296	22328	22160	29012	31818	39589	51907
Ipswich	68120	75515	81121	89784	107681	117528	123301	120447
Mid Suffolk	55100	55447	53148	53168	54521	54264	60722	69787
St. Edmundsbury	49686	49859	45708	44971	51094	55606	71353	86054
Suffolk Coastal	60706	66150	68586	68279	74561	82960	89123	95223
Waveney	65328	71628	78387	74164	74617	77825	90680	99239
Suffolk	370636	391270	397127	398019	439105	467130	538018	596354
East Anglia	1129912	1191545	1209563	1231937	1381515	1469600	1669477	1865021
Amber Valley	75109	84275	89429	93740	103897	102811	105261	109379
Bolsover	48896	70161	72214	73583	73001	75356	72315	70423
Chesterfield	67052	76958	80269	88672	93461	94186	96120	96710
Derby	146728	153509	165394	183663	196256	212720	219582	215736
Erewash	47733	64190	65887	69687	87252	92722	99682	101838
High Peak	65876	72730	74232	74521	71782	70280	79236	82142
NE. Derbyshire	45500	49799	54785	55412	67203	81025	88394	96547
South Derbyshire	39284	42736	42977	45286	54440	55111	60948	67669
West Derbyshire	57252	60839	60312	61486	62745	62596	65073	66485
Derbyshire	593433	675194	705503	746050	810037	846807	886611	906929
Blaby	9309	11391	16119	21964	38688	50539	74242	77210
Charnwood	53494	58333	64147	71542	89351	104032	125596	134204
Harborough	27404	30329	30566	31866	39077	42494	52964	60766

LOCAL AUTH. NAME	1901	1911	1921	1931	1951	1961	1971	1981
Hinckley and Bosworth	36668	42567	44487	49433	61525	65020	75374	87518
Leicester	223970	241980	242415	263691	285626	288065	284208	279791
Melton	25206	27881	27053	28191	32730	34435	38894	43260
NW. Leicestershire	45806	52423	57191	59277	62576	64487	71044	78589
Oadby and Wigston	10153	11499	12453	15671	21576	33577	49780	50569
Rutland	19188	20499	18376	17401	20537	23504	27469	30670
Leicestershire	451199	496899	512807	559036	651687	706153	799571	842577
Boston	35484	37757	38005	40444	45311	47339	48823	52634
East Lindsey	75471	78076	83401	81173	92559	90566	94698	104546
Lincoln	51378	60511	66921	67167	70931	77693	74269	76660
North Kesteven	39046	42120	42886	44721	57939	59742	72720	78527
South Holland	41991	44972	47713	51682	56244	55988	56867	61734
South Kesteven	62669	66392	64299	64844	71781	75048	85560	97600
West Lindsey	54804	57744	55978	54638	61848	62281	70560	75859
Lincolnshire	360844	387573	399203	404669	456613	468657	503497	547560
Corby	5072	5477	5499	5596	21454	40466	52694	52667
Daventry	31602	31821	32016	31818	36072	37354	48091	57656
East Northamptonshire	44796	47151	46369	45680	50561	51720	56739	60843
Kettering	45784	48670	47904	50405	57635	59484	65794	71314
Northampton	98425	101508	101848	106855	115453	123320	133565	156848
South Northamptonshire	33166	33065	32024	31091	37418	41593	55749	64057
Wellingborough	35663	36108	36742	38030	41125	44121	55991	64147
Northamptonshire	294506	303797	302404	309474	359721	398057	468623	527532
Ashfield	53042	68032	76554	80101	91856	94901	101958	106521
Bassetlaw	50119	56721	59830	73325	84636	90295	97434	101970
Broxtowe	34292	39608	45787	50748	76729	86945	98365	102801
Gedling	29631	38465	42960	51139	68200	80568	96275	104134
Mansfield	28576	52280	65383	70811	80064	84892	95394	99349
Newark	44102	47203	47920	64838	73905	83952	98837	104139
Nottingham	245201	266252	264665	277405	307849	311770	300532	271080
Rushcliffe	29142	35197	37649	43964	56932	67669	85775	92587
Nottinghamshire	514107	603761	640749	712330	840174	900989	974573	982631
East Midlands	2214089	2467224	2560666	2731559	3118232	3320663	3632875	3807229
Hartlepool	86433	86003	92080	91556	91788	96708	99512	94359
Langbaurgh	81885	96033	105107	105649	113525	130585	147571	149508
Middlesbrough	85635	99101	110160	120899	134429	149937	158905	149770
Stockton-on-Tees	84236	97435	110616	120426	133527	149267	161778	172138

LOCAL AUTH. NAME	1901	1911	1921	1931	1951	1961	1971	1981
Cleveland	338188	378572	417964	438531	473269	526497	567766	565775
Allerdale	94756	94589	98953	91176	95429	95369	94943	95664
Barrow-in-Furness	70852	74686	86732	76691	77874	75243	75269	72635
Carlisle	78033	78437	80094	83353	97643	100745	100847	100692
Copeland	68689	68254	70271	64746	67724	73519	71794	72788
Eden	46064	44661	43891	44156	43877	42446	41971	43984
South Lakeland	77263	75766	81096	77148	81851	82808	91309	97664
Cumbria	435656	436394	461036	437270	464398	470130	476133	483427
Chester-le-Street	30903	39484	44873	44075	42580	43272	48303	51719
Darlington	50736	62715	70530	75706	89355	93450	98150	97788
Derwentside	82386	105567	111175	110093	102837	99889	92220	88132
Durham	66697	76515	77387	73698	72542	75439	81752	85190
Easington	50318	74843	91141	105780	107347	110237	108234	100717
Sedgefield	58265	74742	80827	75905	77833	84626	88436	92887
Teesdale	29433	31412	32414	27479	28103	26385	24644	24425
Wear Valley	83749	91823	94786	84292	76289	71967	65439	63870
Durham	452483	557098	603129	597030	596889	605263	607174	604728
Alnwick	30330	30333	33450	29620	29893	29812	27931	28734
Berwick-upon-Tweed	34135	32989	33507	30044	29847	27857	25778	26230
Blyth Valley	43735	51010	53558	54650	56456	57241	60615	76787
Castle Morpeth	22640	27124	29147	30245	35745	40789	47630	50570
Tynedale	50230	53309	58576	53813	53158	52063	53144	55087
Wansbeck	38201	56930	65758	66110	67544	66555	64455	62497
Northumberland	219271	251693	273993	264481	272644	274315	279556	299905
Gateshead	184791	220306	235991	235995	222481	223310	224892	211658
Newcastle upon Tyne	274628	306228	317120	330302	346336	338348	308063	277674
North Tyneside	109842	139687	156611	162783	180641	207896	207940	198266
South Tyneside	166791	178783	193951	189193	174726	185111	177000	160551
Sunderland	233264	260309	277479	282673	277207	289181	293797	295096
Tyne and Wear	969317	1105314	1181151	1200944	1201391	1243848	1211694	1143245
North	2414915	2729071	2937273	2938256	3008591	3120053	3142323	3097080
Chester	71512	74932	77612	80711	97417	102053	115608	116157
Congleton	37991	39518	40616	42684	50575	55346	70902	79028
Crewe and Nantwich	74502	79138	80125	80995	89135	91295	97100	98217
Ellesmere Port	11461	18658	23628	31134	42788	56582	78419	81549
Halton	54936	60138	62763	65895	76769	82249	95463	121972

LOCAL AUTH. NAME	1901	1911	1921	1931	1951	1961	1971	1981
Macclesfield	78371	81609	80360	85759	99571	112357	139878	149003
Vane Royal	61381	65049	66547	69926	82934	88326	105909	111521
Warrington	94352	108229	112972	120850	147972	141573	163280	168846
Cheshire	484508	527272	544622	577950	687162	729779	866556	926293
Bolton	253361	271131	267978	267418	254039	251211	259533	260830
Bury	126543	133422	131923	137960	151162	152112	174557	176568
Manchester	649246	719520	735562	766222	702941	661779	543867	449168
Oldham	228068	247911	248895	240603	221055	215484	223985	219817
Rochdale	162657	176354	175739	176691	170449	189649	203148	207255
Salford	307581	333908	343063	338653	305600	294200	279907	243736
Stockport	134045	158602	165293	180746	223473	255817	292271	289730
Tameside	190145	197117	192904	189536	204480	204047	220871	217341
Trafford	95700	121408	129118	155527	205312	223977	227899	221406
Wigan	256518	278897	283321	273744	277688	271633	302963	308927
Greater Manchester	2403868	2638269	2673801	2727104	2716204	2719913	2728997	2594778
Blackburn	172986	179457	170849	165323	148883	143254	141142	141758
Blackpool	52072	64771	102845	107032	147870	153385	151909	147854
Burnley	119338	131578	125976	120134	104622	99317	96560	93779
Chorley	56840	62429	62768	62825	67297	67207	77808	90986
Fylde	24469	30659	39440	39935	54054	58578	67049	68440
Hyndburn	93271	100327	97328	92060	82420	80077	80599	78860
Lancaster	75037	76723	84808	88229	112001	115018	123663	120914
Pendle	87306	104494	106256	101768	90684	86304	85619	85573
Preston	125430	131727	132241	137647	145351	141763	134687	125886
Ribble Valley	35075	37968	38880	41498	42468	43605	51312	51968
Rossendale	85515	84147	79686	77961	69078	65447	61968	64480
South Ribble	30145	34002	36602	42362	55799	68220	86162	97164
West Lancashire	36760	39586	40366	41282	52081	61000	91428	106735
Wyre	31128	37405	42866	52757	65990	78007	94851	97721
Lancashire	1025372	1115274	1160916	1170814	1238599	1261188	1344762	1372118
Knowsley	20740	22056	24935	27309	92962	156607	194610	173356
Liverpool	711683	753831	803493	853985	789208	745471	609904	510306
St. Helens	121751	138291	146450	152585	167310	169518	188762	189909
Sefton	182272	211364	232201	243686	274870	294866	307668	300011
Wirral	196885	252339	290077	309008	338382	351724	355602	339488
Merseyside	1233332	1377879	1497157	1586575	1662733	1718186	1656545	1513070
North West	5147080	5658694	5876496	6062443	6304698	6429066	6596860	6406259

LOCAL AUTH. NAME	1901	1911	1921	1931	1951	1961	1971	1981
Luton	42877	57070	64540	73891	113588	140044	161405	164049
Mid Bedfordshire	46082	47120	48377	49966	63401	69117	89829	102063
North Bedfordshire	60983	66181	67875	69113	90494	103815	124554	132084
South Bedfordshire	23922	26480	28042	29989	45951	69730	88489	106790
Bedfordshire	173864	196850	208835	222958	313434	382706	464277	504986
Bracknall	15858	17589	18889	17996	23187	43763	64141	81885
Newbury	45352	49194	48875	51472	63766	82470	104470	120231
Reading	81340	87826	92410	97135	113975	120508	132945	132037
Slough	17171	21593	24227	38461	73584	92755	99330	97008
Windsor and Maidenhead	57869	61748	67316	69204	83037	107375	124054	130054
Wokingham	18038	21045	23063	27530	44505	63223	99670	113938
Berkshire	235625	258995	274780	301801	402054	510096	624612	675153
Aylesbury Vale	55987	58376	59499	61587	80590	90435	114406	132709
Chiltern	21744	27527	32168	39311	53338	71739	88917	91728
Milton Keynes	35797	38364	37806	36328	43183	48675	66800	123782
South Buckinghamshire	13708	16767	20067	25830	39444	57589	63726	62182
Wycombe	45306	49591	53670	62685	87026	109424	142375	155591
Buckinghamshire	172541	190627	203211	225742	303583	377863	476222	565992
Brighton	127079	135395	148413	148720	158068	163159	161351	146134
Eastbourne	44449	53620	63126	58644	57821	60918	70921	77608
Hastings	66471	62166	67515	66321	65522	66478	72410	74803
Hove	42650	49854	55726	64520	83109	88747	91222	84740
Lewes	33687	35502	37041	40173	49023	56560	72201	77507
Rother	40454	43924	48884	52012	60537	63968	71046	75278
Wealden	55595	62238	65481	67345	80227	86400	108309	116498
East Sussex	410387	442696	486186	497735	554307	586230	647460	652568
Basildon	13153	16038	13217	28464	44201	89667	130581	152301
Braintree	52099	53555	53308	58775	67877	74502	93384	111818
Brentwood	17595	21782	26540	30760	39545	61216	73700	71978
Castle Point	5243	6575	8048	15763	31140	48000	74674	85533
Chelmsford	34338	38715	43994	52928	73618	93683	122829	138318
Colchester	60553	66642	65825	72949	85500	93810	118156	133681
Epping Forest	34812	37444	37452	43322	82679	104367	114099	116204
Harlow	3110	3384	3823	4186	5771	53680	78087	79253
Maldon	22395	24796	26003	25522	28654	31017	40536	47726
Rochford	8327	10468	13840	20516	28997	49350	68469	73540
Southend-on-Sea	38108	77288	113753	129923	151806	165093	162770	156683
Tendring	45181	53600	63141	62165	75522	80381	102413	113819
Thurrock	32427	39199	48380	61168	81287	113120	123837	126870
Uttlesford	37996	38982	36885	36933	42579	45730	54493	61341

LOCAL AUTH. NAME	1901	1911	1921	1931	1951	1961	1971	1981
Essex	405334	488473	554215	643375	839177	1103616	1358028	1469065
Corp. of London	26882	19619	14158	11054	5324	4767	4245	5893
Barking	27225	38881	44627	138006	189430	177092	160800	150175
Barnet	76080	118100	147139	231156	320438	318373	306560	292331
Bexley	53112	59978	76591	95552	205400	209893	217076	214818
Brent	120046	165693	184232	250879	311081	295899	280657	251257
Bromley	100318	116062	126729	164176	267771	293394	305377	294451
Camden	376623	353201	340962	325995	258318	245707	206737	171563
Croydon	143840	188690	212919	270627	310433	323927	333870	316557
Ealing	94985	164694	181545	225673	310690	301646	301108	280042
Enfield	104589	154709	167047	201528	288112	273857	268004	258825
Greenwich	210563	214878	238282	244922	235549	229810	217664	211806
Hackney	388953	384544	378813	363638	265349	257522	220279	180237
Hammersmith	249487	274767	281474	286506	241431	222124	187195	148054
Haringey	208951	271341	285400	307446	277316	259156	240078	203175
Harrow	24106	42030	49271	96711	219494	209083	203215	195999
Havering	25763	33130	38478	77284	192094	245598	247696	240318
Hillingdon	29218	38580	48194	84012	210312	228361	234888	229183
Hounslow	84891	109432	117605	155590	211075	208893	206956	199782
Islington	436413	415288	406983	391738	271002	261232	201874	159754
Kensington and Chelsea	250429	238664	239807	239763	219117	218528	188227	138759
Kingston upon Thames	56417	68731	74409	93408	146615	146010	140525	132411
Lambeth	380707	403882	414743	416259	346964	341624	307516	245739
Lewisham	237852	270292	286979	326899	303071	290582	268474	233225
Merton	61946	98479	114310	157669	200140	189013	177324	164912
Newham	365669	424907	446701	439155	294017	265388	237390	209290
Redbridge	65800	112279	123897	178887	256902	250080	239889	225019
Richmond	94877	123372	141603	161070	188100	180949	174628	157867
Southwark	596238	579100	571305	534586	337638	313413	262138	211708
Sutton	37277	55118	60308	103332	176151	169095	169494	168407
Tower Hamlets	597061	570391	529724	488576	230790	205682	165776	142975
Waltham Forest	198375	257461	267582	283416	275468	248591	234680	215092
Wandsworth	321935	373203	384673	392660	330883	335451	302258	255723
Westminster City	460247	420934	390263	372184	300332	271703	239748	190661
GLC	6506889	7160441	7386755	8110358	8196807	7992443	7452346	6696008
Basingstoke	35958	38838	40080	43826	52750	68324	103427	129899
East Hampshire	31154	42179	40470	46021	58981	63018	79493	89831
Eastleigh	23111	30917	32473	38161	51432	61213	78570	92491
Fareham	14054	16466	18926	22047	42772	58363	80412	88274
Gosport	30500	35191	35830	38673	58531	62512	76125	77276
Hart	17288	20012	21801	24141	31493	37426	61692	75654
Havant	13639	16140	17511	22951	35668	74607	109332	116649
New Forest	39672	45510	49238	60761	86257	107067	130877	145123
Portsmouth	192532	235511	248280	252651	233797	215132	197440	179419
Rushmoor	45417	52618	44911	54371	64622	63191	74873	78107

LOCAL AUTH. NAME	1901	1911	1921	1931	1951	1961	1971	1981
Southampton	130054	151834	167991	183741	190337	205081	215127	204406
Test Valley	31973	39346	37437	43056	58151	61539	79902	90853
Winchester	45160	50414	53393	54469	64817	73186	85734	88385
Hampshire	650507	774974	808335	884872	1029612	1150653	1373008	1456367
Broxbourne	19519	20887	21132	24330	36717	53226	71077	79562
Dacorum	33268	36775	37953	42380	58487	96821	119182	128801
East Hertfordshire	49338	53470	53999	55642	67826	79901	102219	106994
Hertsmere	13189	16995	18715	26963	53298	87821	91190	87752
North Hertfordshire	32842	41274	46941	54315	72008	85481	99415	106986
St. Albans	32779	42898	46696	55993	86626	107105	121204	124867
Stevenage	4199	5268	5438	5911	7215	43014	67084	74381
Three Rivers	15679	18450	19853	25596	59120	77153	80907	77836
Watford	30784	42723	48217	58527	73092	75569	78410	74356
Welwyn Hatfield	10195	11631	11911	23353	47059	81757	93939	93000
Hertfordshire	241797	290373	310860	373313	561445	787850	924632	954535
Medina	49561	53117	54051	53358	57693	56316	64423	67569
South Wight	32857	35069	40615	35096	37932	39436	45089	50623
Isle of Wight	82418	88186	94666	88454	95625	95752	109512	118192
Ashford	42418	44730	46156	49069	56378	61914	79083	85832
Canterbury	56607	59169	65297	70172	82517	91182	110130	116829
Dartford	36557	42780	47220	51074	65792	78334	83333	78236
Dover	80532	85141	84721	91150	92426	93962	98969	100751
Gillingham	46496	56214	58289	61583	70676	72910	86862	93741
Gravesham	47720	50312	55392	60312	71093	84122	96461	95841
Maidstone	61613	64820	67373	73863	88665	97117	121220	130053
Rochester-upon-Medway	78691	85144	86430	86354	101490	117046	139296	143384
Sevenoaks	44366	46768	49904	55605	69752	88237	99535	109402
Shepway	58681	64380	69448	71113	73217	73839	82016	86074
Swale	72796	73398	77812	75953	82293	84345	100897	109506
Thanet	68475	78507	111690	91798	97958	104110	114870	121150
Tonbridge and Malling	45789	48222	50059	51221	61384	69306	93385	96205
Tunbridge Wells	65745	69336	68315	69436	77512	82140	93406	96051
Kent	806488	868927	938112	958701	1091153	1198564	1399463	1463055
Cherwell	41884	42655	40343	42343	61489	69930	94365	106947
Oxford	57773	62711	66984	80242	98544	106168	108824	98521
South Oxfordshire	47659	51275	53745	58572	85376	101023	133624	128596
Vale of White Horse	37708	39523	39978	41380	62244	76875	93325	100749
West Oxfordshire	40728	41780	39191	40149	48699	55764	75036	80266
Oxfordshire	225754	237945	240243	262684	356351	409762	505172	515079

LOCAL AUTH. NAME	1901	1911	1921	1931	1951	1961	1971	1981
Elmbridge	34386	42349	49029	57900	89689	106211	115552	110683
Epsom and Ewell	14513	23866	22808	35053	68102	71147	72305	69230
Guildford	44056	50361	55163	65613	93031	108852	118752	120072
Mole Valley	26038	30005	31353	39642	58871	72126	77531	76614
Reigate and Banstead	45289	52677	54634	65416	92903	115791	119627	116191
Runnymede	25413	27337	29290	34006	55589	70949	75683	71082
Spelthorne	21636	23892	26819	34609	63436	83263	96902	92898
Surrey Heath	14843	22083	23409	27434	34542	44720	66045	76519
Tandridge	30297	37159	40159	47462	64243	75212	79792	75845
Waverley	47615	54575	58576	63861	82073	89749	104108	108901
Woking	21368	28969	31548	35809	47643	67507	75956	81358
Surrey	325456	393270	422787	506800	750122	905530	1002252	999393
Adur	11927	14469	16754	21579	38073	47802	55034	58032
Arun	29988	34637	43439	48462	73464	84162	104583	119206
Chichester	46563	50625	51636	56860	72600	78578	91200	97617
Crawley	3598	3780	8238	8875	11167	54722	68647	73081
Horsham	38245	43693	41920	44163	58447	67050	85639	100647
Mid Sussex	37247	41260	42729	45685	59923	79392	100143	118311
Worthing	24298	32216	37094	46499	69357	80348	88401	91668
West Sussex	191868	220682	241811	272124	383032	492051	593646	658562
South East	10428928	11612439	12170796	13348917	14876702	15993116	16930630	16723955
Bath	70429	73901	73371	73771	81605	83598	84787	79965
Bristol	345945	364916	384474	406392	442777	437538	426774	387977
Kingswood	26589	28540	29902	32073	45725	67061	77925	84045
Northavon	35774	35179	35593	39184	60153	71533	104494	118804
Wansdyke	34037	38950	39008	39173	51069	60151	70980	76322
Woodspring	56119	61047	72109	73305	93237	109069	140932	162295
Avon	568894	602535	634456	663900	774567	828953	905890	909408
Caradon	51426	50174	50806	47690	52837	48508	54145	67894
Carrick	55495	54903	53447	55315	61239	63448	70057	76188
Kerrier	64485	64918	60849	59708	63187	64699	74779	83009
North Cornwall	46887	48992	48791	49266	56034	52379	56489	66189
Penwith	55825	56094	51623	49641	52069	49813	51332	55431
Restormel	46124	50921	53439	54607	58908	62143	72440	79167
Cornwall	320242	326001	318956	316228	344274	340990	379242	430506
East Devon	57947	62248	63815	68102	79487	84226	97215	106320
Exeter	60881	65894	65874	72719	81884	88598	95729	95621

LOCAL AUTH. NAME	1901	1911	1921	1931	1951	1961	1971	1981
Mid Devon	46371	44927	42329	42769	45618	47154	52325	58057
North Devon	55975	57188	61044	57253	63503	62804	70495	78728
Plymouth	208916	224396	227041	228933	226678	230406	239452	243895
South Hams	43639	45626	45198	47012	55354	55515	59898	67861
Teignbridge	57420	59837	62375	65374	75971	79744	90016	95665
Torbay	51334	59270	63147	74034	88311	96293	109257	115582
Torridge	42821	42803	41809	39989	41103	40504	44693	47275
West Devon	36892	37513	36985	36782	38712	37455	39324	42996
Devon	662196	699703	709614	732968	796621	822699	898404	952000
Bournemouth	62372	82136	95394	116429	144435	154207	153854	144803
Christchurch	7317	8835	9781	12710	22232	28680	34291	37708
North Dorset	34395	33642	31401	30408	37205	36050	42333	46479
Poole	28673	40442	45535	59822	82597	92022	107146	118922
Purbeck	16630	18179	24222	24385	28512	31990	36676	40414
West Dorset	60938	62725	61076	61064	67083	68269	74052	78337
Weymouth and Portland	39845	44432	41972	41156	48066	52525	54663	57176
Wimborne	18548	20291	20698	22823	28860	35975	51381	68151
Dorset	268720	310685	330077	368796	458990	499721	554394	591990
Cheltenham	54355	54586	53906	55306	68916	80183	84247	84014
Cotswold	51788	53393	50429	49935	63808	61235	62680	68382
Forest of Dene	54247	55335	57896	57483	61452	62770	65888	72651
Gloucester	57668	60613	60857	63292	74437	82874	90046	92133
Stroud	57569	58264	59553	58910	74466	80125	90445	101356
Tewkesbury	29790	31438	30485	30798	47620	59066	73818	80815
Gloucestershire	305418	313629	313127	315721	390698	426254	467126	499351
Mendip	62306	62605	61284	60887	65770	69781	79312	87030
Sedgemoor	47309	49828	49933	50873	62024	69243	80972	89051
Taunton Deane	54260	56018	55077	56970	69555	73169	81986	86025
West Somerset	22212	23402	24881	26125	28313	28768	29753	32299
Yeovil	82119	84965	83164	86351	99824	104503	114332	130583
Somerset	268205	276820	274337	281204	325484	345462	386356	424988
Kennet	47101	49724	47015	47984	57581	54773	64487	63333
North Wiltshire	55097	54759	52096	53350	82502	86171	94995	102492
Salisbury	60560	65457	69869	72293	89543	91558	101105	100929
Thamesdown	59319	65925	70780	77883	90570	119451	139352	152112
West Wiltshire	48960	50584	51927	51685	66470	70997	86808	99301
Wiltshire	271038	286449	291687	303193	386666	422950	486747	518167
South West	2664713	2815822	2872254	2982010	3477300	3687029	4078159	4326410

LOCAL AUTH. NAME	1901	1911	1921	1931	1951	1961	1971	1981
Bromsgrove	23440	25446	30692	35842	52412	64615	77149	88004
Hereford	21841	23135	23525	24404	32501	40434	46503	47652
Leominster	38637	37557	35959	34796	35498	33240	33224	37196
Malvern Hills	64684	65098	63923	61137	69342	70464	77052	81875
Redditch	19261	21482	22534	22673	29222	34252	40839	66593
South Herefordshire	38856	39199	38683	37709	43661	42623	44364	47511
Worcester	51066	52569	51819	53704	62364	66240	73807	74790
Wychavon	46326	49787	52173	52057	64120	69613	82002	95123
Wyre Forest	45921	45985	45836	49285	63857	70406	85061	91474
Hereford and Worcester	350035	360255	365146	371608	452977	491887	560001	630218
Bridgnorth	33576	33883	31429	31316	41379	42601	47700	50259
North Shropshire	38198	40010	39139	39089	46790	45213	47114	50114
Oswestry	24549	25689	26335	26491	31376	29741	30264	30679
Shrewsbury and Atcham	51798	53834	55228	57205	67962	72885	82395	87218
South Shropshire	36419	36132	35863	34718	34068	32594	32391	33815
The Wrekin	55242	56758	55067	55336	68424	74708	97238	123525
Shropshire	239783	246307	243062	244156	289999	297742	337102	375610
Cannock Chase	33435	38468	42722	45828	54044	60301	79290	84526
East Staffordshire	75722	74038	74696	74871	81315	86857	94423	94862
Lichfield	33885	37040	36775	38103	49862	51833	80360	88454
Newcastle-under-Lyme	75482	82515	84944	88994	104577	114636	119990	117922
South Staffordshire	22874	25501	28568	32524	43290	62101	82794	96493
Stafford	52711	56881	61085	61936	83856	92911	111154	117555
Staffordshire Moorlands	49864	54239	57004	61403	74163	78046	90183	95842
Stoke-on-trent	242761	266342	273624	283131	279867	277251	265258	252351
Tamworth	16675	19082	20720	20257	23180	25429	40285	64315
Staffordshire	603407	654110	680142	707049	794154	849365	963737	1012320
North Warwickshire	24431	28897	31836	33787	37729	43120	58119	59808
Nuneaton	34073	48805	58247	65438	79866	90178	107604	113521
Rugby	38071	45931	52427	55192	67897	75187	83620	86120
Stratford-on-Avon	54414	55853	55699	57659	71857	80972	94523	100431
Warwick	54772	56771	61479	65135	81834	97296	111586	113740
Warickshire	205759	236257	259688	277210	339185	386752	455450	473620
Birmingham	777964	864718	947597	1034020	1160062	1182092	1098085	1006908
Coventry	83217	123736	155756	181420	264616	316024	336387	314124
Dudley	163946	174249	185921	199144	230131	253108	294029	299351
Sandwell	232118	263168	286608	304416	341295	338380	330284	307389
Solihull	21913	26865	29504	42333	94435	136172	191811	198287
Walsall	148188	158817	169593	181035	214899	245697	273456	266123

LOCAL AUTH. NAME	1901	1911	1921	1931	1951	1961	1971	1981
West Midlands (County)	1586709	1779913	1954909	2143088	2546568	2731892	2793288	2644634
West Midlands (Region)	2985693	3276842	3502947	3743111	4422883	4757638	5109578	5136402
Beverley	36678	40682	41600	46426	72330	81399	101349	105698
Boothferry	49328	54290	53230	53802	54269	53982	55178	60290
Cleethorpes	16217	28506	36434	38611	41341	49249	66768	68241
East Yorkshire	48273	50039	58218	54152	62986	63563	65503	74997
Glanford	26591	31912	39295	41050	43931	46316	57517	66761
Grimsby	65027	78325	86475	93207	95717	97978	95541	92147
Holderness	19730	21811	26132	26345	31290	33267	39956	45877
Kingston-upon-Hull	241736	279734	291420	314288	299594	303984	285971	268302
Scunthorpe	18207	24411	27399	33758	54291	67347	70908	66353
Humberside	521787	609708	660205	701640	755753	797083	838692	847666
Craven	44169	45895	45966	45616	46034	44939	46469	47653
Hambleton	47062	48780	51100	50090	56920	58878	67187	74153
Harrogate	77901	86358	91292	93647	108590	115245	127527	139736
Richmondshire	28515	28508	29199	38641	50113	39760	42557	42531
Ryedale	50033	51807	50804	52072	58780	65369	72619	84113
Scarborough	76614	76308	88871	81883	90289	88920	97337	101425
Selby	37503	41443	46237	47472	52706	53634	68695	77212
York	86602	91758	91185	96431	109523	108511	104799	99787
North Yorkshire	448396	470855	494655	505853	572952	575255	627191	666610
Barnsley	142296	181556	187885	205944	218385	222693	225514	224906
Doncaster	81110	113280	149596	216410	245396	267872	281035	288801
Rotherham	106783	140043	161481	178207	205364	226869	243110	251336
Sheffield	474381	528337	568964	572199	583703	585865	572853	536770
South Yorkshire	804571	963215	1067926	1172759	1252847	1303300	1322514	1301813
Bradford	422238	436217	434857	446771	449588	452672	461693	457677
Calderdale	228058	221640	216689	214023	208122	200588	195240	191292
Kirklees	319472	348033	353462	354409	353507	352297	369354	371780
Leeds	584129	612521	621086	652191	696858	714038	738997	704974
Wakefield	192892	233650	249602	271425	277471	285841	302357	311787
West Yorkshire	1746791	1852059	1875695	1938820	1985546	2005434	2067642	2037510
Yorkshire and Humberside	3521545	3895837	4098481	4319072	4567098	4681072	4856039	4853599

LOCAL AUTH. NAME	1901	1911	1921	1931	1951	1961	1971	1981
Alyn and Deeside	24789	31154	35372	38890	48751	51426	65398	72003
Colwyn	23643	27761	34835	34417	38110	38676	45189	48639
Delyn	35521	38191	39885	42829	51283	50756	56881	65140
Glyndwr	37006	37760	37936	37457	39250	38087	37819	40329
Rhuddlan	16017	17927	25867	25849	37605	42044	47524	52338
Wrexham Maelor	76754	85782	88968	89494	98950	101306	105767	111724
Clwyd	213728	238575	262862	268937	313946	322296	358581	390173
Carmarthen	48997	49682	50160	49394	50119	50159	49429	51733
Ceredigion	61078	59880	60881	55184	53278	53648	54882	57372
Dinefwr	33280	42625	45065	45110	41440	38825	36195	36717
Llanelli	53051	68102	79848	84596	80475	79024	76938	75422
Preseli	49156	51686	53185	53886	57059	59621	61130	69323
South Pembrokeshire	38738	38273	38793	33320	33847	34503	37838	39410
Dyfed	284300	310245	327932	321490	316218	315780	316412	329977
Blaenau Gwent	84114	115363	127611	110273	98547	94418	85603	79573
Islwyn	30833	53812	71212	72057	66444	65896	65949	64769
Monmouth	40434	42251	47166	44324	47509	53905	64344	71511
Newport	77208	96325	106882	111812	122443	128449	136822	133698
Torfaen	52941	67754	73645	70635	69756	81035	88423	90133
Gwent	285530	375505	426517	409101	404701	423705	441141	439684
Aberconwy	37615	39934	51785	45974	47851	48532	50878	52503
Arfon	61285	58558	52275	52245	53575	51719	52481	52284
Dwyfor	31476	30842	30711	29123	29099	27478	25902	26285
Meirionnydd	43592	40309	40019	38382	37204	34334	31508	32056
Ynys Mon (Anglesey)	50478	50804	51612	48934	50596	51654	59765	67340
Gwynedd	224446	220449	226403	214659	218324	213719	220535	230468
Cynon Valley	78491	97827	102752	91354	76187	72561	69427	67188
Merthyr Tydfil	75811	90448	90093	80323	69158	67129	63287	60528
Ogwr	60783	86901	103492	98939	104172	111024	123593	129773
Rhondda	115101	154175	163567	142049	111538	100419	88953	81725
Rhymney Valley	47183	88233	105475	102010	95162	95969	101960	105525
Taff-Ely	49112	67394	79890	76036	73866	72550	84624	93127
Mid Glamorgan	426478	584978	645266	590708	530080	519650	531847	537866
Brecknock	39300	42548	43595	42016	41340	39495	37764	40691
Montgomery	55020	53232	51284	48500	46118	44230	43124	48201
Radnor	23400	22676	23538	21350	20121	18536	18284	21575
[illegible]	[illegible]	[illegible]	[illegible]	111866	107578	102260	99173	110467

LOCAL AUTH. NAME	1901	1911	1921	1931	1951	1961	1971	1981
Cardiff	183577	209810	236226	245566	267577	290263	287646	273856
Vale of Glamorgan	48855	58495	67373	70787	83718	90005	102623	110777
South Glamorgan	232432	268306	303600	316354	351294	380267	390269	384633
Afan	26958	39728	50833	50915	53301	60642	59347	54663
Lliw Valley	35008	51811	59428	63229	58409	55652	56283	59745
Neath	44136	60576	68038	71566	72146	70122	67792	66587
Swansea	122139	152290	167178	174507	172677	179930	189824	186199
West Glamorgan	228242	304406	345476	360217	356534	366346	373246	367194
Wales	2012876	2420921	2656474	2593332	2598675	2644023	2731204	2790462
Berwickshire	25550	24504	23560	22114	20662	18337	16995	18092
Ettrick and Lauderdale	37770	38643	35730	35314	34403	33509	32429	31594
Roxburgh	41510	39996	38154	39136	38761	36221	35374	35180
Tweeddale	15196	15283	15495	15192	15317	14166	13681	14382
Borders	120027	118425	112938	111755	109142	102232	98477	99248
Clackmannan	32608	32103	32895	32258	37939	41932	46093	47806
Falkirk	96476	110010	109754	115623	125910	132255	140501	144437
Stirling	56306	62475	64974	63650	69028	70432	76433	80835
Central	185389	204589	207624	211532	232876	244620	263028	273078
Annandale and Eskdale	33420	33345	35197	33664	33624	35347	34592	35338
Nithsdale	43476	43712	49577	50608	55317	56031	56465	56493
Stewartry	31437	30594	25166	24558	24813	23299	22208	23138
Wigtown	36307	35539	33368	31889	34251	31757	29922	30109
Dumfries and Galway	144639	143190	143308	140719	148005	146434	143187	145078
Dumfernline	76033	98569	114196	102190	118465	120003	120530	122232
Kirkcaldy	84858	104785	113609	113419	125405	139617	144955	141861
NE. Fife	57946	64378	65121	60759	62908	61072	61645	62387
Fife	218837	267733	292925	276368	306778	320692	327131	326480
Aberdeen (City)	174146	184028	178700	187326	204101	208054	211960	203612
Banff and Buchan	90309	92194	88014	81839	80307	75100	72854	81446
Gordon	63819	61283	57603	57057	53658	48907	45008	62157
Kincardine and Deeside	41720	39781	40138	35296	36655	33303	33117	47112
Moray	78428	77841	74177	71548	76375	74989	75693	81269
Grampian	448421	455127	438633	433066	451094	440351	438630	470596

LOCAL AUTH. NAME	1901	1911	1921	1931	1951	1961	1971	1981
Badenock and Strathspey	10459	10313	11016	9806	9563	9121	9309	12355
Caithness	37953	35845	31859	28683	24970	29416	29610	27383
Inverness	40404	39201	38266	40120	45686	45848	49760	56557
Lochaber	17021	16290	13765	15499	15613	15910	19193	20539
Nairn	9377	9423	8862	8368	8785	8451	11051	10139
Ross and Cromarty	42026	42885	39068	34442	33653	32698	34855	47305
Skye and Lochalsh	17502	16234	14028	12699	11023	10062	9725	11327
Sutherland	18818	17844	15467	14230	12407	12290	11971	14425
Highland	193559	188035	172328	163846	161702	163796	175473	200030
East Lothian	53300	62252	67232	66773	72802	74431	77406	80187
Edinburgh	406368	415380	432045	449943	478340	484250	476629	436271
Mid Lothian	52847	58033	45444	48029	57481	65683	79744	81661
West Lothian	67206	79649	77946	74525	82254	85799	111843	137373
Lothian	579722	615316	622668	639271	690878	710163	745623	735892
Argyll and Bute	80327	76434	91536	70798	72340	66046	65141	68786
Bearsden and Milngavie	7278	7141	7050	8302	20250	26024	35873	39322
Clydebank	30199	46459	55465	55984	52669	57867	58805	51825
Clydesdale	51759	62787	54431	51123	54415	54625	53524	57361
Cumbernauld and Kilsyth	14988	15292	15277	15433	16826	18663	45632	61707
Cumnock and Doon Valley	41592	41463	41725	40760	46668	52832	48779	45509
Cunninghame	84371	85507	110073	92366	106199	111259	125878	138265
Dumbarton	57884	61385	65557	60260	65990	70477	78806	78041
East Kilbride	25325	30611	24450	22935	14145	40899	74159	82499
Eastwood	19997	26787	12673	17225	38175	43825	49857	53547
Glasgow (City)	940087	976418	1123563	1166779	1174552	1139970	982203	763162
Hamilton	87354	106288	91571	88219	95566	96876	104731	107987
Inverclyde	97900	108534	119615	114115	113734	112458	109365	99966
Kilmarnock and Loudoun	65703	66575	68390	69189	73826	78945	81010	82149
Kyle and Carrick	71433	77937	93223	89547	101175	105076	110476	114463
Monklands	76405	87907	84885	86009	97203	106465	109646	110455
Motherwell	141559	177544	155158	151075	154470	159976	161435	150015
Renfrew	141421	163884	154018	156612	172673	182538	202901	205884
Strathkelvin	43439	50896	41176	43491	52681	59241	77302	86884
Strathclyde	2079017	2269840	2409832	2400223	2523548	2584068	2575514	2397827
Angus	100927	95017	90845	83520	87221	85109	84152	92841
Dundee (City)	185503	188721	182511	188933	189943	195523	197466	180064
Perth and Kinross	113026	114370	115078	111264	119031	117187	115987	118624
Tayside	399455	398109	388433	383716	396194	397820	397605	391529
Orkney	28699	25897	24111	22077	21255	18747	17077	18906
Shetland	28166	27911	25521	21421	19352	17812	17327	26716

LOCAL AUTH. NAME	1901	1911	1921	1931	1951	1961	1971	1981
Western Isles	47647	47606	44177	38986	35591	32609	29891	31766
Islands	104512	101414	93809	82484	76198	69168	64295	77388
Scotland	4473578	4761778	4882498	4842980	5096415	5179344	5228963	5117146

Appendix 6

Census data on magnetic tape

There are many advantages in obtaining SAS census data on magnetic tape: the data only cost one third of the cost of that in paper form and all of the data for over 2000 areas may be stored on one standard length magnetic tape.

OPCS make SAS data available in three different versions of their export format. These are as follows:

ICL 1900 character format – suited for ICL 1900 series computers and 2900 series computers running under DME;
ICL 2900 character format – suited for ICL 2900 series computers running under VME;
IBM EBCDIC character format – suited to IBM and most other computers.

The detailed arrangement of the data on tape is described in *OPCS User Guides* (e.g. *User Guide* 37 is the File Specification for the IBM EBCDIC format; contact OPCS Customer Services for details). The data are normally arranged as logical card images within much larger physical blocks on tape; all the data are stored as integers or as character strings. The data are described internally – hence data for each area are preceded by an area name, etc., and the header records describe whether the data pertain to section 1 (common 100 per cent), 2 (common 10 per cent), 3 (England and Wales 100 per cent), 4 (Wales only 100 per cent) or 5 (Scotland only 100 per cent). All SAS data for EDs and the great bulk of ward data from OPCS are arranged as two files per county, each file being on a separate physical reel of magnetic tape. However, both parliamentary constituencies and districts covering all of Britain can be obtained in two files (100 per cent and 10 per cent data).

These data may be read directly without difficulty by the SASPAC package (see appendix 7); this determines which data are being read and acts accordingly, validating the data in a number of ways. Alternatively, it is not unduly difficult to copy the data to a disk file, edit out area headers, etc. and read the data with standard statistics packages but this requires much more effort and greater skills on the part of the user who also loses the ability of SASPAC to print standard tables, etc.

Appendix 7

Computer software for use with census data

A number of organizations have produced computer programs to handle the 1981 Census SAS data; at the time of writing, no details of the technical organization of other census data have been given but it seems likely that software will be made available to handle them. Essentially the software may be considered under four headings:

i *Software specially created for the SAS data.* The only widely available example in this category is SASPAC, a large and highly unusual computer package written by the Universities of Durham and Edinburgh under contract to the Local Authorities Management Services and Computer Committee (LAMSAC). The package is designed to function on a *very* wide variety of computers (over 150 in total), to be easy to use, to check the data for internal consistency and to provide facilities for selecting cells or areas from the SAS data, carrying out arithmetic and other manipulations on these and printing out census data in a variety of forms. In addition, it has the ability to transform the SAS data into a form which can be used immediately by the standard statistical packages available on most computers in local authorities, in central government and in educational establishments. Details of the package and its availability can be obtained from LAMSAC (see appendix 8).

ii *More general software used with SAS data.* Various computer packages have been or could be modified to handle SAS data. At one extreme, SIA Ltd will be making available a large, general purpose data base package called SIR with interfaces to the SAS. Given the user-friendly organization of 1981 SAS data (appendix 6), it is *possible* for expert users with good facilities to edit the SAS data files and to read the data with standard statistical packages such as the Statistical Package for the Social Sciences (SPSS). Some skill would, however, be required to cope with data suppression and data adjustment (section 2.9.6) and with the variety of special conditions, such as shipping EDs.

SPSS is almost certainly the most widely used statistical package in local government and in educational establishments in Britain, being mounted on a wide variety of computers and well documented (Nie *et al.* 1975). It is distributed from different centres, depending on the type of machine involved: the Program Library Unit at the University of Edinburgh (see appendix 8), for instance, distributes the ICL 2900 version.

Other software which – certainly in principle – can be used to handle SAS data include the ICL FILETAB and PACKAGE X program, particularly commonly used on ICL 1900 computers.

iii *Software available on a bureau basis.* Various firms have made arrangements with OPCS to act as agencies for SAS data and for users to access the data via proprietory software on a bureau basis. Those known at present are CACI Ltd, Geoplan Ltd (specializing in postcoded census data for Britain) and SIA Ltd. Contact points are again given in appendix 8.

iv *Software and bureau facilities for mapping SAS data.* A number of organizations claim to provide mapping of census data for clients (such as Geoplan Ltd) or to be able to provide software for this task. Users should beware: cartographic experience in most such firms is highly limited. Some maps produced from certain organizations are highly misleading (see Chapter 6). Moreover, sophisticated mapping programs are less easy to transfer between computers, much less easy than are statistical packages. Much the best (if rather complex) of the available mapping packages is GIMMS 4, produced by GIMMS Ltd: a simpler package for use on the Apple micro-computer is available from Morgan Fairfield Graphics. Contact addresses are given in appendix 8.

Appendix 8

Contact points

CENSUS MATTERS

Office of Population Censuses and Surveys

OPCS
St Catherine's House
10 Kingsway
London WC2B 6JP

OPCS
Segensworth Road
Titchfield
Fareham
Hants PO15 5RR

Advice on use and dissemination of census results; Census Use Study	Census Division (RES) Room 823 London	(01) 242 0262, extension 2029 or 2024
Advice on table specification; queries on published tables and population bases	Census Division Room 823 London	(01) 242 0262, extension 2008
Census Monitors (general series); 1981 Census County Monitors; Occasional Papers and other OPCS publications	Information Branch (M) Room 806 London	(01) 242 0262, extension 2243
Correspondence arising from Census Monitors	Census Division (M) Room 823 London	(01) 242 0262, extension 2008
Geographical aspects of the Census; computer mapping	Census Division (RES) Room 823 London	(01) 242 0262, extension 2024
Geographical divisions for the Census; Area Master File (area constitutions); boundary definitions and changes	Census Geography Titchfield	(0329) 42511, extension 392

Purchase of Small Area Statistics, special local workplace and migration statistics, extensions of published tables, statistical abstracts, customer-specified tables, maps, prospectuses and User Guides; enquiries about ordering census results and documentation; timetable for census results; census agency agreements	Census Customer Services Titchfield	(0329) 42511, extension 296 or 231
OPCS Library: collections of past and present UK and non-UK census publications; census use collection	Library London	(01) 242 0262, extension 2235
Press enquiries; displays and conferences	Press Office London	(01) 242 0262, extension 2045
Prestel: census information	Press Office London	(01) 242 0262, extension 2040
General enquiries	Census Support Unit Room 823 London	(01) 242 0262, extension 2008

Registrar-General's Office (Scotland)

Customer Services Section
Census Office
Ladywell House
Ladywell Road
Edinburgh EH12 7TF

(031) 334 0380, extension 208 or 254

COMPUTER SOFTWARE FOR CENSUS DATA (see also appendix 7)

Data handling and manipulation programs

Local Authorities Management Service and Computer Committee (LAMSAC)
Vincent House
Vincent Square
London SW1P 2NB

(01) 828 2333

LAMSAC co-ordinated the development of SASPAC, a computer package for handling the SAS data from the 1981 Census. It runs on a very wide range of computers.

Mapping programs

GIMMS Ltd (031) 229 3937
30 Keir Street
Edinburgh EH3 9EU

GIMMS 4 is an extremely widely used and comprehensive package which can produce maps, graphs, histograms, etc. on a wide variety of computer equipment. The cost of GIMMS varies, depending on the type of institution involved.

Morgan Fairfield Graphics (206) 632 1374
PO Box 5457
Seattle, WA 98105
USA

Morgan Fairfield sell a package called MICROMAP II for the Apple II microcomputer. This produces coloured and textured maps, contour maps, 3–D polyhedron or proportional symbol maps, plus statistical charts and graphs as well as perspective views of digital terrain models. The software is written in Applesoft, requires 48k of memory, Apple DOS 3.3 and a 5¼ inch disk drive. Like GIMMS, this is a general-purpose mapping program that is capable of handling census mapping. At the time of writing, MICROMAP II cost $650.

Statistical programs

Almost all statistical mapping programs can be used with census data: consult your computer services manager for details of what is available locally. The simplest solution is to use SASPAC to produce a matrix file which can then be read by statistical programs. Numerous statistical packages are described and contact addresses given in publications by Rowe (see bibliography).

CONSULTANCIES OFFERING CENSUS SERVICES AND DATA

CACI Ltd (01) 404 0834
59/62 High Holborn
London WC1V 6DX

CACI specializes in 'site-planning' applications of and area classifications based on census data using Webber techniques (see Chapter 8).

Geoplan (UK) Ltd (01) 836 8251
4th Floor
141 Drury Lane
London WC2B 5TD

Geoplan specializes in SAS data on postcode sectors, mapping of this and aggregation using it to *ad hoc* areas, plus linkage to other data sets.

SIA Ltd (01) 730 4544
Ebury Gate
23 Lower Belgrave Street
London SW1W 0NW

SIA is a large computer consultancy offering SAS data retrieval, statistical analysis and mapping based on ED and ward-level data. It also acts as an agent for distributing the boundaries of numerous areas digitized by the Department of the Environment.

POSTCODE INFORMATION

The Post Office (01) 432 5589
Marketing Department
Postal Headquarters
22–25 Finsbury Square
London EC2A 1PH

Geoplan (UK) Ltd (01) 836 8251
4th Floor
141 Drury Lane
London WC2B 5TD

Maps of postcode sectors and larger areas may be plotted at 1:50,000 and smaller scales so as to overlay on Ordnance Survey maps.

John Bartholomew and Sons Ltd (031) 667 9341
12 Duncan Street
Edinburgh EH9 1TA

John Bartholomew publish printed maps at postcode district level; other maps are available for postcode sectors. Since these maps are on a different projection to the National Grid, they are not readily used in conjunction with OS maps.

ORGANIZATIONS THAT OFFER DIGITIZING CAPABILITIES AND CAN BE RECOMMENDED

GIMMS Ltd (031) 229 3937
30 Keir Street
Edinburgh EH3 9EU

Graphical Data Capture Ltd (01) 346 4959
262 Regents Park Road
London N3 3HN

Laserscan Ltd (0223) 69872
Science Park
Milton Road
Cambridge CB4 4BH

OTHER RELEVANT ORGANIZATIONS

Census Unit (01) 212 8754
Department of the Environment
2 Marsham Street
London SW1P 3EB

The Department of the Environment (DoE) are major users of Population Census data and have set up a group to meet demand for tabulations (primarily using SASPAC) and maps (using GIMMS) from within DoE. They carried out much of the early work on census tracts and have, over many years, digitized the boundaries of various sets of administrative areas, now available from SIA Ltd.

SSRC Data Archive (0206) 860570
The University of Essex
Wivenhoe Park
Colchester
Essex CO4 3SQ

The Archive is the repository of many social science data bases in computer form and publishes a catalogue of these, together with regular bulletins. It is the centre from which 1981 SAS census data are distributed to those university and polytechnic users who are unable or unwilling to access the data from the London and Manchester national computer centres or from the NUMAC computer in Newcastle, the South Western Regional Computing Centre in Bath, the Regional Computing Organization computer in Edinburgh and the Aberdeen University computer. The Archive is also the only university agency with a complete set of 1971 SAS census data for EDs, held in a portable computer format.

Department of Geography (01) 580 6622
Birkbeck College extension 475
7–15 Gresse Street
London W1P 1PA

The Department has available a complete set of the OPCS ED maps for England and Wales, financed jointly with the University of London Computer Centre. These may be used by members of any educational organization. In addition, the department staff have substantial expertise in handling census data (e.g. see articles by Mohan, Mounsey and Rhind in the bibliography).

Program Library Unit (031) 667 1011
18 Buccleuch Place extension 6756
Edinburgh EH8 9LN

The PLU distributes not only the ICL 2900 version of SPSS and of GIMMS 4, but also a wide range of other programs and, moreover, has long experience in this field.

Bibliography

Aitchison, J. (1981) 'A new approach to null correlation of proportions', *Mathematical Geology* 13 (2), 175–89.

Alderson, M. (1980) 'Cancer mortality in male hairdressers', *Journal of Epidemiology and Community Health*, 34 (3), 182–5.

Alker, H. (1969) 'A typology of ecological fallacies', in Dogan, M. and Rokkan, S. (eds.) *Quantitative Ecological Analysis in the Social Sciences*, London, MIT Press.

Allt, B. (1979) 'The future of social and economic classification', *MRS 22nd Annual Conference Papers*, 241–52.

Anderson, M. (1971) *Family Structure in Nineteenth Century Lancashire*, Cambridge University Press.

Armstrong, A. (1974) *Stability and change in an English county town: a social study of York 1801–1851*, Cambridge University Press.

Australian Bureau of Statistics (1977) *1976 Population Census Information Paper 9(i): Classification of Characteristics,* Canberra, ABS.

Barber, A. (1980) 'Ethnic origin and the labour force', *Department of Employment Gazette*, August, 841–8.

Barnes, R. and Birch, F. (1975) 'Estimating the characteristics of non-respondents in the General Household Survey', *Statistical News*, 30, August, London, HMSO.

Barnett, V. (1976) 'The ordering of multivariate data', *Journal of the Royal Statistical Society, A*, 139 (3), 318–54.

Barnett, V. and Lewis, T. (1978) *Outliers in statistical data,* Chichester, Wiley.

Baxter, R.S. (1976a) 'Parsed data set of British local authority boundaries', *Building Research Estab. Research Note,* N.138/76.

Baxter, R.S. (1976b) *Computer and statistical techniques for planners*, London, Methuen.

Bebbington, A.C. (1978) 'A method of bivariate trimming for robust estimation of the correlation coefficient', *Applied Statistics* 27 (3), 221–6.

Bellamy, J.M. (1978) 'Occupation statistics in the nineteenth century censuses', in Lawton, R. (ed.) *The Census and Social Structure*, London, Cass.

Benjamin, B. (1968) *Demographic Analysis*, London, Allen & Unwin.

Benjamin, B. (1970) *The Population Census*, London, Heinemann, for the Social Science Research Council.

Bennett, R.J. (1981) 'The Rate Support Grant in England and Wales 1967/8–1980/1:

A review of changing emphases and objectives', in Herbert, D. and Johnston, R.J. (eds.) *Geography and the Urban Environment*, 4, London, Wiley.

Berry, B. (1967) Functional Economic Areas and Consolidated Urban Regions of the US. *Final Report of the Social Sciences Research Council Study of Metropolitan Area Classification,* Social Sciences Research Council, New York.

Berry, B.J.L. and Horton, F.E. (1970) *Geographical perspectives on urban systems,* Englewood Cliffs, NJ, Prentice-Hall.

Bertin, J. (1973) *Semiologie graphique: les diagrammes – les reseaux – les cartes*, 2nd edition, Paris, Mouton.

Bertin, J. (1981) *Graphics and graphic information processing*, Berlin & New York, W. de Gruyter.

Bianchi, G., Openshaw, S., Scattoni, P. and Sforzi, F. (1980) 'Problem di zonizzazione: l'identificazione di aree sociali a scala urbana', in *Nuovi contributi allo studio dello sviluppo economica della Toscana*, Firenze, IRPET.

Bickmore, D.P., Shaw, M. and Tulloch, T. (1980) 'Lifestyle on maps', *Geographical Magazine,* LIII, 11, 763–9.

Bliss, C.J. (1970) *Statistics for Biologists*, vol. 2, New York, McGraw-Hill.

Blunden, R. (1975) 'Some findings of the 1971 census post-enumeration survey', *Schedule*, Newsletter of the Census Research Group, 3 (April).

Boston, G. (1980) 'Classification of occupations', *Population Trends*, 20, 9–11.

Bramley, G. and Evans, A. (1981a) 'Block Grant: some unresolved issues', *Policy and Politics*, 9 (2), 173–204.

Bramley, G. and Evans, A. (1981b) *Block Grant Training Package*, School for Advanced Urban Studies, University of Bristol.

Brazier, S. and Hayward, S. (1981) 'Population estimates from the Electoral Register: review article based on experience in Shropshire. Comment', *BURISA*, 49, July 1981, 3–9.

Broome, F.R. and Witiuk, S.W. (1980) 'Census mapping by computer', in Taylor, D.R.F. (ed.) *The Computer in Contemporary Cartography*, Wiley, pp. 191–218.

Brown, N. (1980) 'Postcodes as a building brick for vital statistics', *Population Trends*, 20.

Bulmer, M.I.A. (1980) *Privacy, censuses and surveys*, London, Macmillan.

Burbridge, V. and Robertson, S. (1978a) *Rural indicators study: Indicators relevant to the assessment of socioeconomic problems and priorities in rural Scotland,* Scottish Office Central Research Unit Paper, Scottish Development Department, Edinburgh.

Burbridge, V. and Robertson, S. (1978b) *Rural indicators research: multivariate analysis of District, Islands Area and Parish data,* Scottish Office Central Research Unit Paper, Scottish Development Department, Edinburgh.

Butler, D. and Stokes, D. (1969) *Political Change in Britain*, London, Macmillan.

Buxton, N.K. and Mackay, D.I. (1977) *British Employment Statistics: A Guide to Sources and Methods*, Oxford, Blackwell.

Census 1981, England; H form for private households.

Census Division (1977) 'Planning the Census of Population', *Population Trends*, 10.

Chambers, J.M. (1977) *Computational methods for data analysis*, New York, Wiley.

Champion, A.G. (1976) 'Evolving patterns of population distribution in England and Wales, 1951–71', *IBG Transactions*, New Series 1, 401–20.

Chatfield, C. and Collins, A.J. (1980) *Introduction to multivariate analysis*, London, Chapman and Hall.

CIPFA (1982) *Local Government Comparative Statistics*, London, Chartered Institute of Public Finance and Accountancy Statistical Information Service.

Clarke, J.I. (1972) *Population Geography*, 2nd edition, Oxford, Pergamon.

Clarke, J.I. and Mounsey, H.M. (1981) 'Population redistribution and regional policy in Britain', *OPCS Occasional Paper* 19/3, 1–17.

Cleveland, W.S. and Kleiner, B. (1975) 'A graphical technique for enhancing scatterplots with moving statistics', *Technometrics* 17 (4), 447–54.

Coates, B.E., Johnston, R.J. and Knox, P.L. (1977) *Geography and inequality*, Oxford University Press.

Computer Talk, 9 July 1980.

Coombes, M.G., Dixon, J.S., Goddard, J.B., Openshaw, S. and Taylor, P.J. (1978) 'Towards a more rational consideration of census areal units: daily urban systems in Britain', *Environment and Planning A*, 10, 1179–86.

Coombes, M.G., Dixon, J.S., Goddard, J.B., Openshaw, S. and Taylor, P.J. (1981) 'Functional regions for the Population Census of Great Britain', in Herbert, D. and Johnston, R. (eds.) *Geography and the Urban Environment*, London, Wiley.

Cope, D.R. and Baum, F. (1979) 'The absence of fertility questions from the 1981 Census and its effects on research on fertility patterns', *Eugenics Soc. Bull.*, 11 (2), 41–8.

Coppock, J.T. (1975) 'Maps by line printer', in Davis, J.C. and MacCullagh, M.J. (eds.) *Display and Analysis of Spatial Data*, London, Wiley.

Coulter, J. (1978) 'Grid square census data as a source for the study of deprivation in British conurbations', *Census Research Unit Working Paper*, 13, Department of Geography, University of Durham.

Cox, N.J. and Jones, K. (1981) 'Exploratory data analysis', in Wrigley, N. and Bennett, R.J. *Quantitative Geography: A British View*, 135–43, London, Routledge and Kegan Paul.

CRU/OPCS/GRO(S) (1980) *People in Britain – a census atlas*, London, HMSO.

Daily Telegraph, 21 March 1980, The Rt. Hon. Patrick Jenkin MP.

Davidson, R.N. (1976) 'Social deprivation: an analysis of intercensal change', *Inst. Brit. Geogr. Trans.*, New Series 1, 108–18.

DE (1975) 'The mobility of labour', *Department of Employment Gazette*, 1264–7.

DE (1977) *Employment in metropolitan areas,* Project report, Unit for Manpower Studies, Department of Employment.

Denham, C.J. (1980) 'The Geography of the Census 1971 and 1981', *Population Trends*, 19, 6–12.

DES (1971) *Survey of earnings of qualified manpower in England and Wales 1966–67*, Statistics of Education, Special Series 3, London, HMSO.

Devlin, S.J., Gnanadesikan, R. and Kettenring, J.R. (1975) 'Robust estimation and outlier detection with correlation coefficients', *Biometrika* 62, 531–45.

Dewdney, J.C. (1981) 'The British Census', *CATMOG (Concepts and Techniques in Modern Geography)*, 29.

Dewdney, J.C. and Rhind, D.W. (1975) *People in Durham – a census atlas*, Department of Geography, University of Durham.

DI (1980) *Engineering Our Future: Report Committee of Inquiry into the Engineering Profession* (The Finniston Report), Cmnd 7794, London, HMSO.

Dixon, J.S. and Openshaw, S. (1979) 'FORTRAN subroutines for the functional regionalization of large sparse interaction matrices', *Discussion Paper,* 24, Centre for Urban and Regional Development Studies, University of Newcastle.

DoE (1975a) *The Use of Indicators for Area Action*, Area Improvement Note 10, London, HMSO.

DoE (1975b) *Point in Polygon Project, Stage 1,* London, Department of the Environment Research Report 2.

DoE (1977) *Atlas of the Environment,* London, Department of the Environment.

Drake, M. (1972) 'The Census, 1801–1891', in Wrigley, E.A. (ed.) *Nineteenth Century Society*, Cambridge University Press.

Dugmore, K. (ed.) (1975) 'The Migration and Distribution of Socioeconomic Groups in Greater London: evidence from the 1961, 1966 and 1971 Censuses', *GLC Research Memorandum*, 443.

Duncan, O.D. (1975) *Introduction to structural equation models*, New York, Academic Press.

Duncan, O.D. and Duncan, B. (1955) 'A methodological analysis of segregation indexes', *American Sociological Review* 20, 210–17.

Dunlap, W.P. and Duffy, J.A. (1974) 'A computer program for determining optimal data transformation minimising skew', *Behavioural Research Methods and Instruments*, 6 (1), 48–8.

Edwards, J. (1975) 'Social indicators, urban deprivation and positive discrimination', *Journal of Social Policy*, 4 (3), 275–87.

Ehrenberg, A.S.C. (1975) *Data reduction: analysing and interpreting statistical data*, London, Wiley.

Erickson, B.H. and Nosanchuk, T.A. (1977) *Understanding data*, New York, McGraw-Hill.

Evans, I.S. (1975) 'Discussion of the paper by A.D. Cliff and J.K. Ord, 'Model building and the analysis of spatial pattern in human geography', *Journal of the Royal Statistical Society,* Series B (Methodological) 37 (3), 341–2.

Evans, I.S. (1977) The selection of class intervals, *Inst. Brit. Geogr. Trans.*, New Series 2, 1, 98–124.

Evans, I.S. (1979) 'Relationships between GB census variables at the 1 km aggregate level', in Wrigley, N. (ed.) *Statistical applications in the spatial sciences*, London, Pion, pp. 145–88.

Evans, I.S. (1980) 'British census data and their use in quantitative geography', *Census Research Unit Working Paper* 17, Department of Geography, University of Durham. See also pp. 46–59 in Wrigley, N. and Bennett, R.J. (1981) *Quantitative geography: a British view*, London, Routledge and Kegan Paul.

Evans, I.S. and Jones, K. (1981) 'Ratios', in Wrigley, N. and Bennett, R.J. *Quantitative geography: a British view*, London, Routledge and Kegan Paul, pp. 123–34.

Everitt, B. (1974) *Cluster Analysis*, London, Heinemann.

Ferguson, R. (1978) 'Linear regression in geography', *Concepts and Techniques in Modern Geography* 15, Norwich, Geo Abstracts.

Fields, J. (1970/1) 'The sample cluster: A neglected data source', *Public Opinion Quarterly*, xxxiv, 593–603.

Flaherty, D.H. (1979) *Privacy and government data banks*, Mansell Scientific.
Ford, R.G. (1979) 'An analysis of population turnover', *Area* 11, 127–9.
Fox, A.J. and Goldblatt, P.O. (1982) *Longitudinal study: socio-demographic mortality differentials 1971–75,* Series LS no. 1, London, HMSO.
Francis, K. (1981) 'Census 1981: the impact on local authorities', *Population Trends*, 24, 4–7.
Freedman, D., Pisani, R. and Purves, R. (1978) *Statistics*, New York. W.W. Norton.
Gardiner, V. (1973) 'Univariate distributional characteristics of some morphometric variables', *Geografiska Annaler* A (3–4), 147–53.
Gardiner, V. and Gardiner, G. (1978) 'Analysis of frequency distributions', *Concepts and Techniques in Modern Geography* 19, Norwich, Geo Abstracts.
General Register Office (1956) *Census 1951, England and Wales: Report on Greater London and five other conurbations,* London, HMSO.
Gnanadesikan, R. (1977) *Methods for statistical data analysis of multivariate observations*, New York, Wiley.
Goldblatt, P. and Fox, J. (1978) 'Household mortality from the OPCS Longitudinal Survey', *Population Trends,* 14, 20–7.
Gould, P. (1970) 'Is *Statistix inferens* the geographical name for a wild goose?', *Economic Geography* 46, 439–48.
Gray, P. and Gee, F.A. (1972) 'A quality check on the 1966 ten per cent sample census of England and Wales', *OPCS Social Survey Division*, London, HMSO.
Green, P.J. and Sibson, R. (1978) 'Computing Dirichlet tessalations in the plane', *Computer Journal*, 21 (2), 168–73.
Hakim, C. (1978a) 'Social and community indicators from the Census', *Occasional Paper*, 5, London, OPCS.
Hakim, C. (1978b) 'Data dissemination for the population census', *Occasional Paper*, 6, London, OPCS.
Hakim, C. (1978c) 'Census confidentiality, microdata and census analysis', *Occasional Paper*, 3, London, OPCS.
Hakim, C. (1979a) 'Census confidentiality in Britain', in Bulmer, M.I.A. (ed.) *Censuses, surveys and privacy,* London, Macmillan.
Hakim, C. (1979b) 'The Population Census and its by-products: Data bases for research', *International Journal of Social Science*, xxxi, 342–52.
Hakim, C. (1982) *Secondary analysis in social research*, London, Allen and Unwin.
Hannan, M. (1971) 'Problems of aggregation', in Blalock, H. (ed.) *Causal Models in the Social Sciences*, Chicago, Aldine.
Harley, J.B. (1975) *Ordnance Survey maps – a descriptive manual*, London, HMSO.
Hartwig, F. and Dearing, B.E. (1979) *Exploratory data analysis*, Beverly Hills, Sage. (Qualitative applications in social sciences, 16.)
HM Government (1981) *The review of the government statistical services: Cmnd 8236. Initial study of the Office of Population Censuses and Surveys (annex to Cmnd 8236).*
HMSO (1965a) *The National Plan*, Cmnd 2764, London.
HMSO (1965b) *Registrar General's Quarterly Return for England and Wales*, No. 466, Second Quarter 1965, London.
HMSO (1978) *1981 Census of Population*, Cmnd 7146.
HMSO (1980a) *Classification of Occupations 1980*, London.
HMSO (1980b) *Population projections: area, 1977–1991* (England), Series PP3, No. 3, London.

HMSO (1981a) *Census 1981 Preliminary Report: England and Wales.*

HMSO (1981b) *Census 1981 Preliminary Report: Scotland.*

HMSO (1981c) *Census 1981 Preliminary Report for towns, urban and rural population: England and Wales.*

HMSO (1981d) *Population projections: area, 1979–1991* (England), Series PP3, No. 4, London.

HMSO (1981e) *Government Statistical Services, Cmnd 8236, London, HMSO; Initial Study of the OPCS*, report annexed to Cmnd 8236 (available from OPCS Library).

HMSO (forthcoming) *Longitudinal Study: Background and technical report*, Series LS, London.

Hocking, R.R. (1976) 'The analysis and selection of variables in linear regression', *Biometrics* 32, 1–49.

Hogg, R.V. (1974) 'Adaptive robust procedures: a partial review and some suggestions and theory', *Journal of the American Statistical Association* 69, (348), 909–27.

Hoinville, E. (1980) 'The Relationship between Survey Non-Response and Constituency Characteristics', *SCPR Methodological Working Paper Series*, 21, London, Social and Community Planning Research.

Holtermann, S. (1975a) *Census indicators of urban deprivation, Working Note 6: Great Britain*, DoE, ECUR Division, London (mimeo).

Holtermann, S. (1975b) 'Areas of urban deprivation in Great Britain: an analysis of 1971 census data', *Social Trends* 6, 33–47.

Howe, G.M. (1970) *National Atlas of Disease Mortality in the United Kingdom*, London, Nelson.

Hunt, A.J. (ed.) (1968) 'Population maps of the British Isles, 1961', *Transactions of the Institute of British Geographers* 43.

Imber, V. (1977) *A Classification of the English Personal Social Services Authorities*, DHSS Statistical and Research Report, Series 16, London, HMSO.

ISER (1977) *Census atlas of Newfoundland* 1971, Institute of Social and Economic Research, Memorial University of Newfoundland, St Johns, Newfoundland, Canada.

Jackson, P.W. (1976) *Local Government*, London, Butterworth.

Jarrett, D. (1980) 'Textbooks for introductory quantitative methods in geography', *Journal of Geography in Higher Education* 4 (2), 62–74.

Johnston, R.J. (1967) 'A reconnaissance study of population change in Nidderdale, 1951–61', *Inst. Brit. Geogr. Trans.*, 41, 113–23.

Johnston, R.J. (1969) 'Population movements and metropolitan expansion: London 1960–61', *Inst. Brit. Geogr. Trans.* 46, 69–91.

Johnston, R.J. (1978) *Multivariate statistical analysis in geography*, London, Longman.

Jones, H.J.M., Lawson, H.B. and Newman, D. (1973) 'Population Census: Some recent British developments in methodology', *J. Ryl. Stat. Soc.*, 136 (4), 505–38.

Jones, T.A. (1979) 'Fitting straight lines when both variables are subject to error, I', *Journal of Mathematical Geology* 11 (1), 1–25.

Jones, T.P. and McEvoy, D. (1978) 'Race and space in Cloud Cuckoo Land', *Area* 10 (3), 162–6. Discussion 10 (5) 365–7 and (1979) 11 (1), 82–5, 11 (3), 221–3.

Kaplan, C.P. and van Valey, T.L. (1980) 'Census 80: Continuing the factfinder tradition', *US Dept. of Commerce*, Bureau of the Census, 469–90.

Keates, J. (1973) *Cartographic design and production*, London, Longman.

Kemsley, W.F.F. (1975) 'Family Expenditure Survey: A study of differential response based on a comparison of the 1971 sample with the census', *Statistical News* 31, November, London, HMSO.

Kemsley, W.F.F. (1976) 'National Food Survey: A study of differential response based on a comparison of the 1971 sample with the census', *Statistical News* 35, November, London, HMSO.

Kendall, M.G. (1949) 'Rank and product-moment correlation', *Biometrika* 36, 177–93.

Kendall, M.G. (1975) *Multivariate analysis*, London, Griffin.

Kennett, S. (1978) 'Census Data and Migration Analysis: an appraisal', Paper presented to SSRC conference on census data.

Kermack, K.A. and Haldane, G.B.S (1950) 'Organic correlation and allometry', *Biometrika* 37, 30–41.

Kiernan, K. (1980) 'Patterns of family formation and dissolution', *Occasional Paper* 19/2, OPCS.

Kruskal, J.B. (1968) 'Statistical analysis, special problems of II transformations of data', in Sills, D.L. (ed.) *International Encyclopedia of the Social Sciences*, v.15, 182–93, New York, Macmillan. Reprinted with postscript in Kruskal, W.H. and Taynor, J.M. (eds.) (1978) *International Encyclopedia of Statistics*, v.2, 1044–56, New York, Free Press.

Kruskal, J.B. and Wish, M. (1978) *Multidimensional scaling*, Quantitative applications in the social sciences, 11, Beverly Hills, Sage.

Lambeth Borough Department of Town Planning (1980) 'Bus deficiency areas in Lambeth', *Lambeth LB Research Memo* 10.

Lambeth L.B. (1974) *Lambeth Inner Area Study: labour market study.*

Lamont, D.W. (1979) 'Moves in Glasgow – census data and the study of intra-urban migration: the pattern of population movement in Greater Glasgow 1970–71', *BURISA Newsletter* 37, 12–14.

Langbein, L. and Lichtman, A. (1980) *Ecological inference*, London, Sage.

Launer, R.L. and Wilkinson, G.N. (eds.) (1979) *Robustness in statistics* (Proceedings of an ARO Mathematics Workshop, April 11–12, 1978), New York, Academic Press.

Law, C.M. and Warnes, A.M. (1976) 'The changing geography of the elderly in England and Wales', *IBG Transactions*, New Series, 1, 453–71.

Lawrence, G.R.P. (1979) *Cartographic Methods*, 2nd edition, London, Methuen.

Lawton, R. (ed.) (1978) *The Census and Social Structure*, London, Cass.

Lazarsfeld, P. and Menzel, H. (1965) 'On the relations between individual and collective properties', in Etzioni, A. (ed.) *Complex Organisations*, London, Hart Rinehart and Winston.

Lee, C.H. (1979) *British Regional Employment Statistics 1841–71*, Cambridge University Press.

Lee, T.R. (1978) 'Race, space and scale', *Area* 10, 365–7.

Leete, R. (1978) 'One-parent families: numbers and characteristics', *Population Trends* 13, 4–9.

Lewart, C.R. (1973) 'Algorithm 463. Algorithms scale 1, 2, 3 for determination of scales on computer-generated plots', *Communications, Assoc. Computing Machinery* 16, 639–40.

Linz, J. (1974) 'Ecological Analysis and Survey Data', in Dogan, M. and Rokkan, S. (eds.) *Quantitative Ecological Analysis in the Social Sciences*, London, MIT Press.

Lomas, G. (1974) 'Colour in the census', *New Society* 27, 590.

MacDougall, E.B. (1976) *Computer programming for spatial problems*, London, Edward Arnold.

Manners, A.J. and Rauta, I. (1981) 'Extending the electoral register – 2: two surveys of public acceptability', *OPCS Occasional Paper* 22.

Mark, D.M. and Church, M. (1977) 'On the misuse of regression in earth sciences', *Mathematical Geology* 9 (1), 63–75.

Mark, D.M. and Peucker, T.K. (1978) 'Regression analysis and geographic models', *Canadian Geographer* 22 (1), 51–64. Discussion, ibid, 23 (1), 79–81.

Massey, J.S. (1979) 'Automated production of colour animated movies showing computer-produced maps', *Proceedings of Conference on Computer Graphics and Spatial Analysis,* Adelaide, 13–15 August 1979.

Masters, R. and Shortridge, J. (1981) 'Population estimates from the Electoral Register: review article based on experience in Shropshire', *BURISA* 49, July 1981, 3–9.

Mather, P. (1976) *Computational methods of multivariate analysis in physical geography*, London, Wiley.

de Mellow, R.A. (1979) 'Postcodes in the 1981 Census: Scotland', *BURISA* 41, December 1979.

Meyer, D.R. (1971) 'Factor analysis versus correlation analysis: are substantive interpretations congruent?', *Economic Geography* 47, 336–43.

Mohan, J. (1979) 'The study of grid square census data in the location of hospital facilities; a case study of the Durham Health District', *Census Research Unit Working Paper* 15, Department of Geography, University of Durham.

Monkhouse, F.J. and Wilkinson, H.R. (1971) *Maps and diagrams*, 2nd edition, London, Methuen.

Moore, D.S. (1979) *Statistics: concepts and controversies*, San Francisco, W. H. Freeman.

Moore, E.G. (1979) 'Beyond the Census: data needs and urban policy analysis' in Gale, S. and Olsson, G. (eds.) *Philosophy in Geography*, Reidel, 269–86.

Morgan, C. and Denham, C. (1982) 'Census Small Area Statistics (SAS): measuring change and spatial variation', *Population Trends*, 28.

Morrey, C. (1980) 'Migration assumptions for the 1979 based sub-national population projections', *Statistical News* 51, 6–10, London, HMSO.

Mosimann, J.E. (1962) 'On the compound multinomial distribution, the multivariate distribution, and correlations among proportions', *Biometrika* 49 (1 and 2), 65–82.

Mosteller, F. and Tukey, J.W. (1977) *Data analysis and regression,* Reading (Mass.), Addison-Wesley.

Mounsey, H.M. (1982) 'The cartography of time-changing phenomena: the animated map', Durham University Ph.D. Thesis.

Mounsey, H.M. and Clarke, J.I. (1981) 'Comparison of population changes within Great Britain during 1971–75 and 1975–79', *Census Research Unit Working Paper* 18, Department of Geography, University of Durham.

Muehrcke, P. (1978) *Map use: reading, analysis and interpretation*, Madison, JP Publications.

Nie, N.H., Hull, C.H., Jenkins, J.G., Steinbrenner, K. and Bent, D.H. (1975) *SPSS – Statistical Package for the Social Sciences*, 2nd edition, New York, McGraw-Hill.

Nordlinger, E. (1967) *Working Class Tories*, London, MacGibbon and Kee.

Norris, P. (1980) 'The 1981 Census – the user's perspective', *Census Research Unit Working Paper* 16, Department of Geography, University of Durham.

O'Dell, A. and Parker, J. (1977) *The use of census data to identify and describe housing stress,* Building Research Establishment Current Paper, London, DoE.

Ogilvy, A. (1980) 'Inter-regional migration since 1971: an appraisal of data from the National Health Service Central Register and Labour Force Surveys', *Occasional Paper* 16, London, OPCS.

OPCS (1973) Cohort studies: new developments, *OPCS Studies in Medical and Population Subjects,* 25, London, HMSO.

OPCS (1976) *1971 Census Standard Small Area Statistics (Ward Library: Explanatory Notes)*, London, OPCS.

OPCS (1978/1) *Census Monitor*, CEN 78/1, London, OPCS.

OPCS (1978/2) *Census Monitor*, CEN 78/2, London, OPCS.

OPCS (1978/5) *Census Monitor*, CEN 78/5, London, OPCS.

OPCS (1979) *Census Monitor*, CEN 79/1, London, OPCS.

OPCS (1980a) *1981 Census of Population England and Wales: Discussion Paper: Statistics for grid squares.*

OPCS (1980b) The questions and how the answers are used, *Census Topics*, 5, (11/80).

OPCS (1980c) Local authority population estimates methodology, *OPCS Occasional Paper*, no. 18.

OPCS (1980d) *Population Projections: Area, 1977–1991 (England)*, Series PP3 No. 3, London, HMSO.

OPCS (1980/1) *Census Monitor*, CEN 80/1, London, OPCS.

OPCS (1980/8) *Census Monitor*, CEN 80/8, London, OPCS.

OPCS (1981a) Extending the electoral register – 1: report of the steering committee to the Registrars General, *OPCS Occasional Paper,* no. 20.

OPCS (1981b) *Census of Population England and Wales: Discussion Papers: Special workplace statistics/special migration statistics.*

OPCS (1981c) The revised mid-1971 population estimates for local authorities compared with the original estimates, *OPCS Occasional Paper*, no. 22.

OPCS (1981d) *Census 1981: Preliminary Report, England and Wales*, London, HMSO.

OPCS (1981e) *Population Projections: Area, 1979–1991 (England)*, Series PP3, No. 4, London, HMSO.

OPCS (1981/2) *Census Monitor*, CEN 81/2, London, OPCS.

OPCS (1981/3) *Census Monitor,* CEN 81/3, London, OPCS.

OPCS (1982a) Labour Force Survey 1981, *OPCS Monitor LFS*, 82/1.

OPCS (1982b) *Census of Population. 1971 and 1981 Small Area Statistics: Comparability*, London, OPCS.

OPCS (1982c) 'Editorial: sources of statistics on ethnic minorities', *Population Trends*, 28 (Summer), London, HMSO.

OPCS (1982d) *Census 1981, Definitions, Great Britain,* London, OPCS.

OPCS (1982/3) *Census Monitor*, CEN 82/3, August, London, OPCS.

Openshaw, S. (1974) 'A regionalisation algorithm for large data sets', *Computer Applications*, 3–4, 39–80.

Openshaw, S. (1976) 'A regionalisation procedure for a comparative regional taxonomy of the UK', *Area*, 8, 149–52.

Openshaw, S. (1977) 'A geographical solution to scale and aggregation problems in regions building, partitioning and spatial modelling', *Trans. Inst. Brit. Geogr.*, N.S.2, 459–72.

Openshaw, S. (1978a) 'An empirical study of some zone design criteria', *Environment and Planning A*, 10, 781–94.

Openshaw, S. (1978b) 'An optimal zoning approach to the study of spatially aggregated data', in Masser, I. and Brown, P.J. (eds.) *Spatial Representation and Spatial Interaction*, 95–113, Leiden, Martinus Nijhoff.

Openshaw, S. (1980) 'Menothetic divisive algorithms for classifying large data sets', in Barritt, M.M. and Wishart, D. (eds.) *Proceedings in Computational Statistics, COMPSTAT 1980*, 419–25, Wien, Physica-Verlag.

Openshaw, S. (1981) 'Le probleme de l'aggregation spatiale en geographie', *L'espace geographique*, (forthcoming).

Openshaw, S. and Cullingford, D. (1979) 'Deprived places or deprived people: a study of aggregation effects inherent in area based policies', *Discussion Paper* 28, Centre for Urban and Regional Development Studies, Newcastle University.

Openshaw, S., Cullingford, D. and Gillard, A.A. (1980) 'A critique of the national classification of OPCS/PRAG', *Town Planning Review* 51, 421–39.

Openshaw, S. and Gillard, A.A. (1978) 'On the stability of a spatial classification of census enumeration district data', in Batey, P.W.J. (ed.) *Theory and Method in Urban and Regional Analysis*, 101–19, London, Pion.

Openshaw, S. and Taylor, P.J. (1979) 'A million or so correlation coefficients: three experiments on the modifiable areal unit problem', in Wrigley, N. (ed.) *Statistical Methods in the Spatial Sciences*, 124–44, London, Pion.

Openshaw, S. and Taylor, P.J. (1981) 'The modifiable areal unit problem in geographical analysis', in Bennett, R.J. and Wrigley, N. (ed.) *Quantitative Geography in Britain*, London, Arnold.

Oppenheimer, V.K. (1974) 'The Life Cycle Squeeze: The interaction of men's occupational and family life cycles', *Demography*, 11 (2), 227–45.

Owen, D.W., Dodds, P., Gillespie, A.E. and Mounsey, H.M. (1981) *Employment in the Northern Region*, London, Manpower Services Commission.

Patterson, G. (ed.) (1977) *Monkwearmouth Colliery in 1851*, Durham University Extra-Mural Department.

Peach, C. (1975) *Urban Social Segregation*, London, Oxford University Press.

Peach, C. (1979) 'More on race and space', *Area* 11, 221–3.

Pickett, K.G. (1974) *Sources of official data*, London, Longman.

Pool, I., Abelson, P. and Popkin, A. (1965) *Candidates, Issues and Strategies*, London, MIT Press.

Prandy, K. (1980) 'Residential segregation and ethnic distance in English cities', *Ethnicity* 7 (4), 367–89.

Pringle, D.G. (1980) 'Causal modelling: the Simon-Blalock approach', *Concepts of Techniques in Modern Geography* 27, Norwich, Geo Abstracts.

Rase, W.D. (1980) 'Subroutines for plotting graduated symbol maps', *EDV Report* 2/1980. BfLR, Bonn.

RCGP/OPCS/DHSS (1982) 'Morbidity statistics from general practice 1970–71, socioeconomic analyses', *Studies on Medical and Population Subjects*, 46, London, HMSO.

Redfern, P. (1981a) 'Census 1981 – an historical and international perspective', *Population Trends*, 23 (see also OPCS Occasional Paper no. 25).

Redfern, P. (1981b) 'Census 1981 – an historical and international perspective: 3. Census Geography', *Population Trends*, 24.

Rhind, D.W. (1975) 'Geographical analysis and mapping of the 1971 UK census data', *Census Research Unit Working Paper*, 3, Department of Geography, University of Durham.

Rhind, D.W. (1977) 'Computer aided cartography', *Trans. Inst. Brit. Geogr.*, NS 2.

Rhind, D.W., Evans, I.S. and Dewdney, J.C. (1977) 'The derivation of new variables from population census data', *Census Research Unit Working Paper* 9, Department of Geography, University of Durham.

Rhind, D.W., Evans, I.S. and Visvalingam, M. (1980) 'Making a national atlas of population by computer', *Cartographic Journal* 17, 3–11.

Rhind, D.W. and Hudson, R. (1980) *Land Use*, London, Methuen.

Rhind, D.W., Stanness, K. and Evans, I.S. (1978) 'Population distribution in and around selected British cities', *Census Research Unit Working Paper*, 11, Department of Geography, University of Durham.

Rhind, D.W. and Trewman, T. (1975) 'Automatic cartography and urban data banks – some lessons from the UK', *International Yearbook of Cartography* 15, 143–57.

Robinson, A.H., Sale, R.D. and Morrison, J.L. (1978) *Elements of cartography,* 4th edition, New York, Wiley.

Robinson, G.K. (1950) 'Ecological correlation and the behaviour of individuals', *American Sociological Review*, 15, 351–7.

Rogers, A. (1972) *This Was Their World: Approaches to Local History*, London, BBC.

Rosing, K.E. and Wood, P.A. (1971) *Character of a conurbation. A computer atlas of Birmingham and the Black Country*, University of London Press.

Rothman, J. (1977) 'The development of an income surrogate', in *The General Household Survey 1974*, London, HMSO.

Rowe, B.C. (1980a) *Statistical software for survey research*, Study Group on Computers in Survey Analysis.

Rowe, B.C. (1980b) 'A bibliography of statistical computing', *Statistical Software Newsletter.*

Rowe, B.C. and Scheer, M. (1976) *Computer software for Social Science data*, London, SSRC.

Royal College of General Practitioners/OPCS/DHSS (1982) 'Morbidity statistics from general practice 1970–71, socioeconomic analysis', *Studies on Medical and Population Subjects*, 46, London, HMSO.

Rutter, M. (1980) *15000 Hours*, London, Open Books.

Scheuch, E. (1974) 'Social context and individual behaviour', in Dogan, M. and Rokkan, S. (eds.) *Quantitative Ecological Analysis in the Social Sciences*, London, MIT Press.

Sewell, W. and Armer, J. (1966) 'Neighbourhood context and college plans', *American Sociological Review*, xxxi, 159–68.

Sewell, W. and Orenstein, P. (1965) 'Community of residence and occupational choice', *American Journal of Sociology* 70, 551–63.

Short, J.R. (1978a) 'Residential mobility in the private housing market of Bristol', *Inst. Brit. Geogr. Trans.*, New Series 3, 533–47.

Short, J.R. (1978b) 'Population turnover: problems in analysis and an alternative method', *Area* 10, 231–6.

Showler, B. (1974) 'Employment in Retirement', *Age Concern Manifesto Series* 19.

S.I. 1980 No. 702, *Census Order 1980.*

S.I. 1980 No. 897, *Census Regulations.*

Sibson, R. (1973) 'SLINK: an optimally efficient algorithm for the single linkage clustering method', *Computer Journal*, 16, 30–4.

Silk, J. (1979) *Statistical concepts in geography*, London, George Allen and Unwin.

Sillitoe, K. (1978) 'Ethnic origin: the search for a question', *Population Trends,* 13, 25–30.

Smart, M.W. (1974) 'Labour market areas: uses and definition', *Progress in Planning* 2, 4.

Smith, H.J. (ed.) (1977) *Billingham, Port Clarence and Haverton Hill in 1851*, Durham University Extra-Mural Department.

Sokal, R.R. and Sneath, P.H.A. (1973) *Numerical taxonomy*, San Francisco, Freeman and Company.

Sotto, P. and Donnison, D. (1980) *The good city: a study of urban development and policy in Britain*, London, Heinemann.

SSRC Survey Archive (1981) *Bulletin,* 19, 4.

Stevens, P. and Willis, C.F. (1979) *Race, crime and arrests*, Home Office Research Study 58, London, HMSO.

Studler, D. (1977) 'Social context and attitudes towards coloured immigrants', *British Journal of Sociology*, xxviii, 168–84.

Taylor, D.R.F. (ed.) (1980) *The Computer in Contemporary Cartography*, London, Wiley.

Taylor, P.J. (1977) *Quantitative Methods in Geography*, Boston, Houghton Mifflin.

Taylor, P. and Johnston, R.J. (1979) *The Geography of Elections*, Harmondsworth, Penguin.

Taylor, P.J., Kirby, A.M., Harrop, K.J. and Gudgin, G. (1976) *Atlas of Tyne and Wear*, University of Newcastle, Department of Geography, Research Paper 11.

Thomas, E.N. (1968) 'Maps of residuals from regression', in Berry, B.J.L. and Marble, D.F. (eds.) *Spatial Analysis: A Reader in Statistical Geography*, Englewood Cliffs, NJ, Prentice-Hall, pp. 326–52.

Thompson, M.L. (1978) 'Selection of variables in multiple regression', *International Statistical Review* 46, 1–19 and 129–46.

Till, R. (1973) 'The use of linear regression in geomorphology', *Area* 5 (4), 303–8.

Tillott, P.M. (1972) 'Sources of inaccuracy in the 1851 and 1861 Censuses', in Wrigley, E.A. (ed.) *Nineteenth Century Society*, Cambridge University Press.

The Times, 6 April 1981, The Rt. Hon. Patrick Jenkin MP.

Tobler, W.R. (1973) 'Choropleth maps without class intervals?', *Geographical Analysis* 5, 262–5.

Tukey, J.W. (1970) 'Some further inputs', in Merriam, D.F. (ed.) *Geostatics: A Colloquium*, 163–74, New York, Plenum.

Tukey, J.W. (1977) *Exploratory Data Analysis*, Massachusetts, Addison-Wesley.

United Nations (1967) 'Principles and recommendations for the 1970 population censuses', *Statistical Papers Series M44*, New York, UN Statistical Office.

Unwin, D. (1981) *Introduction to spatial analysis*, London, Methuen.

Valkonen, T. (1969) 'Secondary analysis of survey data with ecological variables', *Social Science Information*, viii, 33–6.

van der Knaap, G.V. and Sleegers, W.F. (1980) 'De structuur van migratiestromen in Nederland: een indeling in Stadsgewesten en Stedelijke systemen', *Deelrapport*, 1 Economisch Geographisch Instituut, Erasmus University, Rotterdam.

Velleman, P.F. and Hoaglin, D.C. (1981) *Applications, Basics and Computing of Exploratory Data Analysis*, Massachusetts, Duxbury Press.

Visvalingam, M. (1975) 'Storage of the 1971 UK census data: some technical considerations', *Census Research Unit Working Paper*,4, Department of Geography, University of Durham.

Visvalingam, M. (1976) 'Chi-square as an alternative to ratios for statistical mapping and analysis', *Census Research Unit Working Paper* 8, Department of Geography, University of Durham.

Visvalingam, M. (1977) 'A locational index for the 1971 kilometre-square population census data for Great Britain', *Census Research Unit Working Paper* 12, Department of Geography, University of Durham.

Visvalingam, M. and Dewdney, J.C. (1977) 'The effects of the size of areal units on ratio and chi-square mapping', *Census Research Unit Working Paper*, 10, Department of Geography, University of Durham.

Visvalingam, M. and Perry, B.J. (1976) 'Storage of the grid-square based 1971 GB census data: checking procedures', *Census Research Unit Working Paper* 7, Department of Geography, University of Durham.

Walter, B. (1980) 'Time-space patterns of second-wave Irish immigration into British towns', *Inst. Brit. Geogr. Trans.*, New Series 5, 297–317.

Waugh, T.C. (1980) 'The development of the GIMMS computer mapping system', in Taylor, D.R.F. (ed.) *The Computer in Contemporary Cartography*, London, Wiley, pp. 219–34.

Webber, R.J. (1977) 'The national classification of residential neighbourhoods: an introduction to the classification of wards and parishes', *PRAG Technical Paper,* 23, Centre for Environmental Studies, London.

Webber, R.J. (1978a) 'Parliamentary constituencies: a socioeconomic classification', *Occasional Paper*, 13, London, OPCS.

Webber, R.J. (1978b) 'An introduction to the OPCS/CES classification of residential neighbourhoods' (mimeo), London, CES.

Webber, R.J. (1980) 'A response to the critique of the national classifications of OPCS/PRAG', *Town Planning Review,* 51, 440–50.

Webber, R.J. and Craig, J. (1976) 'Which local authorities are alike', *Population Trends*, 5, 13–19.

Webber, R.J. and Craig, J. (1978) 'A socioeconomic classification of local authorities in Great Britain', *OPCS Studies in Medical and Population Subjects*, 35, London, HMSO.

Weller, R.H. (1977) 'Wife's employment and cumulative family size in the US, 1970 and 1960', *Demography*, 14, 1, 43–65.

Welton, T.A. (1911) *England's Recent Progress*, London.

Willis, K.G. (1974) *Problems in Migration Analysis*, Farnborough, Saxon House.

Wishart, D. (1969) *Clustan 1A*, University of St. Andrews.

Wishart, D. (1978) *Clustan 1C User Manual*, Program Library Unit, University of Edinburgh.

Woods, R.I. (1976) 'Aspects of the scale problem in the calculation of segregation indexes: London and Birmingham, 1961 and 1971', *Tijdschr. econ. soc. Geogr.* 67, 169–74.

Wrigley, E.A. (ed.) (1972) *Nineteenth Century Society*, Cambridge University Press.

Yule, G.V. and Kendall, M.G. (1950) *An Introduction to the Theory of Statistics*, High Wycombe, Charles Griffin.

Name index

Subject index